The South African Defence Forces in the Border War 1966-1989 offers the first comprehensive analysis of the South African Defence Force's role in the Border War in Namibia and Angola since the end of this conflict in 1989. It investigates the causes of the Border War and follows its progress and escalation in the 1980s. It also considers the broader international context against which this conflict took place.

The author brings vital new information to light gained from documents which have since been declassified. This includes documents from the State Security Council, the department of foreign affairs, the SADF itself, as well as from the Cuban and Soviet governments. It sheds light on the objectives of the National Party government in both Angola and the former Southwest Africa, the SADF's strategy in the war and its cross-border operations in Angola.

To sketch as complete a picture as possible of individual operations, the author not only interviewed several high-ranking SADF officers, but also included information from the Cuban archives and testimonies of Cuban and Russian officers. All the major operations and battles are discussed, including Savannah, Reindeer, Sceptic, Protea and Modular, as well as the battles of Cassinga and Cuito Cuanavale.

Where a battle had no clear winner, the author asks what the aim was of each of the parties involved and whether they succeeded in achieving that goal. In this way, he offers fresh perspectives on long-running and often controversial debates, for instance on who won the battle of Cuito Cuanavale. In the last chapter, the author looks at the objectives of all the parties involved in the war and whether they achieved them. In the process he tries to answer the all-important question: Who won the Border War?

Dr Leopold Scholtz is a senior journalist, political commentator and a highly regarded military expert. He was deputy editor of *Die Burger* until 2007 and is currently the European correspondent for Media24's Afrikaans dailies.

Scholtz obtained his doctor's degree from the University of Leiden and is currently a research fellow at the University of Stellenbosch. He has written four books and over 40 academic articles, most of which are about military history. He was a captain in the Reserve Force of the South African Army until recently.

His books include *Beroemde Suid-Afrikaanse Krygsmanne, Generaal Christiaan de Wet as Veldheer* and *Waarom die Boere die oorlog verloor het*.

THE SADF

IN THE

BORDER WAR

1966–1989

LEOPOLD SCHOLTZ

Helion

Helion & Company Limited
26 Willow Road
Solihull
West Midlands
B91 1UE
England
Tel. 0121 705 3393
Fax 0121 711 4075
Email: info@helion.co.uk
Website: www.helion.co.uk
Twitter: @helionbooks
Visit our blog http://blog.helion.co.uk/

This edition published by Helion & Company 2015
South African edition published in 2013 by Tafelberg, an imprint of NB Publishers, a
Division of Media24 Boeke (Pty) Ltd, South Africa (www.tafelberg.com)

Cover design: Michiel Botha
Book design: Cheymaxim
Editing: Alfred LeMaitre
Proofreading: Lesley Hay-Whitton
Printed by Lightning Source, Milton Keynes, Buckinghamshire

Text © Leopold Scholtz 2013
Maps © Camille Burger
Photos © Documentation Centre of the South African National Defence Force,
UWC-Robben Island Museum Mayibuye Archive, Roland de Vries

ISBN 978 1 909982 76 5

British Library Cataloguing-in-Publication Data.
A catalogue record for this book is available from the British Library.

For details of other military history titles published by Helion & Company Limited
contact the above address, or visit our website: http://www.helion.co.uk.

We always welcome receiving book proposals from prospective authors.

TO MY PARENTS

CONTENTS

LIST OF MAPS

AUTHOR'S NOTE

During the Border War, I worked as a journalist at two Afrikaans newspapers – first at *Beeld* in Johannesburg (1979–1982) and then at *Die Burger* in Cape Town. These newspapers often carried reports of clashes and operations in which the South African Defence Force (SADF) was involved in northern South West Africa or across the border in Angola. Our job was not an easy one, as the Defence Force was rather poor at providing information. As a matter of fact, almost throughout the war there was a measure of tension between the newspapers and the Defence Force; the journalists always wanted more information, while the Defence Force gave as little away as possible.

Apart from the question of whether the Defence Force at the time could have elicited more support from the white population by issuing more information, the relative shortage of facts greatly frustrated me as a military historian. Even then, I had wanted to write a proper independent analysis of the military operations, but this was obviously impossible. The only known facts were those issued by the Defence Force, SWAPO, the MPLA and the Cubans, and the propagandistic nature of their statements made their accuracy highly dubious.

However, a few years ago several web pages started publishing original documents, *inter alia*, of the State Security Council (SSC), the Department of Foreign Affairs, the Defence Force, United States, Cuba and the Soviet Union. To me, this tipped the scales. With the use of additional unpublished documents in the Documentation Centre of the South African National Defence Force (SANDF) and contact with SADF veterans, I decided to tackle this book. It is only a first attempt; as further sources become public, the picture will become even fuller and more nuanced.

I made good friends with several veterans while writing this book. Among them I have to mention especially major generals Roland de Vries and Johann "Dippies" Dippenaar, as well as Ariël Hugo, formerly a second lieutenant with 61 Mechanised Battalion Group and now involved with this unit's veterans' society. They displayed endless patience by reading parts of the manuscript and identifying mistakes. De Vries went to great lengths to write down his observations of several aspects of the Border War especially for me. I am encouraging him to adapt these in book form, as I really think he has an interesting story to tell.

Two more individuals whose patience I have tested to the utmost are Lieutenant Colonel Erika Strydom and Steve de Agrela of the SANDF Documentation Centre, who spent hours finding documents for me. I also conducted personal interviews, or had e-mail correspondence, with the following: General Jannie Geldenhuys; brigadier generals Piet Muller, McGill Alexander and Willem van der Waals; colonels Paul Fouché, CP du Toit, Gerhard Louw, Leon Marais, Jan Malan, André Retief, Gert van Zyl and Ep van Lill; Commandant Dr Jakkie Cilliers of the Institute of Security Studies; Lieutenant Colonel Professor Doctor Abel Esterhuyse of the Military Academy at Saldanha; Major Hans Kriek; and lieutenants Ariël Hugo, Paul Louw, Gert Minnaar and Hubrecht van Dalsen. The maps were kindly drawn by Camille Burger.

To all these people, I want to express my sincerest thanks. Without their help, this book would have been a meagre harvest.

Last but not least, a special mention of my wife, Ingrid Scholtz, who is also a historian. In general, she is my sharpest critic, but also my greatest support. Without her, I am nothing.

Leopold Scholtz,
Delft

INTRODUCTION

This book is primarily a military, rather than a political, history. Politics do feature, insofar as war – as the Prussian military theorist Carl von Clausewitz famously wrote – is a continuation of politics by other means. It is also not a social history, because the impact of the war on South African and other societies is not the main focus and these fields have already been extensively analysed.[1] The book is a history of the armed actions of the combatants – the South African Defence Force (SADF), the People's Liberation Army of Namibia (PLAN, SWAPO's armed force), FAPLA (the armed forces of Angola's MPLA government) and the Cuban military – on the field of battle. It focuses on the levels of security strategy, military strategy, operations and tactics alike.

I have written this book for several reasons. Firstly, there is a continuing and growing interest in the Border War among the South African public, especially the white population, judging by the number of publications seeing the light of day. Many people who participated in the war, mostly in the SADF, have set down their experiences in writing or published them on the Internet, where it is apparently lapped up by both the generation who actually served in the military and a young generation keen to know more of a war they have heard so much about.

Secondly, no comprehensive history of the war has been written yet. Military correspondent Willem Steenkamp did an admirable job with a coffee-table book,[2] published in 1989 when the crack of the guns was still reverberating in the air. Since then, many original SADF and other government documents have been declassified by the SANDF and the Department of Foreign Affairs, and some have been published on the Internet.[3] These have enabled historians to unravel some of the mysteries surrounding aspects of the war. The books by military analyst Helmoed-Römer Heitman and journalist Fred Bridgland, on the last year of South Africa's involvement in Angola, are also noteworthy,[4] but they too appeared in 1990 – too soon after the events for a proper historical perspective to develop.

Thirdly, during the war the SADF – rightly or wrongly – believed that it had to control the flow of information very tightly. While this benefited battle-field security, it also gave rise to an untold number of rumours, many of which persist today. Even now, strange stories circulate about what "really" happened in certain battles. It is perhaps time to put these rumours to rest.

The fourth reason flows from the third. The lack of information during the 1970s and 1980s created a vacuum into which SWAPO, the MPLA, the Cubans and left-wing journalists and academics gratefully stepped. They wrote thousands of newspaper reports, as well as books and scholarly articles, in which SWAPO, MPLA and Cuban propaganda was uncritically repeated as gospel. One cannot blame these three parties for this – propaganda, after all, has always been an intrinsic part of warfare: winning the battle of perception is often as important as winning the shooting war. This is something the SADF and the South African government understood but dimly and never practised properly.

Besides, because of apartheid the South African government had become morally tainted in the eyes of most of the world. Regardless of what government and SADF spokesmen said, the world was not inclined to believe them. Whatever their opponents said was eagerly embraced as the truth. In the process, the SWAPO/MPLA/Cuban propaganda became conventional wisdom. Where possible, it has become time to test these accepted beliefs against original sources.

On the subject of sources: the (non-)availability of sources prevents this book from being balanced. More than 90% of the sources utilised are South African in origin – archival SADF and government documents, accounts by SADF participants, and so on. A few SWAPO sources have become available, but most of these are so propagandist in nature that they are not of much use. The MPLA archives are still firmly shut, although one gets a glimpse of the Angolan decision-making process through Soviet sources, partly unearthed by Russian academic Vladimir Shubin.[5] But Shubin, having been the main Soviet liaison official with the southern African rebel movements, is understandably biased towards them, and his account has to be approached with caution. Some accounts of Soviet advisors among Angolan units at a grassroots level have also been published. These accounts are interesting, but – as with the accounts of most South African participants – they suffer from the fact that the war is viewed through a keyhole.[6]

The only historian who has been admitted to the Cuban archives is an American, Professor Piero Gleijeses, who has done historical writing a great service by lifting the veil on the Cuban side. Unfortunately, because of his uncritical admiration for Fidel Castro, as well as his utter revulsion for apartheid South Africa, one is also forced to read his writings critically.[7]

This book can therefore not be truly balanced, as the accuracy and completeness of the existing accounts from the Soviet and Cuban perspective cannot be guaranteed. One may be able to piece together a battle or operation rather accurately from the South African side, but the picture on the other side of the hill remains obscured. Had it been clearer, it is possible that my interpretation of certain South African actions would also have been somewhat different.

This book is not the final word on the Border War; it is anything but that. While the SADF sources have not nearly been exhausted, in time many more sources will also come to light to fill in the gaps on the Soviet, Angolan, Cuban and SWAPO side. Such new sources may even still turn on its head everything expounded in this book. That is the nature of academic research. This book may best be viewed as an interim report, which could be followed up by either other academics or me – just as long as the political and ideological tail does not wag the academic dog.

There is yet another thing this book is emphatically not. It is not politically correct. To put my cards on the table: I come from a conservative Afrikaner family who sternly believed in God and the National Party. I served in the old SADF Citizen Force and in the new SANDF Reserve Force. However, I have left apartheid behind me and therefore do not feel the urge to defend either the National Party government's ideology or its actions. At the same time, I have no desire to pander to left-wing pressure to interpret in the worst possible light everything done by the previous government and the SADF.

I am an academic historian, not a moral judge. Moral judgments should be left to those who find emotional satisfaction in pronouncing them. My task as a historian is to try to *reconstruct* the past as accurately as I can, to *analyse* the facts as fairly as possible and to *understand* (which is not the same as condoning) as best I can. In the process, I try to steer away from two extremes – on the one hand romanticising the SADF, and on the other blankly condemning everything the previous government and the SADF did. Those who romanticise the SADF in the war usually see any criticism of the military as tantamount to treason.[8] Another variant of this is the belief that whatever the military did was good and wonderful, but that the politicians mucked everything up. Those who have nothing good to say about the SADF are often left-wing politicians, academics and journalists whose criticism is seldom backed up by proper research.

In the course of my analysis, some criticism will be levelled at a number of individuals. Some of them – including SADF members who fought in the war – might ask what gives me the moral right to criticise them, given that I did not see action in the real sense of the word nor was I an eyewitness to the events described and analysed. I can only say that if being an eyewitness were a prerequisite for writing about historical events, then 90% of all history books would be worthless.

The research material is analysed thematically as well as chronologically. The book starts with the rude shock of the failed Operation Savannah. Then I switch to a thematic approach, analysing the development of the SADF's military doctrine and its military and security strategy. This is followed by a chronological analysis of the successive cross-border operations from 1978 to 1984, when there was an attempt at peace negotiations. Three further thematic chapters examine the counterinsurgency war inside South West Africa, SWAPO's exile record and international developments. Then the climax of the war – the so-called Battle of Cuito Cuanavale – is once again discussed chronologically.

A final word: the central theme of the book is that the South African posture was offensive on the tactical, operational and military strategic levels, but defensive on the security-strategic level. My reconstruction of the South African security strategy is that the government wanted primarily to preserve the status quo, but realised that a defensive military strategy and operational and tactical approach would not be sufficient to win the war. Therefore, in a certain sense, the armed actions of the SADF in northern South West Africa and southern Angola may be seen as a counteroffensive.

ABBREVIATIONS

AA	anti-aircraft
APC	armoured personnel carrier
CANU	Caprivi African National Union
CF	Citizen Force
CIA	Central Intelligence Agency
DTA	Democratic Turnhalle Alliance
FAC	forward air controller
FAPA	Fuerza Aéria Popular de Angola (People's Air Force of Angola)
FAPLA	Forças Armadas Populares de Libertação de Angola (People's Armed Forces for the Liberation of Angola)
FAR	Fuerza Aérea Revolucionaria (Cuban air force)
FLEC	Frente para a Libertação do Enclave de Cabinda (Front for the Liberation of the Enclave of Cabinda)
FNLA	Frente Nacional de Libertação de Angola (National Front for the Liberation of Angola)
GOC	general officer commanding
IFV	infantry fighting vehicle
JMC	Joint Monitoring Commission (1984)
JMMC	Joint Military Monitoring Commission (1989–90)
MK	Umkhonto we Sizwe
MPLA	Movimento Popular de Libertação de Angola (Popular Movement for the Liberation of Angola)

MRL	multiple rocket launcher
OAU	Organisation of African Unity
OC	office commanding
OPO	Ovamboland People's Organisation
PLAN	People's Liberation Army of Namibia
SAAF	South African Air Force
SACP	South African Communist Party
SADF	South African Defence Force
SANDF	South African National Defence Force
SAP	South African Police
SSC	State Security Council
SWA	South West Africa (Namibia)
SWANU	South West Africa National Union
SWAPO	South West Africa People's Organization
SWAPOL	South West African Police
SWATF	South West Africa Territorial Force
TRC	Truth and Reconciliation Commission
UAV	unmanned aerial vehicle
UN	United Nations
UNITA	União Nacional para a Independência Total de Angola (National Union for the Total Independence of Angola)
UNTAG	United Nations Transition Assistance Group

1

THE ORIGINS OF THE BORDER WAR

The origins of the Border War may be traced to the annexation of what was then called South West Africa by Germany in 1884. This was much against the wishes of the German Reich Chancellor, Prince Otto von Bismarck, who viewed his country primarily as a European continental power. But he had to give in to the pressure of a powerful lobby, which saw that other European powers – especially Britain and France – had already annexed several prime pieces of land in Africa, and that Germany had to be part of the "Scramble for Africa" if it wanted to count on the international scene. The present-day Tanzania, Rwanda, Burundi, Cameroon and Togo were thus also brought under German rule.[1]

The Germans were no benevolent masters to the indigenous population. Immigration of German (and Afrikaner) settlers was encouraged, and the indigenous people were – as happened in several British colonies as well – confined to "agreed" territories to create space for the settlers. Several uprisings ensued, especially by the Herero people, which were mercilessly suppressed. In 1904, another revolt occurred. In reaction, the German military commander, General Lothar von Trotha, enacted the first genocide of the 20th century. On 2 October 1904, he ordered that the entire Herero people – men, women and children – be driven into the desert to die of hunger and thirst. Some made it to Bechuanaland (now Botswana) or Walvis Bay (a British enclave on the coast), but by far most of the Hereros died. In total, only some 16 000 Hereros survived out of a population of 60 000 to 80 000.[2]

An uprising by the Nama people in the south was also drenched in blood, and by 1907 the German colonial government controlled the entire territory. Many of those who survived were incarcerated in concentration camps, where approximately half of the inmates died. By 1911, the Nama population, which was estimated to be about 15 000 to 20 000 in 1892, had been reduced to 9 800.[3]

In 1914, the First World War broke out, and the new Union of South Africa decided to weigh in on the side of Britain against Germany. South African forces invaded and occupied German South West Africa, and later German East Africa (now Tanzania), in a campaign lasting only a few months. At the Paris Peace Conference at Versailles in 1919, it was decided to turn the German colonies over to members of the victorious Allied coalition to administer in the name of a new international body, the League of Nations. South West Africa (SWA) became a so-called C Mandate territory, to be administered by the Union of South Africa, without the prospect of independence.[4]

An uprising of the Kwanyama clan, the largest among the Ovambo people of the far north, was forcibly put down, although not with the terrible ruthlessness of the German campaigns. King Mandume ya Ndemufayo was killed and the Kwanyama were subdued. "The Ovambos never forgot this thing, just as we Boers never forgot that the Zulus murdered Piet Retief. It is a long story which has nothing to do with communism . . .," Louis Bothma writes.[5] Apparently, this memory played a significant role in SWAPO's uprising against South African rule in the 1960s.

In South West Africa (SWA), South Africa maintained a policy of racial segregation between the indigenous people and the settlers – as was the case in the rest of the colonial world. After the National Party (NP) won power in South Africa in 1948, the policy of apartheid was extended to SWA as well. In accordance with the apartheid idea of partitioning the country into black reserves or "homelands" and "white territories", the so-called Odendaal Commission recommended a similar policy for SWA. Borders were drawn on maps, and it looked like the territory was set to become a mirror image of South Africa.

These plans never came to fruition. Just after the Second World War, the South African government had tried to convince the United Nations (UN), the successor to the League of Nations, to allow it to annex SWA. However, with newly independent India leading the charge, permission was refused due to South Africa's racial policies. South Africa continued to administer SWA "in the spirit of the Mandate", which meant that the territory became, to all intents and purposes, a fifth South African province.

International pressure against South Africa started building up in the 1960s. Liberia and Ethiopia took South Africa to the International Court of Justice in The Hague, arguing that its occupation of SWA was illegal. But in 1966 the court accepted the South African defence that Liberia and Ethiopia had no legal standing in the matter. The General Assembly of the UN reacted by revoking the original League of Nations mandate, and this was ratified by the International Court of Justice in 1971. The SWA matter was fast becoming internationalised, and the South African government could not ignore the trend.

In 1967, the South African Minister of Foreign Affairs, Hilgard Muller, formally accepted that SWA was a separate territory in international law. In 1972, the UN Secretary-General, Kurt Waldheim, and his personal representative, Alfred Escher, visited the territory and elicited from Prime Minister John Vorster a promise that South Africa would not annex SWA. Vorster also undertook to scrap the partitioning of the territory and to keep it together as one international legal entity.[6] Although this was a long way from the international demand for immediate independence, it represented a certain limited movement on the South African side. By negotiating with the UN, Vorster also accepted in practice that the world body had a say in SWA's future. Exactly how South Africa's SWA policy evolved will be analysed in a later chapter.

Organised resistance to South African rule started in 1959 with the founding of the South West Africa National Union (SWANU) and the Ovamboland People's Organization (OPO). The latter was renamed the South West Africa People's Organization (SWAPO) the next year and became the focus of resistance to the South African occupation, while SWANU dwindled into obscurity.[7]

There can be no doubt that South Africa's race discrimination policies contributed considerably to the rise of dissatisfaction among many blacks. The heavy-handed way in which the government suppressed public demonstrations exacerbated black discontent. In December 1959, a protest against the forcible resettlement of Windhoek's black township exploded into violence in the so-called Old Location. The police reacted harshly and shot 11 people dead and wounded 54. As Marion Wallace remarks in her history of Namibia: "This pivotal historical moment thus served further to radicalise the population and to unite opposition to South African rule, as well as causing [Sam] Nujoma and other OPO leaders to take the decision to go into exile."[8]

Pastor Siegfried Groth, a German churchman who in later years became one of SWAPO's greatest critics, wrote of the situation in the 1960s:

Namibian men and women were no longer prepared to accept oppression and humiliation. The prisons in Ovamboland were full to overflowing. Hundreds of people, including women, were whipped in public. The victims had to undress and were then brutally beaten on their buttocks with a six-foot-long palm-tree cane.[9] Anyone who tried to resist the South African dictatorship received electric shock treatment and was imprisoned without trial for months or even years.[10]

This led directly to SWAPO's decision, in 1962, to resort to armed struggle in order to end the South African occupation of SWA, or Namibia, as the country was called by the organisation. However, it was not until September 1966 that the first shots were fired.[11]

The Border War in South West Africa and Angola pitched two armed coalitions against each other in a protracted conflict that lasted 23 years and ended, not with a clear-cut victory for either side, but in a compromise. On the one hand, there was the South African government and its armed force, the South African Defence Force (SADF), in alliance with the Angolan rebel movement União Nacional para a Independência Total de Angola (UNITA), or National Union for the Total Independence of Angola. (A second Angolan rebel movement, the FNLA, was eliminated early on and did not play a meaningful role.) On the other hand, there was the Namibian liberation movement, the South West Africa People's Organization (SWAPO), in alliance with the Movimento Popular de Libertação de Angola (MPLA), or Popular Movement for the Liberation of Angola – recognised as the government of Angola – and the communist dictatorship of Cuban President Fidel Castro, as well as the Soviet Union.

This brought about at least three layers of conflict. One was a civil rights struggle against the South African government's policy of institutionalised race discrimination against black people, better known as apartheid. The second was an anticolonial liberation war for the independence of SWA against the South African occupation of the territory. And lastly, although the first two layers were generated by an indigenous dynamic, there was the global Cold War between the Communist bloc and the West (of which South Africa saw itself as a part) superimposed on it.

It is seductive, especially from an ideological point of view, to interpret the conflict simply as a war against the injustices of apartheid and colonial domination, or resistance against the dangers of communist imperialism. Actually, all three paradigms are valid. The three layers were, as happened elsewhere in the world, fused together so tightly that to try to separate them would be at the cost of truth. If we could bring all three layers together under one roof, it would be that of *revolutionary war*, which manifested itself in insurgency and counterinsurgency warfare.

From a professional military viewpoint, the Border War is also very interesting. It was a revolutionary war, an insurgency and counterinsurgency war, a fast-moving, mobile, conventional war and ended in an attritionist set-piece conventional war. Not many wars have all these characteristics in one. This makes a proper analysis of this war all the more necessary.

The operational area

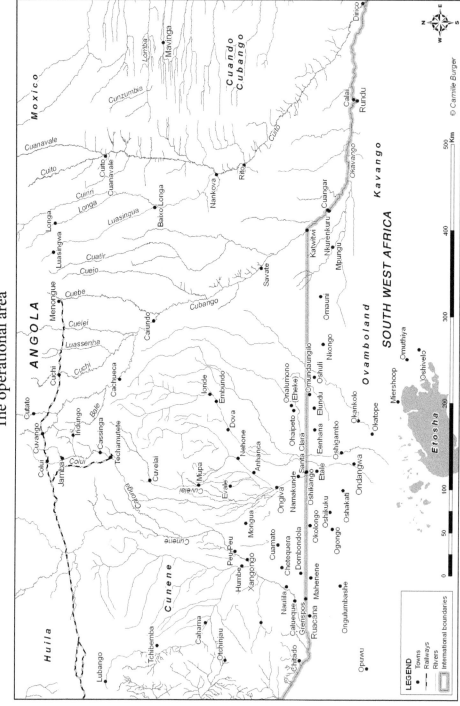

© Camille Burger

2

THE FIRST YEARS
AND OPERATION SAVANNAH

The Border War is generally assumed to have started on 26 August 1966 when a force of 130 men –121 policemen and 9 members of 1 Parachute Battalion hastily attested as temporary policemen in Alouette III helicopters – under the command of Captain (later Colonel) Jan Breytenbach attacked a base of the People's Liberation Army of Namibia (PLAN, SWAPO's armed force) base at Ongulumbashe in Ovambo.[1] Apparently, because of its unwillingness to acknowledge that SWAPO formed a real danger to South African domination in South West Africa, the government decided to entrust the fight against the insurgency not to the Defence Force, but to the South African Police (SAP). This would remain the case until 1974, when the SADF did take over responsibility.

At this stage, the army still suffered from the after-effects of neglect during the post-Second World War era, and particularly from the exodus of experienced English-speaking members. This was a direct result of the policy of the first National Party Minister of Defence, Frans Erasmus, who instituted a kind of affirmative action in favour of Afrikaner officers.[2]

Most of the army's weaponry dated from the Second World War, although a limited modernisation programme had started in the early 1960s.[3] The infantry's Lee-Enfield rifle was replaced with the R1, and the Bren light machine gun (LMG) with an LMG of 7,62-mm calibre. The infantry also had a number of Saracen armoured personnel carriers (APCs) dating from the early 1950s. But their most important antitank weapon was still the old Second World War-vintage six-pounder gun and 3,5-inch rocket launcher (the ENTAC antitank missile was imported in 1966). The process of replacing the old 3-inch mortar with the 81-mm had barely begun. The First World War-vintage Vickers would remain the main medium machine gun for a good decade more. The army had purchased some 206 Centurion tanks from the UK in the 1950s, but quickly sold half of them to Switzerland. For the rest, Shermans and Comets from the Second World War were still operational.

The army did have a useful new armoured car, the Eland – an improved version of the French Panhard – with a 90-mm gun. But the four-wheeled Eland (affectionately known as the "Noddy", due to the way it rocked when riding over uneven terrain) had limited mobility in the African bush, was powered by an inflammable petrol engine instead of diesel, and carried only 20 shells for its gun, so it was not really adequate.[4] The artillery was equipped with light 25-pounder (88-mm) and medium 5,5-inch (140-mm) guns, both dating from before 1945.[5]

The voluntary military service system was replaced in 1962 with a ballot system, according to which some young white men had to serve for nine months. But this was too short a period to train them and then utilise them operationally, and so in 1968 the period of general military service was extended to 12 months. However, most infantry battalions were not very good, a rigid Second World War mentality still being pervasive.

I was trained in 1966 at the old Army Gymnasium in Voortrekkerhoogte, outside Pretoria, and can confirm from experience that my co-members of this unit and I respected only two units – the Gymnasium itself and 1 Parachute Battalion. The Special Forces – the "Recces" – were founded only in 1969.[6] The Gymnasium members would undoubtedly have respected them too!

The fact is that, in 1966, the army was not in a position to fight a war of any kind. Even so, the legacy that would transform the organisation into a highly mobile and battle-hardened force was already present. The army of the 1960s was the descendant of two forefathers, namely, the British Army and the Boer commandos of the 18th and 19th centuries. In terms of its organisation and visible culture, the army was virtually a clone of the British Army: the uniforms, the way in which soldiers marched and saluted, the officers' public manners were all intensely British. The British experience in the Second World War had heavily influenced the army's doctrine, because the senior officers and NCOs were mostly veterans of the Libyan and/or Italian campaigns against the Italians and Germans. Nevertheless, the mounted infantry tradition, the most outstanding legacy of the Boer commandos, was always near the surface. During the occupation of Somalia and Ethiopia in 1940/1941 – the only Second World

War campaign in which South African forces had operated relatively independently – officers such as Major General Dan Pienaar had organised their units into motorised infantry columns, very much like the Boer commandos, and kicked dust into the eyes of the Italians in a whirlwind campaign.[7] After 1975, and the start of cross-border operations in Angola, this mounted infantry tradition would resurface very quickly indeed.

The South African Air Force (SAAF) was equally unprepared for a war. Equipment-wise, the force was relatively well off. In the 1960s, South Africa had acquired a number of GAM Dassault Mirage III aircraft (of which 16 were Mirage IIICZ interceptors, 17 Mirage IIIEZ ground-attack aircraft, as well as several two-seat trainers and reconnaissance aircraft) from France.[8] But by the time the war started to hot up, in 1975, the Mirage III was already obsolescent. Its range was too limited for southern Africa's vast spaces, and sorties sometimes lasted only 40 minutes. Just in time, in 1975, the first of a new batch of Mirage F1s (consisting of 16 F1CZ interceptors and 32 F1AZ ground-attack fighters) was received, although these would become operational only in the course of 1978. Nevertheless, when Major Dick Lord (later Brigadier General) joined the SAAF in the early 1970s from the British Fleet Air Arm, he found a force that "had fallen into the trap of becoming a 'peace-time' air force", so "flying had become rather like the activities of an exclusive aviation club".[9]

The air force had also purchased 16 Blackburn Buccaneer S.Mk.50 and 8 Canberra B (1) Mk 12 and T Mk 4 bombers and trainers in the 1960s, which, together with the Mirages, provided a formidable air strike capability. However, as the 1980s approached, the Buccaneer force had become sadly depleted through accidents. Apparently some senior SAAF officers – again according to Dick Lord – thought they knew better than the British how to maintain and fly the "Buc", with the result that in SAAF service the aircraft had an "abysmal safety record".[10] By April 1978, nine Buccaneers had been lost in flight accidents. When the climax of the Border War came in 1987/1988, only five were left.[11]

The other important asset in the SAAF arsenal was helicopters, without which the army simply wouldn't have been able to fight. A total of 128 Sud-Aviation Alouette III light helicopters had been obtained in different batches since the 1960s.[12] Later on, they would be used in a role they were never designed for, that of helicopter gunship against SWAPO infiltrants in the operational area in northern South West Africa (SWA) and southern Angola. For trooping – critical for the rapid deployment of troops in a counterinsurgency role – a bigger workhorse was needed, and this was found in the form of the Aérospatiale Puma, of which 20 were bought in 1970. Several subsequent batches followed, for a total of 69 by 1978, when a UN weapons embargo was slapped on South Africa. This force was augmented by 16 Aérospatiale Super Frelons. All these helicopters were French in origin.[13]

The other important task of the air force was transport, but the SAAF – with about 40 Second World War-vintage Douglas DC-3 Dakotas, 9 Transall C-160s and 7 Lockheed C-130 Hercules – was not adequately equipped to keep a large army on the move on the battlefield. General Constand Viljoen (later Chief of the SADF) recognised that "we will not be able to haul a significant portion of the logistics load by air" and that it would have to be moved "over land by truck".[14] This inability would prove a substantial limitation on the army's capability to strike deep into Angola for extended periods with large forces.

As for the navy, it would play a rather minor tactical and operational role in the Border War. During the early 1970s, the navy was equipped with two modernised Second World War-vintage destroyers (which were withdrawn from service during the decade), three Type 12 President-class frigates (all bought from Britain), and three French-built Daphne-class submarines. Although the submarines, with their excellent stealth qualities, would be of much use for special force operations, the five major surface ships were not suited to the demands of the Border War. In any case, they were not meant to fulfil South Africa's maritime needs, so much as those of Britain against the background of the Cold War. In the latter half of the decade, Israeli-built strike craft, also eminently suitable for clandestine operations, would begin replacing them as the navy's principal surface vessels.[15]

Early low-level insurgency

The first years of the Border War were very low-key. After having been decimated at Ongulumbashe in 1966, SWAPO did not enter Ovamboland again for some years. The group wiped out here was the first of ten groups that tried to infiltrate Ovamboland through southeastern Angola or through Botswana from Zambia and the only one that actually succeeded in crossing the border. The others were all intercepted and neutralised by the Portuguese before reaching the border.[16]

Instead, the Caprivi Strip, being relatively accessible from Zambia, for the time being became the main battleground. SWAPO had moved its headquarters to Lusaka in 1962, and so Zambia became the main staging ground for the insurgency.[17] This was favourable to South Africa, as the war's centre of gravity proved not to be in Caprivi, but in Ovamboland further west, where 46% of the South West African population lived. Ovamboland was also the area where SWAPO, most of their leaders being Ovambos, would have the best chance of gaining the support and trust of the locals. The Caprivians were loyal to the Caprivi African National Union (CANU), and their support hinged on the precarious alliance between SWAPO and CANU holding up.[18]

Even this route did not bring about much success for SWAPO. Two groups that tried to infiltrate the Caprivi in 1968 were both intercepted, and the insurgents were in rapid order killed or taken prisoner – some fled back to Zambia. Only in 1971 and 1972 did SWAPO try again, this time with somewhat more success.[19] In June 1974, a large group of insurgents infiltrated the Caprivi Strip, but in a battle on 23 June all but six were killed by the SAP. The survivors barely escaped.[20]

The extreme difficulties experienced by SWAPO insurgents at the time were described by one of their field commanders, Rahimisa Kahimise:

> We had to walk a long distance from Zambia through Angola. Some of our people also died in Angola and some missions could not reach Namibia, because they had to fight through Angola . . . the battles we were involved in, most of them were in Angola with the Portuguese . . . by then we had to train new recruits and we also had to fight to get food as we had to walk long distances, and then we had to try and get transport; also after a battle, then you must have more ammunition . . .[21]

The SADF looked on in growing frustration as its role in the fight at Ongulumbashe was publicly denied and the SAP was given the task of nipping in the bud an uprising by what was seen as "a few uppity blacks". The SADF was also denied the chance to get much-needed combat experience in Rhodesia (now Zimbabwe), where the police took the honours of helping the Rhodesians fight their war.[22] Moreover, most of the men employed in patrolling the operational area were riot policemen whose effectiveness was dubious at best. According to historian Annette Seegers, their approach "seems to have been search-and-capture, consistent with policing that aims at a criminal trial". Patrols and hearts-and-mind activities, which later became the key elements of the SADF's counterinsurgency campaign, played a secondary role. The riot policemen were pulled out of SWA in 1968, after which the SAP started a counterinsurgency training course in Pretoria. Until 1972, only whites were employed, but the Rhodesian experience convinced the SAP to recruit black policemen as well.[23]

Although things were fairly quiet on the face of it, the Defence Force was apprehensive. In a confidential report in the early 1970s, senior officers told the Minister of Defence, PW Botha, that the SADF was not adequately prepared for the expected struggle.[24] And so, when several countrywide strikes broke out in South West Africa in 1972 and the police found it impossible to cope with internal security as well as the insurgency, the government at last decided to turn the responsibility for the war over to the military.

In spite of its lack of combat experience, the SADF was better placed to do the job. It had the edge in both manpower and firepower, and had already started training some of its soldiers in counterinsurgency operations in 1960.[25] Several senior-ranking members, such as General CA "Pop" Fraser, had also given considerable attention to the theory of how a counterinsurgency war should be fought. And, as General Constand Viljoen later told writer Hilton Hamann, "we knew the police would not have the capacity to do the job. We wanted to do it. I wanted to give my people the experience of fighting that kind of war because we all knew it was going to come South Africa's way." And, therefore, when the time came, "[w]e jumped at the opportunity . . .".[26]

The military finally took over responsibility for the war on 1 April 1974. It was just in time; barely three weeks later, on 25 April, a coup d'état toppled Portugal's fascist dictatorship. Soon afterwards, that country's new government announced its intention to pull out of its African colonies – Mozambique, Angola and Guinea-Bissau. This changed everything.

Operation Savannah

The South African invasion of Angola in 1975/1976 had profound consequences for the Border War. Although the conflicts in SWA and Angola remained separate in principle, they became ever more intertwined until they finally merged in a spasm of blood-letting.

The particulars of Operation Savannah, as the invasion was called, have been well documented elsewhere.[27] For our purposes, its relevance lies in the fact that Savannah helped to form a certain political and operational pattern that would have considerable importance later on.

The invasion was triggered by the uprising in Lisbon on 25 April 1974, when a group of dissatisfied army officers overthrew the fascist dictatorship of premier Marcelo Caetano. The fall of the Portuguese dictatorship had tremendous strategic consequences for southern Africa. The South African government could no longer use Angola as a buffer territory or count on Portuguese colonial forces to prevent SWAPO fighters from infiltrating South West Africa. The Portuguese, in fact, informed the South Africans that they would no longer be allowed to conduct anti-SWAPO patrols north of the border, and on 26 October the last South African liaison officers attached to the Portuguese forces left Angola.[28]

In his memoirs, SWAPO leader (and later Namibian president) Sam Nujoma wrote perceptively: "Our geographical isolation was over. It was as if a locked door had suddenly swung open. I realized instantly that the struggle was in a new phase . . . For us [it] meant that . . . we could at last make direct attacks across our northern frontier and send in our forces and weapons on a large scale."[29]

To reflect the new reality, SWAPO moved its headquarters from Lusaka to Luanda.[30] At the same time, Tanzanian president Julius Nyerere spearheaded a meeting between Nujoma and MPLA leader Agostinho Neto, which led to a pact between the two movements.[31] For the first time, SWAPO got an important "prerequisite for a successful insurgency, namely a safe border across which he could fall back", as General Jannie Geldenhuys remarked in his memoirs.[32] An optimistic Nujoma told his Soviet contacts in Moscow that he planned "to broaden the area of armed operations, first to the Atlantic coast and then to the centre of the country".[33]

SWAPO moved swiftly to exploit the new possibilities. Within a few months

of the collapse of Portuguese control in southern Angola, the area was swarming with SWAPO armed bands. By November 1974, SWAPO bases of up to
70 men were functioning in the area.[34] From October 1975, SWAPO made its
presence felt in Ovamboland with an incursion by over 500 trained guerrillas.[35]
The SADF responded in August and September with a series of cross-border
operations north of Ovamboland and the Caprivi Strip, known as Operation
Sausage, in which four SWAPO bases were attacked. But although 26 SWAPO
and MPLA fighters were killed, most SWAPO bases were found to be empty,
and the operation did not achieve much.[36]

South African Recces participated in a clandestine operation against SWAPO
in southern Angola in May/June 1974 (in which the SADF suffered its first
combat death, Lieutenant Freddie Zeelie), but this did not do much to hinder
SWAPO's build-up.[37] In a rather short time, the South African security forces
had got into really big trouble.

SWAPO thus succeeded in breaking out of the strategically unimportant
territory of Caprivi. By being able to utilise southern Angola, they were in a
position to infiltrate large bands of guerrillas into Kavango, as well as into the
war's geographic centre of gravity, Ovamboland, greatly enlarging the operational
area and threatening to overstretch the security forces. But SWAPO was even
more ambitious than this. According to David "Ho Chi Minh" Namholo, PLAN's
chief of staff, their strategy "was changed to cross into farming areas, going
to urban areas rather than just being in the north or in Caprivi . . .".[38] Indeed,
sabotage and bomb explosions were soon reported in towns like Windhoek,
Gobabis and Swakopmund.[39]

This in itself was probably enough for the hawks in the SADF to eye the
Angolan border, hot with desire to cross it and clobber SWAPO on the other
side. But although PW Botha sympathised, Prime Minister John Vorster was
a very cautious man, and held back.[40] He relented only when the governments
of the United States (US), Zambia, Zaire and Liberia implored him to move in
and stop the Marxist MPLA from taking power in Luanda.

There is a lot of confusion regarding US pressure on South Africa to intervene in Angola. American historian Piero Gleijeses, who has minutely examined
Cuba's role in the conflict, indicates that US records have been carefully cen-
sored to exclude any proof of collusion with South Africa.[41] But Chester Crocker,

the Reagan administration's point man for Africa, who seems to have had free access to the US archives, writes that not only was America "well aware" of South Africa's intentions, but "our winks and nods formed part of the calculus of Angola's neighbours".[42]

The Alvor Agreement

The political situation in Angola was extremely chaotic. Three anticolonial movements had fought against the Portuguese, namely, the Marxist MPLA under the leadership of Agostinho Neto, the Maoist (later pro-Western) UNITA under Jonas Savimbi, and the ideology-less and corrupt FNLA under Holden Roberto. On 5 January 1975, the three movements signed the so-called Alvor Agreement in Portugal, which granted independence to Angola. The agreement stipulated that a government of national unity had to administer the territory until free and fair elections could be held in October. The date for independence was fixed for 11 November. Although no one will ever really know, some informed observers were of the opinion that UNITA "would win at least a plurality, and possibly a majority, in the elections to be held under the Alvor Agreement".[43]

It is, therefore, interesting to note that Cuban president Fidel Castro told his Bulgarian counterpart, Todor Zhivkov, that the MPLA admitted shortly afterwards "that they have made a mistake agreeing to a coalition government with these people".[44] It became clear that the MPLA had decided to sabotage the Alvor Agreement soon after signing it. In a conversation with the Soviet ambassador to Angola in July 1975, MPLA leader Agostinho Neto described the existence of three liberation movements as "a favourable opportunity for reactionary forces in the country, which in turn was leading to a further intensification of political, social, and economic conflicts". He was in favour of "a tactical alliance" with UNITA, which he described as commanding "no significant military forces" (and was therefore easily controllable). From his side, the Soviet ambassador assured Neto that "[t]he Soviet people are interested in the victory of democratic [read: socialist] forces in Angola".[45]

Judging by its aggressive actions in the months before independence, it may be assumed that the FNLA also had no intention of honouring the Alvor

Agreement. (The FNLA was rather a strange beast. Corrupt and inefficient, it had only one goal – total power. After it was virtually eliminated in 1976, South Africa no longer provided it with support.)

The outgoing Portuguese governor, Admiral Rosa Coutinho, was a committed socialist and actively channelled Portuguese military equipment to the Marxist MPLA.[46] Chester Crocker claimed that Coutinho's actions started even as the Alvor Agreement was being signed. In June of that year, Coutinho secretly visited Havana to coordinate the cooperation between Cuba and the MPLA.[47] As a matter of fact, in 1987, the "Red Admiral", as he became known, openly admitted in a television interview that he never wanted elections to take place, that he worked for an MPLA takeover and that he was the architect of the Cuban intervention.[48]

According to recent research, the ailing Soviet leader Leonid Brezhnev had very little interest in the Angolan situation and gave no strategic leadership to his own government on the matter. However, Fidel Castro used this power vacuum astutely to further his own goals. Nevertheless, the Soviets played along because it gave them a chance to flex their muscles globally and prove that they were as much a superpower as the US. After the Cuban Missile Crisis of 1962, when the Kremlin was humiliated because it did not have a sizeable ocean-going navy, the Soviets developed a navy and strategic airlift capable of projecting their power considerably. They were anxious to experiment and see how far they could go.[49]

Within a few weeks, MPLA forces drove the FLNA out of Luanda, after which UNITA, which had no more than a token presence in the capital, withdrew to the south.

South Africa was drawn hesitantly and incrementally into this cauldron. As an anonymous South African military official who was "present when the decision was made" told US academic Gillian Gunn:

> We had a request from these movements [the MPLA's rivals] for aid, and we decided to expend a relatively small sum initially . . . Our intuitive feeling was that we should have the most friendly power possible on that border . . . We [subsequently] found that our new allies were totally disorganised. They could not utilise cash, so we provided arms.

They could not use the arms, so we sent in officers to train them to use the arms. The training process was too slow, so we handled the weapons ourselves. We got pulled in gradually, needing to commit ourselves more if the past commitment was not to be wasted.[50]

In fact, the Cabinet was deeply divided. Prime Minister John Vorster, who had invested a lot of political capital in a détente policy with black African states – and even had some modest success – was unwilling to jeopardise it. He was supported by the influential head of the Bureau of State Security (popularly known as BOSS), General Hendrik van den Bergh, who felt that securing the Angolan border would be enough to keep SWAPO out. General Constand Viljoen wrote to PW Botha that Van den Bergh saw Angola solely as a political matter. "He says there are no SWAPO terrorists in Angola. This differs from our opinion," he informed Botha.[51] Botha and his generals, therefore, told Vorster that South Africa needed to take the initiative if it wanted to win the war. In the end, Vorster was won over, although his misgivings remained.[52]

Castro's propaganda after the fact was that the South Africans wanted "to rob the Angolan people of its legitimate rights and install a puppet government" and that their aim was "dismembering Angola and robbing it of its independence".[53] He even claimed that he had to intervene in order "to prevent apartheid from being installed in Angola".[54] He raved about the South African "tank columns, blitzkrieg-type, Nazi-type, apartheid style". "Either we would sit idle, and South Africa would take over Angola, or we would make an effort to help."[55]

In fact, the South African objectives were rather modest. In a first operational instruction emanating from the Chief of the SADF, the army was tasked only to help UNITA to win back the areas it had previously controlled.[56] On 24 September, the SADF's final operational approach – a four-phase plan – was laid before the Minister of Defence, PW Botha. This was the beginning of Operation Savannah. The idea, the SADF said, was to carry it out clandestinely and with the minimum number of soldiers. The four phases consisted of the following:

- Aid to the anti-Marxist movements in Angola with regard to battle training, logistics and intelligence;
- Preventing any further advance by the enemy;

- The recapture of all areas occupied by the MPLA and Cubans in their southward march;
- The capture of the southern Angolan harbours.[57]

At the same time, the Chief of the Army, Lieutenant General Magnus Malan, also ordered operations against SWAPO, which had been ensconcing itself in the southern parts of Angola in order to infiltrate southwards over the border. A ceiling of 3 000 men and 600 vehicles of all kinds was placed on the operation.[58]

The strategic aim, as Constand Viljoen explained later, was to employ "a limited war to apply pressure on the OAU [Organisation of African Unity] so they'd put in place a government of national unity", as the Alvor Agreement stipulated. (The OAU was scheduled to meet early in 1976 to deliberate about the matter.) This was done at the request of Savimbi and Roberto "to enable them to remain forces of influence in Angola until the Organisation of African Unity meeting scheduled to take place after the elections".[59] The capture of Luanda by South African forces and the establishment of a UNITA/FLNA government in place of the MPLA was discussed, but rejected. The consensus was that it would entail higher costs than was justified by the prize.[60]

The South African government laboured under the naive idea that all of this could be done in secret. After the first rumours of SADF troops inside Angola hit the international media, PW Botha kept his countrymen in the dark about South Africa's military involvement in the country. However, the government's lack of a clear strategic view, certainly in the first weeks, filtered down to the troops on the ground. Much later Jan Breytenbach would spell out the adverse results for him and his men at the front:

> At the sharp end, during Savannah, we never really knew whether we were to take over the potential SWAPO guerrilla base area by destroying the guerrillas already in residence there, capture as much of Angola as possible before 11 November, attack and take over Luanda, the capital, to install Savimbi . . . or "whatever". As combat soldiers, we hardly knew what the hell was going on and where we were going to. But we went nonetheless.[61]

In the process, several South African battle groups embarked on a series of astonishingly rapid northward advances, flattening everything in their path. As Willem Steenkamp says, the South African commander, Colonel Koos van Heerden, led a "little half-trained army more than 3 100 km up a hostile coast in a mere 33 days of movement, winning every one of the 30 actions he fought, for a cost of five dead (including one South African) and 41 wounded (including 20 South Africans)."[62]

This was a classic rapid advance, reminiscent of the German Army in France in 1940 and the Soviet Union the following year, where the blistering pace of the movement became a weapon in itself. Central Intelligence Agency (CIA) operative John Stockwell wrote of "the most effective military strike force ever seen in black Africa, exploding through the MPLA/Cuban ranks in a blitzkrieg".[63] Jan Breytenbach, in command of one of the battle groups, commented: "The reason Task Force Zulu advanced so rapidly, overrunning one delaying or defensive locality after another, was because FAPLA/Cuban forces were caught off balance when the opening shots were fired. Thereafter they were totally dislocated by never being given a chance to catch their breath, regroup and redeploy into well prepared defensive positions."[64]

But in spite of the military success, things were about to unravel on the political level, and, in the end, this would prove decisive. Although several hundred Cuban advisors and instructors had been in Angola for several months already,[65] Fidel Castro decided to send a large force of Cuban troops to Angola in reaction to the South African invasion without consulting Moscow. The first of these arrived by air in the first week of November, a few days before independence day on 11 November.[66] Within a few weeks, the Cuban contingent grew into a formidable force of 36 000 men and 300 tanks.[67]

South African troops soon clashed with advance elements of the Cuban force. On 23 November, they moved into a Cuban ambush at Ebo and were punished severely. However, a few days later, the SADF took revenge by mauling a Cuban force at Bridge 14, south of Ebo.[68] It is fair to say that the soldiers on both sides developed a healthy respect for each other. Castro noted "serious mistakes" made by his own forces and acknowledged that the South Africans broke through the Cuban lines at least once.[69] At the same time, according to the official South African historian of the operation, the

South Africans noted that the Cubans rarely surrendered and often fought to the death.[70]

On the northern side, the FNLA advanced down towards Luanda with South African artillery support. However, on the morning of the decisive clash, FNLA leader Holden Roberto slept late and started the attack only after the MPLA defenders had had a chance to take up strong positions. Predictably, the attack was a dismal failure, and the South African leader element had to be evacuated by a navy frigate patrolling off the coast of Angola. The battery of 140-mm guns was later extricated via Zaire.[71] This was the end of the South African support for the FNLA.

And so independence day – 11 November – dawned, with the fighting preventing the planned elections from being held. At this point, having installed UNITA safely in its traditional home ground in southern Angola, the South African forces were supposed to withdraw. But it was clear that the job was not yet done and Operation Savannah was not yet over. At the request of the US, France, UNITA and the FLNA, the South African government extended its soldiers' role. They now were ordered to continue the advance to an easily defendable position.[72]

However, the whole initiative was about to come unstuck. On 19 December, the US Senate passed the Clark Amendment, barring aid to groups engaged in military operations in Angola. The idea was to force the South African government to stop aiding the FNLA and UNITA. This sent out a powerful negative signal, although the US government still asked the South Africans to delay their withdrawal until the OAU had assembled in January 1976 for its annual summit in Addis Ababa. The Americans hoped that the OAU member states might decide to censure the Cubans for their intervention.[73]

To be sure, the OAU was split right down the middle, with 22 countries supporting a call for a government of national unity in Angola, in accordance with the Alvor Agreement, and 22 in favour of recognising the MPLA straight away as the country's legitimate government. The OAU member countries' disapproval of the white apartheid government was as intense as their fear of the communist states. The organisation's chairman, President Idi Amin of Uganda, exercised his deciding vote and supported the MPLA.[74] Thus, the fact that the MPLA became the internationally recognised – and therefore legal

– government of Angola was thanks to one of the most brutal dictators Africa has ever known.

With this, the rug was finally pulled out from under the South African government's feet. Its international backing evaporated completely, and so the Cabinet decided to pull out a few days afterwards. Members of 35 Citizen Force units were called up and put into positions on the Angolan side of the border to block a possible Cuban invasion of South West Africa.[75] The South Africans kept a force of 4 000 to 5 000 men at the Calueque water supply dam, until the MPLA promised not to impede the flow of water to the north of SWA, which was dependent on the big dam. Then, by 27 March the last South African troops recrossed the border into SWA. Altogether, 29 of their comrades had been killed in action.[76]

Ominously, the Cubans moved to within striking distance of the South West African border. But Castro stopped there; South African fears that he might invade South West Africa were unfounded. As he explained in a speech in December 1988, "we had men, we had a good number of tanks and cannons, but we didn't have planes or anti-aircraft rockets or much of the equipment we have today!"[77]

The Cuban question

Piero Gleijeses, the only academic ever to have been granted access to the Cuban archives, maintains that South Africa's decision to invade Angola had nothing to do with any Cuban presence in the country, as Pretoria afterwards alleged. In fact, he says, things were the other way round: Cuban dictator Fidel Castro's initiative to intervene in force was in reaction to the South African invasion.[78] Strictly speaking, he is quite correct but the argument loses its relevance when all the facts are taken into account.

Castro's decision to start moving his main force of several thousand men was taken only on 5 November 1975, about two weeks after the South Africans crossed the border on 23 October. But Gleijeses is quite silent about the fact that, by 1974, the Cuba and the USSR (Union of Soviet Socialist Republics, or Soviet Union) had already decided to aid their friends in the MPLA to attain sole power in Angola. The huge quantities of military equipment channelled to the MPLA from late 1974, a flow that accelerated in March 1975, and the hundreds of Soviet and Cuban instructors and military advisors who were sent to Angola, tell their own story.[79] Soviet aid to the MPLA was duly noted in an SADF report, dated 26 April 1975, to PW Botha. It was recommended that South Africa should try to bring the FNLA and UNITA together in an anti-communist alliance.[80] Military involvement was not on the agenda at this stage.

It is now known that the Soviet Union started its military aid to the MPLA in early December 1974, long before the South African involvement was even a glint in PW Botha's eye.[81] Cuba's Deputy Prime Minister, Carlos Rafael Rodrigues, admitted to journalists in January 1976 that 238 military instructors had been sent to Angola in May 1975 to train MPLA fighters – months before the South Africans even entertained the thought of intervening. These were followed by another 200 instructors in August, as well as 1 000 combat troops, armoured cars and trucks aboard three ships, which docked on 4, 5 and 12 October, also well before the South African intervention.[82] The fact that Castro sent the bulk of his army only after the South African invasion cannot alter these facts.

Even Colin Legum, an academic and journalist who is not known for his sympathy with the National Party government, called the assertion that the Cuban intervention was a reaction to the South African invasion "clearly a *post facto* rationalisation".[83]

In a lengthy secret analysis of the Soviet and Cuban involvement in Angola, the CIA's conclusion was that the large-scale military aid coming from the Soviet Union in early 1975 – the report refers to an "escalation of Soviet support" involving "tanks and large mortars" – was not in response to the small amount of aid the FNLA had been getting from China and the US itself. Because the escalation came at a time of relative calm, it could also not be seen "as a response to the immediate battlefield needs of the MPLA". Rather, the Soviet build-up "reflected a decision by the Soviets to try to give their faction in Angola the wherewithal to achieve military dominance". This came about at a stage when the USSR, Cuba and the MPLA all "considered South African intervention unlikely".[84]

Castro's thinking was explained by Brigadier General Rafael del Pino, of the Cuban air force, who defected to the West in 1987. Del Pino was ordered by the Cuban leader in January 1975 to begin preparations for air force involvement. "Castro assumed that the Alvor Accord was going to be honoured by no one, and he wanted to get ahead of the field; he knew that the Chinese and North Koreans were giving aid to the FNLA. The arrangement was that the Soviet Union would send the weapons to Angola and Cuba would send the personnel."[85]

According to another Cuban defector, Juan Benemelis (who at the time was head of the Africa department of the Cuban Foreign Ministry), the first contingent of Cuban instructors reached Angola in March 1975 – months before the South African intervention.[86] Somewhat later, Castro himself admitted, in a secret conversation with Todor Zhivkov, that he had sent arms for 14 000 to 15 000 MPLA fighters in September.[87] On 15 August, he proposed to Moscow that he send Cuban troops to Angola, and requested Soviet logistical help. However, the Soviets did not consider the time to be opportune.[88]

This gives the lie to Cuban propaganda, eagerly disseminated by Gleijeses, that the presence of Cuban troops in Angola was "a legal act", as they "were in Angola at the invitation of the government".[89] When the Cubans intervened, first on a limited scale, and then in earnest in early November, this was done at the request, not of an internationally recognised legal government, but of only *one of three rebel movements*. One could reason that South Africa had no business invading Angola either, but that still does not legitimise the Cuban and Soviet intervention.

The Cuban intervention rested on three factors. The first was Castro's extraordinary ideological worldview. Angola held out little economic or strategic advantage for Cuba itself. But Castro was a true Marxist-Leninist idealist. The liberation struggle (presumably going hand in hand with a socialist revolution) was "the most moral thing in existence", he told East German leader Erich Honecker in 1977. "If the socialist states take the right positions, they could gain a lot of influence. Here is where we can strike heavy blows against the imperialists."[90] And a few weeks later he told a French magazine that Africa was "imperialism's weakest link today . . . If we are militant revolutionaries, we must support the anti-imperialist, antiracist and anticolonialist struggle. Today, Africa has gained great importance. Imperialist domination is not as strong here as it is in Latin America."[91]

Secondly, viewed as a deed of power politics, it came at exactly the right time. The US had been demoralised by its humiliating defeat in Vietnam and was not able to act strongly against the Cubans and Soviets. Castro, with his keen political instinct, surely realised this. And, in the third place, his chief opponent in

Angola was the widely discredited apartheid regime of South Africa. This gave Cuba extra credibility in the eyes of the Third World.

The political consequences

The historical significance of Operation Savannah lies in the patterns it established, patterns that continued to dog the Border War until peace came in 1989. The first of these was that the Cubans proved themselves to be absolute masters of propaganda. Castro immediately launched a huge propaganda offensive, briefing a left-wing Colombian journalist, Gabriel García Márquez, to write an account of Operation Carlota, as the Cuban operation was named.[92] Márquez portrayed the campaign as a huge military triumph for the Cuban army and the MPLA and as a humiliating defeat for the hitherto invincible SADF.

The SADF itself generated a manuscript with a large part of the story, but, in spite of Magnus Malan's support, it was shot down by PW Botha. A British journalist, Robert Moss, produced a more balanced analysis based on the SADF manuscript,[93] but the damage was done – Castro got his blow in first. The fact that the South African government had at first denied the presence of South African troops in Angola did not help its cause. In the eyes of most of the world – including the black populations of SWA and South Africa – these lies destroyed what little credibility Pretoria had. The result was that Castro was widely believed and Botha not.

In actual fact, though, at a tactical level the South Africans performed well. They lost one fight against the Cubans – at Ebo – but won several more. Operationally, they did astoundingly well with the blistering pace of their northward advance. On the levels of military and security strategy, they lost badly due to the changing political situation, over which they had no control. They pulled out, not having been defeated militarily (as Gleijeses asserts),[94] but because they had lost the political fight. But propaganda often has little to do with the facts.

What was true, however, was that South Africa's prestige had been severely dented. Colin Legum pointed out at the time that this had been the first time since 1943 that "the South African Army had been committed to fight in an African war", in which "for the first time in their modern history white South African soldiers ended up as prisoners of war in African hands".[95] A perception took root in Africa that the mighty Boers could be beaten on the battlefield. Castro himself told Todor Zhivkov a few weeks later that "the myth of South Africa" had been exposed. South Africa "is something like Israel in Southern Africa", he said.[96]

Castro's propaganda was also good news to the banned African National Congress (ANC). Its mouthpiece, *Sechaba*, spoke of "wide-spread fear and panic amongst the white population and the racist ruling clique". Thus, "the boast that the South African Army could not be beaten has become a mere propaganda nonsense".[97]

A second pattern that emerged was that the two opposing sides (Cuba and its allies on the one side and South Africa on the other) completely misunderstood each other's motivation and objectives. At the time Castro decided to counter the South African invasion with Operation Carlota, Piero Gleijeses was told by Jorge Risquet Valdés, a senior Cuban official, Castro was convinced that the South Africans wanted to take Luanda itself.[98] Years later, Castro told his biographer: "The objective was for the racist South African forces coming from the south to meet up with [Zairean president] Mobutu's mercenaries from the north and occupy Luanda before Angola proclaimed its independence . . .".[99]

It is only human to ascribe the basest motives to your enemies, and this undoubtedly played a role in the Cuban exaggeration of the South African objectives. But it also had a practical propagandistic effect. When you want to add credibility to your own claims, it helps to make the enemy seem stronger than he really is and to exaggerate his objectives. When analysing the Cuban propaganda victory, this is something to take into account.

According to military historian Sophia du Preez, who had access to all the relevant SADF documents, the capture of Luanda was indeed discussed in South African military circles, but realism prevailed. It was decided that the resources needed for such an operation, and the likely price that would be paid, would be too great and the advantages too small.[100] The Cabinet was advised that a force of 1 500 soldiers would be needed to take Luanda, while casualties were expected to be as high as 40%, which was totally unacceptable.[101]

On the other hand, the South Africans (and the Americans) also misunderstood the Cuban position. For years, both countries would refer in their secret documents to the Cubans as "Soviet surrogate forces". They thought that Castro was simply a puppet dancing on a Soviet string. Piero Gleijeses in general is very partial to Castro, and makes every effort to interpret South African actions in a negative light. But he makes a very convincing case that Castro's decision to intervene in Angola was taken independently of Moscow.[102]

The Cuban intervention and advance towards the South West African border set the alarm bells ringing. There was a real fear in South African government circles that they would invade SWA. From this a third pattern emerged: the fusion of a local anticolonial war with the global Cold War.

Castro had a fine military mind and keen political instincts. He knew that his own army was at the end of a long supply line and that the SAAF held command of the air. In March 1976 he told Todor Zhivkov that his short-term goal was "to reach a political agreement, to avoid a collision, since they out-number us in terms of aircraft and are also much closer to their supply bases". In the middle term, he was looking beyond the consolidation of his victory in Angola to the liberation of Rhodesia and South West Africa. But, he went on, to conquer South West Africa "we will need to advance further inland and sur-round it. However, such action involves our troops invading Namibia and thus bringing negative consequences on the international stage." Nevertheless, the Cuban troops had to stay in Angola "at least until an Angolan army capable of defending its country is set up".[103]

MPLA leader Agostinho Neto was more aggressive. "Our independence will not be complete until South Africa is liberated," he informed a visiting East German official in February 1976. He added: "[W]e will help our brothers in Namibia with all the means at our disposal . . . The struggle will not be over with the liberation of Angola."[104]

Perhaps unknowingly, Neto confirmed South African fears of the commu-nists. Their apprehensions were well founded; Neto had agreed to the training of PLAN insurgents at MPLA army camps, and SWAPO leader Sam Nujoma moved into an Angolan presidential guesthouse in one of Luanda's posh resi-dential areas.[105] In this way a war, which began as a local conflict with its own civil rights and anticolonialist dynamic, irrevocably became part of the broader, global Cold War. Of course, it was far from the most important element of the Cold War, but this did not lessen South African feelings of being under serious and imminent threat.

A fourth pattern that emerged during Savannah was the incremental development of the operation. Jan Breytenbach was quite justified in asking: "Was Operation Savannah the product of a proper analysis of all factors – terrain, weather and enemy capabilities – or was it just the ad hoc chucking together of ideas over beers in some army pub?"[106]

There was no proper analysis; that much has become clear. Neither were there clear political or military objectives from the start; these developed only as South Africa was drawn in deeper. Even so, taking into account what the decision-makers actually knew at the time, plus their general mind-set, it is not surprising that they floundered about. Events developed so fast in Angola that even the Cubans and the Soviets were at times caught unawares.[107]

Lastly, for the time being at least, the Americans lost all the political capital and influence they had with the South African government, who regarded Washington as having left them in the lurch. The full extent of American duplicity would only become known later. Secretary of State Henry Kissinger, for instance, shamelessly denied that the US had encouraged South Africa to intervene in Angola, or that the US even knew about it beforehand. When Chinese leader Mao Zedong expressed uneasiness about South African involvement in December 1975, Kissinger told him: "We are prepared to push South Africa out as soon as an alternative military force can be created."[108]

In January 1977, the Republican administration of Gerald Ford was replaced by the Democrat administration of Jimmy Carter, and relations deteriorated even further. South African suspicion of US machinations did not diminish until President Ronald Reagan took over in 1981, and even then a certain wariness survived.

Operation Savannah did have one lasting advantage for South Africa. The SADF gained a new ally, namely, Jonas Savimbi's UNITA, which had previously supported SWAPO.[109] The liberation movement had made the mistake of treating UNITA supporters harshly, which had angered Savimbi. By the end of 1975, he had rescinded his permission for SWAPO fighters to use UNITA bases in southeastern Angola.[110] "We will never let them operate against the South Africans in Namibia again. Never!" he exclaimed in November 1976 to a British journalist.[111]

The military consequences

On an operational level, the Angolan debacle had negative consequences for South Africa. Firstly, the harshness of the apartheid system and the perceived South African beating at the hands of the Cubans and the MPLA increased support for SWAPO,[112] which moved swiftly to exploit this support and the opportunities it offered. Many young South West Africans crossed the border to join the guerrillas. According to SADF intelligence, SWAPO's military strength increased from about 400 trained guerrillas in 1974 to approximately 2 000 in 1976.[113] From radio intercepts, it became clear to the SADF that Angola had ceded several bases to SWAPO in the south of the country, and that Cuban instructors were training SWAPO fighters. Within a few months, SWAPO was transformed, as Magnus Malan writes, "from a plodding organisation into a powerful, well-trained and well-oiled military machine".[114]

From just south of the Angolan border, where he was engaged in building up what would become 32 Battalion, Jan Breytenbach reported that "the military and political situation in South Angola has deteriorated to such an extent that it presents a critical threat".[115] Military Intelligence established the existence of some 52 SWAPO forward operational bases immediately north of the border.[116]

By 1977, there was an average of a hundred contacts per month between SWAPO insurgents and SADF soldiers. The army estimated that there were about 300 insurgents inside SWA,[117] indicating that SWAPO was very active indeed. "The picture from this time on," Susan Brown writes, "is of regular land-mine casualties among troops in Ovamboland, abduction or assassination of Ovambo headmen, construction workers shot at or injured (South Africa was constructing tarred roads, water towers, pipelines and canals), white construction foremen abducted, stores raided and burned . . ."[118]

SWAPO made use of typical guerrilla tactics – "little more than hit-and-run contacts", as ex-soldier Piet Nortje recounts. "Even when they far outnumbered their opponents, it was customary for them to pour on the heat for a brief period, then disappear into the bush."[119] Bombs were set off in Windhoek and even in Swakopmund and Keetmanshoop.[120] According to SADF planners in May 1977, SWAPO bands were avoiding contact with the security forces and concentrating on "intimidating and activating the local population".[121] It was very effective, and indicative of the extent to which the movement had imbibed the guerrilla doctrines expounded by Marxist strategists like Mao Zedong and Che Guevara.[122]

In order to combat SWAPO, the SADF relied mainly on white conscripts and reservists, often from the cities, who proved to be unsuitable. Being a fair sample of the white community, with the paternalistic and often racist attitudes of the time, they were at a disadvantage in dealing with tribal people in northern SWA. This certainly did not help in winning the loyalty and support of the locals, which meant that the security forces got little or no intelligence, and when they did get it, it was mostly too old to be useful.[123]

According to Eugene de Kock, who was a station commander in Ruacana at the time, SWAPO "seemed to be doing what it liked". In his memoirs, he writes that SWAPO "was ahead of us in most respects". The main reason was that "our troops were not bush-savvy. We took a boy who had just matriculated, gave him a gun, two to three months of basic training – and then threw him in the middle of a country that he did not know, people he did not understand and an enemy that he had never seen. No wonder he did not do very well."[124]

Indeed, how could one expect city boys to track and find guerrillas, who had grown up in the area and knew every bushcraft trick in the book, when they did not want to be found? A typical example of how the conscripts fared is given by a troepie who calls himself "Dennis" and shared online his experience of a patrol in 1979 near Etale in northern SWA:

> The platoon sergeant was not interested in walking any further that day, so we bedded down where we were. We didn't do any protective movement. We stayed where we were. We found a big tree and we slept in a half moon around the tree.

> While we were there, about 45 terrorists actually crept in, and the nearest guy was about 20 feet away from me, and they were also in a half circle around us. Because we were close to a waterhole, there were cattle and we wouldn't have heard them anyway. They dug in about 8 inches and made themselves a little wall in front of them. The guys were armed

with AK47s and RPGs in between them. Then when they had set up,
they looi-ed [hit] us.

I woke up and I thought I was dreaming. There were green and red
tracers flying over my head. I could feel sand actually hitting me from
the bullets that were landing around me. The guy sleeping next to me
on a groundsheet was hit in the leg and in the stomach . . . He was
pretty badly injured, and he was screaming and sitting up. I was trying
to keep him down. I was trying to keep my head as low as possible as
well, with my chin in the ground.

These guys were looi-ing us big time – RPGs were hitting the tree above
us and exploding. I shot off one shot with my R1 and I had a storing
[stoppage] because I had got sand in it while trying not to be hit. I
managed to get hold of the weapon of the guy next to me, and I shot
one shot off and that also had a storing.

By this time, the fire had going down – it only lasted maybe 30 seconds
or a minute – I don't know. Then these terrorists took off and ran.[125]

These shortcomings were caused partly by the SADF's inefficient personnel
system. As Willem Steenkamp explains, large numbers of Citizen Force and
Commando members were regularly called up to man bases and escort convoys.
Time for travel and refresher training "cut the actual operational service to
something over two months . . . and no one stayed long enough in an area to
build up a comprehensive knowledge of people and places . . ."[126]

South African tactics also were clumsy and unwieldy. Jan Breytenbach
relates, with more than a touch of sarcasm, how Operation Kobra was launched
in May 1976 with "masses of infantry"; "[s]upply bases, bursting at the seams,
were set up in the operational area to provide everything from hot showers to
ample issues of daily ration packs . . . It was the biggest deployment of South
African troops since the Second World War. But this huge force did not get a
single kill."[127]

Eugene de Kock observed that the security forces had a disdain for SWAPO at the time because the guerrillas never stood and fought. "The fact that SWAPO soldiers were seldom seen, and resisted getting into set-piece engagements, reinforced the view that they were ineffectual and merely a nuisance. This was not so. SWAPO groups – large ones at that – moved freely around Ovamboland. But, because they could not be found, they did not exist for the security forces."[128]

Recalling that era, a senior SWAPO commander told Susan Brown years later that "the enemy had no influence among the masses . . . During that time, even the SADF were under-trained. They were not specialised in guerrilla tactics. That is why they found it difficult to track down guerrillas during that time; they were not in a position to move in the areas where we used to operate and they got demoralised. At that time we had the upper hand."[129]

SWAPO also moved to broaden the geographical scope of the war. PLAN's chief of staff, David "Ho Chi Minh" Namholo, related: "[Strategy] was changed to cross into farming areas, going to urban areas rather than just being in the north or in Caprivi or in Kavango – to bring the war to the farming areas."[130]

Moreover, SWAPO's freedom of movement meant that they could intimidate the local population by assassinating local pro-South African headmen and officials almost at will. One of the first victims was the "chief minister" of Ovamboland, Filemon Elifas.[131] "Operating in teams of two," Eugene de Kock remembered, "they killed members of the Home Guard and Defence Force and local chiefs".[132] Selective terrorism can be a strong incentive for the locals to support an insurgent force.

The truth is that, by the end of 1977, as Recce member Jack Greeff experienced, "the SADF was losing the war" in SWA.[133] Although the SADF had in excess of 7 000 troops in Ovamboland, against never more than a few hundred SWAPO fighters at any given time,[134] the SADF's "kill ratio" was not impressive. In the period 1966 to 1977, 363 SWAPO guerrillas were killed in action, compared with 88 security force members[135] – a "kill ratio" of only 4,1 to 1, and hopelessly inadequate in a guerrilla conflict. With an estimated 2 000 to 3 000 South West African exiles being trained by SWAPO in Angola, things were not going to get better either.[136]

A rather humorous story told by Breytenbach illustrates the quandary the South Africans found themselves in by early 1978. A major was giving a briefing to some politicians and generals about the situation in the operational area:

So the major picked up his six-foot pointer, walked to the almost blank wall map which was meant to depict the "enemy situation". It covered the whole of Cunene province, in Angola, and all of Ovamboland south of the cutline.

Tentatively he pointed to an insignificant little spot in western Ovambo. "Generals, gentlemen," he said. "This is Ongulumbashe, a former 'terr' base that was discovered in 1966, about twelve years ago. Police and paratroopers attacked the place. They shot the hell out of SWAPO and the survivors scattered all over the place." He swept his pointer over all of the Cunene province and Ovamboland.

"And now we don't know where the f*ck they are!" He stood his pointer in the corner against the wall and sat down.[137]

Beyond that, South African capabilities were eroded because of an interne-cine power struggle between the SADF and the SAP for control of the war and the gathering of intelligence. The matter was only rectified when PW Botha succeeded the police-inclined John Vorster as prime minister and had – as Magnus Malan related – "one of the biggest fights I've ever had in my life" with the police generals.[138]

However, all of this was about to change. In July 1977, Major General Jannie Geldenhuys was appointed GOC South West Africa Command. His orders were "to keep the insurgency at least on such a level that the constitutional develop-ment could take place in an atmosphere of stability and peace".[139] This would prove to be a tall order indeed, given the rampant SWAPO insurgency and the way in which the Savannah campaign had laid bare fundamental weaknesses in the SADF's strategy, doctrine, structure and equipment. Nevertheless, if anyone could do it, this "direct and unpretentious" man – "a soldier's soldier", as Chester Crocker called him[140] – would be it.

3

THE SADF
REINVENTS ITSELF

The failure of Operation Savannah, together with its political fallout, gave rise to a fundamental rethink within the SADF. The campaign exposed a number of organisational, doctrinal, equipment and strategic deficiencies, which had to be addressed rapidly. In fact, the development of a new operational and tactical doctrine was already well under way, as we will see, but Savannah meant that everything had to be accelerated.

Traditionally since 1910, successive South African governments had sought their country's security within the bosom of the British Empire, and later the Commonwealth. Thus, in 1914 Prime Minister General Louis Botha entered the First World War on Britain's side. In the 1930s, Prime Minister General JBM Hertzog fiercely opposed Italy's occupation of Somalia and Ethiopia, and his successor, General Jan Smuts, entered the Second World War on the side of Britain.

By the late 1950s, however, the international situation had started to change. The colonial powers, especially Britain and France, were withdrawing from Africa, and in 1957 Ghana became the first European colony on the continent to gain independence. Not only was the Commonwealth changing from a mainly white club to one dominated by Third World member states, but South Africa's apartheid policy elicited so much international opposition that the country became ever more isolated. Internally, the Sharpeville and Langa shootings of 1960 led to widespread riots. For the first time, whites in South Africa had to face the possibility of a black revolt.

This background naturally gave rise to new thinking in the Defence Force too. And so, in 1960, the General Staff for the first time prepared an analysis of South Africa's altered security situation. The paper identified three threat factors, namely, the ideology of racial equality, the growth of black nationalism and the Soviet Union's plans for world domination.[1] This was the first time that the USSR and communism were identified as threats to South Africa's security.

A new security strategy

The SADF accordingly readied itself for both conventional and counter-insurgency warfare. As the 1969 Defence White Paper explained: "Although an unconventional threat already exists in the form of terrorism, the possibility of a conventional attack is not excluded."[2] This approach was based on a new threat analysis developed by the SADF the previous year. The conventional threats foreseen involved a communist invasion or an invasion under the banner of the UN or the OAU – similar to the Korean War – to wrest SWA from South African control. It was also thought that the Rhodesian question could generate a conventional invasion of the Republic. In the eyes of the SADF strategists, the threat of unconventional war would become acute if the Portuguese colonies and Rhodesia fell.[3] They feared that, if SWA were conquered, the possibility existed that the victors could see such an operation as "just one phase in a campaign to 'liberate' the other white areas as well".[4] The collapse of Portuguese rule in Angola and Mozambique and the failure of Operation Savannah brought the threat much closer to home. It was against this background that South African strategists took a good look at the ideas of the French general André Beaufre (1902–1975).

Beaufre served in Algeria during that territory's war of independence (1954–1962), and based his ideas on counterrevolutionary strategy on the insights he gained there. Although the French won virtually every tactical encounter with the rebels, Beaufre ascribed their defeat to the fact that they could not win over the hearts and minds of the Algerian people. They could not offer the vision of a better future under French rule than an independent Algeria under the rebels. Therefore, he reasoned, the state's strategic objective in a counterinsurgency war should be

> [t]o deprive the enemy of his trump cards. There are two facets to this;
> we must first maintain and increase our prestige, not merely by showing
> we have adequate force available but also by showing the future we hold

out has possibilities; secondly by thoroughgoing reforms we must cut the ground from under the feet of the malcontents.[5]

The answer, according to Beaufre, was a "total strategy", of which the "use of military force is only part of the action. The action is total and it must prepare, assist and exploit the results expected from military operations by suitable operations in the psychological, political, economic and diplomatic fields."[6]

Beaufre also coined the term "total onslaught", which was later often misunderstood. He did not mean that the onslaught was total in its *intensity*, but in its *breadth*. It was total in the sense that it was waged in all fields of life – military, political, diplomatic, economic, religious, cultural, sporting and so on – which was why a "total onslaught" could be countered only by a "total strategy". The answering total strategy is also not total in its intensity, but rather refers to an overarching vision and programme, to which all aspects of government policy (including military action) have to be tailored.

Another point, which became relevant in the Border War context, was Beaufre's discussion of the offensive and defensive approach, where he refined ideas developed by Von Clausewitz.[7] The defensive, Beaufre reasoned, "consists of *accepting the enemy initiative* and rejecting the political arrangement proposed. This attitude can be maintained for a certain length of time but as a rule it does not bring the argument to an end: a defensive attitude cannot lead to any political solution." The defensive, he continued, "can only pay if it leads sooner or later to a *resumption of the initiative*, in other words to some offensive action. *A counter-offensive is essential if submission to the will of the opponent is to be avoided*" (Beaufre's emphasis).[8]

It will become clear how Beaufre's thoughts on the twin elements of *initiative* and *counteroffensive* were translated into action by the South African government's security strategy and the SADF's military strategy. Beaufre visited South Africa in 1974 at the invitation of the South African military attaché in Paris, and even gave a lecture at the Defence Staff College.[9] Under his influence, the Chief of the SADF (and later Minister of Defence), General Magnus Malan, analysed the communist "total onslaught" as being waged against four power bases: political/diplomatic, economic, social/psychological and security.[10] Malan believed that the answer to this total onslaught was a "total strategy" such as

Beaufre proposed. As far as could be established, the first reference to a total strategy was made in the Defence White Paper of 1973, but it was mentioned only in passing.[11] Two years later, the idea started to take root and a more elaborate analysis followed.[12] In 1977, then Defence Minister PW Botha tabled a White Paper in which he identified the Soviet Union as the major culprit in the Angolan and South West African conflict, claiming that South Africa is "involved in a war":

> It is therefore essential that a Total National Strategy be formulated at the highest level. The defence of the Republic of South Africa is not solely the responsibility of the Department of Defence. On the contrary . . . [it] is the combined responsibility of all government departments. This can be taken further – it is the responsibility of the entire population, the nation and every population group.[13]

The total strategy was thus defined as "the comprehensive plan to utilise all the means available to a state according to an integrated pattern in order to achieve the national aims within the framework of the specific policies. A total strategy is, therefore, not confined to a particular sphere, but is applicable at all levels and to all functions of the state structure."[14]

One should not be surprised that it took until 1977 for the government to come up with a coherent and coordinated response to what it perceived as the total onslaught against it. The catalyst was the role of the USSR and Cuba in Angola in the preceding two years. If these two powers had not intervened in 1975, it is likely that the wars and bloodshed up to 1990 would have been much more limited than they eventually were.

On 4 March 1980, the government accepted a top-secret policy document, informally known as the Green Book, in which the total strategy was explained.[15] The threat, according to the document, came primarily from the Soviet Union, which would use "proxy forces" (in other words, the Cubans, SWAPO and the ANC/SACP) against the Republic. This threat was so serious that it could "totally destroy" the country.

The document gave details of policies to be followed on constitutional, social and economic terrain. This followed closely the policy of the Botha government, which was to reform apartheid and to give blacks a stake in the battle against "communist imperialism". The main pillars of apartheid were not really questioned. On the contrary, although the human rights of black South Africans were recognised in theory, this had to be exercised through the so called black homelands. White rule over "white" South Africa had to be safeguarded.

As far as security matters were concerned, a growth in ANC terrorist activity was expected. To combat the threat, South Africa needed to establish a "constellation" of friendly neighbouring states. If this succeeded, the threat of a conventional invasion of the country could be contained to the area north of 10° South. If not, the threat could move southwards to South Africa's neighbours. The document foresaw that South Africa would

> ensure its national security through coordinated offensive pro-active behaviour on all power bases in the strategic and tactic areas. It does not imply that the RSA is striving for aggression against any state or group or is planning any territorial expansion, but if any threat rises from wherever against the RSA, the necessary defensive or pre-emptive operations will have to be conducted against those threats.

Moreover, the prestige of "resistance movements in neighbouring states" had to be promoted "where it is in the RSA's interest".

Based on this thinking, the government divided southern Africa into three strategic categories. The first was the heartland, South Africa and South West Africa. The second consisted of countries of tactical importance, and included Botswana, southern Angola, Zimbabwe, Lesotho, Swaziland and Mozambique south of the Zambezi. The third category was the area regarded as of strategic importance, and which reached as far north as the equator.[16]

A new counterinsurgency doctrine

With SWAPO bands becoming ever more active inside South West Africa, the SADF urgently had to develop a proper counterinsurgency doctrine. The army had started a counterinsurgency training course in 1960, and was also introduced to American doctrine on the matter when then Major Magnus Malan attended a US Army staff course at Fort Leavenworth, Kansas, in 1962.[17] The course taught that "[w]hile a military campaign could delay an insurgency, it could be defeated only by nonmilitary measures designed to win the 'hearts and minds' of the population".[18] Malan later introduced this approach into the SADF.

During the 1960s and early 1970s the army (and SAAF)[19] had observers attached to the Portuguese colonial forces in Angola and Mozambique. The big expert here was Commandant (later Brigadier General) Willem "Kaas" van der Waals,[20] who later wrote a book about the subject.[21] The war in Rhodesia was also studied, especially because several South African units, as well as individual officers and NCOs, had fought clandestinely on the Rhodesian side. As a matter of fact, by late 1979, two companies of 1 Parachute Battalion as well as the entire 3 SA Infantry Battalion were fighting as task forces Yankee, Zulu and X-Ray, respectively, in Rhodesian camouflage uniforms alongside the Rhodesians.[22]

Beaufre was an important source for SADF thinking on the security-strategic level, where people like PW Botha and Magnus Malan moved. But such thinking often went over the heads of practical-minded officers who had to fight a war and kill the enemy. According to General Georg Meiring, a more widely read book was *The Art of Counter-Revolutionary Warfare* by the American military writer John McCuen.[23] McCuen recommends that the counter revolutionary should have clear and encompassing objectives; that the masses, especially the "silent majority", be mobilised against the insurgents; and that the efforts of all state departments be united in a single, overarching and integrated plan.[24]

In general, most officers' interest was limited to the tactical level. The main reason was the traditional contempt for intellectually schooled officers – a quality shared with the British Army. "From the time of Union," Annette Seegers writes, "debates about the Department of Defence held that military experience counted for more than intellectual or staff ability. Staff courses and later joint staff courses at the Defence College favoured those with operational experience ... Even for its elite, the SADF thought theory best ignored."[25]

There were important exceptions, though, such as Lieutenant General CA "Pop" Fraser, Chief of Joint Operations in the 1960s, who in 1969 wrote an unpublished study entitled "Lessons learnt from past revolutionary wars".[26] Fraser had made a study of the available literature about counterinsurgency warfare at the time and had distilled the prevailing insights for his readers.

His fundamental point of departure was "that victory does not come from the clash of two armies on a field of battle". Anticipating PW Botha and Magnus Malan's total strategy approach, he wrote that counterinsurgency warfare had to be conducted "as an interlocking system of actions, political, economic, administrative, psychological, police and military". The revolutionary wages his war by gaining the support of the people. A government can thus be victorious only "by recapturing the support of the masses, and by the complete destruction of that organisation and the eradication of its influence upon the people". Referring to historic examples, Fraser wrote that most counterinsurgency wars were won militarily, but lost politically.[27] Because the objective of both sides is to win over the population itself, "political action remains paramount throughout the war". This means that the interplay between politics and military action is so intricate that the two cannot be separated. "On the contrary, every military and administrative move has to be weighed with regard to its political effects and vice versa". The inescapable conclusion, he emphasised, was "that the overall responsibility should stay with the civilian power at every possible level".[28] He strongly recommended (unspecified) political reforms, and stressed that the locals' life under the government must be perceptibly better than that offered by the insurgents.[29]

Fraser's work was widely studied in the SADF and in government circles. In 1985, President PW Botha wrote a foreword when the main study was distributed to senior officials.[30] In his memoirs, General Jannie Geldenhuys devotes considerable space to Fraser's ideas. "I identified myself intellectually and emotionally with the contents and made the ideas my own," he wrote.[31]

It is thus clear that the South Africans, in theory at any rate, had developed a sophisticated approach to SWAPO's onslaught, which embodied a good understanding of revolutionary guerrilla warfare principles. The question is: to what extent did they practise what they preached?

A return to mobile warfare

The traditional South African method of warfare is based on one overarching concept: mobility. From the 18th century, three factors encouraged this: the vast spaces, a relatively small population and a heavy reliance on militias (called commandos). Individuals could never remain in the field for long periods, as they had to return to their farms to plough or harvest. Campaigns therefore had to be concluded swiftly.

Infantry and cavalry in the European sense had only a limited application in southern Africa; the infantry were not mobile enough to cover the vast distances quickly enough, while cavalry were overly reliant on their horses and could not fight on foot. Thus warfare in this part of the world naturally revolved around *mounted infantry*, that is, fighters able to move around rapidly and across great distances on horseback, and able to shoot from horseback, but who, having entered a battle, would mostly fight on foot.

The mounted infantry commando concept reached its zenith during the Anglo-Boer War (1899–1902), when the Boers mostly outclassed their British counterparts on the tactical and operational levels. It is interesting to note that the British followed the Boer example later in the war by exchanging their infantry and cavalry for mounted infantry, although in general they seldom matched the astounding mobility of the commandos.[32]

This Boer phenomenon never became the subject of military treatises or doctrine. It grew, as it were, out of the ground and simply became second nature. It is, therefore, not surprising that the South African invasion of Italian-occupied Somalia and Ethiopia in 1940/1941 was a classic example of mobile mounted infantry warfare – the horse simply having been exchanged for the lorry. The South Africans achieved great mobility by moving their infantry about in lorries and having them dismount when the need arose. It was, in fact, a sort of motorised Anglo-Boer War.[33]

Of course, after the Somalian and Ethiopian campaigns the South Africans moved to the Western Desert and Italy, where their freedom of movement and independence of decision-making were greatly constrained. South Africa had two infantry divisions in North Africa and an armoured division in Italy, which formed part of the British Eighth Army and later the US Fifth Army. These formations had to do what the senior British and American generals ordered. Moreover, the mountainous terrain of Italy was not conducive to the traditional mobile South African way of war.[34] As Brigadier General George Kruys wrote in a study, during that time "[t]he South African military thus experienced advance, attack, defence and withdrawal actions in largely set-piece operations".[35] It was this experience that dominated the SADF until the 1960s and resulted in a Defence Force still very much in Second World War mode.[36]

Another problem was that few South African officers had practical experience of war. Most were too young to have participated in the Second World War, and the nature of that conflict was very different from the one that was about to begin.[37]

After a new threat analysis in 1968, a series of symposia was held to thrash out the problem. It was decided – against intense resistance, it must be added – to move away from the Second World War set-piece approach to mobile warfare. This was followed by a report of an Officers' Council, which recommended that tactical surprise, commando attacks, strongpoints, infiltration attacks, raids and mobile defence techniques had to form the future nucleus of the army's new operational doctrine of mobile warfare.[38]

These new ideas were, in large measure, based on fresh thinking by a group of younger officers at the Military College in Voortrekkerhoogte, such as Colonel (as he was then) Constand Viljoen, who became commander of the college in 1966. He and others began to see that the old approach would not work, at any rate not in Africa. The problem was that the distances were too great, the spaces too vast and the pool of manpower too small. The old approach would require large armies, which South Africa simply did not have. So the idea grew – as he told an interviewer – that "our whole tactical doctrine is wrong. Then we started with the idea of mobile warfare." This was "based on not to hold ground but to create the design of battle in such a way that you would lure the enemy into [a] killing ground and then [utilise] the superiority of firepower and movement, you would kill him completely. . . . Never think about a battle that could compare with El Alamein, it's completely impossible. In Africa you don't operate that way."[39]

In other words, instead of the *holding* and *occupation of territory* being the fundamental points of departure, factors like rapid movement (mobility), getting into the enemy's rear areas, surprise and misleading the enemy would become instruments to make it impossible or difficult for the enemy to fight in the first place. All these new ideas were tested in exercises, with Land Rovers playing the role of tanks and infantry fighting vehicles (IFVs).[40]

Kruys also highlights the influence of the writings of Frank Kitson, the

British general who came up with the idea of combat groups and combat teams, battalion/regimental-size and company/squadron-size composite, ad hoc units drawn from different corps to provide a balanced force in the field – in other words, armour, infantry, artillery, etc., mixed in a single combat group.[41] This fitted in with the South African tradition of mounted infantry warfare.

By 1975, the SADF reported that the army had "finalised its doctrine for the landward battle"[42] – just in time for Operation Savannah a few months later. The SADF learnt several lessons from Savannah, which Kruys summarises as follows:

- The fog that descended from the political level and obscured the view of the field commanders should be evaded. The aim of future operations would be precisely formulated. Incremental and extended involvement was out; operations would start with sufficient forces and would be of limited endurance.
- It was evident that the SADF was under-equipped for the type of mobile warfare that was being experimented with.
- A heavy armoured car, a proper infantry fighting vehicle (IFV) and modern long-range artillery were needed.
- The concept of combat groups and combat teams drawn from different corps was sound and had to be developed further.
- It was felt that the brigade would become the basic operational combat level for the SADF.[43]

Having a new doctrine is fine, but it has to be implemented to make any difference. For this purpose, at the end of 1973, 1 SA Infantry Battalion (1 SAI) was moved from Oudtshoorn to Bloemfontein to become the test-bed for the new mechanised approach and to be near the armour units with which the mechanised infantry would have to work. The unit, with Commandant Joep Joubert in command, started off with the 30 Saracen armoured personnel carriers the army had at the time. Three years later, amid much excitement, the first Ratel IFVs arrived. The mobile doctrine was developed by then majors Roland de Vries, Tony Savides and Reg Otto (later Lieutenant General and Chief of the Army in the 1990s).[44] De Vries later became one of the army's foremost experts on mobile mixed-arms operations.

The SADF's doctrinal development was furthered by sending several middle-ranking officers on courses with the Israeli Defence Force (IDF), which had amassed considerable experience with mobile mechanised warfare during the wars of 1948/1949, 1967 and 1973, and would expand this in 1982. In 1977, 22 South African officers attended courses at the IDF's combat school, and others followed in subsequent years. Officers who attended mechanised warfare courses in Israel included men who became commanders of elite conventional units like 61 Mechanised Battalion Group (61 Mech), men such as commandants (both later colonels) Gert van Zyl and Ep van Lill.[45] The SADF's tank doctrine was, in addition, much influenced by that of the Israelis.[46]

The SADF took over the Israeli operational planning cycle, as perfected during the Six Day War of 1967 and the October War of 1973. This boils down to simultaneous planning on an integrated basis with free liaison between different staffs. In other words, armour, infantry, artillery, logistics, air force – all involved – would come together and thrash out one or alternative operational plans, which would then be submitted to the senior commanders.[47] This debating procedure was more democratic than rigid decision-making at the top.

The downward devolution of decision-making played an important role for the SADF. As Roland de Vries writes:

> The South African combat leaders were afforded a great measure of initiative down to combat group and combat team [more or less battalion and company/squadron] level. This stimulated independent thought and conduct to a great extent down to ground level. The FAPLA enemy did not have this powerful and flexible attribute. The poor devils had to ask permission for everything and were not allowed to think for themselves.[48]

He points out, though, that things were different for SWAPO and UNITA guerrillas.[49] However, this devolution of power was in sharp contrast to the rigid control in FAPLA and the Cuban army, and helps explain the operational success the SADF repeatedly achieved in its conventional operations inside Angola.

Operation Savannah was indeed the first practical test for the SADF's new doctrine. On an operational and tactical level, it worked very well, although

Savannah was a strategic disaster. After the operation, the Commission of Investigation into the Future Planning of the South African Defence Force was set up, with Jannie Geldenhuys as chairman, for what would, in effect, be a defence review for the 1980s. In the wake of Savannah, the committee report emphasised, among other things, the influence of the "space factor". "Area is the only relatively stable factor as far as the RSA's environmental analysis is concerned," the committee wrote, although it noted that "the space between the RSA and its enemies has narrowed alarmingly". For the SADF's operational doctrine, this meant that "[t]he RSA is a vast country with extended borders and a long coastline. This means that the SADF has to operate in an area and not along a front. This requires special attention to logistics, strategic and tactical mobility, the need for blanket cover, decentralisation of execution and a night-fighting ability."[50]

One prerequisite, as the army realised, was to couple mobility with devastating firepower. As Roland de Vries, at the time second in command of the Army Battle School at Lohatlha, and a junior officer wrote in 1987: "After conducting outflanking manoeuvres or penetrations, the force which has taken the offensive, can attack vital installations behind enemy lines, wreaking havoc. If the enemy's warfare doctrines favour positional rather than mobile warfare, defeat should be imminent and swift." In support of the concept of mobility, they offered a quotation from the British historian Thomas Pakenham about the Anglo-Boer War: "There was one iron law of strategy imprinted on the mind of the Boers like a law of the wild: the answer to superior numbers is superior mobility." With this mobility the objective should be "to out-manoeuvre, rather than engage and become involved in a full-scale confrontation with the enemy".[51]

De Vries, in fact, was one of the foremost SADF thinkers in developing a new mobile warfare doctrine suited to the African battle space. As second in command of 1 SAI in the late 1970s, he – together with Ep van Lill and André Kruger – "developed the training systems, training programmes, training doctrine and *aides-memoire* for mechanised infantry". They tested their ideas in battle simulation exercises at De Brug and Schmidtsdrif, and even involved the air force in order to experiment with the "evolving tactical and operational mobile warfare concepts – one of these being the comfortable utilisation of air support with the close coordination of indirect fire support and ground manoeuvre". He also writes, "We taught our combat leaders situational awareness, thinking one step ahead, fast moving action, leading from the front, quick orders and smoothly attacking from the line of advance."[52]

A new structure and new equipment

Operation Savannah had mixed consequences for the SADF. In Willem Steenkamp's words: "For the South Africans – short of men, short of equipment, their defence force still struggling to wrench itself free from the decades of neglect that had followed World War II – the situation was immensely worrying."[53] Yet it was the army's first experience of mobile warfare in the southern African bush, and as such created a laboratory where the new doctrine could be tested.

One of the most important consequences of Operation Savannah was that it showed the inadequacy of the South African weaponry. Magnus Malan lamented the country's lack of "comparable firepower": "It was a shock to compare the obsolete weaponry of the Defence Force with those of the enemy. This shortcoming needed urgent rectification," he wrote in his memoirs.[54] The need for an infantry fighting vehicle to replace the obsolete Saracen armoured personnel carrier had been identified by 1968,[55] but development really took off in the wake of Operation Savannah.

The fact is that the motorised infantry's main vehicles – Unimog and Bedford trucks – were too soft for the harsh African terrain. A proper infantry fighting vehicle was necessary in order to transform the motorised infantry into mechanised infantry. The four-wheeled Eland armoured cars also found it difficult to move everywhere – the setback at Ebo occurred partly as a result of this deficiency.[56] The army had very little with which to counter Soviet-supplied T-34 and T-54/55 tanks used by FAPLA and the Cubans; the Eland's low-pressure 90-mm gun did not have the necessary penetrative capacity. The Second World War-vintage G-2 140-mm (5,5-inch) gun used by the artillery had a range somewhat shorter than the enemy equivalent – 18 km versus 23 km – while the BM-21 ("Stalin organ") tactical rocket system used by the Cubans was greatly worrying. The need for something similar in the SADF was identified.[57]

A re-equipment programme had started in 1974, but Operation Savannah emphasised the need for rapid action. One of the first breakthroughs was the development of the Ratel IFV. Three years after the prototype saw the light of day, in 1974, the Minister of Defence reported to Parliament that the Ratel had been "successfully industrialised".[58]

The significance of the Ratel can hardly be exaggerated.[59] It was the single most important weapon system in the execution of cross-border operations in Angola. With its six wheels, later equipped with "flat-run" tyres, the Ratel was the army's most mobile vehicle in the bush throughout the 1970s and 1980s. The infantry fighting version was equipped with a rapid-firing 20-mm gun, able to fire both armour-piercing and high-explosive ammunition, and the gunner was able to switch instantly between the two types. It had space for a section of infantry, who could either stand with their upper bodies out of hatches on top or shoot out of portholes in the side of the vehicle.

The infantry could therefore enter the battlefield in an armoured vehicle that had a formidable fighting capability in its own right. When needed, the section could jump out within seconds and fight further on foot. Not only did the Ratel give the infantry a hitherto unheard-of degree of mobility, but it also enabled the troops to enter battles relatively fresh – at any rate, compared with soldiers who had to walk long distances carrying heavy packs to reach the front. Furthermore, the Ratel gave protection against small-arms fire, although not against the formidable Soviet-supplied 23-mm anti-aircraft gun, with which both SWAPO and FAPLA were equipped.

There were various models of the Ratel. Apart from the above-mentioned Ratel 20, there was one with a 90-mm gun, which was basically the Eland 90's turret on top of the Ratel chassis. This model was utilised as an armoured car and as an antitank weapon, and even at times successfully took on the Soviet T-54/55 tank, although its gun was not really up to the task. Against infantry or lightly armoured targets, it was very useful. In close-quarters fighting, as against the T-54/55, its main protection was its formidable mobility, although the lack of a stabilised gun somewhat mitigated this (the Ratel had to stop each time if it wanted to fire accurately, giving up the protection its mobility offered). One could, of course, reason that the dense bush of southern Angola itself acted as a kind of protection, because firing distances were often as little as 30 m. The bush was, in effect, "neutral", as it protected both SWAPO and the Angolans as well as the SADF forces. The decisive factor here was reaction speed. This improved only through intensive training, a field in which the SADF was vastly superior to its adversaries.

Then there was the Ratel Command, which was specially equipped as a mobile headquarters and armed with a 12,7-mm machine gun. Another model became a mobile 81-mm mortar platform, and later on even an antitank missile model was developed. Taking everything into account, the Ratel was probably the best and most flexible weapon system in the army's arsenal, one without which its operations in Angola would have been impossible.

The Ratel was only the second IFV in the world. The first was the Soviet BMP-1, which entered service in 1969. After the BMP-1 and the Ratel, several other countries followed suit, including the US, which developed the Bradley, the British the Warrior and the Germans the Marder.[60] In this regard, the Ratel was a real trailblazer.

To utilise the Ratel, a new breed of infantryman was needed. Hitherto, the South African army had deployed either light or motorised infantry. The new doctrine saw the introduction of mechanised infantry. In January 1977, the Bloemfontein-based 1 SA Infantry, with Joep Joubert in command, was tasked as the training unit for all mechanised infantry. While on deployment in Ovamboland, Joubert had evaluated the possibility of establishing a permanent mechanised combat group in the operational area, and his recommendations led to the formation of Battle Group Juliet, under the command of Commandant Frank Bestbier. At the beginning of 1979, it evolved into 61 Mechanised Battalion Group, which was a totally new kind of animal.[61] Known simply as 61 Mech, the unit consisted of two mechanised infantry companies and an armoured car squadron, as well as its own organic artillery battery, antitank platoon, mortar platoon and combat engineer troop.[62] It became arguably the most experienced conventional warfare unit in the army.

Another weapon system that was a direct result of the lessons learnt in Operation Savannah was the medium G-5 gun (155 mm) and its self-propelled model, the G-6, which replaced the obsolete G-2. The development of the G-5 weapons system started in 1977.[63] The first series production began in 1982, and the G-5/G-6 was continually improved. These guns had a range of

39 km, which is unsurpassed even today.[64] (The range has since been improved to an astounding 75 km.)[65] The BM-21 "Stalin organ" was copied and improved in the form of the Valkiri 127-mm multi-launched rocket system. With its improved artillery, the army became able to shell any opponent accurately and from a distance, without the enemy's being able to counter it.

The lack of a proper anti-aircraft system remained a problem. The Cactus missile system was designed for base protection and fared badly in the bush. The only interim system was the Ystervark – a simple 20-mm rapid-firing gun mounted on the back of a lorry. It was hardly adequate for use against MiG-21s or MiG-23s.

All of this was supplemented with the Olifant Mk 1 main battle tank, which was a drastic modernisation of the old Centurion. The petrol engine was replaced with an adapted Caterpillar diesel engine and a new stabilised 105-mm gun was installed, together with additional armour. The Olifant would form an important fist in the final phase of the war, and was designed as the answer to the Soviet T-62 tank, which was first spotted in southern Africa in the mid-1980s.[66]

The structure of the army was also changed to counter the threat both from within and without. To begin with, national service was extended from one to two years in January 1978 on the advice of a visiting Israeli officer, Colonel Amos Baran.[67] Even so, the SADF struggled with a severe shortage of manpower throughout the war.[68] Doubling the time the troops had to serve meant that they could be thoroughly trained in the first year and that more men would be operationally available during the second. With the SADF's excellent training, this made a huge difference on the battlefield.

Secondly, two types of units were established – area protection and conventional units. The former consisted mainly of commandos (militia) and were organised in regional commands, specialised in counterinsurgency warfare. The latter formed the conventional fist and was organised into two divisions, 7 Motorised Infantry Division and 8 Armoured Division, both consisting of three brigades and other divisional troops. After 1978, these were complemented by 44 Parachute Brigade, with three battalions and other brigade support units. This conventional force was also trained in counterinsurgency warfare.[69]

These units were mostly manned by the Active Citizen Force, which would be called up only when needed or in a crisis. Most of the normal manpower needs were supplied by National Servicemen.

The army's order of battle from the late 1970s onward, therefore, looked like this:[70]

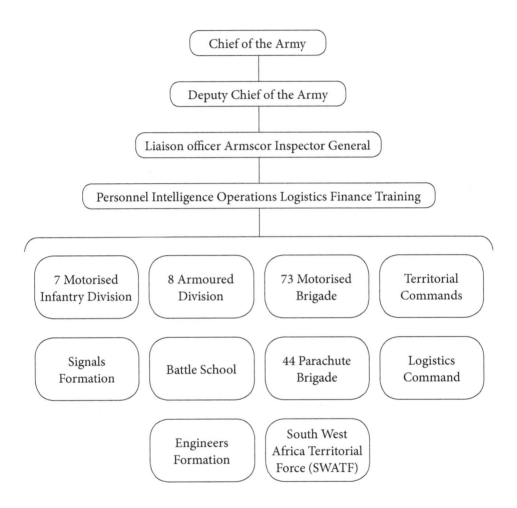

This reinvented SADF went to war in all earnest in the late 1970s.

4

A NEW STRATEGY

On a security-strategic level, South Africa was in an unwinnable situation by the 1970s. Both within South West Africa and internationally, it was regarded as an illegal colonial occupier. Officially, South Africa administrated SWA "in the spirit" of the old League of Nations mandate of 1919 (revoked by the International Court of Justice in 1971), but in practice the territory was run as a fifth province of the Republic. Initially, Pretoria was intent on applying the policy of grand apartheid in SWA, with self-governing and eventually independent homelands for the different black ethnic groups. Petty apartheid – segregation at a grassroots level – was applied assiduously by an army of officials and policemen. This, as we have seen, provided the main cause of dissent and gave rise to SWAPO's insurgency.

Pretoria responded to the challenge with a pragmatism that, in hindsight, was quite surprising. Instead of the usual semi-theological arguments that apartheid was a naturally ordained way to order human relations and a blanket refusal to give up the territory, the government reacted with some flexibility. In 1973, Prime Minister John Vorster declared that the SWA population would have to decide its own future, thereby tacitly accepting that the territory could become independent. He also undertook to abandon the grand apartheid scheme of territorial separation for whites and blacks.[1]

Vorster also received the UN special envoy, Alfred Escher, implicitly acknowledging that the UN had a say in the territory's future. Four years later, a conference between SWA political parties was convened in the Windhoek Turnhalle building, where South West Africans were allowed to decide on the political structures that would govern them. SWAPO viewed the process as a sham, though, and boycotted it. But the apartheid laws were progressively repealed: job reservation was abolished in 1975, along with the hated pass laws and laws forbidding mixed marriages and sex across the colour line, and the principle of equal pay for equal work was accepted in 1978. All of this was a rather adventurous process, seeing that it was still unthinkable in the Republic to contemplate more than just cosmetic changes to apartheid.[2]

In a top-secret assessment, signed by Dr Niel Barnard, director-general of the National Intelligence Service (NIS), it was concluded that white South West Africans had to be convinced "that they cannot demand the same as the whites in the RSA" (with regards to apartheid) and that they had to make "compromises". The "big chasm between white and black aspirations" had to be taken into account in the formation of a united front, wrote Barnard.[3] Looking back on the 1980s, Barnard later told writer Padraig O'Malley, "[t]here is no military solution to any conflict in the world; there are only political solutions".[4]

In the military, the changes were reflected in an ever-increasing number of blacks and coloureds fighting for the South African administration. In 1975, the South African Cape Corps (SACC) was for the first time designated a combat unit, and, later that year, sent a contingent of 190 men to the South West African operational area to take part in counterinsurgency operations. The navy followed suit, while the army established various ethnic-based infantry battalions.[5] The first unit to allow blacks to join the hitherto lily-white SADF was 32 Battalion (consisting of ex-FNLA Angolan fighters). This was followed by 31 Battalion (Bushmen), 101 Battalion (Ovambos), 201 Battalion (East Caprivians), 202 Battalion (Okavango), 203 Battalion (West Caprivians), and 911 Battalion (ethnically mixed). Both 32 Battalion and 101 Battalion were much more than ordinary infantry formations, and effectively grew into motorised infantry brigades. Many blacks also joined the police counterinsurgency unit, Koevoet.

With the exception of 32 Battalion (SADF) and Koevoet (SAP), these units became part of the fast-growing South West Africa Territorial Force (SWATF), an indigenous South West African force under South African command that was founded in August 1980. Whereas SWATF members comprised about 20% of the total South African military presence in 1980, this grew to 51% by 1985. During the 1980s, the force supplied about 70% of the military manpower in the territory – about 30 000 men. More than 90% of these were not white.[6]

The communist threat

The government's more flexible approach in SWA did not mean that the South African government was willing to hand the territory over to SWAPO. During the 1970s and 1980s, the National Party government viewed the USSR as a major threat and Cuba as its surrogate. As Prime Minister PW Botha explained to Parliament in 1980: "The main object . . . under the guidance of the planners in the Kremlin is to overthrow this State and to create chaos in its stead, so that the Kremlin can establish its hegemony here."[7] Botha's Minister of Defence, Magnus Malan, often used a quotation ascribed to Soviet leader Leonid Brezhnev in 1977: "Our goal is to get control over the two great treasuries on which the West depend – the energy treasury of the Persian Gulf and the mineral treasury of Central and Southern Africa."[8]

As far as the USSR's strategy towards South Africa was concerned, a 1981 analysis by Military Intelligence referred to "recent, very credible information" that Moscow expected SWAPO to "tie down" South Africa "through a protracted military struggle in SWA, while the so-called 'united front', of which the ANC onslaught against the RSA forms the other facet, is being developed". Soviet activities in other southern African states, such as Zambia, Botswana, Zimbabwe and Mozambique, confirmed the time scale for the subjugation of southern Africa, which the Soviet Union had shortened "from ten to five years".[9]

These kinds of analyses were, with certain reservations, shared by the Reagan administration. In a 1984 document, the CIA determined the USSR's objectives in southern Africa as a programme "to supplant Western and Chinese influence". Moscow "also seeks to consolidate the emerging leftist, pro-Soviet regimes in Angola and Mozambique, to bring the South-West African People's Organization (SWAPO) to power in Namibia, and ultimately, to undermine the white minority regime in South Africa". Angola, the analysis stated, "is central to these objectives, because it positions the USSR to support and influence Namibian and South African insurgents . . .".

According to the CIA, the Soviets viewed their support for the anti-apartheid struggle in South Africa and SWA "as a central element in their approach to Sub-Saharan Africa over the next decade".[10] "Soviet long-term objectives may also include denial or obstruction of Western access to the region's strategic mineral resources."[11] The document stated that the Soviets sought access to ports for their air and naval forces. In an earlier assessment, the CIA also included the geo-strategic securing of "Soviet sea lines of communication between the European USSR and the Soviet Far East" as a USSR military objective in the region.[12] However, the CIA acknowledged that southern Africa was "largely peripheral to core Soviet security interests and of lower priority than, for example, South Asia and the Middle East".[13]

The main issue here is not whether these analyses were accurate or not. The point is that the NP government believed that South Africa was engaged in an "oorlewingstryd" (struggle for survival), as PW Botha put it.[14] Whoever wants to understand the South African security strategy during the 1970s and 1980s must take the National Party government's fear of the Soviet Union seriously. Rightly or wrongly, this was their point of departure. Their security strategy was therefore in principle *defensive*.[15]

Probably without realising it, Russian academic Vladimir Shubin has since confirmed the South African and American fears about Soviet intentions at the time. In a 2008 book, he rejects the allegation that the Cold War influenced Moscow's strategy towards South Africa, but he apparently understands the term differently from the way it was viewed in the West. He emphasises that Soviet support for African liberation movements was "regarded as part of the world 'anti-imperialist struggle', which was waged by the 'socialist com-munity', 'the national liberation movements' and the 'working class of the capitalist countries' . . . For us the global struggle was not a battle between the two 'superpowers' assisted by their 'satellites' and 'proxies', but a united fight of the world's progressive forces against imperialism." Shubin also notes that the Supreme Council of the MPLA decided in 1982 that South Africa was its "main enemy".[16]

The government's initial security strategy, after PW Botha took over from John Vorster in September 1978, was to try to establish an anti-communist bloc in southern Africa as a counterweight to the Marxist alliance, consisting at the time of Angola and Mozambique, and aided by the USSR and Cuba.[17]

The government's stance on SWA and Angola flowed from this strategy. In fact, South Africa accepted fairly early on that independence for South West Africa was unavoidable. Halfway through 1977, Minister of Foreign Affairs Pik Botha told Rhodesian Prime Minister Ian Smith so during a visit to Salisbury. South African hopes, he said, were pinned "upon the formation of an interim government established to draw up the constitution for an independent Namibia".[18]

But this still did not open a door for SWAPO. Pik Botha wrote to his US counterpart, Secretary of State Alexander Haig, that South Africa strove for an internationally recognised independence for SWA "under a government which does not subscribe to Marxist-Leninist doctrines".[19] During a visit by Haig's Deputy Assistant Secretary of State for Intelligence, Dick Clarke, to South Africa in 1981, Botha explained that his government was not against independence for SWA as such. However, he insisted:

> SWAPO must not be allowed to win an election in South West Africa. We were not prepared to exchange a war on the Kunene for a war on the Orange . . . If South West Africa would be governed by SWAPO, then a serious risk would rise that the Russians could threaten South Africa from the Territory. South Africa would then have to decide to invade the Territory in order to protect its interests. Such a situation would probably be less acceptable to the USA than the status quo. If SWAPO would govern South West Africa, Botswana would directly feel threatened, Dr Savimbi would be eliminated and South Africa would be totally encircled with Russian-inspired powers. If the entire Southern Africa then came under Russian tyranny, the strategic sea route around the Cape and its critical minerals would be lost to the West.[20]

In other words, yes to independence, but a definite no to a communist SWAPO government.[21] "There should be no doubt that South Africa did not want to have the red flag flying in Windhoek," Pik Botha told US Assistant Secretary of State for Africa, Dr Chester Crocker.[22] A top-secret report by the Directorate of Military Intelligence bluntly stated: "The RSA is planning to let the constitutional set-up in SWA develop in such a manner that a pro-SA government comes to power there."[23]

And so, on a security-strategic level, the war became an attempt to win enough time to create the conditions in which SWAPO would lose an election.[24]

At times, the South Africans did try half-heartedly to engage with SWAPO.

General Georg Meiring – who was GOC South West Africa at the time – related to Hilton Hamann how he, Dr Willie van Niekerk (South African Administrator General in SWA), and Foreign Affairs consultant Sean Cleary flew to the Cape Verde Islands in 1985 to try to get SWAPO to participate in a transitional government of national unity. According to Meiring, the guerrilla movement's reaction to this basically boiled down to: "Bugger you!"[25]

To Jannie Geldenhuys, who became one of the SADF's most influential strategic thinkers, the *time* factor was important. In itself, he reasoned, time was neutral – it was on the side of those who utilised it best. Therefore, the important thing was perseverance: "Soviet Russia," he wrote in his memoirs, "would in the long run not be able to keep up its attempt in Angola and with SWAPO. And if they withdrew, the scale would swing radically in our favour."[26] Geldenhuys and the other leading officers in the SADF knew they couldn't win the war against SWAPO (or, for that matter, the ANC) militarily. The most they could do was to stem the tide for a while in order to gain time. It was up to the politicians to utilise that time wisely in order to reach a tolerable political solution, as Constand Viljoen warned the government in the early 1980s.[27]

All of this meant that apartheid, race discrimination and colonial domination diminished, though not vanished, as *casus belli*. What remained was SWAPO's avowed aspiration to convert SWA into a Marxist one-party state (*see* Chapter 10), thereby enabling Pretoria, ironically enough, to present the conflict in the rather more respectable cloak of communist dictatorship versus liberal multiparty democracy. And that, we may surmise, weakened SWAPO and strengthened Pretoria to some extent.

The importance placed upon the military in South Africa's purported struggle for survival may also be seen in the increase in defence spending. From a very low R36 million in 1958/59, it increased to exactly double that in 1961/1962 (R72 million), but concomitant with the first security-strategic analysis conducted in 1961, it suddenly jumped to R129 million in the next financial year. The steady increases then resumed until the Savannah debacle, when the R692 million budgeted for 1974/1975 shot up sharply to R1 043 million for 1975/1976. By 1982/1983, the budget stood at R2 668 million. Put differently, whereas 0,9% of South Africa's Gross National Product (GNP) was allocated to defence in 1969/1970, by 1979/1980 this had risen to 5%.[28]

A strategy for Angola

Major General Jannie Geldenhuys took command in SWA in September 1977. To him and his staff at their headquarters in Windhoek, debating the question of how to turn a losing war into a winning one, things must have looked rather bleak. His orders, as relayed by the Chief of the SADF, General Magnus Malan, were "to keep the level of the insurgency at least at the level necessary to ensure that the constitutional development could take place in an atmosphere of stability and peace."[29] But SWAPO insurgents were infiltrating across the border in sufficient numbers to cause severe headaches to the South Africans, and the army's ham-fisted counterinsurgency operations had practically no success.

The key word was *initiative*. SWAPO had it; the SADF did not. This had to be changed around. But how?

There was a way, and Colonel Jan Breytenbach was the pioneer. Breytenbach took the FNLA troops he had commanded during Operation Savannah to South West Africa, and transformed them into a highly efficient and feared secret unit: 32 Battalion. With these fighters, who spoke Portuguese and the indigenous Angolan languages, he began clandestine cross-border operations against SWAPO soon after the SADF pulled out of Angola in the wake of Operation Savannah. Under his inspired but unorthodox leadership, 32 Battalion struck repeatedly inside Angola and harassed SWAPO in places where it deemed itself safe.

It was his intention, Breytenbach wrote, "to turn the southern Angolan bush into a menacing, hostile environment for SWAPO". In short, he wanted to "out-guerrilla the guerrillas". The purpose was "to get them off balance and keep them on the wrong foot until they began to collapse psychologically and subsequently also militarily".[30] (This approach was behind all SADF cross-border operations in the late 1970s and early 1980s.) The army allowed him to undertake clandestine operations – as the command directive put it, "to deny SWAPO an area of 50 kilometres north of the South West African border".[31] Nevertheless, by the end of 1977 it was clear to the SADF that even 32 Battalion's operations across the border were not enough.[32]

According to James Roherty, Geldenhuys noted, after taking over command in Windhoek,

[t]hat while South Africa was in a *strategic defensive posture* this must be understood in operational terms as requiring aggressive, offensive operations. It would be folly, he informed his superiors in Pretoria, to rely on defensive operations (or a defensive mind-set) in what would certainly be a protracted conflict. It reduces very simply, Geldenhuys argued, to a matter of casualties. The SADF cannot and must not sustain the casualties that would be an inevitable concomitant of manpower-intensive, counterinsurgency and conventional warfare. By carrying the war to the enemy – by inflicting disproportionally heavy casualties – the task becomes manageable. SADF units will have again to be trained in "the way of their forebears".[33]

Geldenhuys's approach, which was built on Breytenbach's example, was adopted by the SADF high command. In a document entitled "The SADF basic doctrine for counter insurgency (rural)", dated November 1977 and generated by the office of the Chief of Staff Operations, it was stated that hitherto the Defence Force's strategic doctrine "was based on defensive reaction". This meant that the insurgents, with their bases outside South Africa's borders, retained the initiative. Because of political considerations, the SADF could not go after them. "Freedom of action was thus largely the prerogative of the enemy and the SADF had perforce to dance to their tune."[34]

This had to change, the document stated. If the SADF remained on the defensive, offensive tactics notwithstanding, "it will not win the war against terrorism". Consequently, the SADF "must now go over to the strategic offensive if it hopes for any success against the communist insurgent strategy being employed against it". The object of such operations should be "destroying the terrorists, their organisation and infrastructure". The basic theme in counter-insurgency strategic doctrine, the document declared, "is to wrest the initiative from the terrorists by offensive action".[35] Here, in a nutshell, is the rationale for the series of cross-border offensives the SADF conducted into Angola in the decade between 1978 and 1988.

This type of posture was in line with South Africa's history. Successive governments had always seen the country's first defence line, not on its northern borders, but far northwards in Africa. This was, for instance, one of the rationales of Prime Minister Jan Smuts in taking South Africa to war against Italy and Germany in 1939.[36] This point of view was, of course, articulated with a view to the threat posed by Fascist Italy and Nazi Germany, but the idea took root that South Africa's true defence line should be as far to the north as possible. And this influenced thinking during the 1970s and 1980s as well.

How did all of this influence South Africa's view of Angola and the war between the MPLA and UNITA? In March 1978, Magnus Malan, then still Chief of the SADF, visited Salisbury and told the Rhodesians that South Africa's course was changing. He said that the military would in future dominate Pretoria's security policy, that a realpolitik approach would be followed, and that the interests of his country would be followed above all else. He said there would be no further compromise regarding South West Africa, and that the idea was to keep southern Angola destabilised, to assist UNITA and to attack SWAPO whenever the opportunity arose.[37]

A year later, Malan's thoughts crystallised in two documents for the State Security Council (SSC), in which a strategy regarding Angola was proposed. The second document made provision for the following: "The political situation in Angola must be kept as unstable and fluid as possible . . ." This aggressive thought was, however, motivated by a defensive purpose: "[T]o ensure the national security of SWA against the Marxist onslaught from without Angola." Therefore, the Angolan government had to be forced to "prevent SWAPO from deploying in South Angola".

The document refers to a future state "when the political situation, especially in South Angola, has improved to the extent that a stable anti-communist government can be brought to power to the advantage of Southern Africa". It further states that the Angolan rebel movements – UNITA, FNLA and FLEC – "should operate under the leadership of UNITA as a united front with the end objective to create an anti-Marxist government in Angola". South Africa also had to support UNITA, according to Malan.[38]

Not everyone agreed with Malan's aggressive stance. The reaction of the Department of Foreign Affairs was distinctly unenthusiastic: whatever their ideological preferences, the Angolan and Mozambican governments were both internationally recognised, and South Africa had to act circumspectly. "Our freedom of movement to bring about changes to the governments of these two countries is limited . . . We have to apply more orthodox diplomatic methods, of which the economic weapon constitutes an important part," the diplomats said.[39]

At about the same time, an agreement was reached between Jonas Savimbi, leader of UNITA, and senior officers of the SADF, according to which UNITA would clear the southeastern part of Angola and restore the lines of communication with South West Africa, while the SADF would take responsibility for the southwestern part.[40] This went hand in hand with a massive SADF aid programme to UNITA. According to a top-secret Military Intelligence report of 1979, South Africa had transferred about 1 400 tonnes of equipment to UNITA in the two previous years. In fact, "UNITA can thank the RSA for about 90% of its present force," the report stated. In addition "[i]f the RSA did not aid UNITA, UNITA would have vanished from the vicinity".[41]

South Africa's limited economic power over Angola may have been another factor that contributed to its more aggressive posture. In the mid-1970s, South Africa had accepted FRELIMO rule in Mozambique and refused to aid attempts by white Portuguese colonialists to prevent the liberation movement from coming to power. In this case, Pretoria had a powerful weapon – Mozambique's integration into the South African-dominated regional economy. Maputo's role as a port city was largely dependent on South African expertise and its position as the nearest import point to the Witwatersrand, South Africa's economic heart. A sizeable portion of the Mozambican working population were migrant labourers in the Republic. After the end of white rule in Rhodesia, South Africa supported the Mozambican rebel movement RENAMO, but this was in part a response to ANC terrorist attacks emanating from Mozambican soil. Its economic leverage enabled South Africa to intimidate Mozambique into signing a non-aggression pact early in 1984, restricting the ANC's ability to operate from that country.

In the case of Angola, South Africa possessed no comparable economic card. The country had its own railways, there were very few Angolan migrant labourers in South Africa, and its oil industry made Angola relatively independent.[42] This meant that not much else but military measures remained for Pretoria to exert pressure on Angola to stop its support for SWAPO. All these considerations meant that the SADF's approach, on the levels of military strategy, operations and tactics, was often aggressive and offensive. Nevertheless, the government remained on the defensive in terms of its security strategy.

The new South African strategy was part of a comprehensive reappraisal of South Africa's geostrategic position, of which the navy became an unfortunate but understandable victim. Traditionally, the navy was, like the rest of the Defence Force, almost a clone of the British mother service. Whereas the army and air force were fast changing their cultures, the navy could still not really be distinguished from the Royal Navy. This did not exactly endear the navy to the army and the air force.

In fact, the navy's posture and force structure were not even driven by South Africa's own needs. In terms of the Simon's Town Agreement of 1955, it was the British who decided what kind of navy South Africa would have, and it had to fit in with their global Cold War strategy. According to the agreement, Britain turned the Simon's Town naval base over to South Africa, in return for the country's playing a role in safeguarding the strategic Cape sea route. The agreement also allowed the navy to purchase anti-submarine frigates and mine-sweepers from Britain.[43] This was the main reason why many in the SADF regarded the navy "as a bit of an 'oddball'" and others even "as a complete anachronism" in the words of Vice Admiral Glen Syndercombe, Chief of the Navy in the 1980s.[44]

But four factors changed all of that. The first was the cancellation of the Simon's Town Agreement by the British Labour government in 1975. The second was the loss of Angola as a buffer territory, which focused strategic thinking very much on the country's continental war needs. Thirdly, there was the retirement, in late 1976, of the Chief of the SADF, Admiral Hugo Biermann, under whose long leadership the navy had fared rather well. He was succeeded by General Magnus Malan who – as did other army generals – viewed the navy and its expensive ships as something of an unaffordable luxury. The fourth factor was the imposition of a UN arms embargo against South Africa. This meant that France cancelled a contract for two corvettes and two submarines, and refused to sell further aircraft as well. Most of the available resources were thereafter used for the development of army and air force weapons systems.

Against this background, the SADF, with input from navy officers, produced two documents, the so-called Mandy and Hogg reports. These questioned the navy's role as custodian of the Cape sea route and, in effect, recommended that the force be transformed to concentrate on coastal defence. At about the same time, Minister of Defence PW Botha announced that South Africa would no longer defend the Cape sea route on behalf of the West.[45] This meant that the navy's frigates would be phased out, and it would concentrate on its new Israeli fast missile strike craft and submarines.[46] As Admiral Syndercombe wrote,

> the frigates, fine ships though they were, were not what we required in our existing operational scenario. We needed small, fast ships with massive surface to surface firepower to present an effective counter to the missile-armed fast attack craft being supplied to the Angolan Navy by the Soviet Union. Their small size also meant that they were difficult to detect, either visually or by radar, while their shallow draft, speed and manoeuvrability gave them the ability to penetrate into restricted waters where other vessels dared not go.[47]

The strike craft and submarines would play a substantial but unsung role in inserting and extracting special force operators behind enemy lines.

Angola: the political objectives

The fact that the proposals in General Malan's strategic reviews of 1979 about an offensive posture towards Angola were formally accepted by the State Security Council elevated them to the level of official, albeit clandestine, policy. That, at least, was the case in 1979. In some SADF documents, there are casual comments that show that the military saw a regime change in Luanda as their eventual goal.[48] But none of these documents presented any operational plan to achieve it. Did it ever go beyond mere proposals? Several considerations suggest it did not.

Firstly, one should remember that the South African state was not a single, monolithic entity. From the outside, US Secretary of George Shultz remarked to President Ronald Reagan that "[t]he South African leadership is of several minds and the military, in particular, is disinclined to take chances or to favour negotiated solutions".[49] Malan's aggressiveness, for instance, was not greeted with whoops of joy by Foreign Affairs officials.

Secondly, the SADF's military strategy shows that all operations up to 1985 were not primarily aimed at FAPLA, the Angolan army, but at SWAPO. In at least one instance, the South African government warned its Angolan counterpart in diplomatic language of an impending SADF cross-border operation, and assured Luanda of South Africa's "consistent policy" that these actions were aimed "solely against SWAPO terrorists and any contact with forces of the People's Republic of Angola is avoided".[50] (Of course, UNITA's guerrilla operations against the MPLA necessitated the deployment of about 50% of SWAPO's forces to help the MPLA, which meant that far fewer SWAPO fighters were available to infiltrate SWA.)[51] The first SADF operations specifically aimed at FAPLA took place only in 1985 and 1986, and then they were on a small, clandestine scale. As we shall see later, the 1987 operation started the same way, suggesting that a forcible regime change in Luanda was not on the immediate military agenda.

Documents in the archive of the Department of Foreign Affairs tend to support this conclusion. In 1984, Pik Botha told Chester Crocker that peace in southern Africa would be impossible if the Soviets took over Angola, as this would help them to take over the entire region. Therefore, it was necessary to achieve "reconciliation" between the MPLA and UNITA; the two had to be forced to talk to each other.[52] On the face of it, it seemed as if South Africa was still committed to the Alvor Agreement of January 1975, according to which the MPLA, the FNLA and UNITA had to form an interim government of national unity to prepare for free elections. But things were not quite that simple.

Although it never happened, President PW Botha and Pik Botha at times actively considered the unilateral recognition of UNITA as the sovereign government of Angola.[53] As Pik Botha explained to a sympathetic Namibian interim government in 1985:

> You can only get Cuban withdrawal if there is reconciliation in Angola. If you get reconciliation in Angola, [President José Eduardo] Dos Santos is finished. The moment they start talking to [UNITA leader Jonas]

> Savimbi, and this is Dr Savimbi's own assessment, we agree, then this present regime in Luanda is finished, and then SWAPO will be finally finished as well.[54]

The South Africans were thus in favour of "reconciliation", of talks between the MPLA and UNITA in the hope of replacing the Marxist MPLA with the friendly UNITA by peaceful means. Not that the South Africans had very much hope of this happening; they and the Americans agreed that "no Angolan party can achieve an outright military victory". If the Cubans were withdrawn, they thought that UNITA could control maybe 60 to 70% of Angola, less if the Cubans stayed on.[55] By 1979, the Directorate of Military Intelligence estimated that UNITA had the support of about 45% of the Angolan population, against 25% for the MPLA.[56] Regardless of its accuracy, the point is that the South Africans were expecting that an election would put UNITA into power in Luanda.

The picture emerging from all of this, then, is that the National Party government would very much have preferred a friendly, anti-communist government under UNITA. Malan's very aggressive stance of 1979, however, was never implemented. It seems as if the South Africans were realistic enough to realise that they did not have the military means to topple the MPLA.

Conversely, South Africa's aid to UNITA proved to be counterproductive in one important regard. The MPLA feared that South Africa was bent on regime change, and therefore aided all South African enemies – SWAPO, the ANC, Zimbabwe and others – in the hope that the fall of the NP government would ease the pressure on Luanda.[57]

The South African strategy was shared, by and large, by the Reagan administration. In a 1987 review of its policy, the White House decided to continue with its attitude, which was "[t]o achieve an equitable internal settlement of the Angolan conflict that affords UNITA a fair share of power". Also, "Soviet and Soviet-proxy influence, military presence and opportunities in Angola and southern Africa" had to be reduced or, if possible, eliminated.[58]

The presence of some 30 000 Cuban troops in Angola obviously complicated things. Fidel Castro, we now know, intervened in 1975 on his own initiative and without informing the Soviets, much less asking their permission.[59] Thereafter, Castro's main reason for staying on was to "protect" the Angolan revolution from the "racist" South Africans, and not so much to help the MPLA win its struggle with UNITA, which he apparently viewed as an internal affair.[60]

Predictably, this is not how the South Africans – or the Americans, for that matter – saw it. In SADF documents, the Cubans are often referred to as "surrogate forces". And so, in 1981, South Africa and the US concluded an informal pact to demand the departure of the Cubans from Angola as a prerequisite for the SADF's withdrawal from Angola and the implementation of Namibian independence – the much-maligned concept of "linkage".[61] In view of the perceived Cuban/Soviet threat, the South Africans definitely saw their military presence in Angola and SWA as defensive in nature.[62] As General Malan – then still Chief of the SADF – explained in 1979 at a meeting of the SSC,

> [t]he question was whether we are going to implement a forward defensive strategy or a close strategy. We want to ensure the RSA's national security outside the RSA . . . If we look at the Rhodesian front, the Mozambican front and the Angolan front, we see that the crisis is coming. The most forward defence line should be outside the Republic. We should be able to choose the time and place.[63]

PW Botha, then still prime minister, agreed. As long as he was prime minister, he assured the meeting, "he was not going to engage South Africa's battle on its own territory. We now know what the Russian intentions are and that they have the ability to bring troops quickly to Southern Africa"[64] – a reference to the influx of Cuban troops into Angola in 1975.

The Americans did not always agree with the South Africans' blunt approach, but there certainly was a convergence of interests, as perceived in Washington and Pretoria. In his memoirs, Chester Crocker explained the US thinking:

> The Cuban troop withdrawal link would bring pressure on Luanda to reconcile with UNITA. It would prevent a Namibia settlement from occurring at UNITA's expense. Cuban withdrawal from Southern Africa was inherently attractive in its own right and in terms of US–Soviet relations. Finally, it would give us the leverage we would need to obtain South African cooperation on Namibian independence.[65]

The question of linkage would become the central issue surrounding the international wrangling about South West Africa and Angola. It would also, in the end, provide the excuse for South Africa to leave SWA, and for Cuba to withdraw its troops from Angola. But all of this lay in the future.

One final point to make is that, obviously, the world looked very different when viewed from Luanda. In 1977, UNITA proclaimed a "Black African and Socialist Republic of Angola" in the areas under its control, but, according to an American researcher, this "was not designed as a secessionist move". Nevertheless, the fear in Luanda was not only that this "UNITA state" would gain international recognition, but that South Africa "was once again attempting to create a 'Great Ovambo State' under its own aegis that would unify the Cuanhama [Kwanyama] speaking communities of northern Namibia and southern Angola". The researcher described "tremendous alarm and paranoia in Luanda". Late in 1978, the Angolan Minister of Defence, Iko Carreira, even publicly alleged that South Africa was on the verge of invading Angola again in order to capture Lubango, Huambo and Luanda itself.[66]

As we have seen, however, this fear did not rest on facts. The story emerging from secret South African documents is very different. But that did not make the fear less real.

5

INTO ANGOLA: REINDEER

By the beginning of 1978, the South African government was in deep trouble on a number of fronts. Only two years before, the black township of Soweto had exploded in an orgy of violence because of anger and resentment about the injustices of apartheid and the petty restrictions it imposed on black South Africans. In late 1977, the UN had imposed an arms embargo on the Republic. The cracks were even beginning to show in the united façade of the governing National Party, which would split within four years. The Vorster government's reach-out programme to black African states had been shattered by the Savannah debacle. In these circumstances, it was logical that the influence of the hawks within government, with Minister of Defence PW Botha at the helm, would increase. This led to a more aggressive strategy, which resulted in a whole series of large and small cross-border operations into Angola and other neighbouring states to smoke out the insurgent movements sheltering there. Within a decade, South Africa would find itself teetering on the brink of an all-out war with Cuba and Angola.

After Operation Savannah, the government at first forbade SADF forces to cross the border into Angola. SAAF aircraft had to take care to stay out of Angolan airspace. An exception was made for 32 Battalion, whose black Angolan soldiers could infiltrate their home country clandestinely and could attack SWAPO in the "shallow" areas near the border without political ramifications. Under Colonel Jan Breytenbach, the unit repeatedly attacked across the border: "We had to get them off balance, take away the initiative and act as the spoiler in their attempts to overrun Ovamboland." As 32 Battalion at this time operated mostly in southeastern Angola, SWAPO vacated the area and moved westwards to Cunene province, where the SADF did not have a big presence.[1] In addition, the Special Forces, the Reconnaissance regiments (generally known as the Recces), carried out small-scale clandestine operations against SWAPO north of the border.[2]

But these actions proved to be insufficient. As Brigadier General As Kleynhans explained: "The area was too big and the border was too long. The terrain made it difficult too, [it was] flat with no natural lookout points. We did not have the capacity to close the border, it always remained permeable."[3] At the end of January 1978, Commandant Gert Nel, who took over from Breytenbach as commander of 32 Battalion, reported that SWAPO "had the initiative in this area [eastern Ovamboland] and also throughout enjoys the support and aid of the local population".[4]

There was only one way to recapture the strategic initiative: escalation. In a report dated 27 February 1978, the first of a series of SADF analyses of the military situation in South West Africa, it was argued that SWAPO had been successful in building up its strength in Ovamboland and the Eastern Caprivi. It was expected that SWAPO would have a force of 5 000 by the end of 1978, although only 1 000 of these were operationally deployable in the short term. Between 250 and 300 insurgents were active in Ovamboland. It therefore became imperative to employ the SADF's full force against SWAPO across the border, instead of relying only on the defensive "hearts and minds" strategy.[5] In fact, Military Intelligence started getting reports of an increasing SWAPO presence in Angola's Cunene province, and it became clear that the area was being developed – in Jan Breytenbach's words – "as an extensive guerrilla base area".[6]

In a second document, undated but apparently written in March or April 1978, it was bluntly stated that the situation in SWA was entering "an unacceptable turn" due to SWAPO's military activity. The movement was becoming "ever more audacious with well-planned operations". SWAPO's political influence was high, and for this to change meaningfully, its "military capability had to be given a knock-out blow".[7]

In his MA thesis on the battle of Cassinga, Brigadier General McGill Alexander summarised a third, even more important, document of 1 April 1978:

> SWAPO was clearly capable of acting in the "traditional terrorist manner", but also where necessary to act more aggressively and in larger groups with the required firepower and mobility in a reasonably

effective way. SWAPO, claimed the document, had established a considerable number of bases in southern Angola from which it conducted military operations across the border as well as doing limited training and delivering logistical support. SWAPO actions north of the border were displaying a tendency to make more use of conventional weapons.

In sharp contrast to this, it was stated in the document, the SADF had concentrated in the past few years on "counter-terrorist" operations and had to a degree fallen into the rut of carrying out specific, elementary actions because it was seldom possible, and was in any case not permitted, to employ the full military potential of the Army and the Air Force against targets. It was further stated that it was militarily unacceptable to allow SWAPO to be trained in safe areas north of the border in order to concentrate for attacks on South Africa in northern Namibia. More than 50% of SWAPO's activities in Namibia, it was claimed, took place in the immediate border areas. The initiative, it was emphasised, therefore remained in the hands of the "terrorists" whilst the SADF was compelled to merely react.[8]

This alarming view was confirmed when the Chief of the SADF, General Magnus Malan, was briefed in Oshakati on 12 April on the worsening security situation in Ovamboland. Not only was SWAPO freely holding well-attended meetings at various places to politicise the locals, but also the youth were being particularly influenced. Intelligence was reporting "open SWAPO support in the rural areas". Militarily, the movement was "acting more purposefully. Moves in big groups. Carries out attacks on the Security Forces. Prepares ambushes and lays mines. Invades territory to the Golden Highway." Some of the attacks were carried out by groups 100 to 150 strong, Malan was told.[9] Several pro-South African headmen were assassinated, land mines exploded, and a bus with 73 passengers (mostly women and children) was hijacked and forced to enter Angola.[10] Something clearly had to be done.

The preparation for this "something" had started some months earlier, on 31 December, when Prime Minister John Vorster met the Minister of Defence, PW Botha, his Foreign Affairs colleague, Pik Botha, the Chief of the SADF,

General Magnus Malan, the Secretary of Foreign Affairs, Brand Fourie, and the Chief of the Army, Lieutenant General Constand Viljoen, at Vorster's holiday home at Oubos, on the Garden Route. There, the intrinsically cautious Vorster was moved to concede the principle of a cross-border operation, provided that he personally approved it.[11]

The South African strategic appreciation was that SWAPO was intensifying its military onslaught in order to strengthen its position in any future negotiations. PW Botha in particular was afraid that this could contribute to a SWAPO victory at the ballot box. Operation Reindeer was meant to tarnish the guerrilla movement's prestige in view of possible internationally supervised elections. Botha felt that SWAPO's military power "had to be broken before elections are held".[12]

By April, it was decided to attack two SWAPO bases in Angola: Cassinga, a mining town about 260 km north of the border, and Chetequera, just 22 km from the border. To SWAPO operatives, Cassinga was known as "Moscow" and Chetequera as "Vietnam". As Cassinga was too far for a conventional mechanised force to reach, destroy and pull back from without an unacceptable confrontation with Angolan and perhaps even Cuban troops, the weapon of choice was a paratroop force. Chetequera, which was seen as a major supply base and a centre for control and planning for operations in western Ovamboland, would be attacked with a mobile conventional ground force. Several other smaller bases just north of the border would be attacked simultaneously.[13]

Unlike Savannah, which was an intervention in the Angolan civil war, Operation Reindeer, and those that followed it (until 1985, at any rate), was aimed primarily at SWAPO. If FAPLA or the Cubans placed themselves in the line of the South African fire, that would be, as it were, collateral damage.

Cassinga: the plan

The parachute assault on Cassinga was preceded by a series of clandestine cross-border operations by 32 Battalion, with the aim of harassing PLAN inside Angola. Patrols were sent out to locate and hit SWAPO concentrations in the "shallow" border areas before they could reach South West Africa.[14] In one of these, elements of 32 Battalion and Reconnaissance commandos paired up to attack

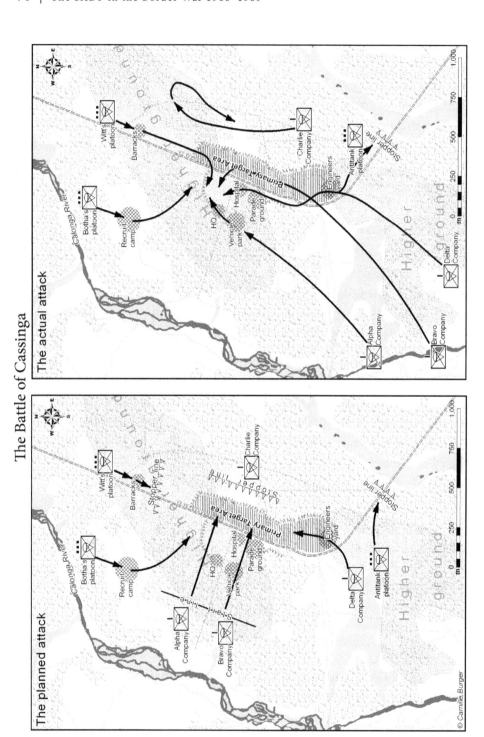

The Battle of Cassinga

The actual attack

The planned attack

© Camille Burger

Eheke, an operational SWAPO headquarters. It was a bitter fight, in which the SADF soldiers suffered heavy losses, but it resulted in SWAPO's eviction. One consequence of this battle was that the SADF realised that the highly trained elite Recces should not be used as infantry; henceforth, they were used mainly for clandestine work such as sabotage and reconnaissance.[15] More importantly, PLAN decided to relocate its headquarters to Cassinga, which was judged safe.[16] This was where the SADF decided to hit SWAPO. The assault would be placed under the command of Colonel Jan Breytenbach, one of the ablest tactical officers in the army.[17]

From a military-historical point of view, the Battle of Cassinga was one of the most interesting engagements of the entire Border War.[18] It was the first, and last, use of the concept of "vertical envelopment", that is, outflanking the enemy by going over his head, instead of around his flanks. The decision was to drop 370 paratroopers, mainly from 2 and 3 Parachute Battalions (both part-time Citizen Force units), as well as an independent platoon from the full-time conscript 1 Parachute Battalion. A company from 3 Para would form the reserve, to be employed only if necessary.

The paratroopers would be dropped by six Lockheed C-130 Hercules and Transall C-160 transport aircraft, with another three C-160s on standby with reserve troops and extra supplies, if needed. The SAAF had the airlift capacity for more troops, but the problem was how to get the men back after the battle. Cassinga had no airstrip, so there was no way to land and extract the troops by fixed-wing transport aircraft. It was a full 260 km inside Angola; therefore walking back was not an option. The plan, therefore, was to send in a force of helicopters to extract them. Breytenbach had originally wanted a force of 450 paratroopers, but the number of troops was restricted on the basis of the available helicopter airlift capacity (19 Super Frelons and Pumas).

The plan was to hit Cassinga hard with a sudden air bombardment by four Canberra and four Buccaneer bombers, immediately followed by a 30-mm cannon strafing attack by two Mirage IIICZ fighters. While the enemy was still reeling from the noise and confusion, the main ground attack force, two companies of paratroopers (Alpha and Bravo) would be dropped west of the target and advance eastwards through the objective. One company (Charlie) would be dropped to the east, the independent platoon to the north and one company (Delta) to the south to act as stopper groups when the PLAN fighters started fleeing. ("We did not really expect them to stand and fight," Breytenbach comments.[19]) A mortar platoon with 60-mm mortars and steel helmets for base plates (there were 12 mortars in total) would be available to support the attack, while an antitank platoon with RPG-7 rockets and antitank mines would be dropped to the south to counter any attempt by the mixed Cuban/FAPLA force at Techamutete to intervene.

At the same time, a so-called helicopter administrative area (code-named Whisky 3) would be established 22 km east of Cassinga to allow the chopper force to land and refuel prior to extracting the paratroopers. After the fight, the choppers would transport half the force (plus a maximum of 16 prisoners) to Whisky 3, return to Cassinga and extract the rest of the soldiers. Then they would be transported back to Eenhana in Ovamboland in two flights.[20]

A few comments about this plan, which posed several risks: Reindeer was a complex, finely tuned operation that depended on various (in themselves reasonable) assumptions and, most importantly, on extremely efficient organisation. The air assets in particular had to be managed almost to the second. For instance, the transport aircraft had to arrive at the target only seconds after the Canberras and Buccaneers had dropped their bombs, which required the juggling of take-off times and time to target. Because the choppers had to be back in SWA before nightfall, the attack had to be finished by midday. An eyeball investigation of the helicopter administrative area's suitability could be undertaken only at daybreak on 4 May. The bombers' attack on Chetequera, which would take place after the assault on Cassinga, had to be factored into the air support plan as well.

In addition, there were two wild cards. The one was a mixed Cuban/FAPLA battle group, based at Techamutete, 15 km south of Cassinga, with a troop of tanks, a mechanised infantry company or two with BTR-152 armoured personnel carriers, plus some motorised infantry and anti-aircraft guns. Planners reckoned that it would take them four hours to reach Cassinga. The tanks, it is true, were Second World War-vintage T-34/85s, and the BTRs were almost equally ancient, but they would still be more than a match for a lightly armed parachute force lacking heavy weapons. The other wild card was the presence of Cuban MiG-21 fighters at the airbases of Lubango and Menongue, both within range.

Essentially, there were many points at which things could go very wrong. Moreover, because each phase was so dependent on the others, any hitch could create a chain reaction and end in a humiliating defeat for the entire mission. Not only would this be catastrophic on a tactical and operational level, but it would also be a major setback to the entire South African war effort.

On the other hand, calculated risk-taking is intrinsically part of war. No operation is ever without risk. The trick is to foresee where things can go wrong, to be flexible and think on your feet, to react quickly enough to unexpected developments, and to build in – in terms of planning, training and equipment – a kind of cushion to absorb unexpected problems when (not if!) they occur. The SADF's "cushion" against the Cuban threat was an antitank platoon and one of the Buccaneer bombers, while a DC-4, fitted with sophisticated ELINT (electronic intelligence) equipment, would act as an airborne early warning system against any MiG interference. Four Mirage IIICZs from 2 Squadron (the famed "Flying Cheetahs") were also added almost at the last minute to counter the threat from the MiGs.

In hindsight, this was woefully inadequate. As we shall see, there were simply not enough ground-attack aircraft on the scene to counter the Cuban threat. The Mirage IIIs were interceptors, not really bombers, and their limited range meant that they could not stay above the battlefield for longer than a few minutes. The four Mirages, which also had to stand in as back-up ground attackers, were also insufficient to counter a determined MiG intervention from Lubango or Menongue. Fortunately, such an intervention never happened, but that changes nothing about the fact that the SADF had too little air capacity at Cassinga.[21]

The ground plan was tactically sound, making maximum use of shock effect and surprise. There would, in effect, be a double surprise. The Calonga River, which flows north–south to the west of the town, formed a natural barrier, and so the SWAPO defences were strongest to the north, east and south. They were not expecting a thrust from the west, and yet this is exactly what Breytenbach and his planners decided to do. Furthermore, being so far from the border, the SWAPO fighters felt safe in Cassinga, and never expected a parachute assault.[22]

When everything is taken into account, the boldness of the operation was an important factor in its eventual success.

Political considerations played an important role in the timing of the operation. South Africa had just accepted UN Security Council Resolution 435, and with it the prospect of Namibian independence and elections under UN supervision. However, the Vorster government still felt the need to project a strong image and to deal SWAPO a heavy blow in order to diminish the rebel movement's capacity to win an election. After all, SWAPO leader Sam Nujoma had only recently proclaimed that his movement was fighting for total power and that elections were unimportant to them (*see* Chapter 10).

The date of Operation Reindeer was shifted repeatedly, until, finally, word came through that the operation was set for 4 May. The paratroopers, who had been training hard in total isolation in the Orange Free State province, were informed of their mission. They then boarded the C-130 and C-160 aircraft and were flown to Grootfontein Air Force Base on 3 May in preparation for the big day – the largest air assault in South African military history.

In order to mislead the enemy, a large combined mechanised infantry and parachute exercise, known as Exercise Kwiksilwer, was laid on at Schmidtsdrif at the same time as the operation. However, the paratroopers and the Ratel troops involved in Operation Reindeer never showed up.

Cassinga: the battle

The Prussian general Helmuth von Moltke (1800–1891) reputedly said that no battle plan ever survives first contact with the enemy. The Battle of Cassinga was no exception. In fact, things began to go wrong even before the first transport aircraft left Bloemspruit Air Force Base for Grootfontein. The aerial-photo interpreters had misjudged the height at which the photos of Cassinga had been taken, and consequently used the wrong scale and got the distances on the ground wrong. Based on this, incorrect information was given to the transport pilots about exactly when to start the paratroop drop. Also, the photographs were about six months old and had been taken in the dry season, when the Calonga River was little more than a trickle. On the day of the attack, the river was full.

At 07h50 the Canberras dropped a total of 1 200 antipersonnel bombs;

they were followed shortly afterwards by the Buccaneers, which dropped 32 high-explosive bombs (450 kg each). This air strike was timed to coincide with the camp's morning mustering parade, and the attack caused enormous carnage on the parade ground. The Buccaneers' ordnance was of Second World War vintage, and exploded with great sound and fury, but signified not very much. It brought down a few buildings and left great craters in which PLAN fighters could take cover and make life difficult for the attackers. The smoke caused by the first attacks obscured the Buccaneer pilots' view, and some of their bombs fell in the bush south of the camp without any effect. Also, the most important part of the base – the heavily defended headquarters complex – was not hit at all, since it had not been identified by the aerial-photo interpreters.

While the Mirages swooped over Cassinga, their 30-mm cannon chattering, the paratroopers commenced their drop, which went awry from the start. Because of the photo interpreters' mistake, the soldiers were dropped too late and had to struggle with a stronger-than-expected northeasterly wind. Instead of landing between the village and the river to its west, a sizeable part of Alpha and Bravo companies landed spread out across the western side of river and to the southwest. About a third to a half of them first had to struggle across the swollen river.

The tactical plan was in a shambles. On the other side, Charlie Company was also dropped late and to the southeast of the target, instead of due east. The two platoons to be dropped to the north landed in the village, right on top of the defenders, while only Delta Company, to the south, came down more or less in their intended landing zone. Breytenbach's forces were therefore in the wrong positions. This also left many gaps through which some SWAPO fighters – including PLAN commander-in-chief Dimo Hamaambo (nom de guerre "Jesus") – promptly escaped. Hamaambo was nowhere to be found for the rest of the day, and his fighters had to battle alone and leaderless.

Any combat parachute drop is followed by a period of confusion – hopefully very short – in which the commander has to establish control over the battle. At Cassinga, Breytenbach had an almost impossible struggle to succeed, but the highly aggressive paratroopers immediately attacked the enemy fighters wherever they found them. Having established the whereabouts of his troops,

Breytenbach proved what an excellent tactician he was. He decided to change the axis of attack – planned to be from west to east – to south to north. A suitable site to cross the river was found, and with Alpha and Bravo companies forming up to the south and southeast of Cassinga, the attack could finally begin, albeit 60 to 90 minutes behind schedule.

This delay had serious consequences. Firstly, it meant that the PLAN fighters had time to recover from the shock and confusion of the air attack. Secondly, the whole tactical plan, daring as it was, depended upon speed. The troops had to be inserted quickly, do the job posthaste and then be extracted. It was cutting things very fine indeed. The delay also would give the Cuban battle group at Techamutete additional time to react.

What is more, unknown to the South Africans, a mechanised combat group of FAPLA tanks, guns and infantry under Cuban officers was also rushing in from the north. Umkhonto we Sizwe (MK) member Joseph Kobo, who was with them, related how they saw everything happening in the distance, but arrived at the battlefield just too late to intervene. Only years later, when he was discussing the matter with Kobo, it dawned on Breytenbach that his force had narrowly escaped being attacked not only from the south, but from the north too.[23] This scenario had not been foreseen during the planning phase.

Meanwhile, from the north, the independent platoon advanced against relatively light opposition, driving the defenders before them, until they encountered their compatriots coming from the opposite direction. Simultaneously, with Alpha Company on the left and Bravo on the right, Breytenbach launched his main attack northwards. It began well, with the attackers making good progress, especially Bravo Company. This force was for a time stopped by heavy machine-gun fire, but the advance of the independent platoon in the north put paid to this.

Alpha came up against formidable defences, especially a mix of at least one 23-mm cannon and some 14,5-mm and 12,7-mm heavy machine guns, which, together with other light machine guns, pinned the South Africans down under a hail of fire. From the north, the defenders' escape route was now cut off, so they stood and fought where they were – either with the desperation of fear or considerable bravery. With accurate rifle and mortar fire, the South Africans killed the SWAPO gun crews several times, but again and again there was no shortage of defenders to take their dead comrades' places and continue firing. Each time the attackers thought the guns were silenced, only to hear the deadly staccato stuttering resume after a few seconds.

In the end, Breytenbach sent two platoons from his reserve in Delta Company in a left flanking attack, which had to clear a whole zigzag trench system metre by metre – a savage, messy and bloody affair. In the process, many civilians, even children, hiding among the fighters in the trenches were also killed. In the chaotic circumstances, nobody could afford to ask questions first. Some of the defenders were women, but armed and in uniform, fighting and dying bravely. At last, the heavy machine guns were silenced, and in Cassinga itself the surviving PLAN defenders started surrendering.

Charlie Company had also cleared the trenches on the eastern outskirts of the town. At this point, another problem cropped up in the form of Brigadier Martiens du Plessis, who had jumped with the paratroop force but had no place in the command structure. However, not only did he appropriate Breytenbach's only radio able to communicate with the operational headquarters at Ondangwa, but he ordered the choppers from Whisky 3 to start the extraction procedure prematurely. Although the climax of the battle was past, Cassinga was not yet totally secured. The decision threw the carefully crafted extraction plan into disarray.

Together with the first wave of helicopters, an unexpected visitor turned up – the dapper, white-haired figure of Lieutenant General Constand Viljoen, Chief of the Army. A real soldier's soldier, he wanted to see and experience things for himself. One cannot but admire him for this, although he arrived in full rank insignia, to the consternation of the officers on the ground.

But more problems loomed to the south. The Cubans and Angolans at Techamutete had awoken to the sounds of battle and were on their way in force. In fact, they were quite slow in reacting. According to a Cuban source, the local commander had to get permission first from the Cuban commanding general in Luanda, and this was slow in coming.[24] Nevertheless, this was even more of a problem than it should have been, as Delta Company, which was supposed to support the antitank platoon exactly against this eventuality, was unilaterally pulled back by Du Plessis and sent off with the first load of troops being evacuated. This left only the antitank platoon, with its nine RPG-7s and 45 rockets, to stop the advance of an entire mechanised battle group. With some paratroopers having been flown out already, the remaining force numbered perhaps 200. It was a very precarious situation.

This problem was exacerbated when the antitank platoon was ordered – it is not known by whom, although it was not Breytenbach – to vacate their carefully chosen ambush position a kilometre south of Cassinga and pull back to a position on the outskirts. When the enemy battle group arrived, they were nevertheless hit with everything the platoon had to offer, and the Cubans and Angolans suffered heavily. But it also meant that the battle group was now on Cassinga's doorstep, and thus a far greater menace than if had they been engaged further away from the town. It would take some time before the helicopters would be able to return, so Breytenbach and his men were, to put it mildly, up the creek without a paddle. The battle was balanced on a knife-edge between success and disaster. Even Constand Viljoen, expecting to be captured, took off his rank insignia and general's beret and hid them.

Breytenbach asked Ondangwa urgently for air support. The problem was that the attack on Chetequera was about to commence, and the bombers were needed for that part of the operation. So the Mirages were scrambled and one Buccaneer diverted to cover the paratroopers. The Mirages, of course, were interceptors and not configured for tank attacks, although the Buccaneer was. What happened next was drama of the highest order. The story is perhaps best taken up by Captain Dries Marais, pilot of the Buccaneer, who flew with navigator Ernie Harvey:

> As I rolled into my dive attack on the tanks, which had by now reached the outskirts of Cassinga, in front of me, just settling into their attack, were the two Mirages. The 30 mm HE rounds of the first one exploded ineffectively on the lead tank and I called out to the second aircraft to leave the tanks alone and go for the personnel carriers. The pilot confirmed my request and the next moment I was overjoyed with pride as I witnessed my closest friend, Major Johan Radloff, whose voice I had immediately recognised, take out three BTRs with a single burst from his twin cannon.
>
> Turning round for another pass, we could see the first tank burning

like a furnace, and on this run, the lead Mirage pilot destroyed no fewer than five BTRs with a long burst, running his shells in movie-like fashion through them. *"Dis hoe die boere skiet, julle ****sems!"* were my thoughts and then our second salvo of 12 rockets, every third one with an armour-piercing head, also struck home.

In a matter of seconds, two tanks and about 16 armoured personnel carriers had been completely destroyed, and then the Mirages were down to their minimum combat fuel and they had to retire leaving us to deal with the rest.

We decided to concentrate on the tanks, and then things started happening. Most of the BTRs were trailing twin-barrelled 14,5-mm anti-aircraft guns, and some of them were now deployed and shooting at us. Even one of the tanks was firing with its main weapon and I remember being amused at the gunner's optimism at hitting a manoeuvring target travelling at 600 knots.

Ernie, on the other hand, was far from amused, as he was not, like me, in a state of aggression and experiencing tunnel vision. Keeping a good look out all around, he was actually aware of several AA [anti-aircraft] positions firing at us. He was even less impressed at my dismissal of the problem, but my whole system was now charged to take out the remaining tanks.

As we turned in again, these two tanks left the road and disappeared into the bush. We destroyed another BTR, but decided to save our ammunition for the tanks. Flying around trying to locate them, I became annoyed with one AA site, which kept up a steady stream of tracer in our direction and decided to take it out. It was, in fact, the gun which had been towed by the BTR we had just destroyed, and to this day I can only have respect for the discipline and courage of the gun crew and some troops who kept up their firing – even with their small arms – until my rockets exploded amongst them, killing the lot and destroying the gun.

As I broke off from this attack, the huge gaggle of helicopters passed underneath us and landed in the pre-planned area to pick up the troops. By this time I had learned that the Chief of the Army, Lieut General Viljoen, was on the ground with them, and that there was grave concern for his safety.

Then, as the helicopters were landing, the remaining two tanks reappeared on the road and started shelling the landing area which was in a shallow depression. Because of this, and the inability of that particular type of tank to lower its gun far enough, they were fortunately over the target, and, calculating that we had 12 rockets left, I asked Ernie to give me only six, leaving another salvo for the other tank.

Timing was critical as the tanks were beginning to find their range. I realised that they HAD to be stopped. It was a textbook, low-angle attack, and the "Buc" was as steady as a rock in the dive. It was like lining up on a trophy kudu bull after a perfect stalk, but when I pulled the trigger, nothing happened – no rockets, not even one.

I jerked the aircraft around, almost in agony, cursing Ernie for having selected the wrong switches. He was quite adamant that he had selected the switches correctly, and then we went in for another attack, but with the same heart-stopping result.

Without really thinking it out, I opened the throttles wide and kept the aircraft in the dive, levelling off at the last moment, and flying over the tank very low and doing nearly Mach One.

Turning, we went in again from the front, this time doing the same thing with the tank once more shooting at us. I assumed that the crew would have no idea that we were out of ammunition, and hoping to intimidate them, we continued to make fast, head-on low level mock attacks. The Buccaneer from close up is an intimidating aircraft. Flying low, it makes a terrific noise compressed into a single instant as a shock wave, and if this had an amplified resonance inside the tank, the crew would have to be well-trained to stay with it, were my thoughts!

Again I can only praise God, for I remember distinctly having felt during those minutes which followed, being an instrument in His hands; myself a perfect part of the aircraft, and He the Pilot. As it was, the tank crews were eventually sufficiently intimidated to once again seek cover in the heavy bush, enabling the helicopters to load their precious cargo and get away safely.[25]

After Marais returned to Grootfontein, an astounding 17 hits were counted on the Buccaneer. This included a 76-mm hit through one of the wings and a 37-mm AA hit through the port wing flap. There were 14,5-mm hits through both engines and a 14,5-mm hit right through the windscreen. Marais received the Honoris Crux for his bravery.

The air attack provided enough cover for the choppers to land and take aboard the South Africans still on the ground. Obviously, the carefully planned order of extraction was thrown to the winds, and everybody scrambled onto any available helicopter, an understandable measure of panic helping them along. The surviving Cuban T-34 was at this stage only 200 m away, but it happened to be on an up-slope and could not depress its gun enough to be accurate. Its shells burst way beyond the South Africans. Some civilians pleaded with the officers to be taken home, claiming they had been abducted. They even tried to clamber aboard, but there was simply no room and the soldiers were the first priority. By then, the Cuban tank was taking pot shots at the choppers.

One Puma, piloted by Major John Church, spotted a soldier left behind, waving forlornly to the departing choppers. Church did not hesitate. He turned back, landed, and not one, but five, paratroopers frantically scrambled aboard. He took off again, this time under heavy small-arms and tank fire. But he got away and flew a final circuit over the mining town to make doubly sure no one had been left behind. The battle was over. Four South African soldiers had died and 12 had been wounded. The Buccaneer that had replaced that of Dries Marais fired a few parting shots, while two Mirages destroyed the last of the Cuban tanks and shot up the town again.

Cassinga: the controversy

The attack on Cassinga was undoubtedly the single most controversial battle of the entire Border War. Subsequent to the battle, a major controversy developed around the nature of the camp at Cassinga. Was it, as SWAPO claimed, a refugee camp housing hundreds of civilians (mainly women and children who had fled, in SWAPO's view, cruel colonial oppression), or was it, as the SADF said, a military planning, logistics and training base? The fact that about 600 people died in the attack made it, whatever the truth, an excellent opportunity for propaganda. Indeed, the smoke still largely obscures the battlefield.

A few days after the attack, SWAPO flew in a number of journalists to view the results of the carnage. One mass grave was already covered, but another was still littered with bodies. Jane Bergerol reported for the BBC and *The Guardian*: "First we saw gaily coloured frocks, blue jeans, shirts and a few uniforms. Then there was the sight of the bodies inside them. Swollen, blood-stained, they were the bodies of young girls, young men, a few older adults, some young children, all apparently recent arrivals from Namibia . . ."[26] Sara Rodriguez from the *Guardian*, a left-wing New York publication, who was also in the party, used similar words to describe the "brightly coloured cotton frocks of young girls, jeans, checkered shirts of the boys, a few khaki uniforms and the swollen bodies of the dead. The victims were mostly very young and had no defence."[27]

These quotations set the scene and became the primary sources for many of the allegations against the SADF. Many other allegations were added later, such as that the SAAF dropped poison gas on the inhabitants of Cassinga, and that the paratroopers indiscriminately bayoneted innocent old people, women and children, even raping women before killing them.[28] The left-wing activist Randolph Vigne wrote: "There was no battle. Botha's troops parachuted in on May 4, slaughtering 600, the great majority of 'other followers' being women and children as revealed by photographs of the great mass graves taken by the international media flown in in May 8."[29]

Piero Gleijeses, who, as we have seen, has trouble hiding his pro-Castro bias, also wrote that "it is more important than ever to remember the crime of Cassinga . . .".[30] British journalist Gavin Cawthra accepted SWAPO's version without any discussion.[31] None of these commentators bothered to examine the evidence. One academic who did, Annemarie Heywood, accepted SWAPO's contention that Cassinga was a refugee camp, but with the qualification that there was a protection unit of 200 to 300 men with two anti-aircraft guns. According to Heywood, Cassinga was not primarily a PLAN establishment, but "was under strict military control and was run on military lines . . ." She also alleged that the South African soldiers killed or bayoneted everyone they could find.[32] Heywood's version was, by and large, echoed by South Africa's Truth and Reconciliation Commission (TRC) in the 1990s.[33]

SWAPO leader Sam Nujoma, displaying a remarkable disregard for facts, told an international conference in 1987 that "heavy bombers and helicopter gunships", which he described as "twelve French-made Mirage jets [sic], British-made Hercules troop carriers [sic] and five helicopters [sic] took part in this operation . . . Chemical weapons, including inflammable phosphate liquid, tear gas and paralysing nerve gas [sic] were also used."[34] (Nujoma did not explain how the SADF paratroopers, who landed immediately after these barbaric weapons were allegedly used, were supposed to have protected themselves from them.) On another occasion, he said that among those "shot and bayoneted to death" were "pregnant women, babies and elderly persons".[35]

On the other hand, South African participants in the attack indignantly denied any wrongdoing. Cassinga was a legitimate military target, populated by PLAN fighters who bravely defended the base, they contended. Lieutenant General Constand Viljoen stated in an interview that Cassinga was "a huge logistics support base" from which it was suspected SWAPO was gathering its forces for an infiltration into SWA to upset the Turnhalle talks (held between the internal South West African parties to discuss the territory's future). "It is true there were some women and children, but completely untrue to say they made up most of those killed. SWAPO had some women in uniform and there were also girlfriends of fighters present. When I was standing at the main objective in Cassinga, there were many buildings around me that were apparently magazines, because they were all exploding," he told a journalist.[36]

Colonel Jan Breytenbach later wrote a book fiercely defending his men from the charges of wanton cruelty and murder. He found "no or very few refugees at the base. The civilians comprised mostly abductees who were forcibly plucked from their neighbourhoods to fill the role of refugees . . ."[37]

So what *was* the nature of Cassinga?

First of all, it should be asked what the SADF planners actually knew – or thought they knew – about Cassinga. The documentary evidence is clear. First of all, the aerial photographs taken by SAAF reconnaissance aircraft and published in several sources show an extensive system of defensive trenches typical of a military installation.[38] This is what the planners saw, and it formed part of the intelligence upon which they based the operation. McGill "Mac" Alexander, a seasoned paratroop officer with considerable operational experience, says that "a spurt of development and extension" was observed in the days leading up to the attack. The "vast array of sophisticated defensive trenches and bunkers" indicated "a defensive force of at least a battalion, which would seem a rather large element to guard a refugee camp. To defend an important operational headquarters or a logistics base, on the other hand, this would be quite realistic."[39]

This inference was backed up by information from PLAN prisoners captured north of the Angolan border by 32 Battalion patrols. They told their interrogators of a base they called "the Farm", where PLAN's commander, Dimo Hamaambo, had his headquarters. After a while, the exact location was discovered by an SAAF Canberra photo-reconnaissance plane from 12 Squadron. Intelligence also discovered the existence of the PLAN base at Chetequera, about 22 km inside Angola, and confirmed it with a Canberra photo sortie.[40]

In a memorandum to convince the SADF leadership that the attack was necessary, it was categorically stated: "No civilians will be involved." Cassinga (referred to by its SADF designation, Alpha), was described as "the operational military headquarters of SWAPO from where all operations against SWA are planned and the execution coordinated. From the base all supplies and weaponry are forwarded to the bases nearer to the front. Here training takes place too. In short, it is probably the most important base of SWAPO in Angola."[41]

Yet another major document, signed by the Chief of Staff Operations and dated 1 April 1978, was silent about the presence of civilians or refugees at Cassinga. The camp was described as PLAN's headquarters, where Hamaambo planned and coordinated all operations in South West Africa from a central operations room. It was also a logistics, training and medical facility, the destruction of which would disrupt SWAPO's operations for at least six months. The population was described "as varying between 300 and 1 200 terrorists and an unknown number of armed women terrorists".[42]

Even the TRC, which in general condemned the National Party government and its institutions, after examining the SADF documents, acknowledged "that the SADF command was convinced that Kassinga [sic] was the planning headquarters of PLAN, and thus a military target of key importance".[43]

It may therefore be stated unequivocally that, whatever the actual composition of the population at Cassinga on 4 May 1978, the SADF was under the impression that what it was attacking was a PLAN military headquarters and base.

But what, then, of the photographs of the mass grave taken a few days after the event? In one widely disseminated photo, one sees a mass of bodies, with a woman in civilian dress lying on top, legs wide. No other women or children are visible. The rest of the bodies appear to be men (recognisable by the unclad upper torsos) and/or women in uniform. Most bodies lie face down. Other photographs show one and two women, respectively, in civilian clothes visible among a host of uniformed men.[44] These photographs are all of the second trench; none are available of the other one, which was already covered up when the journalists arrived on the scene on 8 May.[45] Certainly the available photographic evidence does not back up the claims of "gaily coloured frocks" and "blue jeans", or "the bodies of young girls", even though some of the photos are in colour. In none of the photographs are any children visible, let alone babies.

SWAPO apologists make much of a report by a UNICEF team only a few days before the attack, which alleged that about 70% of the inhabitants of Cassinga were "adolescents, children and infants", while the rest were "essentially adults with very few elderly persons".[46] However, even Annemarie Heywood, who finds it hard to hide her disapproval of the SADF, states that the report is totally wrong about the physical environment: "When describing the Cassinga water supply, this report details arrangements which seem to match those at Chetequera (or possibly elsewhere) but do not make sense for Cassinga."[47]

There is also an interesting report by MK cadre Joseph Kobo, who was in the vicinity when the battle was raging. Kobo, whose job was "supervising supply routes for SWAPO-ANC camps near the border", described Cassinga as "the main SWAPO command post in southern Angola". Kobo happened to witness the assault from a distance and realised, as he wrote later, that SAAF aerial reconnaissance aircraft "had seen the build-up of supplies for an obvious SWAPO infiltration campaign and it was being nailed right on the head". Entering Cassinga after the paratroopers' extraction by helicopter, he saw that it had been razed to the ground. "Six months of logistics work had literally gone up in smoke. Thousands, millions of rounds of ammunition were still exploding . . ." The attack, he went on, had done a lot of damage to SWAPO's war effort. "It had burnt away nearly all the infiltration lines into Namibia. Some of the SWAPO groups on the far side of the border were cut off without resupply and there would be no quick way to re-establish contact."[48]

What Kobo was describing here was clearly not a refugee camp. According to Jan Breytenbach, Kobo told him that PLAN was engaged in a build-up "for an overwhelming incursion by heavily armed SWAPO gangs towards the end of April". The Cubans at Cassinga, together with Dimo Hamaambo, "were at the centre of the planning process".[49]

SWAPO's defence secretary, Peter Nanyemba, wrote in a confidential report about the battle (unearthed by Mac Alexander in the SADF archive) that "[o]ur ground force consisted of about 600 cadres, 300 of whom were fresh from the Hainyeko Training Centre".[50] This was never repeated in public by any SWAPO spokesman.

An American academic, Christian Williams, who has examined SWAPO's atrocities against its own people, discovered that many of the dissidents arrested in 1976 (*see* Chapter 11) had been transferred to Cassinga shortly before the SADF attack. It must rank as one of the highest ironies of war that some of these prisoners were probably killed in the attack. "Also, as became evident in my research interviews, some SWAPO critics who lived in exile quietly question the dominant narrative about Cassinga and describe the camp in ways that resemble the South African alternative version of it," Williams comments.[51]

It should be noted that the SADF never denied that its troops encountered – and killed – women and children during the fighting. There may be something in Mac Alexander's conclusion that one cannot categorically classify "any guerrilla camp as either 'military' or 'civilian'. The nature of a guerrilla or insurgency war is such that the two are inextricably intertwined." This implies "a blurred differentiation between military and civilian activities".[52] The journalist

Willem Steenkamp comes to the same conclusion: "Yes, Cassinga had a strong military presence – not just a small protection element – because it was both a military base and the main PLAN command headquarters. And yes, it did house a large number of civilians of one description or another."[53] Lastly, the TRC also accepted that Cassinga "was thus both a military base and a refugee camp".[54]

The question may, of course, also be approached from the other side. If we accept – as we must, given the evidence – that Cassinga was, among other things, a military base, did SWAPO have any justification for housing civilian refugees there? Is it possible that they were kept there deliberately as human shields against an SADF attack? While it is possible, it does not sound very plausible, given that no SADF attack was expected here. Legalities such as keeping military and civilians apart – as the Geneva Convention stipulates – would hardly play a prominent role in a guerrilla conflict of this nature. On a balance of probabilities, the mixing of troops and civilians was most probably simple ineptitude on SWAPO's part.

The attack on Chetequera

The airborne assault on Cassinga was so dramatic that the second and third phases of Operation Reindeer are often overlooked. Yet, on an operational level, the attack on Chetequera proved to be an even more valuable experience for the SADF. Cassinga was an airborne assault, and was never to be repeated. Chetequera was the first of many operations that employed a mixture of mechanised and motorised infantry, backed by armoured cars and air support. For the attack on other, smaller SWAPO bases closer to the border, an artillery battery with eight 140-mm G-2 guns was also included.

Chetequera would be attacked by Battle Group Juliet,[55] a force spawned mainly by 1 SAI at Bloemfontein. As we saw in Chapter 3, 1 SAI had been transformed into the army's first mechanised infantry unit in 1973, and, as Roland de Vries remembers, "[t]he training for evolving mobile warfare concepts and the appropriate development of South Africa's mechanised infantry systems commenced in all seriousness at Bloemfontein in 1976."[56]

The attack on Chetequera would be preceded by a small operation that was

The attack on Chetequera

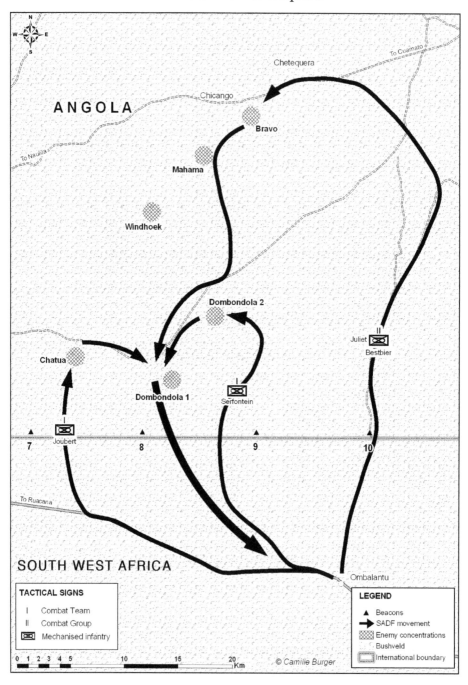

more important than it seems at first glance. This was a foray by Juliet into Angola to try to rescue Sapper Johan van der Mescht, who had been captured by a group of PLAN insurgents only a few days previously. Battle Group Juliet happened to be in Ovamboland to evaluate the new mechanised doctrine and the Ratel under operational conditions, and this presented an excellent opportunity. Under Commandant Joep Joubert, the unit crossed the border posthaste in the vicinity of Eenhana, where the woods were about the densest along the whole border. About 10 km inside Angola, the first SWAPO base was hit. Ep van Lill later remembered:

> As we hit this first base, we were shocked because it was very well camouflaged. When the Ratels got into the trenches, we could not get through or out, as the Ratel at that stage did not have multiwheel drive. The brush badly damaged the air pressure pipes underneath the vehicles. I had to hitch up to six vehicles to each other to pull one out. I looked like a speed cop on the target. Lucky for us, the enemy fled, but it was a very hasty evacuation because the fires still burned and the porridge was still on the fire.[57]

After this, the column attacked a second base, but again SWAPO had already fled. As it was getting dark, the South African column withdrew under cover of artillery fire.[58] In the event, Van der Mescht was not rescued, and remained a prisoner until released in May 1982.[59]

This rather short operation was the very first SADF foray into Angola using mechanised forces. In light of the army's lack of experience with mechanised movements in operational conditions, this was of great importance. According to Major Hans Kriek, Juliet's second in command at the time, doctrine called for the avoidance of land mines at all costs. "Therefore we had to bundu-bash all the way, and that brought about much damage. At times, it was near chaos; in fact, it would have been chaos if it wasn't for the cool leadership of Commandant Joep Joubert."[60]

Van Lill concurs: "Our vehicles were, however, in a bad condition. Everything which could be broken off by the bush, was broken off, and the soft-skinned vehicles were all dents and without windows. Everything was taken to Grootfontein, and there an intense effort was made to repair the vehicles and make them bush-resistant."[61]

For the attack on Chetequera, Battle Group Juliet was put under the command of Commandant Frank Bestbier, Joubert's successor at 1 SAI, an experienced infantry officer who had seen action during Savannah. He would be accompanied by an observer from the Chief of the Army, Commandant (later Major General) Johann "Dippies" Dippenaar, an officer whom we shall meet again later in this book.[62] The unit had 31 Ratels, 23 Eland armoured cars, 9 Buffel armoured personnel carriers and 18 soft-skinned vehicles in the rear echelon. These were divided into three detachments: Combat Team 1, under the command of Major Ep van Lill (one Eland troop and a beefed-up Ratel company); Combat Team 2, under Major PW de Jager (three Eland troops and three support sections in Buffels); and Combat Team 3, under Lieutenant (later Commandant) Mike Muller (one Eland troop, one mechanised infantry platoon and three support sections, plus combat engineers). The formation also had an 81-mm mortar group.

Aerial photographs of Chetequera showed a base with about 200 to 300 men, well dug in with extensive trenches and bunkers, heavy machine guns, mortars and antitank weapons. The photos also showed that the point of gravity of the defences lay in the south. This was logical; any attack would, after all, most probably come from the direction of South West Africa. Therefore, Bestbier decided not to indulge the SWAPO commander, but to attack from the north, where the South Africans were clearly not expected.

The preparation was meticulous. A similar terrain was chosen in Ovamboland, and the SWAPO base was rebuilt there. The attack was repeatedly exercised until everybody knew exactly what to do. Bestbier's operational instruction contained, among other things, strict orders that prisoners had to be taken and that nobody should be killed in cold blood. Shooting prisoners or members of the local population was emphatically out. Fighting with FAPLA or the Cubans had to be avoided.

The idea was that Van Lill's Combat Team 1 would comprise the main punch of the attack. They would attack from the north and push right through to the south. De Jager's Combat Team 2 would cover Van Lill's attack on the western or right flank, its Eland 90s being used more or less in a mobile-artillery role.

Muller's Combat Team 3 would be stationed to the northeast to counter any enemy intervention from that direction. The mechanised infantry would fight mainly from within their Ratels. The attack would start at midday, after a bombardment by the same Canberras and Buccaneers that had brought death to Cassinga that morning. After Chetequera's destruction, the combat group would attack a smaller base at Mahama on the way back.

Things started to go wrong slightly during the march to Chetequera. The combat group moved during the night, but one delay after the other meant that the assembly area for the attack was reached about 90 minutes late. However, the air support was also late, due to the events at Cassinga. At 13h30, the bombers – two Buccaneers, followed by four Canberras – finally went in.

The air attack caused a lot of shock, but relatively little damage, as the bushes cushioned the Canberras' anti-personnel bombs, which did not explode. At this stage, Bestbier discovered that he could not talk to the aircraft to make sure they had completed their task, and another delay ensued. This did not matter much, though, because the enemy fighters were still very much "punch-drunk" when the ground attack went in, according to Van Lill.

Ten minutes after the aircraft were done, the ground troops were unleashed. Van Lill's troops found that their sight was extremely limited due to crops growing in the fields, and they had to form their attack wedge formation on the go. They stormed into the base, but ran into trouble almost immediately. The terrain was very thickly wooded, so that Van Lill had to struggle hard to keep control over his own combat group. The Eland troop, which had to cover his attack from the northwest, found itself 800 m to the south, while the main axis of the advance was about 15° to the east of what it should have been. He could not see more than four of his vehicles at any time, but he succeeded in keeping the momentum going. Some Ratels fell into trenches or got stuck in the huge ant heaps and had to be towed out under heavy machine gun and rifle fire.

A medic, one Forster, remembers: "We flew into the base with the Browning machine gun shooting left, right and centre. Us at the back [of the vehicle] of course were so excited that we shot at any movement the enemy made. A few shots flew over our heads, but it was in vain. We did not allow those unaimed shots to disturb us."[63]

Within 10 minutes, the Ratels drove right through the base in a southerly direction, shooting everything up and trampling a number of SWAPO fighters. At a recoilless 75-mm gun position, an estimated 26 PLAN fighters were killed despite their determined attempts to bring the weapon into action. It was in vain. "The enemy's resistance astonished everyone," Bestbier wrote in his report.[64] The 81-mm mortar group was supposed to give indirect support, but was too late in position to do so. Luckily for the South Africans, they had developed a technique – strictly speaking, illegal – of deploying 60-mm mortars on sandbags on the Ratels' backs, so the absence of 81-mm mortar support did not make that much difference. The terrain was so rough that when Van Lill reached his objective south of the base 11 minutes later, he discovered that only 5 of his 14 Ratels remained entirely serviceable; the tyres on all the others were flat. (At this stage, the Ratel was not yet fitted with flat-run tyres, which would have enabled them to continue.)

Meanwhile, Combat Team 2 (De Jager) moved too far west before changing direction to the south, and consequently missed the northwestern corner of the base. They drew heavy fire, and two South Africans were killed, possibly by friendly fire.[65] Their covering fire – meant to support Van Lill's advance – was also less effective than it was supposed to be because of the dense bush. Not only were they unsure of exactly where their comrades were, they were often unable to see the enemy in the bush. One Eland was shot out, but the others killed enemy fighters by the dozen.

But the battle was far from over. Having reached the objective south of Chetequera, Van Lill had his soldiers debus and move on foot. But he now discovered that his rapid advance had missed quite a number of SWAPO fighters, who started firing at his force from the rear. He had no option: the attack had to be launched all over again, this time in the opposite, northerly direction. And because most of the enemy were concentrated here, it meant heavy going. Van Lill received reinforcements in the form of a mechanised platoon from Combat Team 3. A group of five Alouette III helicopter gunships also joined in the fight, picking off the enemy from the air with their 20-mm cannon. Two were hit by the defenders and had to return to base.

Van Lill witnessed one of his troops grabbing an insurgent's rifle and slapping him hard in the face. When an alarmed Van Lill asked the soldier what the hell he was doing, the man showed him that the enemy fighter had a stoppage, and that he was thus in no danger.

At about 15h15, the base was at last in South African control, after which the rear echelon could move in to resupply the combat teams and render medical aid to wounded SADF and SWAPO personnel. Several women were among the prisoners, many of them clad only in underclothes. Apparently, they had been engaged in calisthenics when the attack started. "What struck me," Van Lill commented many years later, "was that the women were far braver than the men".[66]

The final South African casualty figure was 2 dead and 10 wounded, while more than 200 SWAPO fighters were killed and another 200 were taken prisoner. Among the prisoners were four panic-stricken young women, discovered in a hut, frantically reading aloud from the Bible. "It was not a pleasant task," Bestbier commented.[67]

It was now too late to attack the SWAPO base at Mahama, as planned. The combat group therefore stayed in the bush overnight and returned to their base at Oshivello in Ovamboland the next day.

Cassinga and Chetequera were the most important parts of Operation Reindeer, but there were a number of other attacks on SWAPO bases. Two combat teams under Commandant Chris Serfontein (for some reason generally known as "Swart Hand" or Black Hand) and Joep Joubert, supported by a 140-mm G-2 battery under Major Piet Uys, took on five SWAPO bases near the border, namely, Windhoek, Dombondola 1 and 2, Chatua and Haimona. Additionally, five companies of 32 Battalion under Major (later Brigadier General) Eddie Viljoen would take care of 17 smaller bases further eastwards. All these attacks were unsuccessful, as the bases proved to have been hurriedly evacuated.[68]

Lessons learnt

Tactically, the airborne assault on Cassinga elicited much interest, especially among the airborne community. The United States, United Kingdom, Soviet Union, France, Germany and Israel all had considerable airborne forces, some being airlifted by helicopter, others still parachute-trained. (A group of Israeli officers even visited South Africa – as Jannie Geldenhuys put it – to "find out how the hell we managed to do that operation". The leader of the visitors was Colonel Dan Shomron, commander of the famed Entebbe raid of 1976.)[69]

Cassinga's tactical and operational influence on the Border War itself was, however, next to nil. This was despite the establishment of 44 Parachute Brigade, consisting of three (later four) parachute battalions, with a 120-mm mortar battery and other support troops, all parachute-trained. Provided the SAAF had enough airlift capacity (which was not the case), the whole brigade could be dropped behind enemy lines to create mayhem. But that was not to be. For the remainder of the war, paratroopers were mostly used either as motorised infantry on cross-border operations, or as Romeo Mike (*see* Chapter 9) reaction forces in the counterinsurgency war in northern SWA. Although the brigade's enthusiastic commanders, colonels Jan Breytenbach, Frank Bestbier, Archie Moore and Mac Alexander, attempted to sell the airborne concept to the SADF high command,[70] the way Cassinga had teetered on the brink of a disaster probably weighed too heavily on the generals' minds. So, like the German Oberkommando der Wehrmacht following the parachute assault on Crete in May 1941, the high command came to the conclusion that large-scale parachute operations were too risky.

The landward attack on Chetequera, the baptism of fire for the Ratel, was in fact much more meaningful than Cassinga as a template for future attacks. Chetequera became the prototype of the later large-scale cross-border operations into Angola. The army analysed the performance of the Ratel closely and made several changes to the vehicle based on the experience at Chetequera.[71]

Another problem that cropped up at Cassinga as well as Chetequera was the inadequacy of the South African radio system. Not only did the "pongos" (the army guys) on the ground find it difficult to communicate with supporting aircraft, they also had problems contacting each other. This complicated things unnecessarily. The problem would be solved with new radio equipment, which was procured later.

Operationally, the operation was not as successful as had been hoped. Still, according to the SADF figures, 856 SWAPO fighters were killed and more than 200 taken prisoner (at Chetequera), which meant that SWAPO had lost about a third of its ready military force.[72] But Jan Breytenbach writes of "a general relaxation on the part of the South Africans with no follow-through to maintain the initiative",[73] thereby disregarding an important military principle. Indeed, until July there was a drastic decrease in insurgent activity south of the border, but in the absence of a follow-up, it flared up again considerably.[74]

Another operational consequence was that SWAPO also learnt a few important lessons. Cassinga in particular had been laid out as an orthodox military base, with buildings, roads and a parade ground. Hereafter, bases were spread out over much bigger areas, with covered bunkers replacing buildings and everything being camouflaged. This would make things much more difficult for the South Africans in forthcoming operations. Also, the bases were moved around, which meant that the SADF's intelligence picture became outdated rather quickly.[75]

Another consequence of the operation was the establishment of a permanent mechanised unit in northern SWA, to be used in cross-border operations. Battle Group Juliet was an ad hoc unit, put together especially for the attack on Chetequera. After the event, the idea was to store the equipment at Grootfontein, to be used by another ad hoc unit when the need arose. But obviously this was not as good as having a permanent unit in the area.

And so in October 1978 General Constand Viljoen appointed the first commander of a permanent mechanised conventional warfare unit in the operational area: Commandant Johann "Dippies" Dippenaar. The unit, known as 61 Mechanised Battalion Group, came into being on 1 January 1979, and consisted of two mechanised infantry companies in Ratel 20s, an armoured car troop in Eland 90s (later Ratel 90s) seconded from 1 Special Service Battalion (1 SSB) in Bloemfontein, a 140-mm G-2 battery from 4 Artillery Field Regiment, a support company and a combat engineer troop from 16 Maintenance Unit. In later years, a tank squadron would also be added. The unit was established at a somewhat remote area in Ovamboland, Omuthiya, where the members could shoot, move and exercise to their hearts' content.[76]

Clearly, 61 Mech was a new kind of unit. Instead of the orthodox infantry battalions or armoured/artillery regiments being brought together only on a divisional level, here was an all-arms unit on battalion/regimental level. The unit would have its baptism of fire in June 1980 with Operation Sceptic, and would thereafter be part of every single large cross-border operation until the end of the war. It would also become the template for other similar units – 2 SAI,

4 SAI and 8 SAI – which, in spite of the word "infantry" in their names, could also be classified as mechanised.

Strategically, Reindeer's results were mixed. On the propaganda front, it was a disaster for South Africa. An SADF analysis found that media reporting during the first week was mainly neutral and factual, but then became negative. This was partly due to the fact that South Africa allowed SWAPO and Angola to capture the propaganda high ground by speaking to the media first and announcing that Cassinga was a refugee camp. From there onward, the South Africans continually tried to close the stable door after the horse had bolted. The analysis recommended: "WE MUST SPEAK FIRST. Luanda's first words to the world was that we had attacked a refugee camp. This is the version that was generally accepted by the foreign media."[77] The fact that the movement, objectively speaking, disseminated mainly outright lies and distortions about Cassinga, does not diminish the propaganda feat and the political mileage they extracted from it. SWAPO milked the affair and capitalised on the photographs of the mass graves for years. Throughout the war, SWAPO was light years ahead of the leaden-footed South Africans in terms of propaganda.

This was exacerbated by political developments on an international front. The actions of the South African government were condemned by just about everybody, including the main Western countries. Sam Nujoma, who was in New York for the UN Security Council debate on Namibia, withdrew from all talks and returned to Lusaka, no doubt delighted by the propaganda victory so unexpectedly handed to him.[78]

Nevertheless, Operation Reindeer as a whole was a strategic turning point in the Border War. As Constand Viljoen said, it was Reindeer "which determined the South African military strategy for the next decade: the concept of pre-emptive strikes".[79] The military and the political leaders saw that SWAPO had been dealt a hammer blow and that the concept was strategically and operationally sound. From the South African perspective, the world huffed and puffed, but could not blow South Africa over. And therefore, in Chester Crocker's words, "Angola became the centrepiece of the SADF's anti-SWAPO strategy in the Namibian bush war . . ."[80]

Was Reindeer worth it? The answer will, no doubt, depend on your point of view. On the one hand, it can be reasoned that South Africa squandered a chance for peace, and that the result was a very difficult ten years of war, which brought enormous suffering and hardship. On the other, SWAPO's commitment (*see* Chapter 10) to democracy was extremely doubtful, to put it mildly. It can be said that, by prolonging the war over another decade, the SADF bought time for a better and more durable peace to ripen.

What cannot be denied, in any case, is that the South African government in May 1978 was not yet ready to accept the possibility of free and fair elections under UN supervision, which could bring a SWAPO government to power in Windhoek. As PW Botha wanted, the military option was not yet played out – not by a long chalk. Much more blood and tears would flow in the coming years.

6

THE PATTERN
EVOLVES: SCEPTIC

Immediately after Operation Reindeer, Military Intelligence started to contemplate the possibility of a SWAPO revenge operation. "Trustworthy sources
in Zambia," it was reported, indicated that the movement had taken an oath
to avenge Cassinga and Chetequera. Attacks were expected on targets with
a relatively high population density, such as Ruacana, Oshakati, Ondangwa,
Oshikango, Rundu and – prophetically, as it turned out – Katima Mulilo in the
Caprivi Strip. Reindeer had weakened SWAPO in Angola sufficiently so as to
preclude attacks against well-defended targets. "SWAPO in Zambia has the best
capacity to act against targets in SWA," the analysis stated. Central Ovamboland
and the Caprivi Strip were specifically named as high-risk areas.[1]

The analysts were spot-on. In the early morning hours of 23 August 1978,
SWAPO's revenge came in the form of a series of 122-mm rockets fired from
Zambian soil on the frontier town of Katima Mulilo at the eastern extremity of
the Caprivi Strip. In fact, Military Intelligence knew through radio intercepts
that an attack was coming, and the SADF had frantically prepared countermeasures. The bombardment turned out to be very inaccurate, only two of
the 30-odd rockets falling in Katima itself. One damaged a school in the black
township; the other landed on a dormitory containing sleeping soldiers, killing
ten and wounding another ten. At the same time, a mortar attack was launched
on Wenela base, not far away, but all bombs missed.[2]

The South Africans retaliated at once with everything they had. Within
minutes, a troop of 140-mm guns started a counter-bombardment.
Reinforcements, in the form of paratroopers and additional 140-mm guns,
were flown in from Bloemfontein and Potchefstroom. The previous evening,
the local commander, Commandant AK de Jager, had already organised his
meagre forces into two combat teams, with armoured cars and motorised

infantry supported by the artillery. They crossed the border even as the smoke was still billowing into the air at Katima.

One combat team moved rapidly to a PLAN base about 30 km inside Zambia, but discovered there that the estimated 200 guerrillas had already fled. The other team ran into resistance nearby. With the paratroop reinforcements having arrived, the SADF attacked SWAPO furiously. Alouette gunships circled in the air, taking pot shots at the guerrillas. The South Africans hunkered down for the night, while South African and Zambian artillery and mortars fired at each other. The next day, some of the Zambian bases were blasted by Canberra and Buccaneer bombers. After this, SWAPO scattered in all directions, and, although the pursuit lasted a while longer, there were no more advantages in continuing. By the afternoon of 27 August, all SADF soldiers were safely back in South West Africa. SWAPO's casualties were estimated at 20 dead and an unknown number of wounded.

These events set in motion a process that would cause the rebel movement much grief. To begin with, the attack on Katima coincided with a visit to SWA of the Austrian general Hannes Philipp, the designated commander of the proposed UN peacekeeping force, which had to supervise elections in accordance with Security Council Resolution 435. His SADF counterpart in Windhoek, Major General Jannie Geldenhuys, immediately took advantage of this event to prove to the international community SWAPO's aggressive intentions and its disregard for civilian lives. According to Geldenhuys, the Katima incident led to a "more advantageous climate for cross-border operations".[3]

The SADF exploited this opening to the full. The government – the aggressive PW Botha had by now replaced the cautious John Vorster as prime minister – authorised two cross-border operations, Rekstok (in Angola) and Saffraan (in Zambia), in early March 1979. These came after PLAN launched mortar attacks on SADF bases on 13 and 26 February.[4] Not much has been written about these two operations, except that they were meant to hit SWAPO bases in the shallow area across the borders in Angola and Zambia. Very little action was seen, as SWAPO had already evacuated all its positions, but one of the SAAF's irreplaceable Canberra bombers was shot down by SWAPO anti-aircraft fire.[5]

Some South African officers saw these two operations as failures, but they may have judged them too harshly. According to Geldenhuys, his primary objective was not so much to cause material damage to SWAPO, as to gather information. "The information we got from these operations, made the enemy picture much clearer . . . If these operations did not take place, we would have remained in the dark for much longer. From this time on we could act much more effectively."[6]

Perhaps the most important outcome was a strategic one. Zambia's President Kenneth Kaunda was severely embarrassed by the SWAPO presence on his soil and the forceful SADF response. Consequently, he halted all PLAN military actions. As Geldenhuys put it: "This was the big breakthrough. It made East Caprivi free from insurgence. This was the beginning of the fulfilment of our plan."[7]

When we look at the counterinsurgency war in northern SWA in Chapter 9, the full implications of this decision will become clear. Suffice to say here that this was a prerequisite for Geldenhuys's aspiration to limit the PLAN insurgency to Ovamboland.

The build-up to Operation Sceptic

One result of Operation Rekstok was that SWAPO withdrew its bases from the shallow areas just north of the border to deeper inside Angola.[8] This meant that future South African cross-border operations would have to penetrate considerably deeper into Angola to get at the rebel movement.

A pattern was slowly starting to develop. During the rainy season, a veritable deluge of insurgents would cross the border into South West Africa, taking advantage of the protection afforded by the lush foliage and water in the many streams and rivers. During these months, it was difficult to locate them at their bases in Angola. Therefore the SADF started launching big conventional cross-border operations during the dry winter months when it was easier to move large numbers of vehicles north of the border. The winter was also the time when PLAN regrouped its forces to recuperate and to do retraining, which made it an even more attractive time to attack them.[9]

Another element of this evolving pattern was the SADF's excellent strategic capability to intercept enemy radio communications. Neither SWAPO nor FAPLA nor the Cubans ever realised it, but the vast majority of their radio messages were intercepted and decrypted. As General Georg Meiring, who used to be a signaller himself, said: "If anyone north of us opened their mouths we had it on tape somewhere . . . Our communications interception system was the best in the world at the time." According to him, there never was a single major interception: "Rather, you get a lot of interceptions from which a pattern emerges. Out of that you build your intelligence. Thousands upon thousands of messages were intercepted." He conceded that the Cubans and FAPLA also intercepted SADF messages, but insisted the South African capability was better.[10]

In order to understand the successive SADF cross-border operations during the next few years, it is necessary to say something about PLAN's deployment in Angola. The headquarters of SWAPO's armed force was at Lubango (*see* map on page 6), as was the Tobias Hainyeko Training Centre, where insurgents received their military training. The SWAPO forces were divided into three fronts: Western, Central and Eastern. The Western Front's headquarters was at Cahama, while the Central Front was controlled from Cuvelai and the Eastern Front from Ngluma/Puturunhanga. PLAN also had a so-called mechanised brigade – a grand name for a poorly trained and equipped unit, which existed mainly for its prestige value and had no real place in an insurgency war. The formation, about 2 500 men strong, mostly operated against UNITA as payment to the MPLA for being allowed to use Angolan territory against the "Boers". SWAPO also had four "semi-conventional" battalions of between 100 and 350 men, situated in the general vicinity of Cassinga.[11] This meant that PLAN was mostly stationed in Cunene province in southwestern Angola, and so this was where the South African axe would fall repeatedly.

A tactic often used by SWAPO was to let specially trained guerrillas infiltrate right through the operational area into the "white" farmlands around Grootfontein, Tsumeb and Otavi to terrorise the white farmers and politicise their workers. This happened for the first time on 8 May 1979, when 30 insurgents crossed the cutline (the border between Ovamboland and the white farming area). During that night, they attacked two farm homesteads and killed a grandfather, grandmother and two minor children. This led to 61 Mech's first operational deployment, ironically in a counterinsurgency role rather than in the conventional mobile warfare for which it was created. Armoured cars were deployed in stopper groups on roads in the demarcated area, while infantry carried out follow-up patrols on foot and artillerymen protected the farmhouses. This operation was known as Carrot, as would similar operations be in the following years. In this case, all 30 insurgents were rapidly found and killed or taken prisoner, or managed to escape to Angola.[12]

In February 1980, the insurgents tried again. In a widely publicised case, guerrillas attacked the farmhouse of the Dressel family, 45 km south of Grootfontein, and killed the farmer, Eberhard Dressel. His 15-year-old daughter, Sonja, opened fire on the attackers and shot two dead, after which the others fled.[13] The result was pretty much the same as in 1979: altogether, 31 insurgents died and the rest of the group of 60 were either captured or made their way back to Angola. The SADF suffered two fatalities.[14]

But things were not looking good for the South Africans. In February 1980, the SADF registered 42 land mines – a record number – in Ovamboland.[15] And the SADF learnt that the Soviet Union was pressurising SWAPO to intensify the war. Apparently with this purpose in mind, about 800 PLAN fighters were transferred from Zambia to Cunene province. For the first time, attempts were made to infiltrate Kaokoland (hitherto free of insurgents), while the hydroelectric works at Ruacana (supplying northern SWA with electricity) were also attacked. SWAPO was very far from being beaten. On the contrary, the insurgents were aggressive and spoiling for a fight. Everything pointed to a large-scale guerrilla offensive, although Military Intelligence could not pinpoint exactly what was going to happen.[16]

At the same time, South Africa's strategic position was weakened by the collapse of white rule in Rhodesia. Following the Lancaster House Agreement of December 1979, elections were held in that country in February 1980. Robert Mugabe and Joshua Nkomo's Patriotic Front won an overwhelming majority in the new parliament, with the result that a valuable South African ally was gone. With the transition from white-ruled Rhodesia to independent Zimbabwe, the international focus would now clearly fall on South West Africa. The thinking in SADF circles was that the Rhodesian government had waited too long to strike across its borders, which was one reason for its demise.[17] The arguments advanced in the first months of 1978 in favour of a large cross-border operation were – from the SADF point of view – more valid than ever before.

And thus, in May 1980 the decision was reached: SWAPO had to be taken on and beaten in its lair. The date would be 10 June. The SADF was expressly forbidden to tangle with FAPLA troops. The strategic purpose of the attack was to break down SWAPO's image as a war-winning movement, to show the South West Africans that they should not depend on SWAPO, but that the South African government was dealing the cards, and to pre-empt SWAPO's offensive even before it could start. Operationally, the attackers had to destroy PLAN's command post and headquarters, to disrupt its logistics system, to gain maximum intelligence, and to "eliminate SWAPO terrorists".[18] The base complexes of Chifufua (also known as Smokeshell, or QFL), Ionde, Mulola and Chitumba were to be attacked and destroyed on the first day. Thereafter the force would stay in the vicinity for ten days to follow up and hunt down SWAPO groups that might have escaped. For the operation, known as Operation Sceptic, the invading South African forces were divided into four combat groups:

- The main punch would be provided by 61 Mech (called Combat Group 61 for the duration of the operation), under the command of Commandant Johann Dippenaar. The formation would consist of two mechanised infantry companies, two parachute infantry companies (motorised), an armoured car squadron and support troop, a battery of 140-mm guns, a support company with two antitank platoons as well as a mortar platoon, and a combat engineer troop, together with other support troops.
- The other part of the punch was concentrated in Combat Group 10, under Commandant Chris Serfontein, with two paratroop companies (motorised), one armoured car troop and a support company. His target was Mulola.
- The third element was Combat Group 53 (three motorised infantry companies, two armoured car troops and a support company), under Commandant Jorrie Jordaan.
- Lastly there was Combat Group 54, with five light counterinsurgency infantry companies (including two from 32 Battalion and one from the parabats) and a mortar platoon, all under Commandant Anton van Graan. This group would not be part of the main operation. Van Graan's

light battalion would kick off the operation by securing the area just across the border up to Mulemba for the others to pass through safely. At Mulemba, a temporary base area would be set up where troops would sleep overnight on 9/10 June and from where Smokeshell would be attacked the next day.

The intelligence about Smokeshell was rather deficient – Dippenaar describes the information at his disposal as "very vague".[19] After a while, it became clear that Smokeshell was not so much a base as a complex of 13 positions, spread out over an area of 3 km by 15 km, all of it in dense bush. Each position covered approximately 300 m by 600 m. SWAPO had clearly learnt a lot from Cassinga and Chetequera; Smokeshell was dug in, with the fighters living in foxholes, trenches and covered bunkers, all of which had been excellently camouflaged. This showed a strong Soviet influence. The SADF identified seven anti-aircraft positions, some with the feared 23-mm gun, and the whole complex was manned by an estimated 800 men.[20] (As far as could be ascertained, no women or children were present this time. Had SWAPO learnt its lesson?) The position was, as the crow flies, about 180 km north of the border, but, with winding sandy tracks along which the army would advance, the distance would in fact be about 260 km.[21]

The idea was that Combat Group 61 would lead the way across the border towards Chifufua, with Combat Group 10 in its wake. By noon on 10 June, the attackers were meant to be in place. After an aerial bombardment by the SAAF and a follow-up by 61 Mech's artillery, the South Africans would move in from the east and advance through the complex. It was expected that the enemy would not stand and fight, but would immediately flee westwards. The two parachute companies from Combat Group 61 would be choppered in on the western side to act as stopper groups. Afterwards, the focus of the attack would shift eastwards to the Ionde complex, with four positions and 700 men.[22] And while the assault on Smokeshell took place, Combat Group 10 would take on Mulola, to the south.[23]

Of course, General Constand Viljoen again insisted on being part of the operation, and accompanied Commandant Dippenaar in his command Ratel. As at Cassinga, this would cause discomfort in certain quarters.

The Battle of Smokeshell

The SADF went to considerable lengths to keep PLAN from learning that another big cross-border operation was on the way. The units earmarked for the operation spent approximately ten days before Smokeshell either doing highly visible exercises or counterinsurgency operations in Ovamboland to mislead the enemy.

The SAAF had learnt from Operation Reindeer that air support had to be adequate. For Sceptic, a strong force, consisting of 18 Mirage F1AZ fighter-bombers and 4 Buccaneer and 4 Canberra bombers, was sent to South West Africa. For security reasons – the SAAF feared that people living around Waterkloof Air Force Base, just outside Pretoria, could inform "unfriendly" embassies who could in turn warn Angola and SWAPO about the activity– the aircraft flew there separately and mostly by a roundabout route via Upington.

This makes it all the more difficult to understand why the air force immediately announced its presence in the operational area by attacking both SWAPO's Tobias Hainyeko Training Centre at Lubango and, of all places, Smokeshell itself on 7 June, and again on 9 June, the day before the ground attack. Apparently, they caused little damage.[24] It is not known what SWAPO deduced from this, but it seems a strange way to keep your enemy in the dark about your intentions.

The troops started moving from their bases early on 8 June. The convoy was an impressive sight. When the first vehicles reached Eenhana for a fuel refill, the last ones were just about to leave Omuthiya, the starting point.[25] But, as the previous operations also illustrated, the planned march tempo was too ambitious, thanks to the dense bush and sandy ground. The Eland armoured cars led the way, followed by the Ratels and then the G-2 Magirus Deutz gun tractors. By the time the big tractors were on the move, the tracks had been ploughed up by the Elands and Ratels, with the result that engines overheated, some guns broke loose due to metal fatigue, and delay after delay tested people's tempers. Mulemba, already secured and prepared as a temporary base by Van Graan's Combat Group 54, was reached on the evening of 9 June.[26]

Early the next day, the force moved out again for the 130-km advance to Smokeshell, with Combat Group 61 in a huge convoy of 151 vehicles. The troops were tense, but hyped up. As often happens in battles, things had already

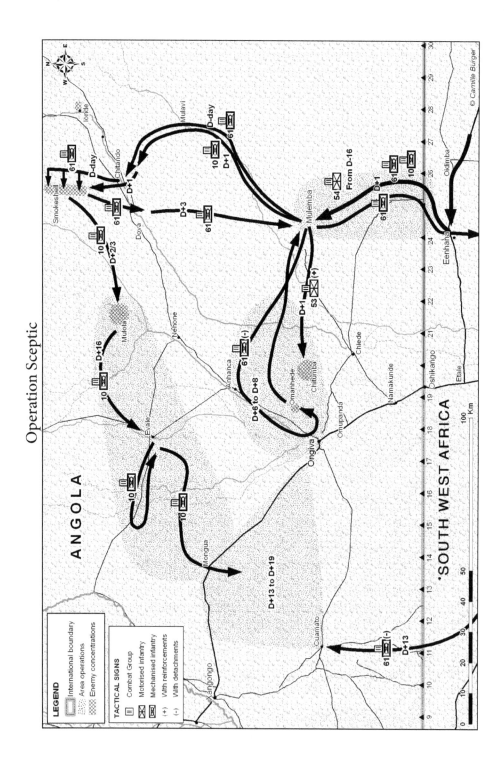

Operation Sceptic

started to go wrong. At Mulemba, helicopters were supposed to pick up the paratroop stopper groups and deliver them to their designated areas west of Smokeshell. But someone had forgotten to organise fuel for the Pumas at Mulemba, which meant an important part of Dippenaar's battle plan could not be executed.

Nevertheless, by 13h15 the rest of the force was in place, the teams all having reported "Ek's hier!" (I'm here!). The SAAF's strike force was present in full strength. Their attack was meant to stun the defenders so that they would offer no or little resistance. However, this raises the question of why the air attack started at 08h00, while the ground attack began only at 12h00, giving the guerrillas ample time to recover. It made no sense, as some of the officers present themselves observed. At any rate, the attack was a failure, with the bombs falling in an empty area to no effect, apart from warning SWAPO that something was brewing.

At 13h15 Dippenaar gave the order: "Laat waai!" (Let rip!) The artillery was supposed to start firing now, but there was only silence. The battery, under the command of Major Tobias Vermaak, was not yet in position. And, when the big guns finally started thundering, their bombardment, like that of the air force, had little effect. In the middle and north of the complex, SWAPO had already evacuated the identified positions or had moved its defence to alternative positions. The bunkers could be destroyed only by a direct hit.

For the assault, Dippenaar had divided his force into six combined-arms combat teams with mechanised and motorised infantry and 90-mm gun support:

- Team 1 (A Company, mechanised infantry, supported by Ratel 90s and mortars), under Major Paul Fouché;
- Team 2 (B Company, mechanised infantry, also supported by Ratel 90s and mortars), under Captain Louis Harmse;
- Team 3 (C Squadron, Eland 90 armoured cars with a support infantry platoon), under Captain Jakes Jacobs;
- Team 4 (parabat company with three stopper groups), under Captain Mac Alexander;
- Team 5 (parabat company with three stopper groups), under Captain Piet Nel;
- Team 6 (reserve), under Major Jab Swart.

The main effort, consisting of Teams 1, 2 and 3, would be launched from west to east, while Teams 4 and 5 were supposed to act as stopper groups on the western side when the insurgents started fleeing. In effect, they were out of the fight due to the aviation fuel blunder. The Elands of Combat Team 3 would be in the north, with Team 1 in the middle and Team 2 in the south. Team 2 would also be supported by 61 Mech's mortar and Ratel 90 antitank platoons.

The attacks by Teams 1 and 3 went like clockwork. Very little resistance was encountered, the defenders – apparently with PLAN commander Dimo Hamaambo among them – having already fled. The question has to be asked whether the SAAF attacks of 7 and 9 June, as well as the early-morning attack on 10 June, were responsible for this. The attackers moved quickly through the complex. Team 1 found it exceedingly difficult to navigate in the dense bush, and after a while found themselves about 800 m north of where they were supposed to be. Team 3 was exactly on target. Both teams found several abandoned anti-aircraft guns. A few skirmishes with fleeing SWAPO fighters ensued, and six of them were killed.

In the south, things went horribly wrong for Team 2. After apparently surprising some SWAPO members at lunch, the team advanced rapidly before making contact with aggressive defences at a previously unknown position. As dictated by mechanised infantry tactical doctrine, Captain Harmse divided his force into a fire support group (a troop of Ratel 90s, a mortar platoon, and a mechanised infantry platoon) and an assault group (two mechanised infantry platoons). He also requested – and got – artillery support. But the support group, once again, walked straight into an anti-aircraft gun position, so that neither the mortar platoon nor the Ratel 90 troop could support the assault group as they were supposed to; they had to fight hard for their own survival. The Ratel 90s even had to use their main guns in close-quarters combat – as little as 30 m at times – and trampled several defenders under their big wheels, while the mortarists had to fight as ordinary infantry.

Meanwhile, the assault group advanced further, not fully realising what was happening to their mates in the support group. SWAPO soldiers were seen running all over the place. As Corporal Gareth Rutherford wrote shortly afterwards, "[t]his was exciting. This was what everybody had been waiting for."

Then, at a shona (an opening in the bush), all hell broke loose. Several anti-aircraft guns, including three 14,5-mm and one deadly 23-mm, suddenly ripped through several Ratels in quick succession. Rutherford wrote:

> Then it happened – not tack tack any more, but doof doof dooooof, doof doof dooooof, about three per second, heavy automatic fire. Memory of the briefing we had back at base, of huge anti-aircraft guns, 4 barrels, 8 ft high, 5 man crew – cutting through a Ratel like butter. I looked up at Gary, our Section Leader, and said, "Gary, do you know what that is?", and he said, "Ja". The booming went on, and we didn't know where it was coming from; what we did know was that it would be tickets if we were hit. Our hearts sank, and our faces must have turned pale as fear turned to terror.[27]

Rifleman WS Bornman remembered that the 23-mm cannon "sounded like a big motorbike's accelerator which one opens quickly and releases again, so rapid did it shoot".[28] And Rifleman Marco Caforio wrote:

> Our Ratel was hit. Suddenly everything went into almost slow motion. Steve Cronjé turned in his seat and opened the hydraulic doors for us to get out, that's when I saw he had been hit in his chest. While I sat staring at Steve in total disbelief, three tracers passed by me inside the Ratel causing shrapnel to bounce around.
>
> I realised at that point that we had just been hit with heavy calibre rounds. I turned to Robert and shouted at him to get out as we were being hit.
>
> I told him to jump. Both of us jumped out of the top hatches. As I came off, I felt a burning sensation in my right hip and my left thigh. I hit the ground with my rifle in hand, where my webbing went to only God knows.
>
> I screamed for Robert, but he didn't answer. I saw him lying about a metre away from me and I crawled to him telling him that I had been

hit. I grabbed him and shook him, his eyes were open but he had already gone. From seeing him lying there my mind snapped and I started shooting at what I didn't know. While I was shooting I could hear AK rounds bouncing off the Ratel.

Crawling from under the Ratel at the back end Van der Vyver, or Van as I called him, was shouting to me: "Caforio, Caforio, jy moet dekking slaan, hulle skiet op jou." I shouted to him: "Waar is die ouens? Waar is almal?" His reply was: "Hulle is almal dood."[29]

Lieutenant Paul Louw, commander of 2 Platoon, which was hit badly, would never forget "the expressions on troops' faces, the crumpled and charcoaled bodies, the smell of burnt human flesh, the smell of diesel early in the morning".[30] Bornman remembered that "the Ratel in which I sat, one smelt just death as it was smeared with the blood of people who had been shot".[31] Twelve South African soldiers died that day, the SADF's largest casualty figure for one day's fighting since 1945.

Those troops who were still unharmed, badly shaken or not, debussed immediately and attacked the enemy positions on foot. Rifleman Andrew McClean took a Bren machine gun, coolly walked towards a 23-mm gun position and shot the crew.[32] The problem was that the assault group and the support group could not render mutual aid, as doctrine called for; both were involved in desperate battles of their own. Reading the eyewitness accounts, one gets the impression that everything must have seemed very surreal at that moment. There was the deep roar of the anti-aircraft guns, the deafening chatter of small-arms fire and the explosions of all sorts of shells. But a job had to be done and the SWAPO fighters had to be killed or driven away.

To complicate matters further, Team 2's rather rattled commander, Louis Harmse, pulled out of the fight and reported to Dippenaar. Harmse stayed with Dippenaar for the rest of the day, leaving his men to continue fighting without their commander. His report did have the advantage of bringing Team 2's serious position to Dippenaar's attention. He immediately took steps to remedy the situation by ordering the reserve Team 6 under Major Jab Swart to go and help Team 2. Team 1 (Paul Fouché), which had already fulfilled its task, was also ordered southwards at 16h30 to reinforce the embattled Team 2. The Elands of Team 3 (Jakes Jacobs) became the new reserve.

WO1 Peet Coetzee from Team 6 described the scene where the Ratels had been "shot and cut to ribbons":

> I . . . witnessed the devastating effects of what a 20-mm [sic; 23 mm] anti-aircraft cannon's armour-piercing rounds could do to a Ratel. It simply went through everything, and that included the occupants sitting inside.
>
> In another Ratel the driver was shot from behind and plastered against the driver's front window. His flesh was protruding through the hole made by the passing round. It was not a pleasant sight and remained with me for a long time . . . I saw a critically wounded guy being made comfortable under a bush in a shady patch, his right arm having been blown off at the armpit with blood squirting out.[33]

Major Jab Swart, commander of Team 6, collected the bodies of some of the South African dead and gathered the remains of Team 2, but then ran into another contact. He swept right through it, firing all the way. Two of his Ratels lost their way, but such was the general mayhem that Swart did not wait to gather them, but continued onward. One Ratel found its way back; the other group spent an anxious night in the bush, fearing a SWAPO attack at any moment.

Dippenaar struggled to maintain his command. It needed a superman to re-establish control in a situation where sight was extremely limited and navigation difficult due to the dense bush, coupled with the shock of the tremendous noise and the losses on the South African side. But Dippenaar was a very good officer. When Major Paul Fouché from Team 1 ran into yet another ambush as he was moving southwards, Dippenaar ordered Jacobs and the Elands of Team 3 forward. Once again, mechanised infantry doctrine kicked in: Fouché pulled back about 200 m to disengage from the ambush and then moved around the enemy's left flank, while Jacobs's armoured cars supported them with their 90-mm guns. At last, everything came together in a textbook attack, and even the air support, in the form of two Impala IIs, was bang on target. In the process, a large number of enemy fighters were killed and two SWAPO prisoners taken. Some of the highly charged troops wanted to kill them, but Constand Viljoen and Johann Dippenaar strictly forbade it, saying, "Shoot at or touch those people [and] you'll be court-martialled!" This was just as well, because the prisoners supplied the South Africans with much valuable information about other targets in the vicinity.

This attack finally broke SWAPO's back. At 17h30 a signal was intercepted: "Enemy infantry had attacked our positions. We tried but we lost conduct of controlling the troops. We are evacuating."[34]

But SWAPO still had a sting in its tail. While moving further southwards in the dark to a spot where they could spend the night, the combat group once again ran into a classic L-shaped ambush. But every South African vehicle brought down maximum fire on the enemy, and this proved too much for the defenders, who broke and ran after about 20 minutes. The night was spent in great anxiety, a massive SWAPO attack being expected any minute. But it never materialised. Most probably, SWAPO was equally, or even more, rattled by the day's carnage.

The sun rose on the morning of 11 June on a scene of utter destruction. Military equipment was strewn about – some destroyed or damaged, some still intact – among dead bodies and the general chaos of war. In the course of the morning, the two companies of paratroops finally arrived in lorries from the echelon area at Mulemba and were used to mop up the area. The mechanised part of Combat Group 61 was by this point very low on fuel and ammunition, and some vehicles even had to be towed, having run dry. A while later, the rear echelon also arrived, as did Combat Group 10 (Chris Serfontein), and the whole Smokeshell complex was examined carefully for survivors and intelligence during the next few days.

At this time, something potentially serious happened. While Dippenaar was moving his headquarters, his command Ratel detonated a double mine. General Constand Viljoen happened to be in the vehicle, but he was thrown clear and was not injured. But at the operations headquarters at Eenhana, where Major General Jannie Geldenhuys was following the progress on radio, there were a few tense minutes until they heard Viljoen was unhurt. This did not stop Geldenhuys from joining Serfontein's combat group just the next day!

In his detailed report, Dippenaar mentions that Viljoen, with "his inexhaustibility and activity was at that stage my biggest worry. The best I can describe General Viljoen is undoubtedly like an ant, because whenever there was a chance, he walked about, looked at equipment and talked to the soldiers. At no stage did he interfere with my command, although, from time to time and when asked, he gave his opinion."[35]

By early afternoon on 13 June, the Smokeshell complex was completely free of SWAPO and in South African possession. Altogether, 267 bodies of PLAN fighters were found and buried, while 10 anti-aircraft guns and huge quantities of ammunition were also taken. Because of the length of the operation, it was judged that the insurgents had evacuated their bases at Ionde and that it would be unnecessary to attack that as well. Then 61 Mech moved back to the base area at Mulemba, where the following day the troops crowded every available radio to listen to the rugby Test between the Springboks and the visiting British Lions. Their day was made when the Boks trounced the Lions 26–9, which made up somewhat for the traumatic battle of four days before.

According to Geldenhuys, a pattern developed during Operation Sceptic that would be repeated later. "Firstly, an ants' nest is kicked open and the ants scatter. Secondly, there is a search around the nest for ants. Smokeshell was the ants' nest. Most cadres swarmed out in little groups to seek refuge at their other nests, or bases. Then a combination of area operations, follow-ups, and search-and-destroy operations were launched to locate and destroy them."[36]

It is not necessary to follow the operations of the next few days in detail. Suffice to say that the South Africans stormed various PLAN bases, but found them empty, hurriedly evacuated after the huge clash at Smokeshell.[37] In the course of these operations, Chris Serfontein and Combat Group 10 also clashed with SWAPO's so-called mechanised brigade north of Xangongo. Apparently, Serfontein came across the enemy rearguard and immediately attacked with two companies, assisted by some SAAF Impalas and mortar fire. Jannie Geldenhuys, who was present, relates that there wasn't really a true fight, as SWAPO immediately broke and fled. Many documents, as well as 76-mm guns and other war materiel, were captured and taken back to South West Africa.[38]

But, on the way back to SWA, something happened to Serfontein's Combat

Group 10 that would be an ominous harbinger of what lay ahead. The plan was for the force to move through the village of Mongua, where it would meet up with Dippenaar's force and return home. What Serfontein did not know was that a company-size mechanised FAPLA force was concentrated there. It appears that the Angolans were as surprised as the South African advance party (travelling in Buffels) when the two parties unexpectedly bumped into each other, but both recovered quickly. The Angolans charged with three BTR-152 armoured personnel carriers, but the South Africans knocked them out in quick succession. Serfontein immediately sent a reinforcement company to the front, and together they counterattacked. An air strike with Mirages followed, and the Angolans fled.[39]

The fight itself was not that remarkable; the South Africans reacted rapidly to an unexpected situation and came out on top. This would happen countless times in the future. What made this fight especially noteworthy is that this was the first time that the SADF and FAPLA had clashed while the South Africans were fighting SWAPO. Given the circumstances, one gets the impression that it was purely incidental – there was no deliberate attempt by FAPLA to intervene in the war between the SADF and PLAN. Nevertheless, a line had been crossed, and within a relatively short time the South Africans would find it more and more difficult to fight against PLAN without coming up against FAPLA as well.

Conclusion

Operation Sceptic, especially the Battle of Smokeshell, was an important development in the Border War. Its predecessors, operations Reindeer, Rekstok and Saffraan, had been limited in scope and time. Sceptic evolved into a much longer operation, during which PLAN was hunted deep within its own rear areas in Angola for about three weeks. Apart from Savannah, this was the biggest and longest operation the SADF had been involved in since 1945.

Another difference from the Battle of Cassinga was that the result at Smokeshell was never really in doubt, in spite of the sudden setback Combat Team 2 suffered in the south of the complex. Although the troops of 61 Mech were highly trained and motivated, they had seen no action before the battle, yet they acquitted themselves well. The members of Louis Harmse's Combat Team 2 in particular would be understandably haunted by their experience for decades to come, but even in the face of death they did what they had to do – they attacked the enemy and defeated him.

Nevertheless, Operation Sceptic laid bare a number of deficiencies in the SADF that had to be remedied. These are addressed below.

Intelligence: Several officers were not satisfied with the intelligence they received about the Smokeshell complex. According to Commandant Dippenaar, there "remained uncertainty about the nature of the target". For instance, even though he knew Smokeshell consisted of 13 bases, it was unclear what "the composition of the enemy" was in each complex.[40] The biggest factor at the time was whether the enemy was dug in or not. The battle plan was based on information that there were only shallow foxholes. The fact that this information was wrong was directly responsible for the problems encountered by Combat Team 2.

The army and SAAF: During this operation the coordination between the SAAF and the army was less than optimal. Firstly, the air attacks in the preceding days either would have warned SWAPO of a planned attack or would have encouraged an evacuation as a precaution against further attacks. Secondly, on the day of the attack on Smokeshell the air attacks were not properly coordinated with the ground assault. Given that the ground forces would reach Smokeshell only later that day, what was the advantage of an early-morning attack? It only gave PLAN time to recover their wits and either prepare for the expected assault or melt away into the dense bush. Reflecting on the battle, Paul Fouché quite correctly wrote in his report: "Air support must be followed up immediately with an attack."[41] Louis Harmse and Jakes Jacobs also criticised the coordination between the air force and the army.[42]

Underestimating your enemy: In his war diary, Commandant Dippenaar states that intelligence had indicated that PLAN would not stand and fight, and that the leaders would flee first.[43] It is true that the defenders of the northern parts of the complex had fled before the attack started, but many of those in the south stood fast and fought courageously. Combat Team 2's attack, with the Ratels' 20-mm guns rattling and the Ratel 90s spewing death and destruction, must have been very frightening. Yet eyewitness accounts tell of SWAPO cadres fighting to the death, spraying the South Africans with deadly fire from 14,5-mm and 23-mm anti-aircraft guns.

In a comment reminiscent of Cassinga, eyewitness Chris de Klerk explained how SWAPO kept at it: "When you shot one terr behind his gun, another jumped in, and if you shoot him another jumps up. If you shot one it didn't mean the weapon didn't work any more – they jumped like rabbits out of those holes, and carried on shooting at you."[44]

It is never a good policy to underestimate your enemy.

Navigation: The terrain in and around Smokeshell was flat and featureless, while dense bush restricted sight and faint paths made navigation difficult. Several times, both during the advance and at the target itself, the South Africans lost their way and floundered about. Once, an SAAF spotter plane guided them back to where they had to be; at other times, they only had a general idea of where they were. This would prove to be an issue for the duration of the war. Only in 1983/1984 did the artillery get a primitive kind of navigation system, along the lines of the Global Positioning System (GPS), which took about 75 minutes to set up.[45]

Equipment: Several equipment problems were identified during Operation Sceptic. Firstly, experience confirmed that the Eland was not really suited to the kind of lightning operations the SADF was conducting. The Eland still burned petrol, whereas all the other vehicles ran on diesel, and its range was considerably less than that of the Ratel (300 km against the 800 km of the Ratel). This made logistics more complicated. During Sceptic, the Elands sometimes ran out of fuel when the Ratels still had more than enough, with the result that the Noddy cars had to be towed.

But even the Ratels gave problems. The accumulation of leaves clogged the air intakes and caused the vehicles to overheat and even to catch fire. More than one 20-mm gun was bent by the vehicle smashing through bushes and trees.

As during Operation Reindeer, the radios gave trouble. Units and sub-units found it difficult to talk to each other; communication with tactical headquarters at Eenhana was problematic; and the SAAF aircraft and the army on the ground could not converse easily.

The artillery dated from the Second World War, and the gunners had trouble calibrating their old guns for accurate fire. Their Magirus Deutz gun tractors overheated, and the old towing equipment sometimes broke down due to metal fatigue.

Operation Sceptic finally proved that the 7,62-mm R1 rifle was not suitable for mechanised operations. It was an excellent weapon, with formidable stopping power, and was very well liked by the troops, but the R1 was too large to be used comfortably from within a Ratel. During his time at the front, General Viljoen carried a 5,56-mm R4, an adaptation of the Israeli Galil rifle, with a folding stock, which would become – and at the time of writing still is – the standard South African Army rifle.

By and large, Sceptic was a valuable learning experience for the SADF and provided several lessons, large and small, which would be applied on forthcoming operations.

One question remains to be answered. Did Sceptic succeed in its objective? The SADF lost 17 soldiers, as well as one Impala light jet bomber and an Alouette III helicopter. The number of PLAN bodies counted were 380. Several hundred tonnes of arms and ammunition were destroyed, and some 150 tonnes, including vehicles and light artillery, were taken back to SWA.[46] SADF Military Intelligence estimated that about 75% of PLAN's transport capacity had been taken or destroyed.[47] The statistics were impressive.

All the sources are unanimous that SWAPO had suffered a substantial reverse: several of its bases were destroyed, its forces were scattered, many fighters were killed and much materiel was destroyed. The South Africans also captured several secret documents, which revealed SWAPO's future plans.

But, despite Operation Sceptic's seemingly conventional nature, it should not be evaluated according to conventional warfare standards. The Border War was essentially a counterinsurgency and guerrilla war, even if the battlefield had been moved from Ovamboland to Cunene province. And in a guerrilla war, reverses like this one are, in the long run, not all that important. After the South Africans had left, PLAN would reoccupy the bases or establish new ones. Their arms and equipment would be replenished – the Kremlin would see to that.

Therefore, although the planned infiltration offensive that gave rise to Operation Sceptic in the first place was disrupted, the effect was temporary. That offensive went ahead, albeit in reduced form. According to Willem Steenkamp,

July saw 65 PLAN fighters killed in Ovamboland, 102 in August and 170 in September,[48] suggesting that Sceptic did not really reduce PLAN's capacity to infiltrate into South West Africa. Indeed, when viewing the statistics, 1980 saw an absolute peak of 1 175 incidents (contacts, ambushes, mines detonated, incidents of intimidation and sabotage). But a total of 1 147 PLAN fighters were also killed (*see* tables in Chapter 9). Could PLAN take the punishment and still continue as an effective force? The next few years would tell.

7

THE SADF SHIFTS GEAR:
PROTEA AND DAISY

As 1981 dawned, the war was still very much hanging in the balance. SWAPO had been hard hit the previous year, but was by no means down. Even though some of its recruits were abducted from South West Africa or otherwise pressed into service, PLAN still got enough reinforcements, and its cadres were aggressive when they clashed head-on with South African forces. The Battle of Smokeshell had shown the SADF that a large-scale, conventional cross-border operation was a difficult and intricate affair, and, when the wolf was attacked in its lair, it had the will and capacity to bite back.

Nevertheless, Operation Sceptic had been an example of what could be achieved. It temporarily relieved the pressure on the counterinsurgency forces fighting the rebels in SWA. SWAPO started recovering in late 1980 and early 1981, by which time the SADF had settled into a two-pronged strategy: a classic counterinsurgency campaign south of the border in South West Africa, and large, pre-emptive conventional strikes north of the border, augmented with countless smaller operations in the so-called shallow areas just inside Angola. The counterinsurgency war inside SWA is discussed in Chapter 9, but it is necessary to mention here that SWAPO's insurgency campaign once again increased in strength in the first half of 1981. Thus, from an SADF viewpoint, the military situation was deteriorating.[1]

Throughout the early months of 1981, several small and not-so-small operations were launched into Angola, mainly by elements of 32 Battalion, and at times by 1 Parachute Battalion as well. In the process, the South Africans observed that FAPLA was becoming ever more aggressive and unwilling to stand aside while the SADF took on PLAN. Nevertheless, for the time being the South African policy remained strict – not to fight FAPLA if it could be helped.[2]

The largest of these operations was Carnation, which lasted from 20 June to early August. As usual, the brunt was borne by 32 Battalion, aided by the paratroopers, while elements of the counterinsurgency battalions in Namibia were also involved at times. The purpose of the operation was to disrupt SWAPO's logistics in the southern regions of Cunene province. It developed into a cat-and-mouse game. PLAN evacuated its bases as the South Africans advanced, dispersing into the bush or running for cover under FAPLA's wing. When the operation petered out, very little had been achieved. Altogether 20 insurgents were killed and 4 captured, while several SWAPO bases were destroyed and its logistics disrupted. In this type of war, however, such advantages are fleeting.[3]

Furthermore, although Carnation (and the smaller Operation Ceiling) succeeded in driving SWAPO further away from the SWA border, with a concomitant reduction in PLAN activity in some areas, this happened only in the central and eastern regions of Ovamboland. In the west, because of the growing integration between SWAPO and FAPLA, PLAN continued its war unabated.[4]

Intelligence indicated a major build-up of SWAPO supplies in Cunene province, and operations inside Angola could not stop the infiltration into South West Africa. In July alone, 277 PLAN fighters were killed south of the border (52 of them in just four days),[5] indicating the rate of SWAPO infiltration. More action was needed.

In May 1981, Major General Charles Lloyd, who had taken over from Jannie Geldenhuys as the ranking SADF officer in South West Africa the previous year, wrote to Constand Viljoen, Chief of the SADF, recommending further strikes against SWAPO inside Angola. He pointed out that SWAPO had evaded SADF forces operating in Angola since Sceptic, quickly evacuating bases whenever they became aware of South Africans in the vicinity, and returning after 48 hours or so when the troops had left. He concluded that the SADF had to operate for longer periods in Angola and dominate a territory, instead of going in after specific bases and leaving again immediately afterwards.[6]

Lloyd observed that SWAPO had sought protection from FAPLA, the Angolan regular army. "Some SWAPO bases are also inside and others near to these FAPLA-controlled areas and so enjoy FAPLA protection. Further SWAPO is served by the same logistic routes as FAPLA." He felt that SWAPO's communication lines across the Cunene River should be permanently broken up. To this end, he urged Viljoen to destroy the combined FAPLA/SWAPO strong-points at Xangongo, Mongua and Ongiva.[7]

That the cooperation between SWAPO and FAPLA was increasing, to the detriment of the SADF, was true. A briefing document compiled after Operation Protea stated that PLAN was logistically fairly independent in the eastern sector, and that FAPLA in this region heeded SADF warnings not to interfere with operations against SWAPO.[8] Indeed, Jan Breytenbach relates that 32 Battalion's commander, Commandant Deon Ferreira, had a fairly cordial relationship with his FAPLA counterpart at Ongiva, Major Alfonso María, and even wrote María a letter thanking him for his cooperation and warning him to stay out of the unit's way. However, further west at Xangongo, the local FAPLA commander was much more aggressive, and constantly harassed SADF patrols in his region.[9] It was there, not coincidentally, that the fusion between PLAN and FAPLA was most intense. The briefing document went on: "SWAPO's logistical system is fully integrated with that of FAPLA, using the main road from Cahama to Xangongo. It is also known that the defensive positions of SWAPO and FAPLA, especially in the Xangongo area, are completely integrated. In the past FAPLA forces in this region have interfered with SF [Security Force] operations against SWAPO."[10] All of this meant that Lloyd's recommendations to attack SWAPO in the central and western sector became all the more urgent.

Preparing for Protea

Operation Protea was even bigger than Sceptic. More than that, it would turn out to be the largest SADF operation of the entire Border War – in many ways even larger than operations Moduler, Hooper and Packer during the climax of the conflict in 1987/1988. An estimated 4 000 troops participated in this operation.[11] Protea was an intricate mechanised operation with many strands, movements and units. It can be difficult to follow, and so, for the sake of clarity, we will identify and separate these strands right away.

Overall command was exercised by Brigadier Rudolf "Witkop" Badenhorst, the officer commanding Sector 10, with his headquarters at Oshakati. For the duration of the operation, the army forces in the operational area were organised into three task forces – Alpha, Bravo and Charlie – each more or less

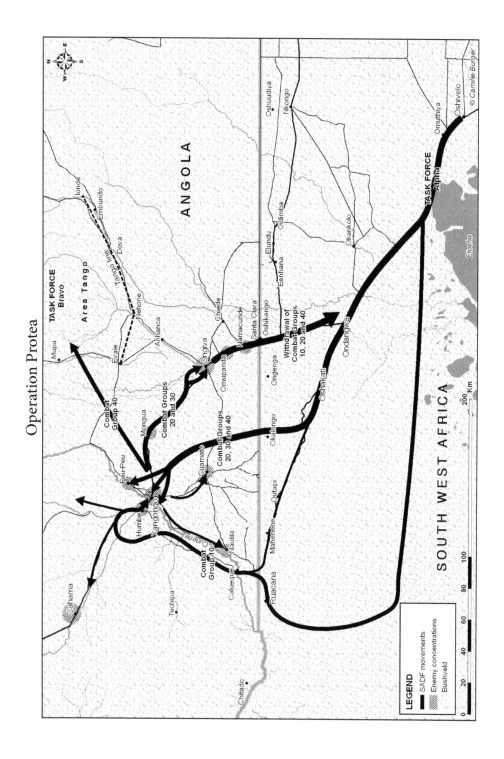

equivalent to a brigade. We can remove Charlie from the picture right away; this force consisted of all the units not involved in the operation and it continued with the counterinsurgency war in northern SWA.

Bravo, under the command of Colonel Vos Benade, would also play a lesser role. Its orders were to conduct area operations in what the SADF called Area Tango, in eastern Cunene province.[12]

The heavy punch of the operation would be provided by Task Force Alpha, a mixed mechanised and motorised infantry force under the command of Colonel Joep Joubert, who would also command the next cross-border operation (Askari) some 29 months later. One of his sub-commanders, Roland de Vries, called him an "an accomplished operational commander" who "understood mechanised warfare".[13] Jan Breytenbach, who did not suffer fools gladly, also had a high opinion of Joubert.[14]

Alpha was in turn divided into four battle groups (for this operation, the term "battle group" was used instead of the standard SADF use of "combat group":[15]

- Battle Group 10 (Commandant Roland de Vries) consisted of a somewhat beefed-down 61 Mechanised Battalion Group – that is, a mechanised infantry company (Ratel 20s), a parachute company (motorised for this operation on Buffels), an armoured car squadron, a mortar platoon, a troop of 140-mm artillery, and a combat engineer troop. One Ratel 20 company and a Ratel 90 troop from the antitank platoon was detached to serve as Task Force Alpha's reserve.
- Battle Group 20 (Commandant Johann "Dippies" Dippenaar, who had also commanded Combat Group 61 during Operation Sceptic). This group was stronger than De Vries's group, with two motorised infantry companies in Buffels, a mechanised infantry company (Ratel 20s), two extra motorised infantry platoons, two armoured car squadrons (Ratel 90s, Eland 90s and Eland 60s), a 140-mm artillery battery, and a combat engineer troop. This force was created specifically for Protea and disbanded afterwards.
- Battle Group 30 (Commandant Chris Serfontein, who had also been involved in Sceptic), was in charge of three motorised infantry companies (Buffels), an armoured car squadron (Eland 90s), a 120-mm mortar battery, an 81-mm mortar platoon and a combat engineer platoon.

- Battle Group 40 (Commandant Deon Ferreira). This force had three motorised infantry companies (Buffels) from 32 Battalion, an armoured car squadron (Eland 90s), a battery of 120-mm mortars, a combat engineer troop and four antitank teams.
- Finally, there was the newly established pathfinder company of 44 Parachute Brigade under the command of Captain (later Colonel) Andreas "Rooies" Velthuizen. Jan Breytenbach, who commanded the brigade, went along for the ride. Nobody really knew what to do with the company, and it operated pretty much on its own.

For the first time in the war, an artillery troop equipped with 127-mm Valkiri multiple rocket launchers (MRLs) was also deployed.[16] This weapon system would prove to be one of the most successful of the war. While only a limited number were available for Protea, they would cause great headaches for their adversaries in future operations.

The air force assembled a fleet of 142 aircraft, the largest concentration of firepower since 1945. The strike force consisted of 12 Mirage F1AZs, 8 Mirage F1CZs, 7 Mirage IIICZs, 6 Mirage IIID2Zs (two-seaters), 16 Impala IIs, 5 Buccaneers and 5 Canberras. This was the last time the Mirage IIICZ would be used operationally, as it was by then obsolete. (Dick Lord calls the Mirage III "the disappointment of the war".)[17] This armada was augmented by various photo-reconnaissance, transport and spotter aircraft, as well as helicopters.

Also, for the first time, the SAAF would employ an unmanned aerial vehicle (UAV) for reconnaissance purposes. At this stage it was known as a "Gharra", but later in the decade it would get the more conventional name of Seeker.[18]

The objective of Operation Protea was "to neutralise SWAPO's military forces in Southern Angola between the Cunene and Kavango rivers . . ." in order to make the movement's war inside SWA more difficult. To achieve this, SWAPO bases at Humbe, Xangongo and Ongiva would be taken out. The operational headquarters of PLAN's northwestern front was located at Xangongo, while Ongiva contained a large logistics base. One of the guidelines for Protea was: "Not to attack any FAPLA positions or troops unless they interfered and the safety of own forces were thus threatened."[19] This proved to be a forlorn hope.

On the "other side of the hill", FAPLA's forces in Cunene province consisted of 2 Division, with its headquarters at Lubango, where SWAPO's military leadership was also ensconced. According to South African intelligence estimates, the division had six brigades, of which three were stationed close enough to pose a threat to the SADF force. There was 21 Brigade at Cahama, which the South Africans suspected was the division's mobile reserve. It would, therefore, have to be closely watched. In addition, 19 Brigade was stationed at Xangongo and Peu-Peu, and 11 Brigade at Ongiva.

The force at Xangongo comprised two infantry battalions, a tank company (or squadron in SADF parlance) with T-34s, an armoured car squadron with BTR-23s, an artillery battery, three 122-mm rocket launchers and seven anti-aircraft guns (which could be used against ground attackers as well), plus a PLAN infantry force. Some of the defences were in reinforced concrete bunkers. FAPLA and SWAPO were integrated to the extent that the one could not be attacked without the other's being hit too. The bulk of the defences, SADF intelligence observed, faced southward.[20]

In light of the SADF's large force, the achievement of operational surprise was out of the question. As Sceptic had shown, PLAN's intelligence system was very good; as soon as Battle Group 61 had penetrated Angola, SWAPO scouts and patrols were aware of it. It would not be any different this time, and the SADF knew it.[21] But, while operational surprise was impossible, tactical surprise was not.

Because the Xangongo defences were oriented toward the south,[22] it was decided that 32 Battalion would assault from the north, where SWAPO/FAPLA obviously did not expect it, while Dippenaar's Battle Group 20, with its heavier punch, would take on the enemy from the east and southeast. At the same time, Battle Group 10 (De Vries) would move on Humbe (6 km west of Xangongo), act as a big stopper group to cut off any PLAN escape across the bridge at Xangongo to the west, and prevent any intervention by FAPLA from the direction of Cahama. It would, at the same time, be well placed to stop FAPLA forces fleeing from Xangongo to Cahama.

For its part, Battle Group 30 (Serfontein) would march on Peu-Peu, to the northeast of Xangongo, and cover the main attack force from that side. A small force of parabats was to be dropped by C-130 far to the north, 15 km south of Techamutete, to act as a tripwire against any possible intervention from that side. (Luckily for the South Africans, nothing happened there.) In this way, the Xangongo battlefield would be isolated. After that, Battle Groups 20 and 30 would march in a southeasterly direction and take Ongiva, while Battle Group 40 (Ferreira) would be transferred to Task Force Bravo. Thereafter the force would be pulled back to South West Africa. The idea was to go in fast, hit the enemy hard, and pull out. The operation would last no longer than 14 days.[23] H-hour was supposed to be 11h00 on 24 August.

Xangongo would not be an easy nut to crack. Military Intelligence had identified "eight clearly identifiable defence complexes/targets", each defended by a mixed force of between 50 and 150 soldiers.[24] After the battle, Ferreira discovered a map in the FAPLA headquarters with all the details of the defences. Breytenbach, who also saw the map, comments:

> It was an elaborate and detailed series of "hedgehog" type strongpoints of a kind developed by the Soviets to use against NATO forces if they had got it into their heads to launch an invasion of Warsaw Pact countries. In a typical and unimaginative fashion, the Soviets took the whole system without a single significant change and transplanted it into the African bush.[25]

The South African plan was sound. It conformed to all operational and tactical principles, especially to do the unexpected and catch the enemy unawares. Also, this time there would be no lapse of several hours between the air attack on the target and the beginning of the ground assault (as had happened at Smokeshell); the troops would move in while the ground was still shaking from the bomb explosions.

There was, however, one strange aspect to the plan. There can be no doubt that 61 Mech was the army's most potent and best-trained unit for conventional mobile operations like Protea. Its predecessor, Battle Group Juliet, had been the trailblazer during Operation Reindeer. The unit was also the mail fist during Sceptic. Now, instead of being the hammer to hit SWAPO at Xangongo, it got a lesser task – guard duty to the west. Furthermore, it was stripped of one of its mechanised infantry companies and its antitank platoon to act as Task Force Alpha's mobile reserve (Combat Team Mamba, under the command of

Commandant Johnny Coetzer). Instead of the normal two troops of artillery, it retained only one. De Vries was not at all impressed,[26] while at least one of his company commanders, Captain (later Brigadier General) Koos Liebenberg, made no bones about his disgust at 61 Mech's treatment in his company report on the operation.[27]

Instead, Battle Group 20 – which had only recently been called into being and could not possibly have reached the same degree of proficiency as 61 Mech – was made the spearpoint. Although Dippenaar was one of the ablest officers in the army, he certainly had a challenging task. There were five different units represented in the combat arm that started to arrive from 7 to 15 August (9 days before D-day). Combat equipment had to be made operational and soldiers had to be married-up and integrated into a combat-ready force.[28]

The Battle of Xangongo

Very early on 23 August, the various battle groups left their bases in South West Africa. With enough provisions for 10 days, they marched to the places where they would cross the border: Battle Group 10 to Ruacana in western Ovamboland, and Battle Groups 20, 30 and 40 to Ombalantu further eastwards. This meant that the invading troops would have a presence on both sides of the Cunene River. They crossed the cutline during the night of 23/24 August, and, under cover of darkness, the troops moved northwards as fast as they could, which, with the dense bush and difficult terrain, was once again not as fast as their commanders would have liked.

PLAN's intelligence was excellent: when Ondangwa Air Force Base was closed shortly before the start of the operation, SWAPO trumpeted the news of an impending operation to the world. One may assume that a flood of messages went back and forth between PLAN and FAPLA. What they did not know, of course, was where the first blows would fall.[29]

In fact, the first blow was dealt by the SAAF. FAPLA had been erecting an early-warning radar system in Cunene province, the presence of which would make it more difficult for South African aircraft to support army troops on the ground. And so, on 23 August, the day before the assault on Xangongo, a forma-tion of Buccaneers, Canberras and Mirage F1s carried out several strikes on the

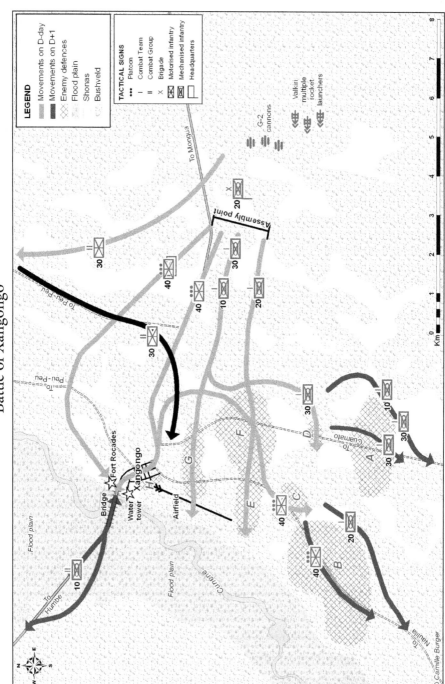

Battle of Xangongo

© Camille Burger

radar installations at Cahama and Chibemba with a mixture of AS-30 guided missiles and bombs. Apparently, not all weapons hit the targets, but the result, nevertheless, was satisfactory from a South African point of view. All radar signals went off the air. This meant that SAAF air supremacy would not be challenged for the duration of Operation Protea.[30]

After crossing the Cunene River at Ruacana, Roland de Vries's Battle Group 10 marched on the town of Humbe, as ordered. The column stormed the town from the northwest, having softened up the target with artillery fire, fully prepared to crush any resistance with brute firepower. Upon spotting a number of fleeing FAPLA soldiers, De Vries decided to hold his fire and let them go. It was just as well, because just then seven Roman Catholic nuns appeared in the company of "the sick and the lame and the lazy". "I would not wish to have borne the brunt of international outcry or be the cause of it for South Africa. South Africa was in enough trouble as it were from the international community," De Vries later remarked.[31]

To the frustration of the South Africans, who were spoiling for a fight, Humbe was otherwise deserted. According to Lieutenant Gert Minnaar, the SWAPO comrades had left in such a hurry that the surprised South Africans found abandoned washing fluttering in the wind. Battle Group 10 then deployed to the west to cover any attempt by FAPLA to intervene from the direction of Cahama.[32] With this, De Vries's first phase was over.

At Ombalantu, Battle Group 40 (Deon Ferreira) led the way, followed by Battle Group 20 (Johann Dippenaar) and Battle Group 30 (Chris Serfontein). This proved to be an unsatisfactory situation, as 40 was less mobile than 20. It caused considerable frustration for Dippenaar, who was champing at the bit and wanted to keep to the schedule. Along the way, Dippenaar tried to overtake Ferreira, but the terrain and bush made it impossible. To add to his impatience, at 09h15 Dippenaar discovered that the column was too far east and had to be rerouted, which meant more time lost. Also, the SAAF air strike was postponed for 15 minutes. H-hour, which was supposed to be at 11h00, was first postponed to 11h30, and finally to 12h00.

At 11h50 the SAAF finally unleashed its bombers. Altogether, six waves of aircraft swooped over the battlefield like angry falcons and mercilessly pounded the intermingled Angolan and PLAN positions on the ground. Jan Breytenbach, who was present with 44 Parachute Brigade's pathfinder company, which attached itself to Battle Group 40 in the northern part of the battlefield, watched how

> [s]teeply diving F-1 Mirages were met by intensive anti-aircraft fire that rose in greenish streams of tracer from the fort area. It was an impressive and disconcerting display of firepower. I knew, as did everybody else, that the same guns would soon be directing their tracers directly at us across open ground that would suddenly appear devoid of cover.[33]

The ground assault commenced immediately, with the FAPLA and PLAN troops still reeling from the shock of the air strike. In the north, Ferreira's 32 Battalion soldiers stormed the defensive positions – mostly trenches and bunkers – on foot. Clearing a trench system is dangerous and hard work; the attackers have to advance using fire and movement, one group covering the other with gunfire while they storm forward, and then jumping into the trenches, throwing hand grenades, shooting the enemy at gunpoint or even clubbing them to death. The battery of 120-mm mortars helped keep the enemy's heads down. After a while, the enemy resistance crumbled and the defenders fled. Battle Group 40 was in possession of all FAPLA and PLAN positions.

In the south, Dippenaar's troops stormed the opposing trenches from the east at 13h25, but found the first ones empty. Apparently, the air strike in the north and the artillery fire had convinced the defenders that it could be bad for their health to stay, and they had taken to their heels. As they moved forward, the attackers started drawing desultory rifle and machine-gun fire, until they were stopped by one of those devastating Soviet 23-mm anti-aircraft guns. Knowing the weapon's fearsome capacity, Dippenaar halted the attack and called for air support.

To his chagrin, it took 40 minutes for the SAAF to respond. The first attack had no effect; the gun continued firing. Dippenaar asked for a second strike, for which he had to wait in growing frustration for another 20 minutes. This one was unsuccessful as well. Dippenaar then lost patience and ordered his artillery to take out the gun. He must almost have had a heart attack when the guns could not silence the enemy either. On top of everything, some of the artillery shells landed on Battle Group 40's troops, wounding 15 of them.

What happened next is best told in the words of Captain Danie Laubscher, the pilot of a Bosbok observation aircraft, who was spotting for the artillery. Laubscher heard about the 23-mm holding up Dippenaar's troops (he thought it was only a 14,5 mm) and flew towards the scene:

> After the second or third sortie of Mirages had no success Spyker [Jacobs, commander of the SAAF Mobile Air Operating Team on the ground] called me ... and asked me to help ... I heard the Mirages – think one of the pilots was Norman Minne – calling "rolling in". I actually picked them up and watched them dive down and fire some 68-mm rockets. The moment they lifted their noses I saw flashes from the ack-ack site as the cannon was firing on the Mirages. It was clear to me that the "vlammies" [jet pilots] were also shooting "blind" as their rockets did not explode close to the target. They rolled in again, the firing from the site stopped, the 68's missed again and the firing from the site started again.
>
> Now I must state here that we were briefed that the only "known" ack-ack at Xangongo were a 14,5 mm. In general we were not too worried about the 14,5 as it was not a very accurate cannon, and flying at 6 000 agl [above ground level] we were relatively safe. However, watching the flashes I realised that it could not be a 14,5 as the rate of fire was much more than what a 14,5 can fire at. Reports from the ground also indicated that it did not sound like a 14,5. But Int [Intelligence] was adamant that it must be a 14,5, so that's what it was.
>
> By now I realised that the FAC [forward air controller] himself wasn't sure exactly where the target was, so I chipped in and said that I'll take control and mark the target with a smoke rocket. The reason why we carried smoke rockets was not to take out the target – that's why we have vlammies in the SAAF – but to mark the vicinity of the target, using it as a reference to explain to the Mirages where the target is and they then take it out. Also Bosbok pilots will tell you that the rockets fired from a Bosbok [are] "extremely" inaccurate – probably due to the low speed (120 to 160 kts) at which they are released. To mark this target

I sort of lobbed a smoke rocket in the general direction. It exploded a distance from the target and I gave corrections to the Mirages. However they missed and I fired another smoke rocket that was bit closer, but still the Mirages could not hit the exact spot. I must come up for the vlammies here – they were basically shooting at my corrections and not at the specific target, as it was very difficult for them to spot it while diving down at 400+ kts.

I realised that the only way to "neutralise" this target was to mark it more accurately, and the only way to do that was to get closer to it. I had a brief discussion with Tinus [the artillery officer] in the back, explaining the situation to him and what I wanted to do. He agreed . . . So rocket pod selected on, pitch full fine to get max speed in the dive, a nice steep wingover and down we went. In the dive I noticed that the cannon was busy firing at me, so I told Tinus to "hang on" as a lot of lead was flying around. For a moment I contemplated selecting ripple mode and firing the remaining 4 smoke rockets but realised that it would be even more confusing for Mirages if there were 4 smoke areas scattered all over southern Angola.

Sometime during the dive I decided that I was probably as close as I would like to be and pulled the trigger. 1 x smoke rocket streaked towards the target. I pulled the nose up into a steep climb and rolled to the left. Looking back at the target I noticed that the smoke of the rocket was coming out of the pit where the ack-ack was deployed. I called the Mirages and told them that the target was right there where my smoke was, only to be told that they were out of ammo and fuel and returning to Ondangwa.

A while later Spyker called me and said that the battle group is busy crossing the road and that the ack-ack was not firing on them. On reaching the specific site they found the gunner sitting in his chair with a 68-mm hole through him where my smoke rocket hit. If there ever was a "mogge troffe" [trust to luck] then this was it. (After the war the SAAF wanted to court martial me and the Army wanted to give me a medal.) Luckily the Army won. What they found was not a 14,5-mm ack-ack cannon, but a ZU23-2 – a much more deadly weapon.[34]

At last, the infantry could advance and take the position – more than two-and-a-half hours after the attack had commenced. For this action, Danie Laubscher received an Honoris Crux.

The armoured cars destroyed at least three 23-mm guns and three tanks. With their fire and movement drill working like an efficient machine, they advanced further, flattening all resistance, and took the airfield. One by one, the bunkers and trenches were stormed and cleared, and they moved on.

Because of the heavy going, late in the afternoon a combat team from Battle Group 30 was ordered to reinforce Dippenaar, who had already thrown his own reserve into the fighting. Compared with what had happened at Smokeshell more than a year ago, command and control was much easier to exercise, although the attack was not exactly a walk in the park. By last light, Battle Groups 40 and 20 were in possession of most of the positions at Xangongo. In excess of 200 of the enemy were killed, against three South Africans from Dippenaar's force. It is not known how many members of Ferreira's battle group (mostly black Angolans) lost their lives.

Serfontein reported that the enemy at Peu-Peu was stirring, and he readied Battle Group 30, which had been placed to the northeast to counter exactly that possibility. A sizeable FAPLA force, consisting of tanks, infantry and artillery, advanced to help their compatriots at Xangongo. Serfontein did not hesitate, and counterattacked. A sharp fight followed, after which the Angolans chose prudence above valour and retreated. Serfontein occupied the town, capturing a staggering 200 to 300 tonnes of ammunition, 120 000 litres of diesel and 90 000 litres of petrol. Three tanks and a large number of armoured cars and armoured personnel carriers, as well as several anti-aircraft guns, were destroyed.[35]

An SADF briefing document about the operation contains this interesting observation: "During the battle at Xangongo, the fiercest resistance was encountered where positions were jointly manned by SWAPO and FAPLA. SWAPO's office in Xangongo was discovered but the leaders had already fled with the

Russians."[36] This suggests two conclusions: firstly, that SWAPO's rank and file fought more determinedly than FAPLA, and secondly, that SWAPO's leaders were not the stuff heroes were made of.

The night that followed was tense. Two separate incidents occurred, one in the north and the other to the south of the target. Breytenbach described the scene in the north, when the combat team of Captain Jan Hougaard opened fire:

> For a moment the enemy, not realising what was going on, were sitting ducks. Then panic set in. Soldiers jumped from their vehicles and fled towards the bridge. A few tried to run the gauntlet in their trucks, but most of them came to flaming grief. Streams of tracer fire pierced the night sky seemingly from every direction, which heightened the chaos.[37]

In the south, Dippenaar moved Battle Group 20 southeast of the target area into a laager. Early in the morning, noises were heard that sounded like a sizeable force with tanks moving in the darkness from the south towards Xangongo. Dippenaar realised that the laager could be the target, and immediately instructed Captain Louis Harmse (the same Harmse we encountered at Smokeshell) to lead two troops of Ratel 90s on foot to the southern side of the laager, where there was a dirt road coming from the south and passing on the side of the laager.

Dippenaar described the deployment as very efficient and quick. With their 90-mm guns, the Ratels spewed fire and death, and soon the enemy vehicles were smoking wrecks. Most of these were loaded with ammunition, which exploded with a thundering noise for more than an hour. The battle group's logistics vehicles, including fuel trucks, were parked in the second row, not far from the explosions. This "was enough to make anyone afraid", Dippenaar commented wryly.[38]

By 12h00 on 25 August, the mop-up operation was just about finished. Shortly afterwards, shooting broke out and Harmse was hit in the chest, dying within minutes. Harmse had blamed himself for the heavy casualties sustained by his team at Smokeshell, and had made every effort to be included in Operation Protea. Whether he was right to reproach himself or not, he had more than redeemed himself and was buried as a brave officer and one who was sorely missed by his men.

An unexpected visitor to the battlefield was Lieutenant General Jannie Geldenhuys, who had been promoted to the position of Chief of the Army. He was especially interested in the performance of the artillery's Valkiri multiple rocket launchers, which were undergoing their baptism of fire in Protea.[39]

Roland de Vries conferred with Joep Joubert, who placed Jan Breytenbach's pathfinder company from 44 Parachute Brigade under De Vries's command and told him to continue covering the SADF force on the western side towards Cahama, where a FAPLA brigade still lurked. De Vries left Commandant Dawid Mentz in command of Xangongo and had Breytenbach's force tag westwards with a combat team from Battle Group 10 under Major Joe Weyers to guard against FAPLA intervening from the direction of Cahama.[40] The combat team encountered signs that the position had been recently vacated by a large enemy force.[41]

During the night, the combat team and the pathfinder company bumped into a much stronger FAPLA force, which was coming from their rear and trying to break through to Cahama. The South Africans promptly attacked and routed the enemy, capturing several 23-mm guns and other vehicles.[42] If the FAPLA brigade commander at Cahama had possessed a spine, this would have been an excellent time to prove it. Only two South African companies, of which one (the pathfinders) was only lightly armed, stood between his brigade and the SADF force at Xangongo. A resolute officer could, at the very least, have created problems for Joubert's task force. But the Angolan commander followed the example of his counterparts at Ongiva and Mongua and sat, as Roland de Vries puts it, "in suspended animation whilst Xangongo was killed".[43]

Be that as it may, the South Africans spent this and the next day in a sweep of the vicinity to destroy other SWAPO bases whose location had been indicated on maps discovered at Xangongo. All the bases were found hastily abandoned,[44] and by 15h00 on 26 August the force began to ready itself for the second major phase of the operation.

The attack on Mongua

Task Force Alpha was now reorganised. Battle Group 10 took over Xangongo to protect the task force against intervention from the direction of Lubango and Cahama. It also had to protect the bridge over the Cunene at Xangongo, an important choke point between eastern and western Cunene province. It was important to keep the bridge in South African hands, as this was the place where Angolan reinforcements would come from the west. The bridge was prepared for demolition, and De Vries decided to transfer his entire force to the east of the bridge. FAPLA's passive stance at Cahama convinced him that he had nothing to fear from that direction.[45]

Battle Group 40 was transferred to Task Force Bravo for area operations eastwards. Battle Groups 20 and 30 moved eastwards towards Mongua and thence southwards to attack Ongiva. Combat Team Mamba (with two companies, under Commandant Johnny Coetzer) was given to Dippenaar's Battle Group 20.[46]

The next major target was Ongiva, to the southeast of Xangongo, and the two battle groups duly set off in that direction. On the way, Combat Team Mamba had to drive a SWAPO/FAPLA force out of Mongua in preparation for the arrival of Battle Groups 20 and 30, as it would not have been wise to attack Ongiva with a sizeable FAPLA force in their rear.[47] Mamba's members had reason to be worried, as Lieutenant Hubrecht van Dalsen remembers afterwards seeing intercepted enemy messages showing that the enemy was considerably stronger that estimated.[48]

Early the next morning, while the Ratels formed up, Valkiri rockets were launched at the enemy positions. An Alouette helicopter, circling in the air as an artillery spotter, radioed that, although the direction was correct, the rockets were exploding before hitting the target. The Ratels started moving forward. Almost immediately, Lieutenant Chris Walls's Ratel became almost unsteerable. Being one of the platoon commanders, he had no time to transfer to another vehicle, and he had to make do with the damaged one. Then the enemy started firing:

> I thought their fire to be perhaps speculative, but then realised that our Alo[uette] spotter was directly above my vehicle at a height of about 150 feet. I turned my sight back to the attack-line to ensure my head wouldn't be whacked by any of the tree branches. As the FAPLA fire intensified, I decided to ask the Alo pilot to back off as I thought that he was giving away our exact position. I looked up for the Alo again and called his sign, only to see him explode above – having been hit by a

ZGU-1 14,5 mm. At the time, we couldn't tell what weapon had struck, but later recovery of the pilot and gunner/engineer bodies and fuselage pieces by Louis Buys (Alpha Company second in command, acting as battle team Mamba's logistics officer and mobile recovery unit) revealed the 14,5 mm entry holes in the rotor blades and fuselage sections.[49]

At this stage, the enemy was not even visible. When the Ratels reached an open road, it was time to quicken the pace. With Corporal Koos Prinsloo's Ratel in the lead, they charged the trees on the other side of the road at full speed. According to aerial photographs, the enemy trenches lay just past the trees. At the trenches, the South Africans encountered the first 14,5-mm gun positions, which were immediately destroyed by fire from a 90-mm gun. Then a few 76-mm guns, firing wildly, were seen. The South Africans were pinned down for half an hour until reinforcements obliterated the enemy guns and mortars with their 90-mm guns.

The South Africans now debussed and stormed forward on foot, while bullets buzzed like angry bees around their heads. With the aid of improvised 60-mm mortars atop the Ratels, the enemy was forced to lay low, and with rifle fire and hand grenades the trenches were cleared one by one. The survivors fled. Mongua was in South African hands, and the advance to Ongiva could continue.

The Battle of Ongiva

Like Xangongo, Ongiva was not an easy target. According to the SADF's intelligence, the town was defended by two infantry battalions, two anti-aircraft battalions with 23-mm guns, a tank company (squadron) with T-34s, an armoured car company (squadron) with BTR-23s, and an artillery battery with 82-mm and 76-mm field guns. The idea was that Dippenaar's troops would assault the town from the northwest and establish a secure base for Serfontein to continue in a second phase in the same direction.[50]

Dippenaar was not very happy with the plan. He felt that the two battle groups should have attacked at the same time, his own from the northwest and Serfontein's from the north.[51] But orders were orders, and he had to carry them out.

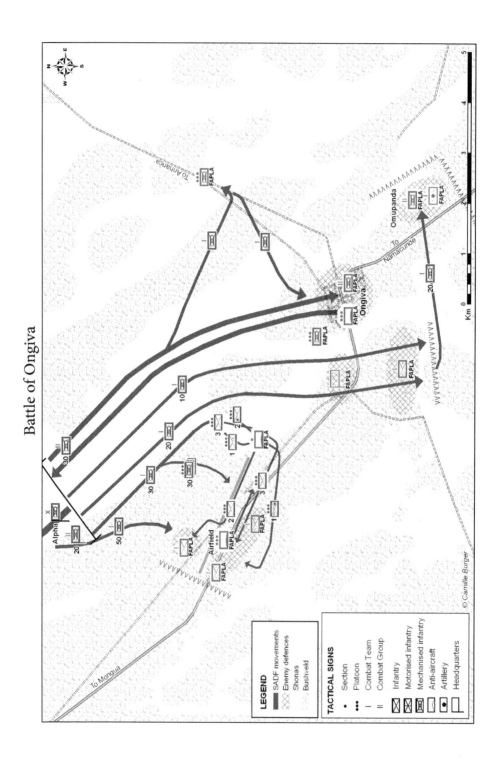

Battle of Ongiva

© Camille Burger

LEGEND

SADF movements
Enemy defences
Shonas
Bushveld

TACTICAL SIGNS

•   Section
:•:   Platoon
—   Combat Team
=   Combat Group

Infantry
Motorised infantry
Mechanised infantry
Anti-aircraft
Artillery
Headquarters

On the evening of 26 August – the attack was due to start the following morning – the SAAF dropped thousands of pamphlets over Ongiva, urging FAPLA soldiers and civilians to leave the town, as the SADF was about to attack SWAPO there. Some civilians did indeed leave, but FAPLA stayed put after its headquarters at Lubango forbade any retreat (as the SADF learnt from intercepted radio messages). PLAN headquarters ordered its fighters to harass the South Africans – in typical guerrilla fashion – from the rear.[52] Whether or not the South West African rebels carried out these orders is not known; if so, it is not reflected in SADF documents. FAPLA received reinforcements in the form of two tanks, two AA guns and two infantry platoons.[53]

Late that night, Dippenaar and Serfontein met with their officers to explain the tactical plan in detail so that everybody would understand exactly what to do.[54] Early the next morning, the killing commenced again with an artillery bombardment, while a total of 20 Mirages, 5 Canberras and 5 Buccaneers attacked the enemy positions with a deafening roar, unleashing rockets and bombs on the airstrip and enemy positions to the west of the town. The enemy fought back determinedly, damaging a Mirage III, which had to turn back to Ondangwa, barely reaching it after a hair-raising flight.[55]

While the explosions were still echoing through the air, Dippenaar unleashed his forces.[56] Three combat teams (10, 20 and 30) and one in reserve (50) were at his disposal. The three teams attacked in different directions, one (30) to the southwest to occupy the airfield, and the other two to the south and southeast. Team 10's advance went like clockwork. A counterattack by three Angolan T-34s caused some anxiety, but two Ratel 90s, commanded by Lieutenant Johan Grové and Candidate Officer Andries Helm, saved the day. Although the thinly armoured Ratel was extremely vulnerable to the T-34's 85-mm gun, by continuous manoeuvring Grové and Helm managed to confuse the FAPLA gunners. Then, when the chance came, they fired together – knocking out the tank. The same happened to a second tank, and the third wisely retreated. A number of the formidable 23-mm anti-aircraft guns gave the South Africans a few problems, but the commander of Team 10, Major JA Victor, called for artillery support and attacked the guns with his infantry. After a while, the enemy broke and fled, after which all meaningful resistance collapsed.

Team 30 (Major Nel van Rensburg) started out well, but was soon pinned down by the withering fire of the anti-aircraft guns. Support from Ratels was not feasible, because the enemy had, very cleverly, stationed troops with RPG-7 rocker launchers near the guns. In the end, supporting mortar fire did the trick, and by 15h30 the troops were in possession of the enemy positions.

The airfield was the target of Combat Team 10 (Major JA Victor), who attacked from east to west along the runway. The enemy resisted fiercely, slowing the South Africans down with their anti-aircraft guns. One of the paratroopers, Granger Korff, recalls:

> "We're taking too much fire, motherfuckers . . . we can't move," I swore at no one in particular. I looked at Stan who also had his head flat against the sand with his ear on the ground. I dared not get up. I dared not move a centimetre. Without moving my head I could see that the whole advance had stopped and was lying prone in a scraggly line. Some had not moved from where they had landed next to the Buffel, which was now very quickly backing away. We were pinned down; we could not move. We could not even look up, never mind shoot back. Sand kicked up around us in terrifying sprays.[57]

At least one T-34 was taken out by a South African armoured car, but the South Africans were held up for two full hours. Artillery fire did not help. One platoon was effectively pinned down and could not advance further. In the course of the fighting, an SAAF photo interpreter discovered that the defending guns were being directed from a radar station on top of a water tower, which was promptly destroyed by fire from a battery of 120-mm mortars. The support platoon then started firing on the defenders from the north, which convinced them to flee. By 14h00, this part of the battle was over.

The South Africans were helped along by the fact that, despite FAPLA having a full company (squadron) of tanks – in other words, 12 to 14 – these machines played a limited role in the fighting. After Ongiva fell, it was discovered that the tanks had been dug in deeply for use as static light artillery, which greatly restricted their trajectories. This negated one of the three main advantages of the tank, namely, movement/shock (the others being protection and firepower).

More importantly, the tanks faced south, while the SADF attack came from the north.

With this, Dippenaar felt that he had carried out his orders by establishing a secure base for Serfontein's Battle Group 30 to take over for the attack on Ongiva town itself. Serfontein duly moved forward, but the going was very tough. First, his force was slowed down by mines, and then by heavy resistance. Also, reports came in of a T-34 tank force threatening Serfontein's infantry force from the east. Joep Joubert sent an urgent request for reinforcements to Roland de Vries, who promptly dispatched Captain Koos Liebenberg and a mechanised infantry company, beefed up with two Ratel 90 troops. Serfontein's 120-mm mortars fired on the advancing T-34s, with one round even detonated right on top of a tank. But mortar bombs are highly explosive in nature, not armour-piercing, and the tank kept going forward. Shortly afterwards, Liebenberg's combat team arrived and swung into action. His orders were to stop the tanks.

Liebenberg rushed forward with his two Ratel 90 troops and met Serfontein at the eastern end of the town, where he saw the enemy tanks approaching. The tanks opened fire. It was already dusk, and he immediately deployed his two troops on both sides of the road leading into Ongiva. It was impossible to fire accurately in the fading light, and the Ratels could manage only speculative fire to discourage the tanks. Only the flashes coming from the enemy guns indicated where they were.

Dusk gave way to pitch darkness, which made things even more unnerving. Then, at Liebenberg's command, all the Ratels fired simultaneously, and suddenly the night was lit up by two great balls of fire a few hundred metres further east. The enemy fire immediately stopped, and Liebenberg assumed that at least two tanks had been destroyed. Serfontein pulled his force back to a position where he could bombard Ongiva the next day.

In spite of the plan to expel the enemy from the battlefield on the first day, 27 August, the job was still not done. It was an uneasy night. The South Africans woke up bleary-eyed and apprehensive, only to discover that the enemy had cleared off. Ongiva town and the entire battlefield were in South African hands. That day and the next were spent clearing up the area, which was littered with destroyed and damaged military equipment. Several hundred enemy bodies had to be buried, documents had to be extracted and secured and the local population had to be handled. Vast quantities of supplies were discovered in the town, a clear indication, in the words of the author of an SADF briefing document, "that these forces were planning future offensive action to the South". The South Africans thankfully refuelled their vehicles and burned whatever fuel remained.[58]

There was another interesting development. During the previous day's fighting, the South Africans had intercepted several radio messages indicating the presence of Soviet advisors, but the information was not precise enough to act upon. Nevertheless, from the point of view of international politics, this was dynamite, because it proved active Soviet participation in the war. Then, on the morning of 28 August a convoy was spotted fleeing Ongiva in a northerly direction.

Major Thinus van Staden, commander of one of the 32 Battalion companies, was in a position to act, and promptly called for air support and prepared an ambush. Mirages and Impalas rolled in and bombed the convoy, while Alouette gunships added their chatter to the melee. Exploding tanks, armoured cars and trucks wreaked havoc. When Van Staden ordered his troops forward to secure the area, they found the bodies of several uniformed Soviet personnel.

Shortly afterwards, they ran into gunfire from a kraal and immediately attacked. Inside the kraal they discovered another two dead Soviet officers and two dead Russian women, together with a dead senior PLAN officer. Sergeant Major Nikolai Feodorovich Pestretsov, understandably shocked and scared out of his wits, was found next to the body of his wife, Galina, and was taken prisoner. Altogether 13 Soviets died that day: of these, three were identified as lieutenant colonels, three as majors, one as a captain, one as a senior lieutenant and one as a sergeant major, while the others were civilians. According to documents found on their bodies, most were military advisors, while there was also a political commissar and a translator.[59]

Elements of Battle Groups 10, 20 and 30 now spread out to attack and destroy other SWAPO bases in the vicinity, but these had all been hurriedly evacuated. The three formations returned to South West Africa on 2 September. Battle Group 10 reverted to being 61 Mech; the other two were disbanded.

Aftermath

Operation Protea was, on the operational and tactical level, a resounding success for the SADF. The statistics are telling: according to the SADF tally, the enemy losses were 831 killed and 25 taken prisoner. In contrast, the SADF mourned the death of only 10 soldiers (four had previously been killed during Operation Carnation) and 64 wounded. Between 3 000 and 4 000 tonnes of military materiel was captured.

Among the equipment taken back to South West Africa (the sources differ) were 6 or 9 T-34 tanks, 3 or 4 PT-76 amphibious reconnaissance tanks, 4 BRDM-2 armoured cars, 2 BM-21 122-mm multiple rocket launchers, 25 or 43 ZIS-3 76-mm field guns, 2 multiple rocket launchers, 16 Soviet ZU-23 23-mm, 17 14,5-mm and 13 Yugoslav M-55 20-mm triple-barrelled anti-aircraft guns, 94 or 97 SA-7 shoulder-launched anti-aircraft missiles, 240 assorted trucks and other vehicles, and about 1 800 small arms. This was in addition to 250 tonnes of ammunition, 490 000 litres of petrol and 120 000 litres of diesel captured and then mostly destroyed. At the same time, the air force destroyed 40 vehicles from the air and damaged a further 50. On their side, the SAAF lost one Alouette III, which was shot down, while a Mirage III, an Impala and a Dakota were damaged but returned to base. One Ratel was destroyed, while several Buffels were damaged by mines.[60]

Jannie Geldenhuys was, from an operational point of view, very satisfied. At a press conference, he told reporters: "Their [PLAN's] command structure, for the time being, has been disrupted and their logistic system is disrupted, and for the moment, ineffective." He thought it would take SWAPO at least a year to recover from the blow it had received from Protea.[61]

What was also apparent was the fact that the South Africans' operational success was due to their mobile warfare doctrine. They moved around fast, kept the enemy hopping and retained the initiative, while FAPLA and SWAPO stayed put in their trenches, "tied down by their own minds and minefields", according to Roland de Vries.[62] Seldom in the Border War was the inherent superiority of manoeuvre over attritional warfare proved so spectacularly.

Protea ushered in two distinct developments in the Border War. The first was that FAPLA, the Angolan army, no longer stayed neutral in the war between the

SADF and PLAN, but intervened forcefully on PLAN's side. This was a serious development, which had to weigh heavily on the minds of the South African decision-makers in terms of future operations. In addition, there was now undeniable evidence of Soviet involvement. This applied not only to their military advisors killed during the operation, but also to the documentary evidence captured. This was potentially even more serious than FAPLA's intervention, as nobody could at this stage know how far the Kremlin was willing to go in aiding the Marxist-Leninist MPLA regime in Luanda. At the same time, there were also signs of increasing Cuban involvement. Enemy MiG-21s had been seen sniffing around during Protea, although they had not actively intervened, no doubt deterred by the powerful SAAF presence. But radio intercepts had revealed chatter in Spanish over the air. Those MiGs were manned by Cuban pilots, which did not bode well for the future.[63]

What effect did Protea have on the ground in SWA? About two months afterward, Major General Lloyd came up with an assessment, stating that SWAPO was now keeping a low profile, and that its strong image had been dented among the South West African civilian population, who now realised that SWAPO could not win the war militarily. Statistical analysis showed sharp decreases in intimidation, sabotage, minelaying and contacts. By 13 October, PLAN had lost a total of 1 195 men that year, which meant that its military capacity had been dented.[64] Indeed, the total casualty figure for 1981 was 1 494,[65] a level the organisation could not sustain indefinitely. Nonetheless, as another assessment by the SADF Chief of Staff Operations stated later that month: "A single operation will have only a limited effect on the internal political situation." Continued operations would be necessary to consolidate the advantages.[66]

In general, the SADF could be very satisfied with the operation. This was the first time its operational and tactical doctrine, the formulation of which had started at the Military College in the 1960s, had come to fruition. From Operation Sceptic, the South Africans had learnt that operational surprise was next to impossible. PLAN's excellent bush telegraph informed its high command as soon as an SADF force crossed the border. What SWAPO's and FAPLA's commanders never knew, however, was exactly where the blow would fall. At Xangongo they apparently never dreamed that the SADF would attack such a relatively densely populated target. And, as the SADF documents show, because the defences were oriented to the south, the South Africans attacked from the north and east. After the fall of Xangongo, commanders in other centres, including Ongiva, had to expect trouble too. Ongiva's defences also faced south, and again the South Africans took them on from the north.

These defences provide another reason for the SADF's success. In typical Russian fashion, they consisted of a series of independent "hedgehog" positions, able to fire in all directions. This was not all bad, for, in contrast with a continuous trench system, one "hedgehog" could be taken with no danger of the others being rolled up from the flank. Each position had to be taken separately. But this left the initiative to the attackers, who would decide where and when the blow would fall. This was illustrated by the use of T-34s dug in as static light artillery, which completely negated the idea of mobile armoured warfare. Roland de Vries commented:

> The static defensive way of fighting was apparently what FAPLA was taught by their Russian advisors. When the South Africans took the entrenched FAPLA forces at Xangongo, Peu-Peu and Humbe on the Cunene River in August 1981 from an unexpected direction, their carefully laid plan collapsed instantly.

> To us who witnessed Operation Protea first hand this was a doctrine copied and then rooted in the teachings of FAPLA's masters. True to form it was characteristic of the then Soviet society, requiring stability, rigid order, respect for tradition and firm authority. "Thou shall not use thy mobile reserve until given the explicit permission to do so" – most of the time never to respond at all or to be deployed too late!

> This was one of the surprise aspects of FAPLA's mobile reserve which was entrenched at Cahama and left untouched by us during Operation Protea. They never took on offensively the very small Combat Team Charlie of Major Joe Weyers of "61". For a little while this minute force lay 15 km to their east, positioned across the Cahama–Xangongo road facing Cahama in a stopping position. For that matter the enemy's mobile reserve not even once probed or reconnoitred in force in the direction

of Xangongo – astonishingly so they remained rooted to the ground during Operation Protea until we left at the end of August. And then they remained there anyway, comfortably in the ground.[67]

At a meeting held to review the operation, Geldenhuys confirmed this view: "The overarching strong point of the SA Army which led to the successes, was the fact that own forces, without exception, attacked from the most unexpected direction. This action surprised, confused, unnerved and ultimately vanquished the enemy."[68]

In contrast to Sceptic, the cooperation with the air force had been good. Enough aircraft were available for continuous close air support or casualty evacuation. Approximately 1 200 sorties had been flown during the operation. As a matter of fact, so much support was available that the air force once complained that the army did not utilise it fully.[69]

The SADF and local civilians

One other aspect of Operation Protea merits our attention. As with the Battle of Cassinga in 1978, this operation elicited considerable pro-SWAPO and pro-MPLA propaganda. As parts of it are sometimes still quoted and used to shape public opinion, it is necessary to look at it briefly.

Joseph Hanlon, a left-wing British journalist and social scientist, wrote a book in 1986 in which he (incorrectly) claimed that the South African advance had been stopped by the Angolans at Cahama. He stated that "[t]owns were flattened and an estimated 130 000 refugees were sent fleeing north" during Operation Protea. "Others were kidnapped and sent to Namibia; cattle were driven to Namibia as well. The idea seemed to be to create a cleared buffer zone; after Operation Protea, several thousand South African troops remained in occupation of a 70-km-deep strip of southern Cunene, including the provincial capital of Ngiva."[70] His sole source for these allegations was a news report published in *The Times* of London on 15 March 1982, almost seven months after the event.

In 1982, Marga Holness, who worked for the Angolan news agency ANGOP at the time, wrote in a booklet that South Africa invaded Angola with 11 000 soldiers (sic), "around 36 Centurion M-41 tanks [sic], 70 AML-90 armoured cars,

200 Ratel, Buffel and Saracen [sic] armoured personnel carriers, heavy artillery, including 155-mm guns [sic], 127 Kentron missiles [sic] and around 90 aircraft and helicopters [sic]". She alleged that the SAAF strafed and bombed "all road traffic", which was "aimed at cutting off supplies to the south, both civilian and military" (sic). Furthermore, Cahama and Chibemba, which Holness calls "urban centres", were "massively bombed", according to her. This "massive use of their air force" brought about "a human tragedy of enormous proportions" – civilian refugees "had to travel for days on foot". An estimated 160 000 people were made homeless, Holness wrote, without referring to any sources.[71]

How accurate are these allegations? During the planning of the operation, the SADF was very much aware of the presence of large numbers of civilians living in or near the target areas.[72] The guidelines imposed on the invading troops included an order to "respect the lives and property of the local population".[73] The orders to the troops on the ground were explicit: "Local population not to be killed unnecessarily and property not to be damaged unnecessarily."[74] According to Roland de Vries, "all churches and civilian concentrations were clearly marked on our maps as zones not to be engaged with fire".[75]

The question is, of course, to what extent these orders were obeyed. Obviously, one cannot state with absolute certainty that every single South African soldier at all times behaved with total courtesy to every civilian. But the impression one gets from the SADF documents – all marked "Uiters Geheim" (top secret), i.e. not meant for public information or propaganda purposes – is that the South African military, by and large, treated the civilians correctly and according to the laws of war.

It is understandable that the civilians were terrified of the fighting, which burst like a sudden torrent over their heads. Several SADF documents relate how troops came across panic-stricken civilians, hiding in houses or structures of some kind. Others fled. However, at Xangongo many of the inhabitants returned the day after the town fell. The SADF distributed food among them and gave medical treatment to those who needed it. While flying over the scene in a helicopter, Jannie Geldenhuys saw a soccer field, and came up with an innovative idea: why not organise a soccer match between the locals and the SADF? The organisation was entrusted to De Vries, whose Battle Group 10 was at the time occupying the village.[76] He recalls:

I was somewhat astounded, but replied as all good mechanised combat commanders usually do: "Yes, sir". I was obviously not going to say to him what I thought of this, and I am still today not prepared to repeat my erstwhile thoughts here in writing. I, of course, had immense respect for him and realised that he had something up his sleeve. He was one of our unusual generals, with amazing insight and a flair for indirectness and creativity.

So, as good commanders occasionally do, I promptly delegated the responsibility for the soccer game to my Garrison Commander Dawid Mentz (who was equally astounded by the order). I told him, "No backchatting". National Service Lieutenant Henri Boshoff was duly appointed as the official referee. I was now free to pursue my duties in overseeing the more military oriented, and to my mind, more important, work at Xangongo.

Needless to say, in true military style of planning excellence and professional execution, the soccer game was a grand success, although "61" lost 3–1. The opposing teams wore their official jerseys. The town spectators turned out to support the local team in high spirits. "61" became the instant and trusted friends of the local community.[77]

According to an official SADF briefing document, the match was attended by 400 to 600 spectators. It adds: "It should be further mentioned that a military town administration was set up, which took care of water and electricity supplies and provided medical attention. Of those seriously wounded, 38 FAPLA/local population members, were flown to Oshakati by helicopter where they received surgery."[78] For the duration of Task Force 10's occupation of Xangongo, Commandant Dawid Mentz became the garrison commander[79] and was therefore responsible for the wellbeing of the civilian population in accordance with the Geneva Convention.

At Ongiva, the SADF also behaved with restraint. We have already seen that the air force distributed thousands of pamphlets before the attack on that town, advising the locals (and FAPLA) to leave before the shooting started.

Many civilians wisely departed, but others stayed.[80] This created considerable problems for the attackers. In his battle report, Dippenaar wrote:

> The Ongiva target area in the vicinity of the military HQ complex is a black living area and covered with locals' houses and farms. After the attack started, it came to light that locals, especially women and children, [sought] shelter in bunkers. This was a very dangerous situation for the local population because mopping up was done by throwing grenades into the bunkers. Obviously, quick adjustments had to be made. Firstly, the troops were warned to use grenades carefully and judiciously in bunkers, and secondly the population was repeatedly warned through loudspeakers to come out to the asphalt road. The locals reacted positively to this and this was also the start of the civic matters effort.[81]

The next day Joep Joubert faced growing chaos as the civilians started plundering the town. It was discovered that the Soviet personnel had lived in considerable luxury while the local population had gone hungry. Serfontein's troops had to intervene when the local bank was stormed. The money inside was made available to SADF civic affairs officers to pay people for information. About 30 tonnes of food previously reserved for FAPLA and PLAN members was donated to the locals. Candidate Officer Andries Helm remembered: "The clothes we found were like mountains. They were still in their bags, in their plastic bags. There were storehouses full of pants, shirts, jackets, boots, caps, anything. We threw everything out at the airfield."[82]

The SADF medics at the scene were overwhelmed by people seeking treatment, and a team of surgeons had to be flown in to assist. Some 30 badly hurt civilians were taken to the local hospital for treatment by SADF medical staff.[83]

While Dippenaar's force was the occupying power in Ongiva, they not only had to restore order and give emergency aid, but also had to get things going again. On 29 August, some officers met with representatives of the town management in an effort to restore the water supply, electricity, transport and policing.[84] "Few of the staff were trained or prepared for this task," Dippenaar remarked in his report.[85] And indeed, during its comprehensive review of the lessons learnt from the conventional operations thus far, "lack of expertise regarding town management" among SADF personnel was identified as one of the gaps. It was recommended that Citizen Force members with appropriate experience be employed to take over the running of towns temporarily occupied by the SADF, while chaplains also had to be pulled in.[86]

Another problem was troops who acted in a manner that caused conflict with the local population. It transpired that a number of soldiers had slaughtered animals belonging to the locals without permission. The SADF briefing document also stated that the plundering of private property should not be permitted under any circumstances, "because it is theft. Orders must be included in Operations Orders."[87]

None of this suggests the expulsion of upwards of 130 000 hapless civilians by the SADF from the target areas around Xangongo, Humbe, Ongiva, Peu-Peu and other places. On the contrary, the picture emerging from these documents is that while individual soldiers were guilty of plundering and slaughtering of animals, the SADF was at pains to treat the civilian population correctly and to ameliorate the hardships necessarily brought about by the war.

Operation Daisy

A treasure trove of documents was captured at Xangongo and Ongiva. From these documents, it was learnt that SWAPO's main command and logistical bases were located at Bambi and Chitequeta, east of Cassinga and Techamutete. It was, therefore, resolved to launch another major incursion to destroy these bases.[88]

Operation Daisy was not as big as Protea and did not have the same operational impact. The target area, about 300 km inside Angola (the furthest the SADF would ever advance into that country), was thought to be heavily defended. Seven targets were identified, with up to 2 000 PLAN fighters thought to be present. FAPLA, too, had strong forces in the vicinity: a brigade with tanks at Caiundo, two battalions at Cassinga, single battalions at Cuvango and Techamutete, and a Cuban regiment (500 men, with armoured cars) at Donga. These SWAPO allies were not thought to be a real threat to the SADF invaders, although the SWAPO forces were expected to flee immediately in the direction of Cassinga and seek refuge with FAPLA. Military Intelligence, quite correctly, expected that SWAPO would be informed the moment the SADF crossed the border.[89]

For this operation, the SADF did not put forward such a strong force as for Protea. The main punch was provided by the full 61 Mechanised Battalion Group under Commandant Roland de Vries, with two mechanised infantry companies, a paratrooper company (motorised), an armoured car squadron, an antitank platoon, an 81-mm mortar platoon and a 120-mm mortar battery. The full 201 Battalion, a motorised infantry unit, would also go along, plus two companies of 1 Parachute Battalion (National Servicemen) and three companies of 3 Parachute Battalion (part-time Citizen Force). In addition, 32 Battalion supplied one company.[90] The air force also provided a relatively strong force.[91]

The operational plan was for 32 Battalion to secure the route to the target area by occupying Ionde and its airstrip and establishing a helicopter landing area. Immediately afterwards, 201 Battalion would move in and conduct area operations (known as Operation Mispel) south of the main target area. While one parachute company would be moved by helicopter to Ionde to act as a mobile reserve, three companies would be dropped north of the main target area to act as stopper groups. The main attack would be carried out by 61 Mech. Altogether, 17 days of area counterinsurgency operations would then follow. Afterwards, 201 Battalion and the 32 Battalion company would cover the withdrawal.[92] The Chief of the Army, Jannie Geldenhuys, showed up when the force departed. He would travel with De Vries in his command Ratel for the entire operation.[93]

In contrast to Protea, very little went right during Operation Daisy. One officer who did not like the plan at all was Colonel Jan Breytenbach, commander of 44 Parachute Brigade. He had two objections. Firstly, he thought that using the paratroopers as stopper groups in a vast open area like this "would be like stopping a flood of water, rushing down a stream bed, with wire mesh . . .". Secondly, he predicted that SWAPO would know as soon as 61 Mech crossed the border with a noisy column and would evacuate the target area. His favourite maxim for situations like this was "find them, fix them and finish them".[94]

Another unhappy officer was Commandant Roland de Vries. He was dissatisfied with the intelligence on which the plans were based. De Vries felt that security would be compromised by the large numbers of troops involved, and that the intelligence was based on assumptions rather than verifiable facts. Sector 10 headquarters, however, felt it was worth taking the chance.[95]

The South African troops left their bases in SWA on 1 November and marched northwards as fast as possible, which was not all that fast; the undergrowth was so thick that the Ratels' front wheels sometimes did not touch the ground! But De Vries's orders were that the attack would commence at the given time. On the way, there was consternation when an extremely dangerous 3-m-long mamba dropped into the Ratel of Major Koos Liebenberg, one of the company commanders. According to Lieutenant Ariël Hugo, this elicited a cacophony that could almost be heard as far as Luanda:

> I would venture to say that the biggest noise came from Major Liebenberg himself as he came down on us because of the noise we were making. I still think he scolded us like that out of fright. Shit, he was angry. But what do you do if such a fellow unexpectedly wants to take a "lift" in Angola? After terrible consternation the snake in the end found his own way out of a door.[96]

The parachute drop went wrong. Before first light on 4 November, the three companies were dropped some distance to the west of the planned drop zone, as the pilots could not distinguish between the Recces' flashing strobes and unexpected veld fires on the ground.[97] A few hours later, 61 Mech stormed Bambi and Chitequeta. Everything went well, except for one small detail – both bases were virtually empty.[98]

As it turned out, Breytenbach and De Vries were both right. The Recces in the target area later reported that they could hear 61 Mech some three hours before their arrival. Apparently, SWAPO also heard the aircraft dropping the parabats. Because of radio communication difficulties, the news that the targets had shifted could be sent only at 03h00 on the morning of the attack, apparently too late to make a difference.[99] In addition, in the closing stages of the operation, soldiers from 32 Battalion captured an important PLAN officer's clerk. He revealed what had become a standard SWAPO procedure: as soon as the SADF column crossed the border, PLAN reconnaissance teams learnt about it and informed their headquarters. This time, the PLAN commanders had guessed correctly what the South African target was, and they had ordered the evacuation of the Chitequeta and Bambi areas.[100]

Before the main force started the attack, early on the morning of 4 November, several Mirages and Buccaneers pounded what they thought was the target. But, of course, it wasn't. The Recces on the ground, who could not communicate with the aircraft, had to watch in frustration as the bombs exploded on empty ground. SWAPO had moved, and its new base came off unscathed. Only at one position was anti-aircraft fire observed. Moreover, it took another 45 minutes after the air attack for 61 Mech to reach the area, during which time the PLAN fighters who were still there took to their heels in a northerly direction. The result was that, when the mechanised column arrived, there was "no resistance". The force swept the whole area, and, although several booby-trapped bunkers and pieces of equipment were found, no enemy was seen. Upon moving westwards to the other target, the force discovered that "there had been no base at all".[101]

Having taken a largely empty base, De Vries immediately ordered his force to move southwards in the direction of Bambi.[102] There they found the entire area "infested with trenches and signs of old SWAPO bases". According to De Vries,

> It was clear that the area was a traditional PLAN strategic base area. At Bambi, inside the old base, three Ratels were immobilised within 15 minutes by mines. We then had to fly in Ratel axles with Super Frelons . . . The first night a small group of terrs walked into our laager unexpectedly from the direction of Techamutete (northwest). They fired at us, but were speedily silenced after Koos Lieb[enberg] ordered his combat team to execute a firebelt action [where all vehicles fire their guns in one direction at once]. The next day we discovered three bodies. One terr shot himself in his throat with his own gun . . .[103]

At a meeting held to review the operation, Breytenbach and De Vries were vindicated. It was acknowledged that both the parachute and the mechanised force had been misused. In a mainly counterinsurgency operation like this, the roles of the two types have to be reversed: the parabats should be the main attack force and the mechanised unit the stopper group. The minutes of the meeting stipulate, *inter alia*: "SWAPO always runs when attacked. Therefore, they can be chased up with a small force, while a bigger, mobile force (vehicles and helis) concentrate on cutting them off on the real escape routes." The use of helicopter gunships and medium artillery (instead of the 120-mm mortars) was also recommended.[104]

For the next two weeks, the South Africans swept through the area in search of SWAPO, but without any success, apart from a few small-scale clashes. By 18 November, the force was back at base after what Jannie Geldenhuys termed "one of the less successful operations". The review meeting agreed that the area operations were "ineffective". Approximately 70 PLAN members and three South African soldiers were killed.[105]

One interesting aspect of the operation was that FAPLA did not intervene. Until the Angolan side of the war is properly recorded, we shall not know why. One can only surmise that the Angolans were not keen for battle after their beating at Xangongo and Ongiva.

Although the ground portion of Operation Daisy was disappointing, the air component caused considerable excitement. Even before the ground attack, the air force had picked up renewed radar activity at Cahama, indicating that the radar station there had been repaired, after being put out of action during Operation Protea a few weeks earlier. So, on 5 November, the station was again attacked by three waves of four Mirage F1s each, which "virtually flattened the entire town and installations", according to the SAAF report. Obviously, the enemy was not very happy about this, and scrambled their MiG-21s, but nothing came of it.[106]

The next day, 7 November 1981, would become a historic day in the annals of the SAAF.[107] Early that morning, South African radar picked up some enemy aircraft moving south from Lubango, possibly threatening the SADF ground forces. Two Mirage F1CZ interceptors, each armed with 30-mm cannon and two Matra 550 heat-seeking air-to-air missiles, were immediately scrambled from Ondangwa Air Force Base. Major Johan Rankin was in the lead, with Lieutenant Johan du Plessis as his wingman. To avoid the enemy radar, they stayed low until they reached the Cunene River, after which they shot up to 25 000 feet in 30 seconds. They detected two MiG-21s about three nautical miles off their port beam, moving southwards. These were flying in a formation with their number one in front, and his wingman about 1 000 to 1 500 m behind, angled off at 30°. The MiGs were apparently unaware of the Mirages. One can imagine how the adrenaline must have pumped through Rankin and Du Plessis. They were about to become engaged in the SAAF's first dogfight since the Korean War.

They jettisoned their drop tanks, making their aircraft more aerodynamic and manoeuvrable. Rankin led Du Plessis in a left turn into a position behind the MiGs. As soon as he got within range of the Angolan wingman, he opened fire with his 30-mm cannon. A hit! Fuel started leaking and a puff of smoke was seen. The Angolans obviously didn't know where this was coming from, and they went into a shallow and hopelessly inadequate left-hand turn, easily enabling the Mirages to stay on their tails. The lead MiG now jettisoned his own drop tanks, after which Du Plessis launched a missile at him. But, to Du Plessis's frustration, the missile malfunctioned (not once did the Matra 550 work properly in action throughout the war).

The apparently inexperienced MiG wingman now made the mistake of attempting to reverse his course, which enabled Rankin to stay on his tail, opening fire with his 30-mm once more. This was the deathblow. The MiG exploded, with Rankin having to take violent evasive action to avoid the burning aircraft. The lead MiG desperately tried to shake off Du Plessis by going down in a spiral, but the South African was not to be shaken off. He launched his second missile, but once again it malfunctioned. He opened fire with his cannon, but it too malfunctioned.

The surviving MiG ran for home and escaped. The pilot of the shot-down MiG was seen to eject, and the Mirages returned home as well.

Conclusion

Operation Protea, and to a lesser extent Operation Daisy, ushered in several clear developments in the Border War. Firstly, it caused the war to escalate. Previously, the fight was primarily between the SADF and PLAN. As we shall see in a later chapter, the South African government was providing aid to UNITA, and thus was indirectly also fighting against FAPLA. But this was not an overt battle. Before Protea, clashes between the SADF and FAPLA had been only sporadic and limited. In a sense, the success of Operation Sceptic made an escalation inevitable. One has to see this from SWAPO's side: in order to survive the SADF's hammer blows, PLAN crept under FAPLA's wing like a chick under a mother hen. At Xangongo and Ongiva, their bases and positions were so mixed up that there was simply no way for the SADF to take on PLAN without getting involved with FAPLA too. This was a first step on a road that almost turned the war against SWAPO into a sideshow and elevated the conflict with the ruling Angolan MPLA to the centre stage.

In the second place, Protea led to a more or less permanent SADF presence in Cunene province. Up to this point, the SADF had invaded the area, hit SWAPO hard, and then pulled back. After Protea, the main conventional forces were pulled back, but counterinsurgency forces stayed behind in order to dominate the territory in cooperation with UNITA. The way in which 32 Battalion had dominated – note, not occupied – eastern Cunene and western Cuando Cubango provinces, making it difficult for SWAPO to infiltrate SWA, was now extended to western Cunene.

For the time being, this did not lead to further battles with FAPLA. SWAPO, Angola and other left-wing countries screamed murder in international political forums, but they did nothing on the ground. In the United Nations, the US vetoed a resolution condemning South Africa for Operation Protea.[108] Cuba, strangely, also sat on its hands; Edward George calls its reaction "uncharacteristically muted".[109]

In a sense, this respect also spilled over to the political arena. In his memoirs, Jannie Geldenhuys noted:

> I had realised previously that almost every time we conducted an operation in Angola, the Cubans and Angolans interpreted our objectives wrongly. They really believed that we were bent on penetrating Angola very deeply. They told me personally later one time that they thought during Operation Protea that we were planning to go much further. To Lubango![110]

Be that as it may, there can be no doubt that SWAPO suffered a series of heavy blows during 1981. Not only did Carnation, Protea and Daisy disrupt their logistics, training and operations; these and other operations hindered PLAN's infiltration of South West Africa. Not that SWAPO gave in; on the contrary, it kept on coming with considerable courage.

8

NO END IN SIGHT: ASKARI

The year 1981 was a hard one for PLAN. The loss of Xangongo, Humbe and Ongiva represented a considerable blow to the rebel movement. The SADF established a more or less permanent presence in the vicinity and patrolled it quite aggressively. A tactical headquarters was established at Ongiva and 32 Battalion ensconced itself at Ionde.[1] As an SADF staff officer wrote, "a semi-permanent (albeit clandestine) presence of light, mobile search-and-destroy teams was maintained up to 100 kms inside Angola to ensure continued disruption of SWAPO's military capabilities".[2] The airfield at Ongiva was repaired and resurfaced by the SAAF for emergency use by South African aircraft.[3] All of this meant that PLAN units had to run the gauntlet for a considerable distance before reaching the Namibian border. And there they were welcomed by more patrols. Although Operation Daisy had been largely a failure, SWAPO nevertheless had to evacuate several strongholds and run for cover. This caused considerable disruption in its plans to infiltrate SWA.

The orders given to a PLAN detachment preparing to infiltrate SWA at about this time are indicative of the problems caused by the SADF's dominance in southern Cunene province:

> The military situation in the area is very tense, and the enemy is in the area. The enemy has mounted a large-scale offensive against us along the whole Northwestern Front up to Xangongo. They can attack you from the rear, from the front, or indeed from all directions at once, at any time, day or night, using ground forces or air power.[4]

But, to give PLAN forces their due, they never gave up and they kept at it, no matter how hard the South Africans hit them. They also tried different tactics

and different routes to outsmart the SADF. In February 1982, the SADF, through
its excellent radio interception service, got wind of a PLAN unit moving down
to the Kaokoland section of the border. PLAN wanted to enter the territory
to the west of the heavily guarded Ovamboland section, thereby outflanking
the South Africans. The people of Kaokoland were not sympathetic towards
SWAPO, since they were not related to the Ovambos. Furthermore, the area
was very sparsely populated. The insurgent units therefore had a rather good
chance of penetrating into Ovamboland from the west without being discovered.

A team of 10 operatives from 5 Reconnaissance Regiment, dressed in PLAN
uniforms, was dispatched on the evening of 9 March to an area around Iona,
north of the Kaokoland border, about 100 km from the Atlantic coast, to take a
look at what was going on. A force of 36 soldiers from 32 Battalion, under the
command of Captain Jan Hougaard, together with two Puma helicopters and
two Alouette III gunships (with the legendary Major Neall Ellis as one of the
pilots) was put on standby at Marienfluss, just south of the border, as a reaction force. These were the opening moves in what was to become one of the
most remarkable clashes in the entire Border War.[5]

After being inserted by a Puma, the Recces (commanded by Sergeant Jose
Dennison) walked through the harsh, arid environment and established themselves at a high point where they could observe the area. They planted a mine in
the road to warn them if the enemy was approaching. Some time later, two vehicles approached and tripped the mine, badly damaging one of them. The other
vehicle trundled away. Of course with this the Recces had exposed themselves.
As could be expected, after a while a PLAN platoon of about 28 heavily armed
men attacked the South Africans. Dennison called for reinforcements, which
shortly arrived in the form of the two Alouettes and a Puma full of 32 Battalion
soldiers. The troops from 32 were put down to act as a stopper group behind the
PLAN fighters, while Ellis and the choppers chased the rebels towards them.
This combination caught the insurgents completely off guard – 21 were killed
and another seven wounded and captured. One escaped.

From the prisoners, the South Africans learnt that there was a sizeable
PLAN force in a base nearby, waiting to cross into SWA. This was dangerous; if
allowed to enter Kaokoland, they would open up a new route into Ovamboland
– the point of gravity of the whole war. If the South Africans wanted to stop the

insurgents, they had to act fast. One of the prisoners, a disillusioned Caprivian, offered to guide them to the SWAPO base.

A radio message was immediately sent to Sector 10 headquarters at Oshakati and a plan was quickly set in motion. Three Pumas flew out another 32 Battalion platoon and an 81-mm mortar section, accompanied by two additional helicopter gunships. Fuel for the helicopters was flown in by C-130 directly to the scene, the big plane landing on the dry, hard flood plain. Everything was in place and Sector 10 ordered an immediate strike, but a thunderstorm broke out and the attack had to be postponed until early the next morning, 13 March.

The choppers took off at first light, and the men waited, their throats tight, mouths dry. The SWAPO camp was easily found, although it was well camouflaged and difficult to recognise from the air. The choppers circled around for seven minutes to make sure, but then the insurgents couldn't take the tension any more and started running. The ground troops were promptly dropped by the Pumas, and the fight was on. Ellis had his gunships open fire on the fleeing guerrillas. He later recounted:

> The first rounds from our choppers stopped the run and the insurgents dived for cover. Then all hell broke loose. I heard a large bang towards the rear of the aircraft as an RPG rocket exploded behind me, while [Captain Angelo] Maranta [another Alouette pilot] shouted over the radio: "SAM launch, six o'clock!" I could see the distinctive thick whitish-grey smoke trail of a SAM-7 twirling up into the sky towards us. I immediately put on more bank to find the firing position.
>
> As I turned through 180 degrees a second SAM-7 was launched towards us. This time it was directed at Maranta. I called hastily "SAM launch: nine o'clock!"
>
> We were so low that by the time I had used my radio the missile was already travelling at Mach 1,5. It passed by harmlessly just in front of his nose.[6]

The South Africans had stirred up a hornet's nest. The SWAPO force was about 200 strong, while the SADF could muster only two platoons and a mortar section on the ground against them. The South Africans, however, had three aces up their sleeve. One was their gunship air support. Secondly, their troops were not just from any unit but from 32 Battalion, one of the most formidable units in the South African Army. Not for nothing were these Angolan refugees called "Os Terriveis", which is Portuguese for "The Terrible Ones". Lastly, the PLAN commander's tactical inexperience showed in his choice of base location – a narrow valley where any attacker would invariably have the high ground.

Nevertheless, the insurgents fought back hard, finding cover in the cracks and crevices in the harsh, dry terrain. Metre by metre, the defenders had to be flushed out of their hiding places. This was bloody and grinding work, involving face-to-face combat, looking the enemy in the eye. Hour after hour, the advance went on relentlessly. One SADF officer and two NCOs were killed, but the enemy fell in scores. During the afternoon, the SADF fighters' ammunition ran out, and they grimly fought on with captured AK-47s. At one point, Sector 10 headquarters unreasonably demanded that Hougaard make a full report; in the end, he had to abandon his troops and fly to Marienfluss to satisfy the request.

The night was spent in great apprehension, since a SWAPO counterattack was expected. But it never came. The next morning, another 24 SADF soldiers were flown in as reinforcements and a few more shots were enough to secure the surrender of the surviving guerrillas.

The rays of the morning sun revealed the full extent of the slaughter: 197 insurgents and three SADF soldiers lay dead on the desert floor.[7] Only seven or eight PLAN survivors were captured – an indication of how hard both sides had fought. The arms cache comprised seven RPG-7 rocket launchers and 1 005 rockets, 648 SKS rifle grenades, 8 000 TM57 and 1 152 TMA3 anti-tank mines, 22 crates of RG3 hand grenades, 463 antipersonnel mines, four SAM-7 missiles, 1 143 60-mm and 309 82-mm mortar bombs, 76 AK-47 rifles with 20 160 rounds of ammunition, 27 B10 antitank recoilless gun rockets, and 37 kg of TNT.[8] Imagine the havoc PLAN could have unleashed, had it been able to get these weapons into Ovamboland!

A day or two later, this action was given the name Operation Super. It was only one of several ongoing SADF actions to retain the military initiative. SWAPO had to be attacked and kept off balance wherever its fighters were.

To prevent them from infiltrating the Xangongo–Humbe–Ongiva area again, several small and medium-sized operations were launched in the vicinity:

- **Operation Makro** (December 1981/January 1982), which was supposed to create and maintain "a no-man's land for SWAPO and FAPLA in the shallow area of southern Angola", according to Commandant Roland de Vries.[9]

- **Operation Meebos 1** (March 1982), which had more or less the same aim. In the process, an element of 2 Parachute Battalion was attacked by a much larger FAPLA force and hastily retreated to Ongiva. There, the parachutists were reinforced by the formidable 61 Mechanised Battalion Group, which advanced aggressively in the direction of Evale, where the FAPLA forces were. As 61 Mech neared the Angolans, the latter took to their heels and returned to Cuvelai, whence they had come.[10]

- **Operation Meebos 2** (July/August 1982). This was a sizeable operation, involving two companies of 32 Battalion, one company from 1 Parachute Battalion, and a company-sized combat team from 61 Mech, with Colonel Jan Pieterse in overall command, his headquarters being at Ongiva. The purpose, in the dry language of the operational instruction, was "to prevent FAPLA from reoccupying Ongiva and Xangongo".[11] (In fact, very little fighting with FAPLA took place. For "FAPLA", read "FAPLA/ PLAN".) The operation was rather frustrating. SWAPO's excellent operational intelligence meant that it was continually a step or two ahead of the SADF. Every time the South Africans located and attacked a SWAPO base, the insurgents were already gone. However, SWAPO fighters were trapped at two locations west of Cassinga, with 106 and 116, respectively, killed in these battles. Mirage F1s also hammered the enemy and contributed considerably to the total PLAN casualty list of 345 men slain. The price, however, was heavy: the loss of an SAAF Puma, with all the occupants – three crew members and 12 troops – killed.[12] No doubt SWAPO's infiltration was disrupted to a certain extent.

In the aftermath of Meebos, there was again considerable excitement for the "vlamgatte" (literally, "flaming holes"; pilots) of 3 Squadron, flying Mirage F1CZ interceptors. On 5 October 1982, Major Johan Rankin – who had shot down an

Angolan MiG-21 during Operation Daisy in 1981 – and Captain Cobus Toerien were escorting a Canberra on a photo-reconnaissance mission. Suddenly the South African radar controller broke in with the message every fighter pilot in the world dreams of: "Two bandits [enemy aircraft, MiG-21s] on an interception course!" With adrenaline pumping and every sense alert, they sent the vulnerable Canberra home and climbed to 30 000 ft. The two formations neared each other at a combined speed that was twice the speed of sound.[13]

The MiGs, flown by lieutenants Raciel Marrero Rodriguez and Gilberto Ortiz Pérez, knew the Mirages were there, because they launched missiles just before the formations crossed. They passed the two SAAF pilots to their right but their missiles missed. The South Africans jettisoned their drop tanks, readying their aircraft for dogfighting, and turned hard right in pursuit, kicking in full afterburner.

Having turned 180°, Rankin and Toerien saw the MiGs in a gentle supersonic turn to the right, outpacing the Mirages. The South Africans had to be quick, otherwise the MiGs would get away, so Rankin turned on his intercept radar in the hope that the Cubans' radar warning receiver would frighten them. It apparently succeeded, and the Cubans, who were most probably inexperienced, reversed their turn. But this only enabled the Mirages to catch up with them. In the turn, Rankin launched a Matra 550 infrared missile at Rodriguez, guided by the MiG's hot tailpipe, but at three kilometres the enemy was too far away. The missile expended all its fuel and dropped to the ground without exploding. Rankin closed to one and a half kilometres and fired a second missile. A desperate Rodriguez entered into a violent split-S manoeuvre, but the missile exploded just behind him.

This was frustratingly bad luck – in action these missiles never performed as advertised. The MiG was damaged, but stayed in the air and ran for home. Later it was learnt that the aircraft made it to Lubango and had to make a forced landing, severely damaging it.

Rankin now closed on the other MiG, flown by Pérez, which executed a similar move as the first one: a split-S to the left. Rankin switched on his two 30-mm cannon and opened fire at 230 m. The MiG exploded directly in front of him, and he flew right through the fireball, inducing a flameout. He had to cut his engine and perform a hot relight. Luckily this succeeded, and he and a frustrated Toerien – who had seen no action – returned to Ondangwa Air Force Base.

Beyond these operations, elements of various units, with 32 Battalion in the forefront, were continually engaged in southern Angola to deny SWAPO a free ride down to the South West African border. The most important of these was probably Operation Dolfyn, the aim of which was to find and destroy PLAN's Eastern Command headquarters north of Cuvelai, as well as to disrupt SWAPO activities in the area. Elements of 61 Mech, 32 Battalion, 4 SAI, 44 Parachute Brigade and a Citizen Force mechanised infantry battalion (Regiment Groot Karoo) were made available for the operation, which took place over an extended period during May and June 1983. The operation consisted of many small contacts, plus one rather big one on 12 June, when a 61 Mech element mistook a sizeable PLAN force for a FAPLA unit. As the standing orders were not to engage FAPLA, except in self-defence, the South Africans did not press home their attack, and the insurgents escaped. By the beginning of July, the operation was over.[14]

Planning for Operation Askari

After Operation Daisy, no large-scale cross-border operation was launched for some time. In April 1983, the Chief of Staff Operations wrote that SWAPO had succeeded in improving its military position in Angola considerably during the previous months. He referred to PLAN's current incursion as "the biggest ever" – which led to Operation Phoenix (*see* Chapter 9) – and stated that the SADF's restraint was leading to a situation where SWAPO would be able "to take the initiative in the war again".[15] As 1983 progressed, the pressure from SWAPO increased, as did the calls from top SADF officers that something had to be done about it. This was the genesis of Operation Askari.

By July, it became clear that something big was in the air. SWAPO withdrew many of its assets inside SWA and the shallow areas of Angola to its main bases at Lubango and Dongo for refresher training. Its so-called Special Unit – about 1 400 men strong, also known as Typhoon – started readying itself for reinfiltration. Recce groups witnessed logistic preparations and supply dumps, including land mines, being built up at Cahama, Cuvelai, Mulondo and Quiteve.

With the approach of the rainy season, it was estimated that this large-scale infiltration would start in January 1984.[16]

As usual, the PLAN and FAPLA forces were fairly integrated, and FAPLA often intervened when SADF patrols clashed with insurgents north of the border.[17] The primary aim of Operation Askari was therefore "to prevent by suitable action the SWAPO Special Unit infiltration to the south" and ensure its destruction as far north as possible.[18] For the operation, the participating South African Army units were divided into five formations:[19]

- Task Force X-Ray, consisting of a beefed-up 61 Mechanised Battalion Group. This formation would have three mechanised infantry companies, an armoured car squadron with Ratel 90s, two troops of Valkiri multiple rocket launchers, a 155-mm G-4 battery,[20] a 140-mm G-2 battery,[21] as well as two anti-aircraft batteries with Ystervark 20-mm guns on Unimog chassis. This formation was commanded by Commandant (later Colonel) Gert van Zyl who would be replaced by Commandant (later Colonel) Ep van Lill in the middle of the operation.

- Task Force Victor, scraped together mainly from Citizen Force regiments of 82 Mechanised Brigade. (This was one of four combat groups of 82 Brigade, taking turns to do border duty. In the brigade it was known as Task Force Delta, but took the designation of Task Force Victor for Operation Askari.) It had two mechanised infantry companies (one from 1 SAI and the other from Regiment Groot Karoo and Regiment De la Rey), an armoured car squadron (Eland 90s) from Regiment Mooirivier and Regiment Molopo, a 140-mm G-2 battery, a Valkiri troop and two anti-aircraft troops. Its commander was Commandant Faan Greyling, in civilian life an Orange Free State farmer from the Wesselsbron district.

- Task Force Echo Victor, with four motorised infantry companies from 32 Battalion. The formation got its name from its commander's initials, Commandant (later Brigadier General) Eddie Viljoen, who was also known as "Big Daddy".

- Combat Team Tango, with a mechanised infantry company from 4 SAI, an armoured car squadron supplied by 1 and 2 Special Service Battalion, and a 140-mm G-2 troop.

- Lastly, the battalion-sized Combat Team Manie, with four platoons of motorised infantry from 202 Battalion and two from 7 SAI, an armoured car squadron (origin not stated), and an 81-mm mortar platoon. This formation was supplied by Sector 20, whereas all the others came from Sector 10.

The plan was that Task Force X-Ray would operate west of the Cunene River and exercise a stranglehold on the garrisons of Quiteve and Cahama to intimidate them into leaving their fortifications. Task Force Victor would do the same east of the river at Cuvelai, while Task Force Echo Victor would act as a cut-off force north of Cuvelai and also destroy SWAPO bases east of the Kavango River. Because of a lack of sources, it is not possible to ascertain what Combat Team Tango's orders were, but Combat Team Manie was to advance from Rundu on Caiundo to confuse and mislead the enemy about the SADF targets. The basic posture in all these cases would be defensive. After that, the area around the Cunene River, Quiteve, Mupa, Vinticette and Ionde had to be dominated by the SADF. In the final phase, a SWAPO infiltration attempt could be thwarted, if necessary.[22] Among the guidelines laid down by Sector 10 was that SWAPO had to be prevented from infiltration altogether *before* the insurgents reached the border. "An infiltration during 1984 must simply not take place. Not even 10 terrorists must succeed in infiltrating," the operational plan stated.[23]

The SAAF would take the form of 4 Canberras, 4 Buccaneers, 10 Impala IIs and 10 Alouette II gunships, with 14 Mirage F1s on standby in South Africa (to be flown over if needed).[24] The whole force would be under the command of Brigadier Joep Joubert, who had commanded Task Force Alpha during Operation Protea. His operational headquarters was established at Xangongo where he would be near the fighting.[25]

A few words about the plan: firstly, Operation Askari would take place much later in the year than was the SADF's habit – in December and January, the rainy season, instead of from May to August. This was quite a gamble, as the rains could make movement difficult, if not impossible, for the heavy army vehicles. The longer the operation continued into January, the more rain could be expected, thereby increasing the risk.

Secondly, the army's mobility was also, once again, restricted by not having vehicles with a uniform cross-country ability. The bulk of the armoured vehicles consisted of the excellent Ratel, as well as the somewhat less mobile Buffel. But the venerable Eland, with its severe disabilities, was still used by one task force's armoured car squadron. And it was discovered that the new (Israeli-manufactured) G-4 gun had all sorts of mobility problems.[26]

Thirdly, the plan's two main pillars – that the FAPLA forces at Quiteve, Cahama, Mulondo and Cuvelai could be intimidated into fleeing, allowing the SADF to dominate the routes along which SWAPO planned to invade SWA – hinged on having enough time available to do the job. If the SADF wanted to neutralise FAPLA quickly, it would have to attack the Angolans with brute force and get it over with. But, for political reasons, the SADF was not especially keen to tangle with FAPLA. South Africa's fight, after all, was with SWAPO. "The military staff responsible for the planning of Op Askari were instructed by the Government that no FAPLA targets could be attacked directly, even if they were obviously providing protection to SWAPO elements – hence the unsatisfactory 'siege' strategy which was eventually adopted," stated an SADF report.[27]

Therefore, the plan was that the operation would start on 9 November and would last for two months. As one of the SADF planning documents stated, to "follow this approach is, of course, time-consuming".[28] In the words of Brigadier Joep Joubert, commander of the operation: "The idea was to isolate them, get them to shoot off all their ammunition and block resupplies. Eventually, it was hoped, the garrisons would wither on the vine and they would have to abandon the towns. Accomplishing their objectives in a week or two would have been impossible, so eight weeks was allowed for the operation."[29]

However, the hostile international situation faced by South Africa meant that the SADF would not get the leeway it needed. On 28 October 1983, less than two weeks before Askari was scheduled to start, the UN Security Council passed a resolution condemning South Africa's role in SWA and Angola and rejecting any link between the South West African question and the Cuban military role in Angola. The US abstained from the vote,[30] indicating that even the support of the Reagan administration had its limits. The Soviet Union and the US both warned the South African government not to push things too far.[31] France also announced that it was suspending its participation in the five-nation Western Contact Group, which was mediating between South Africa and the UN on the question of Namibian independence, and Canada soon followed suit.[32] The operation had to be postponed to 9 December,[33] by which time the deteriorating international situation necessitated a rapid implementation.

The delay gave the troops on the ground precious little time to carry out the plan of gradually pressuring the various FAPLA garrisons to vacate their positions. Besides, after Operation Protea in 1981, the Soviets and Cubans had delivered T-54 and T-55 tanks, as well as a series of ultramodern anti-aircraft missiles, to FAPLA. This would make life much more difficult for the SADF in two respects. Firstly, the army had hitherto come up against only ancient Second World War-vintage T-34 tanks, which were vulnerable to the 90-mm gun on the Ratel and Eland, but, with its thicker armour, the T-54/55 would give the SADF's armoured cars much more trouble. Secondly, the anti-aircraft missiles, in the words of Chester Crocker, made Cunene province "far less vulnerable to SADF air action than it had been two years earlier".[34] By December 1983, FAPLA had completed a two-year training and re-equipment programme and had become much more competent than during Operation Protea. As a matter of fact, Angola was by then spending 35% of its budget on its armed forces, and FAPLA "was starting to resemble a professional army", according to Edward George.[35]

Another factor that had to be taken into consideration was that the enemy was strong in the area where operations would take place. A whole mechanised division, reinforced with Cuban units, about 100 tanks and several batteries of artillery and anti-aircraft weapons (including the very latest Soviet missiles) and PLAN forces, was waiting for the South Africans (who were perhaps 2 000 men strong). However, the Angolan military doctrine was firmly static in nature, while the Cuban policy at this time was emphatically not to tangle with the SADF. As Brigadier Joubert later told Peter Stiff: "Africa is a big piece of ground and it is stupid to prepare defensive positions, if you can be cut off and cannot manoeuvre your own forces. They (FAPLA) fight a totally defensive war . . . [and] cannot act offensively."[36]

Operation Askari

Operation Askari's first drumbeat at the beginning of December was barely audible: the insertion of five Reconnaissance commando teams around the towns of Cahama, Mulondo, Cuvelai and Lubango. They would inform the South African forces throughout about their adversaries' actions and movements.[37] However, South African soldiers got into a contact with PLAN fighters in the vicinity of Cahama and in the skirmish two rebels were killed. With their excellent intelligence system on the ground, the SWAPO leadership apparently realised immediately that a big operation was afoot, and all PLAN units promptly moved to the protection of FAPLA bases.[38]

The second roll of the drums was somewhat louder. On 8 and 9 December, 61 Mech, being the army's premier conventional warfare unit, arrived at Xangongo, and on 11 December advanced to Quiteve, its first target, with two combat teams. The unit stormed the town the next day only to find it deserted. FAPLA had evacuated it. A mountain of supplies – weapons and ammunition, explosives, signals equipment, food and clothes – was seized. There was some excitement when two Angolan tanks, with supporting infantry, were seen advancing from the direction of Mulondo. But air support was requested, and SAAF Mirages swooped down on the FAPLA force, unloading their terrible payload and destroying one of the tanks. The Angolans wisely turned tail and fled back to Mulondo.[39]

With this, 61 Mech had fulfilled the first part of the plan, and it was at this point that Van Zyl was relieved by Ep van Lill.[40] A combat team and a Recce team was sent from Quiteve to harass the FAPLA garrison at Mulondo.[41] The fighting here consisted largely of artillery exchanges, while Mirages and Impalas also struck the Angolans from the air amid heavy anti-aircraft fire. Here the South Africans noticed for the first time ultra-modern Soviet SA-8 and SA-9 anti-aircraft missiles being fired at them – a worrying matter for the SAAF. One Impala was damaged when a missile penetrated its tailpipe without exploding. However, the garrison at Mulondo held its ground and did not run,[42] and the South Africans did not succeed in their objective. The 200 occupants of PLAN's Western Command headquarters, which was situated near Cahama, immediately pulled out and scuttled off to the protection of the FAPLA garrison at Cahama.[43]

Meanwhile, Task Force X-Ray concentrated its attention on Cahama. Van Lill had been briefed by Major General Georg Meiring, GOC South West Africa, to "cut off Camaha's water and lights".[44] Two combat teams

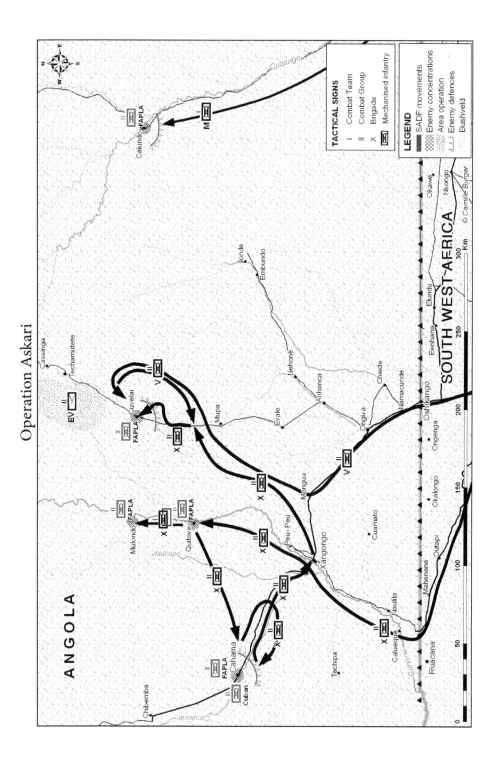

had already been deployed east of Cahama, and a third one to the north to stop enemy intervention from that direction. The task force's strong artillery component – three batteries of G-4 and G-2 guns and Valkiri rocket launchers – was deployed in such a way so as to give the impression that the defenders were being attacked by an entire brigade. The Angolan artillery returned fire, but the South Africans had a sound location system with which to pinpoint the enemy guns, and this enabled them to silence the FAPLA artillery pretty quickly.[45] The South Africans were aided by images transmitted by the Gharra – as the Seeker UAV was known – even though these were blurry and the UAV's range was limited.[46]

An intelligence officer with 61 Mech later reported about the first night's bombardment:

> The artillery were given the order to open fire and the night came alive with gunfire, flashes and noise. It was reminiscent of the artillery barrages of the Western Desert during World War Two but on a slightly smaller scale. From this vantage point FAPLA vehicles with lights blazing were observed moving about from place to place. Suddenly all lights were switched off, also the lights in the town itself. A company of T-55 tanks then deployed forward in front of 61 Mech Bn Gp positions. They were specifically looking for the forward positions so that they could engage the South Africans. The forward elements of 61 Mech Inf Bn Gp then withdrew in the early hours to observe the effects of the artillery bombardment.[47]

This continued for about two-and-a-half weeks. FAPLA's artillery replied in kind and even managed to destroy a Ratel 20 and a gun tractor. There were also several other smaller clashes.[48]

To the east, Task Force Victor's "campers" – as the part-time Citizen Force soldiers were generally known – first marched to Mongua and then to Cuvelai, their target, where they harassed the FAPLA and PLAN garrison, as ordered, and heavy artillery exchanges took place.[49]

Further east, Combat Team Manie carried out its feint towards Caiundo. But the FAPLA garrison there reacted aggressively, attacking an SADF platoon that came too near the defensive perimeter on 18 December. The South Africans were badly mauled, losing eleven: nine dead, one missing (presumed dead) and one taken prisoner. Consequently, SAAF assets had to be diverted to Caiundo, meaning a reduced air effort elsewhere. The South Africans also bombarded the Angolans with 120-mm mortars, but to no avail. The Angolans did not vacate Caiundo, and so the SADF did not succeed in its objective here either.[50]

However, international politics were about to intervene – and not on the side of the invaders. When Jannie Geldenhuys, Chief of the Army, visited the Askari operational headquarters on 20 December, everything seemed on track, and several messages were intercepted from distressed FAPLA garrison commanders calling for reinforcements. Some reinforcements were sent from Lubango, where the FAPLA divisional headquarters was situated, but not enough to make a real difference.

International pressure was building on South Africa to cease Askari. When SADF Chief Constand Viljoen showed up at the front on 24 December, the international furore had changed things considerably. He warned that the operation might not be allowed to continue beyond 31 December. In that case, the operational headquarters officers answered, the nature of the operation had to be changed. Cuvelai was now regarded as a key location in PLAN's infiltration offensive, which meant that something had to be done about the place.[51]

One gets the impression that the SADF was unwilling to withdraw without giving somebody a good walloping. Up to this point, the operation had been very frustrating, without the spectacular victories seen in most previous operations.

The upshot was a change to the South Africans' operational posture, in the form of new orders issued on 28 December. Things now had to be speeded up; the enemy would no longer be subjected to probing attacks and harassment only, but was to be attacked forcefully. Van Lill was ordered to attack Cahama and capture a Soviet-made SA-8 surface-to-air missile launcher, while Greyling's Task Force Victor had to take on the enemy at Cuvelai. All this had to be done before 31 December, after which all offensive action against FAPLA had to stop.[52] The operation was about to get very hot.

Cahama was a tough nut to crack. It had been attacked from the air several times, while South African Army units had also made some probing attacks on its defences. Yet, the defenders never flinched and mostly kept a passive defensive posture. According to SADF intelligence, it was defended by an Angolan brigade and a Cuban battalion, supported by a battery of multiple rocket launchers, 10 T-55 tanks and two batteries of anti-aircraft missiles (SA-8 and SA-9).[53] Van Lill had much less than that, but pressed on regardless:

> On 29 December I received orders to attack Cahama from the south and capture [an] SA-8. On 31 December we carried out a river crossing operation just northwest of Xangongo (this was the first operational river crossing since the Second World War). The Sappers built a Bailey Bridge. The enemy's warning system was good and they waited for us. When we came within range of their artillery, we drew heavy fire. My mortar platoon was in Buffels and a mortar bomb fell inside one Buffel. Two members dead.[54]

According to Brigadier Joep Joubert, there was little cover for the South African attackers, while FAPLA's defences were well developed. This meant that X-Ray's attack stalled before the enemy defence line and could not penetrate it. "Heavy battles were conducted here," he reported.[55] The SAAF also weighed in with Canberras and Impalas, but the Angolan defences were good and casualties seemed to be limited.[56]

Rather to the South Africans' surprise, FAPLA reacted very aggressively, bringing in reinforcements from Lubango, using its artillery extensively and – for the first time in the war – utilising its tanks in mobile charges on the undulating terrain, which was suitable for armoured warfare.[57] As we have seen, in past operations the Angolans had dug in their tanks and used them as light artillery, thereby negating the advantages that their mobility afforded. Additionally, FAPLA had moved beyond the antiquated T-34 tank to the more modern T-54/55.

Van Lill's Ratel 90s had to bear the brunt of the FAPLA tank attack, and for a while things looked quite hairy. This was the first time the Ratel 90, with its inadequate low-velocity 90-mm gun, had come up against the T-55, but the Ratel's vastly superior mobility and the South Africans' excellent training made a big difference. The Angolan attack was beaten off with the destruction of two tanks, but it was not easy.[58] One of the T-55s was hit by the South African artillery in what the battery commander, Major (later Commandant) Dr Jakkie Cilliers, calls "a textbook engagement".[59]

FAPLA's robust defence caused the SADF planners to think twice about continuing the operation against Cahama. Van Lill contacted Joubert and told him that heavy casualties would be incurred if Cahama were to be taken. Joubert ordered him to break off contact and return to Xangongo for another task.[60] In a situation report early in January, it was indeed reported that the SADF "was not equipped and did not plan for a frontal attack".[61]

Clearly the SADF did not succeed in its objective to intimidate FAPLA into leaving Cahama. On the contrary, the South Africans lost this round too.

Task Force Echo Victor (elements of 32 Battalion) had more success. The force discovered quite a few SWAPO bases north of Cuvelai and west of Cassinga and destroyed them all. This in itself, in the words of Colonel Jan Breytenbach, "put paid to SWAPO's planned infiltrations of SWA by their so-called Typhoon units".[62] At that point, Echo Victor was well placed to protect Task Force Victor – the mainly Citizen Force formation – in the vicinity of Cuvelai from the north. This town was also heavily defended, according to SADF intelligence, by a FAPLA brigade, buttressed by 13 T-55 tanks.[63]

But Victor fared even worse than X-Ray, and one misfortune after another befell the formation. In spite of Victor's shadow-boxing in the vicinity of Cuvelai for a few days, the enemy did not budge. In line with the new orders, Victor was now tasked to attack Cuvelai from the northeast. The commander, Commandant Faan Greyling, protested, as he said the route was blocked by the Cuvelai River, which was in flood. But Sector 10 headquarters stood by its orders.

Things went wrong for Victor almost immediately. The SADF vehicles got stuck in almost every stream, and the South Africans were greeted by accurate fire from the feared Soviet-made ZSU-23 anti-aircraft guns, which could slice through the thinly armoured Ratels and Elands like a hot knife through butter. One of the troop commanders apparently lost his nerve, and another officer had to take over that unit in addition to his own. A 23-mm shell hit the Ratel turret of Lieutenant Piet Liebenberg, killing this much-liked officer.[64]

One of the South Africans later reported:

We were in trouble already early on because of faulty intelligence and defective analysis of the tactical situation. Our enemy had most carefully prepared a wide-ranging killing ground. We advanced through brushwood, and suddenly came upon a spooky plain where all the trees were cut off at knee height and we were exposed without any cover.

We were prepared to encounter an opposing force of battalion strength and only learned later that we walked right into the teeth of a brigade. Our intelligence service assured us that no battle tanks would be employed against us, but T-34 and T-55 tanks loomed large and deadly. Our battle group consisted largely of light infantry,[65] by no means in the weight class to slug it out with heavy armour to retain the territory. Our only anti-armour capacity was "Noddy cars", obsolete Eland 90 armoured cars, too low to shoot and scoot in the bushy area on tanks.[66]

What this soldier did not report was what followed. Fearing minefields and more casualties, Greyling ordered a withdrawal. However, the usual careful drill for a withdrawal was ignored by the troops and it allegedly turned into a disorderly rout. With much effort, Greyling managed to restore order and regroup. Sector 10 ordered that the attack be resumed along the same axis, but Greyling refused to do so without proper reconnaissance and planning. The attack was called off.[67] FAPLA was in an excellent position to launch a counterattack at that moment, but its leaders let the opportunity pass.

In his article on the history of Regiment Mooirivier, GJJ Oosthuizen reports even more disturbing facts, based on interviews with eyewitness officers:

After the botched first attack, the groups (mainly two sections) from Regiment Groot Karoo absolutely refused to participate in any further combat. The feeling among the men was that they were always first in the line of fire during an attack and that the attacks were planned in such a way that they were being used as cannon fodder. Major [Kallie] Kallmeyer had the difficult task of convincing the demoralised soldiers to the contrary. Kallmeyer, supported by his enthusiastic armoured vehicle crew, eventually managed to persuade the foot soldiers to continue fighting, but on condition that they received proper orders and were not forced to leave the relative safety of the vehicles prematurely. Kallmeyer also decided to side-step the lieutenants from Regiment Groot Karoo, who no longer had the complete trust of their men, by personally and simultaneously giving orders to the whole combat team.[68]

Greyling also got some of the blame for the failed attack. Seeing that Task Force X-Ray's (61 Mech) attempt to take Cahama had failed, Joubert decided to move this formation to Cuvelai to reinforce Task Force Victor. The commander of 61 Mech, Ep van Lill, was asked to take over command of the renewed attack on Cuvelai from Greyling, as the latter was judged not to be up to the task.[69] Besides, radio intercepts indicated that the FAPLA command at Cuvelai had requested 900 troops as reinforcements. It was not known whether the reinforcements would be FAPLA or Cuban troops.[70]

X-Ray duly "bundu-bashed" via Xangongo to Cuvelai. By now, Van Lill's own troops were already very tired, having been fighting or on the move, almost without rest, for more than three days.[71] Moreover, he had very little time to take Cuvelai, as the international political pressure on South Africa to withdraw from Angola had already become massive. In fact, the order issued on 28 December had stipulated that all offensive action against FAPLA had to cease by midnight on 31 December, but clearly this was impossible. An extension was granted by the political leadership.[72]

Van Lill therefore decided to utilise the "campers" in Task Force Victor, who were relatively fresh, as his main attack force to assault Cuvelai from the southeast. At the same time, the exhausted X-Ray would feint from the south to draw the enemy's tanks away from the real attack. But Victor remained a troublesome formation. Van Lill relates that, while he was still engaged in his orders group, "the Citizen Force members stated that they did not see their way open for another attack". He could, of course, have thrown the book at them and court-martialled the lot, but that would not have solved the immediate problem. He was therefore forced to change his plan. He detached one infantry company from Victor to X-Ray and ordered Victor to draw the enemy away while X-Ray, desperately tired or not, executed the main attack. The two forces would advance together on the gravel road south of Cuvelai. Victor would then make contact with FAPLA, while X-Ray would turn east approximately 10 km from the target.[73]

The attack was preceded by a bombardment by four Canberra bombers, whose strikes were, as an eyewitness reported, "very accurate".[74] Van Lill takes up the story:

> The terrain was densely wooded, and the sky was clouded over with light rain. While "61" was moving to the rendezvous, we came under indirect fire. When I inquired by radio how the force-in-being [Task Force Victor] was coming along, I heard to my dismay that they were following us and not doing what they were supposed to. I ordered them to stay where they were and not to move until further notice. Because navigation was very difficult and GPS was not yet available, my front armoured vehicle (a Ratel 90) got into an enemy minefield.[75] The vehicle was evacuated without casualties and we withdrew to regroup. This was already late in the afternoon, and we were not sure where we were. I asked permission to break contact, as the enemy was again firing on us with T-55s, and to attack again the following morning. This was approved with the proviso that we had to bring down indirect mortar fire all night on the Ratel in the minefield to prevent the enemy from capturing it.[76]

The attack resumed the next day (4 January), and this time everything went according to plan. The enemy was softened up by SAAF air strikes. A radio message was intercepted from the Cuvelai commander, who pleaded with his divisional commander in Lubango to send help. He claimed that the SAAF attack had destroyed 75% of his artillery.[77]

At 08h00, the troops went in. The battle lasted for most of the day, but the Angolan resistance was fierce. The South African artillery supported the attacking troops superbly, firing off some 60 tonnes of ordnance in just a few hours. According to Jakkie Cilliers, the recoil of the guns drove the wheels so deep into the ground that they had to be dug out after the battle.[78] Time and again the enemy's well-dug-in anti-aircraft guns forced the attacking Ratels to retreat, and for a while the whole attack was in the balance.

The courage of a young Alouette pilot, Captain Carl Alberts, played a considerable role in the final SADF victory. Alberts was acting as a spotter for the South African artillery, and several FAPLA guns and positions were taken out with the help of his directions. At one point, when the Ratels were again stopped by enemy fire, Alberts and another Alouette pilot started relieving each other in the role of spotter. An anonymous account (available online) describes the dogged fight:

> One [Alouette] would creep up on the anti-aircraft position at treetop height and pull up. As the anti-aircraft guns fire on him, the other Alouette would be there to determine their position accurately and direct the South African 127-mm [Valkiri] rocket fire from the ground. At one stage Carl, flying at a height of 1 000 feet and without thinking about his own safety as four RPG-4 rockets fired at him simultaneously, accurately fixed their position and gave it to his forces so that they could destroy them.[79]

A little later, a group of 10 Angolan T-55s counterattacked and shot out a Ratel, while another Ratel tripped a mine. Both started burning fiercely. Alberts saw the two vehicles, with some Angolan tanks and infantry milling around close by. He radioed their position to his own artillery, and, within half a minute, the shells exploded right in the middle of the Angolan formation, causing them to pull back hastily. The local platoon commander, 19-year-old Lieutenant Alexander Macaskill, repeatedly ventured into the enemy killing field to rescue five of his comrades in one of the Ratels. For these actions, both Alberts and Macaskill were awarded the Honoris Crux.[80]

Lieutenant Colin Steyn, a descendant of Free State President MT Steyn, was present in a Ratel 90:

> A Ratel 20 mm – call sign 13 Bravo – left to my rear, was hit directly. I remember the white light which shone through the dust and smoke, with the hole which appeared in the right-hand door as the smoke dissipated. An intense fire started inside the vehicle. The team commander opened the hatch. First green smoke burst out, then yellow. The hatch

was closed and opened again. Then I saw the fire inside the Ratel, a white-yellow inferno, and then the thing started to rock and shake, forwards and backwards, due to the explosions within.

I felt how the cold blanket of death came to lay upon me. You don't know what is shooting at you. We were heavily under fire of the enemy artillery.

Suddenly, a T-55 tank stormed them. Steyn loaded an antitank round:

We hit the tank on its turret. A round object flew into the sky. I later learnt that it was the tank's infrared searchlight. But at that time I thought we had fired too high. I ordered: "Three hundred metres, fire!"

The tank was hit and halted. Grey smoke burst out from the turret. After the second shot I succeeded in reporting: "Tank contact!"

Your entire being concentrates on the tank. Behind us, the Ratel with South African soldiers inside was still burning.[81]

By late afternoon, just about all the enemy positions were in South African hands. The enemy fled northwards to Techamutete. The SADF Ratel 90 crews showed their mettle by badly damaging five T-55s. This was more meaningful than it seems, because the low-pressure gun of the Ratel had little penetration ability against the tanks' thick armour. This meant that the Ratel crews had to get very close to a tank to take it out – something that called for considerable skill and courage. Of course, the South Africans were also helped by the fact that the T-55 had a very low profile, which meant that the Angolan gunners could not see their targets over the bushes, while the higher-profile Ratels in turn could see the enemy tanks.[82]

One Ratel was destroyed by a tank, killing the five South Africans inside, one of whom was totally blown apart. In total, the South Africans lost 7 dead and 14 wounded in this battle. Altogether, between 1 December 1983 and 15 January 1984, some 25 South African soldiers died of all causes in Angola and the operational area in northern Namibia. It is not known how many died in Operation Askari itself. The fleeing FAPLA tank crews left behind four more undamaged tanks and many other vehicles. A total of 324 enemy bodies were counted on the battlefield.[83] One welcome addition to the South African arsenal was two SA-9 missile systems, the first time that this ultramodern weapon had fallen into Western hands.[84] This more than made up for the failure to capture an SA-8 system at Cahama. The damaged FAPLA tanks were repaired and taken with the others to 61 Mech's base at Omuthiya in Ovamboland, and were eventually given to UNITA.[85] It was also established that at least six Soviets and eight Cubans had been part of the FAPLA headquarters.[86]

The new Soviet commander in Angola, General Konstantin Kurochkin, was scathing in his criticism of Cuvelai's FAPLA defenders. He reported to Angolan President José Eduardo dos Santos that the defending brigade commander at Cuvelai gave the order to retreat as soon as his communications with headquarters were cut. Kurochkin told Dos Santos that "the brigade ran away not during the combat, but after it. If the brigade had stayed in its positions, South African troops would have retreated"[87] – a statement that, given the SADF's reluctance to incur casualties, may well be true.

Meanwhile, Eddie Viljoen, commander of Task Force Echo Victor, had cleared the area north of Cuvelai. When the final attack on the town took place, he positioned his forces to cut off a northward retreat from it. In the process, his troops tangled with the garrison of Techamutete, who promptly fled. Viljoen was surprised to find himself suddenly the "owner" of the town. When he proudly radioed the news to Joep Joubert, the response was abrupt: "Now who the hell told you to take Techamutete?" After a short silence, Joubert continued: "But now that you are there, you had better stay there!"[88]

Obviously, the poor FAPLA soldiers fleeing the carnage in Cuvelai did not know that "The Terrible Ones" of 32 Battalion had cut off their retreat. They reached Techamutete before first light on the morning of 5 January, dead tired, and suddenly walked into a hail of bullets and shells, also from the formidable 23-mm guns that 32 Battalion had captured there.

Piet Nortje, who was apparently there himself, pictured the scene:

> It looked and sounded like something out of *Star Wars* as burst after burst and bomb after bomb thundered through the darkness. It was

Before the very first battle in the Border War – the attack on the SWAPO base at Ongulumbashe in August 1966 – a number of SADF soldiers in civilian dress scouted the area for the base. They travelled in this bakkie.

The SWAPO base at Cassinga on 4 May 1978 as seen from the air. The smoke indicates where the bombers' ordinance exploded.

An ammunition dump in Cassinga goes up in flames during the SADF assault on this SWAPO base.

The mass grave at Cassinga a few days after the SADF attack. SWAPO claimed that mainly civilians stayed at Cassinga, but except for the woman left in the foreground, the other bodies all seem to be those of young men. Photo credit: UWC-Robben Island Museum Mayibuye Archive.

A parabat guards prisoners during the attack on Cassinga in May 1978.

Colonel Jan Breytenbach (third from the left) consults his officers during the battle of Cassinga. Brigadier Martiens du Plessis stands with his back to the camera.

A group of SADF soldiers somewhere in Angola during Operation Savannah. The uniforms are a little different from those worn during the 1980s.

SADF vehicles at the airfield of Serpa Pinto in Angola (Operation Savannah).

Unita leader Jonas Savimbi with SADF officers during Operation Savannah.

An ideological indoctrination seminar for MPLA members somewhere in South Angola. UNTA (far left on banner) was a Marxist trade union.

South African troops cross a river, most probably during Operation Savannah. The lightning South African advance caused severe headaches for the enemy.

A patrol of 32 Battalion in Angola. Thoughout the war this unit played a prominent role in SADF operations north of the border.

A BTR-152 armoured vehicle, a 76-mm gun and GAZ lorries captured from SWAPO
(Operation Sceptic).

General Constand Viljoen (with his back to the camera) walks towards a Ratel-60 during
Operation Sceptic.

A SAAF pilot lies on a stretcher next to a Puma helicopter. He is most probably Captain Thinus van Rensburg, who was shot down in an Alouette III during Operation Sceptic. He evaded the enemy for a few days before he was found by SADF comrades. General Jannie Geldenhuys is second from left.

Lieutenant General Constand Viljoen inspects a Russian 14,5-mm heavy machine gun (Operation Sceptic).

A Ratel from 2 Platoon, Combat Team 2 (which suffered the most casualties during the Battle of Smokeshell), is towed away. The holes in the armour where it was hit by a Russian 23-mm gun can be seen.

Puma helicopters fly low over the bushy Angolan landscape.

A major part of SWAPO's war in South West Africa consisted of laying land mines. The SADF used the Chubby mine clearance vehicle to find and destroy land mines.

Troops from the Angolan rebel movement UNITA learn to march at a training camp. UNITA was a South African ally throughout the war.

Not only white soldiers fought on South Africa's side in the Border War. It is not known from which unit the troops on the photo are.

A group of senior SADF officers during Operation Protea: General Jannie Geldenhuys is second from the left and Lieutenant General Denis Earp of the SAAF stands with a rucksack between his legs. In the background, with the beret, is Commandant Johann Dippenaar.

A Puma helicopter lifts a damaged Alouette III on the back of a lorry. Due to the international arms embargo against South Africa, the SADF really had to look after its aircraft.

An Alouette III hovers above a Daphne class submarine of the Navy. The submarines played an important role to land special forces behind enemy lines and to extract them again.

An Eland-90 armoured car, popularly known as a "Noddy car". This photo was taken at Xangongo after the town was captured.

Troops on a Ratel-90 guard captured enemy weapons during Operation Protea.

FAPLA trenches at Xangongo. The
South Africans had to storm and "clean
up" several of these trenches.

A FAPLA gun (76 mm) at Xangongo.

A Yugoslav 20-mm three-barreled gun, captured at Xangongo.

SADF officers study a sand model which FAPLA made of its positions at Xangongo
(Operation Protea).

A typical SADF convoy with Buffels in the foreground, a Samil-100 to the back and an Eland-90
to the right.

A G-2 gun (140 mm) behind a Magirus Deutz artillery tractor. From 1985 this obsolete gun from the Second World War was gradually replaced by the formidable G-5.

A SADF sapper gingerly pulls a land mine out of a hole. During the Border War the SADF built up vast mine-clearing expertise.

as if fire was running down the mountain and stars were falling out of the sky. The bombardment was frightening, and then, suddenly, there was silence. Not a sound from the target area and only a shout of "cease fire" to the town's defenders. Then the high-pitched revs of an engine screamed into the night and on the shouted order "Fire!" the deadly pyrotechnical display began again. Once or twice more the mysterious engine was revved to screaming pitch, only to be silenced by another bombardment. Finally, there was nothing more to break the deathly silence.[89]

The engine, it turned out, belonged to the only T-55 to survive the SADF assault on Cuvelai, and was accompanying some fleeing FAPLA infantry. Joubert ordered Van Lill to assemble a strong antitank combat team to reinforce Viljoen at Techamutete, but Van Lill could not comply immediately. He had to inform Joubert that his own force did not have enough fuel left, while Task Force Victor's B echelon (the field logistical unit) refused to come closer than 30 km to the target for fear of the enemy's artillery. Joubert's disgusted response in Afrikaans is difficult to translate: "Dis nou 'n bekakkingswaardige situasie. Los maar" (which translates roughly as "This situation calls for shitting yourself. Leave it."). However, with the enemy out of the way, the fuel trucks turned up the next morning and Van Lill could carry out his orders.[90]

A somewhat amusing sequel to this occurred when Joubert asked Van Lill if he needed anything else. Van Lill, perhaps not expecting that anything would come of it, answered that he really could do with a beer or two. And, lo and behold, two hours later a whole pallet with beer, cold drinks and cigarettes was delivered by parachute from a Dakota.[91]

The final bloody spasm at Techamutete was followed by ten days of area operations to dominate the area in accordance with the original objective. By 13 January, the main forces were back in SWA. Elements of 32 Battalion remained in the vicinity of Cuvelai east of Techamutete to conduct further counter-insurgency operations against PLAN insurgents, and had several firefights in the process. This phase was known as Operation Opsaal, and represented the last – clandestine – phase of Askari.[92]

Some reflections

Operation Askari will not go down in the history books as the SADF's finest hour. This was the first task force or battle group to consist largely of Citizen Force soldiers. In his media briefing, Joubert put a positive spin on Task Force Victor's performance on the battlefield: "For the first time in the history of this conflict the Citizen Force was utilised as a battle group. This was done very successfully; they gained invaluable experience and learnt a lot."[93]

Behind the scenes, different sentiments were expressed. When the SADF reviewed the operation, it was reported that "the morale of the Citizen Force elements was sometimes not good enough and more attention must undoubtedly be given to the Citizen Force leader group". Battle Group Delta (Victor) was bluntly called "the worst battle group in 82 Mechanised Brigade". The armoured car squadron was fine, "but the rest of the personnel was bad".[94] This merited only a fleeting mention at the after-action review meeting, but the words were sharper than spears. At a personnel review, it was also stated that this battle group was "understrength" because of the large number of exemptions given to CF members, and that this applied especially to the leader group.[95]

Several tactical objectives were also not reached. The garrisons of the FAPLA bastions of Cahama, Mulondo, Caiundo and Cuvelai were not intimidated into fleeing. An attack on Cahama was beaten back by an aggressive defence with, for the first time, mobile use of T-55 tanks. At Cuvelai, the SADF was also beaten back at first, and only after concentrating two of the three task forces there did the South Africans achieve their objective and retrieve their honour.

This does not mean that Askari was a failure. The intimidation of the FAPLA garrisons was a secondary aim; the primary aim of the operation was to dominate the approach routes to SWA and prevent SWAPO's big planned infiltration during the 1984 rainy season. This goal the SADF achieved. In an intelligence appraisal, the following conclusions were reached:[96]

- The situation from Cassinga to the South West African border is unsafe for infiltration, and SWAPO appears to be confused and negative.
- The infiltration route has been lengthened from 170 to 270 kilometres, which means that insurgents had to walk an additional 100 kilometres

on foot. Less ammunition, food and supplies could thus be carried. The longer trek also gave the security forces more time to locate and eliminate the insurgents.

- The situation has a negative influence on SWAPO's morale, because the cadres cannot depend on FAPLA.

Indeed, by the end of Askari, "the area south of the Bale River between the Cassinga–Cuvelai Road in the west and the Cubango River in the east had been cleared of SWAPO bases", according to Jan Breytenbach. "So no serious incursions of Owamboland, via this route, took place during 1984 . . . By the end of Operation Askari the South Africans were in control of Cunene province east of the Cunene River and as far north as Cassinga."[97]

The appraisal concluded: "Operation Askari put SWAPO in a weaker tactical situation and brought the Security Forces to the Heartland of SWAPO."[98] This has been confirmed by Canadian academic Susan Brown, who is not at all sympathetic to the SADF's war effort:

> SWAPO's ability to strike at will into the Ovambo area of Namibia now began to diminish rapidly. PLAN combatants, previously based within a few kilometres of the Namibian border, were forced hundreds of kilometres back into the Angolan hinterland. The PLAN headquarters and regional command points came under constant air and ground attack. Forward command posts from which guerrillas operated into Namibia became increasingly insecure if close to the border, with their lines of supply disrupted.

> When SWAPO could no longer establish bases close to the border, this imposed on combatants the need to carry land mines, mortars, automatic rifles, medical equipment and so on hundreds of kilometres on their backs before they even entered Namibia, let alone crossed into white farming areas. This long trek south was impossible without water, so PLAN operations became restricted to the rainy season between November and March . . . This cut into the time combatants were able to stay in Namibia.

This crucially affected their ability to conduct political work among the local population. After 1982, the politicizing role of guerrillas who move continually and easily among the people of Ovamboland, often in civilian clothes, able to communicate and convince, began to wane. The role of combatants was increasingly forced into an exclusively military mould.[99]

But it was naive to think that SWAPO could be prevented completely from an incursion during 1984. As an SADF intelligence appraisal warned: "Although the lengthening of the route through Angola will have a negative effect on SWAPO/Spec Unit's logistical and offensive capacity, SWAPO's capacity to adapt should not be underestimated."[100] Nevertheless, Colonel Dick Lord, air force commander during the operation, sums it up when he says that SWAPO "never succeeded in regaining the offensive capability it had prior to Askari".[101]

At the same time, one has to identify an ominous development since Operation Protea. In having to tangle with FAPLA, South Africa was inadvertently being drawn into the Angolan civil war. After all, any weakening of FAPLA's position could only be to UNITA's advantage. As Chester Crocker put it: "The Angolan civil war became part of a regional war in which the South Africans as well as the Cubans and Soviets were now central players."[102] Dick Lord confirms that "FAPLA grew in stature and evolved into the major factor in our war on SWAPO". With the growing role of the Soviet Union in the Angolan conflict, and to a lesser extent also Cuba, outside factors grew in importance, while South African control over the course of the war diminished.[103]

Without the South Africans' knowing it, their success at Cuvelai almost broke their enemies' spirits. The Cuban commander, General de División (Major General) Leopoldo Cintra Frías, proposed that all three remaining Angolan brigades be withdrawn to the north, where air cover could be provided. (This was part of an intense strategic debate between the Cubans and Soviets about the fundamental course to be taken in the war, which will be discussed in greater detail in Chapter 11.) On 7 January, only three days after the Angolan debacle at Cuvelai, Cuban leader Fidel Castro wrote to Angolan President José Eduardo dos Santos, supporting the Cuban commander's plan. It would have meant that the entire territory south of the railway line between Namibe and

Menongue had to be given up to the SADF. However, the Soviet commander, General Konstantin Kurochkin, steadfastly refused and in the end won the debate. The brigades stayed where they were.[104]

One final puzzle has to be solved. In his memoirs, General Jannie Geldenhuys writes that FAPLA's 11 Brigade and two Cuban battalions sprang to the aid of SWAPO when the latter's headquarters was attacked 5 kilometres from Cuvelai.[105] The problem is that this version is confirmed nowhere in the archival sources.

It is easy to see where it comes from. Several documents, summarising the known intelligence about the enemy deployments in the target area, mention the presence of Cuban units at various places.[106] One source states that two Cuban battalions were sent as reinforcements to Cuvelai, "[b]ut it is unknown whether the Cubans reached Cuvelai".[107] In a document, apparently written early in January 1984, it was recommended that the Chief of the SADF issue a press release on 6 January with the message that the MPLA and Cubans had intervened during South African operations against SWAPO, that this attack was beaten back and that Cuvelai was subsequently captured.[108] This duly happened,[109] but it was not exactly truthful. FAPLA did not intervene, but was attacked by the SADF. No Cubans were involved. Brigadier Joep Joubert also later told Peter Stiff that the only Cubans at Cuvelai were advisors.[110]

Commandant Ep van Lill confirmed much later that he had been *ordered* to tell South African television viewers that his force had been attacked by a Cuban battalion while they were on the heels of SWAPO insurgents, and that he had no alternative. "This was bullshit," he told me bluntly. "It was said for political reasons. There were Cuban advisors, but they fled before we occupied Cuvelai."[111]

Several other lessons were also learnt or re-learnt during Askari. Firstly, the considered opinion within the SADF was that the strangling tactics to force the FAPLA garrisons to evacuate their positions would have worked if there had been enough time. However, politics intervened and prevented the SADF from achieving all of its objectives.[112] Secondly, this would be the last cross-border operation in which the inadequate and obsolete Eland would be used. It really hampered operations.[113] And, thirdly, the army had found that its anti-tank ability was inadequate. The FAPLA tank charges at Cahama really gave the South Africans a scare. New weapons systems were being developed that would come to fruition in 1987.[114]

The presence of T-54/55s on the battlefield, together with the aggressive FAPLA tactics at Cahama, gave the South Africans much food for thought and had a notable sequel. Up to then, the armoured cars had performed well above expectation, and the army believed it could "get away with murder".[115] But when SADF Chief Constand Viljoen visited the front on Christmas Eve, Van Lill told him that his men could not fight that way, as the Ratel 90 and Eland 90 simply could not stand up to the superior armament and armour of the T-54/55. So he asked for tanks, and, a few weeks later, a squadron of Olifant Mk 1 tanks was delivered. The tanks were incorporated into 61 Mech as E Squadron, alongside the mechanised infantry, armoured cars, artillery and other support troops. The tanks arrived too late to be used in Askari, but it was important that FAPLA and PLAN were informed that the SADF had what it took if it became necessary. So Van Lill ordered the tanks straight to the border town of Ruacana, where he staged a huge exercise, aptly named Exercise Ystervuis (Iron Fist).[116]

The tanks became an integral part of 61 Mech, which made the unit the most powerful one in the army at that time. However, because the SADF undertook no further major cross-border operations – at any rate until September 1987 – the tank crews were transferred back to the School of Armour in Bloemfontein, while the tanks were left at 61 Mech's base at Omuthiya. Personnel were flown to Omuthiya from time to time for exercises with the rest of the unit.[117] Besides, FAPLA itself was never seen as a conventional threat to South Africa or SWA,[118] which did not make the full-time retention of South African tanks and their crews in SWA cost-effective. Things would, of course, change during the climactic struggle at the end of 1987.

The Joint Monitoring Commission

Operation Askari had interesting political consequences. It gave rise to a fairly short-lived peace and negotiation process. And, while it failed, the process also proved to be a valuable testing ground, as it were, for the final round of negotiations in 1988.

As was made clear earlier in the chapter, by December 1983 the international climate was very inimical to South Africa and its war effort in South West Africa and Angola. On 5 December, Chester Crocker and South African Foreign Minister Pik Botha met in Rome for the first time in a year. Crocker told Botha rather bluntly "that Washington wanted a significant South African military gesture for a finite period as a means of levering reciprocal moves from Luanda". According to Crocker's memoirs, Botha almost blew his top and "bellowed" that the world could go ahead and impose sanctions for all he cared. But at the same time, Botha was "carefully absorbing the argument and analytical input we provided". It "was obvious Botha saw an opportunity in our Rome message", Crocker says.[119]

Botha needed time to bring PW Botha and the military around, though, and Askari kicked off only three days later. However, just before the full extent of South Africa's foray into Angola became known, on 15 December Pik Botha wrote to UN Secretary-General Javier Pérez de Cuéllar, saying that South Africa was prepared to withdraw all its troops from Angola for an initial period of 30 days, which could be extended. The rider was "that this gesture would be reciprocated by the Angolan Government which would ensure that its own forces, SWAPO and the Cubans would not exploit the resulting situation . . .".[120] This was the heart of the problem, the one that would, in the end, result in the failure of this process.

The initial reaction by both the Angolan government and SWAPO was negative. They said they would accept the proposal only if South Africa promised to start implementing Resolution 435 within 15 days after the 30-day truce. This, of course, was completely unacceptable to South Africa, and for a while the whole initiative looked like a non-starter. But the military pressure caused by Askari, especially the defeat at Cuvelai, made the Angolans wilt. At a meeting with Crocker's assistant, Frank Wisner, on 20/21 January, Angola indicated that that it was willing, as Crocker reported to Pik Botha a week later in person, to "use all its influence with SWAPO to enforce respect for the ceasefire and prevent exploitation of South African withdrawal to reinforce SWAPO's position". Angola also demanded an end to support for UNITA.[121] The Americans also briefed Sam Nujoma, without elevating his movement to the status of a party to the coming agreement[122] – which was, perhaps, a mistake, as we shall see.

This was a potential breakthrough. South Africa's purpose right through the war was to create a situation whereby PLAN could not use Angolan territory as a springboard for infiltration into SWA. This was the basic objective of all the cross-border operations, large and small. If Angola could rein in SWAPO, the South Africans would achieve their objective without further fighting. And, as far as UNITA's alliance with South Africa was concerned, the best that can be said is that international politics is a harsh place where countries do not have permanent friends, only permanent interests.

As an anonymous SADF staff officer, chronicling the history of the Joint Monitoring Commission (JMC), set up to monitor the disengagement process, aptly commented:

> The truth was that the advantages of a negotiated settlement to the hostilities in Angola were becoming more and more apparent to both parties in the conflict. Quite simply, Angola perceived a negotiated settlement as the only means of ensuring an end to the RSA's periodic military adventures on its soil, while the RSA had by now come to accept the fact that a negotiated withdrawal from Angola was the only way to pre-empt the growing calls in the international community for punitive measures against the Republic.[123]

We need not dwell too long on the abortive JMC attempt. It kicked off at a big conference in Lusaka, Zambia, on 16 February 1984, and the minutes show some hard bargaining between the parties. The South African delegation was headed by Jannie Geldenhuys, who summarised the position succinctly by saying that Angola wanted "to establish that there was no South African troop presence in the area in question. South Africa wanted the Commission to verify that there would be no SWAPO and Cuban presence" there. Therefore, a Joint Monitoring Commission, consisting of SADF and FAPLA personnel, was agreed upon to oversee the disengagement process. The JMC's first seat would be Cuvelai; once both sides agreed that there were no SADF soldiers north of the place and no FAPLA, PLAN or Cuban military personnel south of it, the seat could move southwards to Mupa. As the process went on, the JMC could move progressively southwards to Evale, Ongiva and finally to Oshikango on the

South West African border. The SADF and FAPLA would conduct joint patrols to monitor the situation, and a mechanism was established to report and deal with transgressions. The process would start on 1 March and last 30 days, after which all South African troops would be out of Angola.[124] (In fact, all SADF troops, having completed Operation Askari, had already been withdrawn to SWA, but nobody believed it. So the South Africans actually had to send back some units, in order to pull them back visibly.[125])

In a separate chamber, South African ministers Pik Botha and Magnus Malan discussed the political aspects of the JMC with an Angolan delegation headed by that country's Minister of the Interior, Lieutenant Colonel Alexandre (also known as Kito) Rodrigues, and Chester Crocker. President Kenneth Kaunda sat in the chair. It was not difficult to reach consensus.[126]

At first sight, this was a big success for the South Africans. Barely a month before, Prime Minister PW Botha had signed the Nkomati Accord, a non-aggression pact, with President Samora Machel of Mozambique. For a while, it looked as if a general peace was in the air.

But the euphoria was relatively short-lived. The signatories all had widely differing objectives. On the one hand, the South Africans saw the Lusaka Agreement (on the JMC) as the first step to getting the Cubans out of Angola and holding an election in SWA in circumstances in which SWAPO would lose. To them it offered an easing of the international pressure to get rid of apartheid, buying time to sort out the country's internal problems. On the other, the Angolans wanted the South Africans out of their country so that they could get on with the war against UNITA. They had no intention of letting the Cubans go home or of stopping SWAPO from infiltrating SWA after the end of the JMC process.

The subsequent history of the JMC showed that the failure to include SWAPO in the agreement was a fatal flaw. The movement immediately started moving into the areas evacuated by the SADF. The Angolans tried their best to rein in SWAPO, with some success. There were even firefights between FAPLA and PLAN members. But, as time went on, SWAPO's violations of the accord became ever more defiant, and Angola's attempts to stop them ever more lacklustre. The positive atmosphere that characterised the early meetings of the JMC deteriorated into bitter mutual recrimination. The southward movement of the JMC seat was repeatedly delayed, until the South Africans finally pulled out, more than a year after the original timetable, convinced that the exercise held no more advantages due to SWAPO's violations and Angola's visible unwillingness to carry out its promises.[127]

Of course, SWAPO was not a signatory to the agreement, and therefore had no legal obligation to honour it. But Angola did have an obligation to control SWAPO, something that was well within its powers. It did not do so, although SWAPO's attitude caused some irritation in Luanda. When the JMC was disbanded on 16 May 1985, a total of 149 violations of the ceasefire – of which three were transgressions by South Africa – had been registered with the commission. SWAPO was responsible for the rest.[128]

The most probable reason for Angola's about-turn was pressure from Havana and Moscow. Angola did not inform its allies about its negotiations with the hated South Africans and Americans until 21 February; the Soviets and Cubans had to hear about it from the international media. Fidel Castro was dismayed by the idea of the joint SADF/FAPLA patrols, calling it "impermissible and incredible". As he complained to the Soviet military commander in Angola, Konstantin Kurochkin, it would have been much more advantageous to start negotiating in a year or eighteen months, as the communist alliance would by then have adequate anti-aircraft defences and MiG-23 fighters.[129] Castro even summoned Angolan President José Eduardo dos Santos to Havana, where he lectured him sternly on 17 March about his unilateral action. He referred to the Cuban/Angolan agreement of September 1978, which obliged both, as he reminded Dos Santos, to "consult with each other before making decisions or taking actions in the military arena". He continued:

> To speak frankly, since we signed that agreement, you have never consulted us about any decision that was going to affect us; you have almost never informed us beforehand, and only on a few occasions did you inform us after the fact that there had been talks with the United States. At times we learned through our intelligence service in Western Europe that there had been contacts between Angola and South Africa, or between Angola and the United States; at other times we learned of it in the press . . . The final decision was yours, not ours, but at least we could have talked about it beforehand.[130]

In a conversation with Kurochkin, Castro's brother Raúl was even more candid: "They [the Angolans] have already sold out SWAPO and the ANC, and now they are trading our troops."[131]

According to Piero Gleijeses, the Angolan delegation was "contrite": "They acknowledged that they should have consulted their allies; that it had all been a mistake, an oversight; that they were a young state; and that they would be more careful in the future." Castro let the matter rest there; he had, after all, made his point forcefully.[132] The Angolans now clearly realised who the senior partner in the alliance was and who pulled the strings – and it was not them.

These meetings played a large role in the communist alliance's decision to escalate the war during 1985, which we will examine in Chapter 11. Nevertheless, it is logical to assume that Dos Santos's dressing-down by Castro was at least partly responsible for the growing Angolan unwillingness to prevent SWAPO from exploiting the SADF withdrawal and the subsequent failure of the whole process. As a matter of fact, after their meeting Castro and Dos Santos issued a statement in which they, *inter alia*, agreed that the Cubans would leave Angola only after the "unilateral withdrawal of the racist South African troops from Angolan territory", as well as an "end to any act of direct aggression or threat of aggression" by South Africa and the US against Angola. Furthermore, they demanded "the total withdrawal of South African troops" from Namibia.[133] This certainly did not improve the mood of the South African and US governments, who correctly thought that Dos Santos had caved in under pressure. They also agreed not to let things escalate.[134]

Was the Lusaka Agreement worth it, when seen from the South African perspective? According to the staff officer writing the chronicle of the JMC, "the tempo of SWAPO's infiltration into SWA and the number of terrorist incidents inside SWA did not demonstrate a significant decline during the 14 months of the JMC's existence . . ."[135] Colonel Jan Breytenbach was also very sceptical. The JMC was based, he wrote, "on wishful thinking by our Foreign Affairs people and misplaced trust in the integrity of the SWAPO/FAPLA leadership. Because of this and with the connivance of FAPLA, SWAPO got back its former bases on the border. All we got back was square one." He said that the South Africans

still did not appreciate that a defeated enemy must never be allowed the chance to recover, regroup, re-equip, reorganise, retrain and rebuild the morale broken under the strain of battle. Our generals and political leaders seemed not to understand that a defeated enemy must always be pressed, remorselessly and without letting up, until his resolve to carry on fighting collapses.[136]

However, Breytenbach probably views events too much through a military-strategic lens. He had no way of knowing it, but it is clear that the MPLA government in Luanda was, by the beginning of 1984, so war-weary that it was prepared to leave its allies in the lurch. This, after all, was one of the main security-strategic objectives with which the SADF undertook its repeated cross-border operations. If it hadn't been for Castro's intervention and Dos Santos's lack of spine, the Lusaka Agreement might very well have spelled the end of the undeclared war between South Africa and Angola. And that would have put, not South Africa, but SWAPO, back to square one. It was, at the very least, worth a try.

Besides, SWAPO's military back was already largely broken. If one looks at the statistical analysis of the counterinsurgency war inside South West Africa (*see* Chapter 9), it appears clear that, although PLAN – to its credit – never admitted defeat, its efforts became more feeble with every passing year. Besides, though Askari was the last large-scale, brigade-sized cross-border operation aimed at SWAPO, the South Africans did not allow the insurgents north of the border to have it all their own way. A few weeks after the JMC was disbanded, the SADF launched Operation Boswilger (with FAPLA's permission!) to destroy PLAN forces some 10 to 15 km inside Angola. A total of 61 insurgents were killed for the loss of one South African.[137] In March, a government spokesman announced that SADF and SWATF troops would remain up to 40 km inside Angola because the MPLA had not "disciplined" SWAPO as it had promised.[138]

This was followed by Operation Egret in September 1985, in which about 500 men of 101 Battalion attacked a SWAPO base that had earlier been located by men of 32 Battalion. The base was not strongly defended, and only 15 insurgents were killed, although 103 were captured and several large arms caches uncovered. The operation produced a telling document, discovered in the pouch of a PLAN intelligence officer. This was a letter from PLAN's military leadership to a subordinate officer, in which there was a blunt reference to the "unfavourable politico-military situation". The fighters were accused of "undiscipline and poor knowledge" in political, military, economic and operational areas. A series of lectures (read: political indoctrination) was envisaged to rectify the situation.[139] From this, it was clear that SWAPO had big problems.

In both operations – Boswilger and Egret – the Angolans were informed in the early stages, but did not interfere.[140]

Until 1988, the SADF conducted several other cross-border operations, of which little is known, although the days of major operations like Sceptic, Protea and Askari were over. Nevertheless, these smaller operations had a similar negative effect on SWAPO's military capability. In August 1986, the SADF's Chief of Staff Operations reported to Jannie Geldenhuys that about 90% of the PLAN forces had withdrawn to outside the area of Angola in which the SADF was permitted to operate against the movement.[141]

There is evidence that, by the end of 1986 and the beginning of 1987, the SADF was engaged in planning "to create a situation in the Fifth Military Region [Cunene province] of Angola similar to the situation which existed before the Lusaka Accord". In other words, the idea was that the SADF would re-occupy the greater part of Cunene up to Cuvelai and Techamutete, which would entail another large invasion. However, the Commanding General SWA's appreciation was that the situation in the Sixth Military Region (Cuando Cubango province, where UNITA operated) had to be stabilised first. "If this was not going to happen," according to a top-secret SADF briefing document, "it would disadvantage military operations in the Fifth Military Region at a critical stage".[142] This was, of course, the beginning of Operation Moduler, which will be analysed in Chapter 12.

But, before we get to that, there are a number of other aspects of the Border War to be discussed.

9

COUNTERINSURGENCY
IN SOUTH WEST AFRICA

During the mid-1970s, the SADF floundered in its war against PLAN in South West Africa. It encountered the classic problems of a counterinsurgency war – how to identify insurgents hiding among the local population, the wide cultural gap between the locals and the counterinsurgents, and the lack of bushcraft among conscripts. Reading the accounts of troops' experiences during these early years, one is struck by their feelings of helplessness in the face of an enemy they did not understand (and had no specific desire to understand) and the constant PLAN ambushes into which they blundered. Thankfully, PLAN fighters were notoriously bad shots; otherwise the SADF could have been in deep trouble with South Africa's white population, which was the source of its conscripts but who had a low tolerance for casualties.

Flushed with success, SWAPO created a military structure for maximum efficiency. As Sam Nujoma explained:

> We created the eastern Front, covering eastern Caprivi and Kavango; the northeastern Front of eastern Ovamboland; and the northwestern Front of western Ovamboland and the Kaokoveld. All of these Fronts had their own sectors, deep inside the country, within which PLAN combatants operated effectively . . . It was part of our strategy . . . to carry out military offensives on all these fronts at the same time, to confuse and over-stretch the enemy's military power which would result in heavy enemy casualties and expenditure.[1]

This sounds like a fair summary of the situation during the mid-1970s, and is borne out by South African statistics: The number of "incidents" grew from just under 500 in 1978 to more than 900 in 1979. In this last year there were more than 300 firefights with insurgents, almost double that of 1978.[2] However, under the leadership of Jannie Geldenhuys and his successors, the SADF slowly started to turn the tables on SWAPO.

Building on the evolving SADF counterinsurgency doctrine, Geldenhuys and his officers developed a broad strategic approach. They realised that a counterinsurgency war could "not be forced to a speedy end through military action, as your enemy did not present a target on which firepower could be concentrated with decisive effect on a specific place". In his reflections on the war, Geldenhuys identified three situations in which his forces could win: firstly, when the government convinced the population that its cause held more advantages than that of the insurgents (as, indeed, Beaufre and Fraser had preached); secondly, when the insurgents could not make progress despite lengthy operations and lost the support of the population, thereby making negotiations an attractive alternative; and thirdly, when the insurgents' host country (that is, Angola) became war-weary.[3] The third condition was addressed by the cross-border operations described in the previous chapters, but the first two conditions became the yardsticks by which progress in the internal counterinsurgency campaign could be measured.

Internally as much as externally, the security forces needed to wrest the initiative from the insurgents by forcing them to fight on the former's terms. The external operations played a decisive role in achieving this, but it was not enough; SWAPO also had to be beaten south of the border. As the security forces became better equipped – and, as the 1980s approached, also better trained – than the SWAPO guerrillas,[4] firefights more often ended in defeat for the insurgents. The no-go areas that existed in the late 1970s in parts of Ovamboland were slowly eliminated.[5] The SADF came to rely more and more on white and black professionals and less on white conscripts and reservists, who were sometimes not up to the job.

To make it more difficult for PLAN insurgents to cross into SWA, a strip of about a kilometre wide, known as the "cutline", was denuded of vegetation and saturated with anti-personnel mines. A two-metre-high barbed-wire fence was erected along the 450-km border.[6] This did not stop the insurgents, but it did mean that the number of insurgents could be calculated on the basis of the tracks discovered here.

Most importantly, the Defence Force leadership realised SWAPO had to be prevented from increasing the area inside SWA in which it operated. According to Geldenhuys, the main purpose of the SADF's strategy "was to clean Kaokoland, Kavango and the Caprivi . . . If we could attain this goal, we could reduce the widespread insurgent-infested territory until only Ovambo remained. We could then concentrate our efforts there . . ."[7]

SWAPO's first geopolitical setback occurred when President Kenneth Kaunda decided to kick the organisation out of Zambia in 1978 (*see* Chapter 6). This was a breakthrough because it made insurgency in the eastern Caprivi impossible. "This was the beginning of the fulfilment of our plan," Geldenhuys commented.[8] As Major General Georg Meiring (GOC South West Africa) said in 1984, thereafter "SWAPO was no longer a factor in the eastern Caprivi".[9]

Adding to SWAPO's woes, the Caprivian political movement, CANU, broke with its erstwhile ally in 1981, thereby dealing a deathblow to the insurgency there. The fact that SWAPO had allowed Jonas Savimbi's UNITA to become an ally of South Africa now also came into play. As UNITA dominated the whole southeastern corner of Angola, this meant that any attempt to infiltrate western Caprivi and Kavango became fraught with danger. SWAPO did try it, but never really got anywhere. PLAN infiltrated Kavango in 1985 with three groups, but within a few weeks the insurgents were dead, captured or driven out. After that, SWAPO ceased nearly all its operations in Kavango.[10]

To the west, Kaokoland remained hostile to the Ovambo-dominated SWAPO, who tried to enter the territory at least four times. In 1980, the infiltrants were either captured or driven into the desert, where they apparently died of thirst.[11] As we saw in the previous chapter, in February 1982 the SADF got wind of a PLAN concentration north of the border before the infiltration could get under way and an attack was launched by 32 Battalion. The concentration was all but wiped out (Operation Super).[12] SWAPO tried again in 1983 and 1985, but also failed, and never again attempted to activate Kaokoland in force.[13] Once, in early 1984, three groups of PLAN fighters crossed the border from Botswana into Hereroland. This operation failed, too, and the guerrillas withdrew after a while.[14]

That left Ovamboland, SWAPO's heartland, and therefore a very tough nut to crack. Nevertheless, the relatively small size of this territory (only 56 000 ha) made it much easier for the security forces to keep an iron grip on it. SWAPO also made sporadic attempts to infiltrate the white farmlands south of Ovamboland, but these bands were invariably hunted down and wiped out. "And so we reached our goal to limit the insurgency to Ovamboland in a relatively short time," says Geldenhuys.[15]

Structures

Until 1981, the SADF structure in South West Africa was relatively simple. The command was exercised by a major general at what was known as 101 Task Force, a structure originally created for Operation Savannah. It had two regional sub-commands under it: 1 Military Area at Rundu (responsible for counter-insurgency operations in Kavango and the Western Caprivi), and 2 Military Area at Oshakati (Ovamboland and Kaokoland), each under the command of a colonel. The Eastern Caprivi fell under 13 Sub-Area, which technically fell under 1 Military Area, but to all intents and purposes was a separate command.[16]

In 1981, this structure was streamlined. Three operational sectors were established in the north of SWA. These were Sector 10, which covered Kaokoland and Ovamboland, Sector 20 (Okavango and western Caprivi) and Sector 70 (eastern Caprivi). Other sectors covered the "white" areas to the south.[17] The army stationed five so-called modular light infantry battalions in company bases throughout the north, manned mainly by white South African conscripts, who patrolled their own areas, conducted cordon-and-search operations and sweeps, and escorted road convoys. They provided medical and veterinary aid to the locals and sometimes provided troops for external operations.[18] Before this reorganisation, companies were rotated from their mother units in South Africa every three months to the "modular" battalions in SWA, but from then on troops' tours were extended to a year. According to Roland de Vries, this "contributed to a much higher level of active service and training continuity, unit cohesion and overall combat readiness".[19]

Geldenhuys was ordered to establish an indigenous South West African army, the South West Africa Territorial Force (SWATF), when he arrived in Windhoek in 1977. He also established several highly efficient counterinsurgency infantry battalions, of which 101 Battalion was perhaps the most feared by SWAPO insurgents. At its height, 101 Battalion was more akin to a motor-ised infantry brigade than to a battalion, with about 2 000 men on its books.[20] Whereas 101 was manned mainly by Ovambo tribesmen, the members of the much smaller 102 Battalion were from the Kaokoveld; those of 201 and 203 were mainly Bushman trackers; 202 was from Okavango; 701's men came from the eastern Caprivi; and 911 Battalion was a multi-ethnic unit.[21]

New tactics

By the end of the 1970s, Constand Viljoen ordered the SADF to take over the Rhodesian "fireforce" system. The intention was to adapt and perfect it, but the topography of South West Africa was less conducive to the system. In Rhodesia, clandestine observation posts were established on hills in the tribal trust lands from where suspicious movements could be reported on, after which the fire-force units would be called in for the kill. The South West African operational area, however, was flat and densely wooded. Observation posts would be useless. The answer was the ubiquitous infantry platoon patrol.[22] Fewer troops were used for defensive tasks, such as escorting vehicle convoys and guard duties, freeing up men for offensive tasks.[23] Typically, the operational area would be patrolled aggressively and continuously, on foot, on horse, on motorcycles with muffled engines and on mine-resistant infantry vehicles such as the Buffel, Casspir (used by the police counterinsurgency unit Koevoet and 101 Battalion) and, at times, even Ratel IFVs or Eland 90 or 60 armoured cars. Patrols would invari-ably have expert trackers with them, often from the Bushman units, although Koevoet preferred using Ovambos.

When a patrol chanced on the tracks of an enemy band, or received informa-tion from locals about a SWAPO unit in the vicinity, the news would be radioed to the nearest headquarters. (According to General Geldenhuys, about 60 to 75% of these reconnaissance patrols led to contacts with insurgents.)[24] There a "Romeo Mike" (RM) team (the Afrikaans term was "reaksiemag", or reaction force) was on alert. Often the RM would consist of paratroopers, who would be flown in with Puma helicopters, with air support from specially converted Alouette III helicopters equipped with 20-mm cannon. The helicopters mostly proved devas-tating in firefights, but they could stay in the air for only 90 minutes. Therefore, a C-47 Dakota with parachute-equipped troops or a Dakota gunship with a 20-mm cannon would also be used.[25]

In the case of Koevoet and 101 Battalion, the RM would more often than not consist of ground troops, rushing to the battle zone in Casspir vehicles. The insurgents often astounded the pursuing troops with phenomenal feats of physical endurance and excellent bushcraft techniques like anti-tracking or hiding. Anthony Turton remembers one case, while he was attached to Koevoet, in which an injured insurgent was chased for hours, and later even injected himself with morphine to dull the pain: "When he was captured, he was wild-eyed with fatigue and his feet had bones sticking out of them, witness to the combined effect of morphine, combat and commitment."[26] More often than not, the contact would result in some or most of the insurgents being killed or wounded.[27] Both Koevoet and 101 Battalion became highly feared killing machines, with Koevoet achieving the highest "kill ratio" of all units in the war: 3 900 insurgents killed for the loss of 167 Koevoet members.[28]

A pattern that emerged early on was that PLAN infiltrations intensified during the rainy season (December to March). During the dry months, the insurgents would have to carry their water with them – an almost impossible task, given the distance they had to walk – while SADF patrols would keep a close watch on water sources. During the rainy months, the vegetation was lush, giving excellent cover,[29] while the muddy roads made it difficult for the South Africans to operate their vehicles.[30]

Three times – in 1980, 1981 and again in 1982 – SWAPO sent its elite Typhoon or Volcano units to penetrate the "white" agricultural areas south of Ovamboland in the vicinity of Tsumeb, Otavi and Grootfontein. These units had been established after the SADF attack on Cassinga in May 1978 and specialised in sabotage and terrorism.[31] But, although these insurgents gave people living in these areas the jitters, in strategic, operational and tactical terms their efforts were a dismal failure. The SADF in all instances reacted swiftly and with great energy, even calling in Koevoet and a conventional unit like 61 Mech in what became known as Operation Carrot. Time and again, within a few weeks of infiltration, the insurgents had been either killed, captured or driven back into Angola.[32]

Two reports by SWAPO detachment commanders who advanced through Ovambo and Kavango to the "white" area around Grootfontein have survived in the archive of the Department of Foreign Affairs. Both documents make it clear that the detachments were hunted day and night, that the SADF was everywhere, and that the insurgents had to endure great hunger and thirst. Both detachments had to turn back to Angola after a few days, the only practical advantage of the operation being the laying of land mines and failed attacks on isolated farmhouses.[33]

Nevertheless, these incursions greatly worried the South Africans. "The infiltration in 1981 was characterised as a suicide mission," Roland de Vries later wrote. "In 1982 SWAPO had done their homework, they came back better prepared and more dedicated and ferocious. It took the security forces close on two months to find, fix and destroy their special unit of over 156 insurgents."[34]

During the 1982 incursion, PLAN changed its tactics, but made a big mistake. The insurgents moved in big groups and were very aggressive, actively looking for SADF and Koevoet troops to attack. However, the South Africans' much greater firepower meant that the PLAN ambushes invariably ended in defeats with heavy losses.[35] According to Military Intelligence estimates, less than 20% of the insurgents survived to fight another day.[36]

PLAN tried again in 1983, with a major invasion of the "white" farmlands by about a thousand fighters, but with basically the same result. The SADF reacted vigorously and launched a major operation, known as Phoenix, in which a total of 309 insurgents were killed, for the loss of 27 security force members and 33 slain and 161 abducted civilians.[37]

As the war progressed, it became clear that SWAPO was not making much headway. In 1980, Military Intelligence reported that PLAN had been forced by its high casualty rate to shorten its training cycle, which led to a deterioration in its fighting standard. Many fighters could barely handle sophisticated weapons, it was reported.[38] Between January and October 1984, 520 infiltrants died in Ovamboland alone. With the advent of the rainy season in January 1985, another 700 guerrillas crossed the border. Some of them were members of the elite Typhoon unit, and numerous bombs exploded in the next weeks at several places in Ovamboland, mostly at civilian targets. According to SADF figures, by the end of February 157 of the insurgents had been killed; at the end of June, the figure stood at 346. Most of the rest had apparently fled to Angola.[39]

It appeared that SWAPO was in trouble. The interrogation of PLAN prisoners tended to confirm this suspicion,[40] as did an entry in the diary of a dead PLAN commander from January 1983, which simply stated: "Of my group of 60, 43 men wounded and six are missing."[41]

For the next few years, things remained relatively calm, until March 1987, when another major infiltration took place. However, this also ended in a major defeat for SWAPO.[42]

The South African counterinsurgency approach differed from others in one important aspect: the strategy of building so-called protected villages. This strategy was meant to separate the local population from the insurgents – to deny the "fish" the "water" to swim in, according to Mao Zedong's famous metaphor. It had been applied in Vietnam, Rhodesia and the Portuguese territories – where such settlements were known as "aldeamentos". A notorious forerunner was the British concentration camps of the Anglo-Boer War. The SADF considered the possibility of creating protected villages, but, perhaps because of South Africa's history with concentration camps, as well as the negative publicity that protected villages had generated elsewhere, the strategy was never applied in South West Africa.[43]

Looking at the numbers

The statistics certainly tell a fascinating story about how SWAPO's insurgent war stalled after 1979/1980. According to Jannie Geldenhuys, the number of combat contacts with insurgents doubled in 1979 compared with the previous year. However, 85% of those contacts were initiated by the security forces, illustrating their ability to dominate the operational area militarily.[44] In 1981, the percentage was 84%.[45] At the end of 1982, Brigadier (later Major General) Willie Meyer, acting commander of SWATF, said that the number of war-related incidents inside South West Africa in that year had declined by a quarter since the previous year.[46]

By 1987, the army's counterinsurgency strategy was so successful that the security forces became aware of an insurgent's presence south of the cutline only three to six days (the sources differ) after having crossed the border.[47] In SWA, the Defence Force killed 10 to 15 insurgents for every SADF member lost.[48] Tables 1 and 2 tell the story in statistics:[49]

Table 1: Incidents, 1980–1988

Year	1980	1981	1982	1983	1984	1985	1986	1987	1988
Contacts/ambushes	644	545	297	299	307	252	176	213	134
Mines detonated	327	349	311	188	169	170	105	103	101
Intimidation	120	121	102	92	67	98	68	60	33
Sabotage	84	37	46	41	96	136	127	107	112
Total	1 175	1 052	756	620	639	656	476	483	380

Table 2: Mines discovered, 1983–1988

Year	1983	1984	1985	1986	1987	1988
Vehicle mines	89	77	147	328	479	411
Personnel mines	20	142	284	569	569	189
Total	109	219	431	897	1 048	600

These figures show that SWAPO – at least militarily – was not winning the war. The number of contacts decreased markedly through the 1980s, suggesting (together with what we know from other sources) that fewer and fewer insurgents managed to penetrate into SWA. And when they got there, their aggressiveness diminished markedly. In contrast to the late 1970s, when SWAPO actively sought out South African patrols, in the 1980s SWAPO infiltrants tried to evade the SADF and SWATF hunters, and concentrated on sabotage instead – the only statistic that rises in Table 1. Moreover, while the number of mines detonated went down, there was an increase in the number discovered and neutralised before exploding, suggesting that the environment became safer for the SADF patrols and convoys.

US journalist William Claiborne wrote in 1987 that when SADF spokesmen said they were winning the war, "there is evidence to support that assertion".[50] It is understandable, then, that by 1988 the CIA described SWAPO's "military effectiveness" as "minimal".[51] The casualty figures from the period of the insurgency (Table 3) are also interesting:[52]

Table 3: Casualties, 1966–1987

Year	SWAPO losses	SADF losses	"Kill ratio"
1966–1974	363	88	4,1:1
1978	971	44	22,1:1
1979	915	50	18,3:1
1980	1 447	100	14,5:1
1981	1 494	61	24,5:1
1982	1 280	77	16,6:1
1983	913	96	9,5:1
1984	916	39	23,5:1
1985	590	n/a	n/a
1986	645	33	19,5:1
1987	747	72	10,4:1

Of course, cross-border operations contributed greatly to this picture. According to General Geldenhuys, the "kill ratio" on previously planned cross-border operations was 100:1; on general cross-border operations to dominate southern Angola, 30:1; and within SWA, 10:1.[53] Note also that the "kill ratio" decreased somewhat after 1984. This may be explained by the fact that the SADF's focus inside Angola to a certain extent shifted from PLAN to FAPLA, the Angolan army, at this time. Nevertheless, the huge pressure exerted by the SADF south of the border had the effect that PLAN units inside South West Africa had to devote more resources to fighting in order to survive, and their capacity for political work – to mobilise the masses – diminished.

Another interesting statistic is the dwindling numbers of PLAN fighters. In 1977, Military Intelligence estimated that PLAN had a total of 16 000 men. Three years later, the estimate was 12 000 to 14 000 men, of which 4 000 were being trained and just under half were fighting against UNITA or guarding PLAN bases and logistical routes. A total of 400 fighters were known to be south of the border, mainly in Ovamboland.

In July 1985, it was thought that the number of trained PLAN fighters had fallen to 8 500. Of these, a "conventional" brigade of about 3 500 men was engaged in the war against UNITA, another 1 200 in administration and logistics, while 600 were employed at SWAPO's headquarters. This left 1 500 men for the war in SWA. Two years later, this number was down to 1 000.[54] It had become clear that PLAN was in trouble. The Soviet commander in Angola, General Konstantin Kurochkin, complained in 1983 that the SADF had locked up the border so efficiently that "SWAPO practically doesn't receive any reinforcement".[55] Consequently, Major General Willie Meyer could report to a closed meeting in March 1987 that a mere 130 PLAN fighters were estimated to be on the loose in Ovamboland.[56]

While this made matters increasingly difficult for SWAPO, it has to be said that the insurgents kept coming with considerable courage. They even succeeded in bombarding SADF bases at Ondangwa and Eenhana with mortars.[57] But the standoff mortar bombardment of Oshakati, the headquarters of Sector 10, in January 1988, and of the army base at Eenhana, in March the same year, was more or less a last gasp.[58]

Winning hearts and minds

A favourable "kill ratio" is not enough to win an insurgency war. In the end, destroying the enemy combat forces means relatively little if you cannot gain and keep the support of the local population.[59]

In theory, the SADF leadership grasped this very well. In 1983, Constand Viljoen explained at a press conference that "we never count success in terms of the number of heads. We don't think that is important. In this kind of war the number is not important. What is important is whether you can safely protect the area you are defending against the acts of SWAPO."[60]

The SADF thus realised an important aspect of counterinsurgency warfare: the symbiotic relationship between maintaining the safety and the loyalty of the local population. In 1984, Viljoen told an academic audience that "civic action" – which he defined as "medical, educational, agricultural and social assistance . . . to improve the standard of living of the local population" – was "an integral part of any counterinsurgency". He went on to say: "In order to prevent intimidation of members of the population and their subsequent forced cooperation with the revolutionaries, the security forces have to ensure that the safety of the population is continuously guaranteed."[61]

Of course, realising the importance of winning the hearts and minds of the population is one thing. Turning this belief into practice is another. On this point, the South Africans had mixed success. In accordance with the SADF's counterinsurgency doctrine, a "hearts and minds" programme was started in 1974, albeit on a modest scale. As the years went on, more resources were poured into the battle for the South West Africans' loyalty.

When Geldenhuys took over in 1977, SWAPO was already spreading propaganda that the security forces were maltreating, assaulting, raping and torturing the local population in the operational area. The churches and international human-rights organisations soon took up the matter, and a newspaper like the *Namibian* regularly published reports about murders, assaults, rapes, theft and the like by SADF soldiers.[62] SWAPO leader Sam Nujoma even alleged that it was common practice for members of 32, 101 and 102 Battalions to cut off innocent villagers' heads and to get "kopgeld" (head money) from their white officers for it.[63] At an international conference in 1987, Nujoma referred to regular "abductions, detentions, cold-blooded assassinations and wanton destruction of people's property" perpetrated by the South Africans. In fact, he said, "[i]n the course of the last two weeks alone, the occupation army has bombed and set on fire at least 14 local schools in northern Namibia".[64] Even professional diplomats like US ambassador Ed Perkins (who reviled the apartheid government) uncritically reported these kinds of allegations to their governments as the truth.[65] This proves both the effectiveness of SWAPO's propaganda and the importance of propaganda as a weapon of war.

It would be too easy – although not entirely invalid – to try to diminish the impact of these allegations by pointing out that it was in SWAPO's interest to spread such propaganda stories, whether they were true or not. It would have been very surprising if SWAPO had not exploited (and exaggerated) stories, especially since the South Africans were such amateurs at propaganda. Yet the most credible propaganda is based, even if only partly, on fact. Sadly, many stories about maltreatment do have a ring of truth to them.

Even a veteran South African paratroop officer like Brigadier General McGill Alexander, writing about the 1970s, accepts that "the counterinsurgency measures adopted by the SADF were, in the eyes of the local inhabitants, as closely akin to terrorism as anything done by SWAPO". His nuanced and carefully worded view is that "[i]ndividuals and groups of soldiers who ignored or deliberately flaunted [sic; flouted] instructions to treat people humanely exacerbated the situation, as in any war".[66] In these circumstances, it would prove very difficult, if not impossible, for the SADF's civic action programmes to counter the feelings of bitterness and humiliation many black South West Africans felt towards the white South Africans and their cause.

After the war, Jannie Geldenhuys wrote that only 1 to 2% of the allegations about SADF atrocities in South West Africa were true.[67] No doubt he really meant it, but he was not in a position to know about everything that went on at a grassroots level. Several SADF members' accounts of their war experiences make it clear that the general coarsening effect of war did not pass the South Africans by. The official policy notwithstanding, some patrols treated the locals harshly, humiliated them and used violence to extract intelligence about SWAPO fighters.[68] Sometimes troops, disregarding standing regulations, cut off dead insurgents' fingers or ears as trophies.[69]

One of the first things Geldenhuys did after taking command in SWA was to establish a board of inquiry into all such allegations. Where proof could be found, cases were referred to the Attorney General of South West Africa, and this led to several criminal prosecutions.[70] However, the PW Botha government passed a law to indemnify security force members from prosecution when such incidents took place in the course of their duties. This nullified much of the work the official "hearts and minds" policy tried to achieve.[71]

One gets the impression that much depended on individual commanding officers. Some were imbued with the need to win over the people. For instance, in his standing orders to 61 Mech, Roland de Vries emphasised: "The formula is maximum force against the enemy and maximum friendliness, support and understanding towards the local population. As a soldier you must at all times act honourably, command respect and maintain good attitudes."[72] But not all officers shared this opinion; some simply paid lip service to it.[73] In some units, the emphasis was simply on killing as many enemy fighters as possible.[74] As one troepie, serving in Ovamboland in 1978, related: "The ultimate goal for us on the border was to kill terrs. If an unfortunate terr was killed, the body was displayed and the camp celebrated."[75] At the same time, there are also tales of great compassion by SADF soldiers and of SWAPO insurgents' cruelty towards civilians.[76]

The fact that the "hearts and mind" policy was not always followed at a grass-roots level does not mean that the SADF top echelon was not serious about its strategy. After all, they wanted to win the war, and their doctrine dictated an approach whereby the locals should be won over. In fact, a considerable effort was already under way. Apart from troops receiving lectures about the local population and their ways, there were stern orders on how to treat them. Hundreds of conscripts were sent into the operational area as teachers, medics and builders. They built and tarred roads, erected hospitals, clinics and schools, sank boreholes, provided veterinary services, and so forth.[77] Conscripts who had been teachers in civilian life were deployed to teach black children.

As Charles Lloyd, GOC South West Africa, explained (albeit in somewhat propagandistic terms), the idea was "to project an image of the soldier as a man of action but who is nonetheless a friend of the black man and who is prepared to defend him. We want the National Servicemen to teach the black man whilst his rifle is standing in the corner of the classroom."[78] According to an SADF propaganda publication, the number of schools in the operational area increased from 212 in 1962 to 757 twenty years later, and the number of pupils from 32 000 to 172 000.[79] By 1989, fourteen of the 68 hospitals and 31 of the 171 clinics in South West Africa were situated in Ovamboland.[80] There is no reason to doubt these figures, as they tally broadly with other sources.

These efforts had mixed results. In 1981, the correspondent of *The Times* wrote that the SADF's civic action programme had had some success in Kavango and the Caprivi, but that it was an "almost total failure" in Ovamboland.[81] Jannie Geldenhuys also had a fairly nuanced view: the programmes "tended to prevent insurgency from starting in an area but were less successful in countering it if it had already commenced".[82] This is confirmed by Jan Breytenbach, who points out that "most of the Ovambos in eastern Ovamboland, particularly the [majority clan of the] Kwanyamas, were firmly on SWAPO's side. Satisfactory co-operation from the locals was rare and when it existed it had to be dealt with carefully. This changed to some extent when the Hearts and Minds campaign began to take effect, but we never fully weaned them from supporting SWAPO."[83] Nevertheless, according to SADF statistics, the incidence of locals passing on information about SWAPO rose from only 64 in 1983 to more than 2 000 in 1987.[84]

In March 1981, SADF Military Intelligence described SWAPO's support in

SWA as "vloeibaar" (fluid). A secret opinion poll in the previous year indicated that SWAPO might win an election in Ovamboland. According to the analysis, this was partly the result of "hard intimidation", but "entails probably largely soft intimidation and politicisation of the population".[85]

The election results of 1990 confirmed the results of this poll.[86] A whopping 92% of the people in Ovamboland voted for SWAPO, while the organisation got 52% and 40% of the vote, respectively, in the much less pro-SWAPO Kavango and Caprivi.[87] According to Willem Steenkamp, 95% of all SWAPO insurgents caught or killed during the war were Ovambos.[88]

Although the South Africans never really got anywhere in Ovamboland, they did have more success elsewhere. In 1985, Major General Georg Meiring reported that PLAN had suffered such heavy casualties in Kavango the previous year that only 12 PLAN fighters remained there. "The present disposition of the local population is such that it is very difficult for SWAPO to survive, and only in the far west of the Kavango [that is, adjacent to Ovamboland] does SWAPO have a limited following among the population."[89]

One last remark about this matter. Following the example of communist insurgents in China and Vietnam, SWAPO conducted its own campaign of selective terrorism. The fact that the SADF was never able to stop SWAPO infiltration from Angola entirely meant not only that the insurgents could politicise the local population, but also that the South Africans could not adequately shield the locals from SWAPO intimidation and reprisals. Local chiefs and black officials in service of the South African administration were murdered from time to time to impress upon the local population that SWAPO would not tolerate traitors to the cause, and that it would be in their interest to support the movement. The best-known cases were the murders of the Ovambo "chief minister" Filemon Elifas and the Herero chief and Democratic Turnhalle Alliance (DTA) chairman Clemens Kapuuo, but there were many others, as most chiefs tended to support South Africa.[90] In fact, a total of 26 headmen were killed by SWAPO.[91] The SADF kept records of instances where local inhabitants were subjected to intimidation by SWAPO. According to those figures (*see* Table 1, p. 202), intimidation was a central element of SWAPO's strategy.[92] The accuracy of these statistics is, of course, open to discussion, but they confirm anecdotal testimony from other sources.

Writing from a trooper's perspective, Steven Webb (a medic participating in patrols in Ovamboland) tells of villagers being questioned about
SWAPO's whereabouts:

> I watched the individuals being questioned and it was plain to see that
> they were more frightened of their own people than they were of us.
> There was no way the villagers were going to tell us if they had seen or
> even knew where the insurgents were. Their lives depended on it; so
> did ours, but that wasn't their problem. It was the same routine day in
> and day out. We would ask the same old questions and get the same
> old answers.[93]

Another former National Serviceman, Tim Ramsden, has also documented
– and photographed – villages in southern Angola where SWAPO killed the
inhabitants, apparently after torturing them first.[94] In one case, which apparently sent shockwaves through Kavangoland, a SWAPO commander named
Kazangula had nine off-duty members of 202 Battalion "abducted and tortured
before they were either bayoneted or [had] their throats slit". Kazangula, who
was eventually cornered and killed, was described as "a fearsome and merciless
man" by Sisingi "Shorty" Kamongo, a black Koevoet operator.[95]

Black members of the security forces – either army or Koevoet – could expect
no mercy from PLAN fighters. Kamongo also tells of one Festus Kandundu,
who "intimidated the local population with violence and he was well-known
for his relentless retaliation against any person who did not support SWAPO.
He murdered a few locals but his intimidation and terrorism was such that
nobody wanted to say anything because they were scared of retaliation from
SWAPO." If a black army or Koevoet member fell into PLAN's hands, "murder
was on the agenda".[96]

Several times, SWAPO simply abducted schoolchildren to force them
into PLAN service. Some of those forcibly taken in 1978 were transported
to Cassinga, where they pleaded in vain with the South African paratroopers attacking the base to take them home. In 1985, 80 schoolchildren were
abducted, of whom 16 escaped.[97]

According to a letter from the PLAN leadership to political commissars, found on the body of a slain insurgent and dated 17 March 1985, "drastic measures should be taken to regain the support of the masses". It expressly states that "[t]he use of force is allowed on those who do not want to support the organization", but that "[m]urder should be limited only to suspected enemy agents and supporters". The letter continues: "Large numbers of children, if possible a whole village or school, must be captured to rebuild our organization." Atrocities committed by SWAPO must not be exposed, but attributed to the enemy. "Therefore atrocities should not be committed in front of masses."[98]

Sergeant Francois du Toit, a member of Koevoet, told of being sent to a kraal to investigate a shooting: "When we arrived we saw immediately that this was not just a shooting – it was murder, mass murder. Fourteen people lay dead outside the kraal. Women, children and men. Everyone in the kraal was dead. SWAPO came over the border in the afternoon, rounded them up and lined them against the kraal wall . . ."[99]

Incidents like this are difficult to confirm. What can be said with a great deal of certainty is that both sides were guilty of lesser or more serious transgressions, as invariably happens in war. Often, civilians were the grass on which the elephants trampled when they fought each other.

Finally, in his insightful study of revolutionary guerrilla warfare, Thomas X Hammes stresses the point that revolutionaries should disperse their effort and should not expend all their energy on the military front, but utilise the entire range of actions available to them.[100] In the struggle against apartheid, the African National Congress (ANC) understood this very well. After visiting Vietnam in October 1978, the ANC leadership formulated a "four-pillar strategy", consisting of the mobilisation of the masses, the building of underground ANC structures within South Africa, the international isolation of the white minority regime on all fronts (diplomatic, economic, cultural, sport, religious, etc.) and the armed struggle.[101]

This was where SWAPO faltered. Although the movement succeeded in locking the Namibian Council of Churches "into an attitude not to question SWAPO policy",[102] historian Lauren Dobell notes that the SWAPO leadership concentrated on the "diplomatic route in its struggle to liberate Namibia", while the "organization and mobilization of popular resistance at home was neglected by the leadership in exile, as it pursued recognition by the international community of SWAPO's status as the 'sole and authentic representative of the Namibian people' – in that order."[103]

Koevoet

One unit that has attracted much negative publicity is Koevoet (meaning "crowbar"), the counterinsurgency unit of the South African Police. Constand Viljoen, for one, does not mince his words when it comes to Koevoet:

> They had a cruelty about them that certainly didn't further the hearts and minds of the people. In the SADF we made a far greater study of how to win such a war than the Police ever did. They used cruel, crude methods. In whatever we did we always bore in mind the effect it would have on the general population. We realised, in a revolutionary war it is not a case of how many people you kill but rather the battle for the minds of the people.[104]

Jannie Geldenhuys agreed:

> They would, for example, go into an area, "clean" it up, collect the bodies and drag them through the town behind their vehicles. Then they'd be away again, thinking they'd done a hell of a good job. Obviously this kind of thing upset the local population greatly and we'd find we were suddenly getting no more co-operation from the locals.[105]

Georg Meiring criticised Koevoet's command and control system, calling it "stupid". "I hated the way they operated," he said.[106]

This criticism is even echoed by former Koevoet members. In his memoirs, Eugene de Kock, a founding member of Koevoet who later became a notorious government-sanctioned assassin, has documented several instances of human-rights abuses by Koevoet in the early 1980s. He wrote of "a general corruption" in the unit, and refers to an order by Koevoet's commander, Colonel (later Major General) Hans Dreyer, to kill certain SWAPO prisoners whose intelligence value had been exhausted.[107] While acknowledging that Koevoet members "were good bush-fighters" who "probably had the highest kill-count in all of the security forces", another ex-Koevoet member also recognised the possibility that "some of the hundreds or even thousands we racked up weren't terrs but rather civilians who found themselves in the wrong place at the wrong time. The guys in the unit weren't always too choosy. A lot of them ended up in Koevoet because it was the last step before being thrown out of the force or being put in jail."[108] The SADF tried to have Koevoet removed from the operational area, but failed due to a turf war between the ministers of Defence and Police.[109]

Not everybody agrees with this negative view of Koevoet. Colonel Jan Breytenbach and Recce member Jack Greeff wrote highly of the unit,[110] while Peter Stiff praised the unit highly in his book about them: "Most of the accusations originated from the fertile minds of SWAPO's propagandists – some, perhaps, 'confirmed' by nod and wink hints by jealous SADF generals – but few of them could stand up to even superficial scrutiny."[111] The respected military commentator Helmoed-Römer Heitman also rejects the criticism against Koevoet.[112]

Nevertheless, in light of what knowledgeable SADF generals and former Koevoet members had to say about the unit, it seems as if Koevoet, like certain SADF members, sometimes went beyond the bounds of acceptable behaviour. In his memoirs, Sisingi Kamongo recognises that "there were cases where unlawful things took place". However, members who were found guilty of offences against the civilian population were punished:

> Our disciplinary committee was a serious affair. If you were guilty, the *sjambok* [short whip] was taken out for you. Either that or you would be charged and you would have to take your official punishment. Official punishment could get you in jail and out of the unit. Few of us opted for official charges.

> Unfortunately this information was never given to the public. If SWAPO screamed about a mahango patch that was flattened, or kraal walls that were damaged, or of a rape or of an assault, there were enough people willing to send the untested information into the world. Nobody ever

looked to see if it was the truth. As a result we were in a bad situation when the war was over. Many of the unit members went to South Africa or Angola after the war as a result of the false information.

In all the time I was at Koevoet, bad things happened a few times, but never a rape while we were on patrol. The white members were relentless about it. To slap someone was fine but sexual violations were out. That was the one rule that was strictly enforced.[113]

Kamongo acknowledges that, when questioning prisoners, "there were times when we would overstep the boundary". "Sometimes," he says,

an insurgent was stubborn and non-cooperative. We were fighting a war, and did not have a lot of patience with a captured insurgent that killed or intimidated. In some cases a small electric dynamo was used – like the ones that were used in the old telephones. But that was the exception. We would rather beat up an insurgent. We would take a spade from the back of the Blesbok. Not many brave men remained if he was beaten on the buttocks with a spade. After the third or fourth blow the insurgent usually realised we had the whole day to continue, and that he should rather co-operate. Nobody ever died because of this type of interrogation or ended in hospital.

There was a lot of negative propaganda that we had thrown insurgents from helicopters. Why should we? Helicopters were scarce and expensive. If we wanted to kill someone we could rather shoot him. But only once in our team, a captured insurgent was shot. And the result came as a shock. The white policeman was transferred when the whole team asked for his removal from the team. He was threatened with death if he ever did it again.[114]

North of the border, in Angola, things were different. There, "no laws and few rules" applied, and PLAN prisoners were sometimes executed. "I experienced both sides of violence – SWAPO and Koevoet. A life was not worth much.

Sometimes the paperwork was just too much. It is easier to fire a round in the bush," Kamongo writes.[115]

Obviously, Kamongo's views have to be evaluated critically, since his account may not be free of self-justification. But even if he minimises Koevoet's wrong-doings and exaggerates the discipline, one cannot dismiss his views. The truth lies somewhere between those who see Koevoet as the incarnation of Satan and those who refuse to find any fault with the unit. What should not be forgotten is that this was war, and the battlefield has the tendency to turn the seemingly abnormal into something quite logical and normal.

10

SWAPO: THE SEEDS
OF FAILURE

When SWAPO was formed in 1958/1959 it did not have much of an ideology, except a militant anticolonialism. In its first manifesto, the movement spoke of "a free, democratic Government . . . founded upon the will and participation of all the people of our country". It promised to work "for the unification of all the people", "the removal of all forms of oppression such as Apartheid laws", and "universal adult suffrage and direct democratic participation of all inhabitants . . . in all organs of the government". It spoke vaguely of a "reconstruction of the economy, educational and social foundations which will support and maintain the real African independence which our people desire for themselves". In its first party programme, it also called for a "transitional period" under the auspices of the United Nations and "independence not later than 1963". The railways, mining, electrical and fishing industries were to be nationalised and foreign ownership of land was to be abolished.[1]

In 1962, SWAPO took the decision to launch an armed struggle against the South African occupation, and started military training for cadres.[2] The leadership established itself in Lusaka, Zambia. In 1969, while on trial for terrorism, one of SWAPO's leaders, Hermann Toivo ya Toivo, made a statement from the dock, which had a similar symbolic effect to Nelson Mandela's famous statement during the Rivonia trial. Toivo stated:

> We do not now, and will not in the future recognise your right to govern us, to make laws for us under which we had no say; to treat our country as if it were your property; and us as if you were our masters. We have always regarded South Africa as an intruder in our country . . . If you choose to crush us and impose your will on us . . . you will live in security for only so long as your power is greater than ours.[3]

A major influence on the development of the organisation was Sam Nujoma, who ruled SWAPO with an iron fist right from the start. According to Canadian researchers Colin Leys and John S Saul, who have extensively researched the organisation's history in exile, PLAN members soon became dissatisfied with the general lack of efficiency within SWAPO, as well as the perceived corruption of the leadership, its lack of military insight, its dictatorial approach and its unwillingness to listen to constructive ideas.[4]

Then came the influx of thousands of young, mostly idealistic South West Africans who flocked to SWAPO's banners in Zambia and Angola. They were often urbanised, better educated than the old leadership and insistent on playing an important role in the movement. A group calling themselves the "Anti-corruption fighters" issued a statement complaining of "the running of private businesses in Lusaka and the surroundings and in some other Zambian cities". An allegation often made was that some leaders, including Nujoma himself, were selling medicines and blankets supplied by foreign aid donors.

In February 1975, the SWAPO Youth League, in a memorandum, demanded a response from the leadership on issues such as their tendency to treat all questions as treasonous, the movement's constitutional position and its ideology, and the control over administrative and financial matters. There was also resentment at the way SWAPO leaders allegedly took sexual advantage of young female refugees. Thus grassroots pressure built up to make the leadership accountable to the rank and file, and a new congress, taking an unambiguous socialist line, was demanded.[5] Others alleged discrimination against non-Ovambos.[6] Some cadres in Zambia alleged that the SWAPO leadership "are having farms, hotels, shops and bank accounts, that is why they are less interested in the liberation struggle".[7]

One of the dissidents, Otillie Abrahams, later remembered how SWAPO's recognition as the Namibian people's "sole and authentic representative" by the UN had the effect of "suppressing any opposition" within the movement. Anyone who criticised the leadership was "put in a prison camp because you were opposing the leaders". It boosted them "to such an extent that they became little Hitlers".[8]

Such criticism was not appreciated by either Sam Nujoma or his top lieutenants. At the Tanga Conference in 1971, he railed against enemies within the organisation. The enemy's "tactics, methods and power" should be analysed "scientifically and systematically", he said. "We should also be able to know who are our true friends and who are fakes. Above all, we must be vigilant at all times to keep the revolution pure of enemy agents and infiltrators."[9]

These were ominous words. Early in 1976, mutiny broke out among the poorly fed and poorly trained PLAN fighters, who lived in bad conditions in the camps. The rebels arrested two of their leaders and sent a group of 15 representatives to Lusaka to talk to Nujoma and the SWAPO leadership, who refused to see them, so they talked to representatives of the OAU and the Zambian government instead. In a letter, they accused the leadership of "the evil of corruption" and demanded a democratic congress with the power to dismiss the leadership if it so wished.[10]

Finally, Nujoma had enough of these young upstarts. After a few scuffles between the small group of dissidents and Nujoma loyalists, the dissidents were surrounded by three or four battalions of the Zambian army, and disarmed and arrested. Nujoma convinced President Kenneth Kaunda to hold the main dissident leadership incommunicado in a prison in Lusaka. When the news leaked out and a writ of *habeas corpus* was issued by the court to produce the arrested, they were simply flown to Dar es Salaam, Tanzania, where President Julius Nyerere obligingly incarcerated them. They were freed only in May 1978 after much international pressure. Another group of 45 to 50 dissident leaders were simply shot. Inside SWA, SWAPO also took steps to ensure the neutralisation of possible dissidents. Many others were detained and tortured.[11]

In 1976, the movement appointed a commission of investigation, under the leadership of John Ya-Otto, to look into the crisis. The commission, consisting of ten prominent Nujoma loyalists, found that one man, Andreas Shipanga, was to blame. According to the commission's findings, the crisis was the result of "enemy intrigues and infiltration", a "power struggle" with the leadership led by certain members of the SWAPO Youth league and a campaign of "lies, exaggerations and malicious rumours". The blame further fell on "South African-Imperialist (particularly West German) interests". However, the commission also found "official shortcomings and incompetence", a lack of a "sound centrally controlled system of receiving, expending accounting and auditing Party funds", as well as a "tendency to isolate those considered to be trouble makers with a view to silence or punish them".[12]

At a press conference, Nujoma gave no ground. The "problem", he declared, was the result of "a well-controlled, well-financed conspiracy by the South African regime and its imperialist allies, especially West Germany, to destroy SWAPO". The movement "carried out a systematic purge of all the traitors" and also put "tested and reliable cadres" in "a position of responsibility and authority".[13]

More than a thousand SWAPO guerrillas were imprisoned in a Zambian camp for several months, under extremely bad conditions, before some escaped and their position became known. Under pressure, most were transferred to other camps where conditions were slightly better. Some simply disappeared and were never heard of again.[14]

Still, none of these events damaged SWAPO's international standing. Only a few months later, the UN General Assembly recognised SWAPO as "the sole and authentic representative of the Namibian people".[15] That a socialist country like East Germany would dismiss the reports of SWAPO's human-rights abuses as "South African propaganda"[16] was to be expected. But although the governments of Norway, Sweden and Finland were informed about the internal clampdown within SWAPO, they did not curtail or cancel their very generous financial support for the movement, but actually increased it.[17] Otillie Abrahams, who was in exile in Sweden at the time, asked the Swedes why democracy was good for them, but "not for us":

> [T]hey said: "Africa is different." They just told us that we are different! The other thing they said was that "we have to mobilize the Swedish society. The things that you are telling us are not important and if we must put the whole complexity of the argument in front of the Swedish people, they will not understand it." I said that I did not know that the Swedes were such idiots.[18]

According to Pastor Siegfried Groth, a German churchman, the Swedish churches who supported SWAPO knew everything, but did not speak out. They even refused to minister to the needs of those who broke away from the movement. SWAPO demanded – and got – "total obedience" from the clergy both within SWA and internationally .[19]

SWAPO's "Stalinist register"

Still under heavy pressure, SWAPO held a congress in July and August 1976 in Nampundwe, Zambia, where it adopted a new party constitution. But instead of making the party more open, democratic and accountable, as the dissidents had demanded, it transformed SWAPO into an orthodox Marxist-Leninist vanguard party. In the new constitution, SWAPO pledged to combat all forms of ethnic orientation and racism and to "unite all Namibian people, particularly the working class, the peasantry and progressive intellectuals into a vanguard party capable of safe-guarding national independence and of building a classless, non-exploitative society based on the ideals and principles of scientific socialism."

The constitution called on the Namibian people to "fight for unity with the world socialist system and forces for peace and progress throughout the world, and fight against imperialism". The economic vision was that "all means of production and exchange will become the property of the people".[20] In its concomitant National Programme, SWAPO was a bit more circumspect, stating only that "[p]rivate ownership of property and means of production will be allowed only if it serves the interests of the people and is useful to the economic development of Namibia".[21] In another SWAPO publication, it was quite openly stated that

> The ideas of socialist orientation, as stated in the revised political program of SWAPO, have become our way of life, and we have now to grasp this great truth, that the first step in the revolution currently waged by the Namibian proletariat and the working peasants is to raise the two friendly classes in our society to the position of the ruling class which, at the time, is the first step to winning the battle of a people's democracy.[22]

Some observers, while conceding the "Stalinist register" or the "textbook example of Soviet-style phraseology", seek to portray it as a merely opportunistic stance to gain the support of young South West Africans and of the Soviet-bloc weapons suppliers.[23] An American study theorises that Nujoma's stance was "instead intended to allay the anxieties of the sceptical MPLA officials" on whose support SWAPO's insurgency depended.[24] In his memoirs, Nujoma also denies that SWAPO had become a communist organisation.[25]

It is not clear why SWAPO should not simply be taken at its word. After all, most southern African liberation movements, including the MPLA, FRELIMO and the ANC, were at this stage either avowed Marxist-Leninist organisations or dominated by communists.[26] There seems to be no reason to assume that the SWAPO leaders did not mean what they said. Even before the 1976 conference, when Nujoma visited Moscow in December 1974, he confided to his Soviet friends: "We believe in socialism, we want to create a socialist state, but we don't want to announce it."[27] Moreover, from the late 1970s, the movement appointed political commissars in all camps, most of which, in the words of academic Christian Williams, "were trained in scientific socialism and other curricula determined by SWAPO's Soviet allies and were appointed to teach classes in camps".[28]

In 1977, Sam Nujoma let slip SWAPO's true intentions when he was asked by a South African television reporter whether SWAPO would not be "left out in the cold" if a non-SWAPO government took power on independence: "The question of black majority rule is out," he answered. "We are not fighting even for majority rule. We are fighting to seize power in Namibia, for the benefit of the Namibian people. We are revolutionaries. We are not counter-revolutionaries."[29] Afterwards Nujoma complained that he was "quoted out of context".[30] But this was not an aberration. In 1978, he repeated this sentiment in an interview with the German magazine *Der Spiegel*, when he said: "We have fought. We have a right to power. And we shall share that power with no one."[31]

Moses Garoeb, another prominent SWAPO leader, told a conservative West German politician, Alfred Dregger, in 1979: "When SWAPO wins [the war], we will not allow the 'Turnhalle' to exist further as a political unit. Their leaders will be prosecuted. No one will be killed outright, but we will condemn them according to the laws which we will decide." When Dregger asked whether this meant a one-party state with no other political forces allowed, Garoeb answered in the affirmative.[32]

Of course, at this stage the movement already had "laws" stipulating heavy penalties for subverting the revolution. Possibly Garoeb had these in mind when he spoke to Dregger. In September 1977, the SWAPO Central Committee had adopted a document, "Laws Governing the Namibian People's Revolution", which stipulated: "Any propaganda using publications, leaflets, written and oral presentations or any other means to incite to struggle against the SWAPO movement and/or creation and survival of the Namibian state; disruption of the unity of the Namibian people; introduction of inequality among ethnic groups; and resistance to decisions of the SWAPO movement and/or agencies of the new Namibian State shall constitute a felony."[33]

In typical totalitarian fashion, Nujoma declared to the UN Security Council in 1985: "SWAPO leads the nation at home and abroad; it is the people organ-ised . . ."[34] This was in line with SWAPO's Political Constitution, according to which it called itself "the organised political vanguard of the oppressed and exploited people of Namibia". This meant that SWAPO "organises, unites, inspires, orientates and leads" the people. "It is thus the expression and embod-iment of national unity."[35] As late as June 1988, at a Stockholm meeting between SWAPO leaders and influential South West African whites, Hidipo Hamutenya, a member of SWAPO's politburo, denied that a multiparty system was neces-sary for a democracy. Hage Geingob, also on the politburo, maintained that a one-party state did not have to be undemocratic.[36]

SWAPO had clearly become a communist movement. In 1981, Nujoma wrote that the Namibian liberation struggle "identified itself with the Great October Socialist Revolution in Russia",[37] while Moses Garoeb wrote in the same year that the Soviet Union "today embodies the bulwark of social progression in the world".[38] In 1982, a SWAPO publication, *Namibia Today*, propagated the same orthodox Marxist-Leninist two-stage revolution preached by the ANC and South African Communist Party (SACP) – first a bourgeois stage in alli-ance with non-communists (called the "National Democratic Revolution"), but with communists in all important positions, and then the socialist stage when the communists take over all power.[39]

Randolph Vigne, a left-wing SWAPO sympathiser, referred to the fact that "the teachings of Marx, Lenin and Mao" were "expounded in the camps by Political Commissars, full members of the Military Council". The Namibians, he wrote, were "ready for those high principles of Marxism that spread so rapidly through Southern Africa in the 1970s".[40] Only a few months before the fall of the Berlin Wall, Nujoma praised East German leader Erich Honecker's "wise and revolutionary leadership".[41]

SWAPO accepted the constitutional principles for Namibia put forward in 1982 by the five-nation Western Contact Group, thereby acquiescing to a Western-type system, with guarantees for multiple political parties, freedom of speech, an independent judiciary, etc.[42] But this only happened under extreme pressure from the West and did not mean that SWAPO's principles had changed. The movement's political propaganda from the time reinforces the point. "Comrade Lumumba", reportedly the nom de guerre of "PLAN's chief political commissar", wrote in SWAPO's mouthpiece, *The Combatant*, that political education among the masses "should be of class character, be based on the irreconcilable hatred against class enemies, capitalist and imperialist . . ." It should "strengthen the class position of our combatants in the interests of the toiling and exploited, but fighting people of Namibia".[43] The publication also referred to the "racist economy" as being "characteristically capitalist. The workers who produce all the wealth live in poverty." Echoing the views of the South African Communist Party, it said that "this system of capitalist exploitation is operating through the brutal national domination of the African majority".[44] The capitalist system is doomed, it claimed "because of the socio-economic contradictions inherent in it. The tendency in the capitalist system always moves towards socio-economic crisis resulting in a fierce struggle between the working class and the bourgeoisie."[45]

The Combatant also gave ideological lessons to SWAPO members, arguing that ideology furnished a "coherent explanation" of why one system should be preferred above another, and why all social, political and economic action should be "justified in ideology":

> Ideology stipulates preferred values. Capitalists embrace liberalism as an ideology because it justifies capitalism, imperialism and colonialism. Indirectly it justifies racism and apartheid, because they facilitate exploitation and the earning of super-profits. Because of super-profits, capitalist countries will only issue pious statements against apartheid but will never take practical action to end the system.[46]

All of this is nothing if not orthodox Marxism-Leninism. In light of this, one has to wonder why academics so often refuse to accept that, while Nujoma and his lieutenants might have accepted Marxism-Leninism in 1976 partly to please SWAPO's radical youth and its Soviet and Angolan patrons, over the years SWAPO most definitely evolved into a fully fledged communist organisation.

As a matter of fact, CANU leader Mishake Muyongo, who left SWAPO in 1985, told an SADF interrogator after his return to South West Africa that Peter Nanyemba, a prominent SWAPO leader, had tried to convince Sam Nujoma that SWAPO should openly declare itself to be a Marxist-Leninist organisation. Nujoma declined, saying that "it would deter people from Namibia as well as countries which supported the organisation and that the time for such an announcement was not yet ripe".[47]

To be sure, during the late 1980s, when it became clear that the Soviet Union and communism were struggling, SWAPO issued a new policy document in which it abandoned immediate large-scale nationalisation of the economy, although it left the possibility open for the future.[48]

The USSR's role

While the Border War had its own causes and dynamics, it was drawn into the Cold War, the international power struggle between the Eastern Bloc and the free West. Even though Western countries were often somewhat embarrassed to be seen working with apartheid South Africa, by and large they tried to prevent the USSR from using SWAPO and the ANC/SACP to bring southern Africa within the Soviet sphere of influence. It was one of the central pillars of US Assistant State Secretary for Africa Chester Crocker's policy to bring about an independent Namibia without undue Soviet influence.

As for the Soviets, they viewed the Third World – including southern Africa – as a key battleground in the struggle with the West. Secret documents smuggled to the West after the collapse of the Soviet Union in 1991 stated that Nikita Khrushchev (Soviet premier from 1958 to 1964), at the insistence of the KGB, formulated a new policy with regards to the Third World, thereby pulling the Third World from the periphery of Soviet foreign policy to centre stage.[49]

In a secret speech in Moscow in January 1961, Khrushchev announced that his country would force the West "on its knees" through its support of the Third World's "holy" anti-imperialist struggle. This meant support for national liberation movements such as SWAPO and the ANC/SACP. Nikolai Leonov, who later became a prominent KGB official, remembered: "Basically, of course, we were guided by the idea that the destiny of world confrontation between the United States and the Soviet Union, between Capitalism and Socialism, would be resolved in the Third World. This was the basic premise."[50]

Vasili Solodovnikov, one of the architects of the policy, confirmed that the motive was not so much material, as ideological: "We were sure that we were weakening the rich West whose economies were based on colonialism and cheap natural resources." The Cold War, he said, was fought on the backs of Africans, Arabs, Afghans, Vietnamese and Cambodians.[51] The Norwegian Cold War historian Odd Arne Westad confirms that southern Africa's mineral wealth also played a role in Soviet calculations, chiefly by seeking to deny it to the West, but that this played a subsidiary role.[52] Leonid Brezhnev, Khrushchev's successor, thought that the principle of peaceful coexistence between the two power blocs did not apply to the Third World.[53]

As for South Africa, the official Soviet viewpoint was articulated by the magazine *New Perspectives*, the mouthpiece of the World Peace Council, a well-known Soviet front organisation:

> The international community must fully recognize that Apartheid cannot be reformed but must be totally destroyed. The international community must fully respect the right of oppressed people and their national liberation movement to choose their means of struggle, including armed struggle, and lend all assistance needed by them . . .[54]

Hence the USSR and the Soviet bloc became the chief source of international support for SWAPO – not only politically and diplomatically, but especially in terms of weapons and military training. SWAPO (and the ANC/SACP) fitted quite nicely into the Soviet worldview as an instrument to be used in its competition with the US and the West.

This did not necessarily mean that the Kremlin issued orders and that SWAPO simply carried them out. The Soviet Union appreciated the ideological loyalty of the liberation movements it supported, but did not insist on it.[55] Not that it was necessary: in a nuanced secret assessment from 1982, the CIA observed that "[a]s a result of its military assistance, Moscow has gained considerable – but not dominant – influence within SWAPO. As its attempts to dissuade SWAPO from participating in negotiations show, the Soviets have had little success in dictating policy to SWAPO." Nevertheless, the assessment concluded, the Soviets "may have gained additional influence with SWAPO's political leadership. The Soviets have provided ideological and political training for SWAPO cadres . . . In turn, SWAPO delegations have attended the last two Soviet Communist Party congresses."[56] According to PLAN documents placed before US Congressional hearings on Soviet involvement in southern Africa, PLAN officers were trained in "Political Commissarship" in the Soviet Union, East Germany and Cuba.[57]

The SWAPO "spy scare"

SWAPO's internal cohesion started to unravel in the 1980s, partly because of the military difficulties analysed in Chapter 9, but also because of the capricious and dictatorial leadership of Sam Nujoma. "The history of SWAPO in exile," writes Pastor Siegfried Groth, "was riddled with internal crises. Throughout the Sixties, Seventies and Eighties, the liberation movement lurched from one conflict to another, with a continually escalating trend towards violence among the leadership." Groth quotes an anonymous South West African church leader in 1979: "The same process has started in SWAPO which has also happened in Russia under Stalin. Eastern and totalitarian forces are getting stronger and stronger. I am extremely concerned that there will be an era of Stalinism for SWAPO in exile." He also said that the Ovambos were becoming increasingly powerful, while the "moderates, intellectuals and the prudent can no longer hold their own against the 'hard liners' who have seized power".[58]

This had become increasingly true by 1981, when the SWAPO security department was founded on the advice of the Soviet Union, which provided training for its personnel. The organisation was placed under the command of Solomon Hawala, the deputy army commander. As such, he was nominally second to army commander Dimo Hamaambo, but in practice was accountable only to Sam Nujoma. In time, the Security Department grew so powerful that, in 1988, operatives even held and questioned Nujoma's wife, her sister and her brother for some weeks, Nujoma apparently being powerless or unwilling to intervene.[59] The SWAPO leadership developed a culture, Colin Leys and John S Saul write, that "frowned upon spontaneity and debate", and "increasingly defined criticism as disloyalty".[60]

Neither did SWAPO permit debate about its military approach. One of PLAN's commanders, Johannes "Mistake" Gaomab, became worried about the extreme difficulties caused by the SADF's repeated cross-border operations into Angola and wanted to talk about a counter-strategy: "I wanted to change our whole campaign's strategy and tactics," he remembered after the war. "It was not always good that the men had to walk 300 kilometres before they could attack." He therefore proposed "that we create a system whereby our people stayed in the country and fought there, while we supplied them." "But," he went on, "the Military Council was dominated by the old guard, and did not accept any suggestions from below."[61]

In 1982, Anton Katamila, SWAPO's secretary for political mobilisation and orientation, hosted a seminar at Kwanza Sul, Angola, in order to identify and remedy all sorts of bad practices within the organisation. Apparently, those present felt free enough to speak out openly. Shortly afterward, the security department began to arrest those who did not toe the party line.[62]

The security department strengthened its position from 1985, when the so-called spy scare broke out.[63] During this period, about 2 000 SWAPO members were detained, mostly in Angola, but also in Zambia, under suspicion of being South African spies. No one was exempt from suspicion. Even some people working at SWAPO Defence Headquarters were arrested, and by 1985 many of its about 50 members had "disappeared". Most of them were relatively well educated, and had been promoted to their positions by the SWAPO defence secretary, Peter Nanyemba. However, after Nanyemba died in a suspicious car crash, SWAPO's security chief, Solomon Hawala, started targeting them.[64] SWAPO members in Lusaka, London, Paris, Bonn and other places were ordered to watch "a number of videos they would never forget as long as they lived," writes Groth:

> This was the first time they saw the faces of the so-called spies – the
> well-known faces of friends who had fought alongside them for many

years, people who had been loyal, reliable SWAPO members both at home and abroad. They were now confessing their guilt, giving precise details of their lives in Namibia and in exile, their families and how they supposedly became enemy agents. The more the audience saw their faces and heard their voices, the more they were seized by paralysing horror. As part of their confessions, the "spies" gave the names of other freedom fighters who were also under suspicion of espionage. That evening, the unsuspecting audience suddenly began to fear for their own lives as they heard their own names being mentioned and realized that they too, were branded as spies and traitors. They knew that this would lead to imprisonment and torture.[65]

Eventually, hundreds were incarcerated, assaulted, maltreated, raped and tortured, with some dying in the process. And no one was given a fair hearing. Some women prisoners were accused of carrying blades in their vaginas to cut off men's penises.[66] One woman, Ndamona Kali, related how she and her sister were arrested in Cuba, where they were studying, and brought to SWAPO's dungeon in Lubango. She was told to write her autobiography. Then the interrogators started torturing her to make her confess that she was a South African spy. She was ordered to undress:

> They tied my hands and feet. My hands were tied to one end of the horizontal pole and my feet were fastened to the other end. My stomach faced down and my spine was curved. I had terrible pains in my back because of that position. As if this pain was not enough, they started beating me with sticks. I was beaten, I screamed and a woman guard came in and said my screams could be heard outside. A cloth was pushed into my mouth. They said, "Tell what you have been hiding". When I said I was hiding nothing, the beating was continued.[67]

Her sister, Panduleni, who was imprisoned separately, relates how Nujoma himself visited her prison, berating the women

> that we were enemy agents, that we came with poisons to kill the

combatants of PLAN, some of us even tested our poisons, we put them
in the water and food of PLAN combatants, and these people died.
He promised that they would fight more than ever before to liberate
Namibia, and to take us to our mothers and fathers, and we would be
paraded at a revolutionary square where they were going to hoist their
flag and the nation would decide what to do with us.[68]

But, as Philip Steenkamp succinctly puts it, "subsequent evidence makes it
clear that the overwhelming majority were not spies, but simply critics of the
leadership, or just people believed liable to be such critics."[69] In addition, it
appears that educated people were also targeted, as they tended to be more
independent-minded.[70]

When members of the so-called Parents' Committee (who tried to discover
the whereabouts of their loved ones) confronted Nujoma in 1987 in the French
city of Strasbourg, he lost his temper, slapped one of the members and yelled:
"You will die!"[71] No wonder that Norwegian researcher Henning Melber says
"[v]ictims were as liberators often also perpetrators". The fact that "they were
fighting against unjust systems of oppression . . . did not prevent them from
resorting to internal oppression of the worst kind".[72] After the war, SWAPO –
now the government – refused to acknowledge the abuses or to have its dark
past investigated, citing as the reason the need for "reconciliation".[73]

Evidence of these human-rights violations was given to the Namibian Council
of Churches in 1985. But they kept silent for fear of playing into the hands of
the apartheid government. The Parents' Committee described the church-
men's response: "Priest and pastor slandered them, called them agents and
destroyers and accused them of spreading malicious rumour." In his history
of the ANC and SWAPO in exile, Paul Trewhela speaks of "clerical connivance with the SWAPO torture machine".[74] During a visit to southern Africa in
May and June 1988, Groth found it "difficult" to raise the question of SWAPO
dissidents in church circles. "Whenever violations of human rights within the
Namibian liberation movement were at issue, any open-minded discussion
became impossible."[75] Even in 1989, when Groth published a report with his
findings about human-rights abuses within SWAPO, "he was chastised for it
by colleagues in Namibia and Germany".[76] Such responses were all the more

startling, given that SWAPO made it difficult for Christians to confess their religious beliefs openly.[77]

A Soviet diplomat, Alexander Maksyuta, conveyed to Nujoma the USSR's unease regarding the arrests and tortures taking place, apparently without result.[78] According to Christian Williams, other SWAPO allies also "generally accepted and reproduced" the movement's version "despite the fact that some allies had access to contrary information".[79] The Swedish ambassador in Luanda at the time, Sten Rylander, tried to investigate the rumours he had heard, but confessed he was "personally suspicious" about them,

> because all the sources I could find had their roots in apartheid South Africa. And I wrote about that in my reports to the Ministry in Stockholm. It was first in Namibia – after having met a few people that had gone through the torture – that I understood what really had taken place. Bience Gawanas came to my hotel room after I had arrived in 1990 [in Namibia] and for three hours told me, crying, what she had gone through. Bience, as well as most others who were taken to the dungeons in southern Angola, were of course no spies. Many of them were under suspicion because they came from the "wrong" tribe (i.e., from the south of Namibia or south of Ovambo) or because of a good education.[80]

Even in the Western Contact Group – the US, UK, France, Germany and Canada – there was a "ludicrous debate" (in Chester Crocker's words) over "whether it was 'fair' to insist upon democratic checks and balances in Namibia's future constitution". After a while, the "democratically-minded" got their way,[81] but the debate illustrated just how lenient the world was prepared to be with SWAPO.

Only a conservative human-rights group in West Germany, the Internationale Gesellschaft für Menschenrechte (International Society for Human Rights, or IGFM), based in Frankfurt-am-Main, was willing to tell the truth. In a report, based on testimony by people who had been prisoners in SWAPO camps, it accused the movement of human-rights violations. The camps were, in fact, "concentration camps" and "breeding camps", the IGFM said. The report was summarised by a later researcher:

There, people were said to suffer from hunger and poor health. Conditions were especially bad for those who were falsely accused of being "dissidents" or "spies" by leaders motivated by tribal interests and the pursuit of pure power. Women were also badly mistreated, forced to have sex with officials and to bear children, who were taken from them shortly after birth and indoctrinated into the party. Importantly, all these claims were based on the accounts of Namibians who had lived in the camps themselves.[82]

However gruesome these events, the question that must interest us here is how SWAPO's internal difficulties affected its military capabilities. It is true that many SWAPO guerrillas continued fighting, trying to infiltrate SWA, even though they must have known that their chances of success could not have been great. But the brutal suppression of all real or imagined independent thought surely must have dampened their enthusiasm, if not for Namibian independence then for SWAPO itself, and affected their morale. The power of the security department, like that of the KGB in the USSR or the Gestapo in Nazi Germany, was all-encompassing. According to Groth, the atmosphere among exiles

> was poisoned by silence and secrecy. The freedom fighters were surrounded by fear on all sides. They were almost crushed by the weight of rumours, contradictions and uncertainty ... Many leaders were seen in the same light as the Security Service, no longer there to protect and exercise authority, but to oppress and threaten.[83]

Colin Leys and John S Saul write about "the growing Stalinist influence from 1976 onwards". They come to the conclusion that "after 1976 all questioning of policy decisions was delegitimised, so that not even leaders as senior as Hage Geingob (who became democratic Namibia's first Prime Minister) or Lucas Pohamba (Nujoma's successor as President) could get a discussion in the Central Committee of what the security organisation was doing". In the end, they say, "one [anonymous] senior cabinet minister acknowledged to us, 'there was fear everywhere. The Central Committee could not act. We were saved by [the implementation of Security Council Resolution] 435.'"[84]

This last sentence is important, and is buttressed by Leys and Saul's assertion that "SWAPO had all but paralysed itself – for despite its many strengths and its subsequent electoral success, this is hardly too strong a summary of its condition on the eve of the 'peace agreement' that brought SWAPO home and into office after April 1989."[85] The fact is that, by 1989, SWAPO was saved only by its international influence at the UN, and by Cuba and the Soviet Union.[86] Political scientist Elena Torreguitar also comes to the conclusion that "SWAPO was almost annihilated during the spy drama; the leadership was shaken by an internal take-over which lasted many years, almost from 1982 until the eve of the implementation of Res. 435 which saved SWAPO from vanishing entirely."[87]

The movement did not fight for the liberal multiparty democracy Namibia got in 1990. Taking into account the cruelty towards dissidents in its own ranks and the organisation's "Stalinist register", it is clear that SWAPO fought to replace the authoritarian South African rule with a far worse dictatorship. No wonder Leys and Saul, who view SWAPO as having had "a noble cause", recognise that "it was largely external circumstances that dictated SWAPO's acceptance, in the end, of a more formally democratic constitution . . . than its ideological stance in the 1970s had led many observers to expect".[88]

11

CUBA, THE USSR AND
UNITA IN ANGOLA

The civil war in Angola between UNITA and the MPLA had its own dynamic, which must be distinguished from the war between South Africa and SWAPO. The roots of the Angolan civil war lie in the dramatic events of 1974 to 1976 following the Portuguese revolution, but South Africa's shadow nevertheless looms large over the "indigenous" Angolan conflict – almost as large as that of Cuba and the Soviet Union. South Africa played a largely indirect role but had a definite influence on the course of that war.[1] Although we have examined South Africa's intervention in Angola in Operation Savannah (*see* Chapter 2), in order to understand the final climactic confrontation of 1987/1988 it is necessary to take a look at what happened in Angola from 1976 to 1986.

The SADF and UNITA

After the South African withdrawal from Angola at the end of March 1976, UNITA was left largely to fend for itself. With Cuban help, the MPLA captured all the major cities, towns and roads in the south of the country.[2] The rebel movement melted away into the bush, and, under the charismatic but autocratic leadership of Jonas Savimbi, began the slow and difficult task of starting a guerrilla war. In April 1978, when South Africa formally accepted UN Resolution 435, which put forward proposals for a ceasefire and UN-supervised elections, UNITA's difficulties grew as all contact between the SADF and the rebels was broken off. This did not last long; within a few months, the South Africans were once again sending supplies over the border.[3] Within a year or two, the movement was reborn, and its expanding operations throughout the southeastern part of the country began to give the MPLA severe headaches.[4]

The South Africans quickly realised that UNITA could play a key, albeit clandestine, role in their evolving strategy of forward defence. In an analysis early in 1979, SADF Military Intelligence referred to UNITA's renewed operations and identified several advantages for South Africa. When contact was renewed late in 1976, the document stated, UNITA "was a weak and disorganised organisation". The SADF supplied it with 1 400 tonnes of equipment and provided assistance with training and organisation, which meant that "more than 90% of its present force" was due to South African aid. Its operations against the MPLA meant that the Angolan army "could play only a small role against the RSA". Furthermore, a large part of the SWAPO forces were involved in operations against UNITA: "This has had the consequence that these forces could not be utilised against SWA." Also, the fact that SWAPO was unable to activate the Kavango region inside SWA, "could be attributed to UNITA actions in the Cuando Cubango province".[5]

Accordingly, when a senior Military Intelligence officer met Savimbi in March 1979, they agreed that UNITA would take the initiative in Cuando Cubango and eastern Cunene provinces to drive SWAPO out, while the SADF would see to SWAPO in the rest of Cunene.[6] This built on the foundation created by 32 Battalion's guerrilla operations in southern Cuando Cubango province since 1976; the resultant vacuum made it possible for UNITA to re-establish itself in the region.[7] By the early 1980s, the SADF was operating three training camps for UNITA fighters in South West Africa, and a South African liaison officer was based permanently at Savimbi's headquarters.[8]

South Africa's alliance with UNITA arose purely out of self-interest, and its aid to the rebel movement should always be seen in this light. As we have seen, one of the SADF's most important operational objectives inside South West Africa was to limit the war as much as possible to Ovamboland. This made the counterinsurgency war against SWAPO so much easier.[9] The fact that UNITA occupied the entire southeastern corner of Angola made it impossible for SWAPO insurgents to infiltrate into the Caprivi and very difficult for them to infiltrate into Kavango.

In addition, keeping UNITA going presented South Africa with a means of reminding the MPLA of the price for its active aid to SWAPO. In a top-secret memorandum in May 1979, Magnus Malan explicitly wrote that the "ultimate purpose" of South African help to UNITA "was that the MPLA Government [should] prevent SWAPO from deploying in Southern Angola". Therefore, this region had to be kept unstable to "force the MPLA Government to stop its aid to SWAPO".[10]

South Africa was, of course, not the only country to give assistance to UNITA. After a secret meeting in November 1976 between French President Valéry Giscard d'Estaing and UNITA's Foreign Minister, Jorges Sangumba, in Dakar, Senegal, France started supplying arms to the Angolan rebel movement. In addition, according to Savimbi himself, UNITA received arms from China, Kenya, Zaire and Senegal.[11] However, South Africa's support was of the greatest importance.

Cuba's role in Angola

In order to understand Cuba's role in Angola, one must first comprehend the psyche of its leader, Fidel Castro. He was driven by two overriding factors. He was, firstly, an idealist, believing that what he said and did was for the good of mankind, even though he could be ruthless in his pursuit of that which he saw as good. He was also charismatic, arrogant, self-important and very macho. Secondly, he had a romantic view of himself and his Cuban soldiers as knights in shining armour, who would bring freedom to the poor, down-trodden masses of Africa.[12] Castro did not have the freedom of a Western-type multiparty liberal democracy in mind, but rather that of a Marxist-Leninist dictatorship of the proletariat. That was why in 1986 he could, in all earnest, say to the Angolan president: "I believe that in the history of our revolution, *compañero* José Eduardo [dos Santos], our internationalist actions are our most important accomplishments . . ."[13]

The CIA's analysis was probably not far off the mark:

> It is clear that the Cuban leadership sees its foreign assistance pro-
> grams as effective means of achieving foreign policy goals. By aiding
> actual and prospective allies in a tangible way, Cuba satisfies its ideo-
> logical need to promote internationalism, gains prestige as a benefactor
> ostensibly driven by altruistic ideals, and provides sustenance to Fidel

Castro's ego by creating the impression that Cuba is a major actor on the world stage.[14]

Castro's pitiless idealism may have taken him to the brink several times, but he was also a political realist; he always knew when to stop. He not only had good military insight (as he had proved repeatedly during the Cuban revolutionary war in the 1950s and would do again in Angola); he also had a well-developed political nose. His 1975 intervention in Angola was intended to stop the South Africans, but he never wanted to replace Portuguese (or South African) colonialism with Cuban domination. So, in April 1976, following the success of Operation Carlota, Cuba and the MPLA reached an agreement on a gradual reduction in the number of Cuban troops. Within a year, a third of the Cubans had gone home. In 1977, Castro told East German leader Erich Honecker that only 15 000 troops (out of 36 000) would be left in Angola by year's end, and by the end of 1978 this would be reduced to 7 000. But the SADF's air assault on the SWAPO bases of Cassinga and Chetequera (*see* Chapter 5) changed everything, and the Cuban contingent in Angola was again reinforced.[15]

Nonetheless, Castro knew not to go too far. In the years that followed, he restricted his troops mainly to garrison cities and to escorting supply convoys, and seldom allowed them get involved in firefights. Most were stationed in and around Luanda, out of harm's way. Those in southern Angola (about 5 000) were posted as a sort of tripwire along the railway line between Namibe on the Atlantic coast and Menongue, 720 km in the interior and 250 km from the South West African border – well away from the South Africans. They were equipped with tanks, artillery and sophisticated radar and air defences. A few hundred were based south of the railway line, but the official policy was not to operate in Cunene or Cuando Cubango provinces[16] – in other words, to stay far away from the SADF. He compared his army in Angola to "a shield against South Africa's threat"[17]. On a security-strategic level, his posture was – like that of South Africa – defensive.[18]

As Castro himself boasted in a speech in July 1982: "We warn them that if they stage attacks deep into the Republic of Angola and reach our lines, we are going to fight very steadfastly against the fascist, racist South African mercenaries."[19] Of course, he knew that his troops were in positions where the SADF had no reason to go. In effect, he hid behind a smokescreen of tough words and no deeds.

In fact, after Operation Askari ended in January 1984, the Cubans even wanted to have all Angolan troops withdrawn to positions north of the Namibe–Menongue railway line, where air cover could be provided. Castro told President Dos Santos that his aircraft based at Lubango on the railway line could not operate over Cahama, Mulondo and Cuvelai (where the SADF attacked during Operation Askari) "because of too long distances and the superior nature of the South African Air Force". In the end, a compromise was reached between the Cubans and the more aggressive Soviet commanders – in the words of Vladimir Shubin, "several echelons of defence between the front line and the area of deployment of Cuban forces".[20]

"The situation went on for years," Castro defended himself in 1988, "but at the time the balance of forces favoured the South Africans; we had enough forces to defend that line but not to prevent South Africa from intervening in that part of the Angolan territory."[21]

Castro was intelligent enough not to become embroiled in a civil war from which he could not extricate himself. He did not want to meet his Vietnam in Angola. And therefore his troops rarely fought against UNITA and – until 1987 – extremely seldom against the South Africans. They gave advice, supplies and training to FAPLA, but it never really went beyond that.[22] In February 1984, one of Castro's advisors, Jorge Risquet Valdés, wrote that, if the South Africans left Angola and Namibia, "the war against UNITA will become an internal Angolan matter and therefore will have to be fought only by FAPLA, without the participation of our troops".

One reason for this ostensible timidity was Castro's perhaps exaggerated respect for the SAAF's command of the air. As we saw in Chapter 2, this was why he decided, at the beginning of 1976, not to invade SWA following the successful Cuban advance to the border. To a correspondent of the *Washington Post*, he explained that he knew "the South Africans very well, their psychology; we don't underestimate them at all. They have spent a lot of money on weapons in the last ten years. But neither do we overestimate them."[23] As we shall see, the SAAF's ability was also one of the reasons why he continually resisted Soviet pressures to participate in grand offensives against UNITA.

Yet another reason for Castro's inactivity in Angola was the growing unpopularity of the war. In 1987, Brigadier General Rafael del Pino, an air force commander who had fought for several years in Angola and then defected to the United States, told his American interrogators that the Cubans were proud and excited after 1976 because of what was presented to them as a just war: "He told the people that we defeated the South Africans because they were afraid of us. The *povo* [common people] loved that rhetoric . . . He whipped up patriotic sentiments and convinced people that we had an invincible army." But Castro underestimated Jonas Savimbi's stubbornness and unwillingness to give up. In Fred Bridgland's words:

> As the years had gone on he needed success for the MPLA both for his own personal pride and as part of his quest to be an international figure. And, increasingly, he needed the internationalist mission in Angola to distract attention from all the internal economic problems and crises he continued to have in Angola.[24]

With his keen political instinct, Castro was careful not to put his troops too much in harm's way and risk heavy losses. In February 1984, when the Soviet commander in Angola, General Konstantin Kurochkin, expressed to Castro his displeasure at the Cubans' inactivity in the field, the Cuban leader's answer was telling: "In your country the losses may be unnoticeable, but in our small country the human losses become known and have a great effect; therefore we are really trying to avoid losses in Angola."[25]

It is not that the Cubans were not *able* to confront either UNITA or the SADF. According to Castro himself, there were 50 000 Cuban soldiers in Angola by 1988.[26] And, from 1984 onwards, they were increasingly supported by combat aircraft, tanks and artillery. If Castro had really wanted to, he could have caused much trouble for the South African and UNITA leaders. But, largely for political reasons, he held back – at least until late 1987. Yet, at the same time, he wanted the political and ideological prestige that flowed from the "huge" war sacrifice made by a small island, though without making a *real* effort. His biggest investment in this regard was in propaganda. This would happen again in 1987/1988 and afterwards.

Strategic debates

An interesting aspect of the international participation in the Angolan civil war was the differences between the Soviets and Cubans over military strategy. The Soviets were irritated by Castro's stubbornness. As one of the leading Soviet/Africa experts, Karen Brutents, observed: "Fidel Castro wasn't one to obey orders. The Soviet leaders never managed to make him do so."[27]

But they also differed fundamentally about how to confront UNITA. In short, when they took over command in Angola from the Cubans in 1984 after FAPLA's defeat during Operation Askari, the Soviet military were in favour of large-scale conventional offensives with overwhelming firepower to crush the relatively lightly armed UNITA guerrillas, whereas the Cubans favoured a classic counterinsurgency approach. Kurochkin taunted the Cubans that they (in Shubin's words) "were not eager to fight. They were in Angola, but they were avoiding participation in combat, and he felt it was necessary to compel them to be more active in the interest of the cause."[28]

This approach corresponded with Soviet military doctrine. A secret CIA analysis stated that in a war "the Soviet military would attempt to seize the strategic initiative as early as possible, carry the war to the opponents' territory, and destroy the military and political coalition" facing them. This offensive orientation, the analysis went on, "is driven by the Soviet belief that only the strategic offensive offers the possibility of defeating the opponent".[29]

Meanwhile, UNITA, partly with South African aid, was surging through large parts of the country. According to a US military researcher, the MPLA's tactics depended on "periodic campaigns to keep open the principal road networks and regain control of the countryside". He continued:

> These combined-arms sweeps were ill suited to both the terrain and the elusive nature of UNITA's skillful light infantry. As a result, each time the government offensive ended and the MPLA forces withdrew to their bases in the north, the guerrillas simply reoccupied the void. There was never any effort to maintain a permanent government presence in these remote areas, effectively relinquishing them to UNITA by default. By 1983 UNITA had consolidated its hold on extensive portions

of Cuando Cubango and Moxico provinces, operating with nearly unrestricted freedom of action throughout the central region of Angola.[30]

Furthermore, the ever-aggressive Kurochin had set his mind on capturing Mavinga, a strategic town in Cuando Cubango province, held by UNITA, but he was not supported in this by the Cubans, who thought it was becoming an unhealthy idée fixe of his. Castro's attitude was that these operations "couldn't be done unless conditions were created to prevent South Africa's intervention".[31] Exactly what this meant was explained to the Soviets by General Ulises Rosales del Toro, Chief of the Cuban armed forces, at a meeting in Moscow in January 1986: "We must eliminate the impunity with which the South Africans operate, chopping off their hands inside Angola."

Jorge Risquet elaborated: "[O]ur great weakness is that South Africa has air superiority over southern Angola. We must eliminate this." Only then would it become possible to operate against UNITA. It would also facilitate SWAPO's task of infiltrating into Namibia, he said. The Cuban alternative, according to General Leopoldo Cintra Frías, was to operate against UNITA bands in central Angola. He warned against attacking UNITA in an area where the SAAF reigned supreme, but the Soviets would not listen.[32]

Perhaps the more aggressive Soviet attitude was built on the intensive evaluation of SAAF capabilities that they apparently undertook at this time. The conclusion was that this was "generally overestimated". It was specifically mentioned that "South Africa is short of long-range potential . . . and that there are several shortcomings that are likely to become evident if South Africa was put under real pressure".[33]

The Battle of Cangamba (July–August 1983) proved the Cubans right. UNITA decided to attack the Angolan garrison (a brigade, stiffened with some 80 Cuban instructors) of this central Angolan town. The garrison was completely cut off from the outside, and bitter fighting took place in which the defence desperately held and UNITA took heavy casualties. A relief column made slow headway, and Castro became fearful that his instructors would be massacred. In a daring operation, he dispatched a force of helicopters to snatch his own men from under UNITA's noses. The FAPLA garrison was left in the lurch. At the same time, UNITA requested South African help, which arrived in the form of a devastating air strike, by a force of four Buccaneer and four Canberra bombers, escorted by Mirage F1CZ interceptors, blasting Cangamba to bits. The air attack was complemented by a bombardment from an SADF artillery battery with 120-mm mortars. This enabled UNITA to occupy the town at last, only to vacate it shortly afterwards.[34]

Cangamba illustrated several things. Firstly, it vindicated the Cubans' contention that operations within reach of the SAAF were fraught with danger. Secondly, Castro once again pulled off a propaganda coup by transforming his own soldiers' defeat and ignominious flight into a great feat by a force of glorious heroes.[35] Thirdly, the South Africans were initially very skittish about becoming involved in a fight they did not see as their own, and had to be cajoled into it.[36] Fourthly, it led to an escalation of the war: Cuba sent an additional 5 000 troops to Angola, while the Soviet Union sent 10 naval vessels and support ships, including an aircraft carrier, to Luanda in a show of support.[37]

As the CIA analysed the Soviet position, "the Soviets thus see the continuation of the military struggle as their only real option until such time as Savimbi is either gone or UNITA's strength is otherwise diminished. By the same token, Moscow sees a Cuban troop withdrawal before the military balance shifts in Luanda's favour as simply forcing the MPLA into a suicide pact."[38]

After defecting to the US, Cuban Brigadier General Rafael del Pino also told Radio Martí, the free Cuban radio station in Miami, that "we have serious differences with the Soviets on how to employ armaments, how to employ tactics, etc". He referred to the 1985 FAPLA offensive, which the Cubans advised against, but the Soviets remained adamant about: "The [FAPLA] troops were annihilated, and the whole thing was the fault of poor guidance by the Soviet advisers."[39]

Be that as it may, the situation in Angola was changing. The ongoing South African operations in Cunene province, especially Operation Askari in December 1983 and January 1984, were slowly testing Moscow's patience. Just a few weeks before the operation, in late November 1983, the South African ambassador to the United Nations, Kurt von Schirnding, was discreetly contacted by Soviet diplomats. At a secret meeting in a New York hotel, they told him they had a message for Pretoria from Moscow. They warned that their satellites had monitored a South African military build-up near the Angolan border (the preparation for Operation Askari). They noted that South Africa was internationally isolated and that the "Chester Crocker cycle" had now ended – in other words, South Africa should not expect any help from the US. South Africa had to face the facts and pull out of Angola. They did not want to threaten South Africa, they added, but proceeded to do exactly that: the USSR had a friendship treaty with Angola, and would supply "all support necessary" for that country's defence.

They pointed out that the USSR had been only nominally involved in the region up until then. The unspoken threat was that this could change for the worse. They said their rules of engagement could be altered to permit battlefield contact with the SADF. At about the same time, the Americans also warned the South Africans "that Moscow and Havana would raise the stakes, pouring in more men and modern hardware, rather than be humiliated or driven out of Angola by force".[40]

The South African government's answer to this was to proceed with Operation Askari, whereafter the Soviets repeated their warning in public via a statement by TASS, the state news agency.[41] Askari was a watershed of sorts. On the one hand, it led to the short-lived peace process between Angola and South Africa (*see* Chapter 8), but beyond that it convinced the Soviets that they had to solve the Angolan problem militarily. They would not tangle with South Africa for the time being, but UNITA had to be taken out, one way or another.

A few days after Askari, Soviet and Cuban representatives held an emergency meeting in Moscow. As a result, the transfer of new weapons to Angola was drastically accelerated. Anti-aircraft missile systems, such as the sophisticated SA-6 and SA-8, large numbers of T-54/55 and T-62 tanks and armoured personnel carriers and artillery pieces, as well as the formidable MiG-23 and Su-22 fighter and the renowned Mi-25 helicopter gunship, were shipped to Angola, where they were supplied to the MPLA as well as the Cuban troops there. The Cubans sent even more troops, including fighter pilots. The Soviets completely took over the operational control of the war.[42] By 1985, the MPLA arsenal was estimated by SADF Military Intelligence to include the following:

- fighter aircraft: 30 MiG-23, 8 Su-22, 50 MiG-21, 16 MiG-17;
- helicopters: 33 Mi-25, 27 Alouette III, 69 Mi-8 and Mi-17 utility helicopters;
- tanks: 30 T-62, 260 T-55, 150 T-34 (obsolete) and 50 PT-76 light tanks.[43]

By the beginning of 1987, the CIA estimated that a total of 1 200 Soviet and 500 East German military personnel were in Angola as advisors, maintaining complex equipment, setting up an air defence system and training Angolan, PLAN and ANC troops.[44] (In fact, this was an underestimate; the Soviet contingent in Angola numbered about 2 000 men.) Kurochkin was succeeded in 1985 by Lieutenant General L Kuzmenko and in 1987 by Lieutenant General PI Gusev.[45] This build-up created a formidable force by any standards, and one that began to address the Cuban fear of the SADF, and especially the SAAF.

Yet, despite the threat spelled out to Von Schirnding in New York, the Soviet involvement in Angola has to be seen in a global perspective. Angola and South West Africa were not the Kremlin's highest priorities; the standoff with the US and NATO in Western Europe remained the central Soviet strategic concern.[46] Nevertheless, their increasing role in southern Africa was serious enough to the South Africans. And, by 1985, the Soviets were ready to crack the whip on the battlefield.

South Africa is sucked in

In effect, therefore, two separate wars were being fought in Angola. The first was between the SADF and SWAPO; the second was between UNITA on the one side and the MPLA, the Cubans and the Soviets on the other. South Africa did not want to get directly involved in the Angolan civil war any more than was absolutely necessary. Its fight was with SWAPO, and clashes with FAPLA occurred only when the Angolans got in the way, as happened during Operations Protea and Askari. The air support given to UNITA during the Battle of Cangamba was an exception.

However, even before Cangamba, South Africa found itself being sucked into the Angolan civil war. The most important instance was the dramatic Battle of Savate in February 1980. A strange combination of errors make this battle extraordinary. UNITA wanted to capture the border town of Savate, but the brigade-sized FAPLA garrison (more than a thousand soldiers) was too strong for them, and they knew it. So they asked 32 Battalion to help, but told the SADF that the town was defended only by some 300 men.

Three companies from 32 Battalion, six Recce teams and a mortar platoon

(270 men) under Commandant Deon Ferreira duly attacked Savate, but then ran into the entire brigade. The element of surprise was lost when the men bumped into a FAPLA patrol before the attack. Ferreira pressed home his attack, aided by his second in command, Major Eddie Viljoen, in a Bosbok spotter plane. When four Buffel vehicles finally moved in, showering the Angolans with a hailstorm of machine-gun fire, the Angolans broke and ran for their lives. Many ran into the river and drowned or were eaten by crocodiles. Altogether, 39 FAPLA trucks were captured, together with a huge amount of other equipment. The exact FAPLA casualty figure is unknown, but, according to Jan Breytenbach, "hundreds" perished. But 32 Battalion also paid a heavy price, with 15 members killed and 22 wounded – the unit's highest-ever level of casualties. Later, it transpired that there had been a communications blunder and that the SADF high command had never authorised the unit to take part in the battle.[47]

Both Savate and Cangamba were deviations from the usual pattern. However, this was about to change slowly and the two wars would gradually melt into each other. Cangamba in particular proved to be the beginning of a pattern that would eventually lead to an all-out war between South Africa and the Cuban forces in Angola. To South Africa, Cangamba was a limited operation in which no personnel or equipment was lost. Furthermore, while South African involvement was suspected, it happened so quickly and cleanly that nothing could be proven.

In accordance with the military strategy adopted by General Kurochkin, FAPLA started a big conventional offensive in August and September 1985.[48] A strong FAPLA mechanised force, spearheaded by tanks and IFVs and supported by artillery and combat aircraft, advanced from Cuito Cuanavale southeastwards towards Mavinga. The village was important because it had an airstrip that could be developed into an airbase. From there, Jamba – UNITA's headquarters – would be within range. With Mavinga and Jamba occupied, the Russians reasoned, UNITA would to all intents and purposes be knocked out of the war. Soviet advisors were deployed down to battalion level.

The attacking force proved to be lumbering and incapable of rapid movement, while the general disorganised state of the Angolan army made logistics a nightmare. Nevertheless, the firepower was overwhelming, and UNITA soon found that it was no match for FAPLA on a conventional warfare level. Because of UNITA leader Jonas Savimbi's ambitions, the movement was at this stage in the process of transforming an essentially guerrilla army into an army which was partly a semi-conventional and partly a conventional force. Savimbi had been heavily influenced by Mao Zedong's military approach, and he thought that the time was ripe to progress from Mao's first (guerrilla) phase to the second (semi-conventional). This operation proved that he had jumped the gun As a consequence, in Jan Breytenbach's opinion, "it became the South African Army's lot to go to UNITA's assistance and save its skin . . .".[49]

Indeed, within a short time, Savimbi prevailed upon South Africa to bail him out with active military support. This placed the government in a quandary. It did not want to be sucked into someone else's war, but if UNITA was neutralised it would disadvantage South Africa's own war effort. At first, Lieutenant General Neels van Tonder, Chief of Staff Intelligence, believed that UNITA had finally lost its war and that South Africa should cut its losses and withdraw completely from Angola. But, in a dramatic meeting, Savimbi convinced Jannie Geldenhuys to come to his movement's aid; they both then spoke to President PW Botha, who, rather unwillingly, came up with a compromise. Firstly, 28 Squadron's big C-130 and C-160 transport planes were used to switch thousands of UNITA troops rapidly between two fronts (this got the name of Operation Wallpaper). Secondly, a troop of Valkiri 127-mm MRLs and a troop of 120-mm mortars was sent in, protected by elements of 32 Battalion (this was designated Operation Weldmesh). Lastly, the SAAF launched a devastating air strike on FAPLA columns with a strong force consisting of 8 Mirage F1AZs, 6 Mirage F1CZs, 4 Buccaneers, 4 Canberras and 16 Impala IIs, while the Valkiri launchers rained a hailstorm of rockets on the hapless FAPLA troops.[50]

A South African journalist, arriving at the scene shortly afterwards, provides the following graphic description. "Trees have been smashed by heavy vehicles and stripped by shells, and there were hundreds of foxholes, slit trenches and underground bunkers, making the scene reminiscent of a World War I battlefield. The earth was scarred with shell craters and scorched areas where explosions started bush fires. It obviously was a major conventional battle in what until now has been a guerrilla war."[51]

In the end, the SADF benefited greatly from operations Wallpaper and

Weldmesh. The FAPLA offensive was beaten back with heavy losses and UNITA was saved. The SADF participated on a limited scale and suffered no personnel or equipment losses. And, although rumours abounded about alleged SADF involvement, there was little hard evidence. Besides, when the going got tough, the Soviets quickly extracted their advisors by helicopter, leaving the FAPLA troops in the lurch.

An interesting element of the SAAF's participation in this operation was the use of Impala Mk IIs to shoot down Angolan choppers. The South Africans had been informed by UNITA that personnel and supplies were being shuttled to and fro by Mi-25 gunships. In the first part of the operation, two Impalas were directed immediately behind two enemy choppers, shooting down both with their 30-mm cannon. Two days later, four helicopters – two Mi-8s and two Mi-25s – were also bounced from behind, and three were shot down in flames. The pilot of the fourth wrote off his chopper in a controlled crash so as to escape alive.[52]

The intensification of pressure on UNITA contributed to an international development that was not exactly to the liking of the communist alliance. On 6 February, US President Ronald Reagan announced a new approach in his State of the Union speech before Congress. "Freedom is not the sole prerogative of a chosen few," the staunchly anti-communist president said, "it is the universal right of all God's children." He continued: "We must stand by all our democratic allies. And we must not break faith with those who are risking their lives – on every continent, from Afghanistan to Nicaragua – to defy Soviet-supported aggression and secure rights which have been ours from birth."[53]

Reagan never referred to UNITA in the speech. But the new approach was unmistakeable, and was immediately picked up by the media and other observers: Henceforth, the US would aid anti-communist resistance fighters in the Third World. By October of that year, when addressing the UN General Assembly, Reagan went even further, referring specifically to communist interventions in Afghanistan, Cambodia, Ethiopia, Nicaragua – and Angola.[54] At the initiative of certain members of Congress, the Clark Amendment of 1976 was repealed. And, in a series of policy review meetings behind closed doors, the Reagan administration decided to give covert aid, including Stinger anti-aircraft missiles, to UNITA.[55]

In 1986 FAPLA started another offensive along more or less the same lines as the previous year, but it never really got off the ground. This time, it was easier for the South African government to sanction active aid to UNITA, which took the form of Operation Alpha Centauri. First, South African Special Forces destroyed vital supply dumps in the harbour town of Namibe, sinking a Cuban cargo ship, the *Habano*, and damaging two Soviet vessels, the *Kapitan Visblokov* and *Kapitan Chirkov*.[56] Then UNITA (with the help of 32 Battalion, a troop of MRLs and a troop of 155-mm G-5 howitzers) attacked Cuito Cuanavale and destroyed more supplies there. Although the town as such did not fall due to the inexperience and incompetence of the UNITA commander, it did mean the premature end of the FAPLA offensive. (Incidentally, this was the first operational deployment of the famed G-5.)[57] Once again, South Africa had intervened in the Angolan civil war on a limited scale (with no more than 300 to 500 men),[58] without any losses and without the world's being able to point any fingers at the SADF. These three interventions – Cangamba and the operations of 1985 and 1986 – would become important precedents and would help explain South Africa's conduct when FAPLA once again went on the offensive in August 1987.

The climax of the Border War was nigh.

12

OPERATION MODULER: CLASH OF THE TITANS

By the dawn of 1987, the South African government and the SADF had gained considerable political and military experience in dealing with its enemy inside Angola. The South Africans had discovered that allowing PLAN insurgents to utilise Angolan territory freely as their rear area, and to cross the border at will into South West Africa, was the surest way to lose the war. It meant that the enemy had the initiative and that the SADF could only react. Military writers throughout the ages agree that offensive action is the best way to gain the initiative and win a war, and so the South Africans decided to do exactly that. The result was the series of cross-border operations described in previous chapters.

At this point, four observations must be made. Firstly, during this time, the focus shifted to a certain extent in that FAPLA started intervening in the war and at times had to be forced out of the way. Secondly, as we saw in the previous chapter, from 1983 the SADF was slowly drawn into the civil war between the MPLA and UNITA – an example of "mission creep", as the Americans call it. Thirdly, without exception, all the cross-border operations had limited objectives and were of limited duration. The growing international pressure left the SADF with no other option. Lastly, knowing that they would almost always come up against an enemy greater in number, the South Africans had to rely on their superior mobility and an indirect approach.

Typical of this approach was the mechanised warfare doctrine worked out since the 1960s. Several officers were responsible for this, but their ideas were perhaps best expressed by former commander of 61 Mech Colonel Roland de Vries, and, by 1987, the second in command of the Army Battle School at Lohatlha. In that year, De Vries produced two documents that summarised well the thinking of the army's mechanised fraternity. If the leadership had read and internalised these articles, the so-called Battle of

Operational area for Moduler, Hooper and Packer

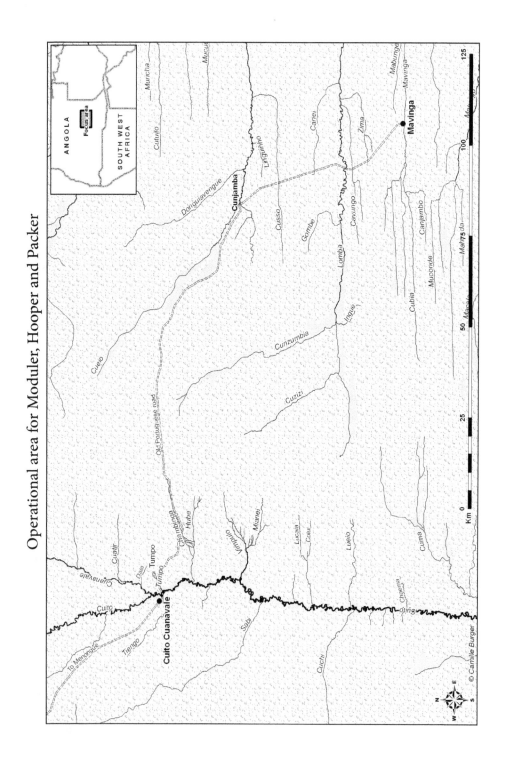

© Camille Burger

Cuito Cuanavale, which would soon unfold, would no doubt have followed a very different course.

De Vries made two extremely important observations which have to be investigated in some detail. The first was the influence on military operations of South Africa's status as international pariah. In a book about mobile warfare he wrote:

> Conflict forms a part of international relations. Taking everything into account, it is doubtful if the superpowers will allow the RSA to conduct protracted conventional battles against its aggressors. International pressure effected during recent cross-border operations on the RSA, is enough proof of this.
>
> Conventional operations which the RSA thus undertakes, will have to be executed extremely fast, and military decisions will have to be forced hastily.[1]

These ideas were shared by the upper echelons of the SADF. In a newspaper interview in March 1986, Jannie Geldenhuys told a journalist that the SADF faced major conventional capabilities across the Republic's borders. In a prophetic observation, he said that "at some point in the near future it may have to engage those forces – and most assuredly alone".[2] De Vries and a co-writer expanded on the argument in an article:

> In a conventional war, the SA Defence Force would be faced by a numerically superior force and would, in all probability, also have to contend with an unfavourable air situation which may develop as a result of the massive build-up of both aircraft and anti-aircraft installations in the Frontline States. Despite their often negative attitude towards the RSA, it is unlikely that the superpowers would allow this country to wage a long-term conventional war against its aggressors for fear of becoming directly involved. Conventional operations on which the RSA may embark, will therefore have to be both swift and decisive and will necessitate expeditious, yet sound and well-founded decision-making.[3]

This fitted in with the experience gained both during and after Operation Savannah. As Brigadier George Kruys put it: "After Savannah, operations were planned in detail in terms of time in, time out and exactly what was to be achieved while in Angola as well as how the operation was to be co-ordinated and executed."[4] This lesson was indeed implemented during all subsequent cross-border operations up to Operation Moduler, which began in an absolute shambles.

According to De Vries, the rapid execution of operations required that mobility be coupled with devastating firepower and an indirect approach. The vast spaces of southern Africa also had to be taken into account. Therefore, as De Vries wrote: "After conducting outflanking manoeuvres or penetrations, the force which has taken the offensive, can attack vital installations behind enemy lines, wreaking havoc. If the enemy's warfare doctrines favour positional rather than mobile warfare, defeat should be imminent and swift."

He identified the following elements as being typical of mobile warfare: movement, quick reaction, surprise, flexibility regarding the utilisation of forces, quick controlled concentration and dispersion, as well as a continuing line of secrecy. The aim of mobile operations was the destruction of enemy forces rather than the taking or occupation of territory; ground was to be held only so long as tactical advantage flowed from it. In such operations, there are no definite lines or fronts.[5]

De Vries also quoted extensively from the works of the British military strategist Sir Basil Liddell Hart, emphasising that the enemy should be attacked where he is *weak*, not strong, where and when he *doesn't* expect it, and that the ideal is to disrupt the enemy through manoeuvre and so undermine his capacity to resist even *before* the shooting starts.[6] The basic purpose of the mobile warfare approach, De Vries explained, is therefore "to outwit the enemy in an ingenious way, rather than being involved in a head-on full-scale confrontation – *Blood is absolutely not the price of victory* [his emphasis]."[7]

This approach did not elicit complete enthusiasm in all quarters of the army. Some officers said he was teaching "his own doctrine" (as opposed to the army's) at Lohatlha. "There were even some officers who allegedly said that they did not understand the 'new' operational concepts that we were then propagating at the Battle School." According to De Vries, "there were some officers in our army who never really understood the operational level of war, nor did they study campaigns and never ever really even understood our own army doctrine; not to mention the creative development of invigorating fresh ones."[8] Indeed, as we shall see, during the final phases of the war, in 1988, the mobile approach would be tragically abandoned in favour of an attritionist mind-set.

One final observation concerns the changing air situation in Angola. During the early 1980s, the SAAF reigned virtually supreme over southern Angola in SADF operations. Twice the Angolan air force tried to intervene, and both times a MiG-21 was shot down. However, as time went by the Angolans became better equipped with anti-aircraft defences – guns as well as missiles – while its radar coverage of the operational area also improved. These improvements limited the SAAF's freedom.[9] In an article published in April 1986, the Chief of the Air Force, Lieutenant General Denis Earp, warned that "as the air umbrella [in Angola] has become more effective, it is obvious that it is becoming increasingly difficult to neutralise it. And unless it is neutralised, no long-range operations in the host country are possible without heavy casualties."[10] The changing situation in the air would make the army's task on the ground considerably more difficult.

The scene is set

The weeks just before and after New Year 1987 saw significant strategic planning taking place in the SADF. On the one hand, it became clear that the advantages of the Lusaka Accord of 1984, when the SADF had agreed to pull out of Angola, had been completely whittled away as SWAPO had filled up the resulting military vacuum in southern Angola and once again infiltrated SWA in considerable numbers. The fact that the South African counterinsurgency forces by this time had the situation south of the border pretty much under control could not prevent this. A decision was therefore taken towards the end of 1986 that the army should "create a situation in the Fifth Military Region of Angola [Cunene province, the battlefield for most of the past SADF operations] which would be similar to the situation which prevailed before the Lusaka Accord".[11] In other words, the SADF would launch another operation similar to Protea or Askari.

Of course, this plan never came to fruition, as it was overtaken by the drama of 1987. Instead, a watered-down operation, designated Firewood, was launched with a battle group consisting of elements of the parabats, Reconnaissance commandos and 101 Battalion, under the command of Colonel James Hills. The force was equipped with Ratel 81s, Casspirs and Buffels. Apparently Eddie Viljoen, at the time Senior Staff Officer: Operations at Sector 10, pleaded with the Chief of the Army, Lieutenant General Kat Liebenberg, to reinforce the battle group with a troop of Valkiri rocket launchers, but the request was refused. According to Viljoen, Liebenberg said: "Man, it's a *terr* in the bush and you trample him with those Casspirs."[12]

On 31 October 1987, PLAN's Northern Command base north of Techamutete was attacked from the west by the Recces and parabats, while 101 Battalion deployed stopper groups to the north, east and south. This time, the PLAN defenders put up a fight and brought in reinforcements from elsewhere. In the end, the base could not be taken.[13] Losses were heavy on both sides. According to a top-secret report to Jannie Geldenhuys, the attackers lost 12 men and 47 were wounded.[14]

In January 1987, the South African intelligence community became aware of a major Soviet airlift during which masses of heavy weapons and military supplies were transported from Tashkent and Moscow to Luanda. The Soviets were withdrawing this equipment from Afghanistan. Anthony Turton, a member of SADF Intelligence, writes:

> This lasted for many months and brought in heavy armour (T-55), BTR-60 APCs, BRDM-2 AFVs and BMP-1 IFVs. These made their way to Cuito Cuanavale in an unprecedented logistics operation on a scale not yet seen in Southern Africa. Intelligence reports indicated that Ilutian [sic; Ilyushin] heavy air transport aircraft were flying into Menongue at around 10 flights a day. These were supported by ground convoys of up to 400 trucks, on a turnaround of six days. This altered the regional balance of power and raised alarm bells within the upper echelons of the security force community.[15]

The SADF pushed several Special Force teams into the vicinity of Tumpo, just across the Cuito River from Cuito Cuanavale, and from March onwards it became clear from their reports that something big was brewing.[16] Military Intelligence intercepted a letter from Angolan President José Eduardo dos Santos to a lobby group in the US, asking them to prepare the climate for an offensive against UNITA. "And from that," a Military Intelligence officer told a researcher, "we clearly deduced that something big was coming." The re-equipping and retraining of FAPLA forces were also signs "of a major offensive being planned".[17]

At this early stage, the South African government still had no idea how to respond. Military Intelligence proposed a "whisper campaign" to leak to French and Portuguese intelligence the message that "South Africa cannot allow a Russian/Cuban-backed MPLA offensive to succeed against UNITA". Beyond that, "dummy equipment" would be placed at Rundu.[18] But there were no concrete plans for actually doing anything. In fact, one gets the distinct impression of a timid response from the generals in Pretoria, who were simply overwhelmed by the speed with which things had escalated. In the process, all the lessons of Operation Savannah were promptly forgotten.

It is important to understand exactly what was at stake here. According to an appraisal by Military Intelligence, the immediate objective of the FAPLA offensive was to advance southeastwards from Cuito Cuanavale to take the town of Mavinga. The airstrip there would give FAPLA a springboard to fly in new supplies and troops and move on to Jamba. Possession of Mavinga would also enable the Angolan air force (FAPA) to bombard Jamba and support the ground advance in that direction. The South Africans' information indicated that FAPLA believed it could take Mavinga within 30 days.[19] Savimbi himself was under no illusions. "It is a question of life or death for UNITA," he told a journalist. "On their side, it is a question of lose and start to negotiate. They will have to talk with us if they fail. On our side, it is lose and disappear."[20]

At the same time, South Africa's primary fight was not so much with Angola as with SWAPO. Although the SADF's posture on the military-strategic, operational and tactical level more often than not was offensive, its security strategy was defensive – above all, the government wanted to safeguard the status quo. Its relations with UNITA must be seen in this light. Throughout the greater part of the decade, UNITA had occupied the southeastern corner of Angola. This made it almost impossible for PLAN fighters to infiltrate Kavango and the Caprivi Strip from Angola. It also aided the SADF counterinsurgency campaign in SWA by largely limiting the war to the relatively small area of Ovamboland. Besides, if UNITA were neutralised, it would also make it easier for ANC fighters to infiltrate South Africa from their camps in Angola via Botswana. All of this the SADF strategists understood very well, and consequently they were alarmed by the possibility that the looming FAPLA offensive could eliminate UNITA.[21] The question was how best to respond.

One of the first officers to understand fully the nature of the threat was Colonel (later Brigadier General) Piet Muller, at this stage commanding Sector 20. Earlier in 1987, Muller had attended a meeting of the General Staff in Windhoek to discuss the unfolding threat in Angola. Supported by Colonel Jock Harris, commander of 32 Battalion, he urged the generals to intervene to save UNITA and presented them with three possible options:

- Ignore the FAPLA advance east of the Cuito River and send in a strong force west of the river to take Menongue in order to cut the attackers' supply lines.
- Take Cuito Cuanavale (rather than Menongue) from the west with the same purpose.
- Meet FAPLA in a head-on clash east of the river in the area where the Angolan advance was taking place.[22]

Muller, supported by Harris, proposed a brigade-sized force to do the job. The aim was to prevent FAPLA from advancing from Cuito Cuanavale and to have the offensive fail before it could even start.[23]

Fred Bridgland mistakenly attributes these plans to a meeting between Muller, Harris and Colonel Fred Oelschig (the SADF liaison officer with UNITA) at Harris's tactical headquarters near Mavinga in August 1987, which he calls "the night of the colonels". As we shall see, that meeting did indeed take place, but, according to Muller, the question of whether the SADF should advance west or east of the Cuito was not discussed at the time.

The choices Muller put before the generals in Windhoek were important. As the picture became clearer, it appeared that a FAPLA force of eight brigades was involved in the operation,[24] of which four would safeguard the rear areas and the other four form the hammer. UNITA was essentially a guerrilla force and was not equipped, structured or trained for conventional warfare. FAPLA was organised along Soviet lines, which meant that each of its brigades was about

1 500 men strong, giving the attacking force a total of about 12 000 soldiers, augmented with artillery, some 80 tanks, numerous armoured vehicles and about 29 fighter-bombers as air support.[25] This was a formidable force by any standard.

An alternative plan put forward was to task 32 Battalion with attacking and destroying the bridge over the Cuito River between Cuito Cuanavale and Tumpo at night and without air cover. As the "butcher's bill" – Jan Breytenbach's words – for such an operation was expected to be in excess of 300 (with no possibility of quick casualty evacuation by air), the idea was wisely dropped.[26] Besides, the Recces also investigated the matter and advised that it would be better to destroy the bridge *after* the offensive had started. Therefore, on the night of 25/26 August, a Recce team of 12 men was dropped 70 km upstream and made its way by canoe to a point near the bridge. After hiding the canoes, the men swam with the current, placing explosives on the pylons. Some of them got away safely, but others were discovered and fired upon. In a moment of high drama, Sergeant Anton Beukman was attacked by a hungry crocodile, which pulled him under the water. Beukman managed to pull out his knife and stabbed the crocodile in the eye. Having learnt that it is unwise to tangle with a South African Recce, the crocodile let go and they all escaped. All 12 members of the group were awarded the Honoris Crux.[27]

Although the explosion damaged 40% of the bridge, the damage was soon repaired. FAPLA had already accumulated sufficient supplies across the river to survive until the bridge was reopened. Thus, the daring Recce operation was an operational failure.[28]

The decision-making process that followed would shape the nature – and outcome – of not only of the campaign of 1987/1988, but also of the war itself. Sadly, it proved to be a study in how *not* to do things.

A first indication that Muller's first two options – to attack either Menongue or Cuito Cuanavale from the west – were not well received by the high command can be seen in a document sent out on 5 June in the name of the Chief of the Army, Lieutenant General Kat Liebenberg. The document recognised that an attack on Menongue could possibly solve the problem militarily, but it was deemed not practicable because of the huge force required, something the army's manpower situation did not allow for. Also, the enemy's air superiority around Cuito Cuanavale would have serious implications for the air force. Thus, the document bluntly warned that "[t]he chances that a real attack on Cuito Cuanavale will be approved, is very limited". Several other options were spelled out, most revolving around small-scale, clandestine aid to UNITA east of the Cuito River. Another option was to allow FAPLA to take Mavinga, and then to launch a counteroffensive with 61 Mech and 32 Battalion to destroy the enemy force.[29]

The document also offers glimpses of the security-strategic thinking prevalent in SADF leadership circles. It stated that no SADF action should elicit revenge attacks inside South West Africa, and – very importantly – "[t]he conflict must not be allowed to escalate beyond the capacity of SWATF or the SADF in general". The following sentence is also significant: "The central idea is thus to let the offensive fail without committing the RSA totally."[30] The central political directive given to the SADF was thus "to support UNITA to stop an offensive against Mavinga".[31]

In the event, Muller's first two options were rejected in favour of the third, to meet FAPLA head-on in the area where its offensive was taking form east of the Cuito. According to Fred Bridgland, the decision was taken by President PW Botha personally:

> His fear, and that of his Cabinet, was of the international outcry that would follow if regular South African troops were perceived to be fighting several hundreds of kilometres inside Angola. For historical and strategic reasons it believed to be sound and just, Pretoria felt its involvement in the Angolan conflict was fully legitimate. But an attack towards Cuito Cuanavale from the west could not have been hidden and substantial casualties would have been inevitable. South Africa was already under heavy international pressure, in the form of sanctions, disinvestment and boycotts of various kinds, over its domestic race laws and the denial of the vote to the black majority. Few countries would be disposed to understand the presence of a major South African military force in the territory of a sovereign black African state: instead, it would be used as another stick to beat a country trying desperately to re-establish international respectability.[32]

Other objections of a more operational nature were discussed in another document, dated 11 June, emanating from the office of the Chief of Staff Operations, Lieutenant General Jan van Loggerenberg. Helmoed-Römer Heitman summarises them as such:

> Taking Cuito Cuanavale would also have raised the problem of what to do with the town after taking it. UNITA would face great difficulty holding it against conventional attack from the west. Taking Cuito Cuanavale would, in fact, require exploitation westwards to defensible terrain to be worthwhile. This would require greater force levels and would also be difficult to do inconspicuously. Holding a town would also bring diplomatic problems, which the government deemed to be unacceptable. Taking it and then withdrawing, would only serve to give the Angolans propaganda ammunition. The Chief of the Army, Lieutenant General "Kat" Liebenberg, summed it up by saying that the SADF would be "like the dog that finally caught the bus".[33]

Besides, as one SADF document put it, one of the objectives of Operation Moduler (the name given to the South African intervention) was clearly political in nature: "[t]o convince the Angolan MPLA government that they should negotiate with UNITA."[34] In other words, an all-out military victory, in which the victors would trample the vanquished underfoot, was not on the cards. Seen from the international and economic perspective, these political arguments do have some merit. However, in the end, all these considerations were progressively abandoned in favour of an open escalation of the SADF's role. But this still lay in the future.

As for the objections raised in the document of 11 June, they show a fundamental inability to understand the doctrine of mobile warfare as propagated by Roland de Vries and others. The occupation of Cuito Cuanavale would have nothing to do with the taking of *territory* – after all, one of De Vries's commandments was that "ground is only held as long as tactical advantage flows from it". It was not the *possession* of a town that mattered, but the fact that FAPLA would be attacked where it was weak – in its rear. Its communication and logistic lines should be severed. In an army that was at the best of times relatively disorganised, the whole offensive could well have withered and died *without* much hard fighting. As De Vries learnt from Liddell Hart, the enemy would have been disrupted and his capacity to resist would have been reduced *before* the battle even started. That was why Cuito Cuanavale had to be taken, not for its own sake.

Why severe casualties were feared, in an operation during which the enemy would be attacked where he was weak and didn't expect it, is incomprehensible. It stood to reason that confronting FAPLA head-on would lead to more casualties.

Tactically and operationally, Cuito Cuanavale was of course not without importance. It had an airstrip that would allow enemy aircraft to be over the battlefield in a matter of minutes. It housed the FAPLA headquarters for the offensive. The supply route – the only proper road in the vicinity, known as the "old Portuguese road" – ran from Menongue through Longa to Cuito Cuanavale, and from there via the bridge over the Cuito River to Mavinga. FAPLA's command and control followed the Soviet system and was highly centralised, and all command lines – ground, artillery, air and logistics – went through Cuito Cuanavale. Taking the village would cut the FAPLA forces in two and paralyse them to a great extent. *Control* over Cuito Cuanavale and its environs – which is not necessarily the same as the permanent *occupation* of the place – would thus accord the SADF important advantages.

Operating west of the Cuito River would bypass the FAPLA concentration to the east of it, conforming to the very important military principle that an enemy has to be taken on where he is *weak*. However, by choosing the eastern option, the South Africans were forced to tackle FAPLA's main force directly. There can be no doubt that the whole operation could have been much easier and less costly if the western option had been chosen.

Another aspect to consider is what Jan Breytenbach quite correctly calls the "fatally flawed incremental nature" of the decision-making process,[35] while Jock Harris writes of "a strange, at times irritating, phenomenon which gave rise to the 'micromanagement of the battlefield' – with generals who moved very near to the battlefront and got involved in tactical decision making". He also mentions in passing some "foolish proposals by outsiders, some of which I am too embarrassed to chronicle".[36] The first of these, at UNITA's request, was the deployment of a Special Forces team to kill enemy tanks. This was an ineffective move, as FAPLA refused to let its tanks operate on their own where they would be vulnerable, but always protected them with an infantry screen, with the result that the tank-killing teams could not get within range.[37] As this was standard operating procedure in any modern army, this South African initiative seems a bit strange.

In accordance with PW Botha's decision, Geldenhuys issued a formal order that the FAPLA offensive had to be halted. UNITA would receive clandestine aid in the form of Special Forces antitank teams, a Valkiri MRL troop and three motorised infantry companies of 32 Battalion – expressly minus the unit's Ratel 90 antitank platoon. Their task would be to delay and, if possible, to halt the offensive. In the meantime, 61 Mech, together with two G-5 batteries, an additional MRL troop and air force support, had to be prepared to go into battle should they be needed.[38] Only Sierra and Foxtrot batteries, the organic artillery elements of the unit, were at that point sent into Angola. Sierra battery left its G-5s at home and converted to 120-mm mortars, while Foxtrot in reality was only an anti-aircraft troop.[39]

Heavy restrictions were placed on the South African troops involved. First of all, UNITA was for the time being not to be told of the possibility of SAAF support. Furthermore, 32 Battalion could only be utilised defensively, and 61 Mech was not to be employed in action without Geldenhuys's permission, the order to prepare for battle notwithstanding. South African soldiers could not be placed in a position where they might be taken prisoner, and SADF equipment was not to be lost to the enemy. The following instruction is significant: "Operations must, where possible, be undertaken as UNITA operations and the possibility to be tracked back to the RSA should be limited to a minimum."[40] If and when SAAF air strikes were allowed, the aircraft could not go nearer than 30 km to Cuito Cuanavale.[41]

At this stage, Operation Moduler was therefore viewed by the government and SADF leadership as similar to the aid given to UNITA during the Battle of Cangamba in 1983, operations Wallpaper and Weldmesh in 1985, and Operation Alpha Centauri in 1986 – it was seen as a limited, small-scale and clandestine operation. The world was not to know. The South African's involvement had to be "plausibly deniable".[42]

In contrast to the earlier operations, additional forces were readied in case this very limited aid proved to be inadequate. Nevertheless, the question has to be asked: in light of the political timidity displayed by the government, and the hesitant and incremental way in which the SADF became involved, was the nature and intensity of the enemy threat at all properly understood? One gets the impression that Pretoria viewed events rather casually. In fact, Jock Harris immediately asked for tanks, a request that was summarily refused.[43]

Even with South African help, though, UNITA could not stop the FAPLA juggernaut. Having stockpiled an enormous amount of supplies, the Angolans started a slow and ponderous advance on 14 August, moving at a rate of about 4 km per day. Although UNITA guerrilla attacks on FAPLA's flanks and rear areas delayed the march, the rebel movement's attempts were brushed off relatively easily. (For instance, while UNITA insurgents destroyed 10 fuel tankers in a supply convoy of 23 tankers on the road between Menongue and Cuito Cuanavale,[44] this did not halt the offensive.) By this time it was clear that FAPLA's advance was spearheaded by four brigades, with another four being kept in reserve east of the Cuito or at Tumpo. By the middle of August, the available elements of 32 Battalion were fully deployed on the southern banks of the Lomba River. UNITA placed three "regular" and four "semi-regular" battalions there.[45] The drums of war would soon begin to beat.

The night of 14 August saw the key meeting at 32 Battalion's forward headquarters near Mavinga, involving colonels Jock Harris (OC 32 Battalion), Fred Oelschig (SADF chief liaison officer with UNITA) and Piet Muller (OC Sector 20, and at this stage in command of the whole operation). This was to be a "long and traumatic night with a lot of heavy arguing"[46] as confirmed by Piet Muller, who describes the meeting as "not as balanced as I would have liked it". They "bumped heads". Muller was impatient, seeing the overwhelming FAPLA force marching inexorably southwards, with UNITA unable to effect more than pinprick attacks. UNITA should do more, he insisted. Oelschig, on the other hand, defended the rebel movement. They were doing all they could, he argued. After several hours of heated debate, the three came to a consensus: some of the SADF reinforcements that were being readied (32 Battalion's Ratel 90 troop, and two artillery batteries, G-5s and 120-mm mortars) would have to be sent in. Muller flew back to his headquarters in Rundu and telephoned Kat Liebenberg in Pretoria to ask him to release the forces.[47]

Liebenberg and Van Loggerenberg flew to Rundu to review the situation, and, after being briefed by Muller, they consented: the requested reinforcements could go in. In addition, the deployment of 61 Mech to the front could proceed, but, as the SADF staff officer chronicling the operation put it, "only on the basis of a last resort in a final decisive battle to destroy the enemy forces in a carefully pre-selected 'killing ground' ".[48] The big guns were flown to Mavinga, while 61 Mech, under the command of Commandant (later Brigadier General) Kobus "Bok" Smit prepared to move to the front at a moment's notice.[49]

This was another step in the slow, incremental involvement of ever more SADF forces in the campaign. The extent of the SADF's hesitancy is shown by a sentence in Army Headquarters' orders to mobilise the artillery, that "the safety of RSA personnel is a higher priority than the success in operations".[50]

Typical of the hesitant South African reaction was the decision not to release the army's other heavy mechanised unit, 4 SA Infantry. It is true that, unlike 61 Mech, 4 SA Infantry was far away at its home base in Middelburg, eastern Transvaal. But, according to its commander, Commandant Leon Marais, the battalion group was already ready for battle in March and could have started the move to Angola at short notice. (In the event, the unit was called in only in October.)[51]

During the next few days, FAPLA continued its slow advance. Harris, as SADF field commander on the scene, desperately had to juggle his pitifully small force in order to slow down the enemy, and, at the same time, prevent any of his men from becoming casualties or falling into enemy hands. After all, he had been expressly forbidden to let that happen. The Valkiri MRLs brought down devastating fire on the enemy and caused a considerable amount of blood to flow, but it was not enough. (The Valkiri MRLs were first used on 19 August.[52] As UNITA did not have such weapons, the Angolans must have realised then that South Africa was involved, which begs the question of how the operation could still have been thought of as clandestine!)

On 28 August, Geldenhuys, Liebenberg and the Chief of the Air Force, Lieutenant General Denis Earp, visited Rundu. There they saw that even the artillery reinforcements would not be enough, and finally decided to lift all restrictions on the offensive use of 61 Mech (minus its tank squadron) and the SAAF. In addition, two motorised infantry companies of 101 Battalion with Casspirs would join the troops already at the front. This in turn required a new formation to coordinate the campaign. This was to be 20 SA Brigade, which was commanded by Colonel Deon Ferreira, a veteran with vast experience and one of the ablest senior officers in the army.[53] He replaced Harris after a row between Harris and SWATF commander Major General Willie Meyer about the tactics to be followed.[54] Ferreira would answer to Colonel Piet Muller as OC Sector 20, who in turn would be responsible to Meyer.[55] Operational command was placed in the hands of Liebenberg, as Chief of the Army.[56]

The decision to release the artillery, 61 Mech and the SAAF was of cardinal importance. It was yet another step in the incremental escalation of the South African involvement in the Angolan civil war, but it also had other implications. From the start, the idea had been to keep everything under wraps, but there simply was no way in which an entire mechanised brigade – 61 Mech alone had about a thousand men and a convoy of 120 to 130 vehicles – with SAAF air support could engage in fierce battles with the Angolan army without the world's finding out about it. Yet, apparently the Botha government still thought it possible.

The point is that the original reasons for rejecting Muller's proposals for a western advance were no longer valid. If the political leadership indeed thought that the operation could still be kept secret – as it seems – they were being exceedingly naive. Towards the end of July, even before 32 Battalion entered Angola in force, the Angolan government told the world press about the SADF's aid to UNITA.[57] In the end, Geldenhuys publicly acknowledged the SADF's role only on 11 November, long after it had become an open secret.[58] The fact is that the strategic situation changed drastically on the day 61 Mech, the G-5 battery and the SAAF were let off the leash.

At that point Muller's original proposals should have been re-evaluated. The plan to send in a sizeable force west of the Cuito and take Cuito Cuanavale from that direction was a viable option. It would have fulfilled the SADF's own mechanised doctrine to a tee. In fact, Cuban air force Brigadier General Rafael del Pino also let it be known "that cutting the Menongue–Cuito Cuanavale supply road was the best and most logical way of stopping the offensive". According to Fred Bridgland, his message was that "[i]t would be a tactical error for the South Africans and UNITA to concentrate their forces on Cuito Cuanavale".[59] It made sense, since the FAPLA brigades had a voracious appetite for supplies; each day, 8 to 10 big Ilyushin-76 cargo aircraft landed at Menongue, and every six days, a huge convoy of 400 vehicles, escorted by two brigades, left Menongue for Cuito Cuanavale.[60]

However, in the naive expectation that a mechanised brigade with artillery and air support could be kept out of sight, the decision was taken to meet the FAPLA offensive head-on – exactly the sort of clash that Roland De Vries (and Liddell Hart) warned against. Apparently De Vries was not read (or understood) in the Presidency or Defence/Army Headquarters. From June to August 1987, the SADF stood at a fork in the road. Its final decision was the first step towards the stalemate of March/April 1988 and Fidel Castro's subsequent propaganda victory.

A final thought on the build-up to Moduler: when 61 Mech, the army's most experienced and potent conventional warfare unit, was released, it crossed over into Angola without the Olifant tanks of E Squadron. It will be remembered that the Olifants had been attached to 61 Mech following Operation Askari, when it was found that the army's Ratel 90s were not really a match for the Angolans' T-54/55 tanks. However, after a while, the tanks were mothballed at 61 Mech's Omuthiya base and the crews returned to the School of Armour in Bloemfontein because no further large-scale cross-border operations took place. Inexplicably, no attempt was made to reconstitute E Squadron, despite the obvious presence of tanks with the FAPLA force.

This, too, was another example of the amateurish and piecemeal way in which the SADF was released into what would become its most important campaign of the entire Border War. Within a few days, the absence of the tanks would be sorely felt.

The Lomba battles

The decision to confront FAPLA east of the Cuito River led to the series of battles at the Lomba River in September/October 1987. In order to understand this confusing jumble properly, the opposing forces' order of battle has

Battles on the Lomba River

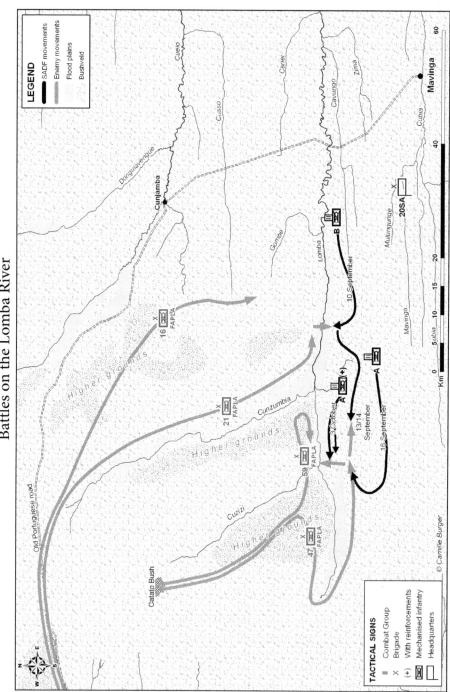

to be outlined. On the one hand, FAPLA had eight brigades of about 1 500 men each, of which two were kept west of the Cuito to safeguard the rear areas and escort supply convoys between Menongue and Cuito Cuanavale. One brigade garrisoned Cuito Cuanavale itself, and one safeguarded the area just east of the river at Tumpo.

Participating in the advance on Mavinga were 16, 21, 47 and 59 Brigades. This meant a total of about 6 000 men and 80 tanks, plus artillery and ample air support from MiG-23s, MiG-21s and Su-22s, protected by numerous SA-6, SA-7, SA-8, SA-9, SA-13 and SA-16 missile batteries – a very powerful force indeed.[61] A small Cuban garrison was stationed in Cuito Cuanavale, but did not participate in the offensive.[62]

The South African force consisted of 61 Mech, a part of 32 Battalion, two companies of 101 Battalion, a G-5 battery, a Valkiri MRL battery and a 120-mm mortar battery – two-and-a-half battalions and an artillery regiment, or perhaps 1 500 men in total. These units were mixed up and then divided into three combat groups:

- Combat Group Alpha (Commandant Kobus Smit), with a mechanised and a motorised infantry company, plus an armoured car squadron, an 81-mm mortar platoon and an anti-aircraft troop;
- Combat Group Bravo (Commandant Robbie Hartslief),[63] with three motorised infantry companies, a Ratel antitank squadron and an 81-mm mortar platoon;
- Combat Group Charlie (Major Dawid Lotter), with a single mechanised infantry company, an antitank platoon and an 81-mm mortar platoon;
- These forces were supported by 20 Artillery Regiment with Quebec Battery (G-5), Papa Battery (MRL) and Sierra Battery (120-mm mortars). These were each protected by an infantry platoon and anti-aircraft weapons.[64]

Of course, 32 Battalion was already in Angola, while 61 Mech's convoy of 126 vehicles arrived on 7 September at its assembly point 25 km southeast of Mavinga.[65] On that same day, Geldenhuys issued a set of guidelines and restrictions, reiterating that "[s]afety of own forces and equipment is of cardinal importance and blatant risks may not be taken". It was again stated that "operations are to be undertaken as UNITA operations and possible tracing to RSA kept to the minimum".[66] It was as if the leadership had still not realised that its troops in Angola were about to engage in a real and bloody shooting match with the enemy.

In addition, the air force transferred 3 Canberra and 4 Buccaneer bombers, 12 Mirage F1AZ fighter-bombers and 8 Mirage F1CZ interceptor fighters to Rundu and Grootfontein air force bases.[67] In addition, 6 Mirage IIICZ interceptors were kept in readiness in South Africa,[68] but in the end these obsolete aircraft were – wisely – not employed.

There were a few thousand UNITA fighters, from its so-called conventional and semi-conventional battalions, but they did not mean much in military terms. As Commandant Johan Lehman, one of the SADF liaison officers with UNITA, bluntly put it: "They were okay, but they couldn't hold. They were fine for a limited type of operations, but certainly nothing conventional."[69] Many SADF officers had a low opinion of UNITA's abilities.[70] Throughout the entire campaign, UNITA played a secondary role, Jonas Savimbi's considerable ego notwithstanding.

As already mentioned, the four FAPLA brigades advanced southeastwards from Cuito Cuanavale, with the village of Mavinga as their immediate operational objective. But, in order to get there, they had to cross the Lomba River, a broad eastward-flowing river up to four to five kilometres across in places. More like a flood plain than a river, the Lomba is not easy to cross. The four brigades moved in groups of two, supporting each other – 16 and 21 to the east, and 47 and 59 to the west.[71]

After a slow start, the Angolans suddenly charged forward, and in a short space of time reached the Lomba on 9 September, looking for places to cross. The western source of the Lomba was rounded by 47 Brigade, which became the first of the four formations to reach a position south of the river. SAAF Mirages, Buccaneers and Canberras started hammering them from the air, while the army artillery also hit them.

Having barely taken over command of 20 SA Brigade, Ferreira had to hit the ground running, for he faced a potentially grave situation. Fortunately, he had excellent information about the enemy's movements, as several Reconnaissance Regiment teams were swarming over the area and the SADF's superb radio interception service worked full time. UNITA also provided some information, but the South Africans' experience throughout the war was that this was very unreliable and best disregarded or treated with great circumspection.

One of the SADF's sources of information was eliminated on 3 September when an SAAF Bosbok light aircraft was shot down by an Angolan SA-8 missile, killing the young pilot, Lieutenant Richard Glynn, as well as the commander of 20 Artillery Regiment, Commandant Johan du Randt. SADF radio intercepts had indicated the presence of a "secret weapon" with the advancing Angolans, but the South Africans did not know what it was.[72] The discovery that the Angolans had this very sophisticated anti-aircraft system came as a huge shock. It made close air support for the South Africans perilous, and the vulnerable Canberra bombers were immediately withdrawn. As a matter of fact, all SAAF bombing was temporarily suspended until it was realised that the so-called toss bombing method they employed was safe enough. This method, used by the British during the Falklands War, meant that the bombers would approach very low over the target, pull up sharply at a predetermined point, release their bombs, and get out right down low. The bombs were thus "tossed" through the air in an arc.

Ferreira's tactical countermoves were self-evident. First of all, he had to prevent 16 and 21 Brigades from crossing the river, as they were closest to Mavinga. Secondly, he had to keep 47 Brigade, already south of the Lomba, from marching further eastwards and joining forces with 59 Brigade, which was still north of the river, though not far away. For the time being, his artillery would be his main weapon, and he stationed it in a position that would cover all four enemy brigades. The 120-mm mortar battery was stationed more to the east, where it could cover the route to Mavinga.

The artillery had been in action for some time and had hurt the enemy considerably, especially making life very difficult for 47 Brigade in its eastward advance south of the river. But the first major clash came on 10 September. The previous day, Robbie Hartslief, commander of Combat Group Bravo, learnt from UNITA that 21 Brigade was crossing the Lomba and had established a bridgehead on the southern shore. This was potentially serious, because the MRL battery was way out to the west, towards the source of the Lomba, where 47 Brigade was advancing. There was only about 24 hours available to withdraw the rocket launchers eastwards and prevent the battery from being cut off.

Luckily for the South Africans, UNITA had previously destroyed the bridge at the place where 21 Brigade was assembling, so crossing the wide river was not a simple task for the Angolans. Hartslief immediately despatched a squadron of Ratel 90s and a company from 101 Battalion to the scene; the Ratels promptly shot out an enemy BTR-60, but the bridgehead stayed in place. Of course, this was dangerous; when Hartslief reported to Ferreira, the latter's reaction was short and to the point: "Take them out!" This was made easier by the arrival of the G-5s from Mavinga. The second company from 101 Battalion was also on the move.

At first light the next morning, Hartslief attacked with his two infantry companies and the Ratel squadron. FAPLA troops were already across the river in battalion strength, and they launched dozens of RPG-7 rockets at the South African Casspirs. However, the two forces were so close that the rockets could not travel the required 15 m to arm themselves, and bounced harmlessly off the Casspirs' armour. The Angolan conscripts were caught unawares by the ferocity of the attack, and within a short time they broke and fled across the flood plain, presenting excellent targets for the SADF troops. Later, 103 rotting bodies were counted at the site.

The South Africans were now subjected to heavy artillery fire from the northern side of the river, 21 Brigade having guessed correctly what was going on. At the same time, three enemy tanks were observed crossing a bridge built by FAPLA sappers. The South African artillery responded, and the morning air rumbled with the roar of the guns and booming explosions of the shells. South African shells burst in the air above the Angolan infantry, causing tremendous carnage.

Major Hannes Nortmann was near the bridge with a squadron of Ratels, some of which were equipped with the experimental ZT3 antitank missile system – so new that it was not yet operational. With the FAPLA tanks approaching, this was perhaps a good moment for an experiment. The Ratel 90s took a few pot shots, but the tanks were too far off and the Ratels' 90-mm guns lacked penetrating power. The first ZT3 missile destroyed a BRDM armoured car and a truck. To Nortmann's surprise, he saw that the enemy force on the south side of the river had now increased to five tanks, and he let fly again with the missiles. Some malfunctioned, but three tanks were taken out. The other two retreated to the north bank. On the South African side, the only casualties were two wounded. Some MiGs bombarded the area furiously, but the South Africans just looked on. The enemy pilots obviously had no idea of what was happening on the ground and completely missed the South Africans. This would become a pattern throughout the campaign.

By nightfall, the situation was completely stabilised. The South African artillery continued to punish any Angolans unfortunate enough to be within range, but the first FAPLA attempt to break through had been beaten off through superior weaponry, training and tactics. The local FAPLA commander complained that the battalion that had crossed the river had been "annihilated", and reported that only two of his ten tanks remained serviceable.[73]

The next step had to be an attack on 47 Brigade, whose eastward advance had been brought to a standstill by harassing South African artillery fire. Intelligence indicated that this formation had pushed two battalions and three PT-76 amphibious light tanks out forward, presumably in an attempt to link up with 59 Brigade. Another battalion and six tanks were halfway between the brigade headquarters and the forward elements, making them well placed to intervene.

On 13 September, Hartslief decided to attack the two forward enemy battalions in a westward direction with two infantry companies in Casspirs (101 Battalion), eight Ratel 90s and four Ratel ZT3s, plus artillery support. The terrain was unlike anything the South Africans had ever encountered. Captain Danie Crowther reminisced about this battle:

> The bush is dense. It's extremely dense. You . . . can't see more than 20m in that bush, which means that your main weapons, your anti-tank weapons, cannot be applied. But terrain is neutral, because it's the same for the other forces as well. What FAPLA did in that situation was these guys were very good at digging, and they dug themselves in. We didn't like that very much. We preferred mobile warfare, and we would rather move to a point where we attack and be able to move out quickly and never get dug in . . . Right, but these guys dug in and 47th was well dug in. Everything was under ground. Good overhead cover, and there they were sitting. So it's a tough nut to crack.[74]

After having trouble at first in locating the enemy, Hartslief ordered the artillery to soften them up, and then charged. UNITA fighters were available as a back-up. Almost immediately a large group of FAPLA men was pinned down against the Lomba. The infantry in the Casspirs let rip with machine-gun fire, while the Ratels spewed anti-personnel grapeshot. Within a short time, 200 Angolans lay dead or dying.

But then Hartslief got a nasty surprise. UNITA's faulty intelligence had led him to expect armoured cars only, but now several enemy tanks raced forward aggressively. The inadequate South African 90-mm guns had great trouble, frequently needing six to eight shots before finding the weak spot just below the tank turret. Besides, the T-54/55s had stabilised guns, so they could fire on the move, whereas the Ratels had to stop and take aim each time before they could shoot. Nevertheless, five enemy tanks were shot out. Four Ratels got stuck, but, despite the confusion, three were recovered. The seven occupants of the fourth, including the highly respected Captain Mac McCallum, were killed by an enemy tank.

Hartslief himself was in the thick of it. A few days later, in an interview, he related how nerve-wracking the fighting was:

> In the meantime, the 2IC, Major [Hannes] Nortmann reported that he saw a tank moving in the direction of the [combat group] headquarters. This tank fired on the vehicle of the commander of the liaison team [with UNITA], Commandant [Bert] Sachse, and Sachse was wounded. The tank fired a shot just to the right of my Ratel, and also fired a shot just behind the ambulance. At that stage I aimed my [90-mm] gun at the tank, which was coming directly at us. At a certain moment the tank swerved to the left and showed its flank at us. I had problems aiming my gun at the tank, as the gunner could not see it due to the tank's camouflage and low profile in the thick brush. I ordered the gunner to fire a shot to blind the tank and get dust between us and him. Then the gunner reported that he could see the tank and fired another two shots, one over and one in front of the tank. The fourth shot was a bull's eye, and we fired another six – altogether seven – bull's eyes on the tank, of which two penetrated the turret. The tank started burning and the crew jumped out, after which we mowed them down.[75]

A new tactic developed spontaneously during this battle, as the Ratel crews discovered that their vehicles could turn more sharply than the enemy tanks. So, whenever they came up against a T-54/55, they turned to get past the tank's flank to reach its vulnerable rear. Obviously, the tank crew would also turn as sharply as they could to prevent this from happening, and so a kind of a "dance of death" (Jan Breytenbach's words)[76] developed, until the Ratels would inevitably get behind the tank and destroy it from there.

Meanwhile, the driver of one of the stuck Ratels became completely frantic with fear and blocked the airwaves with his yelling. After a few minutes, Hannes Nortmann couldn't stand the shouting any more, so he jumped out and ran on foot, armed with only a R-5 rifle and followed by a recovery vehicle, until he spotted the Ratel, which had already been shot out. He looked inside, and what he saw "really didn't look good". He started running back, still followed by the recovery vehicle and passed another Ratel:

> As I got to the Ratel the enemy started to shout at me. I went past the Ratel at the back and got a glimpse of FAPLA boots under the door. I immediately brought my rifle up, firing on automatic, and klapped the guy. As I came around the other side I saw another FAPLA soldier, busy stealing sleeping bags, food etc. from the Ratel, and I shot him too. Actually it was quite difficult to bring him down, because as he was running away, my bullets kept hitting into the tins of food on his back.[77]

At this point, the SADF reserve, in the form of Dawid Lotter's Combat Group Charlie (actually no more than a combat team, equivalent to a beefed-up company) was called in, which made things a bit easier. But the enemy proved to be much stronger than expected, and, after several hours of confused fighting, Hartslief heard that another six enemy tanks were on their way to the battlefield. He decided to call it a day and withdraw. Besides, the 101 Battalion infantry had started fleeing as they had been badly shocked by the tank attacks. They would need to regroup before they would be ready for another battle. Clearly, the extreme violence and chaos of a conventional battle was somewhat different from the counterinsurgency skirmishes against SWAPO to which they were accustomed. (A few weeks afterwards, the SADF acknowledged that

47 members of this unit had been discharged because they objected to being used as "UNITA mercenaries".[78] Probably, this "protest" had something to do with the unit's unpleasant experience on the battlefield.)

Just before midnight on 13 September, Lotter's small force bumped into eight enemy tanks, at a distance of no more than 100 m, and had to withdraw promptly. They were covered by four Ratel 90s led by Lieutenant Johannes Kooij, who personally destroyed two of the enemy behemoths.

Given the ferocity of the fighting, the South African losses were astoundingly light – just seven killed and seven wounded. One Ratel and two Casspirs were lost against five enemy tanks destroyed. Remember that the defending FAPLA force was two or three times the size of the attackers. The SADF estimated some 200 to 300 killed on the other side.[79] More importantly, Ferreira succeeded in his tactical objective: 47 Brigade abandoned all attempts to link up with 59 Brigade.

But 47 Brigade was still south of the Lomba, and while it was there it remained a threat. This time, Ferreira gave the job to Kobus Smit's Combat Group Alpha, while Hartslief was ordered to watch 16 and 21 Brigades to the east. This would be the first time that Alpha, which was based on 61 Mech, would see action. This was remarkable, as General Liebenberg had specifically ordered on 14 September (just two days before the intended attack) that he would only consider "the possible offensive utilisation of 61 (Combat Group A) after proper confirmation of defined objective. After confirmation of defined objective C Army will seek permission for offensive utilisation of air weapon."[80] Even at this late stage, the generals were micromanaging the war from Pretoria, apparently to keep the supposed smoke screen of secrecy in place.

Smit decided on a battle plan truly worthy of Roland de Vries's admonishments: he decided to attack the Angolans from an unexpected direction. He would march past their southern flank and then double back to take them in their rear from the west. The attack was scheduled for 16 September.

But the bush was denser than anything the South Africans had ever seen – one could see no more than 10 to 15 m in any direction. First contact was made only towards midday, instead of early in the morning as expected. Besides, the combat group's navigation was understandably imperfect, with the result that the enemy had time to organise countermeasures. As far as Smit could tell, by late afternoon the only thing his force had knocked out was one mortar pit, and the combat group was floundering about. With one dead and three wounded (one of whom was the armoured car squadron commander, Major PJ Cloete), Smit asked for, and received, permission to break off the attack. After all, 47 Brigade was not going anywhere. Ferreira decided to call off the attack altogether.

The next two weeks were characterised by a stalemate. Incredibly, on 19 September 21 Brigade made another attempt to cross the Lomba at the same place where the first had failed crossing took place on 10 September, making a mockery of all established military principles. Through the interception of FAPLA radio messages, the South Africans knew the enemy was coming and pulled their forces back south of the crossing point in time to evade the inevitable Angolan artillery bombardment. Once again, the G-5s and Valkiri MRLs belched fire and mowed down scores of oncoming enemy soldiers. FAPLA had to call off its attempt. Radio intercepts revealed that 21 Brigade had been ordered to hand over its supplies to 59 Brigade, while 21 Brigade complained that it had no artillery left and that its infantry were dying "like ducks". (The Russian advisors with the brigade tried to leave abruptly by chopper, but were caught by a Valkiri rocket ripple, after which the chopper's radio fell silent.)[81] By this time, according to SADF estimates, FAPLA had lost 844 men, with a further 823 wounded and 22 taken prisoner. Altogether, 13 tanks and 84 other vehicles had been shot out.[82]

The FAPLA objective probably still was to link 47 and 59 Brigade, and Ferreira accordingly decided to make the latter a priority in terms of target acquisition by both the artillery and the SAAF. The continual hammering over the next few days meant that, by the end of the month, 59 Brigade, as well as 21 and 47 Brigades, were judged to be at only 30 to 33% of their original strength. The failure of another attempt by 47 Brigade and 59 Brigade to link up ensured that, for the time being at least, a resumption of the enemy offensive was impossible. But as long as 47 Brigade remained south of the Lomba, it remained a threat. And so Ferreira took the decision to remove this danger once and for all.

The final blow

The idea was to attack 47 Brigade on 5 October. But, as Kobus Smit was readying his forces, Ferreira received intelligence that the enemy was leaving his dug-in positions and moving towards the Lomba, while 59 Brigade was converging from the north of the river. It was clear that 47 Brigade was planning to break out, and so the SADF attack was hastily brought forward to 3 October.[83]

Ferreira knew the enemy's plans. Intercepted radio messages revealed that 47 Brigade's commander had been ordered to abandon the march on Mavinga and return to the northern bank of the river. The officer at first refused, arguing that the battle was not yet lost. Only when he was threatened with a court martial did he comply and start moving his troops to the river.

This presented a unique opportunity. Not only would 47 Brigade be more vulnerable on the move, but the area it would be moving through was less densely wooded than the position from which the SADF had already twice failed to dislodge the Angolans. Ferreira seized the chance to attack FAPLA in a carefully chosen "killing ground", as he signalled to his combat groups.[84]

Ferreira had assembled a relatively strong force for the battle. He placed the small Combat Group Charlie under Smit's command, so that the Commandant now led the whole of 61 Mech – a formidable unit in its own right – plus a motorised company of 32 Battalion. The entire brigade artillery regiment also stood by. In addition, UNITA would provide several units with impressive names – the 3rd and 5th Regular Battalion, the 13th Semi-Regular Battalion and the 275th Penetration Group – but it was an open question whether their fighting power matched their grand descriptions.

Under the guidance of Major Pierre Franken, the forward artillery observer, the SADF G-5s had already pounded the concentration of FAPLA vehicles at the chosen crossing point on 2 October. At daybreak the next day, the South Africans moved out for the attack, advancing in two spearheads. The first consisted of the Ratel 90s beside the river bank, at the edge of the tree line, with a mechanised infantry company in Ratel 20s close behind, while the motorised infantry company brought up the rear to mop up. The second spearhead was Combat Group Charlie's mechanised infantry company as flank and reserve force. They were all guided by UNITA scouts.

First contact took place at 10h17 in the morning. FAPLA, on the move towards the river, was caught completely unawares. Many of the Angolans panicked and tried to cross the river in an undisciplined mass. The Ratel 90s charged them, and once again the Lomba River turned red with the blood of scores of dying men. But then the survivors recovered from the initial shock and started to fight back, causing several anxious moments for Smit. As usual, the Ratel 90s had problems in taking out the Angolan T-54/55s, so their tactics were to encircle single tanks with a Ratel troop (four vehicles) and keep on shooting until the tank was dead. The feared Soviet 23-mm anti-aircraft guns harassed the South Africans until UNITA infantry killed the crews.

The fighting was so intense that by 12h00 the South Africans started running out of ammunition. The Ratels' recoil systems were giving trouble, so Smit pulled back about a kilometre to replenish and regroup. By 14h00 he attacked again, having reinforced his Ratel 90s with one of the troops of the antitank platoon and a mechanised infantry platoon. To prevent 59 Brigade, located north of the river, from coming to the aid of their brothers in arms, the SAAF hit that formation hard with a deluge of bombs. The Angolan air force also tried to support its friends on the ground, but had no success – the SADF did not lose a single soldier or vehicle because of their air attacks.

Intelligence officer Captain Herman Mulder was in the thick of things:

> I have never experienced anything like it. I said goodbye to my life at least six times that day. All the time there was bombing and bombing and bombing. The noise was beyond belief. It was driving me mad. All the time I was thinking: "I just want to get out of this fucking vehicle." . . . I was afraid in the biggest sense you can think of. You know all the time that the next shell might be for you.[85]

Shortly after the attack resumed, elements of the enemy once again broke and tried to escape across the river. Once again, the South African guns killed the panic-stricken FAPLA soldiers in great numbers. One Ratel 90 was hit by an enemy tank, killing its commander, Second Lieutenant Adrian Hind. Smit then had to break off contact a second time to regroup and replenish, while the South African artillery kept throwing its deadly shells at the enemy. Sensing that victory was near, Smit sent in his reserve for a final push, and by 17h00 the Angolans finally threw in the towel. The South African 90-mm guns boomed and the air echoed with the deadly stutter of 20-mm guns, while Valkiri rockets exploded in the air above the fleeing enemy, killing hundreds. The G-5s picked off individual vehicles, adding to the incredible carnage. FAPLA's 47 Brigade was basically wiped out, with more than 600 men killed and dozens of tanks and armoured vehicles taken out. The SADF losses, on the other hand, were incredibly light; only one soldier, Adrian Hind, was killed and one Ratel destroyed.

Interestingly, the South African accounts of the battle are largely supported by that of a Soviet officer serving as an advisor with FAPLA. A few days after the battle, Lieutenant Colonel Igor Anatolevich Zhdarkin reconstructed the day's fighting according to what he had heard from Soviet participants. He confirms that the South Africans attacked three times:

> The brigade suffered three attacks from the South African regular forces. The flight which began after the second attack, turned into panic with the launching of the third.

> There were many reasons for this: the running out of ammunition, as well as the cowardliness of the officers, the absence of precise instructions to the troops engaged, their terror of facing the South Africans and, finally, the fact that on the bank where the brigade stood, across the river Lomba, there was a passage (bridge for crossing). Everybody quickly found out about it and, if it had not existed, perhaps no one would have tried to flee.[86]

Zhdarkin quotes Soviet officers with operational experience, one of whom said that "in Afghanistan, we never experienced such horrors as here". The officer continued: "When the South African artillery began to fire, I felt particularly terrified. However, then came the South African air force and we had very little room on the ground. But the most horrible was when the Angolans turned to flight and began to throw away their equipment . . ." Zhdarkin was also told:

There was terrible panic and confusion all around. The South Africans were shooting all over the place, not sparing ammunition. No one clearly knew whither to run and what to do. The one thing which everyone wanted was to get across to the other bank as quickly as possible. The so-called "commission" for organising the crossing was one of the first to escape.[87]

There was an element of tragicomedy when the SADF and UNITA almost came to blows over a highly sophisticated SA-8 anti-aircraft missile system that was discovered among the equipment abandoned by FAPLA on the battlefield – the first time this system had fallen into Western hands. While the South Africans were anxious to take it apart and study it, UNITA was interested in the prestige of possessing the SA-8 and perhaps sharing its secrets with the Americans. But the SADF stood firm, refusing to surrender the unit to UNITA; the SA-8 was transported to Mavinga and flown out aboard a heavily overloaded C-160 freighter.[88]

On 5 October, the surviving FAPLA forces were ordered to withdraw northwards. The attempt to cross the Lomba, to capture Mavinga and to knock UNITA out of the war had failed dismally. The offensive was over. FAPLA had lost a total of 61 tanks, 53 BTR-60 armoured personnel carriers, 7 BMP-1 infantry fighting vehicles, 23 BRDM-2 reconnaissance patrol vehicles and 20 BM-21 rocket launchers, together with 1 059 men killed and 2 118 wounded. South African casualties totalled just 17 killed and 41 wounded, while three Ratels, two Casspirs, one Bosbok spotter plane (shot down) and Seeker remotely piloted aircraft were lost.[89]

The first phase of Operation Moduler had ended in a decisive victory for South Africa.

13

THE SADF'S PROBLEMATIC CHOICES

For FAPLA, the battle of 3 October 1987 was a painful kick in the teeth. The South Africans had all but destroyed one of its four brigades and badly mauled two more. Within a few days, the Angolans were streaming northwards, away from the SADF. On their side, the South Africans had ample reason to be satisfied. They had claimed victory despite a woefully inadequate force – not even a full brigade – and inadequate weapons (the Ratel 90s versus T-54/55s). With obvious pride, General Jannie Geldenhuys writes:

> From this point there was only one consideration for me: We had already fulfilled our mission. We had hit the enemy offensive totally for a six. However, we could not withdraw immediately. In the short term we had to see to it that the new situation we had created would not be undone. We had to consolidate our gains and prevent the enemy from regrouping and relaunching his offensive.
>
> We could, however, not indefinitely maintain these advantages ourselves. In the longer term we had to leave the area in a way that, if in the future another "yearly" offensive took place, UNITA would be able to beat it off without our help. That is what we wanted to achieve. Nothing more, and nothing less.[1]

The chance to contemplate the future came even before the decisive battle of 3 October. While still planning for that event, Deon Ferreira was called to Mavinga on 29 September to meet a group of top generals and politicians, including President PW Botha, Defence Minister Magnus Malan and his deputy, Wynand Breytenbach.[2]

The presence of the politicians, especially the president, suited the military. Their minds were already busy with the follow-up to the successful defence – a counter offensive. That, of course, fell way outside the parameters set by the government, and this prospect offered a very good chance of turning Botha's head. The party arrived by helicopter, under cover of darkness, late on the evening of 28 September, and the next day Ferreira and various other officers briefed the visitors in considerable detail about what was going on.

Botha took a major decision at the meeting. Perhaps it would be best to tell the story in the words of Major W Dorning, an SADF staff officer tasked to chronicle Operation Moduler:

> In the event, State President Botha emerged from his briefings at 20 Brigade HQ on 29 September impressed enough by what he had seen and heard to give his personal approval for the planning of a more offensive phase of Op Moduler, the aim of which should be the total destruction of the enemy Brigades deployed east of the Cuito River before the onset of the rainy season. The State President in fact made it quite clear that the aim of the new phase of Op Moduler should be to inflict such a crushing blow to the enemy's offensive forces that no offensive would be possible the following year. For this purpose, additional funds would be made available for Op Moduler.
>
> It was of course obvious to CSADF [Chief of the SADF] and his colleagues that if the SADF was to embark on a new, more offensive phase of Op Moduler, additional forces – and especially tanks – would have to be made available to Op Moduler's commanders. The State President, for his part, assured CSADF before departing 20 Brigade HQ on the evening of 29 September that authorisation would be given for the deployment of whatever additional forces CSADF might deem necessary to achieve Op Moduler's new objectives.[3]

The significance of Botha's decision can hardly be overstated. It meant that the political restrictions that had frustrated the South African field officers so much during the first phase of the operation would henceforth be removed. This gives rise to a few questions. Firstly, if the restrictions could now be abandoned so easily, why were they necessary in the first place? After all, nothing had changed in the political-strategic situation since the restrictions were first put in place.

Secondly, did the South African political and military leadership still think that the operation could remain a secret? Geldenhuys waited until 11 November before acknowledging in public that the SADF was involved in a major campaign inside Angola. Thirdly, Botha's very helpful attitude suggests that it was not so much the government that kept the soldiers on a tight leash, but the generals in Pretoria and perhaps Windhoek.

Botha's decision changed the nature of the operation fundamentally. He now decreed that the SADF could undertake a counteroffensive with the purpose of hitting FAPLA so hard that it would not be able to undertake another offensive before the end of 1988. He also authorised the utilisation of whatever forces Geldenhuys deemed necessary. It was just short of a carte blanche, but the SADF commanders never really utilised this freedom of action. We will return to this in due course. For the moment, the question was how Botha's instruction should be translated into operational terms.

Thus, another debate developed around the question of whether a counteroffensive should best be conducted west of the Cuito River, to get into FAPLA's rear areas, or east of it, to drive the FAPLA forces back over the river.

Even before Botha's visit, a document emanating from Kat Liebenberg's office set out the army's thinking. One option mentioned was to assemble a brigade and to advance west of the Cuito River, to attack Cuito Cuanavale from that direction and to have UNITA occupy it until the FAPLA brigades still east of the river could be destroyed. However, according to the document, such an operation would take five to six weeks to organise. Another variant of this option would be not to take Cuito Cuanavale, but merely to threaten it. However, the preferred option was to take the enemy on where he was – east of the river.[4]

In a memorandum to Geldenhuys, Liebenberg outlined that he wanted to force a military decision before 15 December. (This date was important because it marked the end of the service period for the National Servicemen – the conscripts.) An operation in three phases was foreseen, of which the first, stopping the FAPLA offensive, was already completed. The second phase would involve a counteroffensive, while phase three was described as "the launch of an offensive to destroy FAPLA forces east of the Cuito River . . .". Additional forces, in the form of 4 South African Infantry Battalion Group (4 SAI – a mechanised unit similar to 61 Mech) plus a tank squadron and another G-5 battery might be needed for this phase. The document continued: "FAPLA forces east of the Cuito River are pursued till the Cuito River is reached. Then Cuito Cuanavale is placed under artillery fire for a while from all possible sources to cause maximum damage."[5]

Liebenberg also considered attacking Cuito Cuanavale from the west, but he assumed that this would require at least a brigade, the assembly of which would take a minimum of six weeks. Consequently, he decided that the attack on, and occupation of, Cuito Cuanavale should be seen as separate operations. Besides, such an operation would require air strikes against Cuito Cuanavale, Menongue and even Lubango as a first step, which was seen as risky at that stage. The brigade advancing west of the Cuito towards Cuito Cuanavale would then also be vulnerable to enemy air attacks.[6]

Geldenhuys approved Liebenberg's approach, and a few days later Liebenberg issued his formal operational instruction.[7] Three weeks later, a possible fourth phase was added: the capture of Cuito Cuanavale should it prove necessary or convenient. However, the initial three phases had to be completed first.[8] (As far as could be ascertained, there is no mention in any operational instruction hereafter about the possible taking of Cuito Cuanavale from the east, which indicates that it was never seriously entertained.)

At the beginning of October, Roland de Vries was called to Liebenberg's office from the Army Battle School at Lohatlha and informed that he was to leave for Rundu and the Angolan front:

> General Liebenberg then told me that he was seriously contemplating attacking Cuito Cuanavale from the west of the river. This implied the crossing of the Longa River north of Rundu by the main assault force. It also meant that the Cuito River needed to be crossed from east to west by some of the mechanised forces already deployed on the front. In such an instance, he said, I was the designated commander for the main assault force from the West. The enemy brigades deployed to the

east of the Cuito would be fixed by a force under command of Colonel Deon Ferreira . . .

The general carefully explained to me that the attack on Cuito from the west was not a *fait accompli*. All the various operational options for the counteroffensive still required careful and deliberate consideration, for these various courses of action along the western and eastern approaches towards Cuito Cuanavale needed to be thoroughly appreciated. This was part of my work. General Liebenberg emphasised over and over his trepidation at losing unnecessary South African lives and expressed his disquiet at the many lives already lost thus far. Another fear he expressed was the possibility of the war in Angola escalating beyond proportion. The enemy's trump was his overwhelming air force. Main towns in SWA could, if the enemy wanted, be bombed . . .[9]

After arriving in Rundu, De Vries flew to 20 Brigade's headquarters with Brigadier Fido Smit (commander of 7 SA Division), who would now take over as operational commander of Moduler, Colonel Hennie Blaauw, Smit's chief of staff, and Colonel Jean Lausberg (who was appointed OC 20 Artillery Regiment) to talk to Deon Ferreira. It was decided that De Vries, under Smit's supervision, would work out a plan for the western offensive. In this capacity, he and Smit flew to the Cuito and Longa rivers to reconnoitre places where the South Africans could safely cross to the west. They found a ford over the Longa where soft-skinned vehicles could pass through. For tanks and Ratels, the SADF sappers would have to build a bridge.

The plan called for the SAAF to pulverise the enemy air bases of Menongue and Lubango during the opening minutes of the operation, to destroy as many aircraft as possible on the ground and to crater the runways so that aircraft could not use them (as the Israeli air force did on the morning of 5 June 1967, at the start of the Six Day War, when they neutralised the Egyptian air force on the ground). While 32 Battalion tied down the existing FAPLA forces east of the Cuito, 61 Mech would advance westwards, link up with 4 SAI coming from South West Africa, capture the crossing over the Longa, and march northwards. There was only a single FAPLA formation – 13 Brigade – in their way.

The air force, the Recces and UNITA would fix 8 Brigade, which was protecting the FAPLA supply convoys coming from Menongue.[10]

The alternative plan was to create a fluid, mobile battle between the Lomba and the Chambinga and destroy the four enemy brigades one by one. "The success of winning the battle for Chambinga hinged on mobility and manoeuvre," wrote De Vries. "Feint and strike was to become the norm for Chambinga."[11]

Soon afterwards, De Vries and Smit presented their suggestions to Jannie Geldenhuys and the General Staff at Rundu. According to De Vries, both possibilities – advancing west and east of the river – were openly discussed. Geldenhuys (perhaps with PW Botha's virtual carte blanche in mind) even remarked that the political situation might be favourable to the western option.

Colonel (later Lieutenant General) Rinus van Rensburg of the SADF Medical Service remarked that it would be extremely difficult to evacuate wounded soldiers if a full-scale battle developed at Cuito Cuanavale, especially in light of the enemy's superiority in the air. "I could literally and figuratively feel the dampening effect on the spirit of the operational audience," De Vries says. "The loss of more young South African lives lay heavy on the mind . . . I knew from the talking in the army passages that the casualty attrition rate of our young conscripts had become a major political concern."[12] (The later battles at Tumpo took place almost within spitting distance of the proposed battlefield west of Cuito Cuanavale, and the casualty evacuation possibilities were equally difficult, yet that was not seen as an impossibility.)

De Vries says that the possibility that the war could escalate and that heavy casualties could be suffered were important considerations, as was the argument by some that the western option would require two full brigades – a holding force in the east and an assault force in the west. This, it was feared, would have wide-ranging strategic implications, as South Africa still wanted to keep the war limited. After much deliberation, Geldenhuys decided to attack from the east. With this decision, De Vries's planned command of the western force was cancelled, and he was appointed Deon Ferreira's second in command of 20 Brigade.[13]

A few years later, Geldenhuys also said in a press interview that it was decided against "going west over the river, because it would lead to an unnecessary escalation of the war after the mission had been fulfilled already [at the Lomba]." He said he knew there were field commanders "who wanted the Defence Force to act differently, to be aggressive and take Cuito Cuanavale. Those officers did not always understand the guidelines coming from the politicians. Guidelines that Angola should not become South Africa's Vietnam."

Incidentally, in an interview years later, Magnus Malan told the Irish writer Padraig O'Malley that the Americans had somehow heard that the South Africans were considering an attack on Menongue. One of them approached Malan and told him that if the SADF did so they could expect Oshakati to be bombed.[14] This must have had some impact, as the small SAAF was fully engaged on the eastern front and did not have the capacity to protect places like Oshakati and Ondangwa in the west if the enemy decided to attack them.[15]

Logistical challenges may also have influenced the planners' decision-making process. The SADF logistical line was extremely long. It began in Pretoria, going to Rundu via Upington and from there to Mavinga and the front. The distance from Pretoria to Grootfontein by road was 2 268 km, and from Rundu to Mavinga 356 km, but this stage involved extremely challenging jungle terrain.[16] On average, a road trip from Rundu to Mavinga took five days.[17] Many supplies were taken to Mavinga by air, but, as subsequent events proved, the SAAF simply did not have the strategic airlift capacity to keep a full brigade properly supplied.

Lull in the fighting

After deciding to continue the counteroffensive east of the Cuito River, the South Africans hunkered down to plan. Deon Ferreira's force was much better equipped for the counteroffensive than it had been in September, as considerable reinforcements had arrived. (Though, as events would prove, these were still not enough.) On 30 October, 4 SAI arrived south of Mavinga, ready for battle. This unit, a mechanised battalion group similar to 61 Mech, consisted of two mechanised infantry companies (Ratel 20s), an armoured car squadron (Ratel 90s) and a support company (Ratel 90s, Ratel 60s with Milan antitank missiles and Ratel 81s). In addition, the unit had a 120-mm mortar battery, an anti-aircraft troop (Ystervark), a storm pioneer platoon (Ratel 20s) and a combat engineer troop (Ratel 60s). For this operation, a squadron of Olifant Mk 1A tanks (12 vehicles, plus one in reserve), as well as a motorised infantry company from 32 Battalion, was added.

For the first time since 6 SA Division operated in Italy in 1945, South African tanks were about to go into action, under the command of Major (later Colonel) André Retief, who would prove himself an inspiring field commander. The battalion group, probably the strongest and most potent unit in the history of the SADF (1 036 men at the beginning of the operation), was commanded by Commandant Leon Marais, a veteran of operations Protea and Daisy.[18] The artillery was also augmented with another G-5 battery and a troop of three pre-production self-propelled G-6 guns (actually four, but the engine of one broke down and could not be repaired before the guns were withdrawn a few weeks later), together with an additional Valkiri MRL troop.[19]

Captain Danie Crowther, intelligence officer attached to Battle Group Bravo at the time, remembered the excitement in the air when he and his comrades first saw E Squadron's tanks: "We couldn't believe our eyes. I mean, we were fighting all these days, various fights against tanks, we shot out many of those . . . and we never had tanks of our own. Doctrine-wise you fight tanks with tanks, and we didn't do it. This was big-time now."[20]

One is reminded of Ep van Lill's recommendation during Operation Askari that tanks should be deployed to the operational area, as the Ratel 90 was not adequate to counter the Angolan T-54/55. Why were the Olifant tanks brought to the front only now, and why only one squadron? According to one source, when PW Botha visited the front on 29 September 1987, he inquired impatiently why the army did not use its Olifant tanks, since they had been upgraded at great cost. The generals apparently answered that the army never expected to get permission to use them, given the restrictions under which they had to operate. Nevertheless, this gave the green light for a tank squadron to be brought forward.[21]

As far as the second question is concerned, the army poured most of its resources for armour into armoured cars, initially Eland 90s and later Ratel 90s. The School of Armour had only enough conscripts and professionals to man a single tank squadron in the field. Having known since 1984 that tanks would probably be used in the war, this sounds like a very strange situation. And indeed, in a review of the war, it was recommended that the "concept for the utilisation of tanks must be urgently reconsidered". In future, the army would not fight without tanks against tanks, it was said.[22]

To accommodate the reinforcements, a new structure was created: 20 Brigade became 10 Task Force. Deon Ferreira remained the field commander, but he now answered to Fido Smit, who established his headquarters at Rundu. Sector 20 was taken out of the loop and would concentrate once again on the counterinsurgency war against PLAN in Ovamboland. Smit was responsible to SWATF commander Major General Willie Meyer in Windhoek, who in turn answered to army headquarters. The original idea was that Smit would have two brigades at his disposal, but as the western option evaporated, so did one of the brigades: 61 Mech and 4 SAI would fall under Deon Ferreira, 32 Battalion directly under Smit.

Why this unwieldy structure was set up remains a mystery. It never worked well, and when Operation Moduler gave way to Operation Hooper in December 1987, the tactical command, quite rightly, reverted to a brigade headquarters.[23] An ex-officer, who wishes to remain anonymous, told me that Smit's headquarters, which was supposed to take care of the operational level, in practice functioned as a mere post office between Pretoria and the front. The generals in Pretoria called the shots, even in small matters.

Be that as it may, the SADF took the greater part of a month to recuperate, resupply and regroup. The veterans of the Lomba battles were tired and their equipment worn out by the unbelievably difficult conditions. Here, the shortcomings of the South African forces involved in Operation Moduler became evident. It is accepted military doctrine all over the world that a victory has to be followed up as soon as possible, to maintain momentum and keep the enemy off balance. But the South Africans simply couldn't do it; they didn't have the reserves to go on the offensive.[24]

The reinforcements had to be brought up to speed and had to accustom themselves to the densely wooded operational area. The troops also had to get used to the extremely humid heat, to the lack of basic amenities and – above all – to the thousands of giant flies, which attacked everything exposed to the air. Soldiers learnt to keep the flies out of their eyes, noses, ears and mouths by wearing mosquito nets over their bush hats or helmets. Major Dorning writes, for instance, about the thick swarms of flies that harassed personnel at 20 Brigade's headquarters when he arrived there on 19 September:

> Col Ferreira's special brand of humour was to make itself evident during my very first morning in the operations tent. Cmdt Jan Hougaard had the unfortunate yet by no means uncommon experience of swallowing one of the numerous flies which had settled in his "ratpack" breakfast, and as he left the tent spluttering and gasping Col Ferreira protested loudly: "Ag nee, Jan, jy vreet mos al die vlieë op. Gee ons ook 'n gap, man!"[25]

One trooper remembers:

> One thing that bugged everyone was the flies, you couldn't escape them. They lay on you in the hundreds. One day we photographed about 150 flies on Mike Smith's back. They were in your food, at the side of your mouth and trying to drink from your eyes. If you had an open sore then they sat on that. I had scratched my elbow during the MiG incident and now it was infected. This happened to everyone – if you scratched yourself on something it was guaranteed to fester.[26]

In order to understand the coming battles, it is important to visualise the deployment of South African forces at this time (late October). With the reinforcements, the South Africans were reorganised into three combat groups:

- Combat Group Alpha (Kobus Smit was rotated out and replaced by Commandant Mike Muller): 61 Mech minus a mechanised infantry company.
- Combat Group Bravo (Robbie Hartslief): two motorised infantry companies from 32 Battalion and 101 Battalion each, plus 32 Battalion's antitank squadron and support company, and a mechanised infantry company seconded from 61 Mech.
- Combat Group Charlie (Leon Marais): 4 SAI, a tank squadron, plus a motorised infantry company from 32 Battalion.
- 20 Artillery Regiment, which was also reorganised (Colonel Jean

Lausberg). Sierra Battery turned their 120-mm mortars over to Romeo Battery and regained their G-5 guns. The regiment thus consisted of two G-5 batteries, one Valkiri MRL battery and an additional troop, one 120-mm mortar battery and a troop of G-6s.[27]

This brought the total number of South African soldiers to about 3 000 – a strong brigade, but nothing more. It would remain at this level for the rest of the campaign.[28]

Ferreira stationed most of his artillery south of the Mianei River (*see* map on p. 294), covered by Combat Group Bravo. This brought Cuito Cuanavale and its airstrip within range, and on 20 October the big guns started pounding the town.[29] They would continue to do so for many more weeks. The bombardment resulted in the airstrip being abandoned, and the enemy aircraft were withdrawn to Menongue.[30]

In the days that followed, the South African artillery played havoc from afar on the retreating FAPLA forces. As FAPLA withdrew, the range for the SAAF aircraft grew. Whereas the lighter Mirage F1CZ interceptors could take off from Rundu Air Force Base (where work to lengthen the runway was still under way), the Buccaneers and Mirage F1AZs, with their heavy bomb loads, had to depart from Grootfontein Air Force Base, some distance to the south. As the ground war moved northwards, this would become a growing problem, and the SAAF's role diminished.[31] Because of the distance, it was also impossible for radar from Rundu to detect enemy aircraft over the battlefield. The enemy, of course, did not have the same problem.

Nevertheless, the Angolans were highly distressed by the inventive way in which the South Africans operated. On the night of 19 October, for instance, a UNITA reconnaissance team spotted a convoy of FAPLA vehicles approaching the bridge over the Chambinga River. They passed on the information through nine radio relay stations before it reached Commandant Les Rudman, who in turn informed Jean Lausberg. So Lausberg's artillery started bombarding the convoy from 30 km away, with the corrections passed through all the relay stations. The first round reportedly exploded 400 m to the northwest of the bridge, but the second round hit it squarely – such was the quality of the SADF artillerymen. Lausberg told Fred Bridgland:

Rudman said the recce was ecstatic but said the vehicles were still coming. It takes a G-5 shell between 60 and 90 seconds to travel 30 km, so through Rudman's link-up we asked the UNITA man to tell us when vehicles were about 90 seconds from the bridge so we could hit it as one of them arrived. We caused a lot of problems that night, thanks to the UNITA recce and Rudman's radio man.[32]

Radio intercepts confirmed that FAPLA was planning another offensive. From the South African perspective, this clearly had to be forestalled by their own offensive. The decision was to take on the relatively isolated 16 Brigade first. The other brigades were all in positions where they could mutually support each other, whereas 16 Brigade was fairly isolated near the source of the Chambinga River. The SADF's appreciation of the tactical situation was that the unit could be attacked and destroyed before help could arrive.[33] Bravo would keep 21 and 59 Brigades busy in the south to allow Charlie and Alpha to deal with 16 Brigade in the north.[34]

The "Chambinga Gallop"

What happened in the subsequent weeks was, from the South African side, the first properly planned and deliberate action of Operation Moduler. The piece-meal and haphazard way in which the SADF was sucked into the fighting in the beginning gave way to a hard-nosed professional approach, at any rate on a tactical level.

Deon Ferreira stayed at his tactical headquarters near Mavinga to lead his brigade, but he left Roland de Vries as his second in command at Rundu to do the planning.[35] After presenting the plan to the General Staff, who flew to Rundu from Pretoria for the occasion, De Vries and colonels Fred Oelschig and Jean Lausberg went to Mavinga to discuss the plan with UNITA leader Jonas Savimbi.[36]

In order to understand properly what was going on, one has to understand the disposition of the enemy formations and the thinking behind the SADF plan to destroy them. (Refer to the map on page 294 to follow the analysis of the series of battles that now followed.) Having pulled back from the Lomba after their humiliating defeat, the FAPLA forces took the following positions:

- 16 Brigade at the source of the Chambinga River;
- 66 Brigade at the bridge over the Chambinga. This bridge was of vital importance, because it was the only route along which the brigades to the south could escape;
- 59 Brigade at the source of the Vimpulo River;
- an infantry battalion of 66 Brigade at the confluence of the Cuito and Mianei;
- an infantry battalion of 25 Brigade at the source of the Mianei;
- 21 Brigade on the Mianei slightly west of the infantry battalion of 25 Brigade.[37]

Some of the enemy brigades that had been battered at the Lomba had been replaced with fresh ones. These were deployed in a broad defence line from the Chambinga in the north to the Mianei in the south.

De Vries and his staff came up with a clever plan to deal with the FAPLA forces. The idea was to destroy them in accordance with President PW Botha's order to hit the enemy so hard that he would not be able to launch another offensive before the end of 1988. De Vries says the plan was geared to "the maximum destruction of the enemy" and to break his will to fight. The key to the battle, he says, was to "keep the battlefield fluid". Superior mobility was supremely important, as was the need to keep the initiative. Against that, the enemy could only react.[38]

When planning the destruction of the FAPLA forces, De Vries utilised his considerable knowledge of military history. He decided to use as a historical template the Battle of Gazala (May to June 1942), when German Colonel General Erwin Rommel and his Afrika Korps defeated the British Eighth Army before occupying Tobruk in the Libyan Desert. In fact, De Vries had analysed this battle as an example in his book on mobile warfare. He showed that Rommel used part of his force in a full-frontal attack on the British defence lines (which included a South African infantry division) in order to mislead them. Rommel then led his main armoured force around the British southern (i.e. left) flank to threaten their rear, and forced them to retreat in some disarray. The Eighth Army was lucky to escape, but its main armoured forces were destroyed. Elsewhere in his book, De Vries also quoted Liddell Hart: "Choose the line (or course) of least expectation", and "Exploit the line of least resistance".[39] The Battle of Gazala, together with the Eighth Army's subsequent retreat, was later called the "Gazala Gallop"; with this in mind, De Vries named the coming battle the "Chambinga Gallop" for the river where he planned to corner the Angolans.[40]

The battle plan was clearly inspired by Rommel's tactics. Surprise, deception and swiftness of action were important elements. When one looks at a map, it was logical for the South Africans to attack 16 Brigade from the southeast. This is, after all, where most of their forces were concentrated, and one may assume that the Angolans would know this. Therefore, it was decided that Combat Group Alpha (61 Mech minus a mechanised infantry company) would launch a feint attack from that direction. At this stage, 61 Mech's men were already desperately tired, and therefore 4 SAI was given the honour of being the main attacking force. Thus Combat Group Charlie would march around the enemy's left flank and attack them from their rear in the north.[41] At the same time, Combat Group Bravo (32 and 101 Battalion) would fix 59 and 21 Brigades far to the south to prevent them from coming to the aid of 16 Brigade. There was one fly in the ointment: an enemy tank tactical group just north of the Chambinga. And 66 Brigade was about 18 km away, at the bridge over the Chambinga.[42]

The battle would have another advantage on an operational level. Having knocked out 16 Brigade (*see* map on p 294), Alpha and Charlie would then be able to move westwards between the Chambinga and Hube rivers and occupy the bridge over the Chambinga, thereby cutting off 59 and 21 Brigades, who still thought that they could launch their own offensive southwards against the SADF artillery. The possibility of defeating and destroying these two formations[43] underlined the masterful nature of the plan. De Vries reflects with hindsight:

> At that stage, 16 Brigade came out of the appraisal process (in other words, the terrain, own forces, enemy, and the time and space analysis) as the logical target, according to my modest opinion. We had to make the battlefield fluid. Operational paralysis, physical, psychological and sensorial dislocation of the enemy was an underlying objective and formed part of the plan ... Take into account 16 Brigade's strategic position relative to the enemy's command axis, logistical lines and escape route across the Chambinga bridge. 16 Brigade stood out like a

ripe fruit, ready to be plucked. We were very nervous that the enemy would withdraw too soon.[44]

In accordance with De Vries's dicta, the enemy would thus be blindsided once again and attacked where and when he did not expect it, and where he was weakest. At the same time, the impending threat to the South African artillery to the south would be neutralised even before it could really materialise. The plan showed a thorough understanding of mobile warfare and the indirect approach. "In a sense manoeuvre was a goal in itself. Few understood this norm," De Vries writes. "Make the battlefield fluid was our maxim. Feint and strike was the norm."[45]

Put differently, the light infantry of 32 and 101 Battalion would fix 59 and 21 Brigades in position to the south, while the most powerful two units in the South African Army, 61 Mech and 4 SAI, would fall on the relatively isolated 16 Brigade to the north. De Vries explicitly quotes Rommel: "One should endeavour to concentrate one's own forces both in space and time, while at the same time seeking to split the opposing forces and destroy them at different times."[46] This was exactly the plan.

The attack was meticulously prepared.[47] Ferreira had a sand model made of 16 Brigade's positions, and the final coordination between the SADF units was extensively discussed during the evening of Saturday 7 November. Sunday was spent preparing the troops and equipment for the coming battle. This would be the first battle in which the untried troops of 4 SAI would participate.

At 01h00 on the morning of 9 November, Combat Group Alpha launched its diversionary attack from the south. Three hours later Combat Group Charlie moved out of its positions in the north. Artillery shells and rockets shrieked through the air and exploded in the air above the unsuspecting FAPLA troops. At 06h30 the cacophony was augmented by a gaggle of SAAF Mirages releasing pre-fragmented bombs on the enemy, showering red-hot steel shards in all directions, ripping trees, flesh and bones apart indiscriminately.

At 07h00 Alpha's men hit the enemy from the south, making as much noise as they possibly could in order to draw the enemy's attention to them. The Angolan artillery reacted immediately, and the brigade's T-55 tank unit started forming up, presumably for a counterattack. For obvious reasons, Alpha's orders were not to tangle with tanks, and, with his tactical objective achieved, Mike Muller withdrew his men and moved a few kilometres eastwards. His role now changed to that of reserve force.

On the north side, 32 Battalion's Foxtrot Company paved the way, acting as an infantry screen for 4 SAI's armoured vehicles following from behind. The 32 Battalion men felt that the Ratels were too far behind, leaving them exposed as they overran the first trenches and became pinned down by accurate machine-gun and 23-mm cannon fire. (With visibility down to as little as 20 m, it is understandable that the infantry could have felt exposed.) Also, UNITA troops attached to 4 SAI made a lot of noise. Apparently the enemy got wind of this, because an ambush of three T-55s, six 23-mm and two 14,5-mm guns, as well as several other armoured vehicles, was suddenly detected on Combat Group Charlie's left flank. Radio intercepts revealed that the Angolans had become aware of the main attack, and had called in their brigade's tactical group (more or less a squadron of tanks). Leon Marais had to react quickly, because this could have been serious. (Interestingly, the Cubans at 16 Brigade's headquarters immediately withdrew southwards and took two tanks with them. The Soviet advisors called for chopper extraction.)

At this stage, the UNITA guides at the front were contributing considerably to the confusion at Marais's headquarters by providing contradictory and often false intelligence. But, just then, a team of Recces arrived with more accurate information. Marais immediately ordered Major André Retief, commander of the Olifant tanks, to wheel left and engage the FAPLA tanks, supported by A Company's Ratel 20s. The two sub-units integrated themselves and moved forward into what became the first South African tank action since 1945. Within a few minutes, the first T-55 burst into flames, killed by Lieutenant Hein "Mieliepap" Fourie. Eight minutes later, the second followed, taken out by Lieutenant Abrie "Sirkusleeu" Strauss. The big armoured behemoths advanced like unstoppable prehistoric monsters, trampling anyone and everything underfoot and overrunning the defence positions. They showered the fleeing enemy with shells from their big 105-mm guns.

The SADF's G-6s augmented the carnage from afar, and shortly after 09h00 the only enemy left were the dead and dying. The South Africans counted 22 bodies and took two prisoners. A map, showing all the defensive positions

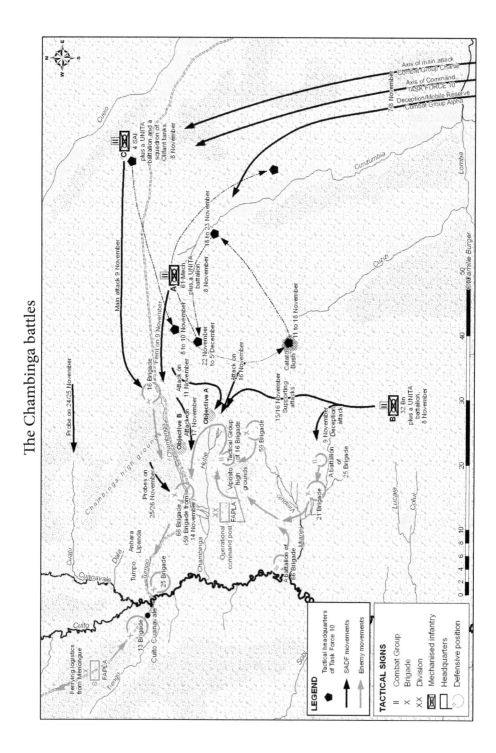

The Chambinga battles

and minefields, was also captured. In addition to the two T-55s destroyed, they also took out four BM-21 rocket launchers, and captured one 14,5-mm and two 23-mm guns, which were given to UNITA. The South Africans suffered no losses at all.

Everything in this action went exactly as in the exercises. Helmoed-Römer Heitman, who listened to the tapes of the squadron command radio network, says they "sound as if they were recorded during a dull exercise".[48]

This action was, of course, a diversion from the actual attack, and valuable time was lost. Nevertheless, 4 SAI started advancing again around 10h00. However, the enemy resistance grew noticeably fiercer (the attackers here became aware of two infantry battalions with about 750 men, ten T-55 tanks and four 14,5-mm and six D30 130-mm guns, as well as six rocket launchers). Fairly accurate indirect enemy artillery fire descended on the attackers, and two men from A Company and one from 32 Battalion were killed. B Company was pinned down, but counterfire by the tanks took the sting out of the enemy fire.

A Ratel 20 from B Company was suddenly confronted by a T-55. The commander kept his cool, and directed a stream of armour-piercing ammunition at the tank. After a few seconds, the tank exploded – probably the first time that a T-55 was destroyed by a mere Ratel 20. But the brave Ratel crew paid dearly, as another tank soon thereafter destroyed their vehicle, killing both the gunner and the driver. In turn, an Olifant took swift revenge by taking out that T-55.

Rifleman Glynn Crookes, also in a Ratel, remembered:

> We landed up at the right end of the squadron and as we came through the thick bush it all opened up and we were immediately faced with an RPG (30m in front of us) and a small troop carrier (50m) of sorts. We immediately set about firing on what was in front of us. It was during this time that a T-55 (150m) that was dug in so that just the turret was above the ground, was at 2 o'clock of our position and well hidden in thick bush, hit us. As I am sure you can imagine that with the hatches closed the visibility was limited, and if it had not been that the [Olifant] tank to our immediate left was traversing their cannon to that area and seen the flame from the T-55 cannon and immediately disabled it, I am sure that I would not be around today.[49]

At this stage, 32 Battalion's infantry reported enemy tanks to the right, and Marais ordered Retief's squadron to wheel right and engage them. One Olifant's track was shot off, but makeshift repairs soon put it back in action. By now, the enemy resistance had diminished, and infantry from A and B companies started cleaning up the bunkers. The surviving enemy troops fled. A South African trooper, with 4 SAI's anti-aircraft guns, described the battlefield after the event:

> The destruction was everywhere around us. The noise, the dust and the smell of death was everywhere. For the first time in my life I saw dead bodies. A head lay on the ground, totally shot off its body, and a body lay halfway out of a ditch. The stink of death was overwhelming. Flies immediately began congregating on the bodies. It was war, and even so, we didn't feel anything any more. We just had to go on.[50]

This action ended with five enemy tanks destroyed and one captured in good working order. The difference between the opposing forces lay mainly in training. The South Africans worked much better as a team, while their reaction time – crucial in a densely wooded environment where the range was sometimes as little as 10 to 15 m – was simply much better than that of their opponents. The old adage "train as you fight" was certainly true of the South African Armoured Corps.

By 12h30 it was clear that the enemy was on the run. Combat Group Charlie's orders were to exploit its advance to a point opposite the source of the Hube River, thereby transforming the battlefield into a killing ground akin to when 47 Brigade was destroyed at the Lomba River on 3 October. The decisive moment of the battle was approaching; the final blow was about to be dealt. But it never happened. Inexplicably, Marais decided to pull back to the original deployment area to resupply his troops.

In his book about 32 Battalion, Jan Breytenbach is scathing about this turn of events. He writes that Deon Ferreira "should have sacked the commander of 4 South African Infantry and replaced him . . . In combat situations one cannot be lenient. The lives of men depend on the commander in actual charge of the battle. Ruthless action should always be taken to rectify failures along the line of command."[51] Bridgland also says Ferreira was "particularly incensed" at Marais's failure to press home the attack.[52]

In personal communications to me, Marais explained that he had to resupply his force, as they had expended most of their ammunition in the two fights. Besides, a FAPLA tactical group – the equivalent of a tank squadron – was just opposite the Chambinga. This force, he reckoned, had become the "main threat".[53]

If one looks only at statistics, it is clear that 4 SAI won the battle handsomely. On 16 Brigade's side, 10 T-54/55s were destroyed and three captured; a BM-21 was destroyed and another captured; one 76-mm gun was destroyed and one captured; two of the feared 23-mm guns were destroyed and three more captured, as were 14 SA-7 and SA-14 anti-aircraft missiles, a 14,5-mm gun and an 82-mm mortar. The Angolans left behind 75 slain soldiers and six prisoners on the battlefield. The South Africans suffered few losses – seven killed and nine wounded. One Ratel 20 was destroyed, and another one damaged. An Olifant had a track damaged.

But winning or losing is not only measured by statistics. The question is whether you achieve what you set out to do. According to Bridgland, the decision to break off Battle Group Charlie's attack "proved to be one of the major mistakes and turning points of the war. It gave FAPLA's forces a reprieve which enabled them to reorganise and make life infinitely more difficult for the SADF than it otherwise would have been."[54]

Marais also complained to me about poor cooperation between the 32 Battalion company and 4 SAI's headquarters, saying that the company communicated directly with Deon Ferreira's headquarters. According to Marais, this contributed to Jan Breytenbach's harsh opinion of 4 SAI's conduct.[55] Nevertheless, the fact is that 16 Brigade got away, and with this 59 and 21 Brigades were saved as well. Had they been destroyed, the war could very well have ended very differently. It was a decisive moment – and the dice fell wrongly for the South Africans.

The second SADF attack

By this time, the Angolans were getting demoralised. In general, they were poorly led and fed. Many had been pressed into service in the first place, either not knowing what they were fighting for or not believing in it. They did not realise that the South Africans on the other side of the hill were often as scared as they were, sometimes swearing as much at "higher authority". The Angolans also attributed mythical capacities to the SADF, especially 32 Battalion. Soviet Lieutenant Colonel Igor Zhdarkin recorded in his diary:

> Something quite incomprehensible is happening now: the Angolan troops are almost completely demoralised; the brigades are on average at 45% strength. For every 10–15 shells launched by the enemy, Angolans are able to send only one, if even that much; our reconnaissance operates poorly; and our enemy knows everything about us. The Angolans fear the South Africans like fire and if they hear that "Buffalo" [32 Battalion] is part of an attack, they throw away all their equipment in panic and flee.[56]

Roland de Vries writes how Deon Ferreira and his staff had rigged high-frequency antennas in the trees at headquarters, hidden under camouflage nets. Here, they heard the course of the 9 November battle, and cheered when André Retief's squadron destroyed the enemy tanks. After the battle, they moved southwestwards to the Catato Bush, south of the battlefield, but failed to realise that an old Portuguese concrete beacon in the centre presented an excellent target for enemy aircraft. De Vries relates the story rather humorously:

> Early one morning two MiG-21s casually sauntered over in our direction and promptly strafed our well-camouflaged Tac HQ position with cannon. It was a surprise low-flying air attack. The shots came up leisurely amongst us. We could see the red star on the helmet of one of the Cuban pilots. The cordite from the aircrafts' firing neatly settled over our position; we could smell and see it. From the radio intercept we discerned that the two Cuban pilots had a suspicion that something eerie was lurking in the shadows below. They talked about "Strata, strata" over the radios – meaning street in Spanish. Later we found that close-by the clear tracks of the Olifant tanks lay to one side of our Tac HQ position. Live and learn. Unwittingly our UNITA friends fired two Stinger missiles at the two MiGs. Vapour trailing endlessly . . . uselessly. The MiGs would be back. The Cuban pilots now knew where we were and they were probably angry. We frowned in the direction of our UNITA compatriots.

I was suddenly very interested in casually deepening my former foxhole with a metal dixie; extremely embarrassing. This was to the utter enjoyment of gunners Jean Lausberg and Frans van Eeden – these two had an extremely deep excavation next to their command Ratel. Their vehicle was being used as the "Fire Coordination Centre". The sequel to our little drama unfolded immediately after we had dragged the somewhat hefty Deon Ferreira from beneath the axle of his own command Ratel. Coen van den Berg, our trusted air support officer in blue, casually sauntered out of the bush with a roll of toilet paper and entrenching tools, tying his belt. Apparently he was caught in a compromising position, white rear shining to heaven like fluorescent "Dayglo", as he took cover in the deep sandy ruts of a Ratel. These little things usually happened to air force officers when they were on mother earth with the "Brown Jobs". I borrowed the small spade.[57]

The South Africans decided to attack again two days later, on 11 November. Once more, an excellent plan was formulated, based on the same principles as the 9 November attack. Firstly, a motorised infantry company from Combat Group Bravo (which was still protecting the artillery south of the Mianei River) would be deployed to attract the attention of FAPLA's 21 and 59 Brigades to prevent them from joining the main battle between Alpha and Charlie and 16 Brigade to the north. Radio intercepts suggested that 16 Brigade expected the next South African attack would come once again from the northeast. Therefore, it was decided that Alpha would launch a feint attack from that direction, hopefully drawing the FAPLA tanks. Meanwhile, Charlie would scissor southwards behind Alpha and hit the enemy from the south. Alpha would then again revert to being a reserve force.[58]

At 06h00 the artillery started with a deluge on the northernmost of the two main positions of 16 Brigade (and SAAF Mirages joined in at 07h00) to create the impression that the attack would come from that direction. But things did not work out exactly as planned, and Combat Group Charlie was once more delayed by the dense bush, which meant that the whole attack had to be delayed several times. An air strike by enemy MiG-23s was wide off the mark, but did not contribute to greater speed. FAPLA used this delay to withdraw from their southernmost position. Combat Group Charlie had to pause and regroup for the advance on the second position, which was held by two infantry battalions, ten T-55s and a mixture of heavy and light artillery.

Charlie was able to start its attack only at 12h25, after six Mirages had dropped their deadly freight on the enemy. But the infantry, having struggled through the dense underbrush on foot for several hours, were dog-tired, and Leon Marais ordered a pause after a request by the commander of A Company. This was exactly what FAPLA was waiting for. The Angolans unleashed a hail of bullets and shells on the unsuspecting South African troops. The situation called for calm nerves and a steady hand, attributes fortunately possessed by Major André Retief, commander of the Olifant squadron. After assessing the situation, he ordered all his tanks to start a so-called firebelt action, whereby all the tanks fired their weapons together in the direction of the enemy. Eight South Africans were wounded here and two killed. The tanks moved forward and integrated with the infantry.

But then radio intercepts revealed that more than 30 enemy tanks had congregated at the source of the Chambinga River. Time was of the essence – the attack had to succeed before these reinforcements could enter the battlefield. After reviewing the situation with Retief and other officers, Marais ordered that the advance resume, with the Ratel 90 squadron covering the force to the right and the antitank platoon and storm pioneers to the left. Then the force bumped head-on into a strong FAPLA tank and infantry force. One Ratel 20 directed a torrent of armour-piercing shells at a T-55 and destroyed it. The gunner, Rifleman MJ Mitton, paid with his life when the Ratel was blown apart by a shell from another T-55's heavy 100-mm gun. The big Olifant guns barked back and destroyed several T-55s, including the one that had killed the Ratel.

The ferocity of the South African attack was too much for the Angolans, who gave way and started withdrawing. Then the South African troops, flushed with victory, drove into a minefield. An Olifant and several Ratels were damaged or destroyed. While the other tanks and Ratels kept up a stream of fire at the enemy, some tank "tiffies" (mechanics) braved the bullets buzzing around their heads and coolly fixed the damaged tank track. Then the enemy fire diminished and FAPLA pulled back.

This was another moment to follow up, but the South Africans were running out of ammunition and the minefield made it difficult to replenish on the battle-field. FAPLA's artillery opened up, raining heavy shells on the attackers. Marais therefore decided to withdraw at about 15h30.

Two 32 Battalion officers, Captain Piet "Boer" van Zyl and Lieutenant De Villiers "Vossie" Vosloo, disobeyed the order after they discovered that one of their wounded comrades had been left behind. It was an iron – if unwritten – law in the unit: no comrade is *ever* left behind. And so Van Zyl and Vosloo ran back towards the front, one covering the other. When they reached the FAPLA trenches, they had to engage in a firefight with the Angolans before they could pick up their badly wounded comrade. They carried him back to the SADF lines, all the while covered by a stream of fire from the Olifants and Ratels. Both men were awarded the Honoris Crux.

Combat Group Alpha tried to marry up with the tanks for a short while to continue the attack, but the momentum was gone, and the sun was going down. The attack was called off.

The South African artillery unleashed a terrible parting shot after an artillery observer reported a FAPLA battalion near the Chambinga bridge. A full ripple of rockets was fired, which exploded above the Angolans' heads, killing or wounding most and destroying about 40 trucks.

FAPLA had again taken a terrible beating, having lost 14 tanks, several other vehicles and 394 men. The South Africans lost five men and 19 were wounded, with two Ratels destroyed and one Olifant damaged but recovered. Igor Zhdarkin wrote in his diary that "at the crossing of the Shambinga [sic] River, groups of soldiers from the 16th Brigade, including those from Tactical Group, were running with and without materiel, with weapons and without weapons, in a great panic and with 'square eyes'."[59] But these statistics do not tell the full story. The fact is that while 16 Brigade had been crippled, it had not been destroyed, and 21 and 59 Brigades were still unscathed. Once again, the South Africans had failed to achieve their objective. Combat Group Bravo launched an attack on 59 Brigade to prevent it from retreating northwards and joining up with the tattered remains of 16 Brigade, but 21 Brigade promptly came to 59's aid, and they withdrew together.

FAPLA's escape

The South Africans' work – to prevent the Angolans from escaping northwards and to destroy their forces east of the Cuito River – was not yet done. It is true that 16 Brigade had been badly mauled, but the remains of this formation got away. Now the challenge was to prevent 21 Brigade and 25 Brigade's single battalion from retreating from their position just north of the Mianei. These two formations had their work cut out for them: they would have to traverse two rivers – the Vimpulo and the Hube, both flowing from east to west, more or less parallel to each other – before they would reach the all-important bridge over the Chambinga. Once they crossed the bridge, they would be home free (*see* map on page 294).

To prevent this, the South Africans put in maximum effort. Combat Group Bravo was placed under Task Force 10's command, together with Alpha and Charlie.[60] The first priority was to establish a defence line at the Vimpulo, the southernmost of the rivers. A series of guard posts was placed at possible fords to see where the enemy wanted to cross, and an ambush – a typical "killing ground", in accordance with army tactical doctrine – would be set up to crush the enemy.

Things began to go wrong from the South African point of view when 21 Brigade surprised everyone by proving that it was capable of resolute and rapid movement, albeit in withdrawing. On the afternoon of 13 November, the Angolans moved like lightning in a northerly direction to the Sandumba ford on the Vimpulo. The SADF Recces picked up their movement, though, and informed Ferreira. He then ordered Battle Group Charlie to move southwestwards as fast as it could (it was a distance of about 20 km) and establish an ambush southeast of the ford. At the same time, Alpha was deployed to the north and Bravo to the south in order to box in the enemy from all directions.

However, in the mad dash through some of the densest bush any of the troops had ever seen, accurate navigation was extremely difficult. As it turned out, Charlie established its ambush *six* kilometres from the Sandumba ford, instead of the planned *two*. And therefore, during the night, the FAPLA force quietly tiptoed its way past the unsuspecting Charlie and crossed the ford.

For the FAPLA force there was still one hurdle left: the Hube. Bravo and Charlie were immediately ordered to move northwards. In this instance, there was no ford over which FAPLA could escape; the force would have to march northeastwards to round the eastern source of the Hube. This was the point at which Bravo and Charlie now converged, while Alpha stayed behind to round up stragglers.

Again things went wrong. Charlie's navigation was inaccurate, and during the night of 15/16 November the formation deployed some distance to the south of the place Deon Ferreira had ordered it to. There the South Africans ran into a minefield, which delayed them quite some time. Also, army doctrine notwithstanding, the formation used flares, and there was much noise as they tried to get out of the minefield, thereby alerting the enemy to their presence.

Nevertheless, when Leon Marais discovered that he was further south of the Hube than he had to be, he redeployed northwestwards to close the gap to the river. Just then, the South Africans bumped into FAPLA. The faulty SADF deployment now meant that the battle became a frontal collision, instead of the South Africans hitting the Angolans in their flank and cornering them against the river, thereby creating the planned killing ground. Fierce fighting broke out. Halfway through the morning, Battle Group Bravo joined them from the south. Several T-54/55s were taken out by Hannes Nortmann's Ratel 90s. The air thundered with the sharp crack of the tank and armoured car guns, while the fearsome stutter of the machine guns and rifles continued in a deadly cacophony. A firebelt action by 4 SAI had to be broken off abruptly when it was discovered that the 32 Battalion company was in the way. Two men were killed by friendly fire.

By 16h30 the South Africans were running out of ammunition, and Leon Marais ordered Charlie to break off the action and move about 12 km away in order to replenish. The order was not received well by anyone, but it was obeyed. Ferreira decided to switch the tanks – which still had enough supplies – to Bravo and continue the attack, while the artillery would pound the Angolans to prevent them from reorganising themselves. It was expected that it would take the Angolans at least six or seven hours to sort themselves out.

But FAPLA again proved that in flight it could move with remarkable speed. In the short time available to them between Charlie pulling out of the fight and Bravo entering it again, the Angolans scarpered eastwards like race-horses. When the South Africans caught on, the Angolans were already around the Hube source, running like hell for the protection of their comrades who were waiting for them at the Chambinga. A thunderstorm helped to hide their escape.

Statistically it was, once again, a grand victory for the SADF. FAPLA lost 131 men, as well as seven T-54/55s, two BM-21 rocket launchers, a BTR-60 armoured car and four trucks. Charlie's losses were 4 men killed and 19 wounded, while two Ratels, a Withings recovery vehicle and a Rinkhals field ambulance were destroyed. Bravo lost two men.

Still, Deon Ferreira did not give up. This time he put Combat Group Alpha in the lead in the hope that it would fare better than Charlie. The idea was to cut the retreating enemy off from the all-important bridge over the Chambinga. But Mars, the god of war, did not smile upon Alpha on 17 November. First, the unit's advance was held up when UNITA incorrectly warned of a major mine-field in front of the unit. More time was lost when an enemy air raid forced Alpha's vehicles under cover. When they started moving forward again, it was too late; the enemy was already at the bridge. Shortly before the Angolans reached it, Ratels from Bravo (again under the command of Hannes Nortmann, who seemed to be everywhere during the entire operation) caught up with the enemy and destroyed two T-55s. The SADF artillery did sterling work, shooting out about 300 FAPLA vehicles, but the enemy had escaped yet again.

The last Moduler fight

The skirmish of 17 November brought Operation Moduler close to its end. The time to release the National Servicemen was rapidly drawing near. The SADF could not keep them on without very good reason, and, in any case, they were on their last legs. "Many of them had seen more action in three months than many South African soldiers saw in the whole of World War II," Deon Ferreira told Fred Bridgland.[61] While this was true, they would be replaced by new recruits who would first have to be brought up to speed with special training in the operational area. Much equipment also needed to be replaced or repaired, which would also require time.[62]

Before any of that could happen, the whole debate of whether the main advance should take place to the west or east of the Cuito flared up again. On 2 November, SWATF headquarters in Windhoek had laid three options before General Liebenberg. These options also had to do with the demobilisation problem:

- It was expected that the existing SADF forces would be fairly exhausted by the time FAPLA was – as planned – destroyed east of the Cuito. "To maintain the momentum of the battle and deny the enemy the opportunity to recuperate/regroup/bring on reinforcements, it is desirable to move in west of the Cuito River with fresh troops for the conclusion of phase 4 [the possible capture of Cuito Cuanavale] . . ." These troops would then be equipped with the weapons from Exercise Sweepslag, which was taking place at the time. At the same time, the present force would be withdrawn together with their equipment.
- Exchange the troops in line. This was deemed undesirable because of logistical difficulties.
- Use the existing forces to finalise phase 4 as well. This had to be considered very carefully in terms of the "political implications, security, morale, etc". (Between the lines one may read, however, that SWATF headquarters was not very enamoured of this option.)[63]

Not everyone agreed. In a memorandum from 20 Brigade headquarters (which presumably reflected Deon Ferreira's views), it was stated that the western option would need an additional brigade, which had to include an entire tank regiment. If this brigade was a Citizen Force formation, it could not be available before 20 December. The earliest date for the start of the operation would be 7 January 1988, which would force it into the rainy season. The second option, changing the troops in line, was also rejected. The third option was the preferred one. The enemy was already 70% defeated, it was stated.[64]

On 18 November, the day after FAPLA escaped at the Chambinga bridge, generals Geldenhuys and Liebenberg met with Admiral Dries Putter, Chief of Staff Intelligence, in Pretoria to discuss the matter. Liebenberg put forward three options of his own: to stop the campaign and withdraw, to exploit the situation east of the Cuito up to the river itself, or to capture Cuito Cuanavale by advancing west of the Cuito. He emphasised that the air situation was becoming problematical: "It must be considered to eliminate Cuito [Cuanavale]."

According to the minutes of the meeting, Geldenhuys's reaction was vague. He agreed that the air threat could become "a decisive factor" and said that it should be investigated how to "put Menongue [air base] out of action". There were certain conditions that had to be fulfilled before South Africa could withdraw. He also added, very importantly: "If Cuito has to be captured from the west, it should be planned to do it with minimum vehicles and maximum troops and artillery fire support." No concrete decisions were minuted.[65]

Fred Bridgland, basing himself on interviews with SADF field commanders (he refers specifically to Robbie Hartslief, Mike Muller and Leon Marais), says that they "argued, more potently than ever, that the logical way to achieve victory was to attack Cuito Cuanavale from the west, isolate all the enemy's eight brigades in and around the town, and then destroy them at the SADF's leisure". They were overruled by the generals. Bridgland says that, at this time, South African diplomats at the United Nations in New York were approached by Cuban diplomats to "explore the possibility of a negotiated settlement". As the government did not want this initiative to fail even before it could take off, he suggests, the western advance option was turned down.[66]

There is ample evidence that the field commanders preferred the western option, but Bridgland has his dates wrong for the Cuban contact in New York. We will discuss this further in Chapter 15, but, according to the two South African diplomats who were involved in this first contact, John Mare and Chris van Melle Kamp, the contact happened only in the second half of February 1988.[67] It could not, therefore, have had any influence on decisions taken in November 1987.

The leadership now decided on one last fling east of the Cuito before sending the troops on their merry way home before Christmas. The purpose was a last attack before demobilisation day on 30 November. The plan, decided upon at a meeting between Liebenberg and the tactical headquarters staff in Rundu, was to attack the FAPLA forces via the Chambinga high ground north of the Chambinga River. The attack would be directed westwards towards the Cuito and the town of Cuito Cuanavale, which lies on the western side of the river. The basic idea was to intimidate the Angolans into withdrawing across the river. The hostilities would begin with an SAAF air strike, after which Battle

Group Alpha would deploy north of the Cuatir River (in other words, to the north of the actual battlefield) as a feint. Then, two UNITA "regular" battalions would attack westwards along the Chambinga – well to the south – after which Battle Group Bravo (with Charlie in reserve) would follow up, supported by the tanks of E Squadron. They would then turn northwards and advance along the Cuito. Finally, Charlie would advance up to the vicinity of the bridge over the Cuito. On a strategic level, it was felt that this last push might just be enough to convince the enemy to start negotiating.[68]

This plan marked a definite deviation from the mobile, indirect approach that had hitherto been followed, in favour of an approach based on attrition. This would continue to a growing degree during operations Hooper and Packer, and its negative consequences will be analysed in the next chapter. As Roland de Vries remarked:

> The war now started feeling to me like a creeping barrage, similar to what was probably experienced when the front on the Somme became bogged down during World War One. What I feared quietly was that if we did not do something soon to wrest the initiative and mobility back from the tightening noose, we would inevitably be drawn into an attrition trap at Cuito. We were gradually allowing ourselves to be hauled into a funnel . . . I mentioned my apprehension to the high-ups a few times. Eventually I realised I had to shut up if I was still interested in further promotion.[69]

The FAPLA defenders were considerably stronger than the SADF attackers. As the Angolans retreated, the brigades that had originally been left in the north to safeguard their rear areas were, as it were, turned into front-line troops. Five brigades – some mauled, but still intact – with some 4 000 to 5 000 men and almost 40 tanks were facing the three South African combat groups with about 3 000 men and 13 tanks. Two more FAPLA brigades, not yet blooded, were in reserve across the river. Normal SADF doctrine demanded that an attack be undertaken with a 3:1 numerical superiority over the defence. But, of course, this rule was never adhered to during the entire Border War; the SADF invariably attacked a numerically superior defence and often won handsomely. The attitude, as an ex-officer who does not want to see his name in print, told me, was basically: "Do what you can with what you have where you are." Also, morale problems were beginning to develop among the SADF troops, especially with their demobilisation not far off.[70]

But the Angolans had other advantages too. First of all, the Chambinga high ground, over which the South Africans elected to attack, favoured the defence. The enemy had ample time in which to prepare his defences. Ominously, a first unit of 300 Cuban soldiers materialised to stiffen the spines of the Angolans. In addition to the dense bush, which already had stymied several South African attacks in the past, the terrain consisted of sandy dunes, which would make any vehicle movement a nightmare.

It had been thought that FAPLA would simply fold and run. But the field commanders on the ground knew better. Fred Bridgland reports:

> Time and again, as this book was researched, these officers . . . asked the author to switch off his tape recorder while they gave him their off-the-record opinions of what they had been asked to do. "Fundamentally stupid", said one highly decorated officer who argued that FAPLA, despite its many shortcomings, had often fought with a degree of determination that South African officers in the field respected.[71]

By the way, this part of the operation meant that another of the early political guidelines – that the SADF was not allowed to operate north of the Chambinga – was tacitly abandoned. This was another indication of the piecemeal way in which the SADF was committed to battle.

The attack took place only on 25 November, so that the South Africans could first replenish their fuel and ammunition and repair their tattered equipment. But very early on that day, things started to go wrong. The dense bush meant that neither the tanks nor the Ratels could even traverse their turrets, which made all fighting impossible. Navigation became extremely difficult. A minefield further slowed Bravo down. By 15h00, Bravo had been able to struggle forward only some 800 m in the previous four hours! They made so much noise that the forward FAPLA elements were able to withdraw in time. During the course of the afternoon, UNITA's "regular" battalions ran into the carefully prepared FAPLA defences. They pushed FAPLA back, but suffered heavy losses in the process. At 17h00, just as Bravo was finally ready to attack, it was smothered in an accurate Angolan artillery bombardment. The Olifants found themselves unable to manoeuvre. Fearing more casualties, and taking into account the late hour, Robbie Hartslief postponed the attack to the following day.

Wisely, it was decided to switch the main thrust of the attack the next day. With the tanks reverting to Charlie, this formation would now lead, with Bravo in support. But this attempt had even less luck. Firstly, FAPLA had reinforced its forces with 10 tanks during the night. Then Charlie was – as became usual by this time – delayed by the dense vegetation and a minefield, while the FAPLA artillery pounded the South Africans from across the river. It simply made no sense to go on, and the whole attack was called off.

Operation Moduler was at an end.

Final thoughts

In the 1979 Currie Cup final, when Western Province played to a draw with arch-rivals Northern Transvaal, captain Morné du Plessis remarked that the outcome was like kissing your sister. This must have been how the men of Combat Groups Alpha, Bravo and Charlie felt after their final battles on 25/26 November. They had beaten the enemy time and again, but frustratingly were just not able to plant the knockout blow.

Nevertheless, the South African political and military leadership had much to reflect on. Operation Moduler turned out to be a victory by points, not a knockout. This was in many ways in spite of, not because of, the leadership in Cape Town and Pretoria. The credit for what was achieved belongs mainly to the field commanders and men.

What did they achieve? Let us catalogue it. FAPLA's attempt to take Mavinga, advance on Jamba and knock UNITA out of the war had failed miserably. The battered FAPLA units were back at Tumpo, whence the offensive had started in July and August. This meant that UNITA would survive as a political lever for South Africa to put pressure on the MPLA government to kick out the Cubans, SWAPO and the ANC from its territory. UNITA's continued occupation of southeastern Angola would continue to make it extremely difficult for SWAPO to infiltrate into the Okavango, thereby compressing the counterinsurgency war into the relatively limited territory of Ovambo. In the process, the South Africans achieved some spectacular victories around the Lomba, especially the devastating hammer blow of 3 October against 47 Brigade. And, although a series of mishaps prevented them from destroying the other Angolan units south of the Chambinga, their tactical plans were impeccable, and they hurt the Angolan formations considerably. In other words, the South African strategic objectives were reached. The statistics were impressive. Enemy losses were approximately 525 killed, and 28 tanks, 10 BTR-60s, 85 logistical vehicles and 3 SA-13 anti-aircraft missile systems destroyed. The South Africans suffered 16 dead and 41 wounded.[72]

This does not mean that everything was hunky-dory. On some levels, the South Africans' handling of their military forces left a lot to be desired. Firstly (and this straddles the military-strategic and political levels), the slow and hesitant way in which South Africa was dawn into the conflict almost defeated its purpose. One can understand *why* this happened. South Africa's fight was not primarily with the MPLA, but with SWAPO. It did not want to become part of the Angolan civil war. But, since 1983, a pattern had slowly developed: UNITA would get into trouble and request South African help; limited help would be given, often grudgingly, but the SADF officers concerned would be strongly constricted by almost impossible guidelines. Such operations had to remain clandestine (or at the very least plausibly deniable); therefore, all objectives had to be reached, and no equipment or men could be lost.

This happened in 1983, and again in 1985 and 1986. And so, when the same thing happened in 1987, only on a bigger scale, the politicians and generals thought they could do the same again. Given their mind-set up to August 1987, they might, therefore, be forgiven for their hesitant attitude up to that point. But then the full extent and import of the FAPLA offensive became known. In particular, when the decision was taken to release 61 Mech, they surely must have realised that the experience of 1983 to 1986 was no longer valid. That was the point at which they should have decided: either we stay out of the fight and take the risk that UNITA be knocked out, or we go in with all the resources needed for the job, defeat the enemy rapidly and pull out. That this decision was eventually taken, during President PW Botha's visit to the front at the end of September 1987, shows that the earlier political fears were invalid, or at least that the advantages were worth the risk.

But, even after this decision, too few forces were committed to the campaign. Only one – albeit strong – additional unit, 4 SAI, was sent, together with a single tank squadron and extra artillery. This was still inadequate. The harsh fact was that the South Africans, on both the operational and tactical level, never had proper reserves available. With, say, two or three more mechanised battalion groups and a full tank regiment, chances are that the FAPLA brigades would not simply have been dealt a series of heavy blows south of the Chambinga, but that they would have been destroyed. The thinking that gave rise to the original slow build-up apparently persisted for many months, and by the end of the campaign the troops indeed felt that they had "kissed their sisters".

This is not all. The decision – confirmed repeatedly – to confront the enemy head-on in the area where he was advancing/retreating, east of the Cuito, does not suggest a proper understanding of the kind of mobile warfare preached by people like Roland de Vries and others. If Piet Muller's advice had been followed from the beginning, if an adequate SADF force had been assembled and sent in west of the Cuito in September 1987 to attack the Angolans in their rear, there can be no doubt that the FAPLA offensive would have been defeated comprehensively, perhaps without much fighting at all.

At the front, there was much frustration. One angry field commander, not wishing to have his name in print, told me: "Whatever options we put to them [the generals], they would always choose the shittiest one." On the ground, he says, he could see no integrated picture for the unfolding of the war and the results the generals wished – military and political – for the western sub-theatre (SWA and Angola). "I believe we were pulled in by circumstances, and upwards nobody sat down and properly re-appraised what we were doing."

This frustration was echoed in an official SADF document on the lessons of the war in Angola. The result of a series of meetings in which officers reviewed the war, the document showed that plans drawn up were repeatedly rejected at the top without reasons. The officers on the ground were also frustrated when requests for the mobilisation of certain units (4 SAI, for example) were rejected and then later approved. "The perception was created that the rejection of previous requests [was] not well considered." Also, the guidelines were changed so often that it resulted in a perception "that there was no decision in advance about what had to be achieved . . .". The repeated rejection of "well-considered plans" also created confusion among commanders about what was expected of them. Moreover, planning groups were not informed of the thinking of the higher headquarters, and they could therefore not understand the need for certain limitations of the operation. That, too, strengthened the perception that the limitations were not well considered.[73]

More than 2000 years ago, the Chinese strategist Sun Tzu, perhaps one of the subtlest military brains in history, wrote: "For to win one hundred victories in one hundred battles is not the acme of skill. To subdue the enemy without fighting is the supreme excellence . . . Thus, those skilled in war subdue the enemy's army without battle."[74] In the same vein, Sir Basil Liddell Hart explained, near the end of his life, that one should never launch an offensive or attack "along the line of natural expectation". To do that would be "to consolidate the opponent's equilibrium, and by stiffening it to augment his resisting power". He came to two conclusions: "The first is that in the face of the overwhelming evidence of history no general is justified in launching his troops to a direct attack upon an enemy firmly in position. The second, that instead of seeking to upset the enemy's equilibrium *by* one's attack, it must be upset *before* a real attack is, or can be successfully, launched . . ."[75]

An offensive west of the Cuito would clearly have upset the enemy's equilibrium *before* the attack even began. And, as Liddell Hart wrote elsewhere, the purpose of strategy is not to overcome resistance: "*Its purpose is to diminish the possibility of resistance*, and it seeks to fulfil this purpose by exploiting the elements of *movement* and *surprise*." In fact, Liddell Hart says, like Sun Tzu, the perfection of operational art would be "to produce a decision *without any serious fighting*".[76] This is exactly what the tactical field commanders did in the series of battles during November 1987. They understood manoeuvre warfare well. Alas, on the operational and strategic level they were let down. Apparently, Sun Tzu and Liddell Hart (and, for that matter, Roland de Vries) were not required reading for those taking decisions in Cape Town or Pretoria. This would have serious negative consequences for the continuation and conclusion of the campaign.

One must emphasise that all of this said in hindsight. But it is also the uncomfortable task of the military historian to use hindsight.

14

THE ROAD TO STALEMATE: OPERATION HOOPER

While the shells were bursting on both sides of the Lomba and at the approaches to the Chambinga, the international political situation was evolving. Following the South African announcement on 11 November that it was engaged in operations in Angola, the UN Security Council condemned "the racist regime of South Africa" for its aggression against Angola. President PW Botha's visit to the front line was also condemned. The UN demanded that South Africa "unconditionally" withdraw its forces from Angola.[1] In a TV interview, the South African Minister of Foreign Affairs, Pik Botha, rejected the demand categorically.[2]

But the UN resolution was indicative of the worsening international climate. Kat Liebenberg – and one may assume that his views were typical of the higher echelons of the military – thought that the SADF would have freedom of action until about 10 December, and that "we shall be forced to withdraw towards the end of December 1987". He felt that a threat to Cuito Cuanavale had to be created "by manoeuvring and movement from the south and southeast", but without engaging in any "decisive battle".[3] This was the genesis of Operation Hooper. Essentially, it meant that the Angolans had to be intimidated into pulling back over the Cuito, as the SADF had tried to do during Operation Askari in 1983/1984. Such a plan did not succeed then, and it is hard to see how it would have succeeded in 1988. In the event, of course, the fighting lasted considerably longer than the end of December.

We will examine the international situation more fully in Chapter 16, but suffice to say here that Fidel Castro was by this time looking for a way out of the Angolan quagmire without losing face. Thus, when he received an urgent appeal for help from the MPLA government in Luanda in early November, he decided on a strategy with three components. Firstly (not in chronological order), he opened up communications with the US and South African governments. Secondly, he got permission from Angolan President José Eduardo dos Santos to take over operational command of the fighting. He also ordered a Cuban tactical group (tanks and mechanised infantry) to Cuito Cuanavale to stiffen Angolan resistance and repeatedly forbade any thought of falling back in the direction of Menongue. These reinforcements were divided among the weakest FAPLA units. Lastly – and most importantly – he dispatched his crack 50 Division from Cuba to Angola; this formation would advance southwards through Cunene province to the South West African border, thereby threatening to outflank those South African units still in the vicinity of Cuito Cuanavale.[4] We shall look at this development more fully in the next chapter, but the import of these decisions now was that the SADF would have to fight for every centimetre of ground. The battleground was considerably smaller than the one south of the Chambinga, with the result that De Vries' "fluid" conditions did not exist. Attrition thus became the name of the game.

The abortive South African attack on 25 November was Operation Moduler's last gasp. The SADF's equipment needed urgent attention. The harsh environment of the preceding weeks had been unlike anything the troops had ever experienced. Their earlier forays into Cunene province had been mostly of limited duration, and in much sparser bush. There was no question of, as in past years, simply taking along enough supplies for 10 to 14 days in the knowledge that they would soon be back at base in northern SWA.

The men, too, were on their last legs. One of the replacements for 61 Mech got a huge fright when he saw those on their way home:

> [W]e were greeted by a phalanx of the wildest, dirtiest-looking people I had ever seen. These guys had not shaved for months, and it looked as though they had not been near water for long. They were wearing filthy overalls and their hair was long. They clapped and cheered as we walked through their ranks to our "new" Ratel. I thought to myself, "These guys look like animals, what the hell have they been doing up there?" As for the Ratel, there was no doubt that it had been through some serious shit over the past few months. It was pretty battered and quite a few things needed fixing before we could even think about taking it into a combat situation.[5]

The South African forces were reorganised. The three combat groups reverted to their "real" names: Combat Group Alpha to 61 Mech, Bravo to 32 Battalion, and Charlie to 4 SAI. Also, 32 Battalion was pulled out to begin preparations for a clandestine operation west of the Cuito – the only concession the generals were prepared to make on cutting off the enemy's communication lines between Menongue and Cuito Cuanavale. In addition to the replacements, a second Olifant tank squadron was sent in. This was manned by Citizen Force soldiers from the Pretoria Regiment under the command of Major Wim Grobler (they were replaced by men from Regiment Molopo after a few weeks). The first squadron was now manned by fresh National Servicemen from the School of Armour in Bloemfontein under the leadership of Major Tim Rudman.

This reorganisation meant that 61 Mech and 4 SAI, together with the two tank squadrons and an artillery regiment (perhaps just over 2 000 men and 24 tanks), would be the only units sent into battle against a vastly superior enemy, consisting of five brigades east of the Cuito and three more to the west.[6] From 13 December, the new operation would get the name of Hooper.[7]

On the Angolan side, FAPLA engaged in a big programme to recruit new soldiers to replace the many hundreds who had fallen against the South African/UNITA forces. There was no time to train them properly, and so they received only elementary training.[8] It would, therefore, appear that the FAPLA forces confronting the SADF at this stage were of an even lower calibre than those that had been defeated so soundly at the Lomba and Chambinga.

At the same time, FAPLA organised its defences rather intelligently. Roland de Vries says that, in contrast to the battles south of the Chambinga, it was now clear that "the principles of defence were implemented by the Cuban masters. There was a clear plan. They had in the meantime learnt and were now desperate."[9] The Angolans stationed their units in three defence lines, each stretching from north to south, one behind the other. Furthest to the east, nearest to the Chambinga high ground, were 21 Brigade in the north, 59 Brigade in the middle and 25 Brigade in the south (*see* map on page 294). Behind that, nearer to the Cuito River, the second line consisted of 16 Brigade in the north, 66 Brigade in the middle at the bridge (with a strong force of 25 tanks), and 3 Tank Battalion in the south. The third defence line lay west of the river, and consisted of 13 Brigade, the Cuban reinforcements that were starting to arrive and a massive array of artillery sited on the high ground, from where they could range far and wide. Only one infantry company was deployed to the south and southwest of Cuito Cuanavale.[10] This, of course, made the Angolans extremely vulnerable to an attack from that direction, but it was not to be.

The battlefield was bordered by the Cuatir River in the north and the Chambinga to the south. The FAPLA defenders had cleverly extended their flanks to the rivers, giving the attackers much less manoeuvring space than had been the case during the November battles south of the Chambinga. There would be no opportunity to "pull a Rommel" on the Angolans by going around their flanks; the South Africans would be forced into frontal attacks on an enemy who had had more than enough time to prepare his defences very carefully. Kat Liebenberg (prophetically, as it turned out) did express his misgivings about "a deliberate attack on, for example, Tumpo in the light of our present capability and the risk connected with high losses".[11] But, given the (political) decision not to launch the offensive in FAPLA's backyard west of the Cuito, the South Africans were forced into the kind of frontal attacks that were a total contradiction of their operational doctrine.

The SADF's task was made more difficult by the virtual sidelining of its excellent radio interception service. Apparently, FAPLA had caught on that the South Africans had been eavesdropping on their radio communications. The bulk of the Angolan communications were now done by telephone, a switch made easier because of the fairly limited area in which their brigades were concentrated.[12]

The first clashes (January 1988)

The South African planning for Operation Hooper took off almost immediately after the failed attack of 25 November. On 26/27 November, a series of intensive planning meetings took place in Rundu between Kat Liebenberg, Fido Smit and the staff of 20 Brigade. Once more the officers on the ground at the front pressed for an advance west of the Cuito to take Cuito Cuanavale from its rear while the bulk of the FAPLA forces were fixed in place east of the river. Once more, this idea was rejected. Liebenberg ordered that FAPLA had to be "fought out of its positions" east of the Cuito. He was, however, prepared to permit a limited, clandestine operation west of the Cuito to threaten the enemy's communication lines between Menongue and Cuito Cuanavale. It was also decided that the SAAF should destroy the bridge over the Cuito with its new H2 "smart" bomb.[13]

With the changeover of the troops completed, Colonel Paul Fouché, a veteran of operations Sceptic and Protea (and well regarded by his colleagues),[14] took over from Deon Ferreira as commander of 20 Brigade. Leon Marais (4 SAI) was replaced by Commandant Jan Malan, and Mike Muller (61 Mech) by Commandant (at the time of writing Brigadier General in the SANDF) Koos Liebenberg, who had distinguished himself during operations Protea and Daisy (*see* Chapter 7).[15] Roland de Vries was posted to Voortrekkerhoogte as commander of the Military College.[16]

Fouché moved his troops to the front as soon as he could and ordered them to shell the enemy to prevent FAPLA from knowing that there would now be a short period of inactivity. The artillery, however, was in bad shape; the logistic apparatus of the SADF simply was not up to supplying a brigade so far from home in such a harsh environment.[17] In addition, there was no single entity in Pretoria, Grootfontein or Rundu that could decide on the priorities for loading trains, lorries or aircraft, taking into account what was needed at the front. Everything was done fairly haphazardly, which led to repeated crises, in spite of superhuman efforts by those directly involved.[18]

On 11 December, Liebenberg issued the formal operational instruction for Operation Hooper, lifting the veil somewhat on how the leadership viewed the immediate future. The basic aim was this: that which had been won should not be squandered again. Therefore, the enemy should either be destroyed east of the river or, at the very least, be pushed back over it with maximum losses, while the SADF should incur the minimum possible losses. In the light of the debate that ensued about the campaign, one of the operational guidelines was telling: "If the opportunity arises to occupy Cuito Cuanavale fairly easily, it should be planned to do it." The South African forces should remain at the front until the enemy is no longer a threat to UNITA, Liebenberg ordered.[19] (Jannie Geldenhuys's assertion after the campaign that Cuito Cuanavale would not be attacked unless it fell into the SADF's hands almost without a fight[20] is, therefore, entirely true.)

However, the newcomers first had to be acclimatised and undergo additional battle training, which meant that the two mechanised units, 61 Mech and 4 SAI, would not be able to attack before 26 December.[21] This meant, of course, that Liebenberg's deadline of 31 December was completely unrealistic, and so the start of the operation was moved to 5 January. In the end, the South Africans stayed in Angola until deep into 1988.

Paul Fouché and his staff drew up a plan for an attack on the FAPLA brigades east of the river, and presented it to Jannie Geldenhuys on 23 December.[22] It boiled down to the following: UNITA would carry out diversionary attacks on 25 Brigade in the south and 59 Brigade in the centre of the outer FAPLA defence line; then 4 SAI would assault 21 Brigade in the north, while 61 Mech at first covered 4 SAI from the south; 61 Mech would slip through the gap between 59 and 21 Brigades while they were fighting for their lives, and advance directly to attack 16 Brigade in the second FAPLA defence line; and finally, 61 Mech – which would have both tank squadrons for this attack – would exploit the breakthrough right to the bridge over the Cuito, or wheel southwards to help UNITA in its fight against 59 and 21 Brigades.[23]

It was an excellent and ambitious plan. Its risk perhaps lay in the fact that Fouché had only two – albeit both fairly powerful – mechanised units at his disposal, giving him no reserves if and when needed. Fouché was confronted by the fact that he could not outflank the enemy; he had no alternative but to attack frontally.[24] But, within those limits, the plan was very intelligent. It utilised feints by 4 SAI in the north and UNITA in the south to the fullest possible extent, while 61 Mech, with the full complement of tanks, would attack the seam between 21 and 59 Brigades, always a weak point in any defensive system. Once through the outer defence line, there was a good chance that 61 Mech could exploit the confusion by advancing to the Cuito bridge to cut off the withdrawal route of the FAPLA formations.

But Geldenhuys rejected the plan, accusing Fouché of being "too aggressive" and risking too many casualties. He told Fouché to rely more on "psychological action", to concentrate the attack on just one enemy brigade and to let UNITA initiate the attacks.[25] Once again, this showed the nervousness of the higher military echelons about being involved in another man's war so deep in another country. In fact, in a confidential review of the lessons of the war, this was explicitly identified as a problem: "Commanders experienced this approval of plans, on the levels on which it happened, as 'looking over the shoulder' because of a lack of confidence in the concerned individual as commander."[26]

Accordingly, a new plan was drawn up. It was decided to concentrate the attack on 21 Brigade in the north of the outer FAPLA defence line. An artillery bombardment would first be used to intimidate FAPLA into leaving its positions. (As an experienced field commander, Fouché was likely doubtful about this scenario.) If artillery did not have the desired effect, UNITA infantry would attack, while the SADF would offer only fire support. If UNITA could not take the enemy positions, 4 SAI (with both Olifant squadrons) would weigh in; once the enemy had been driven away, 4 SAI would withdraw and allow UNITA to occupy the positions, while 61 Mech (with both Ratel 90 squadrons) would cover 4 SAI from the south. This plan was approved, with the understanding that the attackers had to wait for cloudy weather in order to neutralise the enemy command of the air.[27] This was a plan that could, through no fault of the frontline commanders, only be described as timid. While one cannot fault Geldenhuys for his concern for his men, battles are not won by half-measures.

In compliance with the order to use "psychological action", the SADF employed "ground-shout" teams, operating with huge loudspeakers, to exhort the FAPLA soldiers to desert. The artillery also shelled the enemy with pamphlets to the same effect. The "ground-shout" apparently did scare some enemy soldiers, but UNITA told the rather red-faced South Africans that very few FAPLA soldiers could even read, so that the entire pamphlet effort was a waste of time and money.[28]

The attack finally took place on 2 January 1988. After midnight, the South African artillery started a concentrated bombardment of 21 Brigade, and at 02h00 the 81-mm mortars of 4 SAI weighed in as well. Of course, the bombardment did not work, and the enemy did not run away. At 04h45, 4 SAI was ordered to pull back, and plan B kicked in. At 06h00, the SAAF swooped over, releasing its pre-fragmented bombs on the hapless FAPLA soldiers cowering in their bunkers and trenches. Immediately afterwards, UNITA launched its attack, discovering empty forward trenches. Turning southwards, they came under heavy mortar and artillery fire. Recoiling, the UNITA troops withdrew – clearly proving that the movement's forces were more suitable for guerrilla warfare than a deliberate conventional attack in the face of severe defensive fire.[29] The full-scale SADF attack would have to take place after all.

The next day – 3 January – did bring about success of another kind. Two SAAF Buccaneer bombers, escorted by four Mirage F1AZs, took off early in the morning from Grootfontein Air Force Base to attack the Cuito bridge, but turned back when several MiG-23s were detected in the air. Shortly before midday, the South Africans tried again, and this time they were not disturbed. Having reached the target area, one Buccaneer launched an H2 "smart" glide bomb at the bridge. The H2 was steered by the navigator in the rear seat via a TV link, requiring the aircraft to maintain a line-of-sight communication until the bomb hit the target. After several previous attempts had failed, this sortie finally had success. The bomb hit the bridge but did not bring it down, although it blasted a gap of about 20 m and made it temporarily unsuitable for the movement of vehicles and supplies. The Angolans had to establish a pontoon bridge to continue their supply flow, and later repaired the structure. Two MiG-23s took off rapidly from Menongue to intercept the South Africans, but, having acquired the formation of six SAAF aircraft on their radars, they understandably returned to base.[30]

Paul Fouché decided to try again to dislodge 21 Brigade from its positions through a deliberate attack by 4 SAI, aided by UNITA light infantry (the third phase of the plan that started on 2 January). Being somewhat isolated on FAPLA's northern flank, 21 Brigade could expect help only from its southern neighbour, 59 Brigade. To counter this possibility, 61 Mech would cover 4 SAI from that side. To give extra punch to 4 SAI, both tank squadrons were placed under Jan Malan's command, while the two Ratel 90 squadrons were concentrated with Koos Liebenberg's 61 Mech.[31]

The onslaught commenced at 09h45 on 13 January with an SAAF strike and artillery bombardment on 21 Brigade to soften up its defences. At 11h00, 4 SAI's mechanised forces started rolling for what was to become another day full of horror and dying. FAPLA immediately let rip with artillery fire, but the Angolan gunners brought their shells down on empty positions, where the South Africans had earlier drawn attention to themselves as part of a feint. The South Africans had already pinpointed the Angolan artillery positions, and one gun was trained on each known position. As soon as the Angolans opened fire, the designated South African G-5s returned fire, and within minutes the FAPLA guns fell silent.

The dense bush made the advance very difficult, and the first real clash did not take place until the early afternoon. About 20 brave FAPLA defenders stoutly kept the advancing Olifants under rifle fire, jumping out from a bunker, shooting and dashing back. Of course, the AK-47 bullets simply ricocheted off the thick tank hulls. An Olifant advanced up to the bunker, inserted its 105-mm gun into the embrasure and fired a high-explosive shell. What happened to the Angolans does not bear telling.

Having taken the first positions, 4 SAI wheeled northwards to help UNITA on its right flank, where stronger resistance was experienced. The intervention by the South African unit convinced the FAPLA defenders to withdraw. However, when a Ratel detonated a mine and lost a wheel, 4 SAI suddenly found itself in a minefield. Also, the low clouds began to dissipate, and, sure enough, with the sun came a gaggle of angry MiGs. An air attack forced 4 SAI to take cover, but, as usual, the MiGs dropped their bombs wide of the mark. In addition, as soon as the MiGs were spotted, the SADF gunners would fire a 120-mm mortar to mark 21 Brigade's positions with white phosphorus, leading the MiGs to attack their own troops.

The South Africans were now ready for the attack on 21 Brigade's main positions. On 4 SAI's left flank, 61 Mech was prepared to repulse any FAPLA attempt to come to 21 Brigade's aid. The brigade was more or less cut off, the only reinforcements being five extra tanks from 16 Brigade at Tumpo (*see* map on page 342).

The FAPLA positions were cunningly laid out, with strong bunkers and minefields, which made the SADF attack extremely difficult. Two enemy tanks were shot out almost immediately. A BM-21 "Stalin organ" MRL fired its complete complement of rockets horizontally at the South African armour, but, although this slowed down the attackers, none hit a target. The real problem came when the formidable 23-mm cannon joined in. These could not do the tanks any harm, but the Ratels were extremely vulnerable. One 23-mm shell went right though a Ratel turret, missing the gunner's head by a hair's breadth. Two of the 23-mm guns were shot out, and a third T-55 destroyed, after which the surviving two tanks, together with other vehicles, fled southwards, straight into the welcoming arms of 61 Mech. This part of the battle had lasted only 58 minutes. FAPLA simply could not withstand the ferocity of 4 SAI's attack.

A trooper later remembered:

> The sight that greeted us was one out of a Vietnam film. Everything I had seen in the movies was the same – the terrain as well as the chaos. Pretty soon we came upon the enemy positions – lots of trenches and bunkers with T-34 tanks [sic; they were T-54/55s] dug in. We had learned to do bunker and trench clearing drills but here we saw an easier way of doing it – simply drive an Olifant tank up to the bunker, position the 105 mm barrel inside and let off an HE round – no more bunker! . . . The noise inside the Ratel was incredible. The smell of cordite filled the inside. It was incredibly hot inside as we had all the hatches closed and fear and excitement was leaving us all drenched in sweat. I looked over at Mark and he was grinning, shouting to Van der Merwe "soek, soek, soek" [seek, seek, seek]. The Ratels had a much quicker-turning turret than the Olifants so they would watch where the 20 mm cannon were firing and then hit the same target.[32]

The subsequent fighting lasted until after dark, and Jan Malan had to fire star shell with his mortars to illuminate the battlefield, "in spite of", as he put it, "several enemy tanks in flames which lit up the terrain between the bushes considerably. Beyond this, there were terrible explosions the whole time as tank ammunition exploded and big pieces of steel flew around."[33] Ratel 90s of 61 Mech killed three of 21 Brigade's fleeing tanks and four armoured vehicles, but other drivers just thundered through 61 Mech at maximum speed. When the South Africans fired at them, the panic-stricken crews abandoned their vehicles and fled on foot. At one stage, the South Africans observed the surreal sight of about 30 naked FAPLA soldiers stampeding past. Shortly before midnight, silence once more descended on the battlefield. The South Africans and UNITA had taken 21 Brigade's positions, and the brigade had been severely mauled.

The next morning, 4 SAI exploited its victory east of the Cuito and north of the Dala River (*see* map on page 342) and captured numerous pieces of enemy equipment. By midday, the area had been swept clean of the enemy.

An enthusiastic Jan Malan even advanced on the Cuito bridge (with only four tanks, of which one had a faulty gun); when Paul Fouché heard where he was, he ordered Malan to take position east of 21 Brigade's old lines. "The MiGs swarmed in the air, and that morning a host of their parachute-braked bombs fell right in my laager!" Malan remembered years later.[34]

Statistically, it was another big South African victory. Seven FAPLA tanks were destroyed and five captured intact, four armoured cars destroyed and two captured, two rocket launchers, three 23-mm guns and seven logistical vehicles destroyed and three captured. They had also lost about 150 men (dead and captured), against UNITA's 4 dead and 18 wounded. One SADF Ratel 20 was damaged and recovered, and one man wounded (by a comrade who apparently lost his cool). The figures proved that Geldenhuys's fears of high South African casualties were exaggerated.

Operationally, however, it was a draw. Although 21 Brigade's positions had been taken, and a gap punched in the Angolan defence line, these gains could not be exploited properly. As Jan Breytenbach correctly remarks, another unit with two more tank squadrons was actually needed to follow up the tactical gains. But 61 Mech had no tanks, only Ratel 90s, which were not up to the job:

> To put it bluntly, the brigade commander, Colonel Paul Fouché, had been given insufficient combat power to do the job . . . It appears that the coffee-drinking generals . . . had somehow lost sight of the most important principle of war – which demands that an adequate reserve should always be maintained to grasp unexpected opportunities when they present themselves.[35]

Here again, political considerations – the government's understandable unwillingness to be sucked into an Angolan quagmire – collided with operational and tactical necessities. Nevertheless, it is difficult to see why political considerations should have precluded the allocation of a sufficient force to do the job that PW Botha himself had ordered at the end of September 1987. The fault, it seems, does not lie with the government in this case, but with the generals in Pretoria – like Jannie Geldenhuys, who shot down Paul Fouché's original plan as being "too aggressive".

In any event, 4 SAI and 61 Mech withdrew from the battlefield, leaving UNITA to occupy the enemy positions. This made sense, as Jan Malan explained, for the scene was only 16 km from the enemy artillery, which would know exactly where the South Africans were. Besides, swarms of enemy MiGs were in the air; knowing the units' exact position would make the air strikes on target for the first time in the war.[36] It was for this reason that army doctrine called for attackers to fight *through* the objective and not to stop *on* it.

After the battle of 13 January, Castro sent some 200 advisors, officers and NCOs, artillerymen and tankers, as well as arms and equipment technicians and his best pilots from Cuba to the front. From Menongue came a tactical group, consisting of tanks, mechanised infantry and artillery, to remind the demoralised Angolans to fight to the bitter end. Castro was resolved to turn Cuito Cuanavale into a symbol, comparable to Dunkirk (1940), or perhaps to Verdun (1916), where the French general Robert Nivelle uttered the stirring words "*Ils ne passeront pas!*" (They shall not pass!). On 23 January, the South Africans intercepted a radio communication indicating that the Angolan Minister of Defence had ordered the withdrawal of all FAPLA forces from Cuito Cuanavale and the erection of bunkers to defend Menongue.[37] This was exactly what Castro had forbidden.

As Castro put it a few months later in a speech:

> The thing was to protect Cuito Cuanavale, prevent the enemy from annihilating the Angolan troops and taking that position that was becoming a symbol of resistance and of South Africa's success or failure ... Steps were taken not only to stop the South Africans but to turn Cuito Cuanavale into a trap, into a trap the South Africans walked right into![38]

We shall analyse Castro's strategy in the next chapter; suffice to say here that he was losing confidence in the Cuban commander in Angola, General de División (Major General) Arnaldo Ochoa Sánchez. He left Ochoa in command in Luanda, but decided to send one of his confidants, General de División Leopoldo Cintra Frías (affectionately known as "Polo"), to southern Angola. According to Castro's testimony against Ochoa in a (probably trumped-up) drug smuggling court case in 1989, Ochoa had disastrously misjudged the tactical situation at

Cuito Cuanavale, signalling to Havana that the South Africans were on their last legs and that FAPLA could safely withdraw to Menongue to continue the fight against UNITA elsewhere. On 12 January, Castro wrote to Ochoa, refuting these claims and telling him that the SADF was not yet beaten. This, of course, was dramatically proven by the attack of 13 January. In the light of the events of that day, Castro wrote to Ochoa that 59 and 25 Brigades were exposed to the possibility of another breakthrough similar to that at 21 Brigade's positions. Therefore, he gave the following order:

> The defence perimeter east of the river should be reduced by pulling back the 59th and 25th Brigades towards positions that are well forti-fied and closer to the river. These two brigades should cover the east so that the 8th Brigade can resume its mission of supplying food [from Menongue]. The current positions of the 59th and 25th Brigades are very risky, since they are exposed to the possibility of a breakthrough in the area where the 21st Brigade was located. We can't continue running those risks.[39]

Two observations must be made. The first is that Castro was already planning his next move: a march to the South West African border in Cunene, far to the west. He was planning to make the defence of Cuito Cuanavale a heroic symbol, but he knew that the Cunene advance would be the decisive move. He simply wanted to stop the SADF from advancing over the river and taking the town, rather than to force a decision here. Second, it made sense to shorten the FAPLA defence lines in order to make them stronger, thereby making it more difficult for the SADF to break through. This would also bring the South Africans within range of the massed Angolan artillery on the west bank of the Cuito. As we shall see, Castro's assessment was correct. Whatever one may think of his politics, he was a very good tactician and strategist.

But Castro's orders were not immediately carried out. On the contrary, UNITA was not able to resist when FAPLA – 21 Brigade, reinforced with members of 8 Brigade, a fresh formation – advanced again and pushed the UNITA fighters out of 21 Brigade's old positions.[40] On the face of it, the gains of 13 January had been lost, as the enemy defence line was repaired. This did not escape the notice of the SADF troops, and it was left to Major General Willie Meyer, commander of SWATF, to explain lamely that it was – in the words of Fred Bridgland – "sometimes desirable to let an enemy retake a position so that it could be destroyed completely in a later attack!"[41] It was absurd, and it is hard to blame the troops for their low opinion of the generals. Once again, the lack of South African reserves played a role.

Clash of armour: the attack of 14 February

When Jan Malan and Koos Liebenberg were both diagnosed with jaundice and evacuated, Malan's place at 4 SAI was taken by Commandant Cassie Schoeman, while Mike Muller returned to 61 Mech. Paul Fouché departed for Pretoria to mobilise 82 Brigade – a Citizen Force formation – to take the place of 20 Brigade. He was replaced by Colonel Pat McLoughlin.[42]

The reoccupation of 21 Brigade's positions meant, of course, that the 13 January battle had to be refought. But the South Africans realised that an exact repetition would be unwise. The enemy would be well prepared for it. Therefore, 59 Brigade, in the middle of the outer FAPLA defence line, became the main target. It was felt that this formation was the strongest of the three (25 in the south, 59 in the middle and 21 in the north). If 59 Brigade could be defeated, FAPLA might feel impelled to pull the other two brigades back in a general withdrawal to the so-called Tumpo Triangle between the Cuito, Tumpo and Dala rivers. At the same time, UNITA would undertake a feint attack on 21 Brigade, while 61 Mech would position itself between 59 and 21 Brigades in order to cover 4 SAI, the main assault force, from the north.[43]

The date for the attack had to be postponed repeatedly because of the SADF's inability to keep its forces at the front properly supplied. The distances and extreme harshness of the terrain were simply too much for the army's logistics system. In some instances, spare parts for the weapons systems and vehicles had been ordered two months previously, but still had not been delivered. Everything had to be flown in to Mavinga and then laboriously taken by truck to the front. At this stage, Jean Lausberg, for instance, reported that only four of his 16 G-5 guns were serviceable.[44]

Nevertheless, most of the equipment problems were sorted out by 14 February, when the next attack took place. The delay also meant that FAPLA had ample time to make provision for a suitable welcoming committee for the unwanted visitors. Strong defensive positions were prepared, with bunkers, trenches, minefields and carefully plotted fire targets for the massed artillery across the river. The bridge over the Cuito was repaired. A never-ending stream of reinforcements, including troops, tanks and armoured cars, flowed over the bridge each night, when the South African artillery could not take them under fire. It was clear that the next attack would not be easy.

At the same time, the South Africans' numbers were being thinned out by jaundice and malaria.[45]

One trooper later reminisced:

> Mental Status: Really had reached the stage beyond anger, caring etc. Common saying "ek voel fokol" [I feel fuck-all]. There was this total sense of detachment, like as if not much was real, yet everything was very clear, focused, on your survival, nobody talked about home, some days the depression was almost tangible, most times there was a devil-may-care attitude, stalking the camp. This was made worse by the fact that mail, cigarettes and cooldrinks, were only available once every 2–3 weeks, each section got 2 packets of smokes, 1 Coke (flat) and one chocolate, it was then that we took to robbing corpses . . .

> Our main bother was the flies, flies were everywhere in their thousands, during the day one had no peace . . . The flies were so bad, that when doing nothing (most of the time), we would use scarves to cover our faces, both ours and FAPLA scarves were a kind of material with lots of small holes in it. The flies would try to worm their way through these to get at you, it was quite incredible. The worst however was when you had to take a dump. If you sat in one place, they would try to crawl up your arse, the worst feeling in the world, so we would normally dump, hop, dump, hop, wipe and back off. Dunn [a trooper] used to get so pissed off he would use his MAG on them, only made things worse, more shit, more flies. We also used to use explosives, gunpowder etc, to try to wipe out as many as possible with varying degrees of success.

What made it worse was that there was no toilet paper, we used what we could, leaves, grass, papers from ratpacks, letters from home etc.[46]

Early on 14 February the South Africans moved out for the attack. At 08h30, the artillery started belching fire, and about an hour later two battalions of UNITA infantry made first contact with 21 Brigade. This was the final event in convincing the enemy that 21 Brigade would again be the main target. But it wasn't, of course, and the reinforcements previously sent to 21 Brigade thus meant that the defending forces were incorrectly positioned.[47]

To begin with, 4 SAI's main march took it first in the direction of 21 Brigade, as the idea was to assault 59 Brigade on its flank from the north, but this also served to strengthen the impression that 21 Brigade was the intended target. Radio intercepts revealed at this stage that 21 Brigade's troops (remember that a lot of them had lived through the horror of the 13 January fight) started to panic. The panic was magnified by the fact that all the brigade commanders happened to be at a conference in the village of Nancova, west of Cuito Cuanavale.

Because of the dense forest and the constant presence of MiGs in the air, the South African advance was slow, and the enemy perforce was in a constant quandary, not knowing where the blow would fall. By 14h50, both 4 SAI and 61 Mech were in position.

The attack started well. The front positions at both 59 Brigade and 21 Brigade were hastily evacuated, and total panic broke out. Using fire and movement in quick spurts of 50 to 100 m at a time, 4 SAI swept through the 59 Brigade positions without much trouble. Several 23-mm cannon caused some difficulty, but they were promptly shot out by the Olifants and Ratels. An abortive T-55 counterattack was thrown into disarray when the excellent SADF electronic intelligence service jammed the enemy tank radio net. A Ratel 90 destroyed a T-55, and the Olifants killed another four. One Olifant suffered a "cook-off" – a shell exploding in the barrel, splitting it open. A BM-21 rocket launcher launched its missiles horizontally at the South Africans, which was quite scary, but they all missed. The terrified FAPLA troops started running as fast as their legs could carry them in the direction of the river behind them, with many killed by the deluge of bullets and shells.. In an intercepted radio message, 59 Brigade said the morale of the troops was "below zero".

To Fidel Castro, far away in Havana, it seemed as if the South Africans wanted to surround 59 Brigade.[48] It is not known if he had anything to do with what followed, but the enemy reacted intelligently by ordering 3 Tank Battalion and 25 Brigade (with an infantry battalion and four tanks) in the south to counterattack northwards. Pat McLoughlin told 61 Mech to be ready to exploit the breakthrough in the direction of Tumpo. But first the expected counterattack (five tanks were observed coming from Tumpo) had to be dealt with, and 4 SAI was thus ordered to fix them while 61 Mech would spurt southwards and hit them in their flank. In tandem, 61 Mech and 4 SAI now moved southwards, 61 Mech in the west and 4 SAI about 2 km east of it.

What McLoughlin could not know was that these five tanks were part of the reinforcements coming from 25 Brigade, and that they had prepared an ambush for the South Africans just beyond the tree line at the edge of an open shona. These tanks were either wholly or partially manned by Cubans, under the command of Lieutenant Colonel "Ciro" Gómez Betancourt – the first time since the Battle of Cassinga a decade previously that South Africans and Cubans would come eye to eye on the battlefield.

Two things are clear about this confrontation. One, the Cubans did not lack courage. Two, what they had in overabundance was rashness.

The South Africans at first did not see the trap, and moved into the tree line. The Cuban tanks were well camouflaged and covered by the dense jungle, so that they were only detected at distances of some 10 m. Then, instead of waiting until all the Olifants and Ratels were in the trap, some overenthusiastic Cuban tank commanders attacked immediately. According to 61 Mech's official report, the Cubans were "aggressive" and "death-defying", although they were not well handled and attacked "in a mob".

The battle that followed was furious and confusing. For one Ratel 20 (call sign 22 Charlie), confusion reigned when the vehicle was hit, either by fire from the feared 23-mm cannon or by a 105-mm shell from an Olifant.[49] Whatever the source, the effect was devastating, as an eyewitness account confirms:

> We were about 100 m into the bush when we got hit from the side. Suddenly there was a deafening bang. The Ratel pitched from one side to the other; there was smoke everywhere, and then the smell of burning

flesh. Then I saw blood on the inside of the windscreen. Corporal Strauss radioed that we had been hit; he was starting to cry as he thought we had lost men. He was also injured, and so was the gunner. The gunner, driver (me) and the section leader were in full radio contact – I could hear them groaning in pain. Almost suffocating from the smoke, all of us just wanted to get out of the Ratel. We still did not know the full impact of what just happened and we could see nothing. I started to panic. I had no air and I just wanted to get out. I was shit scared!

I wanted to get out through the driver's turret, but I could not, so I opened the side doors. We managed to get out (those of us who were still alive) and lay down on the ground next to the Ratel. Most were badly injured and covered in blood. One buddy, JJ Groenewald, had been hit by shrapnel, opening his throat right up. He almost suffocated in his own blood. The gunner and section leader were also hit by shrapnel in their upper bodies. On the left side of the Ratel were 4 x 23 mm holes, cutting right through the vehicle and exiting through the other side. The troops sitting in the back were hit head on . . . One of my buddies was still sitting upright and buckled in his seat, but his neck was all I could see. No head. The others were all face down, their seatbelts also still fastened. I knew there was no life left there.[50]

One Olifant was also damaged, but was recovered and repaired afterwards. In reaction, Mike Muller decided on a firebelt action to bring down the maximum amount of firepower on the enemy. The noise, the explosion of the shells, the crack of the tank and Ratel 90 guns, and the chatter of the Ratel 20s and machine-gun fire must have been overwhelming. The Cuban commander, very intelligently, kept his tank moving; although it was hit three times, by the end of the day his was the only enemy tank still operational. The torrent of fire from the South Africans did the trick. Seven T-55s, a BTR-60 and three more vehicles were destroyed here, while 14 Cubans were killed in their tanks. About 100 FAPLA soldiers joined them in their version of Valhalla. Bravely, Gómez exploited the South African withdrawal to pick up nine wounded compatriots and take them to his own lines.

A few months later, Fidel Castro claimed that the South Africans' aim to surround the Angolans was "prevented by a desperate counterattack by an Angolan-Cuban tank company". Although the Angolan/Cuban losses were heavy, "this was not in vain for a disaster was averted and time was gained for the Angolan 59th, 25th and 21st Brigades to regroup".[51] This seems correct. In fact, Pat McLoughlin had already ordered 61 Mech to advance towards Tumpo – which, as Castro correctly saw, could have had the result of cutting the three Angolan brigades off – but the counterattack prevented this. And when the counterattack was at last finally defeated, it was already dark. In fact, McLoughlin consulted both Cassie Schoeman and Mike Muller as to whether their units were fit enough to continue the fight the next morning, but too much of their equipment needed attention, and they demurred.[52]

Just after 19h00, McLoughlin ordered 61 Mech and 4 SAI to withdraw. It was too late now to pursue the enemy. In total, more than 500 FAPLA men were killed and 32 Cubans, plus 15 T-55s, 3 BRDM-2s, 1 BMP-1, 4 BTR-60s, 7 23-mm guns, 1 BM-21, 1 SA-13 and 8 trucks were lost. Four South Africans were killed (all in the one Ratel, as described above), 11 wounded and no equipment was lost.[53]

During the night, 21 Brigade withdrew to Tumpo and 59 Brigade crossed the Cuito. The next morning, the enemy command hastily ordered 59 Brigade back to Tumpo, and assembled three battalions for an attack in an attempt to retake 59's positions. The attack was not pressed very hard and was repulsed, which meant that the easternmost FAPLA defence line had, for all practical purposes, disintegrated. The second line, at the Tumpo Triangle, became the only toehold left east of the Cuito.

Interlude

While the South Africans had breached the outer shell of the Cuban/Angolan alliance's defences, the hard inner core was still there. Anybody with intelligence could see that the fighting was heading for a stalemate, and the leadership on both sides tried to deal with it.

In Havana, Fidel Castro observed the successive South African victories with growing anger and frustration. In vain, he bombarded Ochoa with telegrams ordering a withdrawal to the Tumpo Triangle to shorten and strengthen the defence line. He summoned Ochoa to Havana on 31 January to report in person. Ochoa arrived on 5 February, and was promptly sent back, as Castro reported at the general's trial a few months later, "with precise instructions to secure a readjustment of the lines east of the river, the line that was 18 kilometres east, almost out of range of our artillery which was to the west . . .".[54] The day after the 14 February attack, Castro cabled Ochoa that he (Ochoa) had "always underestimated possible enemy action". He added that "here we feel bitter over what happened because it was repeatedly anticipated and warned about".[55]

But still his orders were not carried out. In further messages, Castro revealed his strategic thinking regarding the defence of Cuito Cuanavale, and it is relevant to quote from them in detail. On 20 February, he wrote to Ochoa that it would be a "total disaster" if the South Africans broke through to the Cuito: "Should that happen, it would be hard to hold Cuito [Cuanavale] and the political and moral consequences for FAPLA and the Angolan government would be terrible." On the 21st:

> What would happen if tomorrow the enemy breaks through the line with a powerful attack in the direction of the river? . . . we feel there is a lack of foresight, that those in charge there don't realize the terrible effects on the military and political situation and on morale a disaster with the forces east of the river would have, and we don't even have a few boats to do what the British did with theirs in Dunkirk . . . In our opinion, the formula outlined in my message yesterday should be adopted without further delay, i.e., keep a strongly fortified position with no more than one brigade east of the river, with a staggered line of defence and the tanks at the ready in the rear.[56]

In the event, the problem was solved for Castro by the SADF. Its success on 14 February meant that the defenders were driven back into the Tumpo Triangle, a relatively small area that could be fortified quite heavily, and from where it would be almost impossible to dislodge them.

At the same time, it is clear that Castro completely misunderstood the South African objectives. He thought that they wanted to take Cuito Cuanavale. While this was indeed debated among the SADF generals, staff officers and field commanders, this was done in the context of marching northwards to the *west* of the Cuito River and attacking the town from behind. However, these proposals were turned down every time, as we have seen. All primary sources make it clear that the South African purpose was simply to drive the Angolans over the river, to fortify the Cuito, turn it over to UNITA and go home.[57]

On 29 January, two weeks before the last attack, several generals, among them Jannie Geldenhuys, Jan van Loggerenberg, Denis Earp, Rudolf "Witkop" Badenhorst and Willie Meyer, visited 20 Brigade's tactical headquarters. From the minutes of their meeting with the field commanders it is clear that uneasiness was growing about the length of the South African involvement in another country's war. Geldenhuys impressed on the officers that the South African forces could not stay too long in Angola. But when the SADF withdrew, it had to happen in a way that the enemy could not benefit from it and that the South Africans would not forfeit the advantages they had achieved. More practically, FAPLA had to be driven to the western side of the Cuito, the river had to be built up as defence line, and UNITA had to be empowered to defend this line itself. In his capacity as commander of SWATF, Willie Meyer also emphasised once again the need to keep South African losses to a minimum.[58]

In his memoirs, Geldenhuys relates that this uneasiness was shared by President PW Botha. In two instances, he says, Botha told him in the company of others that the SADF had to finish its job in Angola quickly and come back: "He was serious and firm, but not sharp. When Mr Botha finished talking, you did not have any doubts about what he wanted. He did not want to have a 'Vietnam'. We had to fulfil our mission and withdraw from Angola."[59]

Nevertheless, whatever uneasiness Pretoria and Cape Town might have had, the conditions for withdrawal had not yet been fulfilled. The fighting was not yet over, not by a long shot.

Behind enemy lines

The continuous pressure applied by various SADF field commanders to attack the Angolans from the west in their rear areas did have one effect. The high command decided that 32 Battalion – which would still be known as Combat Group Bravo for this phase – could send a force west of the Cuito. FAPLA supply convoys came from Menongue at regular intervals, making up whatever losses the SADF inflicted. It made no sense to leave them undisturbed. The idea was to disrupt the enemy's command and control, to fix their forces west of the river and even to draw troops from east of the river. A standoff bombardment of the enemy air base at Menongue was also foreseen. But the usual impractical restrictions were reimposed: minimum manpower or equipment losses were to be incurred, and the move had to remain clandestine. No South African was permitted nearer than a kilometre to the main road between Menongue and Cuito Cuanavale.[60]

Following the wrap-up of Operation Moduler in the middle of December, 32 Battalion's men had been pulled back from the front. They spent the next two weeks or so resting, recuperating and re-equipping. The need to cut FAPLA's supply lines was becoming more urgent by the day, but the unit could be ready only after New Year's Day. Therefore, Commandant Jan Hougaard was sent in at the beginning of December with a company of 101 Battalion and a Valkiri battery, as well as a support company with 81-mm mortars, jeep-mounted 106-mm antitank guns and Milan antitank missiles. A number of Recces also joined the makeshift force, which would be aided by UNITA guides and guerrilla units in the vicinity. It was risky to send in such a small force; if they were cornered by the enemy, they would stand no chance.

Hougaard played it safe. He hid his force out of sight in the bush, and at first only guided in several SAAF strikes on the supply convoys coming from Menongue, as well as bombarding them with UNITA's 120-mm mortars to prevent the enemy from knowing that there was an SADF force in their rear. Finally, on 10 January, Hougaard fired two full ripples of rockets at a FAPLA convoy, destroying more than 60 vehicles. From that point onwards, Hougaard told Fred Bridgland, "it was open season on the convoys, hitting them with everything we had whenever good opportunities arose, even putting in UNITA infantry ground attacks right along the road".[61]

By 22 January, Combat Group Bravo was fully recovered, and moved out from Rundu to replace Hougaard's little force. Hougaard had lost only three men: two killed and one wounded when they investigated a booby-trapped MiG that had been shot down. Robbie Hartslief took over and hit at least 16 convoys with his rockets during February, causing considerable carnage along the way.

An American journalist, Karl Maier, was flown by helicopter during February 1988 from Menongue to Cuito Cuanavale. He reported what he saw:

> Down below is a column of hundreds of tanks, armoured cars, fuel trucks and troop carriers weaving slowly in and out of the charred remains of vehicles which have been blown apart by South African jets in strafing runs and UNITA guerrilla attacks. At several points the road is blocked by immense traffic jams, with inevitable crowds of soldiers arguing with each other about how to clear the way. Dozens of tanks are dug in under the trees and behind them are rows of trenches for the ground troops. Every few minutes the MiG-23s scream overhead on their way to the front.[62]

A Cuban journalist, César Gómez Chacón, counted 165 wrecks on this road at about the same time.[63] And Soviet Lieutenant Colonel Igor Zhdarkin remembered seeing the wrecks of 29 petrol tankers, as well as of 350 tanks, armoured cars and trucks on "the road of life",[64] which might as well have been called "the road of death".

In order to coincide with the big assault on 59 Brigade by 4 SAI and 61 Mech on 13 January and to prevent the enemy from hitting the SADF attackers from the air, Hartslief received orders to execute a standoff attack on Menongue air base. On the night preceding the onslaught on 59 Brigade, two ripples of Valkiri rockets were fired at Menongue, and Hartslief immediately moved away to evade the inevitable retaliation. The Angolans never found the culprits, but the results were not encouraging. Only one aircraft was damaged, while seven Cubans and a number of Angolan air force personnel were killed. That afternoon, the MiGs were in the air again to make life difficult for 4 SAI and 61 Mech.[65]

By the beginning of March, the whole force was back at Rundu.

What did this foray achieve? It is clear that a lot more could have been achieved, had the military leadership been willing to think out of the box. But their timidity did not pay off. "I think we succeeded in slowing the logistics operation down," was Hartslief's final assessment. "But that's all. We could have destroyed it, but we weren't given the means or the latitude to do so."[66] In other words, in order to reach the basic objective of forcing the enemy across the river, more frontal attacks were necessary. Now the going would really get tough.

15

STALEMATE AT TUMPO

FAPLA's withdrawal into the Tumpo Triangle resulted in a new ball game for both sides. The area was bordered on the north side by the Dala River, on the south side by the Tumpo River, and on the west by the Cuito. It had a surface of no more than 30 sq km.[1] There was relatively little room to manoeuvre, which meant that the South African Army's strength, which lay in its mobility, was curtailed.

Operationally, the Tumpo Triangle was deemed to be of decisive importance. The staff officer who chronicled Operation Hooper summarised it aptly (and one imagines that this gave an accurate rendering of the feeling at Defence Force and Army Headquarters):

> For the enemy possession of Cuito Cuanavale was more a moral prerequisite than a strategic necessity, as the town could not be occupied and held by own forces [SADF]. Thus was the enemy propaganda surrounding Cuito Cuanavale however that the enemy simply could not afford to surrender the town to the RSA/UNITA forces. For the RSA forces the occupation of Tumpo was the last stumbling block before they could regard their orders as carried out.[2]

A trooper who went through the first two of the three Tumpo battles described the difficult terrain and strong enemy defences: "The positions around Tumpo were now heavily fortified, with FAPLA even clearing large areas of bush so they would be able to see the South African advance and get a clear shot at us as we came in to attack them. They had also laid extensive minefields in front of their positions to stop any advancing force."[3]

The problem was exacerbated by the fact that the enemy artillery – about

80 guns and rocket launchers – was concentrated on the western side of the Cuito, on high ground that gave the gun crews (reportedly mostly Cubans) an excellent view of any advancing enemy.[4] All possible entrance routes from the north, east and south were covered by infantry, supported by tanks, antitank weapons and artillery. A detailed examination of the defences led SADF observers later to conclude that the Cuban/Angolan alliance's plan was to keep any attack force at a distance without engaging in direct contact. Then, when the SADF had lost all mobility, a tank force would launch a devastating counter-attack and wipe out the South Africans.[5] (At this stage, Military Intelligence reported the presence of Cuban T-62 tanks,[6] but these were not used during the battles that followed.) Clearly, the Cubans had learnt through bitter experience that FAPLA could not stand up to a deliberate SADF attack, so they sought to keep the South Africans at a distance through a combination of cunningly laid minefields, well-prepared artillery fire and air strikes.

In any case, the SADF leadership opined that the enemy would not give up his Tumpo bridgehead unless forced to do so, and that he would try to use it again as a springboard for another offensive against Mavinga. Therefore, the planners envisaged a three-stage continuation to Operation Hooper: firstly, FAPLA had to be forced west of the Cuito as soon as possible; secondly, the east bank of the river had to be prepared as an obstacle; and, lastly, FAPLA's preparations to resume the offensive against Mavinga had to be disrupted.[7]

On 19 February, the South Africans learnt that a FAPLA infantry battalion, supported by three tanks, was preparing new positions north of the Dala. Pat McLoughlin, commanding 20 Brigade, could not permit this to happen, and the next day he sent a combat team of 61 Mech to drive the enemy away. The attack succeeded; the enemy positions were still in their formative stage, and FAPLA quickly withdrew. But the South Africans got a foretaste of what they could expect: an Olifant and a Ratel were damaged by mines, while MiGs flew more than 30 strikes against them. The aircraft caused no damage or casualties, but the South Africans were forced to hide under the lush foliage every few minutes as the fighter-bombers screamed over. The South Africans were also severely harassed by enemy artillery fire.[8]

This attack had one other unexpected consequence. Apparently, the troops of 59 Brigade, situated to the south, panicked and fled their own positions when the force north of the Dala was attacked. According to Edward George, who draws on a Cuban account, "the troops were forcibly sent back in the night with orders to resist at all costs". This event led to another "impatient cable from Castro" demanding that the withdrawal he had ordered a few days earlier be carried out immediately. On the night of 24 February, 59 Brigade was finally evacuated from the eastern side of the Cuito to the west, leaving only 25 Brigade to protect the relatively small bridgehead.[9] It was this bridgehead that Castro would now purposely elevate to the position of heroic symbol of a small band of brave fighters standing fearlessly up to the combined might of these "parasitic, racist mercenaries".[10]

It is important to understand another element of the tactical situation: the enemy command of the air. Many accounts make much of the alleged inferiority of the SAAF Mirage F1 vis-à-vis the MiG-23, but – as we shall see in Chapter 17– this is highly exaggerated. The enemy's command of the air was primarily due to geography, a factor over which the SAAF had no control at all.

The fact is that, as the campaign wore on, geography increasingly started to work in favour of the Cubans and Angolans. The biggest and best-equipped SAAF base was at Grootfontein, 500 km south of Cuito Cuanavale. The Cubans and Angolans, on the other hand, could use the air base at Menongue, as the airstrip at Cuito Cuanavale had been effectively knocked out by the South African artillery. As the Angolan army was pushed back northwards, Mirages flying from Grootfontein required 42 minutes to reach the fighting area, which meant that they had fuel for two minutes of fighting before reaching "bingo" state – air force jargon for the minimum amount of fuel needed to get back to base. The SAAF had recently acquired Boeing 707 tanker aircraft, but aerial refuelling operations were still at an early stage and did not have much success in Angola. By contrast, the flight time from Menongue to Tumpo was just nine minutes. With their greater range, the MiG-23s could linger above the battlefield for over an hour, protecting their own troops from South African bombing attacks or looking for targets of opportunity.[11]

The SAAF base at Rundu was closer than Grootfontein, but Rundu's runway was not long enough for the Buccaneers or Mirage F1AZs when heavily laden with bombs. Rundu did house the much lighter Mirage F1CZ fighters while these were in the operational area, and also acted as emergency landing strip for damaged aircraft or those short of fuel on their way back. But the Buccaneers and Mirage F1AZs had to operate from Grootfontein, thereby cutting things very fine indeed.[12]

Dick Lord told Fred Bridgland that the SAAF flew in a more hostile environment than any air force had ever faced. "The Israeli Air Force has never faced such a full range of missiles," Lord said:

> And when its pilots have carried out deep penetration raids it's been on a one-off basis. Our pilots had to go deep day-in, day-out. During Moduler they had to fly to avoid SAM-8s, SAM-13s and SAM-9s as well as the normally expected shoulder-launched SAM-7s, 14s and 16s. During Hooper they also came in range of SAM-6s (computer-controlled missiles with ranges of up to 30 km which can lock on to aircraft as close as 100 m to the ground and up to a height of 18 000 m) and SAM-3 (guided missile used in short-range defence against low-flying aircraft).[13]

Besides, the further north the SAAF aircraft had to operate, the lower they had to fly to avoid enemy radar for as long as possible. They really had to hug the ground.[14]

The first attack at Tumpo

The South Africans tried to mislead the enemy, including making a false move to cross the Cuito south of the battlefield, but there is no indication that the enemy was taken in. And so, on 25 February, the South Africans carried out the first of three attacks on the Tumpo Triangle.

For this attack, 61 Mech was designated as the spearpoint, while UNITA would distract the defenders with feint attacks. The attack force consisted of 61 Mech, with both Olifant tank squadrons (minus a troop), plus a mechanised infantry company (Ratel 20s), two antitank troops (Ratel-ZT3s and Ratel 90s), an anti-aircraft troop (Ystervark 20 mm and SA-7) and a combat engineer detachment. A flanking force was also organised, consisting of a tank troop, an armoured car squadron (Ratel 90s), a mechanised infantry company (Ratel 20s) and a 120-mm mortar group. Three infantry companies from 32 Battalion,

Tumpo

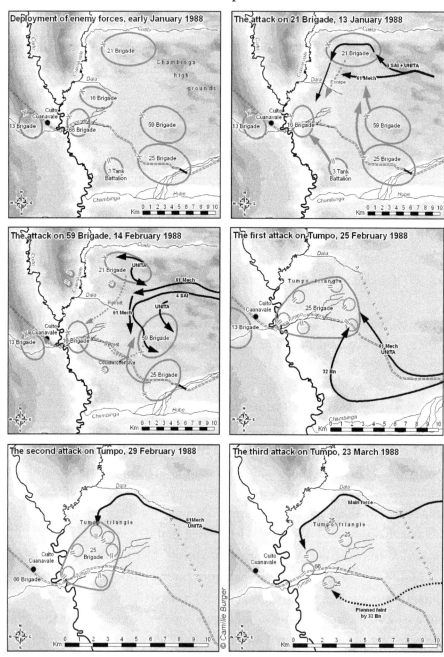

© Camille Burger

under Major Thinus van Staden, would advance on foot. Two UNITA infantry battalions, also on foot (about 1 400 men), would participate, while 4 SAI
was kept in reserve.[15]

The battle plan was simply that 32 Battalion would assault a horseshoe-shaped
FAPLA position in the southeast of the battlefield around the source of the
Tumpo River. When that had been secured, 61 Mech would follow, and together
the two units would clear 25 Brigade from south to north. UNITA would
launch a diversionary attack in the north. The plan had to be approved by Kat
Liebenberg, Jannie Geldenhuys and even the Minister of Defence, Magnus
Malan. Liebenberg stipulated that tanks had to be included in the flanking
force, and that the enemy's formidable 23-mm guns had to be destroyed as
soon as possible through firebelt actions – an illustration of how Pretoria kept
the field commanders on a very short leash.

Before 06h00 on 25 February, 32 Battalion, which had been brought by
vehicle to the Chambinga and had walked northwards through the night,
approached the FAPLA position at the Tumpo source. But all was eerily quiet.
A quick investigation showed that the Angolan soldiers had all fled or were in
the process of fleeing.

This was an early success for the SADF, but it proved to be the only one.
The main force advanced northwestwards inside the tree line as long as it
could, but at a certain stage they had to cross an open flood plain known as
the Anhara Lipanda. Just before moving out into the open, at 09h00, 61 Mech
stumbled upon a previously unknown minefield, and Mike Muller's own tank
was damaged. The advance route had been investigated and marked by Recces,
but the Cubans must have discovered the route markings and laid mines there.
The mine explosion drew the attention of the enemy artillery, which opened
up with everything it had. At the same time, MiGs swarmed in the air above,
making South African counterfire impossible, because the G-5s could not
reveal their positions to the aircraft. And, for reasons already explained, no
South African aircraft challenged the MiGs.

Meanwhile, 59 Brigade's withdrawing soldiers were bunched up together at
the Cuito bridge, making them a perfect target. But the G-5s were only inter-
mittently in action.

Muller was in a quandary, but he was not ready to give up. He ordered the deployment of a Plofadder, an experimental anti-mine device that looked like a long garden hose. The Plofadder was packed with explosives and was launched across a minefield with a rocket fixed to the front end, deploying the whole hose behind it. The charge would then be set off, in theory blasting a corridor through the minefield. But the device refused to detonate – it never worked as advertised during the campaign – and a section of combat engineers, led by Lieutenant Louwtjie Louw, had to go forward and detonate it manually. As the antitank mines were interspersed with antipersonnel mines, this was an extremely dangerous job. All nine sappers received the Southern Cross Medal.

Although a lane was now open, the tanks were further impeded by air strikes and enemy artillery fire, and it was not until 12h26 – after a delay of three hours – that the two tank squadrons were finally through, minus three tanks damaged in the minefield (a fourth was repaired on the battlefield and continued the fight). Undaunted, Muller advanced further to the northwest past the evacuated FAPLA positions, now occupied by 32 Battalion. According to radio intercepts, the Cubans were planning a tank counterattack, but could not carry it out because most of the FAPLA infantry had fled.

By now, 61 Mech was in the open, and at 14h15 the enemy artillery and aircraft unleashed a torrent of fire upon them. Some of the South Africans suspected that an enemy artillery observer was nearby and directing the fire on them. Foolishly, some 32 Battalion troops put down yellow smoke so that 61 Mech would know where they were, which merely served to give the enemy another target to fire at. Now 61 Mech started to take casualties. By 15h00 five Ratels had been hit; one was smashed by a shell from a 130-mm gun, and its commander, Lance-Corporal JJ Botha, lost both his legs. The ops medic coolly amputated his legs right there on the battlefield with a pair of scissors while all sorts of ordnance flew around their ears. Several more soldiers were wounded. Another shell fell directly on a disabled Olifant tank, where the crew was preparing to have it pulled out. The driver could not close his hatch in time and was decapitated. Several MiGs swooped through the air and ditched their bombs on the South Africans, albeit inaccurately.

The attacking force was dead in the water. The enemy was hitting the South Africans effectively, without their being able to fight back in any meaningful way.

When they looked westwards to the enemy, the sun was in their eyes. Shortly before 16h00, Muller bowed to the inevitable and asked for – and received – permission to pull back; 32 Battalion also withdrew, and UNITA, not keen to occupy such exposed positions, fell back as well.

Statistically, it was another handsome SADF victory. FAPLA lost 172 men and the Cubans 10. At least six or seven tanks were destroyed. The South African casualty figures were 4 killed and 10 wounded. (UNITA's casualty figure is unknown.) Several tanks and Ratels were damaged but recovered from the battlefield, and three vehicles were burnt out.

Nevertheless, it cannot be denied that the South Africans had lost. They did not lose against FAPLA, who once again showed very little inclination to fight and die for a cause they neither cared for nor understood. The South Africans were stopped by the Cubans, who cunningly laid the minefield just inside the tree line (where an advance was logical), who manned the artillery, who provided the aircraft pilots, and who planned the whole defence. Like it or not, the Cubans clearly were of a higher standard than FAPLA. Fidel Castro sent his congratulations to the men of 25 and 59 Brigades, but they did not deserve it. It is not known whether he congratulated his own compatriots, who actually saved the day. Having halted the South African tactical momentum, they also broke their operational momentum.

Tumpo 2 (1 March)

At this point, it is perhaps necessary to analyse the opposing sides briefly. Military Intelligence estimated that about 800 Angolan troops from 25 Brigade, supported by seven or ten tanks (the sources differ), three BM-21 rocket launchers and several 23-mm guns, were still occupying a foothold on the eastern bank of the Cuito. (In fact, this was an exaggeration, and this wrong information would play a role in the coming battle.) From the defence dispositions, one may deduce that the enemy expected an attack from the east and northeast, as very little defences were deployed to the south. Whatever the case, the operational objective of Operation Hooper – to drive the enemy over the river – had still not been achieved. Another attack was needed.[16]

By this time, the South Africans were in a bad condition. As we saw in

Chapter 14, the extreme conditions of the area – dense bush, energy-sapping heat, clouds of flies, lack of proper fresh food, disintegrating clothes and boots, lack of washing facilities and the frustratingly slow arrival of spare parts – caused morale to sag. Besides, the troops knew that their time at the front would be up on 8 March, when Operation Hooper would end, and no soldier wants to die or be maimed when the end is in sight.

The equipment was in a deplorable state. A good illustration is to be found in the diary of a tanker: "Repaired damage to tank from Bush Breaking: Left bin smashed, long bin badly damaged, wire bin lost, Ac Ac mounting ripped off, Gun crutch broke off, Rear hull bin lid ripped off, 2 smoke launchers ripped off. 2 of us have bad trots."[17] Mike Muller told Fred Bridgland that the tanks had fought for more than 800 hours and several battles without proper servicing. The necessary equipment was simply not at the front line, in spite of its having been asked for repeatedly: "No other tank in the world could have gone on for that long in those circumstances, and with all that dust, without servicing . . ."[18] This meant that, despite a superhuman effort by the "tiffies" (mechanics), only 12 tanks, 19 Ratel 90s and 12 G-5s could participate in the next attack. In addition, five of the tanks had unserviceable drivers' periscopes. This reduced their fighting capabilities considerably; in battle, the drill called for hatches to be shut, and the lack of periscopes made these five tanks basically blind.[19]

To make things worse, the SADF force had very little in the way of anti-aircraft defences. The army had manually operated 20-mm cannon mounted on the backs of Unimog trucks (known as Ystervarks), but only a lucky shot from one of these would down a fast-moving jet fighter. The air force brought in antiquated Cactus missiles (already some 20 years old), but these were designed for air base defence and could not handle the harsh jungle conditions. They were in theatre for a few weeks, but were withdrawn without having achieved any successes.[20] UNITA, of course, had American-supplied hand-held Stinger anti-aircraft missiles, but these needed proper training to operate, which UNITA often did not have. Although the enemy aircraft stayed high because they feared the Stingers, very few were shot down by them.

The fact is that the South Africans were in no position to undertake another attack. But orders were orders, and over the top they went once again. Actually,

Pat McLoughlin's plan, given the restrictive environment, was a reasonable one. First of all, it was planned to be a night attack. McLoughlin reasoned that the army's superior training in night warfare would give his men an edge over the enemy. In addition, the Cuban/Angolan alliance's artillery would be firing more or less blind in the dark, and the enemy air force would be completely out of the picture. To make doubly sure, he organised a feint attack in the south by elements of 4 SAI, while 61 Mech (with all the available tanks and most of the armoured cars, plus a mechanised infantry company) would sneak up from the northeast and catch the defenders unawares. After a breakthrough had been made, a flank attack would follow. A reserve force, consisting of a Ratel 90 squadron, a mechanised infantry company and an 81-mm mortar platoon would cover the main force from the south. A special UNITA combat team was tasked to destroy the bridge.[21]

Unknown to McLoughlin and Muller, however, the Cubans had reckoned on an attack from the northeast. The night before the attack, they sent out a combat engineer detachment, which laid an extra 150 mines in the path where the attackers were expected.

The attack started promisingly. Because of the southern feint, the enemy did not realise where the main blow was due to fall. Also, rain kept the advancing column – the remaining tanks, 32 Battalion, a combat engineer section with Plofadders, and two UNITA light infantry battalions – hidden for some time and the dark prevented the Cuban MiGs from taking to the air.

When the attacking force reached the assembly point, at about 01h50, it was raining hard. The anti-mine rollers, which had to be attached to the front tanks to clear the way through the minefields, had still not arrived. Mike Muller got permission to postpone the attack to first light.

The tanks advanced slowly to accommodate the UNITA and 32 Battalion infantry on foot. A few shots were directed at them, but the rain and overcast conditions prevented the enemy from realising what was afoot. At 10h43, the troops reached the first forward trenches, which were found empty. Again, a few mortar bombs were aimed at them, but apart from that the battlefield was eerily quiet. Muller denied permission to his tanks to shoot back for fear of alerting the enemy. By late morning, his force was only four kilometres from the Cuito bridge.

It was at this stage that things went awry. The rain stopped, the clouds lifted, and, sure enough, within a few minutes the sky was full of MiGs. At first, the aircraft bombed their own troops, who replied with a barrage of anti-aircraft fire. The tanks advanced further in spurts of 100 m, then 50 m, at a time. But the game was up. Heavy 23-mm and 120-mm mortar fire started coming in. Muller ordered a firebelt action, which had become a very effective SADF tactic. Muller described the scene shortly afterwards to Fred Bridgland:

> I can't begin to describe to you how incredibly heavy the encounter was, but I was assured afterwards by senior officers that in terms of shell volume it was one of the biggest and toughest engagements fought by the SADF since World War II. We fired many hundreds of rounds from the Olifants, the Ratels and our mortars, and gradually we began to pick off their gun positions ...

> Those 23 mm guns were just wiping the UNITA blokes off the tanks. If I close my eyes now, I can still see it clearly. The first 23 mm fire we drew came from the west bank of the Cuito and it went over our heads. Then a burst came between the Olifants and the Ratels. You only *see* the 23 mm tracers. There's so much other noise that you don't hear the shots. In front of my command Ratel there was an Olifant with five UNITA infantrymen sitting on its engine plate. As they jumped off one of them was hit in the face with a 23 mm shell. His head just disintegrated.[22]

The MiGs attacked the South Africans again, but the bombs fell, as usual, far from them. A UNITA Stinger missile blew a MiG out of the sky. This time, the SADF and UNITA did not stop and camouflage themselves against the MiG attacks. Their bravado paid off, as these attacks remained completely inaccurate. Because of the heavy 23-mm fire, Muller swung his force further southwards, while his artillery tried to silence the enemy guns. At 13h25, the South Africans moved into open terrain, and at once deployed in attack for-mation. Again a minefield was encountered, and the 23-mm and 120-mm fire continued unabated. Suddenly a concerted barrage of antitank fire was directed from three sides. When the South Africans reviewed the battle afterwards, it became clear that they had moved into a carefully planned killing area. Both flanks were covered by antitank weapons (including modern Sagger missiles), 23-mm guns and artillery.

Within a few minutes, four tanks had blundered onto mines. Muller stayed calm and ordered another firebelt action, while withdrawing somewhat to review the situation. Here he stayed for about 45 minutes, and by accurate and concentrated fire succeeded in silencing most of the enemy weapons. He then withdrew even further. The turning point came at 14h35, when a Recce reported that the enemy tanks were on the move. This alarmed Muller; after all, he knew from intelligence reports of seven or ten Cuban tanks east of the river. Later, he learnt that the reports were exaggerated, and that only *two* tanks were there. Had he known this, he said subsequently, he would have pressed on with the attack. As it happened, the risk was deemed too great, and he asked permission to withdraw altogether. Only six of his tanks and six G-5s were still serviceable. Remarkably, not a single SADF soldier had been killed. Once again, UNITA's losses are unknown.

As the South African generals were wont to do, a number had assembled at Pat McLoughlin's brigade headquarters, including Jannie Geldenhuys, Kat Liebenberg and Willie Meyer. McLoughlin had to ask the generals for permission to withdraw, and they gave the green light. This would be unheard of in most Western armies, and it completely negated the army's own culture of giving commanders on the battlefield a free hand, provided that they knew what the basic purpose of the battle was and how they fitted into the broader strategic plan (discussed in Chapter 4). Here, a tactical decision, which should have been left to McLoughlin and Muller alone, was referred right up to the Chief of the SADF! This was another example of the way in which the generals micromanaged the last stage of the war.

Once again, the Cuban defence was excellent. The minefields disrupted the South Africans' advance, preventing them from making direct contact with FAPLA. The Cubans then threw every standoff weapon they had – 23-mm cannon, 120-mm mortars, 130-mm artillery, rocket launchers and air strikes – at the SADF forces until the attackers decided to withdraw. In a situation report, the SADF had to admit that the attack had brought "no change to the enemy situation and deployment".[23] As McLoughlin wrote in his war diary on 1 March, just after the attack: "The enemy is strong and clever."[24]

The second attack at Tumpo was effectively the end of Operation Hooper. Both equipment and personnel were spent. It was time for a new team to take over.

Tumpo 3 (23 March)

On 9 March, Pat McLoughlin returned command to Colonel Paul Fouché, who arrived back from Pretoria, where he had mobilised new troops for 82 Mechanised Brigade, a Citizen Force formation. By 13 March, the tattered 20 Brigade was back at Rundu. For the third and final attack on Tumpo, fresh troops from 82 Mechanised Brigade were brought in from South Africa. For the first time since 1984, when an unready Citizen Force battle group had been committed to battle (Operation Askari), the Citizen Force would furnish almost all the troops for Operation Packer, as the attack was designated. For this operation, the headquarters of 82 Mechanised Brigade was activated in command of a makeshift formation consisting of:[25]

- Two Olifant squadrons of Regiment President Steyn, with brand-new tanks. Because the Bloemfontein home of the regimental commander had been flooded in a bad rain storm, he could not go to the front. Commandant (later Colonel) Gerhard Louw of the Army Battle School at Lohatlha, a tank officer who had been tasked to conduct the regiment's refresher training, was therefore ordered to take over command himself.
- A Ratel 90 squadron from Regiment Mooirivier, which took over 61 Mech's battered vehicles.
- Two mechanised infantry battalions, Regiment De la Rey and Regiment Groot Karoo.
- Two artillery batteries (one with G-5s and the other with G-2s) were furnished by Regiment Potchefstroom University. Another battery, with 120-mm mortars, came from 44 Parachute Brigade, and a troop of Valkiri MRLs from 19 Rocket Regiment.
- 32 Battalion remained in theatre, with three motorised rifle companies.
- Several hundred UNITA light infantry on foot.

In other words, the composite 82 Mechanised Brigade looked, in principle, much the same as 20 Brigade, which was now disbanded. The difference is that the formation consisted mostly of Citizen Force soldiers.

Like all difficult activities in life, combat soldiering has to be learnt through tough training. Some aspects of this training remain with the trainees for the rest of their lives; for instance, even old, retired soldiers remember how to salute or to strip a rifle. Other skills, like fire and movement, a tank attack in formation, or bombarding a target kilometres away with artillery or mortars, fade fairly rapidly. Therefore, when reservists are called up for war, they need intensive retraining before they can be committed to battle. During Operation Askari, this was apparently not done properly, with the results described in Chapter 7. Something similar happened during Operation Packer. This was not the fault of the Citizen Force members, many of whom were very brave men. As Gerhard Louw told me, the planners in Pretoria "were simultaneously running out of time and human resources [conscripts]." After all, if everything had gone according to plan in the first place, all operations would have been completed by the end of January 1988.[26]

"We didn't really have enough time to train the men more thoroughly," Louw told Bridgland. "In the nature of things, it takes more time to get men who have been back to civilian life ready for battle than it does career soldiers or National Servicemen ... When the time came to move deep into Angola they still weren't fully operational, mainly because we'd been hampered by ammunition shortages and equipment shortfalls and failures."[27] Apparently the retraining took only five days.[28] In an email to me, Louw went even further:

> To say that the CF troops had had insufficient training was only the tip of the iceberg – they were in no way prepared for what was waiting for them. Beforehand they were as excited as naive children before a picnic; afterwards many were ready for trauma counselling. The fact is, as an officer who chose the Defence Force as a career, I knew what they would go through and pitied them deeply. As a result of this I made unforgivable mistakes, like letting my frustration and doubts [about the attack plan] simmer through to them during information sessions ...[29]

Besides, in the short time available, Louw felt he could not build up the relationship of trust that a commander and his troops need to fight optimally.[30]

In a document discussing the lessons of the campaign, harsh criticism was levelled at the Citizen Force units: "CF conventional training has been neglected a great deal in the past years, and CF units were utilised for the op[eration] which were not up to standard."[31]

On the other hand, the Cuban/Angolan alliance made maximum use of the three-week respite to strengthen its defences, extending its minefields from the Cuanavale River to the Tumpo River to cover every possible approach for an attack. Some of the mines were boosted with 122-mm rocket warheads. As Edward George reports, based on analysis of Cuban sources: "The Cubans deliberately left gaps between the minefields and trained fifteen heavy guns on them, with a further nine behind the main positions and dozens on the opposite bank." Altogether, 15 tanks augmented 25 Brigade's defensive positions, while a further 14 were stationed in the immediate vicinity of the bridge. "They were the most formidable defences the South Africans had faced to date . . ."[32]

The South African plan for the attack was similar to the one for the failed attack of 1 March. Once again, a feint south of the Tumpo River would be carried out, this time by 32 Battalion (reinforced by a mechanised infantry company and other support troops from Regiment Groot Karoo, under the command of the regimental commander, Commandant Dougie Stern). They were tasked to construct a dummy bridgehead south of Cuito Cuanavale. But, although the enemy's reconnaissance teams picked it up, the move had no effect in drawing attention – or troops – away from Tumpo. UNITA would carry out its own feint attack as well. Then the main force, including the two fresh tank squadrons, the remainder of the two mechanised infantry battalions and UNITA troops riding on the backs of the tanks, would attack from the northeast, breaking through to the bridge and destroying it. Then the newly occupied positions would be turned over to UNITA, while the South Africans would withdraw.[33] However, the deception force never even got into action, as the main attack was abandoned before the 32 Battalion men could do anything.

On the face of it, this plan was a mistake. The South African Army (as do other armies) teaches its officers not to renew a failed attack along the same axis unless there are really compelling reasons to do so. But, as both Paul Fouché and Gerhard Louw informed me, the limited Tumpo area was not conducive to attacks from multiple directions. The southern approach, as followed on 25 February, is very sandy, with dunes and dense bush (except for the open Anhara Lipanda), whereas the northern terrain is flatter, on firm ground, with less dense bush, and therefore better suited to the heavy tanks. Nevertheless, neither officer had any faith in the battle plan. As a matter of fact, Fouché told Kat Liebenberg that a night attack by 32 Battalion, supported by the rest of the brigade, was the only other option, but that was turned down. And, as Gerhard Louw relates: "According to (probably very much adapted) oral tradition, the then C Army (General Kat Liebenberg, who was trained in the Special Forces and was a stranger to conventional warfare concepts) said the following about the tactics to be followed to reach the objective: *Why don't you form up the tanks and infantry in an extended line and move forwards, firing until the enemy crosses to the other side of the river?*" Fouché says he was "snookered because of previous limitations and the tactical situation. I was worried about the uninspiring plan and the fact that I had to leave my infantry behind."[34]

Louw says he discussed his misgivings with Brigadier Eddie Webb, who communicated with Liebenberg, but to no avail. Even General Constand Viljoen, the previous Chief of the Defence Force and the original motive force behind the SADF's development of the mobile warfare approach, apparently let it be known that he thought it to be a bad plan, but he had by then retired and was not listened to. At this stage, the SADF leadership still thought that their mission was unfulfilled while FAPLA retained even a small bridgehead east of the Cuito. Given that fact, Fouché and Louw had no other choice. "It was the permanent search for a decisive battle à la Clausewitz," Louw thought.[35]

The main attack force started forming up at 21h00 on the evening of 22 March, moving in two line-ahead formations parallel to each other. But bad luck taunted the South Africans right from the start. First, the guides lost their way, causing a delay. Gerhard Louw wrote to me:

> However, another problem arose while we were crossing Heartbreak Hill (a giant sand dune, covered with vegetation), when part of the medical team requested to break away in order to establish a surgical post. The tents were to be erected – and the post to be protected – by a platoon

of infantry. Apart from the fact that the (civilian, CF, and undoubtedly highly skilled in their profession, but entirely ignorant of war) surgeons complained about the possibility that enemy artillery observers could possibly see the light shining through small tears in the tents' canvas [sic], I was also irritated by the fact that I was never briefed about this diversion and the consequent delay. The advance was stalled against the slopes of the monster dune, and this was where some of the Ratels had to be pulled, either by tanks or recovery vehicles.[36]

Another problem was that a tank with anti-mine rollers (to detonate mines) had overturned, leaving the attackers with only one of these most useful devices. Nevertheless, by 06h00 the advance party was about 10 km from the objective, and all looked well. The South African artillery opened fire, catching unawares a platoon of Cubans who were repairing the forward trenches. But then, while the attack force was moving in the tracks made by Mike Muller's force three weeks earlier, the enemy artillery let rip, and a few minutes afterwards an air strike warning was given. The inexperienced Citizen Force tank crews scattered in all directions, and Gerhard Louw had great trouble reforming them. However, the overcast sky meant that the MiGs could not press home their attack.

After resuming the advance, the first Olifant detonated a mine at 08h35 and was immobilised. Louw's remaining mine-roller tank was ordered forward, but tripped one of the powerful boosted mines. The tank's rear suspension unit was blown off so that the belly was resting on the ground, making recovery impossible. Louw immediately called forward two Plofadder teams, but once again the system had to be set off manually. A path was created through the minefield, and by 12h30 the advance resumed.

But the dust kicked up by the Plofadders had shown the Cubans exactly where the South Africans were, and they started firing with everything they had. The formation started off again, but hit a second minefield, even worse than the first, at 13h44. Three tanks tripped mines almost simultaneously, damaging the vehicles severely. An accurate artillery bombardment descended on them, and numerous shells burst among the attackers. Louw stopped the advance and ordered a firebelt action to suppress the enemy fire. One of the damaged tanks was towed out; the other two were stuck. About a dozen UNITA soldiers from the company riding on the backs of the tanks were killed (not the large numbers suggested in some sources, according to Louw). By this time, Louw says, the Citizen Force leader group

> was confused by the bush and the incessant artillery fire, while the two tank squadrons had lost coherence. I am convinced that the casualties were mostly caused by our own machine guns, fired speculatively in the thick undergrowth by frightened tank crews with hatches firmly battened down . . . It was pitiful to see the UNITA soldiers scrabbling to hide under the bustles at the rear of the tank turrets, trying to keep pace with their turning, and with no enemy in sight.[37]

A South African forward artillery observer described what he saw from his position on the Chambinga high ground:

> When the third attack on Tumpo went in later that morning, we were in the amazing front row seat watching the biggest military showdown in Africa since the Second World War. While I was engaged with registered targets of known artillery positions on the Cuito high ground and watching out for opportunities to take out a BM-21, which kept reappearing in different positions all the time, I was able to see the progress of the battle.
>
> I will never forget the amount of dust and noise generated by the tanks and Ratels during their approach to the target in the morning, and was puzzled by the lack of initial response of FAPLA to the advance. Surely everybody within a 10 km radius would be aware of this approach??!!
>
> But when the response did come at about 08h30, it came in the form over 60 guns opening up with indirect fire upon the advancing SA armour from all over the Cuito high ground and Tumpo Triangle itself. I was sure EVERY available gun was concentrating its fire on the approaching South African force! I did counter battery as best as I could with

the three remaining G-5s but I really don't think I made a dent in the artillery assault FAPLA directed at the oncoming force . . . The thought flashed through my mind that I am glad I wasn't deployed as forward observer with the attacking force!

By 10am the attack was in full swing, and T-55 tanks joined in returning fire on the by then stuck South African force. The attack was stalling in the minefields. We brought G-5 fire down on the positions of the enemy tanks and I think the southern OPO reported a tank knocked out with a direct hit . . . As I was unable to see the tanks directly, I could not tell whether it was as a result of our fire or his (not that it made a difference).[38]

Fred Bridgland quoted Gerhard Louw:

By now the enemy seemed to be throwing everything towards us, including phosphorus bombs. Out of the corner of my eye, I saw missiles whistling over our heads. They had BM-14s and BM-21s firing horizontal rocket salvos at us from the opposite bank. Fortunately all the rockets landed in front of the tanks and the rocket boosters and motors tumbled over our heads and caused no losses. It was a big noise, of course, lots of noise and so much smoke and dust that I could barely see my tanks.

Mortar shells landed all over the place and 23 mm slugs crashed through the sound barrier. We were in danger of being well and truly pinned down in a sea of mines . . .[39]

(Louw later wryly commented to me that Bridgland used "some major poetic licence here. I remember the BM-21 salvo, but not the BM-14s; with regard to the 23 mm guns, I remember the rounds cracking by, but not in the flowery language of Bridgland.")[40] In his account to me, Louw wrote about "tanks in the open – a death's acre – for an indefinite time, in the face of prepared defence positions on the other side of the river, occupied by an enemy who knew that we could cross that river only at one point in a single file."[41]

In reaction, he ordered a short withdrawal to dead ground, where the enemy fire could not do so much damage. He dashed around on foot, unfazed by the amount of lead flying through the air, directing the recovery of the damaged tanks, for which he was later awarded the Honoris Crux. But by this time he had also received notice that the Cuban/Angolan tanks had stirred, while fire from static tanks across the river added to the general mayhem. To complicate things, the cloud cover lifted, and by 13h30 the MiGs were swarming in the air with no Mirages in sight. Louw also discovered that his tanks were running short of fuel.

This was serious. To be caught immobilised in a minefield – heavy, boosted antitank mines interspersed with antipersonnel mines – while heavy artillery pieces, static tanks, mortars and 23-mm guns were throwing everything at you, was to court a devastating defeat. And so by 14h21 Louw had to take the one decision that no commanding officer ever relishes: withdrawal. One of the three disabled tanks could be pulled out by a recovery vehicle, but the other two proved impossible to move, so heavily had their tracks and suspensions been damaged. A fourth was immobilised when it threw a track. Louw took part of the crew aboard, "not realising that the tank was so slightly damaged. This tank was the one-and-only recovered to Luanda – and later to Russia – while the other two remained irrecoverable by either force to this day."[42] A Ratel 20 was also destroyed.

Up to now, it had been an iron law that no prisoner or piece of equipment should ever end up in enemy hands. Seeing that there was no chance to recover the three immobilised Olifants in the hail of fire, Louw requested permission from Paul Fouché to destroy them with South African artillery fire. But Kat Liebenberg, who was also present at Fouché's headquarters, intervened and forbade it. The tanks could be recovered later, he ordered.

Liebenberg's idea was naive. Soon after Louw's men vacated the battlefield, the enemy forces moved in, took possession of one of the three abandoned tanks and – unencumbered by SADF fire – carted it off. This would prove to be a major propaganda coup for Fidel Castro, displaying photographs of the tanks throughout the world as proof of his glorious victory over the "evil racists". For that, Liebenberg must be held directly responsible.

Louw pulled back without having accomplished anything. The third attack on Tumpo had failed. Through what can only described as a miracle, not a single South African soldier died.

Operation Displace

In the wake of the third Battle of Tumpo, the Cuban/Angolan alliance took steps to shore up its defences on the eastern bank of the Cuito even further. Additional forces were brought in from Menongue, and at least 49 extra tanks (including the formidable T-62) and a number of anti-aircraft missile batteries were stationed in the Tumpo Triangle. Forces were also placed in blocking positions southwest of Cuito Cuanavale to guard against a South African attack from that direction. There appeared little chance of eliminating these by a deliberate attack. Wisely, the SADF generals decided to give up and allow the enemy toehold east of the river to remain. On 27 March, it was decided to wind up Operation Packer.[43]

Packer was succeeded by Operation Displace, and 82 Mechanised Brigade was substituted by Combat Group 20, under the command by Commandant Piet Nel of 1 Parachute Battalion. This rather small force consisted of the anti-tank squadron of 32 Battalion, a motorised infantry company of 101 Battalion, a G-5 and a Valkiri battery, and two combat engineer troops. They aggressively simulated the continued existence of 82 Mechanised Brigade and planted thousands of mines along the Cuito to deter the enemy from taking advantage of their weakness. This lasted until the end of August, when all fighting stopped and they returned to South West Africa.[44]

Operation Displace had one big operational advantage. The continued South African presence near Tumpo, according to Chester Crocker, meant that Jannie Geldenhuys

> converted the SADF position at Cuito into a bargaining chip . . . it also helped to deflate the Cuban balloon. Staying at Cuito would avoid the perverse imagery of an SADF withdrawal occurring after Castro's verbal taunts about his new front in the southwest [*see* Chapter 16]. Geldenhuys was determined that there would be no withdrawal until concrete, reciprocal military agreements (including Cuban restraint)

were reached. In other words, Cuban bravado helped keep the SADF engaged at Cuito.[45]

A final conclusion about operations Moduler, Hooper and Packer will have to wait, because the Cuban reaction in southwestern Angola has to be taken into the equation as well. A preliminary conclusion – to be elaborated in the next chapter – would be that the fighting in the province of Cuando Cubango ended in a stalemate.

SADF postmortem

From a military vantage point, one of the most interesting aspects of the SADF was that, throughout the war, it concluded all big operations with a professional postmortem. All senior officers who had participated in the planning and execution of the fighting took part in a comprehensive review, in which no holds were barred and criticism was (relatively) freely given. In a discussion document[46] that served as guide to a meeting to have been held on 16 June 1988 in Pretoria, a number of criticisms were levelled, some of them by implication against the SADF leadership. For instance, it is stated:

> Somewhere something was wrong and the aim of the op[eration] unclear or was changed during the operation. In the beginning it was minimum involvement but it gradually grew to full-scale involvement, but also not sufficient to administer the knockout blow at the right time . . . This, together with the limitation on casualties, the enemy command of the air and the fact that the best course of action could not be followed [a reference to the advance east, instead of west of the Cuito?] led to a protracted campaign against the enemy, who in the end entrenched themselves so strongly east of the Cuito River that they could not be destroyed/removed without a very big attempt (and casualties) . . . There must be reflection about the aim of the op and what the policy of the future should be.

The following is also interesting: "According to policy and doctrine the SA Army only does 'blitzkrieg' ops cross-border, a maximum period of 30 days has been laid down and logistical and other planning is based on it. Present ops are slow and drawn out and last months." This reveals a clear dissatisfaction about the hesitant and incremental way in which the SADF was sucked into the fray, and about the changing aims of the operation. The implication of the last sentence is that the military leadership – in the beginning, at any rate – did not have a clear idea of what they wanted to achieve and, especially, how to do it.

In the same vein (if one knows the background), it is clear that there was discontent about the conduct of the generals who micromanaged tactics. "During the op," the document states, "there was a deviation from the principle that subordinate commanders should have reasonable freedom of conduct . . .". (Years after the war, Jock Harris told a meeting of the Eastern Cape branch of the South African Military History Society: "Political and senior defence intervention was the order of the day, even to tactical level.")[47] By implication, the leadership was reproved because the "principle of concentration of effort was not maintained". There was also the problem of the misuse of the tanks, by pushing them into unswept minefields in front of enemy defence positions. The question was asked whether much more artillery support was not needed at Tumpo.

The document also touched on the unsatisfactory conduct of the Citizen Force troops during Tumpo 3: "CF conventional training has been greatly neglected the last few years, and CF units which were not on standard were utilised for the op." Satisfaction was, however, expressed about the standard of the National Servicemen, and there was deep admiration for the "combat ability, professionalism and experience" of the 32 Battalion members. The morale of the South African troops was mainly good, in spite of the fact that they were not always properly briefed about what was going on in a broader sense.[48]

Commandant Roland de Vries, OC 61
Mechanised Battalion Group.

Lieutenant General Magnus Malan as Chief of
the Army. He later became Chief of the SADF
and Minister of Defence.

General Kat Liebenberg after the war as Chief
of the SADF.

During the war Major General Johann
"Dippies" Dippenaar participated in several
cross-border operations as Commandant
and Colonel.

Major General Jannie Geldenhuys
at his farewell parade as
Commanding General SWA in
Windhoek in 1980. Next to him
is the Administrator General, Dr
Gerrit Viljoen.

Prime Minister John Vorster (on the right) during a visit to the operational area in the 1970s. From
the left: General Magnus Malan (Chief of the SADF), Lieutenant General Constand Viljoen (Chief of
the Army), and PW Botha (Minister of Defence). Botha succeeded Vorster in 1978.

A Ratel-20 ploughs through a wet Angola during Operation Askari. This operation took place in the rainy season which impacted negatively on the SADF's mobility.

South African sappers seek land mines in the north of South West Africa.

Opponents meet during the abortive peace process of 1984: (from the left) Colonel Johann Dippenaar, Colonel Marius Oelschig and an Angolan officer.

Back at the base: these soldiers were probably at a temporary base somewhere in Angola.

Marines of the SA Navy patrol rivers in the operational area. This boat is from the Wenela base.

An unusual sight in a counterinsurgency war – the Buffel mainly transported supplies to patrols, while mounted troops were often used in northern South West Africa because of their mobility.

The "Flossie" transported thousands of South African troops to and from South West Africa. The SAAF had two kinds of "Flossie" – the Lockheed C-130 Hercules as seen on the photo and the Transall C-160.

A Mirage F1CZ fighter of 3 Squadron. Mirages were often utilised in the air above southern Angola.

An unmanned Seeker aircraft which was mostly used for reconnaissance.

Three self-propelled G-6 guns like this one were used to bombard Cuito Cuanavale for a few weeks. Afterwards they were pulled back and displayed at a weapons show in Chili.

Colonel Deon Ferreira, OC 20 Brigade, explain a battle plan during Operation Moduler.

A few Olifant tanks move through the Angolan bush during Operation Hooper in preparation for the assault on FAPLA's 16 Brigade. The tanks gave the South African forces a mailed fist.

Angolan weapons captured during Operation Moduler.

In the Angolan bush taking a bath was an almost unknown luxury. This soldier grabbed the rare chance to wash off the dirt and sweat.

Elands, Ratels and Samils prepare for an operation.

This photo was probably taken in 1988 at a meeting of the Joint Military Monitoring Committee, whose aim was to prevent misunderstandings from scuppering the peace process. Behind the table is from the left Colonel Archie Moore (OC 44 Parachute Brigade), Brigadier Chris Serfontein (OC 10 Division and Sector 10) and Major General Willie Meyer (Commanding General SWA). To the right are Cuban and/or Angolan officers.

This SWAPO soldier was taken prisoner by SADF troops somewhere in Angola.

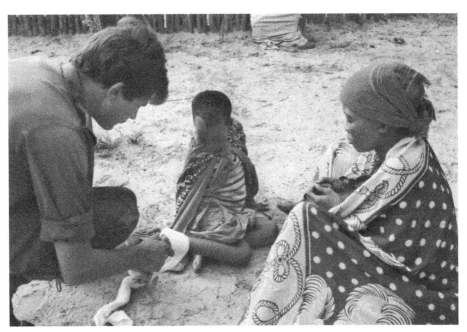

SADF medical personnel accompanied most infantry patrols in northern SWA as part of the intensive hearts and minds campaign to turn the local inhabitants against SWAPO.

Meticulous planning was a hallmark of the SADF. Here an operation is explained to officers to ensure that each of them fully understands where he fits into the broader plan.

UNITA fighters attack FAPLA troops on this photo, but it is unknown where and when it was taken.

Napoleon reputedly said an army marches on its stomach . . . Troops prepare food from their rat packs.

Soldiers use a free moment to braai and put their feet up.

The last spasm of the war: On 27 July 1988 Cuban MiG-23s attacked the Calueque water works. This photo shows the crater one bomb made in the dam wall.

The MiG attack of 27 July also destroyed the big pipes which transported water to the north of South West Africa. Twelve South Africans died in the attack.

The bridge over the Cunene River which was damaged in the Cuban air bombardment on 27 July 1988.

The target area of the last Cuban air attack as seen from the air.

Eleven SADF troops were killed when this Buffel was hit in the Cuban air attack on the Calueque water works.

The war is over! A Ratel-90 is loaded onto the SAS Outeniqua during the final SADF withdrawal from South West Africa.

16

ENDGAME

From September 1987 onwards, FAPLA suffered a series of defeats that severely embarrassed Fidel Castro, and deepened his strategic quandary. By coming to the aid of the socialist MPLA regime in Angola in 1975, Castro had greatly increased his prestige in the Third World, but he could not afford to be sucked into a quagmire, like the Americans in Vietnam. In the late 1970s, therefore, he had started to scale down the Cuban military presence. The spectacular South African paratroop attack on Cassinga in 1978 and the lesser known mechanised attack on Chetequera, however, made withdrawal politically impossible, forcing Castro to strengthen his forces in Angola again.

But Castro's *actions* in Angola were distinct from his *words*, and it may be seen that he opted for a real politician's solution: he threw up a verbal smoke-screen while doing as little as possible. In spite of the tough speeches and dire threats, he limited Cuba's huge military presence in Angola to garrison and training duties. A series of guard posts was set up along the railway line between the harbour town of Namibe and Menongue, capital of Cuando Cubango province. Castro threatened the South Africans with dire consequences if they came near this line, and even depicted it as a defence wall that would save the MPLA from "brutal foreign aggression".[1] One suspects he really thought that the SADF was interested in regime change in Luanda, installing UNITA in the place of the MPLA, rather than in neutralising SWAPO military bases, which were all south of the Namibe–Menongue line. In practice, Castro had a healthy respect for the SADF, and kept his troops out of the South Africans' way.

Fidel Castro's problem

During the early years, there was strong support among Cubans for their country's involvement in Angola. Castro was a charismatic leader, and the people were proud that Cuba was playing such a prominent role on the world stage – far beyond what would be possible in normal circumstances. But things were changing. In the Soviet Union, communism was on its last legs, and Communist Party general secretary Mikhail Gorbachev was engaged in a reform process that, in a few years, would lead to the crumbling of the system. As such, the USSR was already reassessing its relationship with Cuba (and Angola).

Moscow subsidised Cuba with cash, weapons and cheap oil, while the Soviets bought Cuban sugar at 11 times the world price. In fact, Cuba could not have sustained its military intervention in Angola without Soviet aid.[2] The extent of Cuba's dependence on the Soviets was highlighted in a 1993 secret CIA report, which showed that the Cuban economy had contracted by over 35% following the cutting of Soviet subsidies in 1989.[3]

In Cuba, news of the Gorbachev reforms was suppressed or downplayed.[4] "I can tell the imperialists and their theoreticians," Castro defiantly thundered before an audience in Santiago de Cuba on 26 July 1988, "that Cuba will never adopt capitalist methods, styles, philosophies, or idiosyncrasies. This is what I believe." And, while mistakes had to be rectified, "the [Communist] Party's role must not be weakened; it must be strengthened."[5]

It was against this background that Brigadier General Rafael del Pino, a Cuban war hero and Deputy Chief of the Cuban air force, loaded his family into a Cessna aircraft and defected to the United States on 28 May 1987. In a series of interviews with Radio Martí, the free Cuban radio station in Miami, he said that, although the South African invasion of 1975 might have been the trigger for the Cuban military presence in Angola, it had developed into something more. He highlighted three reasons for Cuban involvement:

> First, Angola represents a key strategic point for the Soviet Union in the South Atlantic. Its ports and aerodromes can be refurbished to launch any strategic operation. And the Cubans must somehow pay off the 10 billion rubles that the Soviet Union has given Cuba in armaments, and the huge external debt to the Soviet Union; second, the enormous unemployment that exists in Cuba. You can imagine with the situation as it is in Cuba at the present . . . to suddenly take about 40 000 Cubans

into the country would create an immense problem; third, in recent years, Angola has become a place of punishment, or a place to send difficult officers, i.e., first officers or commanders who do not enjoy the trust of their superior commanders or who have morale problems or problems of command and qualification. The choice of Angola as a place of punishment has created great problems.[6]

He told the radio station that it was openly being said in the Cuban armed forces

> that we are a mercenary army, that we are supporting a group in power [the MPLA] that is amassing fabulous riches in foreign banks, that is vacationing in France and London at the expense of the people; a group that is being kept in power by our arms, because what the Angolans themselves are definitely sure of, as is the power group at the head of the government, is that if we withdraw from Angola, Savimbi will bid us farewell at the airport.[7]

Angola was "a dead-end street," he said. "Angola – many of us military men have discussed this – is Cuba's Vietnam. If there is anybody at all who has any faith in victory, it's only Fidel and Raúl Castro [Fidel's younger brother and Minister of Armed Forces]. I have spoken with officers of my own rank, and among us there is the utter conviction that there is no solution to the case of Angola. It is a lost cause . . ." As for the Angolans themselves, Del Pino continued, they had received the Cubans positively in the 1970s, but this had completely changed:

> The people do not want the Cubans in Angola. We feel bad. The Angolan officers and troops themselves no longer want us there, because they see . . . the poor qualifications of our troops there. And also that our troops will leave them high and dry at the time they most need us, as happened at the Battle of Cangamba . . . The Angolan officers see this, feel it and know it.[8]

What one can distil from this interview is that Fidel Castro was caught up in a war that was becoming increasingly unpopular among both his people and his military. Even his newly appointed commander in Angola, General de División Arnaldo Ochoa Sánchez, allegedly complained that "I have been sent to a lost war to take on the burden of defeat".[9] And there was no immediate prospect of getting out – at least not without huge loss of face. Given Castro's machismo and arrogance, withdrawal was out of the question.

Castro himself boasted that at the end of the 1980s his country had 50 000 soldiers in Angola. Proportionally, he said, this would be equivalent to 1,2 million American or 1,4 million Soviet military sent abroad to fight.[10] In a 1991 speech, Raúl Castro said that altogether 377 031 Cuban military personnel had served in Angola, in addition to almost 50 000 civilians. This amounted to almost 5% of the total population.[11] But no country – least of all one with an inefficient Marxist-Leninist economy – could carry such a burden indefinitely. No wonder Castro wanted out.

Shortly after the war ended, Castro told Chester Crocker that the South Africans had made a strategic mistake when they exploited their victory at the Lomba River by embarking on a counteroffensive. "They created a crisis and forced me to act," he said.[12] It would seem that Castro saw in the South African advance from the Lomba northwards a chance to wriggle out of what had become an untenable war.

Castro recalled that in November 1987 he was in Moscow for the 70th anniversary of the Russian Revolution of 1917 when the news of the SADF's counteroffensive reached him. Between 7 and 15 November, as he put it, "the situation became very much worse due to South Africa's escalation and the danger of their destroying or wiping out the biggest and best group of Angolan troops deployed in Cuito Cuanavale".[13] In the view of the Cuban/Angolan alliance, the SADF wanted to take Cuito Cuanavale and then engineer a regime change. Vladimir Shubin paraphrases the Angolan general R Monteiro ("Ngongo"): "Having captured it and transferred its aviation there, South Africa, using UNITA forces in the central part of Angola [some UNITA units were not far from Luanda] would create a threat to the MPLA government."[14]

Thus, while in Moscow, Castro met with Angolan President José Eduardo dos Santos and the Soviet military. Chester Crocker writes: "Castro later told me that he worked out his plan with Dos Santos on November 7 and then 'informed' the Soviets. Soviet officials confirm that Castro made the big decision around that time, and that his military game plan was greeted with initial Soviet scepticism."[15] Indeed, on 5 December 1987 Gorbachev wrote to Castro that the news of Cuba sending reinforcements to Angola "was for us, I say it bluntly, a real surprise. I find it hard to understand how such a decision could be taken without us."[16]

Immediately after Castro returned to Havana, the situation – from his point of view – became very critical: "[T]he South Africans were on the outskirts of Cuito Cuanavale, the threat was serious and there wasn't a minute to lose." Therefore, on 15 November, he called a joint meeting of the Cuban Communist Party Politburo, the General Staff and the heads of the Revolutionary Armed Forces. A decision was taken to intervene forcefully to counter the South African advance. As Castro elaborated in a speech almost a year later: "The question was, either we make the decision or we face the consequences of letting the South Africans operate with impunity and decide the struggle in Southern Africa militarily."[17] He maintained that the (socialist) "Revolution was at stake", and a defeat here would mean "a major defeat for the Revolution, regardless of how noble, how just and how altruistic the cause".[18]

Castro's strategy

On that day – 15 November – a broad strategy, resting on three pillars, was decided upon. These three pillars were:

- Engaging the Americans and South Africans diplomatically in order to bring an end to the Angolan conflict;
- Strengthening the crumbling FAPLA defences at Cuito Cuanavale;
- Opening up a new theatre of war in southwestern Angola, in Cunene province.

As far as the first is concerned, there are several clues about Castro's thinking in Chester Crocker's memoirs. A senior Soviet official had informed the Americans in late 1987 "that the Cubans now realized that they had to withdraw their troops from Angola". At more or less the same time, the Cuban Deputy Minister of Foreign Affairs, Ricardo Alarcón, confided to a US diplomat that "[t]he Angolans might be worried about the prospect of Cuban troop withdrawal; but no one stood to benefit from it more than the Cubans themselves". Crocker said that "Alarcón expanded on this theme a few days later at a lunch with an American diplomat in Havana: "A settlement would enable Cuba honorably to terminate a very heavy commitment."[19] (In December 1988 Castro would openly declare that "no one has more to gain than Cuba" from bringing the troops home.)[20]

This was an important signal. But, as Castro told Crocker himself a few months afterwards, Cuba was prepared to contribute to a settlement, "but not just any settlement: it must be an honorable one . . ." As Crocker pointed out in his memoirs, this "could only work if both his military and political options appeared to be credible".[21]

There were also other hints. On 29 January 1988, the Angolan Minister of Foreign Affairs, General Afonso Van-Dúnem, informed Chester Crocker – in the presence of Cuban negotiators – that his country was prepared to discuss *total* Cuban withdrawal. A few days later, Castro confirmed this in an interview with an American journalist. This was followed by another meeting on 18 March, when a Cuban delegation explained a proposal to move their troops northwards, away from the war theatre. More importantly, they told the Americans that they had already begun preparations for their withdrawal from Angola. Crocker's apt comment was: "This was on 18 March 1988, *before* Cuban reinforcements had all arrived, *before* the fighting peaked, and *before* Castro proclaimed to the world that he had altered the correlation of forces."[22]

Crocker's observation was confirmed by the Cuban defector Del Pino, whose analysis to the CIA was passed on to the SADF. He told the CIA, according to a secret SADF communication, "that the defeat and the UNITA [sic; SADF] counteroffensive will probably be utilised by Castro to increase his military support [to the MPLA] and thus become a decisive factor in the negotiations."[23]

But the Cuban leader went even further. In the second half of February 1988, while FAPLA was wilting under a series of hammer blows from 20 Brigade, John Mare, a diplomat at the South African Permanent Mission at the United Nations in New York, received an unexpected telephone call.[24] To his amazement, he heard a Cuban voice – also a diplomat – suggesting a confidential meeting. Mare's name had become known to the Cubans following a chance meeting with the Cuban Deputy Foreign Minister in November 1987 at a cocktail party. Mare told the voice that he had to get Ambassador Les

Manley's permission, given the political sensitivities involved. He went to see Manley, who consented: Mare could go and listen to what the Cuban had to say, but he had to take along a colleague, Chris van Melle Kamp, as a witness.

The meeting duly took place at the cocktail bar of the Barclay Intercontinental Hotel in New York. Mare recalled that he "found the atmosphere remarkably relaxed but diplomatically very 'professional', which I appreciated. We shook hands. We ordered something non-alcoholic – coffee, I think. I was pleasantly surprised that their attitude was so friendly/professional and found 'meeting the enemy' extremely interesting. I remember wondering to myself what would result of it . . ."

Mare told me he could not remember the exact words used by the Cubans during the meeting,

> but it was basically that they wanted to establish a channel of communication with SA and together try to (diplomatically) solve problems on the ground in Angola. This was accompanied by some more specific question about some particular place where our forces were in confrontation but I do not think it was a major thing . . . i.e., possibly more like a possible "test case" to see if we could cooperate. The main thing was to ask if we could establish a channel of communication.[25]

Mare could not follow up this contact, as he was posted back to South Africa at the end of February. But Chris van Melle Kamp "thereafter continued being a go-between with various ad hoc meetings with the same Cuban diplomats throughout 1988. These meetings were done with full OK from SA side and Chris always gave feed-back via Ambassador Manley or directly to SA officials . . ."[26]

Elsewhere, Van Melle Kamp confirms "the professional relationship I built up with our Cuban counterpart at the Cuban Mission where he and I and John Mare were the direct channel between Cuba and South Africa and through which the final discussions around Cuito Cuanavale and the final peace treaty and Namibian independence were conveyed".[27]

It wasn't simply the Cubans who were putting out feelers. At approximately the same time, Bavarian premier Franz Josef Strauss visited South Africa. Shortly before, he had been in Moscow, where he had met with Soviet premier Mikhail Gorbachev and Foreign Minister Eduard Shevardnadze. Strauss brought an informal message from them that the USSR was seeking peace.[28]

And, so, when South Africa's Director-General of Foreign Affairs, Neil van Heerden, received a call from Chester Crocker in March 1988, it could not have been entirely unexpected. "Based on a variety of signals," Van Heerden summarised the call, "Washington concluded that a 'window of opportunity' had appeared in Namibia." Van Heerden understood it to mean "the odds are small, but let's try". Crocker said "the Soviets are tired of their extended exposure in southern Africa and wanted out".[29]

Van Heerden flew to Washington to confer with Crocker about the new developments. Crocker reported on a conversation he had with Soviet Deputy Foreign Minister Anatoli Adamishin, which Crocker called an "opaque performance".[30] He told Van Heerden that "the Soviet Union had expressed itself in favour of political settlements to the problems of the Southern African region" (quite a turnaround, as Moscow had insisted on the FAPLA offensive to take Mavinga a few months earlier). It was also clear to Crocker that "the concept of *linkage* had . . . been accepted by the Soviet Union as the basis of any agreement" – another major development that must have caught Van Heerden's attention. Crocker rightly called it "a major shift in their thinking". Ever since 1981, South Africa and the US had insisted that the implementation of UN Resolution 435 (which envisaged a South African withdrawal from SWA) be linked to a complete and verifiable Cuban troop withdrawal from Angola. Ever since that time, Cuba and Angola had insisted that South Africa pull out of Angola and South West Africa *first*, and *then* they would decide among themselves whether the Cuban troops would leave for home (or not).

Crocker gave the South African a document containing Angolan peace proposals and indicated that, while many problems remained, "the document for the first time enshrined the concept of total CTW [combat troop withdrawal]". The Cubans also identified themselves with the document, indicating that it was only an opening bid and that they were prepared to be flexible on some points. Crocker said that it was time to bring the Cubans on board, and encouraged the South Africans to engage them in direct talks. Van Heerden did not respond substantially and simply asked numerous detailed questions.[31] He wrote later that "in time, [we] were given the green light . . . We would attend proximity talks with the Angolans and Cubans under US mediation."[32]

Castro had successfully erected the first pillar of his strategy. He had established Cuba as an influential player without which no peace was possible. This would help him to pull out of Angola while looking like a winner. However, this did not mean that Cuba and the USSR saw eye to eye. Castro had his own agenda. And therefore his diplomatic overtures to the Americans and South Africans were accompanied by the second and third pillars of his strategy. We have already briefly referred to the second pillar, namely, the stiffening of the defence of Cuito Cuanavale. To direct this, he sent one of his confidants, General de División Leopoldo "Polo" Cintra Frías to southern Angola. Another hero of the Cuban Revolution, General de División Arnaldo Ochoa Sánchez, had just been appointed overall Cuban commander in Angola.[33] The Cuban leader wanted to elevate the defence of the town to a symbol of unselfish heroism, where the South African steamroller was at last stopped through pure will-power and tenacity, where the "most glorious page was being written".[34] This would increase his political manoeuvring space to withdraw from an unwinnable war while making it look like a glorious victory.

Thus, by the end of March 1988, after the SADF's third failed attack on the Tumpo Triangle, this second pillar was also well on its way to success. To ensure its success, Castro carefully crafted a myth about the heroic defence of Cuito Cuanavale. This would form the cornerstone of the propaganda that still holds sway with the ANC government and a number of academics.[35]

In May 1998, before a summit of the Non-Aligned Movement in Havana, Castro crowed:

> The battle and its outcome are of historic importance. More than six months have passed and they are far from taking Cuito Cuanavale, and they will not be able to take Cuito Cuanavale. There has been a total change in the balance of power. It is very important to know about this in order to answer a question which many people have in mind: Why does South Africa want to negotiate?
>
> South Africa wants to negotiate because it is fighting a very strong force,

one it had never encountered anywhere before. This is not 1975. The enemy had not been given one single chance. If they had taken Cuito Cuanavale and had annihilated the concentration of troops, what kind of negotiations could we have? We would have to sit down and accept the conditions they would have imposed on us. But this was impossible – everything has changed.[36]

To a certain extent, the second pillar also succeeded. Cuito Cuanavale did not fall. The fact that the SADF had no plans to capture the town did not matter.[37] Castro apparently believed that this was the South African objective, and his brilliant propaganda offensive succeeded in planting that idea firmly in the public mind.

Castro's flanking march

But Castro's strategy also had a third element. Militarily, Cuito Cuanavale would not be the decisive battle.[38] On the contrary, he wanted to tie down the SADF on the Cuito front while making his decisive move far to the west, in Cunene province. This was essentially the same method that Deon Ferreira and Roland de Vries had applied against FAPLA between the Lomba and the Chambinga, but on a far grander scale.

When Castro met with his advisors in Havana on 15 November 1987, the decision was not merely to reinforce Cuito Cuanavale, but to send the crack 50 Division to Angola. This formation, which normally kept watch over the US naval base at Guantanamo Bay, consisted of regulars, not conscripts, and was commanded by Brigadier General Patricio de la Guardia Font.[39] President Dos Santos gave his permission, and also allowed Castro to take over operational command from his headquarters bunker in Havana. The first 9 ships and 20 air freighters, loaded with troops, weapons and war materiel, left Havana on 24 November, and the first elements of 50 Division started moving into Cunene province soon afterwards. To the Cubans, the operation was known as "Maniobra XXXI Aniversario de las FAR". To hide Castro's intentions, the southward movement of troops to Cunene took place on a small scale only, and by the end of January about 3 500 troops were in Cunene. Their presence was promptly detected by South African Military Intelligence, but their purpose was unclear.

Nevertheless, from the beginning of March, Castro prepared to shift to a higher gear. On 6 March he ordered Cintra to move the division southwards, and on 11 March a tank brigade with 40 T-62s reached the town of Chibemba.[40] It appears that the SADF learnt of this southward deployment halfway through April 1988.[41] According to CIA intelligence passed on to the SADF, about 13 300 Cuban troops had been deployed in Cunene province by the end of April. These reinforcements "include Cuba's best combat units, such as the Havana tank regiment". The expectation was that they would be aggressive.[42] By late May, as Crocker reported, "they had established a new southern front running some 250 miles in rough parallel with the Namibian border and coming to within 12 miles of it in some places".[43]

It is important to emphasise that this advance took place largely *after* the bulk of the SADF force at Tumpo had been pulled back and replaced with Piet Nel's Combat Team 20, which had to simulate a larger force. In other words, there never was any question, as the Cubans, the ANC and others have alleged, of the full SADF brigade at Tumpo being cut off. Perhaps the Cuban propaganda is testimony to the success of Combat Team 20's aggressive posture, which made the Cubans think that an entire brigade was still present in the area.

In previous years, Castro had shown a healthy respect for the South African Air Force. He repeatedly cited the SAAF's supremacy in the air as one of the reasons why he did not want to tangle with the SADF. And, therefore, his 15 November meeting also decided, as he explained, "to transfer the most experienced pilots of our air force to Angola, so they could begin to operate in the air from the base at Menongue".[44]

For the same reason, the ground forces advancing southwards in the direction of the South West African border were amply equipped with anti-aircraft guns and 150 SA-8 missile launchers. But the air base at Lubango, capital of Huíla province, was 250 km from the South West African border – too far for Castro's liking. Polo Cintra cut through the red tape and assembled everything for the rebuilding of the airfield at Cahama, and later Xangongo as well. Engineers swarmed over the Angolan air bases to refurbish and lengthen the runways to accommodate the MiG-23s, and to construct bunkers to protect the aircraft from SAAF strikes while on the ground.[45]

From a South African perspective, what made this ominous was that Ruacana,

Ondangwa and Oshakati – all crucial for the counterinsurgency war against SWAPO inside South West Africa – would be well within range of both air bases. The Cubans installed a radar network covering the whole of southern Angola and northern SWA. The purpose was clearly to be able, if necessary, to project Cuban air power into the north of South West Africa.[46]

Within a few weeks, 11 000 to 12 000 heavily armed Cuban soldiers, organised in three task forces, were firmly ensconced in Cunene. They consisted of six rifle regiments of 1 500 to 2 000 men each with tank support, a tank regiment with T-62s and T-55s, an artillery regiment with D-30 artillery and BM-24/BM-21 rocket launchers, an anti-aircraft regiment with missiles, radar and 23-mm guns, three combined Cuban/SWAPO battalions with tank support, and a SWAPO battalion of 300 men. (The Cubans and SWAPO fighters wore the same battle fatigues, making it difficult to differentiate between them.) They were positioned in a big half-circle from Namibe in the northwest, via Chibemba, Cahama and Humbe to Xangongo and Techipa in the south, and thence to Cuvelai and Cassinga in the northeast. Altogether, 200 tanks were present. The best FAPLA units were also moved southwards.[47] According to an SADF estimate, 20 000 of the 50 000 Cuban military personnel in Angola had been deployed in the south.[48]

Castro's strategy was brilliant, and Crocker called it, for obvious reasons, "the grand strategist's classic 'flanking maneuver' ".[49] Castro likened his approach to "a boxer who with his left hand blocks the blow [at Cuito Cuanavale] and with his right – strikes [in the west]".[50] In a speech in December 1998, he explained that the military principle applied was

> that you should not undertake decisive battles on terrain chosen by the enemy; you must wage decisive battles when you choose the terrain and strike the enemy in sensitive and genuinely strategic spots . . . The main idea was to stop them at Cuito Cuanavale and attack them from the southwest. Enough troops were gathered to seriously threaten points of strategic importance for South Africa and strike hard at them on terrain that we, and not the enemy, had chosen.[51]

The South Africans' problem was one of uncertainty: what exactly were Castro's intentions? In theory, with his thousands of troops in Cunene, he could take three different routes: (1) he could keep his forces where they were, as a force in being, as a threat; (2) he could march eastwards inside Angola to cut off the small South African force left at Tumpo; and (3) he could invade northern SWA. Castro was, in effect, confronting the South Africans (in the words of Sir Basil Liddell Hart) "on the horns of a dilemma".[52]

Dick Lord says that the Cuban armoured thrust to the border "was taken very seriously by the SADF".[53] The South Africans were at this stage totally unprepared for a possible invasion of the country. All the conventional formations were engaged at Tumpo or refitting back in SWA and South Africa. The only units available to counter an invasion were lightly armed counterinsurgency infantry battalions and a few troops of obsolete Eland armoured cars.[54] In fact, if Castro had decided then to cross the border, there is very little the SADF could have done to stop him. South West Africa basically lay at his mercy.

Even the Americans were surprised by the size and nature of the Cuban deployment. In a meeting with South African officials – including Magnus Malan and Jannie Geldenhuys – in Cairo at the end of June 1988, Jim Woods, Chester Crocker's equivalent at the Pentagon, said ominously that

> [t]hese were the best units Cuba had, they were armed with advanced equipment, were much tougher and of a higher caliber than any troops seen in Angola before. The troops involved in the southward movement were prepared to take advanced combat positions and were building airfields at Cahama and elsewhere. The main threat in South Western Angola was the full squadron of MiG-23s which had an aggressive posture and capacity.[55]

Woods said that the Cuban units had with them 800 pieces of heavy armour (which sounds like an exaggeration), 400 pieces of light armour, 300 artillery and rocket launchers, 250 air defence weapons, 80 missile launchers, 60 to 70 fixed-wing aircraft, and 20 to 30 helicopter gunships. Woods gave the US appreciation: "It did not appear to be merely a blocking force to prevent South African troop movement into Angola. Initially the US had estimated that this was a political build-up so as to improve the negotiation posture at the talks.

However the force had become too big for that to be the only reason and now it appeared to be an offensive force looking for a fight."

Woods outlined a possible four-point strategy that the Cubans could implement:

- To advance to the border and occupy the Calueque Dam;
- To seek out SADF units in the border area of northern SWA as a result of Castro's belief that South Africa could not absorb as many casualties as Cuba could;
- To take and occupy South African bases in SWA and drive South African forces further south, at the same time driving eastwards along South West African roads to cut off UNITA from the rear;
- To refocus the force currently in the Fifth Military Region (Cunene) against UNITA.

Woods said the intentions of the Cuban thrust would become clearer by mid-July, and that those forces would be in the best shape for an attack in about mid-August. He also said that the Cuban force consisted of between 8 000 and 10 000 men, augmented by 5 000 to 10 000 SWAPO fighters. It was clear that the presence of several thousand armed SWAPO insurgents added to the threat. The area now occupied by the Cubans, which the Angolans called their Fifth Military Region, was exactly the territory that the South Africans had dominated for several years in order to prevent SWAPO infiltration into Ovamboland. As the guerrillas were now integrated with the Cubans at battalion level, it became impossible for the South Africans to fight SWAPO inside Angola without tangling with an aggressive Cuban army.

The last battles

On 18 April, a Cuban unit attacked a group of South African soldiers engaged in a routine operation against SWAPO in Cunene province. The Cubans did it so aggressively that alarm bells went off all over the SADF. The situation was potentially extremely serious, as demonstrated by a series of skirmishes that lasted to the end of June.[56]

On the afternoon of 5 May, a force from 101 Battalion, travelling in

20 Casspirs and two trucks, ran into a Cuban ambush, also in Cunene. Four Casspirs were quickly shot to pieces by RPG-7s. However, the 101 Battalion men reacted immediately with the tactics they had used with great success against PLAN insurgents in SWA: a seemingly disorganised melee, with the Casspirs weaving about, shooting at anything that moved, and trampling everything else. Several Cubans died under the wheels of the Casspirs before the South Africans pulled back at dusk. The Cubans, perhaps shocked by the violent response, did not follow up. Altogether 54 Cubans died, compared with 7 from 101 Battalion. Nevertheless, the Cubans won a huge propaganda coup when a wounded Rifleman, Johan Papenfus, was taken prisoner.

The problem was that there was very little intelligence available about the Cuban/Angolan alliance's order of battle and their positions. Moreover, SWAPO was taking advantage of the build-up north of the border to infiltrate insurgents into Ovamboland. Some of the senior officers at Oshakati wanted to attack the Cubans immediately, but Commandant Jan Hougaard (32 Battalion) convinced them to gather information first. Two three-man Recce teams were inserted over the next few days, following the clash of 5 May. They returned with the news that the Cubans and SWAPO had ensconced themselves strongly at Techipa.

The only unit in the vicinity with some conventional war experience was 32 Battalion, the SADF's ever-willing warhorse, and three companies were hurriedly flown in to Angola. Two were deployed south of Techipa and the third astride the approach to Calueque. (The Calueque reservoir, supplying northern SWA with water, had been protected by an army detachment for several years.) Their orders were to harass the Cubans and act as a kind of tripwire to deter the enemy from advancing nearer to the reservoir and the South West African border until 61 Mech could be brought up and the Cubans driven away.

It didn't happen that way. On 22 May, one of the 32 Battalion companies, under the command of Captain Maurice Devenish, established an ambush near Techipa. But, once the shooting broke out, he discovered that he was facing a strong Cuban formation with tanks and armoured cars, while he had only two 81-mm mortars and two Unimogs. There was only one alternative – to pull out as fast as he could. To make things even worse, both Unimogs were shot out in rapid succession, and his soldiers had to abandon everything and run all the

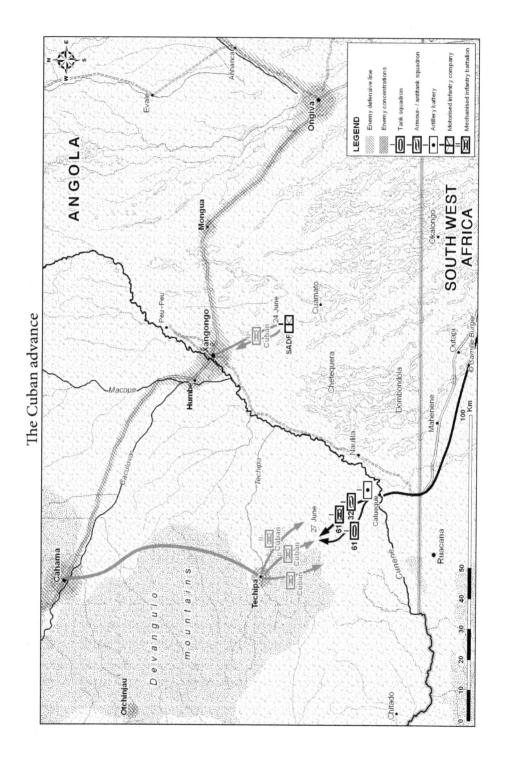

The Cuban advance

way back to Ruacana. Luckily, the 32 Battalion men were invariably extremely fit. The Cubans lost six men, with none lost on the SADF side.

Things were now gearing up for a possible climactic clash. From documents discovered in the Unimogs, the Cubans deduced that the South Africans were planning to attack Techipa. In fact, the outcome of this fight moved the SADF to call off those plans, but the Cubans were not to know this. They therefore decided to pre-empt the South Africans. Referring to Cuban sources, Edward George says that plans for a two-pronged offensive were drawn up: one column would attack southwards from Xangongo and capture Cuamato, 80 km east of Calueque, after which three more columns would strike down from Techipa to take Calueque itself. Two additional missile groups and a tactical group with extra tanks were sent to Techipa.[57]

On 7 June, Fidel Castro cabled his two senior generals in Angola, Ochoa and Cintra, informing them of "the likelihood of a large-scale South African air attack against our advanced units". If this materialised, "plans should be made for a counterattack with every possible plane for the total destruction of the water tank and transformers in Ruacana . . . Plans should also be made for a strike at Ochicata [Oshakati] and nearby airfields [Ondangwa?] . . . The response must be crushing and quick." He also ordered reinforcements to the south, saying: "Decisive moments may be at hand."[58]

The Cuban offensive started on 24 June, when the first column left Xangongo and pushed towards Cuamato. But this force ran into an SADF defence, backed by Ratels and mortars, and a sharp firefight followed in which two Buffels were destroyed. But this was enough to convince the Cubans to fall back to Xangongo.

Obviously, Brigadier Chris Serfontein, commanding Sector 10 in Ovamboland, could not know about the exact Cuban offensive plans, although all his information indicated that the enemy was about to advance southwards. In consultation with his officers, he drew up an excellent tactical plan. By this stage, 61 Mech had arrived with a tank squadron. Also available were four motorised infantry companies and a support company from 32 Battalion, including the unit's antitank troop (in four Ratel 90s and four Ratel ZT3s), three motorised companies from 101 Battalion (in Casspirs), and one motorised company each from 1 Parachute, 202 and 701 Battalions (in Buffels). The artillery support was provided by one battery each of G-5s, G-2s, Valkiris and

120-mm mortars. This force, known as Task Force Zulu, was placed under the command of Colonel Michau Delport.

What the South Africans then did was very interesting indeed. Towards last light on 26 June, Impala aircraft took off from Ondangwa Air Force Base to simulate an air strike on Techipa – the strike Castro was expecting. The timing was carefully planned for 17h00 on a Sunday afternoon, when the enemy's vigilance would be at a low point. Being shortly before nightfall, the strike would also prevent the Cuban MiGs from taking to the air. But as soon as the Impalas were picked up by the Cuban radar, they dived down beneath the radar again, while Jan Hougaard and a few of his men released meteorological balloons that showed up on the Cuban screens as aircraft. The Cubans promptly launched six SA-6 missiles, which were tracked by the South Africans and their positions plotted. Three missile batteries were identified.

Then the large South African guns opened fire. For five horrifying hours, the shells rained down on the Cubans, who suffered terribly. One Cuban battery returned fire, getting off ten shots before falling silent. The original idea was to draw out the Cuban armour and surprise it in an ambush by Task Force Zulu, which had taken up position to the southeast of the Cubans. But the Cubans were apparently so shaken by the bombardment that they were unable to react. At about 22h00 the South Africans, somewhat disappointed by the lack of reaction, withdrew.

But in the light of morning, it was a different story. In Havana, an enraged Castro signalled to Cintra:

> We must respond to today's artillery attack against Techipa. We feel the first step must be a strong air attack against South African camps, military installations and personnel in Calueque and the surrounding area. Avoid as much as possible the loss of civilian life. If the enemy artillery can be located, strike a strong blow at it. We must have at the ready other variants of attack if the circumstances require.[59]

It was as if a bee had stung the Cubans. In three mechanised columns – each with 600 men, supported by 35 tanks – they started advancing towards Calueque. The idea was that they would reach Calueque at the same time as the air strike took place, possibly indicating that they wanted to crush the South Africans and take the storage dam. But the South Africans suspected that something of the kind was afoot, and sent a medium-sized force, consisting of a mechanised infantry company (12 Ratel 20s from 61 Mech, which had been called up from its base in SWA), together with 32 Battalion's antitank troop and eight Ratel 81s, forward from Calueque to see what the Cubans were up to and to prepare an ambush if the enemy was seen to push forward. The column was commanded by Major André Vermeulen, with the ubiquitous Major Hannes Nortmann in charge of the antitank Ratels.

At about 09h00 the South Africans, with Nortmann in the lead, ran into an ambush. A Cuban fired an RPG-7 from as little as 25 m away, and one of the Ratel 90s was immediately destroyed, torn apart by internal explosions. Another Ratel was taken out by a T-55, killing 19-year-old Lieutenant Muller ("Mielie") Meiring. As the area was very bushy, the missile Ratels could not fire, so the burden fell on the Ratel 90s, which, as we have seen time and again, were inadequate against tanks. The surviving Ratels fought back hard, destroying an enemy tank, two tracked 23-mm guns and several trucks. Nortmann was wounded in his neck and hand, but doggedly continued. The South African machine guns and canister shot from the 90-mm guns caused heavy casualties among the Cuban infantry, but it was clear that the South Africans were completely outgunned.

One 61 Mech trooper, Rifleman Hein Groenewald, later described the battle:

> Suddenly, without any Russian weapons in sight, we were fired upon with rifles and heavy RPG-7 fire. We had moved right into the enemy's first line "spotter troops", who move on foot before their combat vehicles.
>
> They hit us with their RPG-7s, and so Second Lieutenant Mielie Meiring's Ratel was hit with an RPG-7. Immediately we shot back with a firebelt action.
>
> The Ratel 81s were in front of us, and as I saw it from my Ratel, they threw unbelievable fire on the enemy with their 81 mm mortars. After the time, it was said that they threw 500+ mortar bombs . . . Our combat

team moved forward and continued firing. In the meantime Second Lieutenant Meiring's body had to be removed, and Ratel 22 and Ratel 22B moved forward through the fire. With great speed the survivors and wounded were taken out and transported backwards. Meiring was already dead when they took him out of the Ratel.[60]

At this stage, the Olifant tank squadron, having been called up hastily by radio, reached the battleground, halfway between Techipa and Calueque (*see* map on page 376). This completely changed the tactical situation, and the tanks killed another T-55 and several other vehicles before the enemy wisely pulled back out of range of the Olifants' 105-mm guns. However, Mike Muller, who was not far off with the rest of 61 Mech, decided not to follow the Cubans, as he had received intelligence that another two Cuban tank squadrons were moving forward to engage the South Africans. Muller got permission to withdraw too. Indeed, two Cuban tank squadrons tried to cut 61 Mech off by outflanking the unit on both sides, but were thwarted by the timely intervention of the South African artillery, which inflicted considerable casualties.

According to SADF estimates, which are impossible to verify, 302 Cuban soldiers died in this clash and the earlier bombardment. (The Cubans acknowledged only 10 dead.)[61] On the South African side, the only death was that of Muller Meiring. The Cubans lost two tanks, two BTR-60s and eight trucks, while the South Africans suffered the loss of two Ratels.

The time now came for the last bloody spasm of the South African–Cuban war. Just before 15h00, several reports came in of enemy aircraft flying very low towards Calueque. But it was too late to do anything about it. In two waves, seven MiG-23s dropped parachute-retarded bombs, clearly aiming for the dam wall, which they hit. Other bombs severely damaged the bridge over the dam. An eighth MiG veered off and dropped its bombs on the water pipeline to Ovamboland. One bomb went astray and killed 11 men from 8 SAI who were standing next to a Buffel watching the drama. (The Cubans claimed that 50 South Africans died.)[62]

Hein Groenewald, whose unit had by then returned to Calueque, witnessed everything:

It wasn't a nice sight. We dived for cover, and everybody dived beneath the Ratel for protection. Some futilely dug in the ground with their hands to get more cover under the Ratel. It was chaos around us [*dis nág rondom ons*], because the MiGs started shooting at us with their cannon and hit us with the bombs. I could see the pilot in his cockpit, so close to us they flew past.

We had never been bombed like this by enemy aircraft in Angola. They continued to shoot accurately and wanted to cause as much damage as possible. It felt like an eternity, and the MiGs turned again and again and came back to us standing next to the dam wall. They hit the dam wall with bombs, which fell left and right of us. Their 23-mm cannon moved us and shots rang out left and right of us . . .

Slowly and shivering, covered in dust, we crawled from under the Ratels. We started running and saw the damage caused. I do not believe that any South African force or groups had been attacked so aggressively before by the enemy's aircraft.[63]

From a professional viewpoint, Dick Lord had great respect for the way in which the mission was carried out. This was different from the inept bombing from safe heights during operations Moduler, Hooper and Packer. "It was a very deliberate, well-planned attack," he told Fred Bridgland. He called it "a very academic attack in which they ignored any threat from our air defences . . .". They dropped 16 bombs, of which six hit their target, "which is not a bad percentage".[64] During the second attack, an audacious Cuban pilot executed a victory roll, reminding the South Africans that they had been caught unawares.

But the Cubans ignored a lesson learnt by more experienced air forces: do not immediately attack the same target again in the face of accurate anti-aircraft fire. This is exactly what the second wave of Cuban MiGs did, and they paid a deadly price. The South African anti-aircraft defences, mainly hand-aimed 20-mm cannon, came to life as the second wave flew over. Two MiGs were hit, and one crashed on its way back to base at Cahama.

The Cubans tried once more to advance in the direction of Ruacana, but ran into extensive minefields and abandoned the attempt. They withdrew to Techipa, while 61 Mech crossed the border back to SWA. That same evening, Kat Liebenberg flew to Oshakati. He told Chris Serfontein to stop all offensive operations against the Cubans in view of the peace negotiations. That was the first time Serfontein had heard of talks.[65]

Jannie Geldenhuys was satisfied with his troops' conduct. "The two incidents at Calueque were executed clinically correctly and in good order," he told a staff meeting a few days later. "The relative losses prove that the Cubans were hurt." He also announced that Chester Crocker had relayed a message from the MPLA government in which they distanced themselves from the Cuban air strike on Calueque.[66] Geldenhuys also communicated to the senior field commanders that he thought the latest series of battles gave South Africa "a definite advantage around the negotiation table", and he congratulated them.[67]

Castro signalled to Ochoa that he had to prepare "a strong blow at enemy bases in northern Namibia", should the South Africans react to the Calueque bombing. "We have already given the first response, so now they must either reconsider or continue the escalation after that."[68]

The South Africans clearly chose not to escalate the fighting. But neither did the Cubans. In the coming months, both sides would *plan* for an escalation, but do nothing to make it possible. "Like scorpions in a bottle, the rival forces avoided each other's sting," Crocker wrote.[69]

There were several rational explanations for the Cuban reticence (we shall discuss the South African position later in the chapter). One was undoubtedly that the broad Cuban strategic objective was to *intimidate* the South Africans in order to get out of the war with honour – not to escalate the fighting. But there also was a second factor, which became known only years after the war: Castro was afraid of South Africa's nuclear weapons.

Over the years, Castro referred several times to South Africa's nuclear capability (which was unconfirmed at the time).[70] But as far as can be ascertained, his first public acknowledgment of the role played by the nuclear threat in his military decision-making in Angola occurred in October 1995, when he addressed a black church audience in Harlem, New York City. He spoke at length about his country's "heroic" involvement in Angola, including the flanking march in 1988, and then said, revealing his uncertainty at the time:

But what is the most extraordinary about this is that South Africa had become a nuclear power by then. And we knew it. We even deployed our forces in such a way that we were taking into account that South Africa had nuclear warheads. The right of the matter was whether they would decide to drop it or not. Who were they going to use the weapon against? Against us? Inside South Africa?[71]

He repeated it more forcefully after his retirement, in his column in the official Cuban newspaper *Granma*, in 2010, when he wrote that

our brave combatants and the military chiefs of our Revolutionary Armed Forces taking part in heroic internationalist missions were close to becoming the victims of nuclear strikes against the Cuban troops deployed close to the Angolan south border from where the South African racist forces – at the time positioned on the Namibian border – had been expelled after the Battle of Cuito Cuanavale.[72]

At times, he said that South Africa had "seven nuclear warheads";[73] at others, he claimed that the "Pentagon, with the consent of the President of the United States, supplied the South African racists through Israel with about 14 nuclear bombs, more powerful than those dropped on the Japanese cities of Hiroshima and Nagasaki . . .".[74] On another occasion he alleged that "the racists were at the point of using them against Cuban and Angolan troops . . .".[75]

Indeed, South Africa's first nuclear devices were built in 1978 and 1979, but these were experimental and not weaponised. The first bomb capable of being delivered by aircraft was completed in 1982. Thereafter, the others followed at a pace of less than one per year, so that South Africa possessed six completed bombs (there was a seventh, which was uncompleted) by the end of 1989.[76] These were designed to be fixed to the SAAF's H2 guided glide bomb (the same one that damaged the bridge at Cuito Cuanavale) and be delivered by Buccaneer aircraft.[77]

However, Castro could not know all of this. Therefore, it is hardly surprising that Jorge Risquet Valdés, a leading Cuban official, investigated the matter during a visit to South Africa at the end of 2010. According to a newspaper report, Risquet and a few colleagues spoke to Pik Botha and asked whether the SADF really had nuclear warheads capable of being fired by artillery (which shows exactly what they were afraid of). "I fully explained that we didn't have such technically advanced stuff, but we did have devices which were comparable to the dirty bombs dropped on Hiroshima and Nagasaki," Botha told the newspaper.[78]

Risquet revealed much about the Cuban fears to Dr Waldo Stumpf, the former chief of South Africa's Atomic Energy Corporation. He wanted to know whether South Africa had ever planned to use its nuclear bombs against the Cuban troops in Angola. He told Stumpf that the Cuban tactics from 1985 were to deploy their forces in Angola in two separate divisions, so that, if one was struck with a nuclear device, the other would survive.[79]

Stumpf explained to the Cubans that the South African strategy regarding nuclear weapons rested on three pillars:

- South Africa would never acknowledge or deny that it had nuclear weapons;
- If a critical threat developed, the country would first inform the US and the UK that it was forced to use these weapons;
- South Africa would then conduct underground tests so that the world could know that it had the capability to produce such weapons.

In reality, one may add a fourth pillar. Stumpf told the Cubans that President PW Botha was adamant that nuclear weapons were only a deterrent, and would *never* actually be used.[80] As Stumpf put it elsewhere: "No offensive tactical application was ever foreseen or intended as it was fully recognised that such an act would bring about political retaliation on a massive scale."[81] It was a powerful bluff.

From all of this it may be clear that the South African nuclear strategy of deliberately being ambivalent in public was a success. It was certainly an important factor, albeit perhaps not the only one, in preventing the Cuban forces from invading South West Africa in May to July 1988.

The South African dilemma

All of this was, of course, not clear at the time. The series of battles between the SADF and the Cubans understandably worried the South Africans, and it is not surprising to learn from the archival sources that they were caught off guard by the Cuban advance. In May, Pik Botha indignantly complained to the Angolans about the Cuban march, calling it "a major thrust" and saying that "South Africa was extremely concerned at this development". If "the opposing forces got too close", he said, "it only required a small spark to set off an explosion".[82] He also sent a message to Mikhail Gorbachev, via Franz Josef Strauss, "that the southward movement of Cuban troops would cause a serious problem at a time when there was a genuine hope for peace".[83]

We know today that the Cubans, in consultation with the Soviets, were never seriously planning to cross the border – although, for obvious reasons, they declined to state this publicly.[84] Chester Crocker tried to prise the information from Risquet, but the wily Cuban preferred to keep the Americans and South Africans guessing.[85] Another Cuban spokesman said in public "that we are not saying that we will not go into Namibia".[86] The problem is that nobody outside the Cuban decision-making circles really knew what their intentions were.

To be sure, the SADF's Directorate of Military Intelligence was not overly alarmed. The early South African appreciation of the enemy's military strategy was that their plan made provision for three mutually supporting phases, though not necessarily following each other. In the first phase, the Cubans would deploy their forces in southwestern Angola in such a way as to tie down the SADF and UNITA there. This would also aid PLAN's activities and strengthen the enemy's power base in the peace negotiations. In phase two, the enemy was expected to establish a base area (though not again at Cuito Cuanavale) with a view to renewing the offensive against Mavinga and Jamba. The third phase would see the launch of the offensive, possibly as early as July/August 1988. The Cubans could be expected to act aggressively in Cunene province in order to build their own prestige.[87]

Some weeks after this appreciation, Military Intelligence again interpreted the Cubans' posture as "predominantly defensive to ensure Angolan territorial integrity and to aid the SWAPO terror onslaught". An invasion of South West Africa was not considered likely, as the Cubans did not underestimate the SADF's capability, and because it would scupper the budding peace talks. According to "a former Cuban general who defected to the US" (probably Rafael del Pino), the Cubans would instead carry out "vengeance air attacks" on "targets like Ruacana and Ondangwa" if the SADF attacked them inside Angola. Also, the USSR agreed to a US request to rein in the Cuban air force if the South Africans similarly refrained from crossing into Angolan airspace.[88] Speaking to South African officers from a safe house in the US, Del Pino indeed assessed the Cuban army as being "not capable of mounting a full-scale attack".[89] At the end of June, the Americans allowed South Africa to interrogate Del Pino. According to Willem van der Waals, who spoke to the Cuban, Del Pino "warned that we should not underestimate Castro. Castro was a relentless adventurer who would not hesitate to launch an air attack on SADF bases in the north of SWA. Plans for that already existed and would be carried out without Soviet support."[90]

In July, formal planning documents on countering a possible Cuban invasion also assumed that the Cubans would rather cover a large-scale SWAPO infiltration into SWA, including the "white" areas south of Ovamboland. This was described as the "most probable" alternative. A full-scale invasion – with the main advance on Ondangwa and supporting attacks on Oshakati and Ruacana – was described as "the most dangerous" alternative. But the implication was that this was less probable.[91]

On the other hand, Jan Breytenbach describes a conversation with Chris Serfontein in Oshakati: "it became apparent he had been extremely worried – and rightly so", as the Cubans were too strong "to suggest it was merely an empty threat".[92] Magnus Malan writes in his memoirs that the most probable interpretation "was that the Cubans wanted to threaten targets inside South West Africa/Namibia from the southwest of Angola and would attack with the least encouragement. These attacks would then give SWAPO the opportunity to take real action in South West Africa/Namibia and declare liberated areas in this country."[93] Even Jannie Geldenhuys, who did not really believe in a Cuban invasion, had to keep such a possibility in mind.[94]

The truth is that Castro had everyone guessing, which is no doubt exactly what he wanted. The third pillar of his strategy – the creation of a new theatre of war – had succeeded.

Contingency planning

As far as the South African planning to counter the Cuban threat was concerned, Geldenhuys describes PW Botha's attitude as follows:

> According to him, we had fulfilled our mission and we did it well. He said he maintained his stance that we should not be sucked into Angola and become a Vietnam case. In the UNITA area we had a valid reason to become involved, but in the southwest we were only interested in the hydro-electrical scheme [at Calueque] and the water supply to South West. The Cubans' adventure in Angola across Kaokoland and Ovambo is a new situation. We do not seek confrontation with the Angolans. Let the Cubans do what they want, keep an eye on them, keep contact, but don't start a new war. Keep your aggressiveness, but don't be arrogant-cocky. Stay cool and exercise self-control.[95]

However, the situation was more complex than that. Several steps were taken in reaction to the Cuban threat. The first came on 7 June, when the first planning group met for the creation of a new formation, known as 10 Division, so named after Sector 10 in SWA.[96] The next day, Geldenhuys announced a partial South African mobilisation. "It had to take care of the necessary force levels if an attack on South West took place, but it also had to address a message to the Cubans about what they could expect," he wrote in his memoirs.[97] This formation was placed under the command of Chris Serfontein, also commander of Sector 10, with Roland de Vries as his chief of staff.[98] The Citizen Force troops who were mobilised had to show up at their units from 22 to 30 July. Refresher training would take place in northern Namibia until 21 August, and by 24 August all units had to be ready for war.[99]

The composition of 10 Division was revealing. The units involved changed over time, but the force level remained much the same:

- 61 Mech, with a tank squadron but without its organic artillery;
- 4 SAI, without tanks or artillery;
- 81 Armoured Brigade (Citizen Force), with a tank regiment (three squadrons), an armoured car regiment (two squadrons), a mechanised infantry

battalion (two companies, plus support company) and various support units;

- 71 Motorised Brigade (Citizen Force), with a mechanised infantry battalion group and a parachute battalion group;
- An artillery brigade, with two batteries of G-5s, two batteries of G-2s, a battery and a troop of Valkiri MRLs and two batteries of 120-mm mortars.[100]

In addition, experienced units like 32 and 101 Battalions could also be drawn upon to act as motorised infantry. This was not only the first operational deployment of a division since 1945, but also the biggest of the entire Border War. It must have comprised at least 10 000 troops.

On 30 May, an operation order was issued for Operation Hilti, designed to defend South West Africa against a possible Cuban attack. Hilti had three sub-operations: Excite (the initial battles with the Cubans already described), Faction and Florentine. At this stage, the purpose was not simply to defend SWA, but, as the order for Operation Faction stated, the army had to "expand the UNITA liberated area in South Angola to extend the old area in dispute east of the Cunene River". This territory was expressly defined as bordered by the Cunene in the west, the Techamutete high ground in the north and the Kavango River in the east. This corresponded to the territory occupied by the SADF at the end of Operation Askari in January 1984. Operation Florentine would involve the establishment of UNITA's authority there.[101] It was expected that this operation would start at the end of August.

According to Roland de Vries, he was summoned to Army Headquarters in May 1988. There Major General Jan Klopper, Chief of Staff Operations, asked him to start contingency planning in case the situation with the Cubans got out of hand. De Vries immediately occupied one of the lecture halls at the Military College and got to work. As one might expect from one of the most prominent exponents of mobile warfare in the SADF, all the attack arrow symbols on the battle map pointed clearly to the rear areas of 50 Division in Cunene. When he joined 10 Division at Oshakati, he summoned the officers on the army's Senior Command and Staff course to help with the planning, as well as to get practical operational experience. "From the terrain appreciation it became evident that Cahama and Xangongo would have to be taken. This was where the main infrastructure and forward airfields of the enemy lay for their Southern Front." Other targets included Lubango and Namibe, indicating that the idea was to go even further than in 1984.[102] True to the SADF's mechanised doctrine – which now apparently once again held sway – it would have been a lightning operation, with a maximum period of 21 days. The area was to have been taken by 31 October, with UNITA firmly entrenched by 31 December.[103]

The SADF planners knew that this was political dynamite. The peace negotiations could obviously be derailed by premature aggressiveness, and in the short term the South Africans had "to maintain a very fine balance between demonstration of power on the one hand and military actions on the other which may lead to confrontation and embarrassment".[104]

According to Roland de Vries, very little intelligence about the enemy was available at this stage. "Serfontein was probably thinking in similar vein as Stonewall Jackson of Chancellorsville had done. Jackson, in facing similar odds during the American Civil War, promptly uttered: 'I was too weak to defend, so I attacked.'"[105] Indeed, the SADF expressly recognised that "[t]he present state of tactical conventional intelligence regarding FAPLA/Cuban forces in the 5th Military Region is not sufficient for the detailed planning of Op[eration] Faction."[106] This seems to have been the reasoning behind the initial offensive nature of the planned Operation Hilti.

As the negotiations gathered momentum, the SADF collected more intelligence about the Cuban order of battle and positions[107] and realised that an offensive would probably be unnecessary and counterproductive. South Africa "should not be the cause of a breakdown in negotiations" because of the possible advantages they held for the country, the SADF leadership ordained.[108] As Magnus Malan told Chester Crocker in Cairo, "while South Africa had selected the killing ground to be north of the SWA border, it might now be preferable to fight inside SWA."[109] Besides, the SADF's intelligence appraisal of the Cuban intentions was that they wanted to tie down the South Africans in Ovamboland and lure them into an attack. "This should serve as trigger for an escalation of the conflict which should spread to SWA territory." Thus, Jannie Geldenhuys wrote to Magnus Malan, "the SADF will not get involved in decisive battles on Angolan territory. Any Cuban threat against the territorial

integrity will, however, be warded off with the necessary action on SWA territory."[110] An advisory group, chaired by Brigadier Eddie Webb, wrote to Jannie
Geldenhuys that "[t]he military balance of power is at present in the enemy's
favour in terms of weaponry and force levels". The group advised that, in the
case of an invasion of Angola, South Africa would be branded as the aggressor, while heavy losses would be endured. There was only a "limited chance to
be successful".[111]

And so, a few days later, on 29 June, Hilti was overtaken by a defensive plan,
Operation Handbag, "to ward off a possible invasion from Angola by Cubans
and/or other force compositions". This defence "does not necessarily have to be
based on the physical SWA border".[112] On 19 July, its place was again taken by a
refined plan, Operation Prone, which had two sub-operations, Linger (counterinsurgency, to combat SWAPO inside SWA) and Pact (a conventional operation,
in the dry official language of the SADF, "to parry an invasion, semi-conventional and/or conventional by the Cubans and/or other force combinations in
the Sector 10 area and so protect SWA's territorial integrity").[113]

There was another reason for the switch from an offensive to a defensive
plan. From top-secret documents in the SANDF Documentation Centre, it is
clear that at this stage the South Africans were simply not able to invade Angola
with such a big force. They had the numbers, but, beyond that, the army and air
force were exhausted. The army reported to the State Security Council (SSC)
that there were "knelpunte" (bottlenecks) with regard to tank and G-5 spare
parts, fuel tankers, lorries, signal equipment and all sorts of vehicle spares.
These would not be solved until well into 1989. Moreover, intensive offensive
operations with two brigades could not be logistically supported (and then only
for two months) before the beginning of December 1988. To send in three brigades would not be possible before July 1989, and then also for two months
only.[114] Presumably the army's stocks had been drained by the intensive fighting during operations Moduler, Hooper and Packer.

The air force was even worse off. The SSC was informed that the SAAF
had only meagre forces available:[115] 4 Mirage F1CZ fighters, 7 Mirage F1AZ
ground-attack aircraft, 4 Mirage IIICZ fighters, 3 Buccaneer bombers, 3 Canberra
bombers, and 10 Impala II light ground-attack aircraft. Of these, the Mirage
IIICZ was so obsolete that it could be utilised for base protection only, while the

Canberra was also obsolete and too vulnerable. The Impala was not equipped for a high-intensity war. (The new Cheetah fighter would not be operational until 1989.)[116] The SAAF had no radar-jamming capability to speak of, and the enemy's extensive radar coverage of southern Angola and even northern SWA, made surprise attacks very difficult, if not impossible. Furthermore, only 20 drop tanks were available for the Mirage F1s, severely limiting their range. There were only nine kits for kicking out "chaff" (bundles of aluminium foil designed to confuse radar) and flares (for misleading enemy radar and heat-seeking missiles), leaving the South African aircraft vulnerable. In addition, there was a shortage of flight personnel. For instance, 3 Squadron (Mirage F1CZs) had only six operational pilots and 2 Squadron (Mirage IIICZs) eight. The cherry on the cake was that these force levels would be available only on D-Day. Battle damage and unserviceability would lessen the levels by 10% per day. The SAAF bluntly warned: "The SAAF attack capability is insufficient to neutralise FAPA [the Angolan air force] effectively on the ground." The final recommendation was not pleasant:

> The small numbers of fighters available, and the dense radar and missile networks which make our aircraft very vulnerable, mean that we cannot neutralise the enemy air force on the ground. Thus we should at all cost avoid a confrontation. If this is not possible, and a confrontation becomes unavoidable, we should go over to the offensive in the knowledge that the Air Force's offensive capability will be neutralised within a short time.

The new defensive plan, therefore, looked much better. Roland De Vries summarised it:

> Lure him in, delay his march in the direction of Tsumeb, create space for manoeuvre, make him suffer losses, grind him down logistically and create bigger military-strategic, political and operational freedom of action. As soon as the time is right, begin a counterattack, go after him into Angola, inside our old playing fields. This was a "game" we knew well.[117]

According to the maps in the detailed SADF battle plan, the idea was for the SADF forces in Sector 10 to withdraw along two routes: one southwards from Ruacana to the edge of the Etosha National Park and thence eastwards; the other southwestwards from Ondangwa and Oshakati. They would then make their stand at the high ground around Tsumeb, create the typical killing ground prescribed by SADF doctrine, and then destroy the invaders in a mobile armoured battle.[118] Plans were also made to evacuate the white population of northern SWA.[119] Chester Crocker talks about the SADF preparing a "killing field" for the Cubans in northern SWA.[120]

In the meantime, the SADF leadership ordered, so-called hot pursuit of PLAN units into Angola could take place, with the proviso that "contact with FAPLA and the Cubans be avoided". No offensive actions against these forces were permitted.[121]

Roland de Vries writes: "It soon became apparent to 10 SA Division that the 50th Cuban Division did not have the will or the heart to launch a major offensive into SWA. Their offensive moves and talks it seemed were more sabre-rattling than anything else."[122] Indeed, the deployment of the Cuban forces, dispersed in a giant half-circle from Namibe in the northwest to Techipa in the south and Cuvelai and Cassinga in the northeast[123] did not suggest a force about to invade South West Africa.

A meeting on 4 July between Magnus Malan, Jannie Geldenhuys and several generals provides a good idea of the SADF's thinking at that time. Geldenhuys referred to the change in the South African approach of not pre-empting a Cuban invasion, but letting the enemy come first. He said that there was a "new strategic approach which boils down to South Angola not being the battlefield, and if there is an escalation of the military situation, the north of South West Africa will be the battlefield . . .". The plan was to disengage in both the west and the east of southern Angola, while helping UNITA to be ready to resist another offensive.[124]

Magnus Malan said he was "not overly optimistic" about the peace negotiations. "Therefore, there should be preparation for a situation if the negotiations do not succeed." If the Cubans cross the border, "we should be ready to attack points north of the border". If the enemy came over the border, "this is a declaration of war and then we act offensively and not just defensively".[125]

For his part, Kat Liebenberg reported on the operational planning in the event of an enemy invasion. He thought the enemy would establish strong bases west and east of the Cunene River, and then deploy reaction forces across the whole front up to the South West African border. From there, SWAPO insurgents would conduct raids on specific targets. But the most dangerous enemy action would be a division-strength invasion, in which two brigades marched on Ondangwa and one on Ruacana. Even then, the enemy would keep half its forces north of the border. However, Liebenberg did not think this likely, due to defective information available to the enemy.[126] In any case, the army's defence plan, he said – though without elaborating – "was based upon deception". (Indeed, through bogus radio traffic and heavy convoy movements 10 Division was simulating a much stronger formation in the hopes of deterring any Cuban adventurism.)[127] Several bases were being prepared as strongpoints, while 61 Mech and 4 SAI had been tasked "to cause confusion by moving in combat teams through the entire area". He added: "The philosophy of the defence plan is: what crosses over [the border], must be cut off and then destroyed." Somewhat later in the discussion, he added that the harbour town of Namibe would be an objective if things got out of hand, because the enemy's logistics had to be cut as far north as possible.[128]

At the same meeting, Denis Earp, Chief of the Air Force, made two points that are relevant for our purposes. The first was that the air force was looking at the possibility of redeploying its aircraft from Ondangwa, near the border, further south to Grootfontein and Windhoek. The second was that possible pre-emptive air strikes, in the case of a threatening enemy attack, were problematic because of the enemy's radar coverage.[129]

Liebenberg's reference to Namibe was confirmed to me by Commandant (later Brigadier General) Mac Alexander, who was a staff officer with 44 Parachute Brigade at the time. Alexander e-mailed me that he and the commander of the brigade, Colonel Archie Moore, were part of the planning group at Oshakati that led to the raising of 10 Division. Alexander saw that almost all of the Cubans' logistics came through Namibe, so he drew up a plan for a simultaneous parachute and amphibious assault on the town. The plan was approved by Kat Liebenberg, with the proviso that the execution would depend on the diplomatic negotiations that were just getting under way, and that it would be carried out only if the Cubans attacked or were seen to be on the verge of attacking. According to Alexander, a strong force of about 1 200 men would be landed in two groups by parachute and from ships. Rapid execution would be essential:

> The Air Force made all their C-130 and C-160 aircraft available, but it was not enough to put the whole force on the ground in one wave. Luckily we trained the Bde shortly before in amphibian operations and some of our people participated in an amphibious exercise at Saldanha Bay. Therefore, we divided the force in two, half jumping and the other half landing from the ships . . .

> Our appraisal of the enemy's air capability was that their fighters would, when flying from Luanda, have no time over target above Namibe, and those at Lubango would have a very limited time. The planning was thus to execute all the landings in one night and that the Navy task force, with the exception of the strike craft, would be over the horizon at first light. The attack would go in at first light, supported by naval gunfire. Specific targets would be destroyed in the objective, including certain harbour facilities, railway facilities and a large part of the railway line itself. The force was large enough to take on the [enemy] elements occupying Namibe and to defend the town against a counter-attack for 72 hours, if necessary. But it all would have been completed in one day, and the withdrawal would have been that night at sea. I would have been throughout on the SAS *Tafelberg*, where the combined HQ would have been.[130]

As Roland de Vries commented: "Namibe was the ideal target to strike at the enemy in depth; so as to cause psychological paralysis and physical disruption of enemy's logistics and command."[131]

A big mechanised exercise was also held at Oshivello in northern SWA during August.[132] This could not have escaped the Cubans' notice. An amphibious landing exercise at Walvis Bay (Exercise Magersfontein), involving the force earmarked for Namibe, also had an impact. In 1989, a "very senior Cuban

army officer" visiting Simon's Town admitted, according to Rear Admiral Chris
Bennett,

> that one of the factors that had finally led to Cuba supporting the ter-
> mination of the conflict with South Africa, was a major Naval Exercise
> (Exercise Magersfontein) conducted from Walvis Bay during 1988. Of
> interest is that the reason for putting on this large, extremely complex
> and highly publicised exercise at such very short notice, was to pass the
> message that the SA Navy was capable of escalating the maritime aspect
> and could also support its fleet fully from a forward base.[133]

Tim Ramsden, a member of 71 Motorised Brigade, wrote that his unit, a Citizen
Force mechanised infantry battalion, exercised conventional warfare attacks
intensively for several weeks during July and August 1988. (The SADF had
absorbed the lessons of operations Askari and Packer, when Citizen Force troops
had been utilised without sufficient retraining.) "It was a spectacular show of
force," he writes, and went on: "Ovamboland was crawling with thousands of
troops, waiting for the green light to steamroller into Angola . . . Every base in
the region was overflowing with troops, all on high alert."[134]

Early in September, Ramsden and his comrades were withdrawn from
Ruacana to Grootfontein, where they were addressed by an unnamed general:

> So what the general said next came like a bombshell and took a few
> moments to sink into our sceptical minds. As a mechanised battalion,
> and then as an armoured brigade, he told us, the plan was for us to
> penetrate 150 kilometres into Angola and capture the FAPLA/Cuban/
> SWAPO base at Xangongo.[135]

As things turned out, all these plans were unnecessary, but they indicate that the
SADF was ready for a fight. At any rate, Castro's purpose, as we know now, was
not to escalate the war, but to get out of Angola without losing face. And therefore he did not go beyond threatening and posturing, knowing that this would
be sufficient to portray himself as the conquering hero. In fact, in August, when
the negotiations had gained considerable momentum, he ordered Ochoa and

Cintra to pull back some units. Probably to hide the move, he told them that "spearhead contingents should stay at Calueque and Ruacana", while a "joint Cuban-Angolan detachment can stay in Techipa". But, he went on, he did not think "the South Africans are eager to resume the hostilities". Thus "[t]he bulk of the forces should pull back to the Cahama–Xangongo line". Nevertheless, in the light of the concentration of a large SADF force in SWA, "[i]t is our duty to be ready for anything".[136]

It is interesting to speculate how the SADF and Cubans would have fared in such a major clash. Up to this stage, there had been only a few direct clashes between the Cuban and the South African armies. The first was during Breytenbach's paratroop assault on Cassinga in May 1978, when the Cubans and South Africans made contact only for a short while; the Cubans were held off by SAAF air strikes. Then there were at least four clashes north of the Chambinga in early 1988. During the first, the Cuban armoured counterattack on 25 February, the Cubans were rash, showing a certain inexperience, but certainly brave and aggressive. And during the three Tumpo battles, when the Cubans directed the defence, they did it very intelligently. The various clashes of May and June 1988 in the south of Cunene province once again proved that they were very aggressive and always prepared to attack, even when it was dangerous, although the South Africans invariably came off best.

In an official US military analysis of the Cuban armed forces, completed in 1979,[137] it is stated that the Cuban soldiers "are literate and well trained", as well as "politically indoctrinated, well disciplined and loyal". The officers "generally are highly motivated, heavily indoctrinated, well trained . . .".[138] "The fundamental Cuban military doctrine, like that of the Soviet Union, is that victory can only be won by offensive action." On the other hand, defence is seen as "an interim measure during which preparations are made for resuming the offensive". When an enemy does not present an assailable flank, the Cubans will execute a frontal attack, but they will, when possible, try to turn the enemy's flanks or to use a "turning movement, which is directed at the enemy's rear areas. The Cubans will combine the envelopment with a frontal attack, using the frontal attack to fix the enemy's forces."[139]

A matter not addressed in the US study is the question of command and control. Because the Cuban army was closely modelled on the Soviet Red Army, one may assume that frontline officers and NCOs had little opportunity to exercise independent initiative in the way the South Africans were trained. However, it is clear that the Cubans had a similar tactical doctrine to the South Africans, and were clearly a different proposition from the mainly inept FAPLA. The conclusion must be that any battle would not have been a walkover for either side and that casualties would have been severe.

The problem would probably have been exacerbated by the fact that 10 Division did not have enough tanks. The operations around Cuito Cuanavale had proved that the war was becoming ever more tank-heavy, and any clash between the Cubans and South Africans would undoubtedly have taken them further down that road. Whereas the Cubans and Angolans had about 200 tanks (including T-62s), 10 Division's order of battle shows one complete tank regiment (35 tanks), plus a tank squadron attached to 61 Mech (13 tanks), giving them a total of just 48 tanks. They also had an armoured car regiment, an armoured car squadron with 61 Mech and 4 SAI respectively, as well as several antitank troops – almost 120 Ratel 90s.[140] If it came to an all-out battle, the South Africans would have needed to introduce at least another tank regiment. They would also have had to change their habit (introduced out of necessity in earlier cross-border operations) of using their very mobile, but vulnerable, armoured cars as ersatz tanks. The armoured cars would have had to be utilised in their proper role, namely, reconnaissance, as well as the rapid exploitation of a breakthrough deep behind the enemy lines.

One last thought: while the battle plan drawn up by Roland de Vries (plus the part drawn up by Mac Alexander) was excellent, it missed a crucial element – air superiority. The fighting north of the Chambinga had shown that the SADF was hamstrung by the enemy's control of the air. That this was not a decisive factor was due to the lush foliage under which the South Africans invariably concealed themselves when the Cubans were in the air, plus the fact that the enemy bombing was terribly inaccurate. But the bush is considerably thinner in northern SWA – the expected battlefield – and would have provided much less cover. And the last Cuban bombing raid of 26 June proved that they were at last prepared to press home their attacks on a low level.

On the other hand, the Cubans would have got into big trouble if they had decided to invade SWA. The South African plan of drawing them in fairly deep into the country would have made their supply lines very long and vulnerable. Chester Crocker, quite rightly, makes the point that the "strategic balance would have shifted sharply in Pretoria's favour had Castro attacked Namibia".[141] Dick Lord's summary appears to be accurate:

> Had they decided to take the risk their forces would have been at the end of a long and tenuous logistic line, much like Rommel, Napoleon and the SADF outside Cuito Cuanavale. Once inside our border the full might of the SADF would have been unleashed upon them. This time the campaign would have been on our home turf with all the attendant advantages.[142]

As Roland de Vries put it: "The South Africans at the operational and tactical level of war were more than ready for the Cubans."[143]

17

THE AIR WAR, 1987–1988

The air war above Angola has, like the ground war, elicited considerable controversy. The radical leftist writer Barry Healy, for instance, states quite categorically (though without presenting evidence) that "Angolan and Cuban MiG-23 pilots swept the South African Air Force from Angolan skies."[1] More importantly, former ANC Cabinet minister Ronnie Kasrils has written: "Soviet MiG-23s had demonstrated their superiority over South Africa's aged Mirage fighters and now that they commanded the skies the network of SADF bases in northern Namibia was at their mercy."[2]

In general, three statements are usually made about the air war during the final stages of the Border War:

- The SAAF had lost air supremacy in Angola by 1987.
- The loss of air supremacy was the direct result of the international arms embargo against South Africa.
- The weakness of the SAAF played a major role in ensuring that the SADF lost the last campaigns in Angola.

Let us investigate the accuracy of these assertions.

The opposing sides

When Cuban forces first intervened in the Angolan civil war in 1975, they were supported by a squadron of nine MiG-17F fighters and one MiG-15UTI trainer of the Fuerza Aérea Revolucionaria (FAR, or Cuban air force). When some more advanced MiG-21MFs arrived somewhat later, the original aircraft were donated to the nascent Angolan air force, better known as Fuerza Aérea Popular de Angola (FAPA). While the Angolan aircraft were deployed against the separatist movement FLEC in the northern enclave of Cabinda, the Cuban MiG-21s were also utilised on the southern front against UNITA and the SADF.[3]

These aircraft remained the main punch in the air on the Angolan/Cuban side until 1984. They were no match for what the South Africans had to offer, but in that year the Cubans and Angolans started receiving the much more advanced MiG-23ML and MiG-23UB. (MiG-23s had been delivered to the FAR in 1978.)[4]

Different sources cite various figures for the Cuban and Angolan air strength, but we may assume that they had anywhere up to a hundred fighters and fighter-bombers.[5] Helmoed-Römer Heitman states that most of the ground-attack work was done by Angolan pilots in MiG-21s, while the top cover and interception fell to Cubans in the MiG-23s.[6] By 1985, according to Fred Bridgland, 80% of the combat pilots were Angolan,[7] although a few pilots from the Soviet Union, East Germany and Romania apparently also participated.[8]

It is, however, an open question how many of these aircraft were serviceable at any given time. Bridgland says that Rafael del Pino told his American hosts that "[s]tandards of command, discipline and technical maintenance . . . began to fall". For instance, Del Pino was sent to Angola in 1984 to investigate "a series of losses of fighter-bombers, transport planes and helicopters in crashes. Many had crashed through sheer carelessness . . ." He also discovered that "the naviga-tion systems of many aircraft had not been inspected or serviced for five years or more and that most of the entries in aircraft service logs were fraudulent".[9]

On the other side, the SAAF was also a formidable force. By the 1980s, the Mirage IIICZ interceptors and IIIEZ ground attackers were already obso-lete, even though they were still utilised in operations Reindeer and Protea. Mirage IIICZs continued to be used by 2 Squadron until the unit received the Cheetah-C in 1993.[10] Throughout the war, the Mirage F1CZ interceptor and the Mirage F1AZ ground attacker remained the mainstay of the SAAF's fighter force.

Comparing the opposing aircraft makes for a fascinating analysis. When the F1 was taken into service, the best fighter available to the Angolans/Cubans was the MiG-21, which was undoubtedly inferior to the F1. Twice, in 1981 and again in 1982, a South African pilot in a F1CZ interceptor – Major Johan Rankin – shot down a MiG-21 with his 30-mm cannon after having damaged another with an air-to-air missile near-miss. However, the MiG-23 was a superior machine. According to Helmoed-Römer Heitman, this model "had more power and speed than the Mirage F1 and also had head-on radar-guided missiles, a major edge over the F1CZ, which had only infrared homing missiles".[11]

On paper, the MiG-23 in most respects had the edge on the Mirage F1. It had a higher maximum speed and could accelerate faster, making it easier to break off from fight whenever the aircraft was at a disadvantage. The Mirage appears to have had a tighter turn, though. And the MiG could fire a radar-guided missile (the R-24) from the front (the effective range in this configuration was 7 to 10 km), while the South African aircraft could fire only from the rear. In 1987/1988, the Mirages were equipped with the French Matra 550 missile and the South African-licensed V3B Kukri air-to-air missile, neither of which was quite up to scratch. The latter had a tendency to detonate on the fleeing enemy's hot tail plume without damaging the aircraft. This happened several times during operations Moduler, Hooper and Packer. Also, the missile could not withstand acceleration manoeuvres involving more than 4 g.[12] The much better V3C became available only shortly after the end of hostilities.[13] The radar-guided Matra 530 was, due to its inadequate performance, never used in Angola.[14] At the same time, the MiG-23 was designed as a high-level bomber interceptor, not as a dogfighter. Chances are that, weapons and pilots being equal, the Mirage was probably better suited to dogfighting.[15]

But there is more to be taken into consideration. When all is said and done, the training, quality and tactics of the pilots inside the cockpits are decisive. Most authoritative sources tend to agree that the SAAF pilots were light years ahead of their poorly trained Angolan counterparts. The Cubans, who did a lot of the operational flying, especially the safer top cover tasks, were also of high quality, although they were not nearly as aggressive as the South Africans.[16] The South Africans held yearly training exercises that involved extensive practice in both ground attack and air combat manoeuvring (ACM, better known as dogfighting). Before being posted to a frontline fighter or bomber squadron, pilots would often have amassed as much as 1 000 flying hours and even have had operational experience in light Impala Mk II ground-attack aircraft. After joining a Mirage squadron, they would have to pass another difficult course before being allowed to fly operationally. By this time, they were comparable to the best in the world. All sources agree that the SAAF fighter pilots in 1987 were very aggressive and eager to fight – everybody wanted to shoot down MiGs.[17] As a matter of fact, Colonel NC Parkins, then SAAF attaché in Washington, reported that, in 1988, the foreign air attachés unanimously voted the South African Air Force the best in the world, with a toss-up between the RAF and Israeli air force for second place.[18] South African and Israeli pilots would from time to time be exchanged, allowing the SAAF to benefit from the vast operational experience amassed by the Israeli air force during decades of conflict with its Arab neighbours.[19]

On the other side, the Cuban and Angolan pilots flew according to Soviet doctrine, which discouraged individual initiative in the air; the crews were strictly subordinated to direction from the ground. Their tactics typically would be to make a fast slashing attack and then use their superior speed to disengage.[20] As Dick Lord, senior SAAF officer in the theatre, told Fred Bridgland: "One thing that worked for us was that FAPA, despite the high quality of its MiG-21s, MiG-23s and Su-22s, was among the worst trained air forces of Africa. And it operated according to rigid Soviet doctrine. Our pilots had freedom of initiative while working within carefully conceived plans. The Angolan Air Force guys were given fixed radar and distance vectors on which to fly from Menongue. As they approached the target they were still directed from Menongue control: 'Steer 145 degrees, hold it steady for 46 nautical miles, now drop your bombs,' that sort of thing."[21]

In principle, the SAAF's aircraft were all irreplaceable due to the international arms embargo against South Africa. It is true that the air force was working up another fighter squadron with brand-new Cheetah-Es, a South African modernisation of the Mirage III, but this unit, 5 Squadron, would not be operational until 1989. And so the SAAF was, right from the beginning, rather skittish in whether, and how, to employ its aircraft.[22] This was an inhibiting factor throughout the campaign.

Aerial encounters

In contrast to the Second World War, the Korean War or the various wars in the Middle East, the South African participation in the war in Angola was not characterised by great aerial battles. In fact, there were only four encounters in the air between South African and Cuban aircraft, and none between South Africans and Angolans. These four encounters are described below.[23]

On 10 September 1987, four South African aircraft were scrambled from Rundu Air Force Base to intercept 10 MiG-23MLs, of which eight were attacking ground forces, while the other two were providing top cover. The South African aircraft arrived on the scene while the MiG attack was still going on. Upon detecting the Mirages, the fighter-bombers immediately fled, while the two escorts turned towards the South Africans. One apparently lost his nerve and made a bad mistake by turning to the left and exposing his tailpipe to Captain Anton van Rensburg's Mirage. Van Rensburg did not waste time, spiralled down after him and launched two Matra 550 heat-seeking missiles. Both tracked beautifully, but a frustrated Van Rensburg had to watch helplessly as the first exploded in the heat plume behind the MiG and the second failed, allowing the MiG to escape. Both MiGs then fled to Menongue, while the Mirages returned to Rundu.

The second encounter went less well for the South Africans. On the morning of 27 September, a SAAF photo-reconnaissance sortie was threatened by a gaggle of MiG-23s, and the Mirages were scrambled in a hurry. This time, two MiGs, piloted by Major Alberto Ley Rivas and First Lieutenant Juan Carlos Chávez Godoy, attacked the Mirages from the front – something they could do with their superior radar and radar-guided missiles. One of the Mirage pilots, Captain Arthur Piercy, later recalled:

> Anyway, the next thing I remember is this MiG coming head-on at me from about my one, two o'clock position. Still turning towards him, I remember flicking the trigger safety over to the cannon position. If he was going to fly through my sights, I was going to squeeze off a few rounds. Unfortunately for me he got off the first shot.

> There was a bright orange flash from his left wing and then this incredibly fast telephone pole came hurtling towards me trailing a solid white smoke trail. What's more is that it was corkscrewing, so I was never sure where it was going.

In all our training we were taught to break towards the missile. This could or should create a tracking problem for the missile and cause it to possibly overshoot.

But faced with reality I found it took a lot of willpower to fly towards something I knew was trying to kill me. However, I kept breaking towards it and I watched it corkscrew over my right wing and disappear behind me. I thought it had missed until I heard a dull thud and felt a light bump on the aircraft. I immediately scanned all the gauges, but there was no indication of any damage. When I looked up again the MiG flew over the canopy and disappeared behind me as well.

I immediately informed the leader that I thought I might have been hit and his reaction was: "OK, let's go home." I did not need a second invitation and I rolled the aircraft onto its back and headed for the ground.

With hindsight it appeared that the whole fight lasted no more than 60 seconds from the time we pitched until I got the "go home" command.[24]

Piercy succeeded in nursing his badly damaged aircraft back to Rundu, but, because his hydraulics were all smashed, he could not brake. The plane overshot the runway and Piercy accidentally ejected. He landed on his back and was partially paralysed for life. The Mirage was repaired and eventually returned to operational flying by cannibalising another one that had crashed. It therefore cannot count as a kill for the Cubans.[25]

The third encounter happened on the morning of 25 February 1988, when a flight of three Mirage F1AZs, piloted by Major Willie van Coppenhagen and Captains Dawid Kleynhans and Reg van Eeden, were intercepted by MiG-23s. The South Africans immediately turned aggressively towards the MiGs, which promptly fled.

A few hours later on the same day, Commandant Johan Rankin, Major Frans Coetzee and Captain Trompie Nel were on another F1AZ bombing sortie, when two MiG-23s, flown by Captain Orlando Carbo and a wingman, positioned themselves on the South Africans' six o'clock position. Again, the

South Africans turned aggressively in to the MiGs, who swept over them. The South Africans went after them, but, because they were configured for ground attack with bombs slowing them down, they could not overtake the fleeing MiGs. Rankin got on Carbo's six o'clock position, launched two missiles and fired his 30-mm cannon, but to no avail. The MiGs used their superior acceleration and speed to escape.

In terms of losses during this period, an apparently well-researched piece by two South African writers documents eight Cuban MiG-23MLs, four MiG-21s, and two Su-22s shot down, apparently by SADF and UNITA ground fire.[26]

Several conclusions may be drawn. Firstly, as far as air-to-air combat is concerned, the war ended inconclusively. Neither side won. Secondly, the South Africans conducted themselves considerably more aggressively in the air than their opponents. In the first and fourth encounters, they were very unlucky not to have shot down the MiGs. Thirdly, this confirms what we already knew on paper, namely, that the MiGs' more advanced avionics and missiles gave them an edge over the Mirage. However, this advantage could very well have been neutralised by the South Africans' better training and more aggressive posture. Lastly, on the basis of these four encounters, it is logical to assume that, had the war in the air continued, the SAAF would have given more than they got.

After the second fight, in which Piercy's aircraft was severely damaged, the South Africans poured considerable energy into developing new tactics to deal with the MiG-23. However, the SAAF command pulled 3 Squadron (the F1CZs, Piercy's unit) back to Waterkloof Air Force Base, outside Pretoria. As Heitman explains: "The distance from Rundu, the nearest air base to the front able to handle Mirages, was too great for the Mirage F1CZs to be effective in their counter-air role. Unable to protect the deployed ground forces, and with no threat to Rundu, there was no justification for keeping a detachment of 3 Squadron at Rundu."[27]

One may, however, surmise that the events of 27 September also played a role in this decision. As Dick Lord explained to Fred Bridgland: "Air-to-air combat was now completely out of the question for us. The FAPA (Angolan Air Force) had too many advantages in terms of speed, range, radar and survivability in the shape of numerous little airstrips they could lob into in the case of emergencies."[28]

Ground attack

With this background, we may now analyse the ground-attack missions on both sides, and especially their effect on the course of the war. The following questions need to be answered:

- To what extent did the Cuban and Angolan air superiority prevent the South Africans from attacking FAPLA on the ground?
- To what extent did the South African ground attacks hamper FAPLA's ground operations?
- To what extent did the SAAF prevent the Cubans/Angolans from attacking the SADF and UNITA on the ground?
- And, lastly, to what extent did the Cuban/Angolan ground attacks hamper the SADF's ground operations?

On the South African side, close air support and battlefield isolation fell to 1 Squadron (with 12 Mirage F1AZs deployed) and 24 Squadron (four Buccaneers). Together, they flew 144 and 32 multi-aircraft strikes, or 683 and 99 sorties, respectively.[29] This was a modest force by any standard.

The answer to the first question is fairly simple. By way of introduction, it must be said that the engagement of 27 September 1987, when Captain Arthur Piercy's Mirage F1CZ was damaged, gave the SAAF a fright. This fight, as well as the one on 10 September – and this was confirmed by the encounter of 25 March 1988 – illustrated that the SAAF's weapons systems on the Mirage F1CZ were not equal to those on the MiG-23. In spite of attempts to come up with improved tactics, and the superiority of the South African pilots, SAAF headquarters decided to recall these aircraft. After all, they were practically irreplaceable, as it would be some months before the first Cheetah-E squadron would become operational. This meant that the bombing raids by the Mirage F1AZs and Buccaneers would have to be made without any fighter protection.

However, Helmoed-Römer Heitman lists a host of strikes flown by 1 and 24 squadrons. His measured conclusion is that the total of 1 185 Cuban sorties flown for top cover, intercept and escort, "had virtually no effect on the SAAF strike programme". In fact, the Mirages "flew several strikes while MiG-23s were prowling above them". He says that they "were also not able to prevent the

SAAF from striking their ground forces at will anywhere in the area, even in the immediate vicinity of Cuito Cuanavale and Menongue. They did, however, force the SAAF to restrict transport operations to the hours of darkness."[30]

As far as the Angolan ground defences are concerned, it is true that they had more than enough state-of-the-art anti-aircraft guns and missiles at their disposal – the deadly ZU-23 gun, for instance, as well as the obsolete SA-2, the somewhat more modern SA-3 and even the latest SA-8 and SA-9 missiles. Right at the beginning of the campaign, on 3 September 1987, an SA-8 destroyed a South African Bosbok spotter aircraft, piloted by Lieutenant Richard Glynn. The presence of this missile system took the SADF totally by surprise, and led to the immediate withdrawal of the by-now-obsolete and vulnerable Canberra bombers from the theatre. This also resulted in a short halt to SAAF aerial bombing, but Commandant Jan Hougaard, who witnessed the South African toss bombing by Mirage and Buccaneer bombers from the ground, assured headquarters that the method worked excellently and caught the enemy by surprise time after time. And so aerial bombing resumed.[31] A few days later, a complete SA-8 system was captured intact and flown to South Africa from Mavinga by an SAAF C-160 cargo plane – the first time this very sophisticated system had fallen into enemy hands.[32]

On 9 February 1988, Major Ed Every was shot down and killed by an Angolan surface-to-air missile during a Mirage F1AZ bombing sortie. (Another F1, flown by Major Willie van Coppenhagen, was lost on 19 March, but the likely cause was an accident.)[33] Nevertheless, just as the MiGs' mastery of the air did not deter the SAAF from attacking FAPLA troops at will, neither did the Angolans' possession of superb Soviet-made anti-aircraft weapons systems. Once, an SA-8 locked on to a Buccaneer, but the lock was quickly broken.[34]

During the whole campaign, South African pilots reported a total of 112 enemy missiles fired at them, in which case for the enemy to have downed only two SAAF aircraft seems truly remarkable. In turn, according to South African intelligence, South African bombing raids were responsible for between 4 000 and 6 000 enemy casualties. Dick Lord reports that Fidel Castro even mentioned the number of 9 000 in a speech to the Cuban parliament.[35]

This success was primarily due to the fact that the SAAF had learnt the toss bombing method from other Western air forces. The attacking pilots would approach the vicinity of the target right down on the deck, and at a predetermined point pull their aircraft up fairly sharply at a predetermined angle. At a predetermined height, they would release their bombs, turn around, dive back to the ground and make for home. If this was done correctly, stick after stick of bombs would smother and obliterate the target, without the enemy radar's being able to lock on to the attacking aircraft. Afterwards, the aircraft sometimes exited as low as 15 m![36]

However safe for the pilots, the major drawback to toss bombing was that it made precision bombing, which is often necessary for close air support, very difficult, especially when the enemy and friendly troops were (as was often the case) very near to each other. (The task of close support was, therefore, successfully taken over by the South African artillery.)[37] The Mirage F1AZ had an excellent laser range-finder and rolling map display, which made dive-bombing very accurate indeed,[38] but this worked only when the plane passed not far from the target. The toss bombing method worked for area bombing, and therefore was more suitable for battlefield isolation – i.e., for preventing supplies and reinforcements, carried by vehicle convoy, from reaching the enemy on the front line.

Early in the battles at the Lomba River, several Angolan formations were hammered hard by SAAF planes and this contributed to the Angolan decision to abandon the effort to cross the river.[39] However, during the battles in the Tumpo Triangle, the South African Army had to do virtually without air support. Therefore, units operating within 39 km of Cuito Cuanavale were warned not to expect any SAAF close air support – interestingly enough, not because of interference from the Cuban and Angolan interceptors, but because of the anti-aircraft systems in and around the place.[40]

Mirage IIIR2Z photo-reconnaissance aircraft often made sorties. They would stay right down at 50 m, rapidly gain height and take their photographs, and exit on the deck. Not one was ever shot down.[41] Other reconnaissance missions were undertaken by 10 Squadron's Seeker UAVs, which beamed television images of the enemy back to the handlers. UAVs played an invaluable role, especially during the Lomba battles, when they – in the words of Dick Lord – "assisted in the identification of suitable targets as the Angolan brigades advanced through the dense bush". Three were shot down, but they were relatively cheap to replace.[42]

Answering the second question (the extent to which South African ground attacks hampered FAPLA ground operations) is less easy because of a lack of sources on the Cuban and Angolan side. According to Gennady Shubin, "Lieutenant Colonel of the reserve Igor Zhdarkin recalls another occasion – the South African planes, flying at a low-level, burned away 29 petrol tankers on the 'road of life' between Menonge [sic] and Cuito-Cuanavale. In total on the road there were over 350 remains of burned out tanks, BTRs, infantry combat vehicles, petrol tankers and trucks."[43]

From intercepted radio messages and Recce reports, it is also clear that the Angolans were at times terribly distressed by the SAAF attacks.[44] Jan Breytenbach reports that FAPLA convoys between Menongue and Cuito Cuanavale were devastated on at least 16 occasions by SAAF Mirage attacks, artillery bombardments or both. He adds: "Results were monitored and confirmed by Recces on the ground, so the figures can be regarded as accurate."[45] At other times, the attacks were inconclusive. On 22 December 1987, for instance, an attack on a supply convoy destroyed only eight out of 318 FAPLA vehicles, including 35 tanks. In contrast, on 9 January, 40 vehicles out of 170 were destroyed by an air strike.[46]

The SADF also repeatedly attempted to destroy the bridge over the Cuito River at Cuito Cuanavale, as it was an important link in the supply route from Namibe to Menongue and thence to the front. Buccaneers and Mirages repeatedly attacked the bridge, were unable to bring it down. Finally, it was destroyed on 3 January 1988 by an H2 guided glide bomb launched from a Buccaneer. However, a pontoon bridge was built alongside the destroyed one, and the movement of supplies went on, albeit at a reduced rate.[47]

It thus appears as if the Angolans were, at times, severely disadvantaged by SAAF operations, but not decisively so. SAAF strikes did help to restrict their supply trains and to curtail their operational and tactical movements. But SAAF attacks were a secondary factor on the battlefield, where FAPLA was defeated by the South African ground forces.

As far as the third question (the extent to which the SAAF prevented the Cubans/Angolans from attacking the SADF and UNITA on the ground) is concerned, the answer is clear. As the SAAF command at the end of September 1987 made a strategic decision not to seek actively to engage the

Cubans or Angolans in the air, they never tried to prevent the enemy from attacking either the South African Army or UNITA on the ground. The Cubans and Angolans had more or less free play. At the same time, Cuban/Angolan aircraft were sometimes destroyed by South African and UNITA ground forces. G-5 artillery bombardment of the airstrip at Cuito Cuanavale, called in by sharp-eyed Recces, more than once destroyed Cuban/Angolan aircraft on the ground. At the end of October 1987, these were withdrawn to Menongue.[48] Nevertheless, having a free hand in the air, Cuban MiGs undertook a total of 1 283 sorties above Cuito Cuanavale between January and March 1988.[49]

The fourth question (the extent to which Cuban/Angolan ground attacks hampered SADF ground operations) requires some discussion. It is clear that the Cuban/Angolan domination of the air caused problems for the South Africans on the ground right from the beginning. When 61 Mech was ordered into Angola at the beginning of September 1987, they moved at first in daylight. As 61 Mech's deputy commander, Major Laurence Maree, related to Fred Bridgland,

> Until Luengue (100 km south of Mavinga) we moved by day. But then we came within range of the enemy MiGs and we had to start moving at night only. It caused lots of problems . . . We stopped at sunrise, spread the convoy, camouflaged everything under the trees and rested all day. At sunset we started again. But only one of our Ratels had night navigation electronics. It would set a course for Mavinga and then weave a way through the forest towards the destination. We had to move very slowly and stop constantly to check by radio that all 126 vehicles were within sight of each other.[50]

This would seem to be fairly representative of South African Army movements throughout the campaign, which generally had to be conducted in the hours of darkness due to the danger of MiG attacks. This turned the resupply of troops at the front into a major headache, and meant that the South African weapons, especially the artillery and tanks, could not be properly maintained. Lack of maintenance and lack of spares caused ever more guns, tanks, armoured cars, trucks, etc., to become unserviceable.[51] Also, throughout the latter part of the campaign the big South African 155-mm G-5 and G-6 guns – arguably the

SADF's key weapons system – had to be moved around continually to avoid MiG strikes.[52]

Generally, the Cuban/Angolan MiGs were in the air in strength, but they caused few casualties.[53] This was due to two factors. The first was that South African Reconnaissance commandos stationed close to Menongue air base would alert SADF ground forces by radio every time the MiGs took off, allowing the troops time to camouflage themselves to avoid detection from the air.[54] Secondly, the Cuban/Angolan pilots had a healthy fear of their adversaries' anti-aircraft weapons – not so much the South Africans' obsolete Cactus missiles or the 20-mm cannon mounted on the backs of Unimog trucks, but UNITA's deadly hand-operated Stinger missiles, which were supplied by the Americans. This meant that they generally released their bombs at a minimum of 6 000 ft and sometimes as high as 16 000 ft. Also, the Cubans and Angolans had to stay high in order to been "seen" by their own radar controllers. This tight control from the ground made their bombing runs highly inaccurate.[55]

Nevertheless, inaccurate or not, the flip side of the coin was that the South Africans had to stop their movements and hide every time the MiGs were overhead. And that certainly hampered their ground operations. During the Lomba battles, the Cuban and Angolan aircraft were not much of a factor. But, as the South Africans advanced northward to the Chambinga high ground and finally the Tumpo Triangle, Menongue was only a few minutes' flight away, and the MiGs could therefore dominate the air totally. Even though only four South African soldiers died and seven were wounded as a result of bombing,[56] many South African accounts mention radio calls of "Victor, victor!" (Afrikaans: "vyandelike vliegtuig", or enemy aircraft) coming through. One troepie remembered: "[T]his call over the radio everyone would pull off the path and into the bushes where we would quickly camouflage them with branches. We heard several MiGs and sometimes we would spot them at high altitude, but they wouldn't see us."[57]

Describing the history of 32 Battalion, Jan Breytenbach also mentions the "unwelcome attention of MiGs" during this series of battles. While the MiG strikes always missed their target, they slowed the South African advance considerably and meant that the element of surprise was lost.[58] Sometimes ground offensives – for instance, the attack on 11 November 1987 – had to be postponed because of MiGs in the sky.[59] Many of the Cuban strikes during this time were flown by "Cuba's finest MiG pilots", as Castro called them, who had been hastily flown to Angola.[60]

Clive Holt's personal memoir of his service with 61 Mech during Operation Hooper makes it clear that MiGs were continually swarming in the air. And although he adamantly states that the air attacks were mostly off target, his account testifies to the way the enemy's mastery of the air made the South African movements on the ground rather difficult at crucial times.[61] During 61 Mech's first attack on the Angolans in the Tumpo Triangle, their artillery support at one stage fell away because of the MiGs in the air. The G-5s could not afford to give away their position to the aircraft, and, for some reason or another, UNITA troops had no Stingers available.[62]

These are all anecdotal pieces of evidence, but typical of what happened throughout the 1987/1988 period. Helmoed-Römer Heitman's conclusion seems inescapable:

> What they [the enemy air attacks] did achieve was to hamper South African operations considerably. It would not be going too far to say that on several occasions it was only the timely arrival of MiGs over a battlefield that prevented the complete destruction of a FAPLA brigade. It was also in large measure because of the MiGs that the small remaining Tumpo bridgehead could be held. If there had been no MiGs overhead, the South African artillery could in time have silenced its opponents on the west bank. The ground forces would then have cleared the east bank of FAPLA. That the MiGs were able to exercise that much influence on the ground battle was largely a result of the remarkable reluctance of the South Africans to accept casualties. A force less concerned with that aspect might have been able to achieve rather more for no appreciably greater number of casualties.[63]

Another aspect of this question is, of course, logistics. The presence of MiG-23 combat air patrols over the operational area meant that supply and medical evacuation flights could normally only be flown at night in very difficult circumstances. The C-130s and C-160s of 28 Squadron, flying between

Grootfontein and the UNITA-controlled airstrip of Mavinga, had to be gone from Mavinga well before daylight or risk being destroyed on the runway by the Angolan/Cuban MiGs. However, the SAAF did not possess enough airlift capability, and so even the frantic efforts of 28 Squadron were not enough, especially as daylight hours could not be utilised. The troops at the front had to contend with shortages of just about everything. This, too, hampered army ground operations, but not decisively so.

The last phase

We have already analysed the final Cuban march to the Namibian border; we may simply add here that some 80 MiG-23s and MiG-21s covered this advance from the air.[64] During this last phase, Cuban aircraft were not challenged in the air at all, the SAAF Mirages and Buccaneers having already been pulled back to South Africa. In the process, the Cuban MiGs crossed the border once or twice and came within 20 km of Oshakati and Ondangwa air force bases. The South Africans had to decide whether to bring back their Mirages, especially after the Cubans established air bases at Xangongo and Cahama, not all that far from the border. As has already been mentioned, the SAAF by this time was fairly exhausted from the intensive operations at Cuito Cuanavale.

Dick Lord explained to Fred Bridgland:

> Although we did think they might attack the bases, the high altitudes they were flying were not conducive to surprise. They were always within our radar cover. I think we made the correct analysis of the extent of the threat. We decided that they wanted to test our pilots' reaction times. For that reason we were reluctant to scramble, but often we couldn't because we didn't have any suitable fighters situated there! (Only Impalas were available.)[65]

Later on, Lord became convinced that these transgressions were the result of navigational errors rather than deliberate provocations. Besides, as a deterrent, the SAAF decided to hold its annual Golden Eagle exercise in northern Namibia, the scenario being attacks from the north. This was done within range of the enemy's long-range radar. Photo-reconnaissance flights were also undertaken to Xangongo and Humbe to lure enemy fighters into the air. However, they stayed on the ground. All of this shows that the SAAF was very much ready to counter any threat from the north.[66]

One question remains: was the international arms embargo against South Africa responsible for the SAAF's problems in Angola? On balance, the answer is a nuanced no. The SAAF frontline fighter, the Mirage F1, became operational a decade before the fighting analysed above. This is not a long time. The French air force, for instance, continued to use the F1 on active operations until 2012, and the type will be withdrawn from service only in 2014.[67] One may also refer to the General Dynamics F-16 (Fighting Falcon), which came into production only a few years after the F1, and is still in service more than 30 years down the line. As a parliamentary journalist, I was told by an Armscor official in the early 1980s that preliminary work had begun on an upgrade of the Mirage III, which eventually became the Cheetah-E and the Cheetah-C. The first three Cheetah-Es were delivered to 5 Squadron in March and April 1988[68] and became operational the following year. The inadequate air-to-air missiles were soon afterwards withdrawn and replaced by the far superior V3C and V4 missiles.[69]

In other words, the renewal of the SAAF's equipment took place pretty much in the normal timeframe one would expect for an air force unhampered by an embargo. In fact, the campaign of 1987/1988 caught the SAAF at an unfortunate time when its aircraft were already outclassed, but before their replacements could reasonably be expected to be operational. The question of how the Cheetah-E, or its final version, the Cheetah-C, would have fared against the MiG-23, cannot, of course, be answered conclusively and will remain a matter for speculation. With the latter's beyond-visual-range capability (radar as well as missiles),[70] we can assume that it would have been more than a match for the Soviet fighter.

But this is guesswork. The only thing one can say for sure is that the SAAF did not see itself as beaten – not by a long shot. But all the plans and speculation were in vain, as the peace negotiations gathered momentum. And it is to this that our attention must now turn.

18

PEACE

On 3 and 4 May 1988, representatives from South Africa, Angola and Cuba met each other in a nondescript hotel in London under Chester Crocker's chairmanship. The South African delegation was led by Foreign Affairs Director-General Neil van Heerden, and included Jannie Geldenhuys. Two leading Angolans – Minister of Foreign Affairs Afonso Van-Dúnem and General António dos Santos França, Deputy Minister of Defence – were among that country's delegates. The Cubans were led by Jorge Risquet Valdés, member of the politburo of the Cuban Communist Party, Carlos Aldana Escalante, the Party's Chief of Ideology, and General Ulises Rosales del Toro, Chief of the Revolutionary Armed Forces.

They were squeezed into "too small a room in the basement around a horseshoe-shaped table", as Van Heerden recalled.[1] This was the first time the South Africans and Cubans – bitter arch-foes – had seen one another in person. It is fair to say that their views of each other were highly coloured, as is generally the case with enemies who do not know or understand one another. Crocker observed: "The isolated South Africans knew little about Soviet thinking and their expertise on the Cubans were the stuff of comic books. Castro knew dangerously little about South African politics . . ."[2]

Beforehand, Van Heerden had agreed with Geldenhuys that the diplomats and soldiers would take one line in the talks, with Foreign Affairs, not Defence, in the driving seat. "In preparatory meetings we pooled our resources and experience from preceding episodes of the Namibian saga. We agreed from the outset that we would stand back to back and guard against being separated from the political level – a healthy principle in bureaucratic survival."[3] This was important, as Foreign Affairs and the SADF did not always see eye to eye, and in fact had a somewhat acerbic relationship at times.

Success was absolutely not guaranteed. Jorge Risquet, "heavily bearded, in khaki fatigues, cap and large cigar" looked every bit like a Cuban caricature. He proved to be a "fiery orator and a bundle of trouble in meetings", which did not make the negotiations any easier.[4] (Risquet's resemblance to a well-known cartoon figure led the South Africans to nickname him "Oom Kaspaas".)[5] On the other hand, Aldana "quickly rose in our estimation," Crocker writes. "He had a feel for reading people and situations; and he was a born craftsman of positive-sum negotiation. The contrast with Risquet was striking."[6]

Looking at the other side, Crocker observed that Van Heerden had "the presence and the dressed-for-success look of a British banker" as well as a "cool reserve and seeming nonchalance".[7] He described Jannie Geldenhuys as "direct and unpretentious", a "soldier's soldier", and "a pro in the diplomacy of war".[8]

But these first London talks, Van Heerden recalled, were "very stiff and formal, with Risquet in particular wild and full of machismo". Fortunately, after Crocker called for a coffee break, the delegates broke up to talk individually, and the tense atmosphere started to relax.[9]

The two top soldiers, Geldenhuys and Rosales, squared off in a sparsely furnished lounge. Rosales remained professional, but his words were laced with menace. For half an hour he warned Geldenhuys, through an interpreter, that the Cubans had concentrated their best troops in Cunene province just north of the South West African border. They were poised to strike. Even the border would not stop them. If the South Africans refused this chance for peace, a full-scale war would break out, a war that the South Africans would lose.[10]

Geldenhuys looked him straight in the eye and refused to be intimidated. He told him that he was the descendant of the same Boer fighters who had held off the overwhelming forces of the British Empire for three years during the Anglo-Boer War. If the Cubans put one foot across the border, it would be "the blackest day in Cuba's military history". Therefore, Geldenhuys told Rosales, let us abandon the threats and concentrate on the matters at hand. "For him, too," Geldenhuys later wrote, "it was a moment of truth. We never regarded each other in completely the same light again."[11]

The main advantage of the meeting was that the enemies had the opportunity to sniff each other, as dogs do when meeting. There was no substantial progress. Both sides agreed that they wanted peace and the implementation of Resolution 435 on Namibian independence, but that was nothing new.

Van-Dúnem reiterated that the "Cuban troops were in Angola as a result of a sovereign decision of the Angolan government. The Angolan and Cuban governments would decide when and if to withdraw when the causes for their presence were removed . . ."[12] After a day and a half's discussions, the meeting broke up, the only positive outcome being an agreement to continue the talks.

Ten days later, the South Africans – now led by Foreign Minister Pik Botha and Defence Minister Magnus Malan – met the Angolans separately in Brazzaville. Botha protested in vain against the Cuban march to the South West African border and raised the question of the supply of water from Calueque – threatened by the Cubans – to northern SWA. Van-Dúnem (in the absence of a Cuban delegation) indicated that his government was prepared to be flexible about the withdrawal of the Cuban troops.[13] This was movement – limited to be sure, but nevertheless movement.

On the brink

The first substantial negotiations took place some six weeks later, on 24 and 25 June in Cairo. Prior to the plenary meeting, the South African and US delegations met separately in the American embassy, where Pentagon official Jim Woods briefed the South Africans – as related in Chapter 16 – about the Cuban advance in Cunene province. Pik Botha, leading the South Africans, thought pessimistically that "this analysis pointed towards war".[14]

The meeting with the Cubans and Angolans was stormy.[15] Pik Botha started with his usual wide-ranging and dramatic speech about Africa being doomed unless its problems were addressed constructively through peace. On behalf of Angola, Afonso Van-Dúnem analysed the South African peace proposals and shot them down one by one. With "a gesticulating and cigar-wielding"[16] Jorge Risquet again in the audience, the relative flexibility Van-Dúnem had displayed in Brazzaville evaporated, and he stated categorically that "Cuban troops would remain in the country because South Africa continued to destroy Angolan territory . . . The troops that should leave were the aggressor troops of South Africa."

Risquet raised the temperature even further, accusing South Africa of arrogance and calling the South African peace proposals "a tasteless joke and totally unrealistic". With apparent reference to the Cuban advance in Cunene, he said that "the South African position was not sustainable in the light of conditions on the ground". Defiantly, he stated: "International guarantees were necessary if Cuban troop withdrawal [was] to take place. South Africa would not get around a conference table that which it failed to achieve on the battlefield." (He was, of course, only echoing Fidel Castro himself, who at this time had said that South Africa was "in no position to demand anything".)[17]

Then Risquet really got going. He demanded an end to South Africa's support for UNITA, and taunted them, as recorded in the minutes: "In reality apartheid was the cause of all problems in southern Africa. According to the UN apartheid was a crime against humanity." He repeated that "the number of Cuban troops in Angola had nothing to do with the South Africans". Thanks to "the internationalist Cuban troops . . . the myth of South Africa's invincibility had forever been destroyed".

All of this was sure to enrage Pik Botha, and Van-Dúnem and Risquet knew it. Botha shot back by saying that "it was not the same Angolan delegation that he had met in Brazzaville", and that he would "need hours to talk about the wrongs in Angola and Cuba". He pointed to the lack of press and religious freedom there, and asked sarcastically when either country had last held an election. He was prepared to discuss South Africa's internal matters, but then those of Cuba and Angola had to be discussed too. He pointed to the progress in the socio-economic position of blacks in South Africa, and said that black taxi owners and hawkers had a higher standard of living than people in Cuba and Angola. More black South Africans than Soviet citizens owned cars. If the Angolans and Cubans wanted to discuss human rights, "it could be done with independent judges or international experts as referees to compare Cuba with South Africa." He invited them all to go to South Africa and see for themselves.

Neil van Heerden later remembered that the talks "were on the brink of collapse".[18] Crocker hastily adjourned the meeting. During the break, Risquet again cornered Botha in the bar: "I am telling you," he thundered, "we are going to introduce 15 000 more Cuban troops". Botha coolly answered: "OK, we will introduce 1 000 more South African troops."

In an interview, Botha told British researcher Sue Onslow:

He took this amiss, by the inadvertent implication that one South African soldier was worth 15 Cuban troops, and lost his temper. I said, "No, no, no. We can both be winners in this war." He was struck by this remark. I went on, "Your leader, Fidel, cannot withdraw unless he can claim something to honour and respect your war and efforts. We undertake Namibian independence in accordance with Resolution 435. Castro can then claim to have succeeded in his purpose. I can tell white voters in South Africa that we have got rid of the Cubans from Angola."

This, Botha told Onslow, "was the turning point".[19] Neil van Heerden wrote that "[w]hen we reconvened a distinctly more constructive approach was in evidence", although he ascribed this to the intervention of a senior Soviet diplomat with the Cubans and Angolans[20] rather than to Botha's altercation with Risquet. Whatever the cause, the minutes of the second day confirm that things proceeded much more positively.

With the help of the Americans, the South Africans worked late into the night to prepare a document containing the principles for a settlement that incorporated some of the Cuban/Angolan ideas.[21] The next morning, Botha introduced the document, stressing that it contained as much as possible of the Cuban and Angolan proposals.[22] He further proposed that the peace process should henceforth proceed on a step-by-step basis. "If the parties tried to achieve too much, too soon, they could run into an impasse," he said.

For his part, Van-Dúnem responded with courtesy and suggested that the parties meet again in two weeks so that experts could try to merge the two sets of proposals into one document. Botha agreed. The fiery Risquet, who had almost derailed the talks with his intemperate outburst, did not utter a single word, which suggests that somebody had got to him. With that, the meeting broke up.

The next day, of course, saw the last climactic battle between the Cubans and SADF between Techipa and Calueque, and for a moment the delegates from all sides must have felt as if time stood still. But everybody kept their nerve. Too much was at stake here, and both the South Africans and the Cubans decided not to escalate the war. Both had looked into the abyss and flinched.

Breakthrough

The next meeting took place in New York on 11 and 12 July.[23] Crocker had pro-posed in Cairo that the politicians stay at home and that the process be taken forward by "no more than six experts" per delegation.[24] This meant that the combative Risquet was left at home and his place as leader of the Cuban delega-tion was taken by the urbane, soft-spoken Carlos Aldana Escalante. Pik Botha also stayed at home and gave the reins to Neil van Heerden. The atmosphere was completely different from the Cairo meeting. When General Van-Dúnem took the floor, one thing he said made the South Africans sit upright: "Angola was not legally bound to bring about Cuban troop withdrawal, but Angola and Cuba had agreed voluntarily to the withdrawal of all Cuban troops from Angola. His delegation had brought to New York firm proposals in this regard." Could this herald a breakthrough? Van Heerden replied diplomatically, repeat-ing Pik Botha's point of view that "success was only possible if there were no losers in the discussions".

After a detailed discussion about the documents containing the peace pro-posals, Aldana ("after some hesitation", we learn from the minutes) started speaking. He delivered a remarkable speech, characterised by its pacific approach. The speech was taken down verbatim and included in its entirety in the South African minutes of the meeting. He told those present that "[w]e now find our-selves closer than ever to an understanding . . ." and that "no one will come out of this or will attempt to come out of this as the winners". Nobody could deny "the contribution made by South Africa . . . to find a responsible and serious settlement to the problem".

His next words struck like hammer blows in a room so silent that you could hear a pin drop:

> We understand that within the framework of the negotiations that we are currently holding, the question of the presence of the Cuban troops bears a relation to the implementation of Resolution 435. Leaving aside rhetoric, we must recognise that there is a linkage. If it is not shown in this document it will be part of it, because there is a linkage. We cannot deny that fact . . .

At other junctures, as we perhaps engaged in controversies, we rejected the concept of linkage. The question was debated in a variety of international fora and the idea was that if Namibia is to be independent, Cuban troops will have to leave Angola. We rejected that and there was great polemics about this. Now we do not deny that if we were to reach a settlement, that settlement would involve the withdrawal of Cuban troops.

For the first time, the Cubans now adopted the South African and US position. Aldana said he was willing to discuss a calendar for the withdrawal, and even to have the withdrawal monitored. He continued:

From our standpoint these are concessions and we are making them on the understanding that it is important that the Government of South Africa understands that these are concessions, otherwise the climate of confidence which we have presently achieved will disappear. It is important to understand that the Government of Angola and the Government of Cuba do not wish to have Cuban troops permanently stationed in Angola. It is not in our interests. In Angola we are acting on our own behalf and what is at stake is the skin of our own people. And nothing could be more honourable than Cuban troop withdrawal from Angola of our own free will . . .

Crocker later wrote that "[t]he air was electric as Van Heerden took the floor" to answer Aldana.[25] The South African diplomat recognised the Angolan and Cuban sensitivities, and he "noted with particular interest" Aldana's words about the linkage between the implementation of Resolution 435 and a Cuban troop withdrawal. He accepted "that all parties should act as sovereign states whose interests had to be taken into account".

The door to peace had swung open. The New York meeting was followed by several others in which the nitty-gritty of the mutual withdrawal was hammered out. Hard negotiations followed, but the deed was basically done. Late in July, the South African, Cuban and Angolan militaries agreed that Cuban troops would not advance further after 9 or 10 August, when the SADF would withdraw its remaining forces from Angola. The water supply from Calueque to SWA would be guaranteed.[26]

In Geneva, a few days later, Van Heerden took the other side by surprise by proposing 1 November as the starting date for the implementation of Resolution 435, and 1 June 1989 as the date for elections in South West Africa. The Cubans would have to have left Angola at that time. Van Heerden also put the presence of the ANC – which occupied several training and logistical camps in Angola – on the table, stating that it was "unacceptable".[27] In response, Angolan President José Eduardo dos Santos informed his South African counterpart, President PW Botha, that he was willing to close down the ANC camps, provided South Africa reciprocated with regard to UNITA camps in SWA.[28] (The SADF had established training camps for UNITA fighters in northern SWA.)

At a press conference on 8 August, Pik Botha, Magnus Malan and Jannie Geldenhuys announced the SADF's withdrawal from Angola. On 22 December, the so-called New York Accords were finally signed by representatives of the Angolan, Cuban and South African governments.[29] After 23 years, the war was almost over.

Who won the "Battle of Cuito Cuanavale"?

At this point, it is perhaps useful to look back on the battles around Cuito Cuanavale and the debate to which these have given rise. Reading the public debates about the "Battle of Cuito Cuanavale" years after the event, one may be forgiven for thinking that the battle about who won is almost as intense as the fighting of 1987/1988 itself. On the one hand, there is a consensus among most left-wing academics and politicians that the SADF lost badly. For instance, Canadian political scientist Isaac Saney called the battle "South Africa's Stalingrad",[30] while former ANC Cabinet minister and MK commissar Ronnie Kasrils has written that there could be no doubt whatsoever "that an epic victory had been won over the apartheid military machine in that embattled country [Angola] . . . constituting a historic turning point in the struggle for liberation".[31] According to Professor Gary Baines, the "Cuban challenge to the SADF's air superiority broke the deadlock on the battlefield in southern Angola and forced the SADF troops to beat a hasty retreat to the Namibian border".[32] In his numerous writings, Piero Gleijeses basically concurs with this interpretation.[33] With the exception of Gleijeses, most writers have neglected to do any in-depth research and have preferred to parrot the view of Fidel Castro. As for Gleijeses, his impressive body of research is tainted by his support for Castro and his distaste for the National Party government in South Africa.[34]

On the other hand, it will come as no surprise that people like Pik Botha, Magnus Malan and Jannie Geldenhuys thought that the SADF had won. In their analyses, they concentrate on the SADF victory at the Lomba River and downplay the later reverses at Tumpo.[35] The figures on which Geldenhuys bases his conclusion are summarised in Table 4:[36]

Table 4: Cuban/FAPLA and SADF losses, 1987–1988

	Cuban/FAPLA losses	SADF losses
Tanks	94	3
Armoured vehicles	100	11
Rocket launchers	34	0
Artillery guns	9	0
Mobile bridges	7	0
Logistical vehicles	389	0
Missile systems	15	0
Radars	5	0
23-mm antitank guns	22	n/a
Fighter aircraft	9	2 (1 shot down, accident)
Light aircraft	0	1
Helicopters	9	0
Men killed	4 785	31

These figures need to be unpacked if we are to answer the question of who won at Cuito Cuanavale. Enemy losses of materiel were mostly well documented by the South Africans and must be considered fairly accurate. The enemy's personnel losses are based upon intercepted radio communications, body counts on the battlefield and estimates, and should also be fairly accurate. As far as Geldenhuys's figure of 31 SADF dead, it must be noted that in general the South Africans could not under-report their own casualties. In a top-secret review of the lessons of the war, it was stated:

Casualties suffered cannot be hidden. Because the next of kin have to be informed at the earliest possible stage of the casualty and in broad terms also have to be informed of the circumstances, it is necessary that the higher HQs should be in possession of the facts surrounding the loss as soon as possible.[37]

For instance, the identities of the four soldiers killed in the battle of 14 February 1988 were immediately flashed from their unit to higher headquarters.[38]

Nevertheless, there is reason to believe that Geldenhuys may have made an honest mistake here. Firstly, the figure of 31 dead may be based on a document by the army medical services analysing the casualty figures – dead and wounded. The number of 31 dead is indeed mentioned. But right at the end it is said that "[t]he above statistic is the version as it extended from 05 August 1987 [to] 11 December 1987".[39] As mentioned, four South African men were killed on 14 February 1988, and another four on 25 February. One soldier drowned at the beginning of that month,[40] and two members of 101 Battalion died in January while Jan Hougaard's small force was harassing FAPLA west of the Cuito. This means that Geldenhuys's figure has to be amended upwards to 42.

Secondly, the total does not include UNITA losses, which were considerable, especially during the final three Tumpo attacks. If these could be included (which they cannot, as nobody bothered to document them), the table would look somewhat less skewed to the detriment of the Angolans and Cubans. But even if one takes UNITA losses into account, there is no doubt that the statistics still support the conclusion of a handsome victory for the SADF. However, we have seen time and again in this study that figures do not tell the whole story. The statistics would tell us that the SADF was much more capable on a tactical level than its adversaries, but, ultimately, other considerations are more decisive. The bottom line is the all-important question: what were the objectives of the opposing sides, and to what extent did they achieve them? I will try to answer these questions systematically.

FAPLA: The strategic objective with which FAPLA started its offensive in August 1987 was to remove UNITA as a military and political factor once and for all. The operational aim was to cross the Lomba, defeat UNITA in battle and take Mavinga, and then to use that village and its landing strip as a spring-board for attacking and occupying UNITA's headquarters at Jamba.

The Angolans failed dismally. Of the four brigades they deployed in the advance to the Lomba, only one reached the southern side (47 Brigade), and that formation was utterly trounced by 61 Mech on 3 October 1987. The others were stopped from crossing the river, and two were badly hurt in the process. They were then driven back from whence they came. Thus, there can be no doubt whatsoever that FAPLA lost badly.

The SADF: From the analysis in the preceding chapters, it must be clear that the SADF had a mixed record during operations Moduler, Hooper and Packer. On a tactical level, it fared excellently. The South African Army equipment was mainly better than that of FAPLA, and its level of training was vastly superior. The SAAF Mirage fighters were marginally inferior to the enemy's MiG-23s, but much more important than this was the fact that the air force was ham-strung by the great distance between its bases and the battlefield.

In spite of the enemy's having the upper hand in the air, the South Africans won every single engagement on the ground whenever they got to grips with the Angolans. (This excludes the final three Tumpo battles, where the SADF tactical advance was stopped by minefields, artillery fire and air attacks before contact with the enemy could be made.) However, on a higher level, the SADF leadership did not always perform well. Until deep into the campaign, the generals naively thought that the South African presence could be kept secret. This entailed placing limitations on the forces involved, which had a disastrous effect on the operational choices made. Among the latter was the decision to tackle the enemy east of the Cuito, where the bulk of their forces were, instead of blindsiding them west of the river.

The SADF strategic objective was to keep UNITA alive in order to impede SWAPO infiltration into Okavangoland and Caprivi and to keep the PLAN insurgency largely confined to Ovamboland, where it could be controlled more easily. In operational terms, this was translated into an order to stop the FAPLA advance. This was highly successful. Then PW Botha ordered the SADF to undertake a counteroffensive and hit FAPLA so hard that it would be unable to repeat its offensive before the end of 1988. Operationally this meant that the Angolan brigades had either to be destroyed or driven across the Cuito. Occupying Cuito Cuanavale was the subject of internal debate, but was decided against.

In this counteroffensive the South Africans again fared well on a tactical level, but the SADF leadership once again decided to maintain its forces east of the river. And when FAPLA was driven back north of the Chambinga, it exchanged its own tried and trusted mobile warfare doctrine for a typical Second World War frontal, attritionist approach – with predictable results.

In the end, FAPLA retained only a small toehold east of the river at Tumpo. And although the South Africans were forced into a series of frontal attacks that were both tactically and operationally unwise, the enemy was effectively boxed in and not able to restart his offensive. As a matter of fact, FAPLA would resume its offensive against UNITA only in 1989/90, which meant that PW Botha's directive was fulfilled.

The Cubans: Tactically, the Cuban and South African armies measured up well against each other. The Cubans were surprisingly aggressive and at times even rash, although the battle-hardened SADF probably had the edge because of its superior doctrine, experience and training. As for the much-vaunted Cuban superiority in the air, this was indeed a problem for the SADF, but never decisively so. The military decisions were forced in the ground operations, not in the air.

From what we have been able to piece together about Fidel Castro's objectives, we know now that he had no interest in escalating the fighting to an all-out war. He wanted to get *out*, not to get deeper *in*. But, cleverly, he did this, to use a colloquial term, by playing chicken. His reinforcements and southward march to the South West African border were intended to *intimidate* the South Africans into giving up and allowing him to bring his troops home while looking like a victor. And he wanted to do it preferably without fighting.

The South Africans did not fall for this ruse completely. They marshalled a strong force inside SWA to prepare a warm reception for the Cubans should they try to cross the border. But can one really say that they were not intimidated at all? That sounds very unlikely. Although their intelligence analyses suggested a Cuban invasion was unlikely, it is well documented that they couldn't, and didn't, really *know*. Besides, the Cuban occupation of Cunene province, which restored SWAPO's ability to infiltrate into SWA without running the gauntlet over hundreds of kilometres, must have played in their minds while the peace negotiations continued. In that sense, the Cuban march to the border must have had at least some results, even if only psychological, at the negotiation table.

Nevertheless, the South Africans did not lose their nerve, and Jannie Geldenhuys and Pik Botha stood up well to the Cuban tactic of intimidation around the margins of the negotiations. It must have become clear to the Cubans that they could proceed only so far with their threats without getting embroiled in an all-out war, which they wanted as little as did the South Africans. Therefore, when Carlos Aldana explicitly accepted the much-maligned linkage between the implementation of Resolution 435 and total Cuban withdrawal from Angola, he probably did it because the Cubans realised that there was a line drawn by the SADF that they should not cross. That became the defining moment. Each side realised that the other side could hurt them greatly in the event of an escalation, and neither side was prepared for that. The negotiations were not exactly plain sailing, but from that moment nobody looked back. Peace was on the horizon, and nobody could afford a failure any more. And with the Soviet Union in retreat, pulling the rug from under SWAPO's feet, handing South West Africa over to a SWAPO government at last became politically affordable to the South African government.

As far as the Cubans and South Africans are concerned, the "Battle of Cuito Cuanavale" was a draw. In a sense, both won and neither lost. Regarding FAPLA and the SADF, the South Africans won so far on points that it was almost a knockout.

April's fool

The peace agreement signed in New York on December 1988 stipulated the following:

- Resolution 435 would be implemented from 1 April 1989 onwards, when a ceasefire would commence. A UN military contingent, the United Nations Transition Assistance Group (UNTAG) would supervise the process.
- The withdrawal of Cuban troops would be carried out in phases, to be completed by July 1991.

- Koevoet and SWATF would be disbanded, and the SADF would be confined to base with no more than 1 500 men.
- SWAPO would remain north of 16° South – that is, far inside Angola.
- Free and fair elections would take place on 1 November 1989 under UN supervision.
- The New York Accords specifically stated: "The Parties shall respect the territorial integrity and inviolability of borders of Namibia and shall ensure that their territories are not used by any State, organization, or person in connection with acts of war, aggression, or violence against the territorial integrity or inviolability of borders of Namibia or any other action which could prevent the execution of UNSCR 435/78."[41]

It all looked positive, actually too good to be true. And indeed, South Africa, Cuba and Angola adhered strictly to the plan. But SWAPO broke it immediately. The organisation had not been asked to sign – as was the case in 1984 – but nevertheless formally accepted the agreement.[42] However, the organisation did not withdraw its fighters to the specified area. South African protests were to no avail.[43]

But more was to come. SADF Military Intelligence learnt that SWAPO was planning to break the agreement and invade South West Africa.[44] On the evening of 31 March, the day before the ceasefire was due to come into effect, Louis Pienaar, the South African Administrator General, the senior civil official in SWA, hosted a dinner for several dignitaries in Windhoek. Pik Botha and Magnus Malan were both there, as was the senior UN civil official, Martti Ahtisaari, and Lieutenant General Prem Chand, commander of UNTAG. Botha had earlier taken Ahtisaari aside and fully briefed him on the South African intelligence picture. He told him that 150 insurgents had already infiltrated into SWA and that 500 to 700 armed fighters were massing immediately north of the border. About 60% of SWAPO's forces were south of the 16th parallel. Ahtisaari thought that SWAPO would have to be exceedingly stupid to violate the peace agreement and he therefore did not believe Botha. He did, however, inform the UN Secretary-General's office of the South African allegations.[45]

During the night and the next day, about 1 200 PLAN guerrillas (according to SADF figures), armed with automatic rifles, antitank rockets and portable anti-aircraft missiles, surged over the border into SWA.[46] Afterwards, SWAPO claimed that it had never crossed the border, that it always had been inside South West Africa, in secret bases about which the South Africans knew nothing.[47] This was a transparent lie; after the first base at Ongulumbashe had been destroyed in August 1966, SWAPO never again had any bases south of the border. The invasion clearly was an attempt to *establish* bases in SWA and create a substantial armed presence so as to influence the local population in the coming election. It was a blatant violation of the peace agreement.

The only force capable of tackling the insurgents was Koevoet, which had officially been disbanded, but whose members were still there as part of the South West African Police (SWAPOL). They still had their Casspirs, though not their heavy weapons (12,7-mm machine guns, 20-mm cannon and 60-mm mortars). Armed mostly with rifles, they charged into the bands crossing the border, suffering heavy losses, but inflicting even higher casualties. The radio waves were alive with screams for air support, but the SAAF Alouettes had also been disarmed, and the politicians did not want to release them unilaterally against the insurgents. Understandably, the policemen on the ground, who could not be aware of the political considerations, were not impressed.[48]

It so happened that the British Prime Minister, Margaret Thatcher, was on an official visit to southern Africa at this time. She had decided to pay a quick visit to SWA to see the British contingent serving with UNTAG. When her aircraft touched down in Windhoek just after midday on 1 April, she was unaware of what was going on. Towards the end of the day she was informed of the situation by Louis Pienaar, who delicately implied that South Africa might halt the implementation of Resolution 435. Pik Botha, meeting her a bit later, said that South Africa needed to release its troops, which were confined to base under the provisions of the peace plan. Thatcher was upset about SWAPO's conduct, but did not want to give her permission for the troops to be released. She warned that deviations from the agreed peace plan, both by SWAPO and South Africa, were not permissible. Botha spoke to Ahtisaari and by phone to UN Secretary-General Javier Pérez de Cuéllar, but they, too, refused to budge.

Botha later described his conversation with Pérez de Cuéllar to his biographer:

I told him: What would you say if I told the world afterwards I phoned you, I asked permission, and you hesitated? And because of your hesitation 435 is now completely off course and all the work of years and years resulted in a break-up? What would you say if I told the world this? And, I said, "I would assume you would not want this to happen, that at last we have reached this point, and it is now at the point of being crushed. In the circumstances, Mr Secretary-General, I am sure you will agree that we must release our troops to stop the SWAPO invasion. Afterwards, you can tell the Security Council, the troops will return to the barracks. This would also be in your interest." Then I put the phone down. I put the assumption to him and accepted that he went along with my assumption. And to Mrs Thatcher I said: "De Cuéllar did not object. So, we are releasing our troops."[49]

Strictly speaking, of course, Botha had taken liberties with Pérez de Cuéllar and Thatcher. But it was an emergency. Not surprisingly, Pérez de Cuéllar put a slightly different spin on things in his report to the Security Council. Pik Botha told him, he wrote, that, as UNTAG was unable to support the police, his government had no choice but "to deploy its military forces once again". He urged Botha "to show the utmost restraint". He also consulted with SWAPO and Angolan representatives, and, on the advice of Ahtisaari and Prem Chand "I authorised them to accept a strictly limited and temporary suspension of the requirement for some units of the South African military to be confined to base . . ."[50]

This meant that the police could start arming its Casspirs again, and that the SAAF Alouette gunships could start giving active air support to the embattled defenders on the ground. Even more importantly, the army was allowed into the fray. Two units, the formidable 101 Battalion and the much smaller Kaokoland-based 102 Battalion – both having been disbanded as part of SWATF – were immediately recalled. The ubiquitous 61 Mech sent in Ratel 90s to beef up the infantry's firepower. The implementation of Resolution 435 was temporarily suspended.[51]

On the morning of 1 April, Kenyan Brigadier General Danny Opande, second in command of UNTAG, raged against SWAPO: "I'm so angry! Such stupidity.

Those poor kids. Murderers, sending them on a suicide mission."[52] During the day, UNTAG representatives were flown to the border area to investigate the situation for themselves. Cedric Thornberry, UNTAG's press spokesman, was present during the interrogation of two SWAPO prisoners.

> These people had not come in to attack bases and strategic installations. They had come to establish bases because of what they had been led to believe was part of the peace process. Somebody had misled them. The idea that SWAPO would come in at ceasefire and establish bases was not part of the peace plan. We had had the whole matter out in 1979 and had told SWAPO, again and again since then, that this was not agreed. We repeated the mantra: they could not expect to gain at the conference table what they had failed to gain on the battlefield; even less so by subterfuge in flagrant breach of a ceasefire agreement. All this was a matter of record over the years.[53]

This tallies with the information supplied by Pik Botha to the UN. On the basis of prisoner interrogations, he informed Pérez de Cuéllar that the insurgents had been informed by their commanders that they would not encounter resistance in South West Africa, as a ceasefire was in force: "Should resistance be encountered, the United Nations would take care of them." By this time (2 April), 4 000 to 5 000 insurgents were poised south of 16°, ready to cross the border.[54] The SADF had also learnt that Sam Nujoma had addressed a gathering of the insurgents at Peu-Peu in Angola on 30 March, before they were sent on their way to the border.[55]

The reaction of the international community towards SWAPO was predominantly negative. The US government condemned the incursion unequivocally, calling it a "direct violation" of the peace accord.[56] Even the chief Cuban negotiator, Carlos Aldana Escalante, informed South Africa that his government viewed the incursion in a serious light and that it was "ready to play a constructive part". The South Africans were referred to "lying statements" by "press agencies" which "attribute responsibility to Cuba for the present situation". In addition, Aldana informed a British diplomat, James Glaze, that SWAPO had "made mistakes".[57] According to Chester Crocker, the "Cubans reported to us that Castro was fit to be tied when informed of the SWAPO fiasco".[58] Peter Stiff cites diplomatic reports that the Cubans were "livid".[59] The Soviet Union and the OAU called for strict adherence to the peace plan.[60]

SWAPO stood alone. But much of the international press remained hostile, unwilling to believe anything emanating from the South African government. On 4 April, Cedric Thornberry, no friend of the South African authorities, wrote in his diary: "The general tone of the press is, however, still hostile, and the further left it is, the more damning. The Western liberal press is giving us an especially hard time." He wrote about a press conference that he conducted, in which he took 58 questions in 55 minutes: "A few were almost screamed, so strong the emotions of some of the journalists. The *Financial Times* man shouted news of some new horror from the north and asked how it felt to have so much blood on our hands. That was felt to be a bit over the top and the conference suddenly calmed down."[61]

The fighting lasted for nine days. Koevoet took the brunt, assisted by soldiers from 101 and 102 Battalions, as well as 61 Mech's Ratel 90s and the SAAF's Alouette gunships. The estimated 1 600 insurgents were hunted mercilessly. The PLAN members stood their ground and often fought back tenaciously, but they were no match for the South Africans' superior firepower. On 8 April, SWAPO leader Sam Nujoma announced that his fighters would withdraw to Angola. The fighting diminished the next day, when the surviving insurgents started fleeing back to Angola. On 28 April, the South Africans announced the final tally: 282 SWAPO fighters had been killed and 38 had been captured. The number of wounded was not given. Altogether 25 South Africans (20 Koevoet and 5 Army) had died in a total of 63 firefights, and 100 had been wounded, while 21 armed vehicles had been knocked out.[62]

On 8 and 9 April, a meeting of the Joint Military Monitoring Commission (JMMC), consisting of South African, Cuban and Angolan representatives, with American and Soviet observers, met at the Mount Etjo game farm. All those present agreed, in differing measures of intensity, that SWAPO was at fault and that the peace process had to continue as agreed.[63] According to Cedric Thornberry, Carlos Aldana said to Pik Botha: "Mr Minister, there are no words in our language or yours to describe what we think of what SWAPO has done last week." Thornberry quoted an anonymous Cuban, who told him that Cuban and Angolan representatives had phoned Sam Nujoma and "bawled him out". Chester Crocker added that, as a result, Nujoma had "just given in" and ordered his fighters back. Pik Botha jokingly told Aldana that the cooperation with Cuba was so good that perhaps the Cubans should reconsider their withdrawal from Angola.[64] Thornberry described the climate at the meeting as follows:

> The camaraderie was evident, with senior officers from the South African, Cuban and Angolan armies – battlefield enemies for more than a decade – chatting, joking, drinking together, cementing a delicate peace through personal bonding. One would have to be obtuse, today, not to feel the strength of the winds of history that are blowing away the anachronisms and debris of the last forty years.[65]

At a meeting of the JMMC in Cape Town towards the end of the month, Cuban military intelligence staff reported that 1 187 PLAN fighters had exfiltrated to Angola, while the SADF put the number at about 850. The Cubans and Angolans estimated that 200 insurgents remained in South West Africa, while the SADF maintained that 400 were still there.[66] Regardless of the final numbers, SWAPO had been humiliated militarily yet again, but politically it would soon experience victory.

The elections

There was one final scare. In the weeks before the November election, rumours abounded that SWAPO was gathering its forces in Angola to invade SWA if the movement should lose the election.[67] The SADF therefore drew up a contingency plan, known as Operation Merlyn. In the case of a renewed SWAPO invasion, the implementation of Resolution 435 would be suspended, and the available forces in South West Africa and Walvis Bay (which remained in South African possession) would be reinforced with extra troops from South Africa. The plan was to protect the airfields at Grootfontein, Ondangwa and Ruacana so that reinforcements could be flown in; pre-emptive attacks would then be carried out north of the border on Xangongo and on SWAPO leaders in the area north of Grootfontein. For this purpose, five SWATF battalions would be reactivated, and three SADF mechanised battalion groups, 32 Battalion, the Cape Corps and 72 Motorised Brigade (Citizen Force) would take on the insurgents. In addition, 44 Parachute Brigade was tasked to relieve Windhoek in case it was taken by SWAPO.[68]

Fortunately, it was never necessary to implement the contingency plan. After SWAPO's treachery, the peace process resumed. There were many mutual accusations of intimidation, many of which were well founded. The SADF tried to organise the anti-SWAPO political parties into a single front.[69] The motto was: "We are *going* to win the election, we *can* win the election and we *have to* win the election!"[70] There were also numerous stories of SWAPO intimidation.[71] Nevertheless, the election campaign proceeded reasonably smoothly, and the voting on 7 to 11 November went off relatively smoothly.

The election results were interesting. Nationwide, SWAPO received 57,3% of the votes, which placed it well short of the two-thirds majority it needed under the peace plan to write the constitution of the new Namibia on its own. This meant that SWAPO had to negotiate with the opposition, a process that produced a Western-type multiparty liberal constitution. Judged by SWAPO's political ideology (*see* Chapter 10), this was not exactly the result the movement's leaders had fought for.

Even more interesting was the geographical breakdown of the results. The South Africans had believed, naively, that their years of investment in winning hearts and minds would pay off. They expected that SWAPO would obtain a majority in Ovamboland itself, but that this would be offset by the movement's unpopularity in the rest of the country.[72] As late as March 1989, Military Intelligence showed the extent of its wishful thinking by reporting that "[t]oday we can confirm that SWAPO support in Ovamboland has decreased markedly". The Democratic Turnhalle Alliance (DTA), the main pro-South African grouping, was reported to be "more highly spoken of than SWAPO".[73] On the other hand, the Department of Foreign Affairs – according to Pik Botha – expected SWAPO to win.[74]

The South Africans were cruelly disillusioned. The final election results showed that SWAPO had gained 92% of all votes cast in Ovamboland, 50% or more in Tsumeb and even Kavango, and 40% in the Caprivi. The DTA got 28,6%, performing best in the south, in Hereroland and in Kaokoland.[75]

With that, the war was finally over. Namibia became independent on

21 March 1990 when the South African flag was lowered and the new Namibian flag hoisted. The guns at last were silent.

19

WHO WON THE BORDER WAR?

In the first chapter we established that the Border War should be seen through the triple prism of a war against racial domination, a war against colonial domination, and as part of the Cold War. In the final chapter, we shall try to dig a little deeper to answer the question posed in the title of the chapter.

Professionally, one of the most interesting aspects of the Border War was that it was an insurgency and counterinsurgency war, a fast-moving mobile conventional war, and, at the end, a set-piece war of attrition, all rolled into one. Shortly before his death, the American military commentator Colonel John J McCuen, whose 1966 book on counterrevolutionary warfare influenced the SADF's counterinsurgency strategy, wrote an article about "hybrid wars". McCuen defined these as "a combination of symmetric and asymmetric war in which intervening forces conduct traditional military operations against enemy military forces and targets while they must simultaneously – and more decisively – attempt to achieve control of the combat zone's indigenous populations by securing and stabilizing them . . .".[1]

He was writing against the background of the wars in Iraq and Afghanistan, where conventional warfare was waged concomitantly with counterinsurgency warfare. The Border War was a little different in that the conventional and counterinsurgency wars were fought – at least from a South African perspective – in separate geographic arenas. The counterinsurgency struggle took place mainly south of the border in SWA, and the conventional operations north of the border in Angola, which makes the Border War, perhaps, a hybrid war of a special kind. The point is that any professional military analysis of the war must take the differing principles of the different types of warfare into account.

As far as counterinsurgency operations are concerned, Mao Zedong famously identified three stages in insurgency warfare. The first phase is typically one where the rebels are weak in numbers, armament and organisation, and are forced to utilise the traditional weapon of the weak: guerrilla warfare. The prime purpose of the guerrilla in this stage is to survive: "The objective of strategic retreat is to conserve military strength and prepare for the counteroffensive. Retreat is necessary because not to retreat a step before the onset of a strong enemy inevitably means to jeopardize the preservation of one's own forces." At the same time the (operational) objective could be to lure the enemy into an area where your support is strong and he tastes "all the bitterness it holds for him".[2]

In the second phase, a strategic stalemate is experienced. This is the longest and most difficult stage, but also the most pivotal. The guerrillas will be dispersed in great numbers in the enemy's rear areas, and they will "launch extensive, fierce guerrilla warfare against enemy-occupied areas, keeping the enemy on the move as far as possible in order to destroy him in mobile warfare . . .".[3]

In the third and final stage, things will progress into a strategic offensive. Mobile warfare will still play an important role, but increasingly there will also be a reliance on conventional warfare. The guerrillas will serve primarily as auxiliaries for the conventional attack forces.[4]

McCuen built upon Mao's stages, but took things a step further. He identified *four* phases: subversion, terror, guerrilla warfare and mobile warfare. The trick, he wrote – as summarised by Professor Annette Seegers – was "to arrest the progression in its prevailing phase, then force the guerrillas back into an earlier phase".[5]

It is, of course, not strictly necessary that Mao's third (or McCuen's fourth) stage be reached for the insurgents to win. In the Portuguese African colonies and in Rhodesia, the war never progressed beyond Mao's first (or McCuen's third) phase. But, in the end that did not matter much, because the insurgents drew the conflict out into such a protracted war that they broke down the counterinsurgents' political will to win.

In South West Africa, PLAN also never progressed beyond Mao's first and McCuen's third stage. There was a time, in the mid-1970s, when PLAN's insurgency war in SWA was going well. The guerrillas ran rings around the white SADF conscripts, mostly city boys, and it is clear that the military command at that stage did not have the foggiest idea how to tackle the problem. But, slowly, the tide turned. It turned primarily because of the insights of the GOC South

West Africa, Major General Jannie Geldenhuys, who saw that the war had to be fought much more professionally. It was Geldenhuys who laid the foundations of a winning strategy.

On the one hand, Geldenhuys correctly assumed that PLAN had to be taken on in its safe base areas inside Angola *before* the insurgents crossed the border into SWA. In this way, the fangs of the insurgency could be drawn to a great extent in a way that would not be possible south of the border. This resulted in several large-scale and smaller cross-border operations with highly mobile mechanised forces, which gave the SADF the opportunity to practise its mobile warfare doctrine.

Inside South West Africa, great emphasis was placed on keeping PLAN's insurgency geographically limited to Ovamboland. This succeeded. PLAN never could activate Okavangoland, the Caprivi and Kaokoland to the extent that it activated Ovamboland. Attempts to spread the war through terrorism to the "white" farmlands south of Ovamboland, and to Windhoek, Grootfontein, Keetmanshoop and other towns were dealt with severely by the SADF, and the unfortunate insurgents were killed, taken prisoner or driven back.

Even in Ovamboland, SWAPO's heartland, the insurgents were increasingly harried as the 1980s wore on. The area was swamped with infantry patrols, augmented with Romeo Mike forces, which smoked out the guerrillas before they could politicise the locals too much. And a big effort was made to capture the hearts and minds of the people.

This strategy, together with SWAPO's internal problems, ensured that PLAN was largely a spent force by 1988. But was this enough for the South Africans to win the war?

The operations in Angola must be judged on a different level. The mobile doctrine developed at the initiative of Constand Viljoen in the 1960s, and fleshed out by men like Roland de Vries in the 1980s, is worthy of study in any military-educational setup. This doctrine was based on two factors: firstly, the African battle space was vast; and, secondly, there were simply not enough troops available. In other words, the set-piece linear approach followed by the Allies in Europe during the Second World War was totally wrong for Africa. Here, the vast open spaces could – as in the Western Desert in 1941/1942 – be compared to the sea, and the mobile mechanised armies to ships that had to be manoeuvred around each other. As in naval battles, possession of territory is irrelevant, unless it affords one tactical or operational advantages. The best approach is, therefore, to outmanoeuvre your opponent, lure him into a killing field and destroy him there. Most importantly, the doctrine demanded that the unexpected be done, that the enemy be attacked in his weakest spots, where and when he did not expect it. As Roland de Vries's book on mobile warfare makes clear, this doctrine borrowed much from military thinkers like Sir Basil Liddell Hart, Sun Tzu, Erwin Rommel and Heinz Guderian, but also from the Boers' experience in the Anglo-Boer War.

Indeed, up to Operation Askari in 1983/1984, this doctrine was assiduously followed in the SADF. The problem is that too few officers had read De Vries, Liddell Hart or other writers. Typical of the lightweight, anti-intellectual approach taken by many officers is a piece by the late Brigadier General JNR ("Junior") Botha, in which he furiously attacks me because I had the audacity to distil some principles of warfare from the writings of Carl von Clausewitz, Liddell Hart and others and to use these in a 1998 critique of the SADF's operational approach during operations Moduler, Hooper and Packer. He wrote: "The theories of these writers, and many others, are precisely that: theories. They have never been tested in a real war. They are distanced so far from reality that they are simply of academic importance!"[6] Objectively speaking, this is complete nonsense. That he also alleged that there never was a "Battle of Cuito Cuanavale"[7] does not help.

The question is, of course, to what extent Botha's approach was typical of the SADF's higher command spheres. After all, he was a senior staff officer at Army Headquarters during operations Moduler, Hooper and Packer. Did this kind of thinking influence the wrong operational decisions made by the SADF high command during 1987/1988? This question cannot be answered here; not enough sources are available. And perhaps too many reputations may suffer. The fact is that the SADF's superb mobile doctrine was thrown out of the window in 1988 and exchanged for a typical Second World War-type approach – precisely the one wisely discarded in the 1960s.

The fundamental question

Who won the war in the end? The conclusions often differ so widely that one would think people are talking about different wars. On the one hand, a serious academic like Timothy Stapleton writes, quite categorically, that "South Africa lost the long 'Border War' in Namibia and Angola", but does not substantiate his conclusion.[8] On the other hand, not surprisingly, Magnus Malan writes in his memoirs that few countries could equal South Africa's military successes. "The outstanding achievement is that we did not suffer a defeat once during this long physical struggle."[9] One could quote many similar opinions.

In the end, however, there has to be some objective measure with which to come to a conclusion. This is not an easy task, because this war was not one where anyone with an atlas could more or less follow the advance or withdrawal of the opposing sides by looking up the places mentioned in the official press statements. The Border War was different. There were no front lines, no permanent occupation of places or capitals. Leaders did not cower in bunkers and not a single one committed suicide. Inside SWA, it was a counterinsurgency war, a battle for the hearts and minds of the South West African people. Across the border in Angola, it was a fast-moving mobile war with ever-changing positions, and possession of territory as such was not an objective.

So, how to determine who won? The only way is to identify the war aims of all the parties concerned – the *real* war aims, not the caricatures painted by opponents on all sides – and then to analyse to what extent these were reached. Let us examine the aims of the communist alliance members first, and then take a look at those of South Africa.

SWAPO

SWAPO's primary war aim was to end the South African occupation – as it was seen – to establish an independent Namibia, and to occupy the seat of government itself. But it did not end there. SWAPO wanted a one-party socialist system in which no opposition would be allowed and in which the state would control economic activity. While it formally accepted the international peace plan, which envisaged a Western-type liberal multiparty democratic system, the evidence in Chapter 10 of this book makes it clear that the movement remained wedded to the idea of a socialist dictatorship.

When CANU leader Mishake Muyongo broke his movement's alliance with SWAPO, he was interviewed by a South African officer. Muyongo, who used to be in the heart of SWAPO's leadership, had some interesting tales to tell. In the period 1978/1979, when it looked for a time that the implementation of UN Resolution 435 was at hand, he said, SWAPO appointed personnel to take care of its interests. But, as the interviewing officer recorded:

> Weapons had to be cached near the places where the [UN] monitor forces would have had bases. Places subject [in other words, Muyongo] could remember, were Oshakati, Oshivello, Oshikango, Katima Mulilo, Rundu, Grootfontein, Tsumeb and Windhoek. 125 black Cubans had already been earmarked for special training as saboteurs and assassins. Their tasks would be to infiltrate before the ceasefire into SWA with the aid of internal leaders of SWAPO under cover of clandestines [?], together with trained Ovambo terrs and lay low. Some of these Cubans would also return to SWA as refugees. Attacks would be carried out on members of the monitor force, leaders be eliminated and the RSA be blamed. The reason for black Cubans is because they would not elicit suspicion as refugees. With the disruption of the election the rest of the Cubans would occupy Ovambo[land] and systematically work down to Windhoek. Provision was then also made for the establishment of a Cuban force in Zambia. Subject reports that the sea would not be utilised as route because Walvis Bay belongs to the RSA. Shortly afterwards subject heard that the specialists had started with their training. In this way the Cubans would hand power to SWAPO.[10]

For a long time, the movement laboured under the illusion that it could defeat the South Africans militarily, whereupon it would march victoriously up the Windhoek Kaiserstrasse and occupy the government buildings. Even after the war, Sam Nujoma wrote in his memoirs that his forces "had never, since the launching of the armed liberation struggle ... been overrun".[11] But this is typical of the "partial, highly selective versions of the past"[12] (as Professor Christopher

Saunders writes) bandied about by Nujoma and other SWAPO leaders. In the end, SWAPO did not win the military struggle in that way. Events far outside South West Africa – in South Africa, Angola, Cuba, America and the Soviet Union – brought about a situation in which Sam Nujoma and his lieutenants were forced to participate in a democratic election on a level playing field.

It is true that SWAPO went on to win the 1989 election with a decisive majority, but it fell short of the two-thirds majority it needed to write a constitution to its liking. It had to be satisfied with exactly the sort of liberal multiparty political system with limits on government power that it wanted to avoid. Nujoma became president, but not a dictator for life. The distinction is important. The opening of the Berlin Wall and the collapse of communism as a global political power factor shortly afterwards also meant that SWAPO could not preside over a transformation to a socialist economy.

In other words, SWAPO fell far short of most of its main war aims. At the same time, having become a more or less functional democracy, it may be reasoned that Namibia came off best.

The MPLA and UNITA

Like SWAPO, the MPLA believed in a Marxist-Leninist one-party dictatorship with a socialist economy. Egged on by the Soviet Union and Cuba, it refused to grant UNITA and the FNLA a place at the transitional government's table in 1975, and this was the primary cause of the protracted civil war with UNITA. This is not to say that UNITA was any more democratic in nature than the MPLA, but recognising UNITA and Jonas Savimbi's undeniable faults does not mean that the MPLA was on the side of the angels. Also, the fact that the MPLA was internationally recognised as the legal Angolan government in 1976 does not make its forcible investment with power morally legitimate.

The MPLA's war aims were to consolidate its own power, to neutralise the FNLA and UNITA and to drive out the South Africans. On the other hand, UNITA wanted to force the MPLA to hold elections, which it believed it could win.

The MPLA succeeded in some respects. The FNLA, an inefficient, corrupt movement led by the incompetent Holden Roberto, was knocked out early.

UNITA, aided by South Africa, stubbornly held on. In the end, the same international developments that resolved the South West African question also led to the solution of the Angolan problem. Free and fair elections were held in 1992, which UNITA lost. Alleging electoral fraud, Savimbi went back to the bush and fought on until he was killed in 2002. Then Angola at last came to rest. The collapse of the Soviet Union meant that the MPLA's Marxist orientation was largely abandoned. UNITA reorganised itself as a legal political party, and the country is more or less a democracy – albeit brittle – although the MPLA still forms the government.

The conclusion, therefore, must be that both the MPLA and UNITA also fell well short of their war aims.

Cuba

We have seen that Cuban dictator Fidel Castro was politically and militarily very astute. He also was charismatic and, seen from his own perspective, an idealist who really thought that he was doing good for mankind. At the same time, his pitiless idealism brooked no opposition or deviant thought at all. Not only did he mercilessly crush all opposition and freedom of thought in his own country, but this was indeed the system he wished to safeguard in Angola by his armed intervention. At the same time, the heightened prestige this engendered in certain circles fed his megalomania. It is one of the greatest ironies (and mysteries) of the war that this dictator, who killed all freedom and imprisoned democrats in his own country, actually thought that he was bringing freedom to the oppressed masses of Africa – and that many politicians and academics, from whom one might expect better, still worship him for it.

The true character of Castro's rule was nowhere better illustrated than in the trial of the Cuban commander in Angola, General de División Arnaldo Ochoa Sánchez, on drug-smuggling charges. Ochoa had been a hero of the Cuban Revolution right from the beginning, and his distinguished career included fighting not only in Angola, but also in the October War of 1973 against Israel and in Ethiopia in 1977. The problem with this arrogant but very charismatic general, who was worshipped by his troops, was probably that he aroused Castro's jealousy. Castro, therefore, kept him as much as possible on foreign assignments far from home, which, ironically, only enhanced his political prestige. In the end, it apparently became too much for Castro, who viewed Ochoa as a political threat. The trial of 1989, in which he was convicted, sentenced to death and executed, was designed, as the US National Intelligence Council interpreted it in a secret report, to "[e]liminate a popular and distinguished general who had somehow threatened the regime's authority".[13]

Castro's basic war aim was, as he saw it, to protect the Angolan communist revolution from the South Africans. He once even threatened that Cuba would stay in Angola for 30 years if necessary and that his troops would not leave until South Africa had dismantled apartheid.[14] After the first phase of the war (1975–1976), having ensconced the MPLA in Luanda by force, the civil war between the MPLA and UNITA was not a priority for him any more. Nevertheless, as US political scientist Owen Ellison Kahn wrote in 1987, the effect of Cuba's military presence in Angola "is in prolonging the civil war, making the MPLA and UNITA less willing to negotiate a settlement".[15] This is an interesting riposte to those who like to point the accusing finger exclusively at South Africa.

At the same time, Castro was a born politician. He understood well how to conjure up the image of his small country's hard work and selfless sacrifice in order to increase its international standing and prestige, while actually doing as little as possible. (In fact, Angola paid Cuba about US$300 million per year for its military and civilian aid. This cost was offset by Angola's oil sales, but after 1986, when the oil price fell from US$45 to US$13 per barrel, the Angolans could not pay any more, while Cuba's own economic circumstances made the war unaffordable.)[16] Therefore, from 1976 to 1987, Cuban troops were largely kept out of harm's way, and seldom saw action. The official death toll is 2 016, although Edward George cites credible sources in Havana that about 3 800 Cuban soldiers died in Angola[17] – still a low figure for 16 years of war.

The problem was that, while the low casualties muted criticism at home, there seemed to be no end, no exit strategy, to Castro's war in Africa. Being endowed with sensitive political antennae, he realised that he had to get out sooner or later. But, whatever the real facts on the ground, his withdrawal had to be made to look like a glorious victory. Ironically, the humiliating defeat of his Angolan allies at the Lomba and Chambinga rivers in September to November 1987 gave him the opening he needed. With consummate political skill, he took the gap and got clean away with it. He elevated the defence of Cuito Cuanavale to a heroic super-legend, and succeeded in convincing large parts of the world that the invincible SADF juggernaut had been decisively beaten there.

And then he blindsided the South Africans (and the Americans) by sending his crack 50 Division into Cunene province and southwards to the South West African border, brilliantly creating the *illusion* of a threat. It is true that the South Africans did not panic and prepared a warm welcome for any Cuban crossing the border into SWA. But there can be no doubt that this illusion, at the very least, concentrated the minds of the South African negotiators, and that this was a contributing factor in the compromise peace treaty that followed.

One does not have to be a political or ideological supporter of Castro to acknowledge that he came off much better than the objective correlation of power seemed to allow him, say, at the beginning of 1988. Although ruthless, power-hungry, cruel and vain, he also was a brilliant politician and strategist who extricated his country through the eye of a needle from a seemingly unwinnable war.

The Soviet Union

For the Soviet Union, the basic strategic objective of its involvement in the wars in Angola and SWA – and the ANC/SACP's campaign in South Africa, for that matter – was based on the 1961 Kremlin decision to elevate the Third World to the main terrain of conflict with the West.[18] After all, it could hardly start a war in Europe for fear of igniting a nuclear war, so the chosen field of rivalry was at the fringes of the world. But by the 1980s, the idealism of the Russian Revolution of 1917 was long gone. As Dmitry Furman, a Cold War historian, puts it:

> In its last years, the Soviet Union had lost many of its ideals, was in a state of decay and did not quite understand what it was fighting for. It had completely forgotten about the "victory of Communism all over the world" and attempted to protect itself against old age and death, whose coming it felt somewhere in the depth of its consciousness, with missiles.[19]

In his brilliant study about why the Soviet Union collapsed, Robert Strayer takes things a step further. Referring to the "stagnation of the Soviet economy", he writes:

> Soviet achievements in the international arena had become costly burdens by the early 1980s. Third World involvements in Angola, Ethiopia and Nicaragua irritated the United States, while producing few benefits for the Soviet Union. Cuba, at one time a promising communist outpost in the western hemisphere, had become a drain on the Soviet economy to the tune of almost $5 billion a year . . . By the early 1980s, then, the worsening Soviet international position had magnified the country's domestic problems and provided even greater incentives for some change in direction.[20]

Of course, the war in Angola was not wholly without advantages to the Kremlin, certainly in the beginning. In the first ten years of its independence, Angola imported about $4,5 billion worth of weapons, of which 90% came from the Soviet Union.[21] (The weapons used by the Cubans in Angola were, however, provided cost-free by Moscow.)[22] Also, having a foothold in southern Africa held strategic advantages, like access to naval bases, political influence in Africa, etc.[23] But, by the end of the 1980s it became clear even in the Kremlin that these wars, on balance, had a net disadvantage. One of the chief Kremlin ideologues, Karen Brutents, afterwards called it "one of the most stupid actions in the foreign policy of the Soviet Union":

> The Soviet involvement cost the Soviet Union dearly, financially. What did we seek in Angola? They were very rich: Gas, oil, diamonds – but we didn't get anything from them. We sat there, protecting them from the South Africans, and at the same time the Americans were pumping their oil in Cabinda, we were draining ourselves of our own blood.[24]

It would be a hopeless exaggeration to say that the Angolan war – and, by extension, the SADF's role in it – brought down the Soviet Union. Indeed, in 1983, US Undersecretary of State for Political Affairs Lawrence Eagleburger wrote to Pik Botha that the Soviets "have apparently decided not to make southern Africa a major priority in their overall strategy for the time being".[25] Other factors, such as the general ideological decay, the loss of belief in the final victory of socialism, the notoriously inefficient economic system, the unaffordable weapons race with America, and the costly war in Afghanistan, occupied centre stage. But certainly the Angolan war – and therefore also the SADF – did play a subsidiary role.

South Africa

Reduced to its absolute core, the South African war aim was simply the perpetuation of the status quo. The PW Botha government wanted to "modernise" apartheid, to reduce the suffering of blacks in both South Africa and SWA, and to co-opt important black allies in order to retain enough influence in order to keep pulling all the important strings. For this to happen, the liberation movements – SWAPO in SWA and the exiled ANC/SACP alliance, with the Soviet Union and Cuba behind them – had to be defeated. The communists had to be prevented from taking power through the barrel of a gun.

Therefore, the government supported UNITA to facilitate its own war against SWAPO. An additional strategic goal of its repeated cross-border operations into Angola from 1978 was, amongst others, to force the MPLA to start negotiating with UNITA in order to bring about power-sharing between the two as a first step towards free elections. The South African expectation was that the MPLA would lose hands down, causing a chain reaction: a UNITA government in Luanda would then kick SWAPO out, which in turn would facilitate an election defeat for the movement in an independent Namibia, and the installation of a government sympathetic to South Africa. And finally, a SWAPO defeat in SWA would make a government victory over the ANC/SACP much easier.

To what extent did the South African strategy succeed? In important respects, it failed. SWAPO won the elections of 1989 in Namibia. After PW Botha was rather unceremoniously toppled from power in a palace revolution inside the governing National Party the same year, his place was taken by FW de Klerk, who unbanned the ANC/SACP early in 1990. A period of negotiations followed, after which the ANC/SACP finally took power in 1994. By 1999, the once-mighty National Party was a shadow of its former self and three years later ceased to exist. On the face of it, the NP government lost the war.

Yet, at the same time, neither SWAPO nor the ANC/SACP succeeded in obtaining the unfettered power they had fought for. On the contrary, they were forced to become governments subject to a constitution, while their power was kept in check by various other power centres both within the political system as such and civil society.

The National Party government certainly did not win the war, but neither did it lose it. The end result, quite ironically, was the kind of liberal multiparty democracy with checks and balances that neither side had fought for. In this process, the SADF played a crucial role. Although the SADF, like any military in any country, was a political instrument utilised by the government, the men in uniform succeeded in winning time that allowed for the communist threat to dissipate. And when that finally happened, the transfer of power to SWAPO and the ANC/SACP ceased to be the existential threat the government had perceived it to be.

Economically, it would have been difficult for South Africa to continue the war indefinitely. During the 1980 to 1989 period, annual economic growth averaged only 1%, compared with the 3% increase per year in the size of the black population.[26] At the same time, military expenditure went through the roof – from 0,9% of GDP (or 6,6% of total state expenditure) in 1960/1961[27] to 3,9% and 15,3%, respectively, by 1984/1985.[28] With economic problems mounting, aggravated by international sanctions, South Africa also needed a way out.

After the war, General Constand Viljoen, obviously with the advantage of hindsight, told Padraig O'Malley:

> The aim was never to win that war . . . The aim was to check the expansionism of communism in southern Africa and that they [the SADF] did. In fact I have always maintained that in three places in the world the international communism got defeated. The one was here, southern Africa, the other one was in the Middle East where they could never really subject Israel, and the other one was Afghanistan where the Afghan rebels dealt with the whole situation of the expansionism of communism from Russia. I think those three spheres, three operational

spheres, caused the collapse of communism and therefore I always maintain that what we have done in Angola was not in vain and I want to emphasise it was never aimed at winning that war.[29]

When one takes everything into account, that seems to be an acceptable summary of the outcome of the war. It is perhaps a fair conclusion to say that, strangely enough, no one really lost the war, and that, in a way, all parties could step out of the conflict regarding themselves as winners.

How did the opponents measure up to each other?

Once again, we have to look at the performance of the individual parties.

SWAPO

Obviously, SWAPO – or PLAN, the movement's army – should not be judged in the same light as, say, the SADF, FAPLA or the Cuban army. Although it possessed units with the grand description of "mechanised brigades", this was in theory only; PLAN never had any conventional warfare capability worth the name. It was intended, structured, trained and equipped as a guerrilla army with the purpose of fighting a protracted insurgency in South West Africa, and must be judged as such.

As a guerrilla army, PLAN did well at a grassroots level. The insurgents' bushcraft was superb, and it was all but impossible for white conscripts to follow their spoor. Only when the SADF started employing Ovambo and Bushman trackers did the survival chances of the insurgents diminish. They were often very brave and determined, and impressed their adversaries with their extreme stamina and perseverance. Sometimes the pursuers chanced on syringes, showing that the insurgents injected themselves with painkillers or drugs in order to keep going under inhuman conditions. And, when cornered, PLAN fighters were very dangerous. Their only deficiency on a tactical level was that they were mostly poor shots, not correcting for the AK-47's tendency to buck upwards when fired in automatic mode. This saved many a trooper's life.

This also applied to PLAN fighters when attacked in their bases in Angola.

We have highlighted several instances where PLAN members fought with commendable courage to the death. They deserve to be remembered with honour.

It is a fact that many South African soldiers had great respect for their PLAN counterparts. Jannie Geldenhuys thought that if "they were in a tight spot they were good fighters. They were experts at escape and evasion. I recall many occasions when troops and junior commanders told me SWAPO cadres were better fighters than FAPLA and the Cubans and, if they had the chance, they'd rather engage FAPLA than PLAN."[30] Jan Breytenbach agreed, judging PLAN fighters "to be worthy opponents in the field".[31] And Willem Steenkamp wrote of them:

> Militarily, the insurgents had pronounced weak and strong points. The average PLAN insurgent was often good at fieldcraft, camouflage and anti-trenching techniques, and capable of extreme feats of physical endurance, even when wounded. From beginning to end, however, the rank-and-file insurgent was never as thoroughly schooled in the fighting skills as he should have been, even at the height of the war, in the early 1980s.[32]

The Soviet general Konstantin Kurochkin was also impressed with their "high revolutionary spirit, organisation and discipline".[33]

At the same time, PLAN's leadership appeared to be rather deficient. When threatened, the officers tended to run away, leaving their men in the lurch. This happened, for instance, at Cassinga in 1978 and again at Smokeshell two years later. The sparse accounts by PLAN members at times also contain harsh criticism of the officer class.[34] But the greatest deficiency appears to have been at strategic level. Sam Nujoma was politically astute in the sense that he knew how to manipulate SWAPO for his own political survival. Beyond that he was a dour Stalinist with a penchant for spouting (and perhaps believing) propaganda. Historian Christopher Saunders says that there is "much myth in the way Nujoma portrays the war" in his memoirs, providing "a bland and highly distorted account".[35]

Far from being sensitive to the desire of young South West Africans for an open, democratic liberation movement where their voices would be heard, Nujoma transformed it into – as Saunders puts it – "a military culture, strongly hierarchical, authoritarian and closed".[36] It became a dictatorial movement where questions or doubts were punished, where power was wielded in an arbitrary fashion, and where thousands of innocent people were accused of being apartheid spies, imprisoned, assaulted, sexually abused, tortured, even killed. There is evidence that this culture of fear and uncertainty, akin to that which Stalin fostered in the Soviet Union, in the end paralysed SWAPO politically and brought its war effort almost to a standstill. Had international developments not brought about a political acceleration in 1988, chances are that the movement could have collapsed completely.

FAPLA

FAPLA was perhaps one of the most inefficient armies of modern times. In the mid-1980s, Konstantin Kurochkin wrote dismissively of the FAPLA soldiers' low morale and bad discipline. He noted their weak intelligence, the leakage of information to UNITA and the huge gap between the officers and men, and how some officers even stole their subordinates' food.[37] And Edward George has recorded the Cuban military's "complaints about the incompetence and indiscipline of the FAPLA troops".[38]

As the war developed, FAPLA acquired more and better weaponry from the USSR, while Soviet and Cuban instructors went to great lengths to train Angolan soldiers. But the average FAPLA soldier – there was a fair chance that he would have been forced into military service – did not know why he was fighting, nor did he understand the cause. Many soldiers made a show of fighting, but in reality simply tried to survive.

The officer corps was even worse. Their mind-set was firmly defensive. Before 1985, they mostly let their adversaries take the initiative and attack them; they simply tried to ward off the attacks. Even when their opponents were vulnerable, as the invading SADF battle groups were during Operation Protea from the direction of the FAPLA fortress of Cahama, they sat on their hands and let chance after chance slide away.

After FAPLA's crushing defeat at Cuvelai during Operation Askari, a series of aggressive Soviet generals took over operational command in Angola, and induced FAPLA at last in 1985 and 1986 to take the initiative and start an offensive. It was a shambles, due to the army's generally disorganised state and the amateurish state of its logistics support. Even small interventions by South African troops were sufficient to stop the Angolans in their tracks.

Things were different by 1987, when more South Africans were needed to fight the FAPLA advance. But even a woefully inadequate SADF force succeeded in smashing the offensive decisively. And, right to the end of the campaign, the South Africans won every single clash with the Angolans hands down.

The Cubans

Not having really fought to any recognisable extent in Angola, the Cubans were not terribly experienced when they clashed with the SADF near Cuito Cuanavale in early 1988. They had had a brush with the South Africans at Cassinga in 1978, but, beyond that, Fidel Castro had kept them as far away from harm as he possibly could during all their years in Angola.

However, after a series of humiliating FAPLA defeats at the Lomba and Chambinga rivers, the Cubans took over operational command from the Soviets and sent a small number of officers and NCOs to stiffen the spines of the Angolans at Cuito Cuanavale. In the single heavy clash that took place between South Africans and Cubans, on 14 February 1988, the latter proved that they were nothing like FAPLA. They were courageous and aggressive, even rash, and the officers who took over command at Cuito Cuanavale conducted a very intelligent defence. They saw that FAPLA was never able to withstand the fury of a South African attack. Therefore, through the astute placement of minefields, utilisation of the high ground on the west bank of the Cuito for their massed artillery, and air attacks when the weather allowed, they prevented the South African attackers from even making contact with FAPLA. And each time the South Africans reeled back with a bloody nose.

In the clashes of April, May and June 1988 in Cunene province, the Cubans proved themselves to be well trained, well motivated and aggressive to the point of rashness. Allowing for the limited exposure their troops had in the war, they fared rather well.

UNITA

Like PLAN, UNITA was primarily a guerrilla army and should be evaluated as such. As a guerrilla army, it was good. It mostly ran rings around FAPLA, and, by 1987, it either dominated or challenged MPLA authority in much of the Angolan countryside. Granted, much of this was due to the aid UNITA received from South Africa, in the form of training and captured FAPLA weaponry, as well as American-supplied weapons – the latter during the late 1980s. But UNITA fighters were much better motivated and trained than their FAPLA counterparts.

This is not to say that UNITA was perfect; it was flawed in many respects. Especially during operations Moduler, Hooper and Packer, South African troops learnt not to trust UNITA fighters alongside them too much. Often, the intelligence they received from UNITA was faulty, sometimes due to the unwillingness of the UNITA fighters to risk their skins.

Besides, UNITA leader Jonas Savimbi was too impatient. He tried far too soon to transform his movement from a guerrilla army into a conventional force, and unfortunately the captured heavy weapons – tanks and artillery – he received from the SADF encouraged him in his delusions. The fact is that UNITA never measured up to FAPLA in conventional warfare terms – not because of inferior human material, but because the Soviets saw to it that FAPLA's conventional firepower remained overwhelming.

The SADF

When evaluating the SADF's performance in the Border War, one should perhaps make a distinction between the forces on the battlefield and the high-ranking leadership. The SADF was basically a conscript force, overwhelmingly dependent on National Servicemen, with a skeleton of career soldiers. In South West Africa, these were supplemented with indigenous units of professionals, plus Angolan refugees (32 Battalion). The police counterinsurgency unit Koevoet also played a controversial role. An additional source of manpower was the Citizen Force, men who had to return to military duty for certain periods following completion of their National Service.

The dependence on conscripts had certain disadvantages. Troops were not in uniform by choice – the alternative was either to emigrate or go to jail. They had no particular desire to be subjected to verbal abuse by NCOs or to get into firefights where they might die or get wounded. Nevertheless, the combat units were mostly well trained, well equipped and well led. The officer class was generally respected. Of course, complaining about military life was a favourite activity of National Servicemen and Citizen Force members (something they shared with soldiers all over the world), but many also viewed their military service as a rite of passage to manhood and were proud of their prowess.

The dependence on conscripts also meant that, throughout the war, the SADF leadership was very skittish about losses. This was nothing new; historically, the limited numbers of white soldiers available meant that South African commanders were often unwilling to take initiatives that might involve high casualties. During the Border War this, too, formed a stumbling block.

The very best units were mainly manned by professionals, such as the Reconnaissance regiments – the crème de la crème, as good as any other special forces in the world. Next were elite units like the Parachute Battalions and supporting troops of 44 Parachute Brigade. On a par with them were units with mostly black soldiers, such as 32 and 101 Battalion. These units carried a disproportionate load in the war.

Different, but not inferior, were the heavy mechanised units like 61 Mech and 4 SAI, which provided the heavy punch during semi-conventional and conventional cross-border operations. Because of the thoughtful, intellectual analysis of modern mobile warfare provided by the mechanised brotherhood – Constand Viljoen, Roland de Vries, Johann "Dippies" Dippenaar and others – these units punched well above their weight.

Unfortunately, the Citizen Force units often did not fare well. This is always a dilemma with reservists, as it is unavoidable that some of their military skills will erode, requiring intensive retraining. The SADF did not always realise this sufficiently, with the result that Citizen Force formations, through no fault of their own, at times did not quite measure up during high-pressure conventional operations.

In general, the combat elements of the SADF fought very competently indeed. An authoritative study of modern warfare by James F Dunnigan (published in

1993) ranked the SADF very highly. Dunnigan compiled a list of all the armed forces in the world, which he ranked in various fields. He also gave a percentage point to the quality of each, "determined by evaluating historical performance". One may, therefore, assume that the historical record of the 20th century, including the two world wars and the Border War, is taken into account. The SADF was ranked first in Africa, with a percentage of 68. Only one country in the world got a higher figure – Germany, with 75%. Other countries that fared well were Japan (63%), Australia (61%), Israel (55%), and Britain (53%). Angola got 18% and Cuba 16%.[39]

The South Africans stood head and shoulders above their opponents in the Border War. However, Dunnigan probably gives Cuba insufficient acknowledgement. In the few instances when Cuban troops clashed with the South Africans, they performed rather well, even though the SADF always had the edge.

When evaluating the military-strategic leadership of the SADF, one must be rather more nuanced. The strategy for the counterinsurgency war in South West Africa was excellent. The doctrine was superb, taking into account the necessity to concentrate on the hearts and minds of the population rather than on killing the enemy, although not all units adhered very strictly to this. That the Ovambo population in particular could not, in the end, be weaned from SWAPO, was due to factors beyond the control of the SADF. The way in which Jannie Geldenhuys turned a virtually lost war around in the late 1970s, establishing a firm basis on which his successors could build, deserves greater recognition.

General officers like Constand Viljoen and Geldenhuys also realised that the fight had to be taken to the enemy and that the concept of *initiative* was crucial. The cross-border operations played an extremely important role in keeping PLAN at bay and in preventing SWAPO from taking power in SWA through the barrel of a gun. But the military-strategic leadership during operations Moduler, Hooper and Packer could have been much better and was probably responsible for the lack of a decisive outcome. During this time, there was frequent tension between the frontline officers and the generals in their headquarters. Geldenhuys, however, played a key role during the peace negotiations of 1988. He and Foreign Affairs Director-General Neil van Heerden proved to be a duo with consummate negotiation skills who played a mediocre hand extremely well.

Although the war ended in a draw, the peace was far better than could have been expected.

Was it all worth it?

A question one encounters repeatedly in newspaper and magazine articles, published letters and contributions to online discussions, is whether the Border War was worth it. This is a question that has to be treated with great sensitivity. Some people lost loved ones – sons, brothers, fathers, husbands – in the war. Others who fought in the war were scarred for life, physically and/or psychologically. Some still smell the burnt human flesh or decomposing bodies and hear the screams of dying men. For them, it is impossible to forget it. The plethora of reminiscences, published either in printed form or on the Internet, is meant, in part, to rid the writers of these ghosts of the past.[40]

These victims of war will surely answer the above question differently from a historian like me who can coolly look at sources and bases his analysis purely on facts and logic. War is a brutal and cruel business, and the pain and suffering it causes cannot simply be reduced to cold facts. Even so, it is the uncomfortable duty of the historian to look beyond individual suffering and to see the wood instead of the trees. Therefore, with the greatest of respect for the victims on all sides of the war, here is an imperfect attempt at an answer.

It would, of course, have been easier if the Border War, like the Second World War, had ended in a clear-cut victory. But it didn't. Nevertheless, a very important object of war – that is to say, if the decision-makers are wise – is a peace that is better than the situation before the war.

The peace that South Africans and Namibians experience today is certainly not perfect. But perfect peace probably does not exist. The NP government's old enemies, SWAPO, the MPLA and the ANC/SACP, rule in Namibia, Angola and South Africa. The white establishment in South Africa is still coming to terms with the loss of political power. In South Africa, members of minority groups are discriminated against by a ruling party that is forgetting its non-racial ethos and exchanging it for an aggressive, race-based African nationalism. Violent crime is rampant and state corruption is increasing. Service delivery, especially on a local level, is collapsing in places.

No, the peace we have is far from perfect. But how did South Africa and South West Africa look during the 1980s? What would have happened if SWAPO and the ANC had taken power by force in – say – the late 1970s or early 1980s? To know whether the war was worth it, these questions will need answers as well.

In Chapter 10, we looked at SWAPO's agenda for an independent Namibia – simply put, a dictatorship with no room for an opposition or deviant thinking, as the movement made pretty clear through its cruel treatment of internal dissidents. Based on the complete lack of internal freedom and democracy, as well as the arbitrary and dictatorial leadership displayed by Sam Nujoma and his lieutenants, a Namibia "liberated" by SWAPO would have been a very oppressive place.

Imperfect as the present democracies in both Namibia and South Africa may be, they are a far cry from the systems that SWAPO and the ANC/SACP fought for. No wonder that Lauren Dobell, no friend of the National Party government, acknowledges about the 1988 negotiations: "Of all parties concerned, it was SWAPO, excluded from the talks, that conceded the most."[41] Press freedom (vigorously exercised by independent media) is entrenched in the constitutions of both countries, even though elements in both governments would very much like to curtail it. The courts are independent and, by and large, take their role as custodians of the constitutions very seriously, even though the ruling parties do not like it. A vigorous civil society exists in both Namibia and South Africa, even though the governments would like to bring everybody to heel. And in both countries democrats are vigilant and ring the alarm bells every time those in power launch another onslaught against our freedoms.

For this, we have to thank, amongst others, the SADF and everyone who fought in it. Some – perhaps many – individual officers and soldiers may have in fact fought to entrench apartheid. But, objectively speaking, even they helped to win time for the politicians to work out a political solution. And the fact is that a political solution was impossible as long as the shadow of a communist dictatorship hung large over SWAPO and the ANC/SACP. Only when the Soviet Union lost its stomach for world revolution and the economic and military tools to produce it – and of course when the Berlin Wall crumbled and the Soviet Union fell apart – could the white South African government afford to give up its monopoly on power. Only then were the fangs of the communist beast finally drawn.

Ironic as it might seem, regardless of the motivation of individual officers and soldiers fighting in the SADF, their historical role was to make possible a better peace for South Africa. Not a perfect peace, not by a long shot, but one that has a fighting chance of success, as long as everyone keeps in mind John Philpot Curran's famous adage, which should apply to every democracy: "The condition upon which God hath given liberty to man is eternal vigilance."

In a nutshell there we have, in a sense, the continuation of the battles of the Border War by other means. Whether they knew and meant it or not, those men who sacrificed so much during the war helped to establish freedom and democracy in southern Africa. That battle must now be continued, albeit with other means, or else the sacrifices really will have been in vain.

NOTES

INTRODUCTION

1   Cf. for example Gary Baines and Peter Vale (eds.): *Beyond the Border War. New Perspectives on Southern Africa's Late-Cold War Conflicts* (Pretoria, Unisa, 2008); Gary Baines: "Breaking rank: Secrets, silences and stories of South Africa's Border War", at www.inter-disciplinary.net/ptb/wvw/wvw4/baines%20 paper.pdf; Graeme Callister: "Compliance, compulsion and contest: Aspects of military conscription in South Africa, 1952–1992" (unpublished MA thesis, University of Stellenbosch, 2007); Rialize Ferreira and Ian Liebenberg: "The impact of war on Angola and South Africa: Two Southern African case studies" (*Journal for Contemporary History*, 31/3, 2006, pp. 42–73).

2   Willem Steenkamp: *South Africa's Border War 1966–1989*.

3   Cf. www.61mech.org.za; www.aluka.org/ page/about/historyMission.jsp; www. disa.ukzn.ac.za/index.php?option=com_ content&view=article&id=44&Itemid=61.

4   Helmoed-Römer Heitman: *War in Angola. The Final South African Phase*; Fred Bridgland: *The War for Africa. Twelve Months that Transformed a Continent*.

5   Vladimir Shubin: *The Hot "Cold War". The USSR in Southern Africa*.

6   Gennady Shubin and Andrei Tokarev: *Bush War. The Road to Cuito Cuanavale. Soviet Soldiers' Accounts of the Angolan War*.

7   Cf. Leopold Scholtz: "The standard of research on the Battle of Cuito Cuanavale, 1987–1988" (*Scientia Militaria*, 39/1, 2011, pp. 123–129.

8   The late Brigadier General JNR ("Junior") Botha's attack on me must be seen in this light. Cf. Junior Botha: "Suidoos-Angola 1987–89 in perspektief: Castro, Von Clausewitz en Liddell Hart", in Jannie Geldenhuys (ed.): *Ons was Daar. Wenners van die Oorlog om Suider-Afrika*, pp. 525–532.

CHAPTER 1

1   Cf. Hans-Ulrich Wehler: *Bismarck und der Imperialismus* (Munich, Kiepenhauer und Witsch, 1969), passim.

2   The entire drama is vividly related by Jeremy Sarkin: *Germany's Genocide of the Herero. Kaiser Wilhelm II, his General, his Settlers, his Soldiers*, passim. Cf. also Peter H Katjavivi: *A History of Resistance in Namibia*, pp. 9–10.

3   Marion Wallace: *A History of Namibia. From the Beginning to 1990*, pp. 172–177; Katjavivi: *A History of Resistance in Namibia*, p. 10.

4   "A" mandates could attain independence in the short term, "B" mandates in the long term, while "C" mandates were seen as so undeveloped that independence had to be deferred to some unspecified time far in the future.

5   Louis Bothma: *Anderkant Cuito. 'n Reisverhaal van die Grensoorlog*, p. 18. Cf. also Wallace: *A History of Namibia*, pp. 207–210.

6   Wallace: *A History of Namibia*, p. 277; James Barber and John Barratt: *South Africa's Foreign Policy. The Search for Status and Security 1945–1988*, p. 127.

7   Katjavivi: *A History of Resistance in Namibia*, pp. 22 and 41–49.

8   Wallace: *A History of Namibia*, p. 254. Cf. Katjavivi: *A History of Resistance in Namibia*, pp. 48–49.

9   It is relevant to mention here that this practice was outlawed by a court of law. Cf. Wallace: *A History of Namibia*, pp. 277–278.

10 Siegfried Groth: *Namibia – The Wall of Silence. The Dark Days of the Liberation Struggle*, p. 33.

11 Katjavivi: *A History of Resistance in Namibia*, pp. 59–60.

CHAPTER 2

1   Peter Stiff: *The Silent War. South African Recce*

Operations 1969–1994, pp. 36–37; Dick Lord: From Fledgling to Eagle. The South African Air Force during the Border War, pp. 44–48; LJ Bothma: Die Buffel Struikel. 'n Storie van 32 Bataljon en sy Mense, p. 23. The day's events and background have been described by Paul J Els: Ongulumbashe. Die begin van die bosoorlog.

2 Roger S Boulter: "Afrikaner nationalism in action: FC Erasmus and South Africa's defence forces 1948–1959 (Nations and Nationalism, 6/3, pp. 437–459).

3 White Paper on Defence and Armaments Supply, 1975, pp. 11–12, par. 30.

4 Evert Jordaan: "The role of South African armour in South West Africa/Namibia and Angola, 1975–1989" (Journal of Contemporary History, 31/3, 2006, p. 166).

5 Clive Wilsworth: First In, Last Out. The South African Artillery in Action 1975–1988, p. 22.

6 Paul J Els: We Fear Naught but God. The Story of the South African Special Forces, "The Recces", pp. 8–9.

7 Cf. James Ambrose Brown: The War of a Hundred Days. Springboks in Somalia and Abyssinia 1940–41.

8 Winston Brent: Cheetah. "Guardians of the Nation", p. 5.

9 Dick Lord: From Tailhooker to Mudmover, pp. 192–193.

10 Lord: From Tailhooker to Mudmover, p. 196.

11 Anton Dyason: "Blackburn Buccaneer S.Mk.50 SAAF", at http://newsite.ipmssa.za.org/content/view/111/28/1/0/.

12 Monster Wilkins: Chopper Pilot. The Adventures and Experiences of Monster Wilkins, pp. 144–147.

13 Wilkins: Chopper Pilot, pp. 149–150; Paul Dubois: "Puma SA 330 in SAAF service", at www.sa-transport.co.za/aircraft/puma_sa_330.html.

14 James Michael Roherty: State Security in South Africa. Civil-Military Relations under P.W. Botha, p. 104.

15 Chris Bennett: Three Frigates. The South African Navy Comes of Age, pp. 5–8; André Wessels: "The South African Navy during the years of conflict in Southern Africa, 1966–1989" (Journal of Contemporary History, 31/3, 2006, pp. 284–290).

16 Sophia du Preez: Avontuur in Angola. Die verhaal van Suid-Afrika se soldate in Angola 1975–1976, p. 20.

17 Susan Brown: "Diplomacy by other means. Swapo's liberation war", in Colin Leys and John S Saul (eds.): Namibia's Liberation Struggle. The Two-Edged Sword, p. 21.

18 Steenkamp: South Africa's Border War 1966–1989, p. 21.

19 Brown: "Diplomacy by other means. SWAPO's liberation war", in Leys and Saul: Namibia's Liberation Struggle, p. 21.

20 Du Preez: Avontuur in Angola, p. 21.

21 Katjavivi: A History of Resistance in Namibia, p. 85.

22 Cf. Hilton Hamann: Days of the Generals. The Untold Story of South Africa's Apartheid-era Military Generals, p. 9.

23 Annette Seegers: The Military in the Making of Modern South Africa, pp. 137–138; Francis Toase: "The South African Army: The campaign in South West Africa/Namibia since 1966", in Ian FW Beckett and John Pimlott (eds.): Armed Forces & Modern Counter-Insurgency, pp. 202–203.

24 Dirk de Villiers and Johanna de Villiers: PW, p. 236.

25 Cf. Jannie Geldenhuys: Dié wat gewen het. Feite en fabels van die Bosoorlog, p. 64.

26 Hamann: Days of the Generals, pp. 9 and 64.

27 Cf. F. du Toit Spies: Angola. Operasie Savannah 1975–1976; Du Preez: Avontuur in Angola. ; Stiff: The Silent War, ch. 9; Steenkamp: South Africa's Border War 1966–1989, pp. 36–74; Willem Steenkamp: Borderstrike! South Africa into Angola 1975–1980, pp. 60–206; Hamann: Days of the Generals, chapters 1 and 2. The Cuban side of the story is told by Piero Gleijeses: Conflicting Missions. Havana, Washington, Pretoria, passim.

28 Gleijeses: Conflicting Missions, p. 273.

29 Sam Nujoma: Where Others Wavered. The Autobiography of Sam Nujoma, pp. 228–229.

30 Nujoma: Where Others Wavered, p. 234.

31 GM Saunders: "The foreign policy of Angola under Agostinho Neto" (unpublished MA thesis, Naval Postgraduate School, Monterey, Dec. 1983), p. 65.

32 Geldenhuys: Dié wat gewen het, p. 45.

33 Shubin: The Hot "Cold War", p. 213.

34 Gleijeses: Conflicting Missions, p. 273.

35 Brown: "Diplomacy by other means", in Leys and Saul (eds.): *Namibia's Liberation Struggle*, p. 21; Helmoed-Römer Heitman: *South African Armed Forces*, p. 146; Du Preez: *Avontuur in Angola*, p. 22.

36 Spies: *Operasie Savannah*, pp. 43–44; Gleijeses: *Conflicting Missions*, p. 295.

37 Stiff: *The Silent War*, pp. 53–55.

38 Brown: "Diplomacy by other means", in Leys and Saul (eds.): *Namibia's Liberation Struggle*, p. 24.

39 Cf. Peter Stiff: *The Covert War. Koevoet Operations Namibia 1979-1989*, pp. 21–22; Eugene de Kock: *A Long Night's Damage. Working for the Apartheid State*, p. 66.

40 Steenkamp: *Borderstrike!*, pp. 51–52.

41 Gleijeses: *Conflicting Missions*, p. 291.

42 Chester Crocker: *High Noon in Southern Africa. Making Peace in a Rough Neighborhood*, p. 49.

43 Chas W Freeman: "The Angola/Namibia accords" (*Foreign Affairs*, 68/3, Summer 1989, p. 127).

44 Minutes of conversation between Castro and Zhivkov, 11.3.1976, at http://www. wilsoncenter.org/digital-archive.

45 "Soviet Ambassador to the People's Republic of Angola EI Afanasenko, Memorandum of Conversation with President of the Movement for the Popular Liberation of Angola Agostinho Neto", 21.7.1975, at http:// www.wilsoncenter.org/digital-archive.

46 CIA: "Soviet and Cuban intervention in the Angolan Civil War", March 1977, p. 10.

47 Crocker: *High Noon in Southern Africa*, p. 47.

48 Georgie Geyer: "Proud he gave Angola to Marxists" (*Gettysburg Times*, 14.7.1988); Fred Bridgland: "Angola and the West", in Al J Venter (ed.): *Challenge. Southern Africa within the Revolutionary Context*, p.123; Du Preez: *Avontuur in Angola*, p. 10.

49 Vladislav M Zubok: *A Failed Empire: The Soviet Union in the Cold War from Stalin to Gorbachev*, pp. 249 and 252–253.

50 Gillian Gunn: "The legacy of Angola", in Thomas G Weiss and James G Blight (eds.): *The Suffering Grass. Superpowers and Regional Conflict in Southern Africa and the Caribbean*, pp. 49–50.

51 De Villiers and De Villiers: *PW*, p. 275.

52 Steenkamp: *Borderstrike!*, pp. 51–52.

53 Speech by Fidel Castro, 2.12.2005, at emba. cubaminrex.cu/Default.aspx?tabid=15937.

54 Transcript of Swedish documentary film, *History will absolve me*, lanic.utexas.edu/ project/castro/db/1977/19770723.html.

55 Barbara Walters: "An interview with Fidel Castro" (*Foreign Policy*, no. 28, autumn 1977, p. 39).

56 Du Preez: *Avontuur in Angola*, p.27.

57 Ibid., p. 30. Cf. Magnus Malan: *My lewe saam met die SA Weermag*, p. 124; Piet Nortje: *32 Battalion. The Inside Story of South Africa's Elite Fighting Unit*, p. 17; Hamann: *Days of the Generals*, p. 15.

58 Malan: *My lewe saam met die SA Weermag*, pp. 124–125.

59 Hamann: *Days of the Generals*, pp. 32 and 24. Cf. Spies: *Operasie Savannah*, p. 147.

60 Spies: *Operasie Savannah*, p. 150. Cf. also Malan: *My lewe saam met die SA Weermag*, p. 123.

61 Jan Breytenbach: *Eagle Strike! The Story of the Controversial Airborne Assault on Cassinga 1978*, p. 17.

62 Steenkamp: *Borderstrike!*, p. 164.

63 John Stockwell: *In Search of Enemies A CIA Story*, p. 191.

64 Breytenbach: *Eagle Strike!*, p. 10.

65 "Speech by Dr Fidel Castro Ruz, President of the Republic of Cuba, at the ceremony commemorating the 30th anniversary of the Cuban Military Mission in Angola and the 49th anniversary of the landing of the 'Granma', Revolutionary Armed Forces Day", 2.12. 2005, at emba.cubaminrex.cu/Default. aspx?tabid=15937.

66 Gleijeses: *Conflicting Missions*, pp. 305–308.

67 Minutes of a conversation between Fidel Castro and Erich Honecker, 3.4.1977, at http://macua.blogs.com/files/castro-in-africa. doc

68 Spies: *Operasie Savannah*, ch. 16.

69 Minutes of conversation between Fidel Castro and Todor Zhivkov, 11.3.1976, at http://www.wilsoncenter.org/index. cfm?topic_id=1409&fuseaction=va2. document&identifier=E9026DDC-423B-763D-D4131E66A2A26461&sort=Collection& item=Cuba%20in%20the%20Cold%20War.

70 Spies: *Operasie Savannah*, p. 108.

71 Bennett: *Three Frigates*, pp. 159–173.

72 Du Preez: *Avontuur in Angola*, p. 36.

73 "Former South African Foreign Minister RF 'Pik' Botha in an interview with Dr Sue Onslow (LSE IDEAS Fellow), Pretoria, 15th July 2008", p. 3, at www2.lse.ac.uk/IDEAS/programmes/africaProgrammes/pdfs/bothaInterview.pdf.; Malan: *My lewe saam met die SA Weermag*, p. 134.

74 Spies: *Operasie Savannah*, pp. 264–266.

75 Spies: *Operasie Savannah*, p. 220; Du Preez: *Avontuur in Angola*, p. 277. Cf. Willem Steenkamp: *Adeus Angola*, passim, for a personal report of a Citizen Force infantry regiment's experiences.

76 Steenkamp: *South Africa's Border War 1966–1989*, p. 60.

77 Castro: "Paying our debt to humanity", in Isaac Deutschmann (ed.): *Changing the History of Africa. Angola and Namibia*, 5.12.1988, pp. 110–111.

78 Piero Gleijeses: *Conflicting Missions*, pp. 254–262.

79 CIA Directorate of Intelligence: "Soviet and Cuban intervention in the Angolan Civil War", March 1977, pp. 9 and 10–12; John A Marcum: "Lessons of Angola" (*Foreign Affairs*, 54/3, April 1976, p. 413); Stockwell: *In Search of Enemies*, pp. 68–69.

80 De Villiers and De Villiers: *PW*, p. 247.

81 Zubok: *A Failed Empire*, p. 252.

82 Fred Bridgland: *Jonas Savimbi. A Key to Africa*, pp.451–452.

83 Quoted in Bridgland: *Jonas Savimbi*, p. 453.

84 CIA: "Soviet and Cuban intervention in the Angolan Civil War", March 1977, pp. 11, 13 and 18.

85 Bridgland: "Angola and the West", in Venter (ed.): *Challenge*, p. 123.

86 Ibid., p. 124.

87 "Minutes of the meeting between Politburo of the Central Committee of the Bulgarian Communist Party and Comrade Fidel Castro – First Secretary of the Central Committee of the Cuban Communist Party and Prime Minister of the Revolutionary Government of Republic of Cuba", 11.3.1976, at http://www.wilsoncenter.org/digital-archive.

88 Odd Arne Westad: "Moscow and the Angolan crisis, 1974–1976: A new pattern of intervention" (*Cold War International History Project Bulletin*, 8–9, Winter 1996–1997, p. 25).

89 Piero Gleijeses: "Moscow's Proxy? Cuba and Africa 1975–1988" (*Journal of Cold War Studies*, 8/2, Spring 2006, pp. 26 and 40–41).

90 "Fidel Castro's 1977 Southern Africa tour: A report to Honecker", 3.4.1977, at macua.blogs.com/files/castro-in-africa.doc.

91 Fidel Castro: Interview with *Afrique-Asie*, 5.5.1977, at lanic.utexas.edu/project/castro/db/1977/19770506.html.

92 Gabriel García Márquez: "Operation Carlota", at http://emba.cubaminrex.cu/Default.aspx?tabid=21658.

93 WS van der Waals: "Lewensverhaal: Willem Stephanus van der Waals", p. 122 (unpublished memoirs, with permission from the author).

94 Gleijeses: *Conflicting Missions*, p. 341.

95 Quoted in Robin Hallett: "The South African intervention in Angola 1975–76", (*African Affairs*, 77/308, July 1978, p. 349).

96 Minutes of conversation between Castro and Zhivkov, 11.3.1976, at http://www.wilsoncenter.org/digital-archive.

97 "The ANC says hands off Angola!" (*Sechaba*, 3rd quarter, 1976, p.11).

98 Gleijeses: *Conflicting Missions*, p. 305.

99 Fidel Castro (with Ignacio Ramonet): *My Life. A Spoken Autobiography*, p. 318.

100 Du Preez: *Avontuur in Angola*, p. 35.

101 De Villiers and De Villiers: *PW*, p. 264. Cf. also Steenkamp: *South Africa's Border War 1966–1989*, p. 54; Stiff: *The Silent War*, p. 119.

102 Gleijeses: *Conflicting Missions*, pp. 305–307.

103 Conference between Castro and Zhivkov, 11.3.1976, at http://www.wilsoncenter.org/digital-archive.

104 Gleijeses: *Conflicting Missions*, p. 345.

105 Saunders: "The foreign policy of Angola under Agostinho Neto", p. 70.

106 Jan Breytenbach: *Buffalo Soldiers*, p. 124.

107 Gleijeses: *Conflicting Missions*, pp. 305–307; Edward George: *The Cuban Intervention in Angola 1965 to 1991*, pp. 65–77, 73–80.

108 "Memorandum of Conversation",

3.12.1975, at http://www.gwu.edu/~nsarchiv/ NSAEBB/NSAEBB67/gleijeses4.pdf.

109 Cf. Saunders: "The foreign policy of Angola under Agostinho Neto", pp. 61–62. For SWAPO's early alliance with UNITA, see David Lush: "Brothers in-arms" (*Insight Namibia*, at www.insight.com.na/article/full/1157/03-02-2011/brothers-in-arms.html).

110 Heitman: *South African Armed Forces*, p, 147.

111 Bridgland: *Jonas Savimbi*, pp. 229–230 and 237. Cf. also Hamann: *Days of the Generals*, p. 69.

112 Brown: "Diplomacy by other means", in Leys and Saul (eds.): *Namibia's Liberation Struggle*, p. 23; Nujoma: *Where Others Wavered*, p. 229; Groth: *Namibia – The Wall of Silence*, p. 33.

113 Heitman: *South African Armed Forces*, p. 146.

114 Malan: *My lewe saam met die SA Weermag*, p. 141.

115 Nortje: *32 Battalion*, p. 41.

116 Breytenbach: *Buffalo Soldiers*, p. 184.

117 Willem Steenkamp: "South Africa's Border War", in Venter (ed.): *Challenge*, p.195; Steenkamp: *South Africa's Border War 1966–1989*, p. 70.

118 Brown: "Diplomacy by other means", in Leys and Saul (eds.): *Namibia's Liberation Struggle*, p. 25.

119 Nortje: *32 Battalion*, p. 113.

120 De Kock: *A Long Night's Damage*, p. 66; Heitman: *South African Armed Forces*, p. 148.

121 Steenkamp: *South Africa's Border War 1966–1989*, p. 68.

122 Andreas Shipanga: *In Search of Freedom*, p. 50.

123 Cf. Breytenbach: *Buffalo Soldiers*, p. 200.

124 De Kock: *A Long Night's Damage*, p. 65. Cf. Brigadier General McGill Alexander's opinion in his MA thesis, "The Cassinga Raid" (unpublished MA thesis, Unisa, July 2003), p. 40.

125 Dennis Finch: "11 Commando (1979–1980) Etali, Okatope, Nkurunkuru and Grootfontein", at http://sadf.sentinelprojects.com/bG-2/Finch.html.

126 Steenkamp: *South Africa's Border War 1966–1989*, p. 61.

127 Breytenbach: *Buffalo Soldiers*, p. 149. Cf. also Steenkamp: *South Africa's Border War 1966–1989*, p. 63.

128 De Kock: *A Long Night's Damage*, p. 66. This was Operation Kobra, launched in May 1976. Cf. Toase: "The South African Army: The campaign in South West Africa/Namibia since 1966", in Beckett and Pimlott (eds.): *Armed Forces & Modern Counter-Insurgency*, p. 210.

129 Brown: "Diplomacy by other means", in Leys and Saul (eds.): *Namibia's Liberation Struggle*, p. 27.

130 Ibid., p. 24.

131 Ibid., p. 25.

132 De Kock: *A Long Night's Damage*, p. 66.

133 Jack Greeff: *A Greater Share of Honour*, p. 78.

134 Alexander: "The Cassinga Raid" (unpublished MA thesis, Unisa, 2003), p. 40.

135 Steenkamp: *SA's Border War 1966–1989*, p. 71.

136 Hamann: *Days of the Generals*, p. 9.

137 Breytenbach: *Eagle Strike!*, p. 93.

138 Hamann: *Days of the Generals*, pp. 7–9.

139 Geldenhuys: *Dié wat gewen het*, p. 49.

140 Crocker: *High Noon in Southern Africa*, p. 117.

CHAPTER 3

1 Kriek van der Merwe: *Die Suid-Afrikaanse Leër-Gevegskool. Ontstaan en Ontwikkeling: 1978 tot 1996*, p.13. Cf. *White Paper on Defence and Armament Supply, 1977*, par. 10–11.

2 *White Paper on Defence and Armament Supply, April 1969*, p. 3, par. 15. This approach was again taken in the Defence and Armament Supply White Paper of 1973 (p. 5, par. 9).

3 Kriek: *Die Suid-Afrikaanse Leër-Gevegskool*, pp. 15–17; De Villiers and De Villiers: *PW*, pp. 225–227.

4 "'n Strategiese konsep vir die RSA", par. 71.18 (MV-B, Group 2, Box 152).

5 André Beaufre: *Introduction to Strategy*, p. 125.

6 André Beaufre: *Strategy of Action*, p. 110.

7 Cf. Carl von Clausewitz: *Vom Kriege*, VI/1, p. 371.

8 Beaufre: *Strategy of Action*, p. 121.

9 Roherty: *State Security in South Africa*, p. 61.

10 Magnus Malan: "Die aanslag teen Suid-Afrika" (*Strategic Review for Southern Africa*, 2/1980, pp. 8–11).

11 *White Paper on Defence and Armament Supply*, 1973, p. 1 (preface by PW Botha).

12 *White Paper on Defence and Armament Supply*, 1973, p. 4, par. 3 and 4.

13 *White Paper on Defence and Armament Supply*, 1977, p. 4, par. 2.

14 Ibid., p. 5, par. 6.

15 "Die RSA se belange en die RSA-regering se doel, doelstellings en beleid vir ordelike regering", 11.8.1980 (Aluka online archive).

16 Ibid., 5.7.1; Malan: *My lewe saam met die SA Weermag*, p. 155.

17 Malan: *My lewe saam met die SA Weermag*, 43.

18 Timothy J Stapleton: *A Military History of South Africa. From the Dutch-Khoi Wars to the End of Apartheid*, p. 155.

19 Lord: *From Fledgling to Eagle*, pp. 53 and 58; Wilkins: *Chopper Pilot*, pp. 80-91.

20 Cf. Seegers: *The Military in the Making of the Modern South Africa*, p. 141.

21 WS van der Waals: *Portugal's War in Angola 1961-1974*, passim.

22 Unpublished memoir by Roland de Vries; Greeff: *A Greater Share of Honour*, pp. 48-49; Lord: *From Fledgling to Eagle*, pp. 59-63 and 469; Stiff: *The Silent War*, ch. 15-16; John W Turner: *Continent Ablaze. Insurgency Wars in Africa 1960 to the Present*, p. 84.

23 JJ McCuen: *The Art of Counter-Revolutionary Warfare. The Strategy of Counter-Insurgency*, passim. Meiring's view was reported by Gavin Cawthra: *Brutal Force. The Apartheid War Machine*, p. 29.

24 Seegers: *The Military in the Making of the Modern South Africa*, pp. 140-141.

25 Ibid., p. 141.

26 I thank Dr Stephen Ellis of the African Studies Centre at the University of Leiden for kindly making a copy of Fraser's study available to me.

27 CA Fraser: "Lessons learnt from past revolutionary wars", pp. 1-2.

28 Ibid., pp. 4-5.

29 Ibid., p. 15.

30 *Truth and Reconciliation Commission of South Africa Report*, II, par. 158.

31 Geldenhuys: *Dié wat gewen het*, p. 64.

32 *Vide* Leopold Scholtz: *Why the Boers lost the War*, passim.

33 Brown: *The War of a Hundred Days*, passim.

34 Cf. Jack Kros: *War in Italy. With the South Africans from Taranto to the Alps* for a history of 6 SA Armoured Division's war in Italy, 1944-45.

35 George Kruys: "Doctrine development in the South African armed forces up to the 1980s", in M Hough and L du Plessis (eds.): *Selected Military Issues with Specific Reference to the Republic of South Africa*, p. 9.

36 Interview with Constand Viljoen, 26.7.1988, at www.nelsonmandela.org/omalley/index.php/site/q/03lv00017/04lv00344/05lv01183/06lv01209.htm.

37 Geldenhuys: *Dié wat gewen het*, pp. 63-64.

38 Kriek: *Die Suid-Afrikaanse Leër-Gevegskool*, pp. 17-18; Kruys: "Doctrine development in the South African armed forces up to the 1980s", in Hough and Du Plessis (eds.): *Selected Military Issues with Specific Reference to the Republic of South Africa*, p. 11.

39 Interview with Constand Viljoen, 26.7.1998.

40 Kruys: "Doctrine development in the South African armed forces up to the 1980s", in Hough and Du Plessis (eds.): *Selected Military Issues with Specific Reference to the Republic of South Africa*, p. 12.

41 Ibid.

42 *White Paper on Defence and Armament Supply*, 1975, p. 10, par. 37.

43 Kruys: "Doctrine development in the South African armed forces up to the 1980s", in Hough and Du Plessis (eds.): *Selected Military Issues with Specific Reference to the Republic of South Africa*, pp. 13-14.

44 Personal memoir by Roland de Vries; e-mail from Ep van Lill, 6.5.2011.

45 Interview with Colonel Gert van Zyl, 21.4.2006; unpublished memoir by Roland de Vries in author's possession; Sasha Polakow-Suransky: *The Unspoken Alliance. Israel's Secret Relationship with Apartheid South Africa*, pp. 97, 103 and 144. Cf. Greeff: *A Greater Share of Honour*, p. 105.

46 Jordaan: "The role of South African armour in South West Africa/Namibia and Angola: 1975-1989", pp. 169-170.

47 Unpublished memoir by Roland de Vries.

48 Ibid.

49   Ibid.

50   Roherty: *State Security in South Africa*, pp. 102–103.

51   R de Vries and Gl McCaig: "Mobile Warfare in Southern Africa", (August 1987, pp. 12 en 13–14).

52   Unpublished memoir by Roland de Vries.

53   Steenkamp: *South Africa's Border War 1966–1989*, p.61.

54   Malan: *My lewe saam met die SA Weermag*, p. 143.

55   Kriek: *Die Suid-Afrikaanse Leër-Gevegskool*, p. 17.

56   Cf. Du Preez: *Avontuur in Angola*, pp. 144–145.

57   Wilsworth: *First In, Last Out*, pp. 142 and 193.

58   *White Paper on Defence and Armament Supply*, 1977, p. 27.

59   For the technical aspects surrounding the Ratel, vide Helmoed-Römer Heitman: *Krygstuig van Suid-Afrika*, pp. 47–54.

60   Cf. "BMP-1 Infantry Fighting Vehicle (Russia)", at www.historyofwar.org/articles/weapons_bmp1.html.

61   Frank Bestbier: "1978", at www.61mech.org.za/years/1978.

62   Johann Dippenaar: "1979", at www.61mech.org.za/years/1979.

63   An Israeli-designed 155-mm howitzer, the G-4, was a stop-gap measure. It was used in action on only one occasion during Operation Askari in December 1983 and January 1984. Wilsworth: *First In, Last Out*, pp. 132–138

64   IB Greeff: "South Africa's modern Long Tom" (*Military History Journal*, 9/1, June 1992).

65   Bastiaan Verhoek: "Denel shatters artillery records" (*South African Soldier*, July 2006, p. 13).

66   Cf. *White Paper on Defence and Armament Supply*, 1986, p. 12.

67   Polakow-Suransky: *The Unspoken Alliance*, p. 97; Nortje: *32 Battalion*, p. 125.

68   *White Paper on Defence and Armament Supply*, 1977, p. 18; *White Paper on Defence and Armament Supply*, 1979, p. 5; Merran Willis Phillips: "The End Conscription Campaign 1983–1988. A Study of White Extra-Parliamentary Opposition to Apartheid" (unpublished MA thesis, Unisa, 2002, pp. 6–22).

69   Cf. Malan: *My lewe saam met die SA Weermag*, p. 97

70   *White Paper on the Organization and Functions of the South African Defence Force and the Armaments Corporation of South Africa*, 1984, p. 35, par. 234.

CHAPTER 4

1   Brown: "Diplomacy by other means – SWAPO's liberation war", in Leys and Saul (eds.): *Namibia's Liberation Struggle*, p. 22.

2   Cf. Wallace: *A History of Namibia*, p. 287; Loraine Gordon, Suzanne Blignaut, Carole Cooper and Linda Ensor: *Survey of Race Relations in South Africa, 1978*, pp. 517–518. For a (negative) SWAPO view on these developments see Katjavivi: *A History of Resistance in Namibia*, pp. 84–103.

3   MI/204/3/N4/2, "SWA/N: Uitbouing van die interne demokratiese partye tot 'n effektiewe, daadkragtige politieke teenvoeter vir SWAPO", 22.5.1981 (61 Mech online archive).

4   Interview with Neil Barnard, 17.9.1998, at www.nelsonmandela.org/omalley/index.php/site/q/03lv00017/04lv00344/05lv01183/06lv01252.htm.

5   Stapleton: *A Military History of South Africa*, pp. 155–156.

6   *White Paper on Defence and Armaments Supply*, 1986, p. 30, par. 142; Geldenhuys: *Dié wat gewen het*, pp. 75 and 77. Cf. also Philip H Frankel: *Pretoria's Praetorians. Civil-Military Relations in South Affrica*, pp. 116–123; Kenneth W Grundy: *Soldiers without Politics. Blacks in the South African Armed Forces*, pp. 252–267.

7   Quoted in Robert Scott Jaster: *The Defence of White Power. South African Policy under Pressure*, p. 91. Cf. also Daan Prinsloo: *Stem uit die Wildernis. 'n Biografie van oud-pres. PW Botha*, p. 133.

8   *Witskrif oor Verdediging en Krygstuigvoorsiening*, 1984, p. 1, paragraaf 3; Malan: *My lewe saam met die SA Weermag*, p. 67.

9   MI/204/3/A6/1: "Moontlike implikasies van optrede teen SWAPO in Angola", 3.6.1981, par. 4 (61 Mech online archive). Cf. also

White Paper on Defence and Armament Supply, 1981, p. 1, par. 4, where the same allegation is made.

10   CIA: "Soviet policy and Africa", 23.2.1981, p. 9.

11   CIA: "Moscow's response to the diplomatic challenge in Southern Africa", 5.1.1984.

12   CIA: "Soviet policy and Africa", 23.2.1981, p. 2.

13   CIA: "Soviet policies in Southern Africa", 13.2.1985, p. 9.

14   Disa, Minutes of State Security Council Meeting, 28.1.1980, at www.disa. ukzn.ac.za/index.php?option=com_ content&view=article&id=44&Itemid=61.

15   Cf. Disa, "Riglyne vir die Staatsveiligheidsraad om 'n langtermyn nasionale strategie ten opsigte van selfverdedigingsaksies te formuleer, bylae A", attached to minutes of State Security Council, 12.2.1979, at www. disa.ukzn.ac.za/index.php? option=com_displaydc&recordID=min 19790212.040.024.079.

16   Shubin: *The Hot "Cold War"*, pp. 3 and 82.

17   Cf. "SVR guidelines for ZR: The Republic of South Africa's national security objectives, policy and guidelines", in Sue Onslow: "Documents. South Africa and Zimbabwe-Rhodesian independence, 1979–1980, document 3 (*Cold War History*, 7/2, p. 310).

18   Sue Onslow: "South Africa and the Owen/ Vance Plan of 1977" (*South African Historical Journal*, 51/2004, p. 135).

19   Pik Botha – Al Haig, 19.5.1981 (Aluka online archive). Cf. also Brand Fourie: *Brandpunte*, pp. 176–178. In a secret planning document in January 1980, the SADF spelled it out rather crudely: "The RSA plans to have the political system in SWA in such a manner that a pro-SA government be put in power there." See MI/204/3/A6/1: "Aanwending van UNITA om RSA doelwitte te bevredig", 24.1.1980 (61 Mech online archive).

20   Pik Botha – Cabinet colleagues, 23.6.1981 (Aluka online archive). Cf. Fourie: *Brandpunte*, pp. 178–183; Crocker: *High Noon in Southern Africa*, pp. 98–102.

21   In February 1979 the Security Council even decided to formulate a strategy that would lead SWAPO to renounce Resolution 435. In hindsight this was very naive. See "SVR

riglyne vir 'n Suidelike Afrika-strategie: SWA en Angola", 12.2.1979, par. 5(a)(1)(i) (HIS/ AMI, Group 6, Box 125).

22   "Summary notes of a meeting between a South African and a Unites States delegation on the question of South West Africa: Geneva, 21 April 1986", p. 2 (Aluka online archive). Cf. also Richard Leonard: *South Africa at War. White Power and the Crisis in Southern Africa*, pp. 250–251; Susan Cullinan: "Military policy and the Namibian dispute" (South African Research Service: *South African Review*, I, p. 34).

23   MI/204/3/A6/1: "Aanwending van UNITA om RSA doelwitte te bevredig", 24.1.1980 (61 Mech online archive), par. 4, 24.1.1980 (61 Mech online archive).

24   In 1978, part of PW Botha's reasoning for unleashing Operation Reindeer on SWAPO was: "Die SWAPO-mag moes gebreek word voordat verkiesing gehou word." Cf. De Villiers and De Villiers: *PW*, p. 341. Cf. Geldenhuys: *Dié wat gewen het*, p. 49.

25   Hamann: *Days of the Generals*, pp. 78–79.

26   Geldenhuys: *Dié wat gewen het*, p. 72.

27   Hamann: *Days of the Generals*, pp. 54–57.

28   Frankel: *Pretoria's Praetorians*, pp. 72–73.

29   Geldenhuys: *Dié wat gewen het*, p. 49.

30   Breytenbach: *Buffalo Soldiers*, p. 179.

31   Nortje: *32 Battalion*, p. 44.

32   Alexander: "The Cassinga Raid", pp. 35–36.

33   Roherty: *State Security in South Africa*, p. 102.

34   HS Ops/305/1/1/2, "The SADF basic doctrine for counter insurgency (rural)", November 1977, par. 5 (document provided by Lt. Col. Prof. Dr Abel Esterhuyse).

35   Ibid., par. 5, 6, 9 and 40.

36   Roherty: *State Security in South Africa*, p.50.

37   Ken Flower: *Serving Secretly. Rhodesia's CIO Chief on Record*, p. 257.

38   Disa, Memorandum HSAW – Voorsitter van die SVR Werkkomitee, 15.3.1979, at www. disa.ukzn.ac.za/index.php?option=com_ displaydc&recordID=mem19790315. 040.024.079. Cf. *TRC Report*, II, p. 55.

39   Sue Onslow: Documents (P Killen, 19.1.1979).

40   *TRC Report*, II, p. 57.

41   MI/203/4/0502: "Angola: Unita invloed op die Angolese situasie en RSA-hulp sedert

Operasie Savannah", par. 21, 22 and 28, 15.2.1979 (61 Mech online archive).

42 Owen Ellison Kahn: "Cuba's impact on Southern Africa (*Journal of Interamerican Studies and World Affairs*, 29/3, Autumn 1987, р. 43).

43 See the agreement in *White Paper: Exchanges of Letters on Defence Matters between the Governments of the Union of South Africa and the United Kingdom*, June 1955.

44 Glen Syndercombe: "Positive Aspects of Actions of the SADF and in particular the SA Navy in the 1980s", at navy.org.za/pages/syndercombe; Wessels: "The South African Navy during the years of conflict in Southern Africa, 1966–1989" (*Journal of Contemporary History*, 31/3, 2006, p. 285).

45 Rear Admiral Chris Bennett discussed all of this extensively in his *Three Frigates*, pp. 177–184. Cf. Thean Potgieter: "The geopolitical role of the South African Navy in the South African sphere of influence after the Second World War" (*Strategic Review for Southern Africa*, June 2002).

46 Wessels: "The South African Navy during the years of conflict in Southern Africa, 1966–1989" (*Journal of Contemporary History*, 31/3, December 2006, pp. 295–296).

47 Syndercombe: "Positive Aspects of Actions of the SADF and in Particular the SA Navy in the 1980s", at navy.org.za/pages/syndercombe.

48 Cf. for instance Appendix G in operation instruction 32/88: "Landwaartse konvensionele operasionele plan: Op Pact", s.d., par. 4 (document provided by Roland de Vries); "Lesse geleer tydens konvensionele operasies in die westelike subteater", s.d., Appendix A, Introduction, par. 7 (document provided by Roland de Vries); ST/310/4/Kassala/3: "Angola: Unita strategie", par. 2, 11.11.1985 (group 4, box 160, p. 23).

49 Margaret Thatcher Foundation: "Shultz memo for Reagan", 6.6.1983, at www.margaretthatcher.org/archive/displaydocument.asp?docid=110535.

50 SA government – Angolan government, 3.4.1981 (Aluka online archive).

51 MI/203/4/0502: "Angola: Unita invloed op die Angolese situasie en RSA-hulp sedert Operasie Savannah", par. 5, 15.2.1979

(61 Mech online archive); "Angola group discussion: Oaklands, Virginia", 18.3.1983, p. 15 (Aluka online archive).

52 "Minutes of a meeting between Pik Botha and Chester Crocker", 27.1.1984, p. 3; "Minutes of a meeting between Pik Botha and Robert McFarlane, US National Security Advisor," 8.8.1985, p. 4 (Aluka online archive).

53 "Minutes of a meeting between Pik Botha and Chester Crocker", 31.10.1984, p. 6 (Aluka online archive).

54 "Samesprekings: Staatspresident met Kabinet van die Oorgangsregering van Nasionale Eenheid (Orne) van SWA", 21.5.1985, p. 11 (Aluka online archive).

55 "Bilateral consultations between the Republic of South Africa and the United States", 17–18.3.1983, par. 6 (Aluka online archive). The SADF Directorate of Military Intelligence concurred: Cf. MI/204/3/A6/1: "Aanwending van UNITA om RSA doelwitte te bevredig", par. 14, 24.1.1980 (61 Mech online archive).

56 MI/203/4/0502: "Angola: Unita invloed op die Angolese situasie en RSA-hulp sedert Operasie Savannah", par. 14, 15.2.1979 (61 Mech online archive).

57 Assis Malaquias: "Angola's foreign policy since independence: The search for domestic security" (*African Security Review*, 9/3, 2000, pp. 34–46).

58 "United States policy towards Angola", National Security-Decision Directive Number 274, 7 May, 1987, at www.gwu.edu/~nsarchiv/nsa/publications/DOC_readers/saread/sa870507.jpg.

59 Gleijeses: *Conflicting Missions*, p. 307.

60 Gleijeses: "Moscow's Proxy? Cuba and Africa 1975–1988" (*Journal of Cold War Studies*, 8/2, Spring 2006, p. 25).

61 Pik Botha described the agreement in some detail to his cabinet colleagues. Cf. Pik Botha – Cabinet colleagues, 23.6.1981 (Aluka online archive); Fourie: *Brandpunte*, pp. 178–183.

62 "Meeting between South Africa and Angola, Ilha do Sal, Cape Verde", 7.12.1982, passim (Aluka online archive).

63 "Minutes of the State Security Council", 28.1.1980 (Disa online archive).

64 Ibid.
65 Crocker: *High Noon in Southern Africa*, p. 65.
66 Saunders: "The foreign policy of Angola under Agostinho Neto", pp. 73–74, 76 and 88.

CHAPTER 5

1   Breytenbach: *Buffalo Soldiers*, pp. 179 and 185. Cf. Nortje: *32 Battalion*, pp. 99–128; Bothma: *Die Buffel Struikel*, p. 255.
2   Stiff: *The Silent War*, pp. 192–193; Els: *We Fear Naught but God*, pp. 222–228; Breytenbach: *Buffalo Soldiers*, pp. 184–185.
3   Lieneke de Visser: "Winning the Hearts and Minds. Legitimacy in the Namibian Border War" (unpublished MA thesis, University of Utrecht, August 2010), p. 14.
4   Bothma: *Die Buffel Struikel*, p. 186.
5   *TRC Report*, II, p. 47.
6   Breytenbach: *Eagle Strike!*, p. 65.
7   "Voorlegging oor die noodsaaklikheid van oorwoë militêre operasies teen SWAPO in Angola", n.d. (61 Mech online archive).
8   Alexander: "The Cassinga Raid" (unpublished MA thesis, Unisa, July 2003), p. 38.
9   "Voorligting: H Leër 12 Apr. 78" (61 Mech online archive).
10 Some of them were later discovered among the "refugees" at Cassinga.
11 CJ Nöthling: "Operasie Reindeer", pp. 5–6 (61 Mech online archive).
12 De Villiers and De Villiers: *PW*, pp. 340–341.
13 Frank Bestbier: "Dagboek Veggroep Juliet", p. 1 (61 Mech online archive); Nöthling: "Operasie Reindeer", p. 11–13 (61 Mech online archive).
14 Breytenbach: *Buffalo Soldiers*, p. 179.
15 Stiff: *The Silent War*, pp. 193–201; Els: *We Fear Naught but God*, pp. 46–52; Breytenbach: *Buffalo Soldiers*, pp. 204–206; Bothma: *Die Buffel Struikel*, ch. 5.
16 Breytenbach: *Eagle Strike!*, p. 100; Greeff: *A Greater Share of Honour*, pp. 38–46; Joseph Kobo: *Waiting in the Wing*, p. 133.
17 Brigadier Martiens du Plessis, who was appointed OC of 44 Parachute Brigade, later falsely claimed that he was in overall command of the Cassinga attack. There had been a long history of enmity between him and Breytenbach. Although he jumped into the battle at Cassinga all sources categorically state that Breytenbach was in command. In fact it is claimed that Du Plessis's presence led to some irritation since he interfered in Breytenbach's handling of the battle, to the detriment of the South Africans.
18 Unless otherwise stated the description of the battle is taken from the following sources: Breytenbach: *Eagle Strike!*, passim; Steenkamp: *Borderstrike!*, book 3, chapters 1–2 and 4–17; Alexander: "The Cassinga raid"; Mike McWilliams: *Battle for Cassinga: South Africa's Controversial Cross-Border Raid, Angola 1978*, passim; and Nöthling: "Operasie Reindeer", chapters 1, 2 and 4 (61 Mech online archive). The Air Force's contribution is chronicled by Dick Lord: *From Fledgling to Eagle*, pp. 81–87 and Monster Wilkens: *Chopper Pilot*, pp. 96–99. There are numerous accounts from SWAPO's side, but few are really useful. Many accounts come across as outright propaganda, while others clearly show military ignorance. Alexander and Breytenbach have discussed these at length.
19 Breytenbach: *Eagle Strike!*, pp. 147–148.
20 "Voorligting oor Operasie Reindeer", n.d. (61 Mech online archive).
21 In this regard I share the views expressed by Willem Steenkamp (*Borderstrike!*, pp. 348–349).
22 Kobo: *Waiting in the Wing*, pp. 133–134.
23 Ibid., pp. 141–143; Breytenbach: *Eagle Strike!*, pp. 365–367.
24 "El attaque a Cassinga (1)", at http://laultimaguerra.com/2009/10/27/el-ataque-a-cassinga-i/.
25 Dries Marais: "Buccaneer to the rescue", at www.avcollect.com/marais.htm.
26 Annemarie Heywood: *The Cassinga Event*, p. 46.
27 Quoted by Alexander: "The Cassinga raid", p. 170.
28 Dale Lautenbach: "Namibia recalls its bloody past" (*Sowetan*, 26.5.1992); SWAPO: *Massacre at Kassinga*, p. 17. (In fact, the South African army had abolished bayonets a few years before. Cf. Breytenbach: *Eagle Strike!*, pp. 118–119.)
29 Quoted by Brady Ridgway: "No evidence to support Vigne's claims on Cassinga" (*Sunday Independent*, 20.1.2008).
30 Piero Gleijeses: "The massacre of Cassinga",

at http://amadlandawonye.wikispaces.com/
page/diff/The+Massacre+of+Cassinga%
2C+Piero+Gleijeses/657945.

31 Cawthra: *Brutal Force*, p. 149.

32 Heywood: *The Cassinga Event*,
pp. 15–22 and 33–34.

33 *TRC Report*, II, p. 50.

34 "Statement by Sam Nujoma, leader of
SWAPO: Dialogue between the Southern
African liberation movements (ANC, PAC
and SWAPO) and the Churches, Lusaka,
Zambia", 4.8.5.1987 (Aluka online archive).
Cf. "Thank you, Cuba" (*New African*,
April 2008).

35 Sam Nujoma: "Foreword", in Mvula ya
Nangolo and Tor Sellström: *Kassinga. A
Story Untold*, pp. v-vi. Cf. "Thank you,
Cuba" (*New African*, April 2008).

36 "Battle of Cassinga still rages", (The
*Star*19.5.2007).

37 Breytenbach: *Eagle Strike!*, p. 211.

38 Ibid., pp. 409–414; Alexander: "The
Cassinga Raid", appendix A to chapter 3. An
SAAF aerial photograph analyst involved
in the planning devotes several pages in
his book to an extensive analysis of the
photographs. See Peet Coetzee: *Special
Forces "Jam Stealer". The Memoirs of a
Specialist who served in Special Forces and
Defence Force of South Africa*, pp. 43–69.

39 Alexander: "The Cassinga raid", p. 55.

40 Breytenbach: *Eagle Strike!*, pp. 97–98.

41 "Voorlegging oor die noodsaaklikheid van
oorwoë militêre operasies teen SWAPO
in Angola", n.d., par. 11–12 (61 Mech
online archive).

42 Alexander: "The Cassinga raid", pp. 53–54.

43 *TRC Report*, II, p. 53.

44 Alexander: "The Cassinga raid", appendix
9B-6 and 9B-7.

45 Heywood: *The Cassinga Event*, p. 7.

46 I Fall: *Report on a Mission to SWAPO
Centres for Namibian Refugees in Angola
from 10 to 14 April 1978*, p. 6.

47 Heywood: *The Cassinga Event*, p. 6.

48 Kobo: *Waiting in the Wing*, pp. 133, 139,
141 and 142.

49 Breytenbach: *Eagle Strike!*, p. 208.

50 Alexander: "The Cassinga raid",
pp. 132–133.

51 Christian A Williams: "Exile history: An

ethnography of the SWAPO camps and the
Namibian question" (unpublished D Phil
thesis, University of Michigan, 2009), p. 64.

52 Alexander: "The Cassinga raid", pp. 64–65.
Alexander was mercilessly attacked by
Colonel Jan Breytenbach, Captain Tommie
Lamprecht and others, who alleged that he
"accused the paratroopers and aircrews of
massacring civilians at Cassinga" and of
treating "the unadulterated rubbish released
by SWAPO and Co with reverence", while
"regarding the evidence supplied by his fellow
paratroopers with suspicious circumspection".
(Breytenbach: *Eagle Strike!*, p. xv). I regard
Breytenbach very highly as an operational
commander, but here he perhaps protests
too much and incorrectly attributes certain
viewpoints to Alexander. Breytenbach and
the other critics do not seem to understand
that Alexander merely followed academic
procedure. Alexander defended himself very
well – see McGill Alexander: "Response
to Tommie Lamprecht and others" (*Army
Talk Magazine*, March, 2008, pp. 6–13).
Furthermore, Breytenbach acknowledges
in his book that there were women and
civilians at Cassinga, in the same way as there
were civilians at the SADF headquarters at
Oshakati and Rundu in the north of Namibia.
(Breytenbach: *Eagle Strike!*, pp. 146–147.)

53 Steenkamp: *Borderstrike!*, p. 227.

54 *TRC Report*, II, p. 50.

55 The formation was named after its first
commander, Commandant Joep Joubert, call
sign "Juliet Juliet".

56 Personal memoir by Roland de Vries.

57 E-mail from Ep van Lill, 6.5.2011.

58 Ibid.

59 Bothma: *Die Buffel Struikel*, p. 268.

60 E-mail from Hans Kriek, 13.1.2011. Cf.
Bothma: *Die Buffel Struikel*, pp. 205–211.

61 E-mail from Ep van Lill, 6.5.2011.

62 Unless stated otherwise, the following analysis
is based on ops order 1/1978, battle group
Juliet, 30.4.1978 (61 Mech online archive); ops
order 2/1978, battle Group Juliet, 30.4.1978
(61 Mech online archive); Bestbier: "Dagboek
Veggroep Juliet", passim (61 Mech online
archive); Frank Bestbier: "Verslag: Ops
Reindeer: Aanval op teiken Bravo, 4 Mei
1978", 12.5.1978 (61 Mech online archive); Ep

van Lill: "Geskiedenis Ops Reindeer", 8.5.1978 (61 Mech online archive); Nöthling: "Operasie Reindeer", chapter 3 (61 Mech online archive); e-mail from Ep van Lill, 6.5.2011; Steenkamp: *Borderstrike!*, Book 2, chapters 3 and 12-16.

63 Quoted by Bestbier: "Dagboek Veggroep Juliet", p. 10 (61 Mech online archive).

64 Bestbier: "Dagboek Veggroep Juliet", p. 11 (61 Mech online archive).

65 Bothma: *Anderkant Cuito*, p. 58; e-mail from Ep van Lill, 6.5.2011.

66 E-mail from Ep van Lill, 6.5.2011.

67 Bestbier: "Dagboek Veggroep Juliet", p. 20 (61 Mech online archive).

68 Unless otherwise stated, this section is based on Nöthling: "Operation Reindeer", pp. 33-38; Steenkamp: *Borderstrike!*, pp. 340-343; Breytenbach: *Buffalo Soldiers*, pp. 209-210; Nortje: *32 Battalion*, pp. 128-132; Bothma: *Die Buffel Struikel*, 224-227; Wilsworth: *First In, Last Out*, pp. 160-162.

69 Polakow-Suransky: *The Unspoken Alliance*, pp. 131 and 272.

70 Cf. Breytenbach: *Eagle Strike!*, pp. 453-477 for a discussion of 44 Parachute Brigade.

71 Personal memoir by Roland de Vries.

72 Nortje: *32 Battalion*, p. 135; Alexander: "The Cassinga raid", p. 176.

73 Breytenbach: *Buffalo Soldiers*, p. 210.

74 Alexander: "The Cassinga raid", p. 178.

75 Georg Meiring: "Current SWAPO activity in South West Africa" (*Strategic Review for Southern Africa*, 1/1985, p. 9); Geldenhuys: *Dié wat gewen het*, p. 85.

76 Dippenaar: "1979", at www.61mech.org.za/years/1979.

77 "Media analysis: Operation Reindeer", p. 3, par. 14a (61 Mech online archive).

78 Alexander: "The Cassinga raid", p. 168.

79 Ibid., p. 179.

80 Crocker: *High Noon in Southern Africa*, p. 57.

CHAPTER 6

1 Intelligence report WF/227/11.5.1978 (61 Mech online archive).

2 Unless otherwise stated, this section is based on Steenkamp: *Borderstrike!*, pp. 366-382; Geldenhuys: *Dié wat gewen het*, pp. 80-85; Lord: *From Fledgling to Eagle*, pp. 90-91; Wilsworth: *First In, Last Out*, pp. 169-170;

Tinus de Jager: "Caprivi April 1977-Desember 1979 – die grens", in Geldenhuys (ed.): *Ons was Daar*, pp. 89-92.

3 Geldenhuys: *Dié wat gewen het*, p. 85.

4 Saunders: "The foreign policy of Angola under Agostinho Neto", p. 90.

5 Lord: *From Fledgling to Eagle*, pp. 109-112; Heitman: *South African Armed Forces*, pp. 152-153; a anonymous SADF soldier wrote about his experience (or lack of it) during this operation. See Anonymous.: "Operation Safraan Southern Zambia 1979", at www.samagte.co.za/phpbbs/viewtopic.php?f=50&t=452.

6 Geldenhuys: *Dié wat gewen het*, p. 87.

7 Ibid., p. 90.

8 Heitman: *South African War Machine*, p. 155.

9 RS Lord: "Operation Askari. A sub-commander's retrospective view of the operation" (*Militaria*, 22/4, 1992, p. 1).

10 Hamann: *Days of the Generals*, pp. 66-67. Cf. also Colin Leys and John S Saul: "SWAPO: The politics of exile", in Leys and Saul (eds.): *Namibia's Liberation Struggle*, p. 55.

11 Nortje: *32 Battalion*, pp. 7-8.

12 Johann Dippenaar: "Operation Carrot, 1979", at www.61mech.org.za/operations/3-operation-carrot.

13 Roland de Vries: "Operation Carrot, 1980", at www.61mech.org.za/operations/4-operation-carrot.

14 Geldenhuys: *Dié wat gewen het*, pp. 94-95; Steenkamp: *South Africa's Border War 1966-1989*, p. 90.

15 Heitman: *South African Armed Forces*, p, 154.

16 Johann Dippenaar: War Diary, Battle Group 61, Operation Sceptic, n.d. par. 1-2 (61 Mech online archive).

17 Anon.: "Platform for peace: The history of the Joint Monitoring Commission from the South African perspective", p. 3 (Aluka online archive).

18 Information about the objective of the operation and the composition of the invading force derived from Johann Dippenaar: War diary, Battle Group 61, Operation Sceptic, n.d., par. 3-6 (61 Mech online archive); Steenkamp: *Borderstrike!*, pp. 392-394; Geldenhuys: *Dié wat gewen het*, pp. 94-95; Nortje: *32 Battalion*, pp. 153-154; Wilsworth: *First In, Last Out*, pp. 184-186.

19 Dippenaar: "Operation Sceptic" (61 Mech online archive).

20 A SWAPO publication says 900 men. See Oswin O Namakalu: *Armed Liberation Struggle. Some Accounts of PLAN's Combat Operations*, p. 83.

21 Dippenaar: War diary, Battle Group 61, Operation Sceptic, n.d., par. 39–40 (61 Mech online archive).

22 Dippenaar: War diary, Battle Group 61, Operation Sceptic, n.d., par. 42 (61 Mech online archive)

23 Dippenaar: "Operation Sceptic", at www.61mech.org.za/operations/5-operation-sceptic.

24 Lord: *From Fledgling to Eagle*, pp. 148–158; Nortje: *32 Battalion*, pp. 155–156.

25 Coetzee: *Special Forces "Jam Stealer"*, p. 182.

26 Unless stated otherwise, the analysis of the Battle of Smokeshell is drawn from the following sources: Dippenaar: War diary, Battle Group 61, Operation Sceptic, n.d., par. 44–125; "Nabetragtingsverslag: Ops Sceptic, Artillerie", n.d.; "Nabetragtingsverslag: Ops Sceptic, log/pers: 61 Bn Gp", n.d. (61 Mech online archive); "Nabetragtingsverslag: Ops Sceptic, LWT bedryfsprobleme", n.d. (61 Mech online archive); "Nabetragtingsverslag: Ops Sceptic, Vegspan 1", n.d. (61 Mech online archive); "Nabetragtingsverslag: Ops Sceptic, Vegspan 2", n.d. (61 Mech online archive); "Nabetragtingsverslag: Ops Sceptic, Vegspan 3", n.d. (61 Mech online archive); "Nabetragtingsverslag: logistiek/personeel stats", n.d. (61 Mech online archive); Steenkamp: *Borderstrike!*, pp. 390–430; Heitman: *South African War Machine*, p. 155; Nortje: *32 Battalion*, pp. 155–156; Geldenhuys: *Dié wat gewen het*, p. 95; Wilsworth: *First In, Last Out*, pp. 187–191; Lord: *From Fledgling to Eagle*, pp. 148–159.

27 Personal memoir of Corporal Gareth Rutherford, at www.61mech.org.za/operations/5-operation-sceptic.

28 WS Bornman: "Op Sceptic – Ratel 21 se kanonnier se herinneringe", at http://www.61mech.org.za/operations/5-operation-sceptic#stories-photos.

29 Marco Caforio: "Op Sceptic – my story of Smokeshell", at www.61mech.org.za/operations/5-operation-sceptic.

30 Paul Louw: "Op Sceptic: Tweede luitenant Paul Louw van roepsein 21 se storie", at www.61mech.org.za/operations/5-operation-sceptic.

31 Bornman: "Op Sceptic – Ratel 21 se kanonnier se herinneringe".

32 Louis Bothma: "Die pyn lê nog vlak" (*Die Burger*, 10.6.2008).

33 Coetzee: *Special Forces "Jam Stealer"*, pp. 192–193.

34 Heitman: *South African Armed Forces*, p. 155.

35 Dippenaar: War diary, Battle Group 61, Operation Sceptic, n.d., par. 135 (61 Mech online archive).

36 Geldenhuys: *Dié wat gewen het*, pp. 95–96.

37 Johannes "Mistake" Gaomab: "With the People's Liberation Army of Namibia in Angola", in Colin Leys en Susan Brown (eds.): *Life Histories of Namibia. Living through the Liberation Struggle*, p. 67.

38 Geldenhuys: *Dié wat gewen het*, pp. 97–98; Dippenaar: War diary, Battle Group 61, Operation Sceptic, n.d., par. 154–216; Steenkamp: *Borderstrike!*, pp. 440–448.

39 Steenkamp: *Borderstrike!*, pp.449–452; Nortje: *32 Battalion*, p. 156.

40 Dippenaar: "Operation Sceptic" (61 Mech online archive).

41 Fouché: "Nabetragtingsverslag: Ops Sceptic, Vegspan 1", par. 26 (61 Mech online archive).

42 Harmse: "Nabetragtingsverslag: Ops Sceptic, Vegspan 2", n.d., par. 5 (61 Mech online archive); Jacobs: "Nabetragtingsverslag: Ops Sceptic, Vegspan 3", n.d., par. 2 (61 Mech online archive).

43 Dippenaar: War diary, Battle Group 61, Operation Sceptic, n.d., par. 40 (61 Mech online archive).

44 Steenkamp: *Borderstrike!*, p. 416.

45 Wilsworth: *First In, Last Out*, p. 226.

46 Heitman: *South African Armed Forces*, p. 157; Nortje: *32 Battalion*, p. 156.

47 Military Intelligence: "Die militêre bedreiging en die RSA", par. 60. I thank Lieutenant-Colonel Prof. Dr. Abel Esterhuyse for this reference.

48 Steenkamp: *South Africa's Border War 1966–1989*, pp. 94–95.

CHAPTER 7

1 Geldenhuys: *Dié wat gewen het*, p. 114.

2   Breytenbach: *Buffalo Soldiers*, pp. 220–221; Nortje: *32 Battalion*, pp. 158–159 and 165–166. See Granger Korff: *19 with a Bullet. A South African Paratrooper in Angola*, pp. 174–191, for a personal account of one of these clashes with FAPLA.

3   H Leër/IG/305/3/1: "Notule: Nabetragtingskonferensie Operasie Protea, 9 en 10 September 1981 te Grootfontein", 23.10.1981, par. 8 (61 Mech online archive). Nortje: *32 Battalion*, pp. 166–169; Heitman: *South African Armed Forces*, pp. 158–159.

4   MI/309/4 Protea: "Briefing: Op Protea", 9.11.1981., par. 5–6 (61 Mech online archive).

5   Heitman: *South African Armed Forces*, p. 159; Geldenhuys: *Dié wat Gewen het*, p. 114.

6   CJ Lloyd: "Voorgestelde ops ontwerp vir eksterne ops in Suid-Angola (aanhangsel A by Bevelvoerdersdagboek, Veggroep 20)", d.d. May 1981 (61 Mech online archive).

7   Ibid.

8   MI/309/4 Protea: "Briefing: Op Protea", 9.11.1981, par. 2 (61 Mech online archive).

9   Breytenbach: *Buffalo Soldiers*, p. 220.

10 MI/309/4 Protea: "Briefing: Op Protea", 9.11.1981, par. 3 (61 Mech online archive).

11 Nortje: *32 Battalion*, p. 169. Marion Wallace (*A History of Namibia*, p. 297) alleges that 10 000 troops participated, which is highly exaggerated. Like much of the book, it is unclear what her source is.

12 MI/309/4 Protea: "Briefing: Op Protea", 9.11.1981, par. 9 (61 Mech online archive); H Leër/IG/305/3/1: "Notule: Nabetragtingskonferensie Operasie Protea, 9 en 10 September 1981 te Grootfontein", 23.10.1981, par. 6 (61 Mech online archive).

13 Unpublished memoir by Roland de Vries.

14 Breytenbach: *Buffalo Soldiers*, p. 242.

15 Roland de Vries: "OPSO 1/81: Ops Protea", 14.8.1981, p. 2 (provided by Roland de Vries); "War Diary of Charlie Squadron of 61 Mechanised Battalion Group", entry of 5.8.1981 (provided by Roland de Vries); Johann Dippenaar: "OPSO 1/81, 309/1 Oef. Konyn", 8.8.1981, par. 4, (61 Mech online archive);

Dippenaar: "Operasie Protea: Veggroep 20 bevelvoerdersdagboek", par. 4 (61 Mech online archive); Nortje: *32 Battalion*, p. 169; Breytenbach: *Buffalo Soldiers*, p. 223.

16 Wilsworth: *First In, Last Out*, pp. 201–202.

17 Lord: *From Fledgling to Eagle*, p. 220.

18 "Inligtingsnabetragting: Ops Protea: Leër HK", Sept. 1981, par. 3.

19 MI/309/4 Protea: "Briefing: Op Protea", 9.11.1981, par. 8 (61 Mech online archive).

20 "Bevelswaardering: Yankee Suid (aanhangsel I by bevelvoedersdagboek Veggroep 20", 4.8.1981, par. 1–9 (61 Mech online archive); "Situasie: Aanhangsel A by OPSO 1/81", n.d., par. 1a and 1b (61 Mech online archive).

21 "Tak[tiese] waard[ering]: Yankee Suid, aanhangsel J, bevelvoerdersdagboek Veggroep 20", 5.8.1981, par. 36, (61 Mech online archive).

22 "Tak[tiese] waard[ering]: Yankee Suid", 5.8.1981, par. 5 (61 Mech online archive).

23 MI/309/4 Protea: "Briefing: Op. Protea", 9.11.1981, par. 13; Dippenaar: "OPSO 1/81, 309/1 Oef. Konyn", 8.8.1981 par. 5 and 6 (61 Mech online archive); Dippenaar: "Operasie Protea: Veggroep 20 bevelvoerdersdagboek", map on p. 12b (61 Mech online archive); De Vries: "OPSO 1/81: Ops Protea", 14.8.1981, p. 3 (provided by Roland de Vries); AFB Grootfontein – 10 Forward Air Controller Post, 26.8.1981 (61 Mech online archive); Breytenbach: *Buffalo Soldiers*, pp. 223–224.

24 "Situasie: Aanhangsel A by OPSO 1/81", n.d., par. 1(b)(iii)(f)(f) and 1(c) (61 Mech online archive).

25 Breytenbach: *Buffalo Soldiers*, p. 226.

26 E-mail from Roland de Vries, 17.1.2011.

27 Koos Liebenberg: "Chronologiese volgorde Operasie Protea", n.d. (61 Mech online archive).

28 E-mail from Johann Dippenaar, 7.3.2011.

29 Unless stated otherwise, the analysis of the Battle of Xangongo is based on the following sources: MI/309/4 Protea: "Briefing: Op Protea", 9.11.1981 par. 14–19; (61 Mech online archive); "H Leër nabetragting: Op Protea", 9.12.1981 (61 Mech online archive); Dippenaar: "Operasie Protea: Veggroep 20 bevelvoerdersdagboek" par. 57–89 (61 Mech online archive); Koos Liebenberg: "Chronologiese volgorde Operasie Protea"

par. 15–22 (61 Mech online archive); "War Diary of Charlie Squadron of 61 Mech", entries of 24–25.8.1981 (provided by Roland de Vries); Jan Breytenbach: "44 Parachute Brigade's pathfinder company during Operation Protea" (61 Mech online archive); Breytenbach: *Buffalo Soldiers*, pp. 222–228; Nortje: *32 Battalion*, pp. 169–176;Wilsworth: *First In, Last Out*, pp. 194–216; Lord: *From Fledgling to Eagle*, pp. 167–187; Heitman: *South African Armed Forces*, pp. 159–164; Steenkamp: *South Africa's Border War 1966–1989*, pp. 88–89; Stiff: *The Silent War*, pp. 352–357; Geldenhuys: *Dié wat gewen het*, pp. 114–120; personal memoir by Roland de Vries.

30 H Leër/IG/305/3/1: "Notule: Nabetragtingskonferensie Operasie Protea, 9 en 10 September 1981 te Grootfontein", 23.10.1981, par. 9 (61 Mech online archive); Lord: *From Fledgling to Eagle*, pp. 169–171.

31 Unpublished memoir by Roland de Vries.

32 Gert Minnaar: "Op Protea – Humbe was nie net rustig gewees nie", at http://www.61mech. org.za/stories/65?height=400&width=400. Cf. also Chris Gildenhuys: "A personal account and experience – 30 years on", at www.61mech.org.za/ stories/168?height=400&width=400.

33 Breytenbach: *Buffalo Soldiers*, p. 224.

34 Danie Laubscher: "Bosbok over Xangongo – Operation Protea", 13.10.2010, at www. flyafrica.info/forums/showthread.php?30477-Bosbok-over-Xangongo-Ops-Protea/ page3.

35 MI/309/4 Protea: "Briefing: Op Protea", 9.11.1981, par. 19; (61 Mech online archive); Ops HQ – H Army, situation report as of 10h00, 26.8.1981 (61 Mech online archive).

36 MI/309/4 Protea: "Briefing: Op Protea", 9.11.1981, par. 19 (61 Mech online archive).

37 Breytenbach: *Buffalo Soldiers*, p. 227.

38 Dippenaar: "Operasie Protea: Veggroep 20 bevelvoerdersdagboek", par. 82 (61 Mech online archive).

39 Geldenhuys: *Dié wat Gewen het*, pp. 116–117.

40 Jacques du Randt: "61 Meg Ops Protea", unpublished memoir in author's possession.

41 "War Diary of Charlie Squadron, 61 Mech", entry of 5.8.1981 (provided by Roland de Vries).

42 From Breytenbach's account ("44 Parachute Brigade's pathfinder company during Operation Protea", 61 Mech online archive) one would think that the pathfinder company fought all alone. However, Roland de Vries's unpublished memoir makes it clear that Weyers's combat team has to share in the honour of routing the enemy. This is confirmed by Charlie Squadron's War Diary, entry of 25.8.1981 (provided by Roland de Vries); another unpublished account by Lieutenant Jacques du Randt, "61 Meg Ops Protea", in author's possession, as well as Gildenhuys: "A personal account and experience – 30 years on".

43 Unpublished memoir by Roland de Vries.

44 Ops HQ – H Army, situation report as of 13h30, 26.8.1981 (61 Mech online archive).

45 Unpublished memoir by Roland de Vries.

46 Dippenaar: "Operasie Protea: Veggroep 20 bevelvoerdersdagboek", paragraaf 90 and 97 (61 Mech online archive); MI/309/4 Protea: "Briefing: Op Protea", 9.11.1981, paragraaf 20 (61 Mech online archive); Dippenaar: "MO vir aanval op Ongiva van 'n bandopname af getranskribeer", 26.8.1981, paragraaf 13 (61 Mech online archive).

47 Ops HQ – H SADF, situation report at 15h00, 25.8.1981 (61 Mech online archive).

48 E-mail from van Hubrecht van Dalsen, 16.2.2011.

49 Ops HQ-H SADF, situation report at 15h00, 25.8.1981 (61 Mech online archive).

50 "Tak[tiese] waard[ering]: Aanval op Charlie [Ongiva]", 9.8.1981 par. 20–21 (61 Mech online archive); "Bevelswaard[ering]: Aanval Charlie [Ongiva]", 9.8.1981 par. 1–2 and 7 (61 Mech online archive); "Op[erasie] Instr[uksie] 1: Aanh[angsel] H by OPSO 1/81", n.d., par. 4 (61 Mech online archive); Koos Liebenberg: "Chronologiese volgorde Operasie Protea", n.d., par. 36 (61 Mech online archive); Dippenaar: "MO vir aanval op Ongiva van 'n bandopname af getranskribeer", 26.8.1981, par. 13 (61 Mech online archive).

51 Dippenaar: "Operasie Protea: Veggroep 20 bevelvoerdersdagboek", par. 113 (61 Mech online archive).

52 MI/309/4 Protea: "Briefing: Op Protea", 9.11.1981 par. 21–22 (61 Mech online archive); Nortje: *32 Battalion*, p. 173.

53 Dippenaar: "MO vir aanval op Ongiva van 'n bandopname af getranskribeer", 26.8.1981, par. 8 (61 Mech online archive).

54 Ibid.

55 "Notule van nabetragtingsvergadering Operasie Protea, 9 en 10 September 1981", 23.10.1981, par. 9 (61 Mech online archive); Wilsworth: *First In, Last Out*, p. 209; Lord: *From Fledgling to Eagle*, pp. 175–177.

56 Unless otherwise stated, the analysis of the Battle of Ongiva is based on the following sources: Dippenaar: "Operasie Protea: Veggroep 20 bevelvoerdersdagboek", par. 90 (61 Mech online archive); MI/309/4 Protea: "Briefing: Op Protea", 9.11.1981, par. 20 (61 Mech online archive); Liebenberg: "Chronologiese volgorde Operasie Protea", n.d., par. 36 (61 Mech online archive); unpublished memoir by Roland de Vries; Wilsworth: *First In, Last Out*, pp. 209–213; Nortje: *32 Battalion*, pp. 174–175; Breytenbach: *Buffalo Soldiers*, pp. 226–228; Lord: *From Fledgling to Eagle*, pp. 175–181; Johan Groré: "Ratel teen tenk", at www.samagte.co.za/weermag/hc/grove.html; Johan van Rensburg: "Piloot tot Peg-Leg tot PostNet", in Geldenhuys (ed.): *Ons was Daar*, p. 113.

57 Korff: *19 with a Bullet*, p. 263.

58 MI/309/4 Protea: "Briefing: Op Protea", 9.11.1981 par. 31–32 (61 Mech online archive).

59 Ops HQ – C SADF and C Army, 2.9.1981 (61 Mech online archive). Van Staden's account was written up by Jim Hooper at http://veridical.co.za/default.aspx?tabid=1112. Cf. also Bazil Newham: "Operasie Protea – teerpad en maanlig", in Geldenhuys (ed.): *Ons was Daar*, pp.105–106.

60 H Leër/IG/305/3/1: "Notule van nabetragtingsvergadering, Operasie Protea, 9 en 10 September 1981 te Grootfontein", 23.10.1981, par. 11 (61 Mech online archive); "Memorandum: Effek van Operasie Protea op die SWA/N konfliksituasie", October 1981, par. 9 (61 Mech online archive); Nortje: *32 Battalion*, p. 176.

61 Cited in Morgan Norval: *Death in the Desert. The Namibian Tragedy*, p. 149.

62 Unpublished memoir by Roland de Vries.

63 Lord: *From Fledgling to Eagle*, p. 187.

64 HS Ops 309/4, Chief of Staff Ops – Chief of Staff Intelligence, "Memorandum: Effek van Operasie Protea op die SWA/N konfliksituasie", October 1981 par. 9 and 16 (61 Mech online archive).

65 Heitman: *South African Armed Forces*, p. 164.

66 HS Ops 309/4, Chief of Staff Ops – Chief of Staff Intelligence, "Effek van Operasie Protea op die SWA/N konfliksituasie", 30 October 1981 (61 Mech online archive).

67 Ibid.

68 H Leër/IG/305/3/1: "Notule van nabetragtingsvergadering, Operasie Protea, 9 en 10 September 1981 te Grootfontein 23.10.1981", par. 67 (61 Mech online archive)

69 Ibid. par. 9 and 31 (61 Mech online archive); "Aanhangsel M by nabetragtingsdokument, Oktober 1981" (61 Mech online archive).

70 Joseph Hanlon: *Beggar your Neighbours. Apartheid Power in South Africa*, p. 159.

71 Marga Holness: *Apartheid's War against Angola*, pp. 19–20.

72 "Tak[tiese] waard[ering]: Yankee Suid", 5.8.1981 par. 2d, 3e, 4d and 39c; "Bevelswaardering: Yankee Suid", 4.8.1981, par. 2 (61 Mech online archive).

73 MI/309/4 Protea: "Briefing: Op Protea", 9.11.1981, par. 8 (61 Mech online archive); H Leër/IG/305/3/1: "Notule nabetragtingskonferensie Operasie Protea, 9 en 10 September 1981 te Grootfontein", 23.10.1981, par. 5 (61 Mech online archive).

74 "Bevelswaardering: Yankee Suid", 4.8.1981, par. 21 (61 Mech online archive).

75 Unpublished memoir by Roland de Vries.

76 MI/309/4 Protea: "Briefing: Op Protea", 9.11.1981, par. 16 (61 Mech online archive); Geldenhuys: *Dié wat gewen het*, p. 117.

77 Roland de Vries: "Kaptein Payne en Sokker", in Geldenhuys (ed.): *Ons was Daar*, pp. 117–118.

78 MI/309/4 Protea: "Briefing: Op Protea", 9.11.1981, par. 17 (61 Mech online archive).

79 Unpublished memoir by Roland de Vries.

80 MI/309/4 Protea: "Briefing: Op Protea", 9.11.1981 par. 22 and 27 (61 Mech online archive).

81 Dippenaar: "Operasie Protea: Veggroep 20 bevelvoerdersdagboek", par. 109 (61 Mech online archive)

82 Grové: "Ratel teen tenk".

83 MI/309/4 Protea: "Briefing: Op Protea",
9.11.1981 par. 27–29 (61 Mech online
archive); Dippenaar: "Operasie Protea:
Veggroep 20 bevelvoerdersdagboek"
par. 116–117 (61 Mech online archive);
H Leër/IG/305/3/1: "Notule van
nabetragtingsvergadering, Operasie
Protea, 9 en 10 September te Grootfontein",
par. 11 (61 Mech online archive).

84 "Notule van Ondjiva-dorpsbestuur gehou
op 29 Augustus 1981 te Ondjiva" (61 Mech
online archive).

85 Dippenaar: "Operasie Protea: Veggroep
20 bevelvoerdersdagboek", par. 121
(61 Mech online archive).

86 H Leër/IG/305/3/1: "Notule van
nabetragtingsvergadering, Operasie Protea,
9 en 10 September 1981 te Grootfontein",
par. 20 (61 Mech online archive);
"Aanhangsel C by nabetragtingsdokument:
Burgersake", Oktober 1981, par. 11
(61 Mech online archive).

87 "Aanhangsel C by nabetragtingsdokument:
Burgersake", Oktober 1981, par.
12 (61 Mech online archive); H
Leër/IG/305/3/1: "Notule van
nabetragtingsvergadering, Operasie
Protea, 9 en 10 September 1981 te
Grootfontein, par. 34 (61 Mech online
archive). Cf also Breytenbach: *Buffalo
Soldiers*, pp. 212–213.

88 Geldenhuys: *Dié wat gewen het*, p. 115;
Nortje: *32 Battalion*, pp. 178–179; Lord:
From Fledgling to Eagle, p. 187.

89 "Inligtingsplan vir Ops Daisy", Okt.
1981, par. 2 (61 Mech online archive);
"Op instr 14/81: Op Afval", 22.10.1981,
par. 1 (61 Mech online archive);
"Operasie instruksie 21/81: Operasie
Daisy", 22.10.1981, par. 1. (61 Mech
online archive).

90 "Ops no 2/81: Op Daisy: Aanv[al] op
Doelw[it] Daisy en daaropvolgende
gebiedsops tot D plus 17", Oktober 1981,
par. 2 (61 Mech online archive). According
to Roland de Vries the entire force formed
a convoy of 55 km long.

91 The force included 12 Mirage F1AZs,
8 Mirage F1CZs and 10 Impala Mk IIs for
day operations and 4 for night operations,
as well as 3 Buccaneers. In addition,

there were 21 helicopters, 6 C-130s/C-160s,
4 Dakotas and 9 Bosboks. "Summary of Air
Force participation in Op Daisy", n.d., par. 2
(61 Mech online archive).

92 "Ops no 2/81: Op Daisy: Aanv[al] op
Doelw[it] Daisy en daaropvolgende
gebiedsops tot D plus 17", Oktober 1981, par.
2 (61 Mech online archive).

93 Geldenhuys: *Dié wat gewen het*, pp.120–121.

94 Breytenbach: *Eagle Strike!*, p.468.

95 E-mail from Roland de Vries, 16.2.2009.

96 Ariël Hugo: "Op Daisy – navigasie met
Operasie Daisy", at www.61mech.org.za/
operations/8-operation-daisy.

97 "Notule van 'n nabetragtingskonferensie t.o.v.
Op Daisy gehou by HK Sektor 10", 25.11.1981,
par. 31 (61 Mech online archive); "Special
report" par. 57–59 (61 Mech online archive);
"Summary of Air Force participation in Op
Daisy", n.d., par. 6 (61 Mech online archive).

98 Emails from Roland de Vries, 16.2.2011, and
Ariël Hugo, 17.2.2011.

99 "Notule van 'n nabetragtingskonferensie
t.o.v. Op Daisy gehou by HK Sektor 10",
25.11.1981, par. 2 (61 Mech online archive);
"Special report" par. 36–37 and 65–68
(61 Mech online archive).

100 Nortje: *32 Battalion*, p. 179.

101 "Notule van 'n nabetragtingskonferensie
t.o.v. Op Daisy gehou by HK Sektor 10",
25.11.1981, par. 3 (61 Mech online archive);
"Special report" par. 43–51 and 71 (61 Mech
online archive); "Summary of Air Force
participation in Op Daisy", n.d., par. 7
(61 Mech online archive).

102 On the way Ariël Hugo's platoon ran into a
contact with PLAN insurgents, in which a
32 Battalion officer, Lieutenant G van Zyl,
and a UNITA major were killed. Corporal
JL Potgieter heroically floored his own Ratel
gunner, saving his life, but dying in the
process. In the end, SWAPO's resistance was
broken when a Rifleman Swanepoel stormed
in on his own and shot the defenders.
Ariël Hugo: "Op Daisy – Held van sy tyd:
Korporaal JL Potgieter", at www.61mech.org.
za/operations/8-operation-daisy.

103 E-mail from Roland de Vries, 16.2.2011.

104 "Notule van 'n nabetragtingskonferensie
t.o.v. Op Daisy gehou by HK Sektor 10",
25.11.1981, par. 4 (61 Mech online archive).

105 "Notule van 'n nabetragtingskonferensie t.o.v. Op Daisy gehou by HK Sektor 10", 25.11.1981, par. 4 (61 Mech online archive); Geldenhuys: *Dié wat gewen het*, p. 120; Steenkamp: *South Africa's Border War 1966-1989*, p. 99.

106 "Summary of Air Force participation in Op Daisy", n.d., par. 9 (61 Mech online archive).

107 The description of this aerial combat is based on the following sources: "Summary of Air Force participation in Op Daisy", n.d., par. 11 (61 Mech online archive); AFB Ondangwa – WAC (Int), 6.11.1981 (61 Mech online archive); Lord: *From Fledgling to Eagle*, pp. 193-194.

108 Crocker: *High Noon in Southern Africa*, p. 105.

109 George: *The Cuban Intervention in Angola*, p. 141.

110 Geldenhuys: *Dié wat gewen het*, p. 202.

CHAPTER 8

1 Breytenbach: *Buffalo Soldiers*, p. 239.

2 Military Information Bureau, SADF: "'Platform for peace': The history of the Joint Monitoring Commission from the South African perspective", p. 4 (Aluka online archive).

3 Lord: *From Fledgling to Eagle*, p. 310.

4 Namakalu: *Armed Liberation Struggle*, p. 99.

5 This description is based on the following sources: Breytenbach: *Buffalo Soldiers*, pp. 229-234; Nortje: *32 Battalion*, pp. 181-185; Stiff: *The Silent War*, pp. 358-361; Els: *We Fear Naught but God*, pp. 168-171; Heitman: *South African Armed Forces*, p. 166; Al J Venter: *The Chopper Boys. Helicopter Warfare in Africa*, pp. 195-203.

6 Venter: *The Chopper Boys*, p. 201.

7 Louis Bothma (*Anderkant Cuito*, p. 53) says that the SADF "adapted" the SWAPO number of dead upwards, although the SADF casualty figure of three dead is correct. He does not cite any source. The figure cited in the text comes from Piet Nortje's book *32 Battalion*, which is based on contemporary SADF reports. Until evidence to the contrary is presented, this figure has to be accepted.

8 Nortje: *32 Battalion*, p, 184. As Nortje's book is based on SADF archival material, these statistics seem credible.

9 Unpublished memoir by Roland de Vries.

10 Ibid.

11 "OPSO 1.1982 Op Meebos", 11.7.1982, par. 4 (61 Mech online archive).

12 Venter: *The Chopper Boys*, pp. 177-190; Heitman: *South African Armed Forces*, p. 166; Steenkamp: *South Africa's Border War 1966-1989* p. 103; Lord: *From Fledgling to Eagle*, pp. 211-214; Geldenhuys: *Dié wat gewen het*, pp. 115-116.

13 This description is based on Lord: *From Fledgling to Eagle*, pp. 215-217; "Listing of Cuban losses in Angola and Ethiopia", at www.ejection-history.org.uk/country-by-country/cuba.htm. A Cuban source (Rubén Urribarres: "Cuban MiG-21 in action", at www.urrib2000.narod.ru/EqMiG-21a-e.html) denies that Rankin actually shot down the MiG, but the photographic evidence (see Lord, p. 217) is decisive. Urribarres's writings are not to be trusted in the light of their propagandistic nature.

14 SWS3/309/1/Op Plan: "Bevestigende notas: Samesprekings op beplanning: bastion 19 April 1983", 21.4.1983 (61 Mech online archive); HS Ops/D Ops/309/1: "Op instr 1/1983: Op Dolfyn", 28.4.1983 (61 Mech online archive); 309/1/Op Dolfyn: "Kontakontleding: Veggroep Bravo: 12 Junie 1983 te 781527WN", 23.6.1983 (61 Mech online archive); Gert van Zyl: "Operation Dolfyn", at www.61mech.org.za/operations/12-operation-dolfyn; Nortje: *32 Battalion*, pp. 192-193; Lord: *From Fledgling to Eagle*, p. 264.

15 HS Ops/309/4/Rekstok: "Notas vir motivering van uitbreiding van huidige ops optrede in S Angola", 15.4.1983 (61 Mech online archive).

16 H Leër/D Ops/309/1: H Leër – BG SWA et al, 27.10.1984 (61 Mech online archive); "Inligtingsaanhangsel A by Sektor 20 op instr 4/83", 30.11.1983, par. 1 (61 Mech online archive); "Op Askari", n.d. par. 1-4 (61 Mech online archive); Dudley Wall: *Operation Askari 1983-1984, Southern Angola*, p. 1, at www.warinangola.com/Default.aspx?tabid=1173.

17 Transcript of press conference by General Constand Viljoen, 26.12.1983, pp. 1-2 (61 Mech online archive); transcript of press conference by General Viljoen and Lieutenant

General Ian Gleeson, 29.12.1983, pp. 1–2
(61 Mech online archive); "Operasionele
voorligting Op Askari", n.d. par. 1–2. Cf. also
Geldenhuys: *Dié wat gewen het*, p. 122.

18 H Leër – BG SWA et al, 28.10.1984 (61 Mech
online archive); Sektor 10/309/1 Op Askari:
"Op plan: Op Askari", 23.9.1983 par. 21–35;
"Operasie instruksie 5/83: Operasie Askari",
19.10.1983, par. 3 (61 Mech online archive);
"Operasionele voorligting Op Askari", n.d.
par. 1–3 (61 Mech online archive).

19 "Sektor 10: Op Askari Des 1983-Jan 1984",
briefing by Brigadier General Joep Joubert,
n.d., (61 Mech online archive); "Operasionele
voorligting op Askari", n.d. par. 6–7 and
26–27; Sector 20 HQ: "Op instr 4/83 Op
Askari", 30.11.1983 par. 4 and 6; Breytenbach:
Buffalo Soldiers, pp. 243–244.

20 This was an Israeli gun, which proved to be
no success. It was never used on an operation
again. See Wilsworth: *First In, Last Out*,
p. 225.

21 Under the command of Major Jakkie
Cilliers, who later became Director of the
authoritative Institute of Security Studies
in Pretoria.

22 H Leër/D Ops/309/1 – Op instr 13/83,
27.10.1983, par. 3 (61 Mech online archive);
"Nabetragting: Op Askari", n.d., par. 6
(61 Mech online archive).

23 "Op plan: Op Askari", 23.9.1983 par. 4 and 20
(61 Mech online archive).

24 "Voorligtingsnotas Op Askari: Minister van
Verdediging", n.d., p. 2 (61 Mech online
archive).

25 Lord: "Operation Askari. A sub-commander's
retrospective view of the operation"
(*Militaria*, 22/4, 1992, p. 2).

26 Wilsworth: *First In, Last Out*, pp. 232–233.

27 Military Information Bureau, SADF:
"'Platform for peace': The history of the Joint
Monitoring Commission from the South
African perspective", pp. 5 and 7 (Aluka
online archive).

28 "Nabetragting Op Askari", n.d., par. 6
(61 Mech online archive).

29 Stiff: *The Silent War*, p. 366.

30 Crocker: *High Noon in Southern Africa*,
pp. 178–179.

31 Crocker: *High Noon in Southern Africa*,
pp. 170 and 180; Steenkamp: *South Africa's*

Border War 1966–1989, pp. 112–113;
Bridgland: *Jonas Savimbi*, pp. 424–425.

32 Pieter Wolvaardt, Tom Wheeler and Werner
Scholtz (eds.): *From Verwoerd to Mandela.
South African Diplomats Remember*, I, p. 276.

33 "Nabetragting Op Askari", n.d. par.
8–9 (61 Mech online archive); Military
Information Bureau, SADF: "'Platform for
peace': The history of the Joint Monitoring
Commission from the South African
perspective", p. 7 (Aluka online archive).

34 Crocker: *High Noon in Southern Africa*,
p. 171.

35 George: *The Cuban Intervention in Angola*,
p. 180.

36 Stiff: *The Silent War*, p. 364.

37 Lord: *From Fledgling to Eagle*, p. 302.

38 "Op Askari", n.d., par. 8 (61 Mech
online archive).

39 "Operasionele Voorligting: Op Askari" par.
7–8 (61 Mech online archive); Gert van Zyl:
"Operation Askari", at http://www.61mech.
org.za/operations/13-operation-askari..

40 E-mail from Ep van Lill, 16.4.2011.

41 "Operasionele Voorligting: Op Askari", par. 10
(61 Mech online archive).

42 "Operasionele Voorligting: Op Askari" par.
10–11 (61 Mech online archive); transcript
of press conference by General Constand
Viljoen, 29.12.1983 (61 Mech online archive);
Lord: *From Fledgling to Eagle*, pp. 304–305.

43 Transcript of press conference by General
Constand Viljoen, 29.12.1983 (61 Mech
online archive).

44 E-mail from Ep van Lill, 16.3.2011.

45 "Operasionele Voorligting: Op Askari", par. 12
(61 Mech online archive); Tak HK Taakmag
X-Ray – Sektor 10, 17.12.1983 (61 Mech
online archive); Wilsworth: *First In, Last Out*,
pp. 231–232.

46 "Notule van nabetragting, Op Askari fase
2, gehou op 27 Januarie 1984 om 10h30,
AG saal, Oshakati", par. 8 (61 Mech
online archive).

47 Wall: *Operation Askari 1983–1984, Southern
Angola*, p. 7.

48 Ibid.

49 "Operasionele voorligting Op Askari", n.d.
par. 31–32 and 35 (61 Mech online archive);
GJJ Oosthuizen: "Regiment Mooirivier,
Potchefstroom: Grensdienservarings van

'n pantserburgermageenheid, 1975–1988" (*Joernaal vir Eietydse Geskiedenis*, 31/3, Dec. 2006, p. 205).

50 Sektor 20 – H Leër, 19.12.1983 (61 Mech online archive); DF – Sektor 10, 29.12.1983 (61 Mech online archive); Lord: *From Fledgling to Eagle*, p. 306; Wilsworth: *First In, Last Out*, pp. 234–235.

51 "Nabetragting Op Askari" n.d. par. 12–16 (61 Mech online archive); "Op Askari", n.d., par. 8 (61 Mech online archive); Stiff: *The Silent War*, pp. 366–367.

52 "Nabetragting Op Askari" n.d., par. 17 (61 Mech online archive); e-mail from EP Van Lill, 16.3.2011; Oosthuizen: "Regiment Mooirivier, Potchefstroom: Grensdienservarings van 'n pantserburgermageenheid, 1975–1988" (*Joernaal vir Eietydse Geskiedenis*, 31/3, Dec. 2006, p. 206).

53 "Op Askari", n.d., par. 7 (61 Mech online archive).

54 E-mail from Ep van Lill, 16.3.2011.

55 "Sektor 10: Op Askari, Des. 1983–Jan 1984" (61 Mech online archive).

56 Wall: *Operation Askari 1983–1984, Southern Angola*, p. 11.

57 HS Ops/309/4/Askari, Sitrap op Askari, n.d., par. 2 (61 Mech online archive); "Op Askari", n.d., par. 8 (61 Mech online archive); "Operasionele voorligting Op Askari", n.d., par. 24 (61 Mech online archive).

58 E-mail from Ep van Lill, 16.3.2011; HS Ops/309/4/Askari, Sitrap op Askari, n.d., par. 2 (61 Mech online archive); Colin Steyn: "Angola – Operasie Askari – Die Slag van Cuvelai", in Geldenhuys (ed.): *Ons was Daar*, pp. 148–150.

59 E-mail from Jakkie Cilliers, 7.5.2011.

60 E-mail from Ep van Lill, 16.3.2011.

61 HS Ops/309/4/Askari, Sitrap Op Askari, n.d., par. 2 (61 Mech online archive).

62 "Operasionele voorligting Op Askari", n.d. par. 27–30 and 33–34 (61 Mech online archive); Breytenbach: *Buffalo Soldiers*, p. 244. Cf. also Nortje: *32 Battalion*, pp. 194–196.

63 "Op Askari", n.d., par. 7 (61 Mech online archive).

64 Oosthuizen: "Regiment Mooirivier, Potchefstroom: Grensdienservarings van 'n pantserburgermageenheid, 1975–1988",

(*Joernaal vir Eietydse Geskiedenis*, 31/3, Dec. 2006, pp. 206–207); Gustav Venter: "Gaan sê vir Professor Ben Liebenberg", at www.61mech. org.za/operations/13-operation-askari.

65 In fact, there were no light infantry, but mechanised infantry – also no match for tanks. In addition, there is no record of T-34 tanks at Cuvelai, only T-55s.

66 Gustav Venter: "Gaan sê vir Professor Ben Liebenberg", at www.61mech.org.za/ operations/13-operation-askari.

67 Oosthuizen: "Regiment Mooirivier, Potchefstroom: Grensdienservarings van 'n pantserburgermageenheid, 1975–1988", (*Joernaal vir Eietydse Geskiedenis*, 31/3, Dec. 2002), p. 207).

68 Oosthuizen: "Regiment Mooirivier and South African transborder operations into Angola during 1975/76 and 1983/84" (*Historia* 49/1, May 2004, p. 150).

69 E-mail from Ep van Lill, 16.3.2011.

70 "Operasionele voorligting Op Askari", n.d., par. 25 (61 Mech online archive).

71 E-mail from Ep van Lill, 16.3.2011.

72 "Nabetragting Op Askari", n.d., par. 23 (61 Mech online archive).

73 E-mail from Ep van Lill, 16.3.2011.

74 Wall: *Operation Askari 1983–1984, Southern Angola*, p. 17.

75 According to what Task Force Victor officers told GJJ Oosthuizen, Van Lill "got hopelessly lost". See Oosthuizen: "Regiment Mooirivier and South African transborder operations in Angola during 1975/76 and 1983/84" (*Historia* 49/1, May 2004, p. 150).

76 E-mail from Ep van Lill, 16.3.2011.

77 Lord: *From Fledgling to Eagle*, p. 309.

78 E-mail from Jakkie Cilliers, 7.5.2011.

79 Anonymous: "Kapt. Carl Friedrich Wilhelm Alberts", at www.samagte.co.za/weermag/hc/ alberts.html.

80 Ibid.;Wall: *Operation Askari 1983–1984, Southern Angola*, p. 19, at www.warinangola. com/Default.aspx?tabid=1173.

81 Colin Steyn: "Angola – Operasie Askari – Die Slag van Cuvelai", in Geldenhuys (ed.): *Ons was Daar*, p. 152.

82 E-mail from Ep van Lill, 16.3.2011.

83 "Operasionele voorligting Op Askari", n.d. par. 39–40 (61 Mech online archive); "Operasie Askari (fase 2) personeelverliese 1 Desember

1983 tot 15 Januarie 1984", n.d. (61 Mech online archive).

84 "SAW buit Russiese missielstelsel" (*Paratus*, February 1984); "Operasionele voorligting Op Askari", n.d., par. 41 (61 Mech online archive); Wall: *Operation Askari 1983–1984, Southern Angola*, p. 20.

85 Lord: *From Fledgling to Eagle*, pp. 319–321; e-mail from Colonel André Retief, 25.4.2011.

86 Wall: *Operation Askari 1983–1984, Southern Angola*, p. 22.

87 Shubin: *The Hot "Cold War"*, p. 285, footnote 137.

88 Breytenbach: *Buffalo Soldiers*, p. 245; Nortje: *32 Battalion*, p. 197.

89 Nortje: *32 Battalion*, p. 197.

90 E-mail from Ep van Lill, 16.3.2011.

91 Ibid.

92 Nortje: *32 Battalion*, pp. 199–200.

93 "Op Askari, Des 1983–Jan 1984" (61 Mech online archive).

94 "Notule van nabetragting, Op Askari fase 2, gehou op 27 Januarie 1984 om 10h30, AG saal, Oshakati" par. 9 and 14 (61 Mech online archive).

95 "Aanhangsel H by nasbetragting Op Askari Fase 2, nabetragting personeel)", n.d. (61 Mech online archive).

96 "Operasionele voorligting Op Askari", n.d., par. 49 (61 Mech online archive). Cf. also "Invloed Op Askari op SWAPO/Spes Unit", n.d. par. 2 and 3 (61 Mech online archive).

97 Breytenbach: *Buffalo Soldiers*, pp. 244 and 247. Cf. also Nortje: *32 Battalion*, pp. 193–199.

98 "Invloed Op Askari op SWAPO/Spes Unit", n.d., par. 4 (61 Mech online archive).

99 Brown: "Diplomacy by other means", in Leys and Saul (eds.): *Namibia's Liberation Struggle*, p. 32. Cf. also Breytenbach: *Buffalo Soldiers*, p. 191.

100 "Invloed Op Askari op SWAPO/Spes Unit", n.d., par. 2 (61 Mech online archive).

101 Lord: *From Fledgling to Eagle*, p. 318.

102 Crocker: *High Noon in Southern Africa*, p. 57.

103 Lord: *From Fledgling to Eagle*, p. 318.

104 Vladimir Shubin: "The USSR and Southern Africa during the Cold War", at www2.spbo. unibo.it/dpis/centroafricamedioriente/ Shubin_OP1.pdf.

105 Geldenhuys: *Dié wat gewen het*, p. 122.

106 Cf. "Aanhangsel B by OPSO 6/83: vy situasie", Nov. 1983, par. 14 (61 Mech online archive); Sektor 20 – H Leër, 19.12.1983, par. 3 (61 Mech online archive); "Op Askari", n.d., par. 7 (61 Mech online archive);

107 "Op Askari", n.d., par. 8 (61 Mech online archive).

108 HS Ops/309/4/Askari, n.d., par. 8 (61 Mech online archive).

109 Press release in the name of General Constand Viljoen, 6.1.1983 (61 Mech online archive).

110 Stiff: *The Silent War*, p. 367.

111 E-mail from Ep van Lill, 16.4.2011.

112 "Notule van nabetragting, Op Askari fase 2, gehou op 27 Januarie 1984 om 10h30, AG saal, Oshakati", par. 14 (61 Mech online archive).

113 Ibid., par. 16 (61 Mech online archive).

114 Ibid, par. 19 (61 Mech online archive).

115 Jordaan: "The role of South African armour in South West Africa/Namibia and Angola: 1975–1989" (*Journal for Contemporary History*, 31/3, December 2006, p. 165).

116 E-mail from Ep van Lill, 18.4.2011. According to Sergeant Dion Rossouw, one of the armour members taking the tanks to Namibia, the exercise followed only a few weeks after their arrival at 61 Mech. Cf. Dion Rossouw: "1984 – Second deployment of SADF tanks to the SWA operational area", at www.61mech.org.za/ years/1984#stories-photos.

117 E-mail from Colonel André Retief, 25.4.2011.

118 Constand Viljoen: "The conventional threat to the RSA and SWA" (*Strategic Review for Southern Africa*, December 1984, p. 7).

119 Crocker: *High Noon in Southern Africa*, pp. 188–189.

120 The full letter is quoted by Military Information Bureau, SADF: " 'Platform for peace': The history of the Joint Monitoring Commission from the South African perspective", pp. 8–9 (Aluka online archive).

121 "Summarised minutes of discussions between South African and United States delegations", 27.1.1984 (Aluka online archive).

122 Crocker: *High Noon in Southern Africa*, p. 193.

123 Military Information Bureau, SADF: "'Platform for peace': The history of the Joint Monitoring Commission from the South African perspective", p. 11 (Aluka online archive).

124 "First meeting of the South African/Angolan Joint Monitoring Commission", Lusaka, 16.2.1984 (Aluka online archive); "Points of agreement reached during the trilateral meeting on the establishment of the Joint Monitoring Commission", Mulungushi, Lusaka, 16.2.1984; (Aluka online archive); Military Information Bureau, SADF: "'Platform for peace': The history of the Joint Monitoring Commission from the South African perspective", pp. 15–16 (Aluka online archive).

125 Geldenhuys: Dié wat gewen het, pp. 124–125.

126 Military Information Bureau, SADF: "'Platform for peace': The history of the Joint Monitoring Commission from the South African perspective", p. 19 (Aluka online archive); Crocker: High Noon in Southern Africa, pp. 194–196.

127 For a full chronicle of the process, cf. Military Information Bureau, SADF: "'Platform for peace': The history of the Joint Monitoring Commission from the South African perspective", passim (Aluka online archive).

128 Military Information Bureau, SADF: "'Platform for peace': The history of the Joint Monitoring Commission from the South African perspective", pp. 105–121 (Aluka online archive).

129 Shubin: The Hot "Cold War", pp. 98–100.

130 Gleijeses: "Moscow's proxy? Cuba and Africa 1975–1988" (Journal of Cold War Studies, 8/2, Spring 2006, p. 28).

131 Shubin: The Hot "Cold War", p. 98.

132 Gleijeses: "Moscow's proxy? Cuba and Africa 1975–1988" (Journal of Cold War Studies, 8/2, Spring 2006, p. 28)

133 "Free translation of the text of the joint declaration issued by Fidel Castro, President of Cuba, and José Eduardo dos Santos, President of Angola, on the occasion of the latter's visit to Cuba on 19 March 1984" (Aluka online archive).

134 Cf. "Meeting between the Honourable RF Botha, Minister of Foreign Affairs and Ambassador H Nickel of the United States: Cape Town, Mar. 20, 1984" (Aluka online archive); "Letter from CA Crocker to RF Botha", 21.3.1984 (Aluka online archive); "Meeting between Minister RF Botha, Minister of Foreign Affairs and Ambassador H Nickel of the United States: Cape Town: 21 March 1984" (Aluka online archive).

135 Military Information Bureau, SADF: "'Platform for peace': The history of the Joint Monitoring Commission from the South African perspective", p. 186 (Aluka online archive).

136 Breytenbach: Buffalo Soldiers, p. 248.

137 Military Information Bureau, SADF: "'Platform for peace': The history of the Joint Monitoring Commission from the South African perspective", p. 84 (Aluka online archive); Steenkamp: South Africa's Border War 1966-1989, p. 133.

138 Steenkamp: South Africa's Border War 1966-1989, p. 127.

139 Ibid., p. 134.

140 Jaster: The Defence of White Power, p. 97.

141 HS Ops/TS/309/4-Cinema: "Uitbreiding van gebied waarin Cinema uitgevoer word", 29.8.1986 (Group 4, Box 160, H SAW 309/4, p. 22).

142 "Voorligting aan senior offisiere van die SAW oor Operasie Moduler/Hooper", n.d., par. 7 (61 Mech online archive).

CHAPTER 9

1 Nujoma: Where Others Wavered, pp. 315–316.

2 Steenkamp: South Africa's Border War 1966-1989, p. 86.

3 Geldenhuys: Dié wat gewen het, p. 65.

4 Steenkamp: SA's Border War, p. 190.

5 Brown: "Diplomacy by other means", in Leys and Saul (eds.): Namibia's Liberation Struggle, p. 29.

6 Alexander: "The Cassinga raid" (unpublished MA thesis, Unisa, 2003), pp. 27 and 29.

7 Geldenhuys: Dié wat gewen het, p. 68.

8 Ibid., p 90.

9 Meiring: "Current SWAPO activity in South West Africa" (Strategic Review for Southern Africa, 1/1985, p. 8).

10 Geldenhuys: Dié wat gewen het, pp. 132–133; Stiff: The Covert War, p. 250.

11 Gaomab: "With the People's Liberation Army of Namibia in Angola", in Leys and Brown (eds.): *Life Histories of Namibia*, pp. 65–67.

12 Nortje: *32 Battalion*, pp. 181–185; Stiff: *The Covert War*, pp. 124–128.

13 Geldenhuys: *Dié wat gewen het*, pp. 132–133; Stiff: *The Covert War*, pp. 210–213.

14 Geldenhuys: *Dié wat gewen het*, p. 133.

15 Ibid, pp. 90–91. Cf. also pp. 94–95 and 133; Steenkamp: *SA's Border War 1966-1989*, pp. 101 and 107.

16 Alexander: "The Cassinga Raid", pp. 31–32; Geldenhuys: *Dié wat gewen het*, p. 59.

17 Turner: *Continent Ablaze*, p. 39.

18 Helmoed-Römer Heitman: *Modern African Wars (3). South-West Africa*, p. 15.

19 Unpublished memoir by Roland de Vries. Cf. also Alexander: "The Cassinga raid" (unpublished MA thesis, Unisa, 2003), p. 32.

20 Steenkamp: *South Africa's Border War 1966-1989*, p. 204.

21 Turner: *Continent Ablaze*, pp. 74–76.

22 Abel Esterhuyse and Evert Jordaan: "The South African Defence Force and Counterinsurgency, 1966–1990", in Deane-Peter Baker and Evert Jordaan (eds.): *South Africa and Contemporary Counterinsurgency. Roots, Practices, Concepts*, pp. 111–113.

23 Geldenhuys: *Dié wat gewen het*, p. 69.

24 Ibid., pp. 78–79.

25 Lord: *From Fledgling to Eagle*, p. 245; Stiff: *The Covert War*, p. 267.

26 AR Turton: *Shaking Hands with Billy. The Private Memoirs of Anthony Richard Turton*, p. 96.

27 For an analysis of the "Romeo Mike" tactics, cf. Venter (ed.): *The Chopper Boys*, pp. 127–168; Ian Uys: *Bushman Soldiers. Their Alpha and Omega*, p. 134; Turner: *Continent Ablaze*, pp. 34–55; Alexander: "The Cassinga Raid", pp. 33–34.

28 Heitman: *South African Armed Forces*, p. 112.

29 Geldenhuys: *Dié wat gewen het*, pp. 67–68.

30 Alexander: "The Cassinga Raid", p. 34.

31 Gaomab: "With the People's Liberation Army of Namibia in Angola", in Leys and Brown (eds.): *Life Histories of Namibia*, p. 64.

32 Cf. South African Research Service: *South African Review*, I, p. 40; Geldenhuys: *Dié wat gewen het*, pp. 94–95.

33 "Report issued by groups J-11 and D-10 from their mission down south", 22.3.1980 (Aluka online archive); "Report and information given by group M-4 commander cde Kapoko from their mission in Grootfontein area", 23.3.1980 (Aluka online archive).

34 Personal memoir by Roland de Vries.

35 Arn Durand: *Zulu Zulu Golf. Life and Death with Koevoet*, pp. 216–217. Cf. also Stiff: *The Covert War*, pp. 152–165.

36 Stiff: *The Covert War*, p. 164.

37 Geldenhuys: *Dié wat gewen het*, p. 116; Stiff: *The Covert War*, pp. 184–185; Lord: *From Fledgling to Eagle*, p. 258; Gert van Zyl: "Operation Phoenix", at www.61mech.org.za/operations/11-operation-phoenix.

38 Directorate of Military Intelligence: "Die militêre bedreiging teen die RSA", 13.3.1981, par. 29 and 60. (HIS AMI, Group 3, Box 404).

39 Steenkamp: *South Africa's Border War 1966-1989*, pp. 124–127; Heitman: *South African Armed Forces*, pp. 173–175.

40 Cf. "Ondervragingsverslag van Josef Gerbert Ashipara", n.d. [1984] (61 Mech online archive).

41 Stiff: *The Covert War*, p. 182.

42 Ibid., pp. 285–288.

43 Nortje: *32 Battalion*, pp. 185–188.

44 Geldenhuys: *Dié wat gewen het*, p. 87.

45 *White Paper on Defence and Armament Supply*, 1982, p. 6.

46 South African Research Service: *South African Review. Same Foundations, New Facades?* p. 39.

47 Lord: *From Fledgling to Eagle*, p. 386; Steenkamp: *SA's Border War 1966-1989*, p. 145.

48 Sheryl Raine: "Army Chief shuns defensive strategy" (*Star*, 29.6.1983).

49 Frontline Fellowship: "Special Report March 1989: South West Africa Namibia and 435", at www.sabwv.co.za/media.php?choice=article. The figures tally with those given by Major General Georg Meiring in a paper in 1985. See Meiring: "Current SWAPO activity in South West Africa" (*Strategic Review for Southern Africa*, 1/1985, pp. 8–15). Essentially the same figures appear in PRH Snyman: *Beeld van die SWA Gebiedsmag*, p. 24.

50 William Claiborne: "Namibia's forgotten bush war" (*Washington Post*, 16.6.1987).

51 CIA: "Soviet and Cuban objectives and activity in Southern Africa through 1988" Feruary 1988, p. 6.

52 Compiled from different sources.

53 Geldenhuys: *Dié wat gewen het*, pp. 69–70.

54 Directorate of Military Intelligence: "Die militêre bedreiging teen die RSA", 13.3.1981, par. 29 and 60. (HIS AMI, Group 3, Box 404); Heitman: *South African Armed Forces*, pp. 174 and 176; Steenkamp: *South Africa's Border War 1966–1989*, p. 133; Claiborne: "Namibia's forgotten bush war".

55 Shubin: *The Hot "Cold War"*, p. 88.

56 "Vergadering van die AG-werkgroep op 19 en 20 Maart 1987, Kaapstad", pp. 4–6 (Aluka online archive).

57 Brown: "Diplomacy by other means", in Leys and Saul (eds.): *Namibia's Liberation Struggle*, p. 32.

58 Stiff: *The Covert War*, pp. 293–294, 299–300 and 317.

59 There is a considerable body of literature about this. Cf. amongst others, David Galula: *Counterinsurgency Warfare. Theory and Practice*; John A. Nagl: *Learning to Eat Soup with a Knife. Counterinsurgency Lessons from Malaya and Vietnam* (Chicago, University of Chicago Press, 2006); David Kilcullen: *The Accidental Guerrilla. Fighting Small Wars in the Midst of a Big One* (Oxford, Oxford University Press, 2009); Thomas X Hammes: *The Sling and the Stone. On War in the 21st Century*; Thomas Rid and Thomas Keaney: *Understanding Counterinsurgency. Doctrine, Operations, and Challenges* (London, Routledge, 2010).

60 Transcript of press conference by General Constand Viljoen, 29.12.1983 (61 Mech online archive).

61 CL Viljoen: "Revolutionary warfare and counter-insurgency", in M Hough (ed.): *Revolutionary Warfare and Counter-Insurgency*, p. 5.

62 Cf. for example Nujoma: *Where Others Wavered*, p. 321; Leonard: *South Africa at War*, pp. 69–72; Denis Herbstein and John Evenson: *The Devils are Among Us. The War for Namibia*, p. 105; Groth: *Namibia:*

The Wall of Silence, pp. 28–31; Barbara König: *Namibia, the Ravages of War. South Africa's Onslaught on the Namibian People*, pp. 46–47; Katjavivi: *A History of Resistance in Namibia*, p. 89. Examples of sworn statements by Namibians alleging to have been brutalised by the security forces are published in Heike Becker: "Narratives of War and Survival from Northern Namibia: The Liberation War in Postcolonial Namibian writing", in Chris van der Merwe and Rolf Wolfswinkel (eds.): *Telling wounds. Narrative, Trauma & Memory working through the SA Armed Conflicts of the 20th Century*, pp. 201–208; Leys and Brown (eds.): *Histories of Namibia*, p. 60.

63 Nujoma: *Where Others Wavered*, pp. 321–322. No confirmation could be discovered from any credible source for this allegation.

64 "Statement by Sam Nujoma, leader of SWAPO: Dialogue between the Southern African liberation movements (ANC, PAC and SWAPO) and the Churches, Lusaka, Zambia", 4.8.5.1987 (Aluka online archive).

65 Cf. Edward Perkins: *Mr. Ambassador. Warrior for Peace*, p. 414.

66 Alexander: "The Raid on Cassinga", p. 34.

67 Geldenhuys: *Dié wat gewen het*, p. 135.

68 De Kock: *A Long Night's Damage*, pp. 79, 81–87; Steven Webb: *Ops Medic: A National Serviceman's Border War*, p. 219. Cf. also the opinion of Lieutenant-Colonel Sarel Karsten in De Visser: "Winning the Hearts and Minds" (unpublished MA thesis, University of Utrecht, August 2010), p. 13.

69 Korff: *19 with a Bullet*, pp. 121–124.

70 Steenkamp: *South Africa's Border War 1966–1989*, p. 69.

71 *TRC Report*, III, p. 14.

72 "Eenheid staande order", 61 Gemeganiseerde Bataljongroep, par. 56 (61 Mech online archive).

73 De Visser: "Winning the Hearts and Minds" (unpublished MA thesis, University of Utrecht, August 2010), p. 43.

74 Lieneke De Visser: "Winning hearts and minds in the Namibian Border War" (*Scientia Militaria*, 39/1, 2011, p. 93).

75 MJ le Roux: "Armour, 1978–1979", at http://sadf.sentinelprojects.com/bG-2/Tinuslr.html.

76 Paul: *Parabat*, pp. 90–91; Korff: *19 with a Bullet*, pp. 115 and 199–202.

77 Geldenhuys: *Dié wat gewen het*, p. 68; Malan: *My lewe saam met die SA Weermag*, pp. 105–109; Steenkamp: *SA's Border War 1966–1989*, p. 67.

78 South African Research Service: *South African Review*, I, p. 44.

79 JA Visser: *The South African Defence Force's Contribution to the Development of South West Africa*, p. 7.

80 Turner: *Continent Ablaze*, p. 81.

81 Steenkamp: *SA's Border War 1966–1989*, p. 97.

82 Hamann: *Days of the Generals*, p. 74; Geldenhuys: *Dié wat gewen het*, p. 68.

83 Breytenbach: *Buffalo Soldiers*, p. 196.

84 ASJ Kleynhans: *Die Stryd teen Terreur in SWA/Namibië 1957–1987*, p. 22. Cf. also William Claiborne: "Namibia's forgotten bush war".

85 Directorate of Military Intelligence: "Die militêre bedreiging teen die RSA", 13.3.1981, par. 29 and 60. (HS AMI, Group 3, Box 404).

86 Of course, in the internal election of 1978, an event boycotted by SWAPO, a countrywide voting percentage of 78% was attained, but there is some doubt as to how free the Ovambos especially felt to vote or abstain as they wished. Steenkamp: *SA's Border War 1966–1989*, p. 83.

87 De Visser: "Winning hearts and minds in the Namibian Border War" (*Scientia Militaria*, 39/1, 2011, pp. 87–88).

88 Steenkamp: *South Africa's Border War 1966–1989*, p. 18.

89 Meiring: "Current SWAPO activity in South West Africa" (*Strategic Review for Southern Africa*, 1/1985, p. 12.

90 Cf. Colin Leys and John S Saul: "Introduction", in Leys and Saul (eds.): *Namibia's Liberation Struggle*, p. 15; Steenkamp: *SA's Border War 1966–1989*, pp. 74–75 and 76; Louis Bothma: *Die Buffel Struikel*, pp. 222–223.

91 De Visser: "Winning the Hearts and Minds" (unpublished MA thesis, University of Utrecht, August 2010), p.14. Cf. also Breytenbach: *Buffalo Soldiers*, p. 201.

92 Frontline Fellowship: "Special Report March 1989: South West Africa Namibia and 435". Cf. also Henning Melber: "Liberation and democracy in Southern Africa: The case of Namibia" (*Discussion Paper 10*, Nordiska Afrikainstitutet, Uppsala, 2001), p. 20.

93 Webb: *Ops Medic*, p. 113.

94 Tim Ramsden: *Border-Line Insanity*, pp. 162–166.

95 Sisingi Kamongo and Leon Bezuidenhout: *Skadus in die Sand*, pp. 51–52.

96 Kamongo and Bezuidenhout: *Skadus in die Sand*, pp. 57–59. Kandundu was also tracked down and killed by the security forces.

97 Steenkamp: *South Africa's Border War 1966–1989*, p. 128.

98 Jim Hooper: *Koevoet! The Inside Story*, pp. 126–127.

99 Kamongo and Bezuidenhout: *Skadu's in die Sand*, p. 241. Cf. also Durand: *Zulu Zulu Golf*, pp. 65–66.

100 Hammes: *The Sling and the Stone*, pp. 213–214.

101 Anthea Jeffery: *People's War. New Light on the Struggle for South Africa*, pp. 25–39.

102 Philip Steenkamp: "The Churches", in Leys and Saul (eds.): *Namibia's Liberation Struggle*, p. 107.

103 Lauren Dobell: *SWAPO's Struggle for Namibia, 1960–1991. War by Other Means*, p. 20.

104 Hamann: *Days of the Generals*, p. 65.

105 Ibid., p. 65.

106 Ibid., pp. 65–66.

107 De Kock: *A Long Night's Damage*, pp. 68, 73, 74, 79, 80, 82.

108 Hamann: *Days of the Generals*, p. 64.

109 De Visser: "Winning the Hearts and Minds" (unpublished MA thesis, University of Utrecht, August 2010), p. 42.

110 Breytenbach: *Buffalo Soldiers*, pp. 211–212; Greeff: *A Greater Share of Honour*, p. 77.

111 Stiff: *The Covert War*, p. 492.

112 Heitman: *South African Armed Forces*, pp. 112–118.

113 Kamongo and Bezuidenhout: *Skadus in die Sand*, pp. 103–104.

114 Ibid., pp. 117–118.

115 Ibid., p. 127.

CHAPTER 10

1   Katjavivi: *A History of Resistance in Namibia*, pp. 45–46; Dobell: *SWAPO's Struggle for Namibia*, p. 30.

2   Brown: "Diplomacy by other means – SWAPO's liberation war", in Leys and Saul (eds.): *Namibia's Liberation Struggle The Liberation Struggle for Namibia*, p. 20.

3   The full text may be found in SWAPO: *To be Born a Nation. The Liberation Struggle for Namibia*, pp. 311–326.

4   Leys and Saul: "SWAPO: The politics of exile", in Leys and Saul (eds.): *Namibia's Liberation Struggle*, pp. 43–44.

5   Leys and Saul: "SWAPO: The politics of exile", in Leys and Saul (eds.): *Namibia's Liberation Struggle*, pp. 48 and 60–61 (notes 32, 36 and 40).

6   Groth: *Namibia — The Wall of Silence*, pp. 101–102 and 105.

7   Dobell: *SWAPO's Struggle for Namibia*, p. 51.

8   Interview with Otillie Abrahams by Tor Sellström, at www.liberationafrica.se/intervstories/interviews/abrahams/index.xml?by-country=1&node-id=2238869971–39.

9   "Speech by Sam Nujoma to SWAPO consultative conference in Tanga, Tanzania", in SWAPO: *The Namibian Documentation*, no pagination.

10 Leys and Saul: "SWAPO: The politics of exile", in Leys and Saul (eds.): *Namibia's Liberation Struggle*, p. 49.

11 Cf. Shipanga: *In Search of Freedom*, ch. 23–31; Dobell: *SWAPO's Struggle for Namibia*, pp. 47–51; Groth: *Namibia - The Wall of Silence*, pp. 55–66; Saul and Leys: "SWAPO. The Politics of Exile", in Leys and Saul (eds.): *Namibia's Liberation Struggle*, pp. 48–53; Colin Leys and John S Saul: "Liberation without democracy? The SWAPO crisis of 1976" (*Journal of Southern African Studies*, 20/1, March 1994, pp. 123–147). For a SWAPO view of the crisis, see Katjavivi: *A History of Resistance in Namibia*, pp. 105–108.

12 Williams: "Exile history" (unpublished D Phil dissertation, University of Michigan, 2009), p. 112; Leys and Saul: "SWAPO: The politics of exile", in Leys and Saul (eds.): *Namibia's Liberation Struggle*, pp. 50–51; Dobell: *SWAPO's Struggle for Namibia*, pp. 53–55.

13 Williams: "Exile history" (unpublished D Phil dissertation, University of Michigan, 2009), p. 113. Williams (pp. 132–136) also highlights that the SWAPO leadership actively utilised many members' belief in witchcraft to portray dissidents as witches.

14 Williams: "Exile history" (unpublished D Phil dissertation, University of Michigan, 2009), pp. 117–118.

15 Katjavivi: *A History of Resistance in Namibia*, p. 100.

16 Toni Weis: "The politics machine: On the concept of 'solidarity' in the East German support for SWAPO" (*Journal of Southern African Studies*, 37/2, 2011).

17 Eva Helene Østbye: "The Namibian liberation struggle: Direct Norwegian support to SWAPO", in Tore Linné Eriksen (ed.): *Norway and National Liberation in Southern Africa*, pp. 98–104; Tor Sellström: "SWAPO of Namibia: Tentative steps towards firm relations", in Tor Sellström (ed.): *Sweden and National Liberation in Southern Africa*, II, *Solidarity and Assistance, 1970-1994*, p. 246.

18 Interview with Otillie Abrahams by Tor Sellström.

19 Groth: *Namibia — The Wall of Silence*, pp. 42 and 70.

20 SWAPO: "Political Programme of the South West Africa People's Organization. Adopted by the meeting of the Central Committee, Lusaka, July 28 – Aug. 1, 1976", p. 6.

21 Dobell: *SWAPO's Struggle for Namibia*, p. 61.

22 Quoted in Richard H Shultz: *The Soviet Union and Revolutionary Warfare. Principles, Practices and Regional Comparisons*, p. 142.

23 Cf. Dobell: *SWAPO's Struggle for Namibia*, p. 58; Leys and Saul: "SWAPO. The Politics of Exile", in Leys and Saul (eds.): *Namibia's Liberation Struggle*, p. 52; Herbstein and Evenson: *The Devils are Among Us*, pp. 47–49; Groth: *Namibia — The Wall of Silence*, pp. 131, 135 and 152; Wallace: *A History of Namibia*, p. 282. Cf. also Katjavivi: *A History of Resistance in Namibia*, p. 109. However, Kimmo Kiljunen acknowledges unequivocally that "SWAPO's programme is socialist in character". Cf. "The ideology of national liberation", in Reginald H Green (ed.): *Namibia, The Last Colony*, p. 185.

24 Saunders: "The foreign policy of Angola under Agostinho Neto", p. 65.

25 Nujoma: *Where Others Wavered*, pp. 247–248.

26 Cf. Leopold Scholtz and Ingrid Scholtz: "Die ontstaan en ontwikkeling van die SAKP se tweefase-revolusiemodel" (*Tydskrif vir Geesteswetenskappe* 30/3 and 30/4, September and December 2004).

27 Shubin: *The Hot "Cold War"*, p. 213.

28 Williams: "Exile history" (unpublished DPhil dissertation, University of Michigan, 2009), p. 136n.

29 Steenkamp: *The South African Border War 1966–1989*, p. 74.

30 Annemarie Heywood (who accepts his excuse) provided the entire interview in her book about the South African assault on Cassinga, from which it is quite clear that he was *not* quoted out of context. Heywood: *The Cassinga Event*, pp. 79–82.

31 Quoted by Henning von Löwis of Menar: *Namibia im Ost-West-Konflikt*, p. 37.

32 Fritz Sitte: *Schicksalfrage Namibia*, p. 91. In the early 1980s, SWAPO also torpedoed a plan to introduce the West German system of voting ("one man, two votes") in Namibia as an "imperialist plot". Cf. Crocker: *High Noon in Southern Africa*, pp. 122–123.

33 Leys and Saul (eds.): "SWAPO: The politics of exile", in Leys and Saul: *Namibia's Liberation Struggle*, p. 63, note 63.

34 Yuri Gorbunov (ed.): *Namibia, a Struggle for Independence. A collection of Articles, Documents and Speeches*, p. 117.

35 SWAPO: *To be Born a Nation*, p. 257.

36 Dobell: *SWAPO's Struggle for Namibia*, p. 86.

37 Gorbunov (ed.): *Namibia, a Struggle for Independence*, p. 10.

38 Sitte: *Schicksalfrage Namibia*, p. 90.

39 Quoted in William Heuva: "Voices in the liberation struggle. Discourse and ideology in the SWAPO exile media", in Henning Melber (ed.): *Re-examining Liberation in Namibia. Political Culture since Independence*, p. 32. Cf also Peter Vanneman: "Soviet foreign policy for Angola/Namibia in the 1980s: a Strategy of coercive diplomacy", in Owen Ellison Kahn (ed.): *Disengagement from Southwest Africa. Prospects for Peace in Angola & Namibia*, p. 142.

40 Randolph Vigne: "SWAPO of Namibia: A

movement in Exile" (*Third World Quarterly*, 9/1, January 1987, p. 98).

41 Weis: "The politics machine: On the concept of 'solidarity' in the East German support for SWAPO" (*Journal of Southern African Studies*, 37/2, 2011).

42 Crocker: *High Noon in Southern Africa*, p. 128; Dobell: *SWAPO's Struggle for Namibia*, p. 71.

43 Herbstein and Evenson: *The Devils are Among Us*, p. 41. One cadre reported that his study in Poland in the 1960s was characterised by Marxist-Leninist theory "as a compulsory subject". Cf. Marcus Schivute: *Go and Come Home. A Namibian Story into Exile and Back*, p. 40.

44 Anonymous: "Self-defeating lies exposed" (*The Combatant*, June 1986).

45 Anonymous: "Cassinga massacre: a product of imperialism" (*The Combatant*, May 1986).

46 Quoted in Heuva: "Voices in the liberation struggle. Discourse and ideology in the SWAPO exile media", in Melber (ed.): *Re-examining Liberation in Namibia*, pp. 29–30.

47 Interrogation report of Mishake Muyongo by Major CA Beukes, n.d., pp. 7–8 (61 Mech online archive).

48 Dobell: *SWAPO's Struggle for Namibia*, pp. 87–89.

49 Christopher Andrew and Vasili Mitrokhin: *The Mitrokhin Archive, II. The KGB and the World*, p. 9. Cf. also Odd Arne Westad: *The Global Cold War*, p. 214; Robert Service: *Comrades! Communism: A World History*, p. 319.

50 Andrew and Mitrokhin: *The Mitrokhin Archive, II*, pp. 9–10. Odd Arne Westad confirms on the basis of original documents that the KGB was the chief architect of the Third World strategy of the Kremlin. Cf. Westad: "Moscow and the Angolan crisis, 1974–1976: A new pattern of intervention" (*Cold War International History Project Bulletin* 8–9, Winter 1996–1997, p. 22). Vladimir Shubin denies (without substantiation) that the Soviet Union saw its relations with the Third World as part of the Cold War. See Vladimir Shubin: *ANC. A View from Moscow*, p. 401.

51 David Pryce-Jones: *The War that Never Was.*

The Fall of the Soviet Empire 1985-1991, p. 116.

52 Westad: "Moscow and the Angolan crisis, 1974-1976: A new pattern of intervention" (*Cold War International History Project Bulletin 8-9*, Winter 1996-1997, pp. 21-22).

53 John Lewis Gaddis: *The Cold War*, p. 187.

54 Shultz: *The Soviet Union and Revolutionary Warfare*, p. 127.

55 Cf. Shubin: *The Hot "Cold War"*, p. 16.

56 CIA: "Moscow and the Namibia peace process", April 1982, p. 8 (at www.foia.cia.gov/browse_docs_full.asp).

57 Shultz: *The Soviet Union and Revolutionary Warfare*, pp. 141-142.

58 Groth: *Namibia – The Wall of Silence*, pp. 100 and 101-102.

59 Leys and Saul: "SWAPO: The politics of exile", in Leys and Saul (eds.): *Namibia's Liberation Struggle*, pp. 55-56.

60 Leys and Saul: "Introduction", in Leys and Saul (eds.): *Namibia's Liberation Struggle*, p. 5.

61 Gaomab: "With the People's Liberation Army of Namibia in Angola", in Leys and Brown (eds.): *Life Histories of Namibia*, p. 70.

62 Ibid., p. 68.

63 It is important to note that the ANC at the same time and in roughly the same vicinity went through a similar purge, complete with witch-hunts, concentration camps, torture and other human-rights abuses. But while the ANC later more or less came clean, SWAPO swept everything under the carpet. It must still be investigated whether there was a causal relationship between the two.

64 Williams: "Exile history" (unpublished D Phil dissertation, University of Michigan, 2009), pp. 145-146; Leys and Saul (eds.): *Namibia's Liberation Struggle*, p. 65, note 80; "With the People's Liberation Army of Namibia in Angola", in Leys and Brown (eds.): *Life Histories of Namibia*, pp. 70-71.

65 Groth: *Namibia – The Wall of Silence*, p. 105.

66 Paul Trewhela: *Inside Quatro. Uncovering the Exile History of the ANC and SWAPO*, p. 149.

67 Ibid., pp. 150-161.

68 Ibid., p. 153. Several similar eyewitness accounts were recorded by Groth: *Namibia – The Wall of Silence*, pp. 114-129. Cf. also the account by Gaomab: "With the People's Liberation Army of Namibia in Angola", in Leys and Brown (eds.): *Life Histories of Namibia*, p. 73.

69 Steenkamp: "The Churches", in Leys and Saul (eds.): *Namibia's Liberation Struggle*, p. 106.

70 Elena Torreguitar: *National Liberation Movements in Office. Forging Democracy with African Adjectives in Namibia*, p. 242.

71 Hooper: *Koevoet*, p. 26.

72 Melber: *Re-examining Liberation in Namibia*, p. 144.

73 Colin Leys: "Lubango and after", in Colin Leys: *The Next Liberation Struggle: Capitalism, Socialism and Democracy in Southern Africa*, ch. 5.

74 Trewhela: *Inside Quatro*, p. 167.

75 Groth: *Namibia – The Wall of Silence*, p. 74.

76 Williams: "Exile history" (unpublished D Phil dissertation, University of Michigan, 2009), p. 199.

77 Groth: *Namibia – The Wall of Silence*, p. 82.

78 Shubin: *The Hot "Cold War"*, p.228.

79 Williams: "Exile history" (unpublished D Phil dissertation, University of Michigan, 2009), p. 158.

80 Interview with Sten Rylander by Lennart Wohgemuth, at www.liberationafrica.se/intervstories/interviews/rylander_s/index.xml?by-country=1&node-id=2238869971-39.

81 Crocker: *High Noon in Southern Africa*, p. 122.

82 Williams: "Exile history" (unpublished D Phil dissertation, University of Michigan, 2009), p. 20.

83 Groth: *Namibia – The Wall of Silence*, p. 103.

84 Leys and Saul: "Liberation without democracy?" (*Journal of Southern African Studies*, 20/1, March 1994, p. 145).

85 Ibid.

86 Leys and Saul: *Namibia's Liberation Struggle*, pp. 56-57.

87 Torreguitar: *National Liberation Movements in Office*, p. 283.

88 Leys and Saul (eds.): "Introduction", in Leys and Saul: *Namibia's Liberation Struggle*, p. 3.

CHAPTER 11

1 W James Martin III: *A Political History of the Civil War in Angola 1974–1990*, chapter 6.

2 Saunders: "The foreign policy of Angola under Agostinho Neto", p. 67.

3 Bridgland: *Jonas Savimbi*, p. 275.

4 Military Intelligence: "Military Situation in Angola", n.d. [1980] (61 Mech online archive).

5 MI/203/4/0502: "Angola: Unita invloed op die Angolese situasie en RSA-hulp sedert Operasie Savannah", 15.2.1979 (61 Mech online archive). Cf. also Meiring: "Current SWAPO activity in South West Africa" (*Strategic Review for Southern Africa*, 2/1985, p. 15); Leys and Saul: "SWAPO: The politics of exile", in Leys and Saul (eds.): *Namibia's Liberation Struggle*, p. 55; Turner: *Continent Ablaze*, p. 35; Steenkamp: *South Africa's Border War 1966–1989*, p. 110.

6 *TRC Report*, II, p. 57, par. 56.

7 Breytenbach: *Eagle Strike!*, pp. 104–105.

8 George: *The Cuban Intervention in Angola*, p. 165.

9 Geldenhuys: *Dié wat gewen het*, p. 68.

10 HSAW/NGBS/303/5/11/2: "Korttermynstrategie vir Angola", 15.3.1979 (Disa online archive). Cf. also Crocker: *High Noon in Southern Africa*, p. 56.

11 Saunders: "The foreign policy of Angola under Agostinho Neto", p. 73.

12 Cf. pp. 21–24 in chapter 2.

13 Quoted by Piero Gleijeses: *The Cuban Drumbeat. Castro's Worldview: Cuban Foreign Policy in a Hostile World*, p. 59.

14 CIA: "Soviet policy and Africa", February 1981, p. 8.

15 "Fidel Castro's 1977 Southern Africa tour: A report to Honecker", 3.4.1977; Aluka, "Cuba-Angola declaration", 4.2.1982; Deutschmann (ed.): *Changing the History of Africa*, p. 106 (speech by Castro, 5.12.1988); George: *The Cuban Intervention in Angola*, pp. 116–117.

16 Ibid., pp. 120 and 152–153; Bridgland: *Jonas Savimbi*, pp. 237 and 270.

17 Deutschmann (ed.): *Changing the History of Africa*, p. 106 (speech by Castro, 5.12.1988).

18 Cf. "Transcript of Meeting between U.S. Secretary of State Alexander M. Haig, Jr., and Cuban Vice Premier Carlos Rafael Rodriguez, Mexico City, 23.11.1981, at www.wilsoncenter.org/index.cfm?topic_id=1409&fuseaction=va2.document&identifier=5034EF21–96B6–175C–9C45700AE8493D87&sort=Subject&item=Contras.

19 Speech by Fidel Castro, 26.7.1982, at lanic.utexas.edu/project/castro/db/1982/19820726.html.

20 Shubin: *The Hot "Cold War"*, pp. 94–96.

21 Deutschmann (ed.): *Changing the History of Africa*, p. 106 (speech by Castro, 5.12.1988).

22 Ibid., p. 94 (interview with Castro in *Washington Post*, 30.1.1985).

23 Ibid., p. 99 (interview with Castro in *Washington Post*, 30.1.1985).

24 Bridgland: *The War for Africa*, pp. 20–21.

25 Shubin: *The Hot "Cold War"*, pp. 97–98. Cf. also George: *The Cuban Intervention in Angola*, p. 122.

26 *Case 1/1989*, p. 380 (testimony by Fidel Castro, 23.7.1989).

27 CNN interview with Karen Brutents, at www.cnn.com/SPECIALS/cold.war/episodes/17/interviews/brutents/.

28 Shubin: *The Hot "Cold War"*, p. 97.

29 CIA: "The nature of Soviet military doctrine", January 1989, pp. 1–2. http://www.foia.cia.gov/docs/DOC_0000499601/DOC_0000499601.pdf.

30 William A DePalo Jr.: "Cuban internationalism: The Angola Experience, 1985–1988" (*Parameters*, 23, Autumn 1993), p. 65.

31 Deutschmann (ed.): *Changing the History of Africa*, p. 107 (speech by Castro, 5.12.1988).

32 Gleijeses: "Moscow's Proxy? Cuba and Africa 1975–1988", pp. 32–35.

33 Lord: *From Fledgling to Eagle*, pp. 327–329.

34 Ibid., pp. 289–294; George: *The Cuban Intervention in Angola*, pp. 166–170; Wilsworth: *First In, Last Out*, p. 220.

35 Cf. Fidel Castro: "The battle of the truth and Martin Blandino's book," three parts, at http://monthlyreview.org/castro/2008/10/09/the-battle-of-the-truth-and-martin-blandino%E2%80%99s-book/ http://monthlyreview.org/castro/2008/10/12/the-truth-in-battle-and-martin-blandino%E2%80%99s-book-part-ii/ http://monthlyreview.org/castro/2008/10/14/the-battle-of-the-truth-and-martin-blandinos-book-part-3-and-final/

36 Lord: *From Fledgling to Eagle*, p. 290.

37 George: *The Cuban Intervention in Angola*, pp. 166–170.

38 CIA: "Soviet policies in Southern Africa", February 1985, pp. 13–14.

39 *General Del Pino Speaks. Military Dissension in Castro's Cuba.* The Cuban-American National Foundation, pp. 24–25.

40 Crocker: *High Noon in Southern Africa*, pp. 170 and 180; Steenkamp: *South Africa's Border War 1966-1989*, pp. 112–113; Bridgland: *Jonas Savimbi*, pp. 424–425.

41 Vanneman: "Soviet foreign policy for Angola/Namibia in the 1980s: a Strategy of coercive diplomacy", in Kahn (ed.): *Disengagement from Southwest Africa*, p. 73.

42 George: *The Cuban Intervention in Angola*, p. 183; CIA: "Soviet military support to Angola: Intentions and prospects, 24.10.1985, p. 8; Crocker: *High Noon in Southern Africa*, p. 196; Vanneman: "Soviet foreign policy for Angola/Namibia in the 1980s: a Strategy of coercive diplomacy", in Kahn (ed.): *Disengagement from Southwest Africa*, pp. 73–74.

43 Bridgland: *Jonas Savimbi*, p. 443.

44 CIA: "Soviet foreign military assistance", May 1987, p. 23.

45 Shubin: *The Hot "Cold War"*, p. 104.

46 CIA: "Soviet and Cuban objectives and activity in Southern Africa through 1988", February 1988, p. 6.

47 Breytenbach: *Buffalo Soldiers*, pp. 215–218; Nortje: *32 Battalion*, pp. 147–153; Bothma: *Die Buffel Struikel*, pp. 258–261.

48 The following paragraphs about the 1985 offensive are based on the following sources: Breytenbach: *Buffalo Soldiers*, pp. 254–256; Steenkamp: *South Africa's Border War 1966-1989*, pp. 133 and 135; Lord: *From Fledgling to Eagle*, pp. 347–359; Heitman: *War in Angola*, pp. 13–16; Bridgland: *The War for Africa*, pp. 15–16; George: *The Cuban Intervention in Angola*, pp. 193–195; Wilsworth: *First In, Last Out*, pp. 241–246; Vanneman: "Soviet foreign policy for Angola/Namibia in the 1980s: a Strategy of coercive diplomacy", in Kahn (ed.): *Disengagement from Southwest Africa*, p. 75.

49 Breytenbach: *Buffalo Soldiers*, p. 252.

50 Lord: *From Fledgling to Eagle*, pp. 347–355;

51 Quoted in Jaster: *The Defence of White Power*, p. 99.

52 Venter: *The Chopper Boys*, pp. 163–168; Lord: *From Fledgling to Eagle*, pp. 355–358.

53 Full text of the speech at www. presidency.ucsb.edu/ws/index. php?pid=38069#axzz1OyCwkIL6.

54 Full text of speech at www.reagan.utexas.edu/ archives/speeches/1985/102485a.htm.

55 Crocker: *High Noon in Southern Africa*, pp. 293–299.

56 Stiff: *The Silent War*, pp. 534–535; George: *The Cuban Intervention in Angola*, p. 198.

57 Breytenbach: *Buffalo Soldiers*, pp. 266–271; Steenkamp: *South Africa's Border War 1966-1989*, pp. 144–145; Heitman: *War in Angola*, pp. 17–19; Bridgland: *The War for Africa*, pp. 17–18; George: *The Cuban Intervention in Angola*, pp. 197–199; Wilsworth: *First In, Last Out*, pp. 247–260; JA Laubscher: " 'n Briljante debuut: Operasie Alpha Centauri 1986", in Geldenhuys (ed.): *Ons was Daar*, pp. 191–205.

58 Garrett Ernst Eriksen: "Forged in flames: The SADF experience of the Battles of Cuito Cuanavale 1987-1988" (History honours thesis, Rhodes University, 2010), p. 50, at www.scribd.com/doc/48564518/ Forged-in-Flames.

CHAPTER 12

1 Roland de Vries: *Mobiele Oorlogvoering. 'n Perspektief vir Suider-Afrika*, p. xix.

2 Roherty: *State Security in South Africa*, p. 146.

3 De Vries and McCaig: "Mobile warfare in Southern Africa" (*Strategic Review for Southern Africa*, Aug. 1987, p. 11).

4 Kruys: "Doctrine development in the South African armed forces up to the 1980s", in Hough and Du Plessis (eds.): *Selected Military Issues with Specific Reference to the Republic of South Africa*, p. 13.

5 De Vries: *Mobiele Oorlogvoering*, pp. 136–137.

6 Ibid., ch. 6.

7 Ibid., p. xxii

8 Unpublished memoir by Roland de Vries.

9 Lord: *From Fledgling to Eagle*, pp. 330–331.

10 Denis Earp: "The Role of Air Power in

Southern Africa" (*Strategic Review for Southern Africa*, April 1986, p. 34).

11 "Voorligting aan senior offisiere van die SAW oor Operasie Moduler/Hooper", n.d., p. 6 (61 Mech online archive).

12 Bothma: *Anderkant Cuito*, p. 99.

13 Ibid., pp. 99–101.

14 "Firewood B: Personeelverliese", n.d. (group 4, box 160, HSAW 310/4, p. 57). *Anderkant Cuito* mentions 19 dead and 64 wounded. It is possible that some wounded died after the report was compiled.

15 Turton: *Shaking Hands with Billy*, p. 153. Cf. also Heitman: *War in Angola*, p. 20; Geldenhuys: *Dié wat gewen het*, p. 162; Robert Scott Jaster: *The 1988 Peace Accords and the Future of South-Western Africa*, Adelphi Papers 253, p. 17.

16 "Voorligting aan senior offisiere van die SAW oor Operasie Moduler/Hooper", n.d., p. 3 (61 Mech online archive); Bridgland: *The War for Africa*, p. 27.

17 Eriksen: "Forged in flames" (History honours thesis, Rhodes University, 2010), p. 50, at www.scribd.com/doc/48564518/Forged-in-Flames.

18 ST/310/Coronation: "Operations Asterix and Luxor: Establishing the perception amongst MPLA of SADF intervention against an offensive", 31.5.1987 (group 4, HSAW 310/4, Box 160, pp. 54–55).

19 "Lesse geleer tydens konvensionele operasies in die westelike subteater", p. A-1 (document provided by Roland de Vries); "Voorligting aan senior offisiere van die SAW oor Operasie Moduler/Hooper", n.d., pp. 4–5 (61 Mech online archive)

20 William Claiborne: "Angolan rebels prepare for expected offensive" (*Washington Post*, 6.8.1987).

21 "Voorligting aan senior offisiere van die SAW oor Operasie Moduler/Hooper", n.d., p. 9 (61 Mech online archive); HQ 20 Bde – C Army and GOC SWATF, n.d. (61 Mech online archive); "Lesse geleer tydens konvensionele operasies in die westelike subteater", pp. A-1-2 (document provided by Roland de Vries); HK 20 Bde. – H Leër & BG SWA, n.d. (61 Mech online archive); Geldenhuys: *Dié wat gewen het*, p. 167; Freeman: "The Angola/Namibian accords (*Foreign Affairs*, 68/3, Summer 1989, p. 129).

22 Interview with Brigadier General (ret.) Piet Muller, 3.6.2011.

23 W Dorning: "A concise history of Operation Moduler (phase one) May–October 1987" (unpublished SADF document), appendix C, interview with Colonel Jock Harris, 24.9.1987).

24 Bridgland: *The War for Africa*, p. 29.

25 "Lesse geleer tydens konvensionele operasies in die westelike subteater", Inleiding, Aanhangsel A, par. 5 (document provided by Roland de Vries); HS Ops/UG/310/4/3: "Op Moduler sitrap", contained in HSAW 3 – HSAW, 21.8.1987 (group 4, box 160, HSAW 310/4. p. 56).

26 Breytenbach: *Buffalo Soldiers*, pp. 272–273.

27 The story is told in considerable detail in Anton Beukman: "Operation Coolidge II – 4 Verkenningsregiment", in Geldenhuys (ed.): *Ons was daar*, pp. 27–33.

28 "Voorligting aan senior offisiere van die SAW oor Operasie Moduler/Hooper", n.d., p. 19 (61 Mech online archive); HS Ops/UG/310/4: "Terugvoering: HSAW riglyne mbt SAW optredes in SO Angola", 14.9.1987, par. 4 (group 4, box 160, HSAW 310/4. p. 117).

29 H Leër/D OPS/309/1, "Beplanning: Op Modular", 5.6.1987 par. 6–15 (61 Mech online archive).

30 Ibid. par. 16 and 5.

31 "Voorligting aan senior offisiere van die SAW oor Operasie Moduler/Hooper", n.d., par. 8 (61 Mech online archive).

32 Bridgland: *The War for Africa*, p. 32. Cf. also Lord: *From Fledgling to Eagle*, p. 394.

33 Heitman: *War in Angola*, pp. 30–31. Cf. also Gerhard JJ Oosthuizen: "Die Suid-Afrikaanse Weermag en Transgrensoperasie Moduler, fase 1: Die Fapla-offensief teen Unita, Augustus–Oktober 1987" (*New Contree*, no. 60, November 2010, p. 47).

34 AMI/IO/328/6/3: "Komopsplan: Op Modular", 17.9.1987 (61 Mech online archive).

35 Breytenbach: *Buffalo Soldiers*, p. 273.

36 Jock Harris: "Ek is verbaas", in Geldenhuys (ed.): *Ons was Daar*, p. 265–267. Cf. also Dick Lord: "Oorsig van Ops Moduler, Hooper en Packer Suidoos-Angola", in Geldenhuys (ed.): *Ons was Daar*, p. 384.

37 "Voorligting aan senior offisiere van die SAW oor Operasie Moduler/Hooper", n.d., p. 16

(61 Mech online archive); Dorning: "A concise history of Operation Moduler" (unpublished SADF document), p. 10.

38 Dorning: "A concise history of Operation Moduler" (unpublished SADF document), pp. 11–13; H Leër/D OPS/309/1 "Op Instr 18/87: Op Moduler", 22.6.1987 par. 5–6 (61 Mech online archive); "Voorligting aan senior offisiere van die SAW oor Operasie Moduler/Hooper", n.d., pp. 8–9 (61 Mech online archive).

39 Kobus Smit: "Operation Modular", at www.61mech.org.za/operations/19-operation-modular.

40 HS Ops/UG/309/4 Coronation, "Opsinstruksie 11/87: Walene", 17.6.1987 par. 6–11 (61 Mech online archive). Cf also Dorning: "A concise history of Operation Moduler" (unpublished SADF document), p. 15.

41 LMH/TS/SSO Ops Plan/309/4Moduler: "Ops Direktief 29/76: Ops Moduler", 22.6.1987, par. 7 (61 Mech online archive).

42 Bridgland: The War for Africa, p. 33.

43 Bothma: Anderkant Cuito, pp. 118–119.

44 Shubin and Tokarev (eds.): Bush War. (interview with Colonel Vyacheslav Aleksandrovich Mityaev), p. 25.

45 Dorning: "A concise history of Operation Moduler" (unpublished SADF document), pp. 20–25; "Voorligting aan senior offisiere van die SAW oor Operasie Moduler/Hooper", n.d., p. 10 (61 Mech online archive).

46 Bridgland: The War for Africa, p. 32.

47 Interview with Piet Muller, 3.6.2011. Cf also Dorning: "A concise history of Operation Moduler" (unpublished SADF document), pp. 24–25; Bridgland: The War for Africa, p. 32.

48 Dorning: "A concise history of Operation Moduler" (unpublished SADF document), pp. 26–27.

49 Smit: "Operation Moduler", at www.61mech.org.za/operations/19-operation-modular; Dorning: "A concise history of Operation Moduler" (unpublished SADF document), p. 30.

50 Wilsworth: First In, Last Out, p. 267.

51 E-mail from Leon Marais, 8.9.2011.

52 Nortje: 32 Battalion, p. 236.

53 Dorning: "A concise history of Operation Moduler" (unpublished SADF document), pp. 34 and 39; "Voorligting aan senior offisiere van die SAW oor Operasie Moduler/Hooper", n.d., p. 20 (61 Mech online archive).

54 Bothma: Anderkant Cuito, p. 119.

55 Heitman: War in Angola, p. 31.

56 HS Ops/UG/309/4 Coronation, "Opsinstruksie 11/87: Walene", 17.6.1987, par. 5 (61 Mech online archive).

57 Michael Parks: "S. African-led forces fight in Angola; battles may signal expansion of Pretoria's military operations" (Washington Post, 29.7.1987).

58 "Genl. Geldenhuys meld tenks, stralers en helikopters in stryd" (Die Burger, 12.11.1987); John Battersby: "South Africa acknowledges its troops aided Angolan rebels" (New York Times, 12.11.1987).

59 Bridgland: The War for Africa, p. 32.

60 Ibid., p. 45.

61 "Lesse geleer tydens konvensionele operasies in die westelike subteater", Inleiding, Aanhangsel A, par. 5 (document provided by Roland de Vries); HS Ops/UG/310/4/3: "Op Moduler sitrap", contained in HSAW 3 – HSAW, 21.8.1987 (group 4, box 160, HSAW 310/4. p. 56).

62 Shubin and Tokarev (eds.): Bush War (interview with Colonel Vyacheslav Aleksandrovich Mityaev), p. 30.

63 This competent and brave officer became the new SANDF's foremost expert on peace support operations after the war. Nevertheless, he was passed over as commander of the SANDF's quick reaction force because of the pale colour of his skin in favour of an inexperienced ex-MK officer with the correct pigmentation and political connections. He resigned with the rank of Colonel and later tragically committed suicide.

64 Dorning: "A concise history of Operation Moduler" (unpublished SADF document), pp. 41–42.

65 Bridgland: The War for Africa, p. 121.

66 C SADF – C Army, 7.9.1987 (61 Mech online archive).

67 Heitman: War in Angola, pp. 311 and 319.

68 LMH/TS/SSO OPS PLAN/309/4/Moduler "Ops Direktief 29/87: Ops Moduler", 22.6.1987, par. 9 (61 Mech online archive).

69 Eriksen: "Forged in flames" (History honours thesis, Rhodes University, 2010),

p. 75, at www.scribd.com/doc/48564518/
Forged-in-Flames.

70 Cf. 309/1 Op Moduler: "Kronologiese
verloop van gevegte oos van Quito rivier
oor die periode 8 Nov tot 17 Nov 1987,
Veggroep C", 19.11.1987, par. 26 (document
provided by Leon Marais).

71 Unless otherwise stated, the analysis of
the Lomba River battles is based on the
following sources: Dorning: "A concise
history of Operation Moduler", pp. 34–71,
plus Dorning's interviews with colonels
Fred Oelschig, Jock Harris, commandants
Jan van der Westhuizen, Robbie Hartslief,
Les Rudman, and majors Theo Wilken,
Hannes Nortmann (appendixes A-I);
"Voorligting aan senior offisiere van die
SAW oor Operasie Moduler/Hooper",
n.d., pp. 14–27 (61 Mech online archive);
Bridgland: *The War for Africa*, pp. 44–164;
Heitman: *War in Angola*, pp. 46–78;
Breytenbach: *Buffalo Soldiers*, pp. 273–
283; Nortje: *32 Battalion*, pp. 233–241;
Wilsworth: *First In, Last Out*, pp. 261–285;
Stiff: *The Silent War*, pp. 544–548; Eriksen:
"Forged in flames" (History honours thesis,
Rhodes University, 2010), pp. 50–55, at
www.scribd.com/doc/48564518/Forged-
in-Flames; Harris: "Ek is verbaas", in
Geldenhuys (ed.): *Ons was Daar*, pp.
266–268.

72 Eriksen: "Forged in flames" (History
honours thesis, Rhodes University, 2010),
p. 71, at www.scribd.com/doc/48564518/
Forged-in-Flames.

73 HS Ops/UG/310/4/3: "Op Moduler sitrap",
15.9.1987 (group 4, box 160, HSAW 310/4,
p. 102).

74 Eriksen: "Forged in flames" (BA Honours
thesis, Rhodes University), pp. 54–55.

75 Dorning: "A concise history of Operation
Moduler" (unpublished SADF document),
appendix F, p. 5, interview with
Commandant Robbie Hartslief, 30.9.1987.

76 Breytenbach: *Buffalo Soldiers*, p. 278.

77 Dorning: "A concise history of Operation
Moduler" (unpublished SADF document),
appendix H, p. 8, interview with Major
Hannes Nortmann, 27.9.1987.

78 Jaster: *The Defence of White Power*,
pp. 102–103.

79 HS Ops/UG/310/4/3: "Op Moduler sitrap"
par. 2 and 3, contained in HSAW 3 –
HSAW, 14.9.1987 (group 4, HSAW 310/4,
pp. 95 and 98).

80 H Leër – BG SWA, 14.9.1987 (61 Mech
online archive).

81 HS Ops/UG/310/4: "Op Moduler
sitrap", contained in HSAW 3 – HSAW,
21.9.1987 (group 4, box 160. HSAW 310/4,
pp. 111–113).

82 Oosthuizen: "Die Suid-Afrikaanse
Weermag en Transgrensoperasie
Moduler, fase 1" (*New Contree*, no. 60,
November 2010, p. 55).

83 Unless otherwise stated, the analysis of this
battle is based on the following sources:
Dorning: "A concise history of Operation
Moduler" (unpublished SADF document),
pp. 74–77; Ops 581: Op Modular: Plan vir
Veggp A se optrede teen 47 Bde", contained
in 20 Brigade HQ – Tactical HQ, Rundu,
3.10.1987 (61 Mech online archive); Smit:
"Operation Modular", at www.61mech.
org.za/operations/19-operation-modular;
Bridgland: *The War for Africa*, pp. 136–
149; Heitman: *War in Angola*, pp. 73–78;
Breytenbach: *Buffalo Soldiers*, pp. 281–283;
Wilsworth: *First In, Last Out*, pp. 282–284.

84 20 Brigade – Battle Groups A, B and
C, Sept. 1987 – exact date not known
(61 Mech online archive).

85 Bridgland: *The War for Africa*, p. 139.

86 Igor Anatolevich Zhdarkin: "Cuito
Cuanavale – Notes from the Trenches,"
diary entry of 14.10.1987, in Shubin and
Tokarev (eds.): *Bush War*, p. 40.

87 Ibid., p. 41.

88 The full story is told by Lord: *From
Fledgling to Eagle*, pp. 418–423; Bridgland:
The War for Africa, pp. 150–150; Eriksen:
"Forged in flames" (History honours thesis,
Rhodes University, 2010), p. 70–72, at
www.scribd.com/doc/48564518/Forged-
in-Flames; Greg Mills and David Williams:
7 Battles that Shaped South Africa,
pp. 175–178.

89 Lord: *From Fledgling to Eagle*, p. 411.

CHAPTER 13

1   Geldenhuys: *Dié wat gewen het*, p. 172.

Cf. also interview with Magnus Malan, 30.10.2001, at www.nelsonmandela.org/omalley/index.php/site/q/03lv00017/04lv00344/05lv01388/06lv01401.htm.

2 Dorning: "A concise history of Operation Moduler", (unpublished SADF document), p. 71.

3 Ibid., p. 72. Cf. also Malan: *My lewe saam met die SA Weermag*, p. 272.

4 H Leër/D OPS/309/1 Op Moduler: "Voorstelle mbt voortgesette deelname aan Op Moduler", 25.9.1987 par. 11–13 (61 Mech online archive).

5 H Leër/D Ops/309/1/Moduler: "Beslissingsvoordrag aan H SAW oor voortgesette SAW deelname aan Op Moduler", n.d. (61 Mech online Archive).

6 H Leër/D Ops/309/1/Op Moduler/Hooper: "Voorligting aan senior offisiere van die SAW oor Operasie Moduler/Hooper", n.d., p. 16 (61 Mech online archive).

7 H Leër/D Ops/309/1 Op Moduler Op instr 24/78, contained in C Army – SWATF, 7.10.1987 (61 Mech online archive); H Leër/D Ops/309/1/Moduler: "Beslissingsvoordrag aan H SAW oor voorgesette SAW deelname aan Op Moduler", n.d.

8 Heitman: *War in Angola*, p. 109; GJJ Oosthuizen: "Die Suid-Afrikaanse Weermag en die 'stryd' om Cuito Cuanavale: Fases 2, 3 en 4 van Operasie Moduler, Oktober–Desember 1987 [deel 2]" (*New Contree*, 61/2011, p. 35).

9 Unpublished memoir by Roland de Vries.

10 Ibid.

11 Ibid.

12 Ibid.

13 Ibid. Cf. also Heitman: *War in Angola*, p. 93.

14 Interview with Magnus Malan, 30.10.2001.

15 Siebrits: "24 Eskader – Per Noctem Per Diem", in Geldenhuys (ed.): *Ons was Daar*, pp. 236–237.

16 Unpublished memoir by Roland de Vries.

17 "Voorligting aan senior offisiere van die SAW oor Operasie Moduler/Hooper", n.d., p. 6 (61 Mech online archive).

18 309/1 Op Moduler: "Kronologiese verloop van gevegte oos van Quito rivier oor die periode 8 Nov tot 17 Nov 1987", 19.11.1988, par. 5 (document provided by Leon Marais); e-mail from Leon Marais, 8.9.2011.

19 Heitman: *War in Angola*, pp. 113–155; Bridgland: *The War for Africa*, pp. 182–183.

20 Eriksen: "Forged in flames" (History Honours thesis, Rhodes University), p. 58.

21 Jordaan: "The role of South African armour in South West Africa/Namibia and Angola, 1975–1989" (*Journal of Contemporary History*, 31/3, 2006, p. 175).

22 "Lesse geleer tydens konvensionele operasies in die westelike subteater", chapter 20, par. 7 (document provided by Roland de Vries).

23 Ibid., chapter 1, par. 5 (document provided by Roland de Vries); H Leër/D Opl/G/309/1: "Nabetragting Modular/Hooper/Packer", 30.5.1988, Appendix C, par. 1 (document provided by Roland de Vries); Heitman: *War in Angola*, p. 106.

24 "Lesse geleer tydens konvensionele operasies in die westelike subteater", chapter 1, par. 13 (document provided by Roland de Vries). In a review after the war, this was identified as a large deficiency in the army. It was also recommended that mechanised battalion groups be augmented with a third mechanised infantry company.

25 Dorning: "A concise history of Operation Moduler", (unpublished SADF document), p. 7.

26 Damian French: "1 SAI – Ratels in Op Hooper (1987–1988)", at sadf.sentinelprojects.com/bG-2/dfrench.html.

27 Heitman: *War in Angola*, pp. 105, 114 and 120; Bridgland: *The War for Africa*, p. 183; Breytenbach: *Buffalo Soldiers*, pp. 284–285; Nortje: *32 Battalion*, pp. 241–242; Wilsworth: *First In, Last Out*, p. 286.

28 Geldenhuys: *Dié wat gewen het*, p. 187.

29 Wilsworth: *First In, Last Out*, p. 288.

30 Heitman: *War in Angola*, p. 108.

31 Cf. Leopold Scholtz: "The air war over Angola, 1987–1988: An analysis" (*Journal for Contemporary History*, 33/3, February 2009, pp. 237–265).

32 Bridgland: *The War for Africa*, p. 181. The story is also told by Heitman: *War in Angola*, pp. 99–100, and Wilsworth: *First In, Last Out*, p. 287.

33 E-mail from Roland de Vries, 9.7.2011; Heitman: *War in Angola*, pp. 117–118 and 121.

34 Unpublished memoir by Roland de Vries.

35 E-mail from Roland de Vries, 28.6.2011.

36 Unpublished memoir by Roland de Vries.

37 Ibid.

38 Ibid.

39 De Vries: *Mobiele Oorlogvoering*, pp. 50–52 and 88.

40 E-mail from Roland de Vries, 28.6.2011.

41 309/1 Op Moduler, "Kronologiese verloop van gevegte oos van Quito rivier oor die periode 8 Nov tot 17 Nov 1987", 19.11.1988, par. 11 (document provided by Leon Marais); unpublished memoir by Roland de Vries.

42 Unpublished memoir by Roland de Vries.

43 Heitman: *War in Angola*, pp. 121–122; Bridgland: *The War for Africa*, p. 188.

44 E-mail from Roland de Vries, 9.7.2011.

45 Unpublished memoir by Roland de Vries.

46 Ibid.

47 Unless stated otherwise, the analysis of this battle is based on the following sources: 309/1 Op Moduler, "Kronologiese verloop van gevegte oos van Quito rivier oor die periode 8 Nov tot 17 Nov 1987", 19.11.1988 par. 12–36 (document provided by Leon Marais); Heitman: *War in Africa*, pp. 122–130; Bridgland: *The War for Africa*, pp. 192–198; Breytenbach: *Buffalo Soldiers*, pp. 284–285; Nortje: *32 Battalion*, pp. 242–243; Martin Teubes: "Met elke geveg uit hul loopgrawe verdryf", in Geldenhuys (ed.): *Ons was Daar*, pp. 300–302. Roland de Vries also kindly provided a personal analysis of the series of Chambinga battles (17 pages!) to me.

48 Heitman: *War in Angola*, p. 125.

49 Online discussion, 11.1.2011, at www.veridical.co.za/default. aspx?tabid=590&forumid =27&postid=129&view=topic.

50 Rob Jefferies: "Lugafweerbrokkies", in Geldenhuys (ed.): *Ons was Daar*, pp. 270–271.

51 Breytenbach: *Buffalo Soldiers*, p. 285.

52 Bridgland: *The War for Africa*, p. 198.

53 E-mails from Leon Marais, 13.6.2011 and 8.9.2011.

54 Bridgland: *The War for Africa*, p. 198.

55 E-mail from Leon Marais, 8.9.2011.

56 Zhdarkin: "Cuito Cuanavale: Notes from the Trenches", diary entry of 11.11.1987, in Shubin and Tokarev (eds.): *Bush War*, p. 57.

57 Unpublished memoir by Roland de Vries.

58 Unless otherwise stated, the analysis of this battle is based on the following sources:; 309/1 Op Moduler: "Kronologiese verloop van gevegte oos van Quito rivier oor die periode 8 Nov tot 17 Nov 1987, Veggroep C", 19.11.1987 par. 41–53 (document provided by Leon Marais); Heitman: *War in Angola*, pp. 132–139; Bridgland: *The War for Africa*, pp. 200–209; Breytenbach: *Buffalo Soldiers*, pp. 286–290; Nortje: *32 Battalion*, p. 243; unpublished memoir by Roland de Vries.

59 Zhdarkin: "Cuito Cuanavale: Notes from the Trenches", diary entry of 12.11.1987, in Shubin and Tokarev (eds.): *Bush War*, p. 59.

60 Unless otherwise mentioned, the analysis of 21 Brigade's escape is based on 309/1 Op Moduler: "Kronologiese verloop van gevegte oos van Quito rivier oor die periode 8 Nov tot 17 Nov 1987, Veggroep C", 19.11.1987 par. 54–65 (document provided by Leon Marais); Bridgland: *The War for Africa*, pp. 215–224; Heitman: *War in Angola*, pp. 140–155; Breytenbach: *Buffalo Soldiers*, pp. 290–293; Nortje: *32 Battalion*, pp. 243–244; unpublished memoir by Roland de Vries.

61 Bridgland: *The War for Africa*, p. 227.

62 Brigadier Frank Bestbier: "Memorandum: Demobilisasie Op Moduler Des 1987", 28.10.1987 (61 Mech online archive).

63 SWAGM – H Leër, 2.11.1987 (61 Mech online archive).

64 20 Brigade HQ – Tac HQ Rundu, n.d. (61 Mech online archive).

65 H SAW/309/1/Op Moduler: "Bevestigende notas Op Modular: H SAW kantoor", 18.11.1987. Jan Breytenbach (*Buffalo Soldiers*, p. 297) alleges that the General Staff decided to accept Liebenberg's third option – advancing west of the Cuito – but it is not clear what his sources are. The sources I have seen do not support his conclusion.

66 Bridgland: *The War for Africa*, pp. 227–228.

67 E-mail correspondence with John Mare, 13.7.2011. Mare and Van Melle Kamp consulted each other about the date of the Cuban contact, and Mare reported that they were "99% sure".

68 Unless stated otherwise, the analysis of this battle is based on the following sources: Tak HK 10 – Veggp A/B/C, 23.11.1987 (document provided by Roland de Vries); Heitman: *War in Angola*, pp. 157–168; Bridgland: *The War for Africa*, pp. 229–232; Breytenbach: *Buffalo Soldiers*, pp. 297–298; unpublished memoir by Roland de Vries.

69 Unpublished personal memoir by Roland de Vries.

70 "Voorligting aan senior offisiere van die SAW oor Operasie Moduler/Hooper", s.d., par. 31 (61 Mech online archive).

71 Bridgland: *The War for Africa*, p. 230.

72 "Voorligting aan senior offisiere van die SAW oor Operasie Moduler/Hooper", s.d., par. 27 (61 Mech online archive).

73 "Lesse geleer tydens konvensionele operasies in die westelike subteater", chapter 1 par. 7 and 8 (document provided by Roland de Vries).

74 Sun Tzu: *The Art of War*, p. 25.

75 BH Liddell Hart: *Memoirs*, I, p. 163.

76 BH Liddell Hart: *Strategy*, pp. 337–339.

CHAPTER 14

1   Resolution 602 (1987), 25.11.1987, at http://daccess-dds-ny.un.org/doc/RESOLUTION/GEN/NR0/524/74/IMG/NR052474.pdf?OpenElement.

2   Theresa Papenfus: *Pik Botha en sy Tyd*, pp. 531–532.

3   SWAGM VHK 309/1 (Op Moduler) Memorandum: "Op beplanning volgens H Leër riglyne", 8.12.1987, par. 2 (61 Mech online archive).

4   George: *The Cuban Intervention in Angola*, pp. 200–211 and 215–216; SWAGM – H SAW, H Leër, "Kub magspeile in Angola", 10.2.1988 (61 Mech online archive).

5   Clive Holt: *At Thy Call we did not Falter. A Frontline Account of the 1988 Angolan War, as Seen Through the Eyes of a Conscripted Soldier*, p. 32.

6   Heitman: *War in Angola*, pp. 176–177; Bridgland: *The War for Africa*, pp. 256–257.

7   Anon.: "Gesamentlike militêre aksies deur RSA en UNITA magte teen FAPLA magte in die sesde militêre streek van Angola vanaf Desember 1987 tot Maart 1988", par. 4 (61 Mech online archive).

8   Ibid., par. 12 (61 Mech online archive).

9   E-mail from Roland de Vries, 24.7.2011.

10 Anon.: "Gesamentlike militêre aksies deur RSA en UNITA magte teen FAPLA magte in die sesde militêre streek van Angola vanaf Desember 1987 tot Maart 1988", par. 13 (61 Mech online archive).

11 SWAGM VHK 309/1 (Op Moduler) Memorandum: "Op beplanning volgens H Leër riglyne", 8.12.1987, par. 2 (61 Mech online archive).

12 Anon.: "Gesamentlike militêre aksies deur RSA en UNITA magte teen FAPLA magte in die sesde militêre streek van Angola vanaf Desember 1987 tot Maart 1988", par. 13 (61 Mech online archive).

13 Ibid. par. 14–16 (61 Mech online archive).

14 Cf. Breytenbach: *Buffalo Soldiers*, p. 302; e-mail from Roland de Vries, 4.8.2011.

15 Heitman: *War in Angola*, p. 176.

16 Unpublished personal memoir by Roland de Vries.

17 Anon.: "Gesamentlike militêre aksies deur RSA en UNITA magte teen FAPLA magte in die sesde militêre streek van Angola vanaf Desember 1987 tot Maart 1988" par. 31–36 (61 Mech online archive).

18 "Lesse geleer tydens konvensionele operasies in die westelike subteater", chapter 1 par. 15 and 20 (document provided by Roland de Vries).

19 Anon.: "Gesamentlike militêre aksies deur RSA en UNITA magte teen FAPLA magte in die sesde militêre streek van Angola vanaf Desember 1987 tot Maart 1988", par. 40 (61 Mech online archive).

20 Steenkamp: *South Africa's Border War 1966–1989*, p. 152; Marga Ley: "Jannie Geldenhuys: 'Ek en Castro het nie saamgesweer'" (*Beeld*, 12.11.1992); Geldenhuys: "Veterane van die Koue Oorlog, insluitend die diensplig-generasie, oor waarheid en propaganda" (full text in author's possession); Geldenhuys: *Dié wat gewen het*, pp. 179 and 191; Geldenhuys: *South Africa is fantastik*, pp. 129–137.

21 Anon.: "Gesamentlike militêre aksies deur RSA en UNITA magte teen FAPLA magte

in die sesde militêre streek van Angola vanaf Desember 1987 tot Maart 1988", par. 45 (61 Mech online archive).

22 According to the official SADF chronicle of Operation Hooper (ibid., par. 89) (61 Mech online archive), the plan was presented to Kat Liebenberg, but Paul Fouché (e-mail, 3.8.2011) is quite adamant that it was Jannie Geldenhuys.

23 309/1: "Op Hooper", contained in 20 Brigade – Tac HQ Rundu, 22.12.1987 (61 Mech online archive).

24 E-mail from Paul Fouché. 12.8.2011.

25 Anon.: "Gesamentlike militêre aksies deur RSA en UNITA magte teen FAPLA magte in die sesde militêre streek van Angola vanaf Desember 1987 tot Maart 1988", par. 89 (61 Mech online archive); e-mail from Paul Fouché, 3.8.2011.

26 "Lesse geleer tydens konvensionele operasies in die westelike subteater", chapter 18, par. 10 (document provided by Roland de Vries).

27 Anon.: "Gesamentlike militêre aksies deur RSA en UNITA magte teen FAPLA magte in die sesde militêre streek van Angola vanaf Desember 1987 tot Maart 1988" par. 89, 93, 112 and 139 (61 Mech online archive).

28 Ibid., par. 113 (61 Mech online archive).

29 Ibid. par. 152–171 (61 Mech online archive).

30 Ibid. par. 172–178 (61 Mech online archive); Lord: From Fledgling to Eagle, pp. 428–434; Bridgland: The War for Africa, pp. 269–271; Siebrits: "24 Eskader Per Noctem Per Diem", in Geldenhuys (ed.): Ons was Daar, pp. 239–241.

31 The analysis of the 13 January battle is based on the following sources: Anon.: "Gesamentlike militêre aksies deur RSA en UNITA magte teen FAPLA magte in die sesde militêre streek van Angola vanaf Desember 1987 tot Maart 1988" par. 251–290 (61 Mech online archive); "Voorligting aan senior offisiere van die SAW oor Operasie Moduler/Hooper", n.d., pp. 41–42 (61 Mech online archive); HS Ops/310/4/3: "Op Hooper sitrap", contained in HSAW 3 – HSAW, 18.1.1988 (group 4, box 160, pp. 139–141); Heitman: War in Angola, pp. 206–213; Bridgland: The War for Africa, pp. 263–267; Breytenbach: Buffalo Soldiers, pp. 301–302; Wilsworth: First In, Last Out, pp. 316–317.

32 French: "1 SAI – Ratels in Op Hooper (1987–1988), at sadf.sentinelprojects.com/bG-2/dfrench.html.

33 E-mail from Jan Malan, 25.7.2011.

34 Ibid.

35 Breytenbach: Buffalo Soldiers, p. 301.

36 E-mail from Jan Malan, 25.7.2011.

37 Anon.: "Gesamentlike militêre aksies deur RSA en UNITA magte teen FAPLA magte in die sesde militêre streek van Angola vanaf Desember 1987 tot Maart 1988", par. 336 (61 Mech online archive).

38 Deutschmann (ed.): Changing the History of Africa, pp. 109–110 (speech by Castro, 5.12.1988).

39 Case 1/1989 (testimony by Fidel Castro in the court case against Ochoa, 12.7.1989), pp. 381 and 385.

40 "Voorligting aan senior offisiere van die SAW oor Operasie Moduler/Hooper", n.d., p. 43 (61 Mech online archive).

41 Anon.: "Gesamentlike militêre aksies deur RSA en UNITA magte teen FAPLA magte in die sesde militêre streek van Angola vanaf Desember 1987 tot Maart 1988" par. 303, 317–322 and 333 (61 Mech online archive); Bridgland: The War for Africa, p. 267.

42 Anon.: "Gesamentlike militêre aksies deur RSA en UNITA magte teen FAPLA magte in die sesde militêre streek van Angola vanaf Desember 1987 tot Maart 1988", par. 323 (61 Mech online archive); Bridgland: The War for Africa, p. 272.

43 Anon.: "Gesamentlike militêre aksies deur RSA en UNITA magte teen FAPLA magte in die sesde militêre streek van Angola vanaf Desember 1987 tot Maart 1988" par. 335 and 348 (61 Mech online archive)

44 Ibid., par. 302 (61 Mech online archive); Bridgland: The War for Africa, p. 273.

45 Anon.: "Gesamentlike militêre aksies deur RSA en UNITA magte teen FAPLA magte in die sesde militêre streek van Angola vanaf Desember 1987 tot Maart 1988" par. 336, 358, 362, 365 and 386 (61 Mech online archive).

46 D Kirkman: "7th South African Infantry Battalion: Memories of my SADF experiences", at www.samagte.co.za/phpbbs/viewtopic.php?f=17&t=439.

47 The analysis of the 14 February attack is based on the following sources: 61 Mech – 20 Tac

HQ, 15.2.1987 (61 Mech online archive);
Anon.: "Gesamentlike militêre aksies deur
RSA en UNITA magte teen FAPLA magte
in die sesde militêre streek van Angola vanaf
Desember 1987 tot Maart 1988" par. 429–485
(61 Mech online archive); "Voorligting aan
senior offisiere van die SAW oor Operasie
Moduler/Hooper", n.d., pp. 45–48 (61 Mech
online archive); Heitman: *War in Angola*,
pp. 227–235; Bridgland: *The War for Africa*,
pp. 272–282; Breytenbach: *Buffalo Soldiers*,
pp. 302–304; George: *The Cuban Intervention
in Angola*, pp. 221–223.

48 *Case 1/1989* (testimony by Fidel Castro,
12.7.1989), p. 386.

49 Hein Groenewald: "Roepsein 22C en 1988 se
Valentynsdag", at www.61mech.org.za/
operations/20-operation-hooper.

50 Holt: *At Thy Call we did not Falter*, p. 78
(story of Hein Groenewald).

51 *Case 1/1989* (testimony by Fidel Castro,
12.7.1989), p. 386.

52 Anon.: "Gesamentlike militêre aksies deur
RSA en UNITA magte teen FAPLA magte
in die sesde militêre streek van Angola vanaf
Desember 1987 tot Maart 1988", par. 473
(61 Mech online archive).

53 One Cuban account (Rubén Urribarres:
"Tanques y otra tégnica enemiga" ["Enemy
tanks and other techniques"], at www.
urrib2000.narod.ru/Tanques3.html) alleges
that the SADF attacked with 40 Olifant tanks,
of which 10 were destroyed. This author,
however, is notorious for his propagandistic
take on the war and need never be
taken serious.

54 *Case 1/1989* (testimony by Fidel Castro,
12.7.1989), p. 386.

55 Ibid., p. 386.

56 Ibid., p. 387–388.

57 Cf. Leopold Scholtz: "The South African
Strategic and Operational Objectives in
Angola, 1987–1988" (*Scientia Militaria*, 38/1,
2010, pp. 68–98).

58 Anon.: "Gesamentlike militêre aksies deur
RSA en UNITA magte teen FAPLA magte
in die sesde militêre streek van Angola vanaf
Desember 1987 tot Maart 1988" par. 367–368
(61 Mech online archive).

59 Geldenhuys: *Dié wat Gewen het*, p. 177.

60 The following analysis is based on TM HK

10 – Bde HK 20, 20.2.1988; THK10 – Bde
HK 20, n.d. (both documents provided
by Roland de Vries); Heitman: *War in
Angola*, pp. 236–240; Bridgland: *The War for
Africa*, pp. 244–253 and 286–293; Nortje:
32 Battalion, pp. 245–247; Wilsworth: *First
In, Last Out*, pp. 320–333.

61 Bridgland: *The War for Africa*, p. 250.

62 Karl Maier: *Angola: Promises and Lies*, p. 27.

63 George: *The Cuban Intervention in Angola*,
p. 327, footnote 39.

64 Shubin and Tokarev (eds.): *Bush War*, p. 197,
footnote 39.

65 HS Ops/UG/310/4/3: "Op Hooper Sitrap",
contained in HSAW 3 – HSAW, 26.2.1988
(group 4, box 160, p. 176).

66 Bridgland: *The War for Africa*, p. 292.

CHAPTER 15

1 Bridgland: *The War for Africa*, p. 294.

2 Anon.: "Gesamentlike militêre aksies deur
die RSA en Unita magte teen FAPLA magte
in die Sesde Militêre Streek van Angola
vanaf Desember 1987 tot Maart 1988" par.
512 and 514–515 (61 Mech online archive).

3 Holt: *At Thy Call we did not Falter*,
pp. 84–85.

4 Heitman: *War in Angola*, p. 244.

5 Anon.: "Gesamentlike militêre aksies deur
RSA en UNITA magte teen FAPLA magte
in die sesde militêre streek van Angola vanaf
Desember 1987 tot Maart 1988" par. 519 (61
Mech online archive).

6 "Voorligting aan senior offisiere van die
SAW oor Operasie Moduler/Hooper", n.d.,
p. 40 (61 Mech online archive).

7 GG/SG – Bev. Med. Kmdmt. SWA,
19.2.1988 (61 Mech online archive).

8 Anon.: "Gesamentlike militêre aksies deur
RSA en UNITA magte teen FAPLA magte
in die sesde militêre streek van Angola
vanaf Desember 1987 tot Maart 1988" par.
498–508 (61 Mech online archive); Heitman:
War in Angola, pp. 242–243; Bridgland: *The
War for Africa*, p. 283; George: *The Cuban
Intervention in Angola*, pp. 224–225.

9 George: *The Cuban Intervention in Angola*,
p. 225.

10 Jaster: *The Defence of White Power*, p. 95.

11 Cf. Lord: *From Fledgling to Eagle*, p. 426;

Heitman: *War in Angola*, p. 312; Bridgland: *The War for Africa*, pp. 261–262.

12 Heitman: *War in Angola*, pp. 48–49; Lord: *From Fledgling to Eagle*, p. 425.

13 Bridgland: *The War for Africa*, p. 261.

14 Ibid, p. 262.

15 The analysis of the battle is based on the following sources: Anon.: "Gesamentlike militêre aksies deur RSA en UNITA magte teen FAPLA magte in die sesde militêre streek van Angola vanaf Desember 1987 tot Maart 1988" par. 529–569 (61 Mech online archive); "Voorligting aan senior offisiere van die SAW oor Operasie Moduler/Hooper", n.d., pp. 50–53 (61 Mech online archive); CS Ops/310/4/3: "Op Hooper Sitrep Primary Report", contained in CSADF 3 – CSADF, 15.2.1988 (group 4, box 160, HSAW 310/4, pp. 189–191); HS Ops/UG/310/4/3: "Op Hooper Sitrap", contained in HSAW 3 – HSAW, 26.2.1988 (group 4, box 160, pp. 174–175); Heitman: *War in Angola*, pp. 245–254; Bridgland: *The War for Africa*, pp. 294–307; Breytenbach: *Buffalo Soldiers*, pp. 304–306; Nortje: *32 Battalion*, p. 246; Wilsworth: *First In, Last Out*, pp. 337–338; Holt: *At Thy Call we did not Falter*, pp. 89–100; George: *The Cuban Intervention in Angola*, pp. 225–227.

16 Anon.: "Gesamentlike militêre aksies deur RSA en UNITA magte teen FAPLA magte in die sesde militêre streek van Angola vanaf Desember 1987 tot Maart 1988" par. 571, 581 and 589 (61 Mech online archive).

17 William Surmon: "School of Armour – 4 SAI – Operation Hooper (1987–1988), diary entry of 3.1.1988, at uk.geocities.com/ sasolboy/abenstxt.html.

18 Bridgland: *The War for Africa*, p. 311.

19 Anon.: "Gesamentlike militêre aksies deur RSA en UNITA magte teen FAPLA magte in die sesde militêre streek van Angola vanaf Desember 1987 tot Maart 1988" par. 590, 594 and 597 (61 Mech online archive).

20 Ibid., par. 570 (61 Mech online archive).

21 This analysis is based on Anon: "Gesamentlike militêre aksies deur RSA en UNITA magte teen FAPLA magte in die sesde militêre streek van Angola vanaf Desember 1987 tot Maart 1988" par. 582–634 (61 Mech online archive);

"Voorligting aan senior offisiere van die SAW oor Operasie Moduler/Hooper", n.d., pp. 53–54 (61 Mech online archive); Aanhangsel B by Ops/558/02 Mar 88: "Aanval op Tumpo 1.3.88 volgorde van gebeure" (group 4, box 160, HSAW 310/4, p. 205); Heitman: *War in Angola*, pp. 255–262; Bridgland: *The War for Africa*, pp. 308–314; Breytenbach: *Buffalo Soldiers*, p. 306; George: *The Cuban Intervention in Angola*, pp. 227–230.

22 Bridgland: *The War for Africa*, p. 311.

23 HS Ops/UG/310/4/3: "Op Hooper Sitrap", contained in HSAW 3 – HSAW, 2.3.1988 (group 4, box 160, p. 209).

24 Anon.: "Gesamentlike militêre aksies deur RSA en UNITA magte teen FAPLA magte in die sesde militêre streek van Angola vanaf Desember 1987 tot Maart 1988", par. 626 (61 Mech online archive).

25 Bridgland: *The War for Africa*, pp. 321–324; Heitman: *War in Africa*, p. 266; Wilsworth: *First In, Last Out*, pp. 340–343; GJJ Oosthuizen: "The final phase of South African transborder operations into Angola: Regiment Mooi River and Operations Modular, Hooper, Packer and Displace (Handbag), 1987–1988" (*Journal of Contemporary History*, 28/2, 2003, p. 100).

26 E-mail from Gerhard Louw, 17.8.2011.

27 Bridgland: *The War for Africa*, p. 321.

28 "H Leër/D OPL/G/309/1: Nabetragting Modular/Hooper/Packer", 30.5.1988, appendix M, par. 5 (document provided by Roland de Vries).

29 E-mail from Gerhard Louw, 12.8.2011.

30 Ibid.

31 H Leër/D Opl/G/309/1: "Nabetragting Modular/Hooper/Packer", 30.5.1988, Appendix B, par. 3 (document provided by Roland de Vries).

32 George: *The Cuban Intervention in Angola*, p. 232.

33 The analysis of this battle is based on the following sources: HS Ops/UG/310/4/3: "Verslag: Aanval 82 Meg Bde op Tumpo op 23 Mrt 88", contained in HSAW 3 – HSAW, 24.3.1988 (group 3, box 160, HSAW 310/4, pp. 223–229); HS Ops/UG/310/4/3: "Op Packer sitrap", contained in HSAW 3 – HSAW, 28.3.1988 (group 3, box 160, HSAW 310/4,

pp. 230–232); Heitman: *War in Angola*,
pp. 274–280; Bridgland: *The War for Africa*,
pp. 323–333; Breytenbach: *Buffalo Soldiers*,
pp. 307–309; Nortje: *32 Battalion*, pp. 247–
249; Oosthuizen: "The final phase of South
African transborder operations into Angola"
(*Journal of Contemporary History*, 28/2, 2003,
pp. 100–104); George: *The Cuban Intervention
in Angola*, pp. 232–233.

34 E-mails from Paul Fouché, 11.8.2011 and
Gerhard Louw, 12.8.2001.

35 E-mail from Gerhard Louw, 12.8.2001.

36 E-mail from Gerhard Louw, 17.8.2011.

37 Ibid.

38 Johan Schoeman, at www.warinangola.com/
default.aspx?tabid=590&forumid=43&
postid=295&view=topic (posted on
24.11.2009).

39 Bridgland: *The War for Africa*, p. 328.

40 E-mail from Gerhard Louw, 17.8.2011.

41 E-mail from Gerhard Louw, 12.8.2011.

42 Ibid. Cf. also HS Ops/UG/410/4/3: "Op
Packer Sitrap", contained in HSAW 3 – HSAW
milsek, 29.3.1988 (group 4, box 160, p. 234).

43 Heitman: *War in Angola*, pp. 281–284.

44 Ibid., pp. 285–294; Geldenhuys: *Dié wat
gewen het*, p. 176.

45 Crocker: *High Noon in Southern Africa*,
p. 370.

46 "H Leër/D OPL/G/309/1: Nabetragting
Modular/Hooper/Packer", 30.5.1988
(document provided by Roland de Vries).

47 SA Military History Society: "Newsletter No
1 October 2009", at http://samilitaryhistory.
org/9/p09octne.html.

48 "H Leër/D OPL/G/309/1: Nabetragting
Modular/Hooper/Packer", 30.5.1988
(document provided by Roland de Vries).

CHAPTER 16

1 Cf. Deutschmann (ed.): *Changing the History
of Africa* (interview with Fidel Castro in
the *Washington Post*, 30.1.1985), p. 94;
Case 1/1989, (testimony by Fidel Castro,
12.7.1989), p. 381.

2 Gabriel Marcella and Daniel S Papp: "The
Soviet-Cuban relationship: symbiotic or
parasitic?", in Robert H Donaldson (ed.): *The
Soviet Union in the Third World: Successes
and Failures*, pp. 57–58; Mervyn J Bain:

"Cuba-Soviet relations in the Gorbachev era"
(*Journal of Latin American Studies*, 37/2005,
p. 777).

3 CIA: Cuba: "The Outlook for Castro and
Beyond", August 1993, p. 1.

4 Cf. George Black: "Toward victory always,
but when?" (*The Nation*, 24.10.1988,
pp. 384–385).

5 "Castro Moncada Barracks anniversary
speech", 26.7.1988, at http://lanic.utexas.edu/
project/castro/db/1988/19880726.html.

6 *General Del Pino Speaks*. The Cuban-
American National Foundation, p. 12. That
a posting to Angola was used as punishment
is confirmed by Jaime Suchlicki, researcher
at the Research Institute for Cuban Studies
in Miami, in his *The Cuban Military under
Castro*, p. 116.

7 *General Del Pino Speaks*. The Cuban-
American National Foundation, pp. 13–14.

8 Ibid., p. 17.

9 *Case 1/1989* (testimony by Raúl Castro,
26.6.1989), p. 51.

10 *Case 1/1989* (testimony by Fidel Castro,
12.7.1989), p. 380.

11 George: *The Cuban Intervention in Angola*,
pp. 324 (note 1) and 143.

12 Crocker: *High Noon in Southern Africa*,
p. 365.

13 *Case 1/1989* (testimony of Fidel Castro,
12.7.1989), p. 381.

14 Shubin: *The Hot "Cold War"*, p. 105.

15 Crocker: *High Noon in Southern Africa*,
p. 365.

16 Gleijeses: *The Cuban Drumbeat*, p. 62.

17 *Case 1/1989* (testimony of Fidel Castro,
12.7.1989), p. 381; Deutschmann: *Changing
the History of Africa*, pp. 108–109 (speech
by Castro, 5.12.1988); George: *The Cuban
Intervention in Angola*, p. 211.

18 *Case 1/1989* (testimony of Fidel Castro,
12.7.1989), p. 394.

19 Crocker: *High Noon in Southern Africa*,
pp. 361–362.

20 Deutschmann (ed.): *Changing the History of
Africa* (speech by Fidel Castro, 5.12.1988),
p. 114.

21 Crocker: *High Noon in Southern Africa*,
pp. 355 and 368. Cf. also Geldenhuys: *Dié
wat gewen het*, p. 181.

22 Crocker: *High Noon in Southern Africa*,

p. 384. Cf. also "Interview with Maria Shriver", 28.2.1988, at http://lanic.utexas.edu/project/castro/db/1988/19880228-1.html.

23 HSAW 2 – HSAW 3: "Kubaanse betrokkenheid in Angola", par. 5, 25.4.1988 (group 4, box 160, HSAW 310/4, p. 266).

24 In his contribution to an anthology of South African diplomats' reminiscences, Mare writes that the Cuban mission phoned him "in 1987" (cf. Wolvaardt, Wheeler and Scholtz (eds.): *From Verwoerd to Mandela*, III, pp. 142–143). However, on reflection and after discussing it with his colleague Chris van Melle Kamp, he e-mailed me to say, "I am 99% sure that I received the telephone call from the Cuban diplomats … in mid/late February 1988" (e-mail, 13.7.2011).

25 E-mail from John Mare, 13.7.2001.

26 Ibid.

27 Wolvaardt, Wheeler and Scholtz (eds.): *From Verwoerd to Mandela*, III, p. 232.

28 Papenfus: *Pik Botha en sy Tyd*, pp. 532–533.

29 Wolvaardt, Wheeler and Scholtz (eds.): *From Verwoerd to Mandela*, I, p. 281 (reminiscences of Neil van Heerden).

30 Crocker: *High Noon in Southern Africa*, p. 386.

31 "Meeting between Director-General N.P. van Heerden and Dr. C. Crocker, Assistant Secretary of State in Washington on 30 March 1988" (Aluka online archive). Cf. also Crocker: *High Noon in Southern Africa*, pp. 386–390.

32 Wolvaardt, Wheeler and Scholtz (eds.): *From Verwoerd to Mandela*, p. 282 (reminiscences of Neil van Heerden).

33 *Case 1/1989* (testimony by Fidel Castro, 12.7.1989), pp. 379–380.

34 Ibid., p. 394.

35 Cf. Scholtz: "The standard of research on the Battle of Cuito Cuanavale, 1987–1988" (*Scientia Militaria*, 39/1, 2001, pp. 115–137).

36 Isaac Deutschmann: "Preface", in Deutschmann (ed.): *Changing the History of Africa*, p. viii.

37 Cf. Scholtz: "The South African strategic and operational objectives in Angola, 1987–1988" (*Scientia Militaria*, 38/1, 2010, pp. 68–98).

38 Deutschmann (ed.): *Changing the History*

of Africa, p. 109 (speech by Fidel Castro, 5.12.1988).

39 Roland de Vries: "Operation Prone – the operation that never was" (unpublished memoir in author's possession).

40 *Case 1/1989*, (testimony by Fidel Castro, 12.7.1989), p. 389; George: *The Cuban Intervention in Angola*, pp. 215–216 and 236; SWS2/inl/203/4: "Kub magspeile in Angola", SWAGM 21 – HSAW2, 10.2.1988 (61 Mech online archive).

41 HSAW 2 – HSAW 3: "Militêre situasie in Angola", 14.4.1988 (group 4, box 160, HSAW 310/4, pp. 257–258).

42 HSAW 2 – HSAW 3: "Kubaanse betrokkenheid in Angola", par. 9, 25.4.1988 (group 4, box 160, HSAW 310/4, pp. 261–263).

43 Crocker: *High Noon in Southern Africa*, p. 367.

44 Deutschmann (ed.): *Changing the History of Africa* (speech by Fidel Castro, 5.12.1988), p. 109.

45 *Case 1/1989* (testimony by Fidel Castro, 12.7.1989), pp. 389 and 391; Deutschmann (ed.): *Changing the History of Africa* (speech by Fidel Castro, 5.12.1988), p. 111; George: *The Cuban Intervention in Angola*, p. 237.

46 Lord: *From Fledgling to Eagle*, pp. 447–448.

47 CSADF/310/4: "Implementation Res 435: Military aspects", 14.9.1988 (Group 4, box 160, HSAW/3009/4, p. 228); George: *The Cuban Intervention in Angola*, p. 239; Crocker: *High Noon in Southern Africa*, p. 367; Breytenbach: *Buffalo Soldiers*, p. 316; Heitman: *War in Angola*, p. 296; Nortje: *32 Battalion*, p. 249; Geldenhuys: *Dié wat gewen het*, pp. 189–190; De Vries: "Operation Prone – the operation that never was" (unpublished memoir in author's possession).

48 CSADF/310/4: "Implementation Res 435: Military aspects", 14.9.1988 (group 4, box 160, HSAW/3009/4, p. 228).

49 Crocker: *High Noon in Southern Africa*, pp. 366–367.

50 Gleijeses: "Moscow's Proxy? Cuba and Africa 1975–1988" (*Journal of Cold War Studies*, 8/2, Spring 2006, p. 37).

51 Deutschmann (ed.): *Changing the History of Africa*, pp. 109–110 (speech by Fidel Castro, 5.12.1988).

52 Liddell Hart: *Strategy*, pp. 348–349.

53 Lord: *From Fledgling to Eagle*, p. 447.

54 Cf. Breytenbach: *Buffalo Soldiers*, p. 316.

55 "Summary minutes of a meeting held at the US embassy in Cairo on 24 June 1988 between the South African and US delegations to the Cairo talks" (Aluka online archive).

56 Unless stated otherwise, the following analysis of the Cuban-South African clashes is based on MI/204/3/A6/8, Wakefull – Alle atts & verts, 29.6.1988 (61 Mech online archive); Heitman: *War in Angola*, pp. 295–307; Bridgland: *The War for Africa*, pp. 341–364; Breytenbach: *Buffalo Soldiers*, pp. 315–324; Nortje: *32 Battalion*, pp. 249–253; Wilsworth: *First In, Last Out*, pp. 343–358; Geldenhuys: *Dié wat gewen het*, pp. 192–201; George: *The Cuban Intervention in Angola*, pp. 236–246; Crocker: *High Noon in Southern Africa*, pp. 371–372; G.H.F. Swanepoel: "Teikenvaslegging deur middel van misleiding", in Geldenhuys (ed.): *Ons was Daar*, pp. 457–459.

57 George: *The Cuban Intervention in Angola*, p. 242.

58 *Case 1/1989*, (testimony by Fidel Castro, 12.7.1989), p. 390.

59 Ibid., p. 391.

60 Hein Groenewald: "Op Excite – Calueque gedurende Junie 1988: Die laaste aanval in Angola", submitted 1.4.2010, at www.61mech.org.za/operations/22-operation-excite#stories-photos.

61 Piero Gleijeses: "Cuba and the Independence of Namibia" (*Cold War History*, 7/2, May 2007, p. 295); Crocker: *High Noon in Southern Africa*, p. 372.

62 Gleijeses: "Cuba and the Independence of Namibia" (*Cold War History*, 7/2, May 2007, p. 295).

63 Groenewald: "Op Excite – Calueque gedurende Junie 1988: Die laaste aanval in Angola", submitted 1.4.2010.

64 Bridgland: *The War for Africa*, pp. 361–362.

65 Chris Serfontein: "Die Calueque-voorpos – Techipa", in Geldenhuys (ed.): *Ons was Daar*, p. 425.

66 MS/UG/309/1 "Bevestigende notas oor vergadering op 4 Jul 88 oor ops en krygstuig-aangeleenthede met betrekking tot Noord-SWA en Suid-Angola", par. 4, 5.7.1988 (61 Mech online archive).

67 HS Ops – H Leër, HLM, GG and BG Spesmagte, 15.7.1988 (Group 4, Box 160, H SAW 3009/4, p. 118).

68 *Case 1/1989*, (testimony by Fidel Castro, 12.7.1989), p. 391.

69 Crocker: *High Noon in Southern Africa*, p. 371.

70 Cf. "Closing of the WPC presidential committee meeting", 23.4.1981, at http://lanic.utexas.edu/project/castro/db/1981/19810421.html; "Paris meeting on South Africa", 21.5.1981, at http://lanic.utexas.edu/project/castro/db/1981/19810521.html; "Castro speaks at closing of European solidarity meeting", 16.12.1993, at http://lanic.utexas.edu/project/castro/db/1993/19931216.html.

71 "Excerpt from Fidel Castro's address to Abyssinian Baptist Church in Harlem", 23.10.1995, at http://www.hartford-hwp.com/archives/43b/022.html.

72 Fidel Castro: "Finding out the truth in time" (*Granma*, 28.6.2010, at http://www.granma.cu/ingles/reflections-i/28jun-Reflections.html).

73 "Castro addresses U.S. Friendship Caravan", 21.9.1996, at http://lanic.utexas.edu/project/castro/db/1996/19960921.html.

74 Castro: "Finding out the truth in time" (*Granma*, 28.6.2010, at http://www.granma.cu/ingles/reflections-i/28jun-Reflections.html).

75 "Apartheid govt wanted to nuke Cuban troops", 14.12.2010, at www.politicsweb.co.za/politicsweb/view/politicsweb/en/page71654?oid=215328&sn=Detail&pid=71616.

76 Waldo Stumpf: "Birth and death of the South African nuclear weapons programme", at www.fas.org/nuke/guide/rsa/nuke/stumpf.htm.

77 Peter Liberman: "The rise and fall of the South African bomb" (*International Security*, 26/2, Autumn 2001, p. 54).

78 Jan-Jan Joubert: "Kuba het SA se kernvermoë totaal oorskat" (*Rapport*, 4.1.2011).

79 Ibid.

80 Ibid. Cf. also Liberman: "The rise and fall of the South African bomb" (*International Security*, 26/2, Autumn 2001, p. 56).

81 Stumpf: "Birth and death of the South African nuclear weapons programme".

82 "Summary minutes of the bilateral meeting held in Brazzaville on Friday 13 May between delegations from the Governments of the Republic of South Africa and the People's Republic of Angola" (Aluka online archive).

83 "Summary minutes of a meeting held at the United States Embassy in Cairo, June 24, 1988 between the South African and United States delegations" (Aluka online archive).

84 Shubin: *The Hot "Cold War"*, p. 111; Crocker: *High Noon in Southern Africa*, p. 367.

85 Gleijeses: "Moscow's Proxy? Cuba and Africa 1975–1988", pp. 41–41); Crocker: *High Noon in Southern Africa*, p. 399.

86 Peter Vanneman: *Soviet Strategy in Southern Africa*, p. 38.

87 H Leër/D Ops/310/4 – Hilti: "Op instr 21/88 Op Hilti", 30.5.1988 par. 3–7 (document provided by Roland de Vries). Cf. also Geldenhuys: *Dié wat gewen het*, pp. 190–191.

88 Chief Army – Sector 20 HQ, 24.6.1988 (61 Mech online archive).

89 Bridgland: *The War for Africa*, p. 345.

90 Van der Waals: "Lewensverhaal: Willem Stephanus van der Waals", p. 210 (unpublished memoirs, with permission from the author).

91 "Ops order: Op Prone", 19.7.1988, byvoegsels 3 en 4, aanhangsel A" (document provided by Roland de Vries).

92 Breytenbach: *Buffalo Soldiers*, p. 316.

93 Malan: *My lewe saam met die SA Weermag*, p. 296.

94 Geldenhuys: *Dié wat gewen het*, pp. 190–191.

95 Ibid., pp. 191–192.

96 "Lesse geleer tydens konvensionele operasies in die westelike subteater", chapter 1, par. 24 (document provided by Roland de Vries).

97 Geldenhuys: *Dié wat gewen het*, pp. 195–196.

98 Unpublished personal memoir by Roland de Vries.

99 D Ops/310/4/Hilti: Director Operations – C Army, 1 June 1988 (document provided by Roland de Vries).

100 "Lesse geleer tydens konvensionele operasies in die westelike subteater", appendix A with chapter 1; "Aanhangsel A by H Leër/ D Ops/310/4 – Hilti: Op instr 21/88: Magsamestellings SA Leër Op Hilti", 27.5.1988 (document provided by Roland de Vries).

101 H Leër/D Ops/309/4 – Hilti: "Op instr 21/88 Op Hilti", 30.5.1988 par. 15–17, 19 and 23 (document provided by Roland de Vries). "Lesse geleer tydens konvensionele operasies in die westelike subteater", chapter 1, par. 31 (document provided by Roland de Vries).

102 De Vries: "Operation Prone – the operation that never was" (unpublished memoir in author's possession).

103 H Leër/D Ops/309/4 – Hilti: "Op instr 21/88 Op Hilti", 30.5.1988 par. 17 and 19 (document provided by Roland de Vries).

104 H Leër/D Ops/309/4 – Hilti: "Op instr 21/88 Op Hilti", 30.5.1988, par. 37 (document provided by Roland de Vries).

105 De Vries: "Operation Prone – the operation that never was" (unpublished memoir in author's possession).

106 10 Div/DS2/205/1/Excite: "Insamelingsplan: Op Excite 13 Jun 88 tot 27 Jul 88", 13.6.1988, par. 1 (document provided by Roland de Vries). Cf also "Inl vereistes: Op Hilti", Jun 1988, par. 1 (document provided by Roland de Vries).

107 HSAW advisory group – HSAW and HS Ops: "Werksdokument 22: Waardering van situasie waar onderhandelinge om KTO afbreek", 26.9.1988, par. 1 (group 4, box 160, HSAW 310/4, p. 31).

108 CS Ops/310/4 Hilti: "Operation instruction 7/88 Midrand", 29.6.1988 (group 4, box 160, HSAW 3009/4, p. 97). Cf. also "Lesse geleer tydens konvensionele operasies in die westelike subteater", chapter 1, par. 31 (document provided by Roland de Vries); De Vries: "Operation Prone: the operation that never was" (unpublished memoir).

109 "Summary minutes of a meeting held at the United States embassy in Cairo, June 24, 1988, between the South African and United States delegations" (Aluka online archive).

110 HSAW – Minister of Defence, 9.9.1988 (group 4, box 160, HSAW 310/4, pp. 23–24).

111 HSAW advisory group – HSAW and H Ops: "Werksdokument 22: Waardering van situasie waar onderhandelinge om KTO afbreek", 26.9.1988 par. 11 and 15 (group 4, box 160, HSAW 310/4, pp. 28–29).

112 HS Ops/UG/304/1/3: "Beplanningsinstruksie 2/88: Gebeurlikheidsbeplanning SWA: Operasie

Handbag", 29.6.1988 (group 4, box 160, H SAW 3009/4, p. 94).

113 "Lesse geleer tydens konvensionele operasies in die westelike subteater", chapter 1, par. 26 (document provided by Roland de Vries).

114 H Leër/D Ops/309/4 – Prone: "Notas vir aanbieding aan SVR mbt operasies in Suid Angola: SA Leër", Julie 1988 (group 4, box 160, HSAW 3009/4, pp. 133–134).

115 Addendum C to HS Ops/D Ops/UG/309/4 – Prone: "SALM deelname aan die landgeveg", July 1988 (group 4, box 160, HSAW 3009/4, pp. 127–131); Addendum D to HS Ops/D Ops/UG/309/4 – Prone: "SALM outonome operasionele vermoë" (group 4, box 160, HSAW 3009/4, pp.122–126).

116 In September 1989, the SAAF reported that it had 8 F1AZs, 5 F1CZs, 2 Canberras, 1 Buccaneer, 12 Impalas, and 5 Cheetahs available for Operation Merlyn, which was meant to ward off a SWAPO invasion in case that movement refused to accept an election defeat. Cf. Addendum A to Merlyn Ops instruction /89: "Merlyn Lugmag Plan", Sept. 1989, par. 5 (61 Mech online archive).

117 Unpublished personal memoir by Roland de Vries. The detailed battle plan was set out in a comprehensive document, drawn up by De Vries: "10 Div oorlegplan: Op Prone", 26.8.1988 (provided by Roland de Vries).

118 "10 Div oorlegplan: Op Prone", 26.8.1988 (document provided by Roland de Vries).

119 "Lesse geleer tydens konvensionele operasies in die westelike subteater", chapter 1, par. 29 (document provided by Roland de Vries).

120 Crocker: *High Noon in Southern Africa*, p. 372.

121 HS Ops – H Leër, HLM, H Vloot, GG, and BG Spesmagte, 19.7.1988 (group 4, box 160, HSAW 3009/4, pp. 120–121.)

122 De Vries: "Operation Prone: The operation that never was" (unpublished memoir).

123 George: *The Cuban Intervention in Angola*, pp. 239–241.

124 MS/UG/309/1 "Bevestigende notas oor vergadering op 4 Jul 88 oor ops en krygstuig-aangeleenthede met betrekking tot Noord-SWA en Suid-Angola" par. 2 and 3, 5.7.1988 (61 Mech online archive).

125 Ibid. par. 5–14 and 33, 5.7.1988 (61 Mech online archive).

126 Ibid. par. 15–16, 5.7.1988 (61 Mech online archive).

127 De Vries: "Operation Prone: The operation that never was" (unpublished memoir in author's possession).

128 MS/UG/309/1 "Bevestigende notas oor vergadering op 4 Jul 88 oor ops en krygstuig-aangeleenthede met betrekking tot Noord-SWA en Suid-Angola", par. 17 and 33, 5.7.1988 (61 Mech online archive).

129 Ibid.

130 E-mail from McGill Alexander, 14.6.2011.

131 De Vries: "Operation Prone: the operation that never was" (unpublished memoir in author's possession).

132 Andreas Velthuizen: "Applying military force for political ends: South Africa in South-Western Africa, 1987–1988" (unpublished MA thesis, Unisa, 1991), p. 107.

133 Bennett: *Three Frigates*, p. 178.

134 Ramsden: *Border-Line Insanity*, pp. 265 and 269–270.

135 Ibid., p. 275.

136 *Case 1/1989*, (testimony by Fidel Castro, 12.7.1989), p. 392.

137 See www.hsdl.org/?view&doc=28649& coll=limited.

138 Defense Intelligence Agency: *Handbook of the Cuban Armed Forces*, pp. 2–11 and 2–12.

139 Ibid., p. 5–24 and 5–25.

140 CS Ops/TS/309/4 Hilti: "Force levels SA Army: Op Hilti", 7.6.1988 (group 4, box 160, HSAW 3009/4, pp. 100–101).

141 Crocker: *High Noon in Southern Africa*, p. 367.

142 Lord: *From Fledgling to Eagle, p. 447.*

143 De Vries: "Operation Prone – the operation that never was" (unpublished memoir in author's possession).

CHAPTER 17

1 Barry Healy: "Cuito Cuanavale: Cuba strikes for Africa's freedom" (*Green Left Weekly*, issue 755, 18.6.2008).

2 Ronnie Kasrils: "Turning point at Cuito Cuanavale" (*Mail & Guardian*, 23.3.2008).

3 Rubén Urribarres: The MiG-17 Fresco in Cuba, at www.geocities.com/urrib2000/ EqMiG17-e.html; Tom Cooper and Jonathan Kyzer: "Angola: Claims & reality about SAAF

4 Heitman: *War in Angola*, pp. 12 and 13.
5 Bridgland: *The War for Africa*, p. 17; Vanneman: *Soviet Strategy in Southern Africa*, p. 52; Heitman: *War in Angola*, p. 22, Table 13: "Major Air Force and Air Defense Force Equipment, 1988", at lcweb2.loc.gov/frd/cs/angola/ao_appen.html.
6 Heitman: *War in Angola*, p. 329.
7 Bridgland: *The War for Africa*, p. 15.
8 Cooper and Kyzer: "Angola: Claims & reality about SAAF losses", at www.acig.org/artman/publish/article_184.shtml.
9 Bridgland: *The War for Africa*, pp. 23 and 24.
10 Brent: *Cheetah*, p. 96.
11 Helmoed-Römer Heitman: "Equipment of the Border War" (*Journal of Contemporary History*, 31/3, Dec. 2006), p. 106.
12 Cooper and Kyzer: "Angola: Claims & reality about SAAF losses", at www.acig.org/artman/publish/article_184.shtml.
13 Lord: *From Fledgling to Eagle*, pp. 403 and 513.
14 "The Kukri air-to-air missile: The sword is drawn", at www.aessa.org.za/articles/kukri.doc.
15 Cf. Heitman: *War in Angola*, p. 329.
16 Ibid., *War in Angola*, p. 329.
17 Lord: *From Fledgling to Eagle*, p. 402.
18 NC Parkins: "Faster, better and higher. The image of the S.A. Air Force as viewed by a veteran", at http://www.rhodesia.nl/parkins.htm.
19 Lord: *From Fledgling to Eagle*, p. 158.
20 Cooper and Kyzer: "Angola: Claims & reality about SAAF losses", at www.acig.org/artman/publish/article_184.shtml.
21 Bridgland: *The War in Africa*, p. 262.
22 Cf. Heitman: *War in Angola*, p. 48.
23 Lord: *From Fledgling to Eagle*, pp. 401–402, 405–406 and 439–440; Heitman: *War in Angola*, pp. 319–320; Bridgland: *The War for Africa*, pp. 104 and 108; Cooper and Kyzer: "Angola: Claims & reality about SAAF losses", at www.acig.org/artman/publish/article_184.shtml. The Cuban viewpoint may be found on an unofficial Cuban website, but it is not clear how authoritative it is. Cf. Rubén Urribarres: "A Cuban MiG-23 in Angola, II: Air superiority missions", at www.geocities.com/urrib2000/EqMiG-23aa-e.html.
24 Arthur Piercy: "A SAAF Pilot", at http://www.urrib2000.narod.ru/ArticPiercy2.html. He also told his story in detail elsewhere. Cf. Piercy: "Operasies Moduler en Hooper – in die lug", in Geldenhuys (ed.): *Ons was Daar*, pp. 249–253.
25 Cooper and Kyzer: "Angola: Claims & reality about SAAF losses", at www.acig.org/artman/publish/article_184.shtml; Heitman: *War in Angola*, pp. 71 and 73.
26 Cooper and Kyzer: "Angola: Claims & reality about SAAF losses", at www.acig.org/artman/publish/article_184.shtml.
27 Heitman: *War in Angola*, p. 321.
28 Bridgland: *The War for Africa*, p. 262.
29 Heitman: *War in Angola*, p. 311.
30 Ibid., pp. 313 and 328.
31 Ibid., pp. 49, 53–54 and 55.
32 Lord: *From Fledgling to Eagle*, pp. 414–423; Nortje: *32 Battalion*, p. 241; Bridgland: *The War for Africa*, pp. 150–160.
33 Lord: *From Fledgling to Eagle*, pp. 438–439 and 441–442; Breytenbach: *Buffalo Soldiers*, p. 313.
34 Heitman: *War in Angola*, p. 313; Pikkie Siebrits: "24 Eskader – Per Noctem Per Diem", in Geldenhuys (ed.): *Ons was Daar*, p. 236.
35 Lord: *From Fledgling to Eagle*, p. 443.
36 Cf. Lord: *From Fledgling to Eagle*, pp. 428–434; Bridgland: *The War for Africa*, pp. 49–51.
37 Cf. for instance Bridgland: *The War for Africa*, pp. 75 and 84.
38 The writer witnessed this himself during a demonstration at Lohatlha Army Battle School in 1996. A tank would fire a smoke shell which would explode a few hundred yards away and became the target for the Mirages. Their bombs landed within 5–10 m of the target, more than adequate to destroy it. (Of course, the Cheetah-Cs with their even more advanced equipment were even better, but that is beside the point.)
39 Bridgland: *The War for Africa*, pp. 49, 100–101 and 140–141.
40 Heitman: *War in Angola*, p. 94.
41 Bridgland: *The War for Africa*, p. 49.

42 Ibid., p. 116; Heitman: *War in Angola*, pp. 325–326; Lord: *From Fledgling to Eagle*, pp. 399–400.

43 Gennady Shubin (ed.): *The Memoirs of Veterans of the War in Angola,* footnote 39.

44 Bridgland: *The War for Africa*, pp. 177 and 247; Heitman: *War in Angola*, pp. 69, 95, 164 and 183.

45 Breytenbach: *Buffalo Soldiers*, p.312.

46 Bridgland: *The War for Africa*, pp. 246 and 250.

47 Lord: *From Fledgling to Eagle*, pp. 428–434.

48 Cf. Ibid., p. 180; Heitman: *War in Angola*, pp. 107–108.

49 Rubén Urribarres: "Los MiG-21 Fishbed de Cuba en acción", at www.geocities.com/urrib2000/EqMiG-21a.html.

50 Bridgland: *The War for Africa*, pp. 119–120.

51 Heitman: *War in Angola*, p. 102.

52 Bridgland: *The War for Africa*, p. 175.

53 Cf. for instance Ibid., pp. 143 and 196.

54 Ibid., p. 67.

55 Heitman: *War in Angola*, pp. 110 and 329. Cf. also Breytenbach: *Buffalo Soldiers*, p. 277, and Bridgland: *The War for Africa*, pp. 85, 162, 262 and 273.

56 Lord: *From Fledgling to Eagle*, p. 443.

57 French: "1 SAI – Ratels in Op Hooper (1987–1988)", at uk.geocities.com/sadf_history1/dfrench.html.

58 Breytenbach: *Buffalo Soldiers*, p. 286.

59 Heitman: *War in Angola*, p. 132.

60 George: *The Cuban Intervention in Angola*, p. 215.

61 Holt: *At Thy Call we did not Falter*, p. 87 and 89–98. Cf. also Bridgland: *The War for Africa*, pp. 212 and 274; Heitman: *War in Angola*, p. 227.

62 Bridgland: *The War for Africa*, p. 297.

63 Heitman: *War in Angola*, p. 328. Cf. also pp. 250–251, 259–262, 279–280 and 283.

64 Urribarres: "Los MiG-21 Fishbed de Cuba en acción", at www.geocities.com/urrib2000/EqMiG21a.html.

65 Bridgland: *The War for Africa*, pp. 344 and 360.

66 Lord: *From Fledgling to Eagle*, p. 448.

67 Jean-Sebastien Seytre: "Au revoir Reims" (*Air Forces Monthly*, September 2011, p. 95); "Last French Mirage F1CRs leave Kandahar" (*Air Forces Monthly*, October 2011, p. 11).

68 Brent: *Cheetah*, p. 80.

69 "Mirage F1AZ/CZ ordinance", at newsite. ipmssa.za.org/content/view/149/28/1/5.

70 Divan Muller: "Cheetah phasing out function" (*African Pilot*, 7/5, May 2008).

CHAPTER 18

1 Wolvaardt, Wheeler and Scholtz (eds.): *From Verwoerd to Mandela*, I, p. 284 (reminiscences of Neil van Heerden).

2 Crocker: *High Noon in Southern Africa*, p. 358.

3 Ibid.

4 Wolvaardt, Wheeler and Scholtz (eds.): *From Verwoerd to Mandela*, I, p. 283 (reminiscences of Neil van Heerden).

5 Geldenhuys: *Dié wat gewen het*, p. 208.

6 Crocker: *High Noon in Southern Africa*, p. 399.

7 Ibid., p. 387.

8 Ibid., pp. 117 and 407.

9 Ibid., p. 182; Wolvaardt, Wheeler and Scholtz (eds.): *From Verwoerd to Mandela*, I, p. 283 (reminiscences of Neil van Heerden).

10 Geldenhuys: *Dié wat gewen het*, pp. 1–2.

11 Ibid., pp. 1–3 and 193. Cf. also Crocker: *High Noon in Southern Africa*, p. 399.

12 "Summary minutes of exploratory discussions held in London, May 3–4, 1988 between a South African Delegation and an Angolan Delegation, facilitated by a delegation of the Unites States" (Aluka online archive). The quotation appears on p. 6.

13 "Summary minutes of the Bilateral Meeting held in Brazzaville, May 13, 1988 between delegations from the governments of the Republic of South Africa and the People's Republic of Angola" (Aluka online archive).

14 "Summary minutes of a meeting held at the United States embassy in Cairo, June 24, 1988, between the South African and United States delegations" (Aluka online archive).

15 "Summary minutes of a meeting between the Republic of South Africa, and Angolan/Cuban delegation and the United States of America as mediator on the question of SWA/Namibia and Angola: Cairo, June 24–25, 1988" (Aluka online archive). Cf. also Crocker: *High Noon in Southern Africa*, p. 428.

16 Wolvaardt, Wheeler and Scholtz (eds.): *From Verwoerd to Mandela*, I, p. 284 (reminiscences of Neil van Heerden).

17 Vanneman: *Soviet Strategy in Southern Africa*, p. 38.

18 Wolvaardt, Wheeler and Scholtz (eds.): *From Verwoerd to Mandela*, I, p. 284 (reminiscences of Neil van Heerden).

19 "Former South African Foreign Minister RF 'Pik' Botha in an interview with Dr Sue Onslow (LSE IDEAS Fellow), Pretoria, 15th July 2008", p. 3, at www2.lse.ac.uk/IDEAS/ programmes/africaProgramme/pdfs/ bothaInterview.pdf.

20 Wolvaardt, Wheeler and Scholtz (eds.): *From Verwoerd to Mandela*, I, p. 284 (reminiscences of Neil van Heerden).

21 Ibid.; Crocker: *High Noon in Southern Africa*, p. 428.

22 "Summary minutes of a meeting between the Republic of South Africa, and Angolan/Cuban delegation and the United States of America as mediator on the question of SWA/Namibia and Angola: Cairo, June 24–25, 1988" (Aluka online archive). Cf. also Crocker: *High Noon in Southern Africa*, pp. 428–429; Geldenhuys: *Dié wat gewen het*, pp. 196–197.

23 "Summary minutes of a meeting held in New York on July 11–12, 1988 between a South African delegation and an Angolan delegation, facilitated by the Unites States" (Aluka online archive).

24 "Summary minutes of a meeting between the Republic of South Africa, and Angolan/Cuban delegation and the United States of America as mediator on the question of SWA/Namibia and Angola: Cairo, June 24–25, 1988" (Aluka online archive).

25 Crocker: *High Noon in Southern Africa*, p. 400.

26 "Summary of points of agreement and others discussed at the South African and Cuban/ Angolan military meetings: Sal Island, Cape Verde: 22 and 23 July, 1988" (Aluka online archive).

27 "Minutes of plenary meetings held in Geneva, Aug. 2–5, 1988" (Aluka online archive).

28 "Notes of the conversations with his Excellency, Pres. J.E. Dos Santos on Sep. 23, 1988 to be conveyed directly to His Excellency, President P.W. Botha" (Aluka online archive).

29 Papenfus: *Pik Botha en sy Tyd*, pp. 549–550.

30 Isaac Saney: "African Stalingrad: The Cuban revolution, internationalism and the end of apartheid" (*Latin American Perspectives* 33/81, 2006, p. 101).

31 Kasrils: "Turning point at Cuito Cuanavale".

32 Gary Baines: "Challenging the boundaries, breaking the silences", in Baines and Vale (eds.): *Beyond the Border War*, p. 4.

33 Cf. Gleijeses: "Moscow's proxy? Cuba and Africa 1975–1988" (*Journal of Cold War Studies*, 8/2, Spring 2006, p. 37); Gleijeses: "Conflicting versions: Cuba, the United States and Angola", in Manuela Franco (ed.): *Portugal, os Estados Unidos e a África Austral*, pp. 119–35; Gleijeses: "Cuba and the independence of Namibia" (*Cold War History*, 7/2, May 2007); Gleijeses: *The Cuban Drumbeat*; Gleijeses: "Cuito Cuanavale revisited" (*Mail & Guardian*, 6–12.7.2007).

34 Cf. my analysis – Scholtz: "The standard of research on the Battle of Cuito Cuanavale, 1987–1988" (*Scientia Militaria*, 39/1, 2011, pp. 115–137).

35 Jannie Geldenhuys' viewpoint is expressed in Steenkamp: *South Africa's Border War 1966–1989*, p. 152; Marga Ley: "Jannie Geldenhuys: 'Ek en Castro het nie saamgesweer'" (*Beeld*, 12.11.1992); Geldenhuys: *Dié wat gewen het*, pp. 179 and 191. Magnus Malan's contribution can be found in his memoirs, *My lewe saam met die SA Weermag*, pp.272–273.

36 Geldenhuys: *Dié wat gewen het*, p. 177.

37 "Lesse geleer tydens konvensionele operasies in die westelike subteater", chapter 18, par. 8 (document provided by Roland de Vries).

38 Ops 309/3: "Spes sitrap", 61 Meg Bn – 20 Tak HK, 15.2.1988, par. 4 (61 Mech online archive).

39 Addendum G to Med 20/UG/309/1 Op Moduler par. 1 and 16, dated February 1988 (61 Mech online archive).

40 CS Ops/310/4/3: "Op Hooper sitrep", par. 3, contained in CSADF 3 – CSADF, 3.2.1988 (group 4, box 160, HSAW 310/4, p. 155).

41 "Tripartite agreement", 22.12.1988, at http:// lcweb2.loc.gov/frd/cs/angola/ao_appnb. html. Cf. further "The Geneva protocol", 5.8.1988, at www.c-r.org/our-work/accord/ angola/geneva-protocol.php.

42 "Remarks by the Secretary-General at informal consultations in the Security

Council today (Namibia)", 3.4.1989, pp 8–9 (Aluka online archive).

43 Geldenhuys: *Dié wat gewen het*, pp. 213–214; Papenfus: *Pik Botha en sy Tyd*, p. 578.

44 Geldenhuys: *Dié wat gewen het*, p. 214.

45 "Remarks by the Secretary-General at informal consultations in the Security Council today (Namibia)", 3.4.1989, p. 1 (Aluka online archive); Peter Stiff: *Nine Days of War. Namibia – Before, During and After*, pp. 72–73; Papenfus: *Pik Botha en sy Tyd*, p. 579.

46 H Leër/D Ops/309/4 – Merlyn: "Aanbiedingsnotas oor Op Agree en Op Merlyn: Situasie in SWA 14 April 89" (HSAW/3009/4, pp. 271–272, box 160).

47 Cf. Nujoma: *Where Others Wavered*, p. 395 ff.

48 Peter Stiff has documented the nine days' fighting in great detail. Cf. Stiff: *Nine Days of War*, passim; Stiff: *The Covert War*, pp. 350–466. There is also a detailed report in the SANDF Documentation Centre. Cf. H Leër/D Ops/309/4 – Merlyn: "Aanbiedingsnotas oor Op Agree en Op Merlyn: Situasie in SWA 14 April 89" (HSAW/3009/4, pp. 262–272, box 160). For SWAPO's version, cf. Namakulu: *Armed Liberation Struggle*, pp. 121–136.

49 Papenfus: *Pik Botha en sy Tyd*, p. 581.

50 "Remarks by the Secretary-General at informal consultations in the Security Council today (Namibia)", 3.4.1989, p. 4 (Aluka online archive).

51 Stiff: *Nine Days of War*, pp. 96–97 and 103–104.

52 Cedric Thornberry: *A Nation is Born. The Inside Story of Namibia's Independence*, p. 98 (diary entry, 1.4.1989).

53 Thornberry: *A Nation is Born*, p. 99 (diary entry, 1.4.1989). Cf. also "Remarks by the Secretary-General at informal consultations in the Security Council today (Namibia)", 3.4.1989, p. 1 (Aluka online archive); Wolvaardt, Wheeler and Scholtz (eds.): *From Verwoerd to Mandela*, I, pp. 292–293 (reminiscences of Carl von Hirschberg).

54 Pik Botha – Perez de Cuellar, 2.4.1989 (Aluka online archive).

55 H Leër/D Ops/309/4 – Merlyn: "Aanbiedingsnotas oor Op Agree en Op

Merlyn: Situasie in SWA 14 April 89" (group 4, box 160, HSAW/3009/4, p. 272).

56 "Transition to independence marred in Namibia", State Department statement, 3.4.1989 (*Department of State Bulletin*, June 1989).

57 Carlos Aldana – Neil van Heerden, 6.4.1989 (Aluka online archive).

58 Crocker: *High Noon in Southern Africa*, p. 422.

59 Stiff: *Nine Days of War*, pp. 216 and 220.

60 "The crisis unfolds (chronology of UN participation in Namibian peace negotiations)" (*UN Chronicle*, June 1989).

61 Thornberry: *A Nation is Born*, p. 105 (diary entry, 4.4.1989).

62 Stiff: *Nine Days of War*, pp. 220 and 231.

63 Ibid., pp. 220–224; Papenfus: *Pik Botha en sy Tyd*, pp. 584–585

64 Thornberry: *A Nation is Born*, p. 113 (diary entry, 9.4.1989).

65 Thornberry: *A Nation is Born*, pp. 113–114 (diary entry, 9.4.1989).

66 "Report by the joint intelligence staff on the current state of SWAPO withdrawal from South West Africa/Namibia and from southern Angola", Addendum B to "Draft summary of the third regular meeting of the Joint Commission in Cape Town", 27–29.4.1989 (group 4, box 160, HSAW 3009/4, pp. 287–288).

67 Stiff: *Nine Days of War*, pp. 298–299.

68 HS Ops/UG/309/4/Op Merlyn: "Operasie instruksie no 8/89: Operasie Merlyn", 4.8.1989 (group 4, box 160, HSAW 3009/4, pp. 221–224); Op instr: Riglyne vir beplanning Op Merlyn, 18.8.1989 (61 Mech online archive); HS Ops/309/4/ Op Merlyn "Operasie instruksie nr 12/89: Operasie Merlyn", 16.10.1989 (group 4, boc 160, HSAW 3009/4, p. 226).

69 "Op Heyday: Verkiesingsplan: Notas vir H Leër", 30.1.1989 (group 4, box 160, HSAW 3009/4, pp. 182–184).

70 Addendum A to HS Ops/ UG/309/4Agree: "Opdragte en riglyne vir beplanning en uitvoering", 6.2.1989 (group 4, box 160, HSAW/3009/4, pp. 337–363. The quote comes from p. 337.

71 Cf. Kamongo and Bezuidenhout: *Skadu's in die Sand*, pp. 215–216.

72 Cf. Hamann: *Days of the Generals*, pp. 178–179.

73 Intelligence report, 1.3.1989 (Aluka online archive).

74 Pik Botha: "Bosoorlog: Daar was geen ander uitweg nie" (*Rapport*, 19.12.2009).

75 Wallace: *A History of Namibia*, p. 306; De Visser: "Winning hearts and minds in the Namibian Border War" (*Scientia Militaria*, 39/1, 2011, pp. 87–88).

CHAPTER 19

1 John J McCuen: "Hybrid wars" (*Military Review*, March-April 2008, p. 108).

2 Mao Zedong: "Problems of Strategy in China's Revolutionary War" in Mao Zedong: *Selected Military Writings*, pp. 113–115.

3 Mao Zedong: "On Protracted War" in Mao Zedong: *Selected Military Writings*, pp. 212–214.

4 Ibid., p. 214.

5 Seegers: *The Military in the Making of South Africa*, p. 140.

6 Junior Botha: "Suidoos-Angola 1987–89 in perspektief: Castro, Von Clausewitz en Liddell Hart" in Geldenhuys (ed.): *Ons was Daar*, p. 525.

7 Botha: "Samevatting van Operasies Moduler, Hooper en Packer" in Geldenhuys (ed.): *Ons was Daar*, p. 401.

8 Stapleton: *A Military History of South Africa*, p. 185.

9 Malan: *My lewe saam met die SA Weermag*, pp. 446–447.

10 Major CA Beukes: "Ondervragingsverslag: Mishake Albert Muyongo", n.d. [1985], par. 15 (61 Mech online archive).

11 Nujoma: *Where Others Wavered*, p. 389.

12 Christopher Saunders: "History and the armed struggle", in Henning Melber (ed.): *Transitions in Namibia. Which Changes for Whom?*, p. 26.

13 Brian Latell: "Fidel Castro's deepening crisis. The implications of the 'Ochoa-De la Guardia Affair'" (National Intelligence Council, 13.7.1989).

14 Castro: "We will stay until Namibia is independent", in Deutschmann (ed.): *Changing the History of Africa*, p. 104; Crocker: *High Noon in Southern Africa*, p. 335.

15 Kahn: "Cuba's impact on Southern Africa" (*Journal of Interamerican Studies and World Affairs*, 29/3, Autumn 1987, p. 48).

16 Pamela S Falk: "Cuba in Africa" (*Foreign Affairs*, 65/5, Summer 1987, p. 1095).

17 George: *The Cuban Intervention in Angola*, p. 268.

18 Andrew and Mitrokhin: *The Mitrokhin Archive, II*, p. 9.

19 Dmitry Furman: "A silent cold war" (*Russia in Global Affairs*, 4/2, April-June 2006, pp. 69–70).

20 Robert W Strayer: *Why did the Soviet Union Collapse? Understanding Historical Change*, p. 81.

21 Crocker: *High Noon in Southern Africa*, p. 52.

22 Gleijeses: "Moscow's Proxy? Cuba and Africa 1975–1988" (*Journal of Cold War Studies*, 8/2, Spring 2006, p. 44).

23 Shubin: *The Hot "Cold War"*, p. 72.

24 CNN interview with Karen Brutents, at www.cnn.com/SPECIALS/cold.war/episodes/17/interviews/brutents/.

25 Lawrence S Eagleburger – Pik Botha, 15.2.1983 (Aluka online archive).

26 Jaster. *The 1988 Peace Accords and the Future of South-Western Africa*, pp. 130–131.

27 *White Paper on Defence and Armament Supply*, 1969, p. 2, par. 3.

28 *White Paper on Defence and Armament Supply*, 1986, p. 25, par. 121.

29 Interview with Constand Viljoen by Padraig O'Malley, 26.7.1998, at www.nelsonmandela.org/omalley/index.php/site/q/03lv00017/04lv00344/05lv01183/06lv01209.htm.

30 Hamann: *Days of the Generals*, p. 77.

31 Breytenbach: *Eagle Strike!*, p. 63.

32 Steenkamp: *South Africa's Border War 1966–1989*, p. 190.

33 Shubin: *The Hot "Cold War"*, p. 80.

34 Cf. for instance Johannes "Mistake" Gaomab: "With the People's Liberation

Army of Namibia in Angola", in Leys and Brown (eds.): *Life Histories of Namibia*, p. 70; Schivute: *Go and Come Home*, p. 63.

35 Saunders: "History and the armed struggle: From anti-colonial propaganda to 'patriotic history'?", in Melber (ed.): *Transitions in Namibia*, p. 25.

36 Ibid., p. 24.

37 Shubin: *The Hot "Cold War"*, pp. 78 and 101.

38 George: *The Cuban Intervention in Angola*, p. 155.

39 James F Dunnigan: *How to Make War. A Comprehensive Guide to Modern Warfare for the Post-Cold War Era*, pp. 587–594.

40 The extent to which some soldiers were scarred psychologically can be understood by reading military psychologists' and psychiatrists' memoirs. Cf. Antony Feinstein: *Battle Scarred. Hidden Costs of the Border War*, passim; "André" [pseud.]: "Psychologist 1", at sadf.sentinelprojects.com/propat/4andre.html; Clive Wills: "Doctor", at sadf.sentinelprojects.com/propat/5cw.html; Barry Fowler: "1 Military Hospital", at http://sadf.sentinelprojects.com/1mil/introtoc.html.

41 Dobell: *SWAPO's Struggle for Namibia*, p. 75.

LIST OF SOURCES

A. Primary sources

1. Books

Cloete, Bertie: Pionne. Hermanus, Hemel & See, 2009.

Coetzee, Peet: Special Forces "Jam Stealer". The Memoirs of a Specialist who served in Special Forces and the Defence Force of South Africa. N.p., Peet Coetzee, 2008.

De Kock, Eugene: A Long Night's Damage. Working for the Apartheid State. Saxonwold, Contra, 1998.

Deutschmann, Isaac (ed.): Changing the History of Africa. Angola and Namibia. Melbourne, Ocean, 1989.

Durand, Arn: Zulu Zulu Golf. Life and Death with Koevoet. Cape Town, Zebra, 2011.

Geldenhuys, Jannie: Dié wat gewen het. Feite en Fabels van die Bosoorlog, 2nd ed. Pretoria, Litera, 2007.

Geldenhuys, Jannie (ed.): Ons was Daar. Wenners van die Oorlog om Suider-Afrika. Pretoria, Kraal, 2011.

Feinstein, Anthony: Battle Scarred. Hidden Costs of the Border War. Cape Town, Tafelberg, 2011.

Flower, Ken: Serving Secretly. Rhodesia's CIO Chief on Record. Alberton, Galago, 1987.

Holt, Clive: At Thy Call we did not Falter. A Frontline Account of the 1988 Angolan War, as Seen Through the Eyes of a Conscripted Soldier. Cape Town, Zebra, 2005.

Kamongo, Sisingi and Bezuidenhout, Leon: Skadu's in die Sand. Pinetown, 30° South, 2011.

Kasrils, Ronnie: Armed & Dangerous. From Undercover Struggle to Freedom, 2nd edition. Johannesburg, Jonathan Ball, 1998.

Kobo, Joseph: Waiting in the Wing. Milton Keynes, Nelson Word, 1994.

Korff, Granger: 19 with a Bullet. A South African Paratrooper in Angola. Johannesburg, 30° South, 2009.

Malan, Magnus: My lewe saam met die SA Weermag. Pretoria, Protea, 2006.

Nujoma, Sam: Where Others Wavered. The Autobiography of Sam Nujoma. London, Panaf, 2001.

Ramsden, Tim: Border-Line Insanity. Alberton, Galago, 2009.

Schivute, Marcus: Go and Come Home. A Namibian Story into Exile and Back. Windhoek, Gamsberg, 1997.

Shipanga, Andreas: In Search of Freedom. Gibraltar, Ashanti, 1989.

Stockwell, John: In Search of Enemies. A CIA Story. London, Futura, 1979.

SWAPO: To be Born a Nation. The Liberation Struggle for Namibia. London, SWAPO Dept. Of Information and Publicity, 1981.

Thornberry, Cedric: A Nation is Born. The Inside Story of Namibia's Independence. Windhoek, Gamsberg, 2005.

Wall, Dudley: Operation Askari 1983-1984, Southern Angola, at www.warinangola.com/Default. aspx?tabid=1173.

Webb, Steven: Ops Medic: A National Serviceman's Border War. Alberton, Galago, 2008.

Wilkins, Monster: Chopper Pilot. The Adventures and Experiences of Monster Wilkins. Nelspruit, Freeworld, 2000.

Wolvaardt, Pieter, Wheeler, Tom and Scholtz, Werner (eds.): From Verwoerd to Mandela. South African Diplomats Remember, three volumes. Pretoria, Crink, 2010.

2. Articles

"André": "Psychologist 1", at sadf.sentinelprojects. com/propat/4andre.html.

Anonymous: "5 SAI (1969)", at http://sadf. sentinelprojects.com/bg1/5sai69.html.

Anonymous: "Cassinga massacre: a product of imperialism" (The Combatant, May 1986).

Anonymous: "El attaque a Cassinga (1)", at http://laultimaguerra.com/2009/10/27/ el-ataque-a-cassinga-i/.

Anonymous: "Kapt. Carl Friedich Wilhelm Alberts", at www.samagte.co.za/weermag/hc/alberts.html.

Anonymous.: "Operation Saffraan Southern Zambia 1979", at www.samagte.co.za/phpbbs/viewtopic. php?f=50&t=452.

Anonymous: "Self-defeating lies exposed" (The Combatant, June 1986).

Anonymous.: "The adventure of a lifetime", at sadf. sentinelprojects.com/bG-2/LP1.html.

Anonymous: "The A.N.C. says hands off Angola!" (Sechaba, 3rd quarter, 1976, p. 11).

Anonymous: "Victory Day: Glorious holiday for mankind" (The Combatant, May 1986).

Battersby, John: "Angola lags in drive on U.S.-backed rebels" (New York Times, 14.9.1987).

Battersby, John: "South Africa acknowledges its troops aided Angolan rebels" (New York Times, 12.11.1987).

Bestbier, Frank: "1978", at www.61mech.org.za/years/1978.

Bornman, WS: "Op Sceptic – Ratel 21 se kanonnier se herinneringe", at http://www.61mech.org.za/operations/5-operation-sceptic#stories-photos.

Botha, Pik: "Bosoorlog: Daar was geen ander uitweg nie" (Rapport, 19.12.2009).

Caforio, Marco: "Op Sceptic – my story of Smokeshell", at www.61mech.org.za/operations/5-operation-sceptic.

De Vries, Roland: "Operation Carrot, 1980", at www.61mech.org.za/operations/4-operation-carrot.

De Vries, Roland: various unpublished writings, to be consolidated in a book, in author's possession.

Dippenaar, Johann: "1979", at www.61mech.org.za/years/1979.

Finch, Dennis: "11 Commando (1979-1980) Etali, Okatope, Nkurunkuru and Grootfontein", at http://sadf.sentinelprojects.com/bG-2/Finch.html.

Fowler, Barry: "1 Military Hospital", at http://sadf.sentinelprojects.com/1mil/introtoc.html.

French, Damian: "1 SAI – Ratels in Op Hooper (1987-1988)", at uk.geocities.com/sadf_history1/dfrench.html.

Gibson, Erika: "Jannie Geldenhuys: 'Ek en Castro het nie saamgesweer'. Die waarheid oor wat gebeur het by Cuito Cuanavale ná beweringe in boek deur Chester Crocker" (Beeld, 12.11.1992).

Gildenhuys, Chris: "Op Protea: A Personal Account and Experience – 30 Years On", at www.61mech.org.za/stories/168?height=400&width=400.

Groenewald, Hein: "Op Excite – Calueque gedurende Junie 1988: Die laaste aanval in Angola", at www.61mech.org.za/operations/22-operation-excite#stories-photos.

Groenewald, Hein: "Roepsein 22C en 1988 se Valentynsdag", at www.61mech.org.za/operations/20-operation-hooper.

Grové, Johan: "Ratel teen tenk", at www.samagte.co.za/weermag/hc/grove.html.

Hare, Simon: "Operation Askari", at http://sa-soldier.com/data/index.htm.

Hooper, Jim: "We've got a Russian!", at http://veridical.co.za/default.aspx?tabid=1112.

Hugo, Ariël: "Op Daisy – Held van sy tyd: Korporaal J.L. Potgieter", at www.61mech.org.za/operations/8-operation-daisy.

Hugo, Ariël: "Op Daisy – navigasie met Operasie Daisy", at www.61mech.org.za/operations/8-operation-daisy.

Kirkman, D: "7th South African Infantry Battalion: Memories of my SADF experiences", at www.samagte.co.za/phpbbs/viewtopic.php?f=17&t=439.

Laubscher, Danie: "Bosbok over Xangongo – Operation Protea", 13.10.2010, at www.flyafrica.info/forums/showthread.php?30477-Bosbok-over-Xangongo-Ops-Protea/page3.

Le Roux, MJ: "Armour, 1978-1979", at http://sadf.sentinelprojects.com/bG-2/Tinuslr.html.

Lord, RS: "Operation Askari. A sub-commander's retrospective view of the operation" (Militaria, 22/4, 1992).

Louw, Paul: "Op Sceptic: Tweede luitenant Paul Louw van roepsein 21 se storie", at www.61mech.org.za/operations/5-operation-sceptic.

Marais, Dries: "Buccaneer to the rescue", at www.avcollect.com/marais.htm.

Minnaar, Gert: "Op Protea – Humbe was nie net rustig gewees nie", at http://www.61mech.org.za/stories/65?height=400&width=400.

Parks, Michael: "S. African-led forces fight in Angola; battles may signal expansion of Pretoria's military operations" (Washington Post, 29.7.1987).

Piercy, Arthur: "A SAAF Pilot", at www.geocities.com/urrib2000/ArticPiercy2.html.

Raine, Sheryl: "Army Chief shuns defensive strategy" (Star, 29.6.1983).

Rossouw, Dion: "1984 – Second deployment of SADF tanks to the SWA operational area", at www.61mech.org.za/years/1984#stories-photos.

Rutherford, Gareth: Personal memoir, at www.61mech.org.za/operations/5-operation-sceptic.

SA Military History Society: "Newsletter No 1 October 2009, at http://samilitaryhistory.org/9/p09octne.html.

Schoeman, Johan: online discussion at www.warinangola.com/default.aspx?tabid=590&forumid=43&postid=295&view=topic.

Stumpf, Waldo: "Birth and death of the South African nuclear weapons programme", at www.fas.org/nuke/guide/rsa/nuke/stumpf.htm.

Surmon, William: "School of Armour – 4 SAI – Operation Hooper (1987-1988)", at uk.geocities.com/sasolboy/abenstxt.html.

Terrero, Ivan: "El vuelo inolvidable de Juan Francisco Doval" (Granma, 1.12.2005), at www.granma.cu/ESPANOL/2005/diciembre/juev1/49piloto.html.

Van Dalsen, Hubrecht and Walls, Chris: "Op Protea – The fight for Mongua and the story of its FAPLA HQ flag", at http://www.61mech.org.za/operations/7-operation-protea.

Van Zyl, Gert: "Operation Askari", at http://www.61mech.org.za/operations/13-operation-askari.

Van Zyl, Gert: "Operation Phoenix", at www.61mech.org.za/operations/11-operation-phoenix.

Vermaak, Hugo: "Herinneringe aan Operasie Askari", at http://www.61mech.org.za/operations/13-operation-askari.

Vigne, Randolph: "SWAPO of Namibia: A movement in Exile" (Third World Quarterly, 9/1, January 1987).

Walters, Barbara: "An interview with Fidel Castro" (Foreign Policy, no. 28, autumn 1977).

Wills, Clive: "Doctor", at sadf.sentinelprojects.com/propat/5cw.html.

3. Published documents

Anonymous article about the battle at Bridge 14 without title, at http://laultimaguerra. com/2010/01/29/la-batalla-del-puente-14-version de-un-combatiente-cubano.

Anonymous: "Countdown", at www.lenoury.net/ beetlecrusher/dc03.html.

Anonymous: "Services School & 5 SA Infantry Ladysmith, Etale & Oshikango (1976 – 1977)", at www.samagte.co.za/phpbbs/viewtopic. php?f=211&t=350.

Brink, Mike: "Weekends, missions and other Border War stories", at www.zs6meg.co.za/ borderstories07.htm.

Case 1/1989. Havana, José Marti, 1989.

Castro, Fidel: Castro Speech Database, at http:// lanic.utexas.edu/la/cb/cuba/castro.html.

CIA: "Cuba: The Outlook for Castro and Beyond", August 1993.

CIA: "Moscow and the Namibia peace process", April 1982

CIA: "Moscow's response to the diplomatic challenge in Southern Africa", January 1984.

CIA: "Soviet and Cuban intervention in the Angolan Civil War", March 1977.

CIA: "Soviet and Cuban objectives and activity in Southern Africa through 1988", February 1988.

CIA: "Soviet policies in Southern Africa", February 1985.

CIA: "Soviet policy and Africa", February 1981.

CIA: "The nature of Soviet military doctrine", January 1989.

"Cobus": "Parabat" (www.geocities.com/ sadfbook/2cobuc.htm?200611).

CNN: "CNN interview with Karen Brutents", at www.cnn.com/SPECIALS/cold.war/episodes/17/ interviews/brutents/.

Crookes, Glynn: Online discussion, 11.1.2011, at www.veridical.co.za/default. aspx?tabid=590&forumid=27&postid=129 &view=topic.

Defense Intelligence Agency: *Handbook of the Cuban Armed Forces*. N.p., April 1979.

Fall, I: *Report on a Mission to SWAPO Centres for Namibian Refugees in Angola from 10 to 14 April 1978*. Brazzaville, UNICEF Area Office, 2.5.1978.

"Fidel Castro's 1977 Southern Africa tour: A report to Honecker", 3.4.1977, at macua.blogs.com/files/ castro-in-africa.doc.

Fidel Castro: Speech, 2.12.2005, at emba. cubaminrex.cu/Default.aspx?tabid=15937.

General Del Pino Speaks. Military Dissension in Castro's Cuba. N.p., The Cuban-American National Foundation, 1987.

Gorbunov, Yuri (ed.): *Namibia: a Struggle for Independence. A Collection of Articles, Documents and Speeches*. Moscow, Progress, 1988.

Frontline Fellowship: "Special Report March 1989: South West Africa Namibia and 435", at www. sabwv.co.za/media.php?choice=article.

Interview with Constand Viljoen, 26.7.1998, at www.nelsonmandela.org/omalley/index.

php/site/q/03lv00017/04lv00344/05lv01183/0 6lv01209.htm.

Interview with Magnus Malan, 30.10.2001, at www. nelsonmandela.org/omalley/index.php/site/q/03lv0 0017/04lv00344/05lv01388/06lv01401.htm.

Interview with Neil Barnard, 17.9.1998, at www. nelsonmandela.org/omalley/index.php/site/q/03lv0 0017/04lv00344/05lv01183/06lv01252.htm.

Interview with Otillie Abrahams by Tor Sellström, at www.liberationafrica.se/intervstories/interviews/ abrahams/index.xml?by-country=1&node -id=2238869971-39.

Interview with Sten Rylander by Lennart Wohgemuth, at www.liberationafrica.se/ intervstories/interviews/rylander_s/index. xml?by-country=1&node-id=2238869971-39.

"Interview with SWAPO President Comrade Sam Nujoma" (*Dawn*, May 1979).

Latell, Brian: "Fidel Castro's deepening crisis. The implications of the 'Ochoa-De la Guardia Affair'" (National Intelligence Council, 13.7.1989).

Margaret Thatcher Foundation: "Shultz memo for Reagan", 6.6.1983, at www.margaretthatcher.org/ archive/displaydocument.asp?docid=110535.

"Memorandum of Conversation" [between Gerald Ford, Henry Kissinger and Deng Xiaoping], 3.12.1975, at http://www.gwu.edu/~nsarchiv/ NSAEBB/NSAEBB67/gleijeses4.pdf

"Minutes of the meeting between Politburo of the Central Committee of the Bulgarian Communist Party and Comrade Fidel Castro – First Secretary of the Central Committee of the Cuban Communist Party and Prime Minister of the Revolutionary Government of Republic of Cuba", 11.3.1976, at http://www.wilsoncenter.org/ digital-archive.

Onslow, Sue: "Documents. South Africa and Zimbabwe-Rhodesian independence, 1979-1980, (*Cold War History*, 7/2).

Onslow, Sue: "Former South African Foreign Minister R.F. 'Pik' Botha in an interview with dr. Sue Onslow (LSE IDEAS Fellow), Pretoria, 15th July 2008", at www2.lse.ac.uk/ IDEAS/programmes/africaProgramme/pdfs/ bothaInterview.pdf.

"Petraeus outlines Afghanistan strategy", transcript of speech at panel discussion, Munich, 8.2.2009, at www.weeklystandard.com/weblogs/ TWSFP/2009/02/petraeus_outlines_afghanistan. asp.

"Soviet Ambassador to the People's Republic of Angola EI Afanasenko, Memorandum of Conversation with President of the Movement for the Popular Liberation of Angola Agostinho Neto", 21.7.1975, at http://www.wilsoncenter.org/ digital-archive.

"Speech by Dr Fidel Castro Ruz, President of the Republic of Cuba, at the ceremony commemorating the 30th anniversary of the Cuban Military Mission in Angola and the 49th anniversary of the landing of the 'Granma', Revolutionary Armed Forces Day", 2.12. 2005, at emba.cubaminrex.cu/Default.aspx?tabid=15937.

SWAPO: "Political Programme of the South West Africa People's Organization. Adopted by the meeting of the Central Committee, Lusaka, July 28 – Aug. 1, 1976".

SWAPO: *The Namibian Documentation*. N.p. n.d.

"The Geneva protocol", 5.8.1988, at www.c-r.org/our-work/accord/angola/geneva-protocol.php.

The Truth Legion: *Greater South Africa: Plans for a better World. The Speeches of General the Right Honourable J.C. Smuts* (Johannesburg, The Truth Legion, 1940).

Toivo Ya Toivo, Hermann: "SWAPO leads Namibia", at www.nelsonmandela.org/omalley/index.php/site/q/03lv01538/04lv020 09/05lv02010/06lv02028/07lv02029.htm.

"Transcript of Meeting between U.S. Secretary of State Alexander M. Haig, Jr., and Cuban Vice Premier Carlos Rafael Rodriguez, Mexico City", 23.11.1981, at www.wilsoncenter.org/index.cfm?topic_id=1409&fuseaction=va2.document&identifier=5034EF21-96B6-175C-9C45700AE8493D87&sort=Subject&item=Alexander Haig.

Transcript of Swedish documentary film, *History Will Absolve Me*, at lanic.utexas.edu/project/castro/db/1977/19770723.html.

"Tripartite agreement", 22.12.1988, at www.c-r.org/our-work/accord/angola/tripartite-agreement.php.

"United States policy towards Angola". National Security-Decision Directive Number 274, 7 May, 1987, at www.gwu.edu/~nsarchiv/nsa/publications/DOC_readers/saread/sa870507.jpg.

USSR Report, International Affairs, 12.8.1985, p. 38, at www.dtic.mil/cgi-bin/GetTRDoc?AD=ADA367354&Location=U2&doc=GetTRDoc.pdf.

White Paper: Exchanges of Letters on Defence Matters between the Governments of the Union of South Africa and the United Kingdom, June 1955.

White Paper on Defence and Armament Supply, April 1969.

White Paper on Defence and Armament Supply, 1973.

White Paper on Defence and Armament Supply, 1975.

White Paper on Defence and Armament Supply, 1977.

White Paper on Defence and Armament Supply, 1979.

White Paper on Defence and Armament Supply, 1981.

White Paper on Defence and Armament Supply, 1982.

White paper on Defence and Armaments Supply, 1984.

White Paper on Defence and Armaments Supply, 1986.

White Paper on the Organisation and Functions of the South African Defence Force and the Arms Corporation of South Africa Limited, 1984.

4. Unpublished documents

4.1 SANDF Documentation Centre

Diverse, Group 2, Box 2.
Diverse, Group 2, Box 152.
Group 4, Box 160.
Group 6, Box 125.

4.2 61 Mech online archive (only the parts mentioned in endnotes)

Operation Askari index at http://www.61mech.org.za/media/tag/operation-askari

Operation Carrot index at http://www.61mech.org.za/media/tag/operation-carrot

Operation Daisy index at http://www.61mech.org.za/media/tag/operation-daisy

Operation Dolfyn index at http://www.61mech.org.za/media/tag/operation-dolfyn

Operation Excite index at http://www.61mech.org.za/media/tag/operation-excite

Operation Hilti index at http://www.61mech.org.za/media/tag/operation-hilti

Operation Hooper index at http://www.61mech.org.za/media/tag/operation-hooper

Operation Meebos index at http://www.61mech.org.za/media/tag/operation-meebos

Operation Merlyn index at http://www.61mech.org.za/media/tag/operation-merlyn

Operation Moduler index at http://www.61mech.org.za/media/tag/operation-modular

Operation Packer index at http://www.61mech.org.za/media/tag/operation-packer

Operation Protea index at http://www.61mech.org.za/media/tag/operation-protea

Operation Reindeer index at http://www.61mech.org.za/media/tag/operation-reindeer

Operation Sceptic index at http://www.61mech.org.za/media/tag/operation-sceptic

Year 1979 index at http://www.61mech.org.za/media/tag/year-1979

Year 1980 index at http://www.61mech.org.za/media/tag/year-1980

Year 1981 index at http://www.61mech.org.za/media/tag/year-1981

Year 1984 index at http://www.61mech.org.za/media/tag/year-1984

Year 1985 index at http://www.61mech.org.za/media/tag/year-1985

Year 1986 index at http://www.61mech.org.za/media/tag/year-1986

Year 1987 index at http://www.61mech.org.za/media/tag/year-1987

Year 1988 index at http://www.61mech.org.za/media/tag/year-1987

4.3 Aluka online archive

Documents from the South African Department of Foreign Affairs, 1962-1990, selected by Professor Christopher Saunders, UCT. Index at http://www.aluka.org.ez.sun.ac.za/action/doBrowse?sa=xst&t=2067&br=tax-collections%7Cpart-of%7Ccollection-minor.

4.4 Digital Innovation South Africa (Disa)
online archive
Various documents from the State Security
Council and the South African Department
of Foreign Affairs, 1962-1989. Index at www.
disa.ukzn.ac.za/index.php?option=com_
content&view=frontpage&Itemid=30.

4.5 Other
Du Plessis, Louis: "Rewolusionêre
oorlogvoering", 1977 (kindly provided by
Colonel Prof. Dr Louis Du Plessis).
Fraser, CA: "Lessons from past revolutionary
wars", 1969 (kindly provided by Professor
Stephen Ellis of the University of Leiden).
Fraser, CA: "The strategy of the revolutionary",
1969 (paper before the SAIIA, n.d.).
309/1 Op Moduler: "Kronologiese verloop
van gevegte oos van Quito rivier oor die
periode 8 Nov tot 17 Nov 1987", 19.11.1988
(document provided by Leon Marais).
Roland de Vries documentary collection:
Various documents regarding Operations
Protea, Moduler, Hilti and Prone, 1981-1988.
General De Vries has also written hundreds
of pages of reminiscences and analyses of the
operations he was involved with, which he
has, very unselfishly, shared with the author.

One understands that this will, in time,
culminate in a book.

4.6 Personal interviews
Brigadier General Piet Muller
Colonel Gert van Zyl

4.7 E-mail correspondence
Brigadier General McGill Alexander
Brigadier General Willem van der Waals
Colonel André Retief
Colonel CP du Toit
Colonel Ep van Lill
Colonel Gerhard Louw
Colonel Jan Malan
Colonel Leon Marais
Colonel Paul Fouché
Commandant Doctor Jakkie Cilliers
General Jannie Geldenhuys
Lieutenant Ariël Hugo
Lieutenant Colonel Professor Doctor
Abel Esterhuyse
Lieutenant Gert Minnaar
Lieutenant Hubrecht van Dalsen
Lieutenant Paul Louw
Major General Johann Dippenaar
Major General Roland de Vries
Major Hans Kriek

B. Secondary sources

1. Books

Andrew, Christopher and Mitrokhin, Vasili: *The
Mitrokhin Archive, II. The KGB and the World.*
London, Allen Lane, 2005.
Baines, Gary and Vale, Peter (eds.): *Beyond the Border
War. New Perspectives on Southern Africa's Late-
Cold War Conflicts.* Pretoria, Unisa, 2008.
Baker, Deane-Peter and Jordaan, Evert (eds.): *South
Africa and Contemporary Counterinsurgency.
Roots, Practices, Prospects.* Cape Town, UCT
Press, 2010.
Barber, James and Barratt, John: *South Africa's
Foreign Policy. The Search for Status and Security
1945-1988.* Cambridge, Cambridge University
Press, 1990.
Beaufre, André: *Introduction to Strategy.* London,
Praeger, 1965.
Beaufre, André: *Strategy of Action.* London,
Faber, 1967.
Beckett, Ian FW & Pimlott, John (eds.): *Armed Forces
& Modern Counter-Insurgency.* London, Croom
Helm, 1985.
Bennett, Chris: *Three Frigates. The South African Navy
comes of Age.* Durban, Just Done, 2006.
Bothma, LJ: *Die Buffel Struikel. 'n Storie van
32 Bataljon en sy Mense.* Langenhovenpark, LJ
Bothma, 2006.

Bothma, Louis: *Anderkant Cuito. 'n Reisverhaal
van die Grensoorlog.* Langenhovenpark, LJ
Bothma, 2011.
Brent, Winston: *Cheetah. "Guardians of the Nation".*
Nelspruit, Freeworld, 2008.
Breytenbach, Jan: *Buffalo Soldiers. The Story of
South Africa's 32 Battalion 1975-1993.* Alberton,
Galago, 2002.
Breytenbach, Jan: *Eagle Strike! The Story of the
Controversial Airborne Assault on Cassinga 1978.*
Sandton, Manie Grové, 2008.
Bridgland, Fred: *Jonas Savimbi. A Key to Africa.* New
York, Macmillan, 1986.
Bridgland, Fred: *The War for Africa. Twelve
Months that Transformed a Continent.* Gibraltar,
Ashanti, 1990.
Brown, James Ambrose: *The War of a Hundred Days.
Springboks in Somalia and Abyssinia 1940-41.*
Johannesburg, Ashanti, 1990.
Castro, Fidel (with Ignacio Ramonet): *My Life. A
Spoken Autobiography.* London, Allen Lane, 2007.
Cawthra, Gavin: *Brutal Force. The Apartheid War
Machine.* London, International Defence and Aid
Fund, 1986.
Cilliers, JK: *Counter-Insurgency in Rhodesia.* London,
Croom Helm, 1985.

Clancy, Tom: *Armoured Warfare. A Guided Tour of an Armoured Cavalry Regiment*. London, HarperCollins, 1996.

Cock, Jacklyn and Nathan, Laurie (eds.): *War and Society. The Militarisation of South Africa*. Cape Town, David Philip, 1989.

Crocker, Chester: *High Noon in Southern Africa. Making Peace in a Rough Neighborhood*. Johannesburg, Jonathan Ball, 1992.

De Villiers, Dirk and De Villiers, Johanna: *PW*. Cape Town, Tafelberg, 1984.

De Vries, Roland: *Mobiele Oorlogvoering. 'n Perspektief vir Suider-Afrika*. Menlopark, F.J.N. Harman, 1987.

Dobell, Lauren: *SWAPO's Struggle for Namibia, 1960-1991. War by Other Means*. Basel, Schlettwein, 1998.

Donaldson, Robert H: (ed.): *The Soviet Union in the Third World: Successes and Failures*. Boulder, Westview, 1981.

Dunnigan, James F: *How to Make War. A Comprehensive Guide to Modern Warfare for the Post-Cold War Era*, 3rd edition. London, Harper Perennial, 1993.

Du Preez, Sophia: *Avontuur in Angola. Die verhaal van Suid-Afrika se Soldate in Angola 1975-1976*. Pretoria, Van Schaik, 1989.

Els, Paul J: *Ongulumbashe. Die Begin van die Bosoorlog*. N.p., PelsA, 2004.

Els, Paul J: *We Fear Naught but God. The Story of the South African Special Forces, "The Recces"*. Johannesburg, Covos Day, 2000.

Eriksen, Garrett Ernst: "Forged in flames: The SADF experience of the Battles of Cuito Cuanavale 1987-1988" (History honours thesis). Rhodes University, 2010, at www.scribd.com/doc/48564518/Forged-in-Flames.

Eriksen, Tore Linné (ed.): *Norway and National Liberation in Southern Africa*. Stockholm, Nordiska Afrikainstitutet, 2000.

Franco, Manuela (ed.): *Portugal, os Estados Unidos e a África Austral*. Lisbon, Instituto Portugués das Relaçoes Internacionais, 2006.

Frankel, Philip H: *Pretoria's Praetorians. Civil-Military Relations in South Africa*. Cambridge, Cambridge University Press, 1984.

Gaddis, John Lewis: *The Cold War*. New York, Penguin, 2005.

Galula, David: *Counterinsurgency Warfare. Theory and Practice*. Westport, Praeger, 2006.

George, Edward: *The Cuban Intervention in Angola, 1965-1991*. London, Frank Cass, 2005.

Gleijeses, Piero: *Conflicting Missions. Havana, Washington, Pretoria*. Alberton, Galago, 2003.

Gleijeses, Piero: *The Cuban Drumbeat. Castro's Worldview: Cuban Foreign Policy in a Hostile World*. London, Seagull, 2009.

Greeff, Jack: *A Greater Share of Honour*. Ellisras, Ntomeni, 2001.

Green, Reginald H (ed.): *Namibia. The Last Colony*. Michigan, Longman, 1981.

Groth, Siegfried: *Namibia – The Wall of Silence. The Dark Days of the Liberation Struggle*. Wuppertal, Hammer, 1995.

Grundy, Kenneth W: *Soldiers without Politics. Blacks in the South African Armed Forces*. Berkeley, University of California Press, 1983.

Hamann, Hilton: *Days of the Generals. The Untold Story of South Africa's Apartheid-era Military Generals*. Cape Town, Zebra, 2001.

Hammes, Thomas X: *The Sling and the Stone. On War in the 21st Century*. St. Paul, Zenith, 2004.

Hanlon, Joseph: *Beggar your Neighbours. Apartheid Power in South Africa*. London, James Currey, 1986.

Heitman, Helmoed-Römer: *Krygstuig van Suid-Afrika*. Cape Town, Struik, 1988.

Heitman, Helmoed-Römer: *Modern African Wars (3). South-West Africa*. Oxford, Osprey, 1991.

Heitman, Helmoed-Römer: *South African Armed Forces*. Cape Town, Buffalo, 1990.

Heitman, Helmoed-Römer: *South African War Machine*. Johannesburg, Bison, 1985.

Heitman, Helmoed-Römer: *War in Angola. The Final South African Phase*. Gibraltar, Ashanti, 1990.

Herbstein, Denis and Evenson, John: *The Devils are Among Us. The War for Namibia*. London, Zed, 1989.

Heywood, Annemarie: *The Cassinga Event*. Windhoek, National Archives of Namibia, 1994.

Holness, Marga: *Apartheid's War against Angola*. New York, United Nations, 1983.

Hooper, Jim: *Koevoet! The Inside Story*. Johannesburg, Southern, 1988.

Hough, M (ed.): *Revolutionary Warfare and Counter-Insurgency*. ISSUP ad hoc publication no. 17, March 1984.

Hough, M and Van der Merwe, M: *Contemporary Air Strategy*. ISSUP ad hoc publication no. 23, Institute for Strategic Studies, August 1985.

Jaster, Robert Scott: *The 1988 Peace Accords and the Future of South-Western Africa*. Adelphi Papers 253, International Institute for Strategic Studies, London, Autumn 1990.

Jaster, Robert Scott: *The Defence of White Power. South African Policy under Pressure*. New York, St Martin, 1988.

Jeffery, Anthea: *People's War. New Light on the Struggle for South Africa*. Johannesburg, Jonathan Ball, 2010.

Kahn, Owen Ellison (ed.): *Disengagement from Southwest Africa. Prospects for Peace in Angola & Namibia*. New Brunswick, NJ, Transaction, 1991.

Katjavivi, Peter H: *A History of Resistance in Namibia*. London, James Currey, 1988.

Kleynhans, ASJ: *Die Stryd teen Terreur in SWA/Namibië 1957-1987*. Windhoek, SWA–Gebiedsmag, 1988.

König, Barbara: *Namibia, the Ravages of War. South Africa's Onslaught on the Namibian People*. London, International Defence and Aid Fund, 1983.

Kros, Jack: *War in Italy. With the South Africans from Taranto to the Alps*. Rivonia, Ashanti, 1992.

Leonard, Richard: *South Africa at War. White Power and the Crisis in Southern Africa*. Craighall, Ad Donker, 1983.

Leonhard, Robert: *The Art of Maneuver. Maneuver-Warfare Theory and AirLand Battle*. Novato, Presidio, 1991.

Leonhard, Wolfgang: *The Kremlin and the West. A Realistic Approach*. London, W.W. Norton, 1986.

Leys, Colin and Brown, Susan (eds.): *Life Histories of Namibia. Living through the Liberation Struggle*. London, Merlin, 2005.

Leys, Colin and Saul, John S: *Namibia's Liberation Struggle. The Two-Edged Sword*. London, James Currey, 1995.

Liddell Hart, BH: *Memoirs*. London, Cassell, 1965.

Liddell Hart, BH: *Strategy*. New York, Praeger, 1954.

Lord, Dick: *From Fledgling to Eagle. The South African Air Force during the Border War*. Johannesburg, 30° South, 2008.

Lord, Dick: *From Tailhooker to Mudmover*. Johannesburg, 30° South, 2009.

Lord, Dick: *Vlamgat. The Story of the Mirage F1 in the South African Air Force*. Weltevreden Park, Covos Day, 2000.

Löwis of Menar, Henning von: *Namibia im Ost-West-Konflikt*. Cologne, Verlag Wissenschaft und Politik, 1983.

Maier, Karl: *Angola: Promises and Lies*. London, Serif, 1996.

Mao, Zedong: *Selected Military Writings*. Peking, Foreign Languages Press, 1963.

Martin, W James III: *A Political History of the Civil War in Angola 1974-1990*. New Brunswick, NJ, Transaction, 1992.

McCuen, JJ: *The Art of Counter-Revolutionary Warfare. The Strategy of Counter-Insurgency*. London, Faber & Faber, 1966.

McWilliams, Mike: *Battle for Cassinga. South Africa's Controversial Cross-Border Raid, Angola 1978*. Pinetown, 30° South, 2011.

Melber, Henning: *Liberation and Democracy in Southern Africa: The Case of Namibia. Discussion Paper 10*. Uppsala, Nordiska Afrikainstitutet, 2001.

Melber, Henning (ed.): *Re-examining Liberation in Namibia. Political Culture since Independence*. Uppsala, Nordiska Afrikainstitutet, 2003.

Melber, Henning: *Transitions in Namibia*. Uppsala, Nordiska Afrikainstitutet, 2001.

Mills, Greg and Williams, David: *7 Battles that Shaped South Africa*. Cape Town, Tafelberg, 2006.

Morgan, Daniel: *Wars of National Liberation*. London, Cassell, 2001.

Namakalu, Oswin O: *Armed Liberation Struggle. Some Accounts of PLAN's Combat Operations*. Windhoek, Gamsberg, 2004.

Nangolo, Mvula ya and Sellström, Tor: *Kassinga. A Story Untold*. Windhoek, Namibia Book Development Council, 1995.

Nortje, Piet: *32 Battalion. The Inside Story of South Africa's Elite Fighting Unit*. Cape Town, Zebra, 2003.

Norval, Norman: *Death in the Desert. The Namibian Tragedy*. Washington DC, Selous Foundation Press, 1989.

Orkin, Mark (ed.): *Sanctions against Apartheid*. Claremont, David Philip, 1989.

Orpen, Neil: *Total Defence*. Cape Town, Nasionale Boekhandel, 1967.

Papenfus, Theresa: *Pik Botha en Sy Tyd*. Pretoria, Litera, 2011.

Paul, Mathew: *Parabat. Personal Accounts of Paratroopers in Combat Situations in South Africa's History*. Johannesburg, Covos Day, 2001.

Perkins, Edward: *Mr. Ambassador. Warrior for Peace*. Norman, University of Oklahoma Press, 2006.

Polakow-Suransky, Sasha: *The Unspoken Alliance. Israel's Secret Relationship with Apartheid South Africa*. New York, Pantheon, 2010.

Prinsloo, Daan: *Stem uit die Wildernis. 'n Biografie van oud-pres. PW Botha*. Mossel Bay, Vaandel, 1997.

Pryce-Jones, David: *The War that Never Was. The Fall of the Soviet Empire 1985-1991*. London, Weidenfeld & Nicolson, 1995.

Roherty, James Michael: *State Security in South Africa. Civil-Military Relations under P.W. Botha*. New York, M.E. Sharpe, 1992.

Sarkin, J: *Germany's Genocide of the Herero. Kaiser Wilhelm II, his General, his Settlers, his Soldiers*. Woodbridge, James Currey, 2011.

Scholtz, Leopold: *Why the Boers lost the War*. Basingstoke, Palgrave Macmillan, 2006.

Schoultz, Lars: *That Infernal Little Cuban Republic. The United States and the Cuban Revolution*. Chapel Hill, University of North Carolina Press, 2009.

Seegers, Annette: *The Military in the Making of Modern South Africa*. London, Tauris, 1996.

Sellström. Tor (ed.): *Sweden and National Liberation in Southern Africa, II. Solidarity and Assistance, 1970-1994*. Stockholm, Nordiska Afrikainstitutet, 2000.

Service, Robert: *Comrades! Communism: A World History*. Cambridge, Harvard University Press, 2010.

Shubin, Gennady and Tokarev, Andrei: *Bush War. The Road to Cuito Cuanavale. Soviet Soldiers' Accounts of the Angolan War*. Auckland Park, Jacana, 2001.

Shubin, Gennady: *The Memoirs of the Veterans of the War in Angola*. Moscow, Memories, 2007.

Shubin, Vladimir: *ANC. A View from Moscow*. Bellville, Mayibuye, 1999.

Shubin, Vladimir: *The Hot "Cold War". The USSR in Southern Africa*. London, Pluto, 2008.

Shultz, Richard H: *The Soviet Union and Revolutionary Warfare. Principles, Practices and Regional Comparisons*. n.p., Hoover Institution, 1988.

Sitte, Fritz: *Schicksalsfrage Namibia*. Vienna, Styria, 1983.

Spies, F du Toit: *Angola. Operasie Savannah 1975-1976*. Pretoria, SA Defence Force Directorate Public Relations, 1989.

Stapleton, Timothy J: *A Military History of South Africa. From the Dutch-Khoi Wars to the End of Apartheid*. Santa Barbara CA, Praeger, 2010.

Steenkamp, Willem: *Adeus Angola*. Cape Town, Howard Timmins, 1976.

Steenkamp, Willem: *Borderstrike! South Africa into Angola 1975-1980*. N.p., Just Done, 2006.

Steenkamp, Willem: *South Africa's Border War 1966-1989*. Gibraltar, Ashanti, 1989.

Stiff, Peter: *Nine Days of War. Namibia – Before, During and After*. Alberton, Lemur, 1999.

Stiff, Peter: *The Covert War. Koevoet Operations Namibia 1979-1989*. Alberton, Galago, 2004.

Stiff, Peter: *The Silent War. South African Recce Operations 1969-1994.* Alberton, Galago, 1999.

Strayer, Robert W: *Why did the Soviet Union Collapse? Understanding Historical Change.* New York, ME Sharpe, 1998.

Suchlicki, Jaime (ed.): *The Cuban Military under Castro.* Miami, University of Miami Press, 1989.

SWAPO: *Massacre at Kassinga.* N.p., SWAPO publicity department, 1978.

Torreguitar, Elena: *National Liberation Movements in Office. Forging Democracy with African Adjectives in Namibia.* Frankfurt am Main, Peter Lang, 1979.

Trewhela, Paul: *Inside Quatro. Uncovering the Exile History of the ANC and SWAPO.* Auckland Park, Jacana, 2009.

Truth and Reconciliation Commission of South Africa Report, II. n.p., n.d.

Turner, John W: *Continent Ablaze. Insurgency Wars in Africa 1960 to the Present.* Johannesburg, Jonathan Ball, 1998.

Turton, AR: *Shaking Hands with Billy. The Private Memoirs of Anthony Richard Turton.* Durban, Just Done, 2010.

Uys, Ian: *Bushman Soldiers. Their Alpha and Omega.* Germiston, Fortress, 1993.

Van der Merwe, Kriek: *Die Suid-Afrikaanse Leër-Gevegskool. Ontstaan en Ontwikkeling: 1978 tot 1996.* Postmasburg, SA Leërgevegskool, 1996.

Vanneman, Peter: *Soviet Strategy in Southern Africa.* n.p., Hoover Press, 1990.

Venter, Al J (ed.): *Challenge. Southern Africa within the Revolutionary Context.* Gibraltar, Ashanti, 1989.

Venter, Al J (ed.): *The Chopper Boys. Helicopter Warfare in Africa.* Halfway House, Southern, 1994.

Visser, JA: *The South African Defence Force's Contribution to the Development of South West Africa.* Pretoria, SADF Military Information Bureau, 1984.

Von Clausewitz, Carl: *Vom Kriege.* Berlin, Ullstein, 1999.

Wallace, Marion: *A History of Namibia. From the Beginning to 1990.* London, C. Hurst, 2011.

Wehler, Hans-Ulrich: *Bismarck und der Imperialismus.* Munich, Kiepenhauer und Witsch, 1969.

Weiss, Thomas G and Blight, James G (eds.): *The Suffering Grass. Superpowers and Regional Conflict in Southern Africa and the Caribbean.* London, Lynne Riener, 1992.

Westad, Odd Arne: *The Global Cold War.* Cambridge, Cambridge University Press, 2007.

White, Rowland: *Phoenix Squadron.* London, Bantam, 2009.

Williams, David W: *Op die Grens 1965-1990. Wit Mans se Militêre Ervaring.* Cape Town, Tafelberg, 2008.

Wilsworth, Clive: *First In, Last Out. The South African Artillery in Action 1975-1988.* Johannesburg, 30° South, 2010.

Zubok, Vladislav M: *A Failed Empire: The Soviet Union in the Cold War from Stalin to Gorbachev.* Chapel Hill, University of North Carolina University Press, 2007.

2. Articles

Anonymous: "Apartheid govt wanted to nuke Cuban troops", 14.12.2010, at www.politicsweb. co.za/politicsweb/view/politicsweb/en/ page71654?oid=215328&sn=Detail&pid=71616.

Anonymous: "BMP-1 Infantry Fighting Vehicle (Russia)", at www.historyofwar.org/articles/ weapons_bmp1.html.

Anonymous: "Last French Mirage F1CRs leave Kandahar" (*Air Forces Monthly,* October 2011).

Anonymous: "Mirage F1AZ/CZ ordinance", at newsite.ipmssa.za.org/content/view/149/28/1/5.

Anonymous: "The Kukri air-to-air missile: The sword is drawn", at www.aessa.org.za/articles/ kukri.doc.

Bain, Mervyn J: "Cuba-Soviet relations in the Gorbachev era" (*Journal of Latin American Studies,* 37/2005).

Baines, Gary: "Conflicting memories, competing narratives and complicating histories: Revisiting the Cassinga controversy" (*The Journal of Namibian Studies,* 6/2009).

Baines, Gary: "Partial sources colour the Cassinga story" (*Sunday Independent,* 17.2.2008).

Black, George: "Toward victory always, but when?" (*The Nation,* 24.10.1988).

Bothma, Louis: "Die pyn lê nog vlak" (*Die Burger,* 10.6.2008).

Boulter, Roger S: "Afrikaner nationalism in action: FC Erasmus and South Africa's defence forces 1948-1959 (*Nations and Nationalism,* 6/3).

Campbell, Horace: "Cuito Cuanavale – a tribute to Fidel Castro and the African Revolution" (*Socialist Unity,* 9.6.2008).

Castro, Fidel: "The battle of the truth and Martin Blandino's book," three parts, at www. embacubaqatar.com/fidel091008e.html; embacu. cubaminrex.cu/Default.aspx?tabid=9123; www. telepinar.co.cu/ving/index.php/200810153858/ Reflection-by-Fidel/reflections-by-comrade-fidel-the-battle-of-the-truth-and-martin-blandinos-book-part-iii-and-final.html.

Claiborne, William: "Angolan rebels prepare for expected offensive" (*Washington Post,* 6.8.1987).

Claiborne, William: "Namibia's forgotten bush war" (*Washington Post,* 16.6.1987).

Clark, Marsh and Hawthorne, Peter: "Namibia: A droning, no-win conflict" (*Time Magazine,* 2.3.1981).

Cockburn, Alexander: "Beat the devil" (*The Nation,* 1.5.1989).

Cooper, Tom and Kyzer, Jonathan: "Angola: Claims & reality about SAAF losses", at www.acig.org/ artman/publish/article_184.shtml.

DePalo, William A Jr.: "Cuban internationalism: The Angola Experience, 1985-1988 (*Parameters,* 23, Autumn 1993).

De Visser, Lieneke: "Winning hearts and minds in the Namibian Border War" (*Scientia Militaria,* 39/1, 2011).

De Vries, R and McCaig, GI: "Mobile Warfare in Southern Africa" (*Strategic Review for Southern Africa,* August 1987).

Du Randt, Jacques: "61 Meg Ops Protea" (unpublished memoir in author's possession).

Dyason, Anton: "Blackburn Buccaneer S.Mk.50 SAAF", at http://newsite.ipmssa.za.org/content/view/111/28/1/0/.

Earp, Denis: "The Role of Air Power in Southern Africa" (*Strategic Review for Southern Africa*, April 1986).

Ellis, Stephen: "The historical significance of South Africa's Third Force" (*Journal of Southern African Studies*, 24/2, June 1998).

Falk, Pamela S: "Cuba in Africa" (*Foreign Affairs*, 65/5, Summer 1987).

Farnham, Barbara: "Reagan and the Gorbachev revolution: Perceiving the end of threat" (*Political Science Quarterly*, 116/2, Summer 2001).

Ferreira, Rialize and Liebenberg, Ian: "The impact of war on Angola and South Africa: Two Southern African case studies" (*Journal for Contemporary History*, 31/3, 2006).

Freeman, Chas W: "The Angola/Namibia accords" (*Foreign Affairs*, 68/3, Summer 1989).

Furman, Dmitry: "A silent cold war" (*Russia in Global Affairs*, 4/2, April-June 2006).

Geldenhuys, Deon: "Castro's Cuba: The defiant deviant" (*Unisa Latin American Report*, 20/2, 2004).

Gleijeses, Piero: "Cuba and the Independence of Namibia" (*Cold War History*, 7/2, May 2007)

Gleijeses, Piero: "Cuito Cuanavale revisited" (*Mail & Guardian*, 6-12.7.2007)

Gleijeses, Piero: "Moscow's Proxy? Cuba and Africa 1975-1988" (*Journal of Cold War Studies*, 8/2, Spring 2006).

Gleijeses, Piero: "The massacre of Cassinga", at http://amadlandawonye.wikispaces.com/page/diff/The+Massacre+of+Cassinga%2C+Piero+Gleijeses/657945.

Greeff, IB: "South Africa's modern Long Tom" (*Military History Journal*, 9/1, June 1992).

Hallett, Robin: "The South African intervention in Angola 1975-76", (*African Affairs*, 77/308, July 1978).

Healy, Barry: "Cuito Cuanavale: Cuba strikes for Africa's freedom" (*Green Left Weekly*, issue 755, 18.6.2008).

Heitman, Helmoed-Römer: "Equipment of the Border War" (*Journal of Contemporary History*, 31/3, Dec. 2006).

Jordaan, Evert: "The role of South African armour in South West Africa/Namibia and Angola, 1975-1989" (*Journal of Contemporary History*, 31/3, Dec. 2006).

Joubert, Jan-Jan: "Kuba het SA se kernvermoë totaal oorskat" (*Rapport*, 4.1.2011).

Kahn, Owen Ellison: "Cuba's impact on Southern Africa" (*Journal of Interamerican Studies and World Affairs*, 29/3, Autumn 1987).

Kasrils, Ronnie: "Turning point at Cuito Cuanavale" (*Mail & Guardian*, 23.3.2008).

Kruys, George: "Doctrine development in the South African armed forces up to the 1980s", in M. Hough and L. Du Plessis (eds.): *Selected Military Issues with Specific Reference to the Republic of South Africa* (ISSUP ad hoc publication no. 38).

Lautenbach, Dale: "Namibia recalls its bloody past" (*Sowetan*, 26.5.1992).

Leys, Colin and Saul, John S: "Liberation without democracy? The SWAPO crisis of 1976" (*Journal of Southern African Studies*, 20/1, March 1994).

Liberman, Peter: "The rise and fall of the South African bomb" (*International Security*, 26/2, Autumn 2001).

Lord, Dick: "SAAF fighter involvement in the Border War, 1965-1988" (*Journal of Contemporary History*, 31/3, Dec. 2006).

Lush, David: "Brothers-in-arms" (*Insight Namibia*, at www.insight.com.na/article/full/1157/03-02-2011/brothers-in-arms.html).

Malan, Magnus: "Die aanslag teen Suid-Afrika" (*Strategic Review for Southern Africa*, 2/1980).

Malaquias, Assis: "Angola's foreign policy since independence: The search for domestic security" (*African Security Review*, 9/3, 2000).

Marcum, John A: "Lessons of Angola" (*Foreign Affairs*, 54/3, April 1976).

Márquez, Gabriel García: "Operation Carlota" at http://emba.cubaminrex.cu/Default.aspx?tabid=21658.

McCuen, John J: "Hybrid wars" (*Military Review*, March-April 2008).

Meiring, Georg: "Current SWAPO activity in South West Africa" (*Strategic Review for Southern Africa*, 1/1985).

Mortimer, Brigadier DJ: "Conventional deterrence with specific reference to the RSA" (*Strategic Review for Southern Africa*, May 1980).

Muller, Divan: "Cheetah phasing out function" (*African Pilot*, 7/5, May 2008).

Onslow, Sue: " 'Noises off': South Africa and the Lancaster House Settlement 1979-1980" (*Journal of Southern African Studies*, 35/2, June 2009).

Onslow, Sue: "South Africa and the Owen/Vance Plan of 1977" (*South African Historical Journal*, 51/2004).

Oosthuizen, GJJ: "Die Suid-Afrikaanse Weermag en die 'stryd' om Cuito Cuanavale: Fases 2, 3 en 4 van Operasie Moduler, Oktober-Desember 1987 [deel 2]" (*New Contree*, 61/2011).

Oosthuizen, Gerhard JJ: "Die Suid-Afrikaanse Weermag en Transgrensoperasie Moduler, fase 1: Die Fapla-offensief teen Unita, Augustus-Oktober 1987" (*New Contree*, 60/November 2010).

Oosthuizen, GJJ: "Regiment Mooirivier, Potchefstroom: Grensdienservarings van 'n pantserburgermageenheid, 1975-1988" (*Joernaal vir Eietydse Geskiedenis*, 31/3, Dec. 2006).

Oosthuizen, GJJ: "Regiment Mooirivier and South African transborder operations into Angola during 1975/76 and 1983/84" (*Historia* 49/1, May 2004, p. 150).

Oosthuizen, GJJ: "The final phase of South African transborder operations into Angola: Regiment Mooi River and Operations Modular, Hooper, Packer and Displace (Handbag), 1987-1988" (*Journal of Contemporary History*, 28/2, 2003).

Owen, Robert C: "Counterrevolution in Namibia" (*Aerospace Power Journal*, Winter 1987-88, at www.airpower.maxwell.af.mil/airchronicled/apj87/owen.html).

Parkins, NC: "Faster, Higher and Better. The Image of the S.A. Air Force as Viewed By a Veteran", at http://www.rhodesia.nl/parkins.htm.

Potgieter, Thean: "The geopolitical role of the South African Navy in the South African sphere of influence after the Second World War" (*Strategic Review for Southern Africa*, June 2002).

Ridgway, Brady: "No evidence to support Vigne's claims on Cassinga" (*Sunday Independent*, 20.1.2008).

Saney, Isaac: "African Stalingrad: The Cuban revolution, internationalism and the end of apartheid" (*Latin American Perspectives* 33/81, 2006).

Scholtz, Leopold: "Cuito Cuanavale: Wie het regtig gewen?" (*Scientia Militaria*, 28/1, 1998).

Scholtz, Leopold: "Die ontwikkeling van die SA Leër in die Grensoorlog, 1966-1989" (*Joernaal vir Eietydse Geskiedenis*, 31/3, Dec. 2006).

Scholtz, Leopold: "Lessons from the Southern African Wars: A Counterinsurgency Analysis" (*Journal of Contemporary History*, 36/2, Sept. 2011).

Scholtz, Leopold: "'n Strategiese en operasionele beoordeling van die SAW se oorgrens-operasies in Angola, 1975-1988" (*Joernaal vir Eietydse Geskiedenis*, 33/3, Feb. 2009).

Scholtz, Leopold: "The air war over Angola, 1987-1988: An analysis" (*Journal for Contemporary History*, 33/3, Feb. 2009).

Scholtz, Leopold: "The Namibian Border War: An appraisal of the South African strategy" (*Scientia Militaria* 34/1, 2006).

Scholtz, Leopold: "The South African Strategic and Operational Objectives in Angola, 1987-1988 (*Scientia Militaria*, 38/1, 2010).

Scholtz, Leopold: "The standard of research on the Battle of Cuito Cuanavale, 1987-1988" (*Scientia Militaria*, 39/1, 2011).

Scholtz, Leopold and Scholtz, Ingrid: "Die ANC/ SAKP in Angola: 'n gevallestudie rakende interne demokrasie" (*Historia*, 54/1, May 2009).

Scholtz, Leopold and Scholtz, Ingrid: "Die ontstaan en ontwikkeling van die SAKP se tweefase-revolusiemodel" (*Tydskrif vir Geesteswetenskappe* 30/3 and 30/4, Sept. and Dec. 2004).

Seytre, Jean-Sebastien: "Au revoir Reims" (*Air Forces Monthly*, Sept. 2011.)

Shubin, Vladimir: "The USSR and Southern Africa during the Cold War", at www2.spbo.unibo.it/dpis/centroafricamedioriente/Shubin_OP1.pdf.

Syndercombe, Glen: "Positive Aspects of Actions of the SADF and in Particular the SA Navy in the 1980's", at navy.org.za/pages/syndercombe.

Urribarres, Rubén: "A Cuban MiG-23 in Angola, II: Air superiority missions", at www.geocities.com/urrib2000/EqMiG-23aa-e.html.

Urribarres, Rubén: "Cuban MiG-21 in action", at www.urrib2000.narod.ru/EqMiG-21a-e.html.

Urribarres, Rubén: "Tanques y otra tégnica enemiga" ["Enemy tanks and other techniques"], at www.urrib2000.narod.ru/Tanques3.html.

Urribarres, Rubén: The MiG-17 Fresco in Cuba, at www.geocities.com/urrib2000/EqMiG17-e.html.

Van Zyl, Gert: "Operation Dolfyn", at www.61mech.org.za/operations/12-operation-dolfyn.

Verhoek, Bastiaan: "Denel shatters artillery records" (*South African Soldier*, July 2006).

Viljoen, Constand: "The conventional threat to the RSA and SWA" (*Strategic Review for Southern Africa*, Dec. 1984).

Vreÿ, François and Jordaan, Evert: "Operational strategy and the South African way of war: The way forward" (*Strategic Review for Southern Africa*, XXVIII/1, May 2006).

Weis, Toni: "The politics machine: On the concept of 'solidarity' in the East German support for SWAPO" (*Journal of Southern African Studies*, 37/2, 2011).

Wessels, André: "The South African Navy during the years of conflict in Southern Africa, 1966-1989" (*Journal of Contemporary History*, 31/3, 2006).

Westad, Odd Arne: "Moscow and the Angolan crisis, 1974-1976: A new pattern of intervention" (*Cold War International History Project Bulletin*, 8-9, Winter 1996-1997).

3. Unpublished theses and documents

Callister, Graeme: "Compliance, compulsion and contest: Aspects of military conscription in South Africa, 1952-1992". Unpublished MA thesis, University of Stellenbosch, 2007.

De Visser, Lieneke: "Winning the Hearts and Minds. Legitimacy in the Namibian Border War". Unpublished MA thesis, University of Utrecht, August 2010.

Dorning, W: "A concise history of Operation Moduler (phase one) May-October 1987". Unpublished SADF document, 1987.

Phillips, Merran Willis: "The End Conscription Campaign 1983-1988. A Study of White Extra-Parliamentary Opposition to Apartheid". Unpublished MA thesis, Pretoria, Unisa, 2002.

Saunders, GM: "The foreign policy of Angola under Agostinho Neto". Unpublished MA thesis, Monterey CA, Naval Postgraduate School, Dec. 1983.

Velthuizen, Andreas: "Applying military force for political ends: South Africa in South-Western Africa, 1987-1988". Unpublished MA thesis, Pretoria, Unisa, 1991.

Williams, Christian A: "Exile history: An ethnography of the SWAPO camps and the Namibian question". Unpublished D Phil dissertation, University of Michigan, 2009.

INDEX

D

E

F

CPSIA information can be obtained
at www.ICGtesting.com
Printed in the USA
BVHW04s0952110818
523998BV00002B/11/P